The Rites of the Catholic Church as Revised by the Second Vatican Ecumenical Council

THE RITES
OF THE
CATHOLIC CHURCH

as Revised by Decree of the
Second Vatican Ecumenical Council
and Published
by Authority of Pope Paul VI

STUDY EDITION

English translation
prepared by
The International Commission
on English in the Liturgy

PUEBLO PUBLISHING CO

New York

Concordat cum originali:
Terence Cardinal Cooke
Archbishop of New York

Published by authority of the Bishop's Committee on the Liturgy.

Pastoral Care of the Sick approved by the National Conference of Catholic Bishops for use in the dioceses of the United States of America, November 18, 1982. Confirmed by the Congregation for the Sacraments and Divine Worship, December 11, 1982 (Prot. No. CD 1207/82).

Design: Frank Kacmarcik

ISBN: 0-916134-15-6

Printed in the United States of America.

CONTENTS

PREFACE

The Roman Ritual has undergone numerous revisions since the edition of Pope Paul V, of 1614. Now, in response to the directives of the Second Vatican Ecumenical Council, a new edition has been undertaken by the Holy See. One of the animating principles that has guided the preparation of the new rites is to encourage the people of God to understand and participate more fully in these sacred celebrations.

The matter is clearly stated in the Instruction on the Proper Implementation of the Constitution on the Sacred Liturgy (*Inter Oecumenici,* September 26, 1964), no. 5:

"It is essential that everybody be persuaded that the scope of the Constitution on the Sacred Liturgy is not limited merely to the changing of liturgical rites and texts. Rather its aim is to foster the formation of the faithful and that pastoral activity of which the liturgy is the summit and source (see Const., Art. 10). The changes in the liturgy which have already been introduced or which will be introduced later, have this same end in view."

The Constitution on the Sacred Liturgy (*Sacrosanctum Concilium*) itself points out:

"Mother Church earnestly desires that all the faithful should be led to that full, conscious, and active participation in liturgical celebrations which is demanded by the very nature of the liturgy, and to which the Christian people, 'a chosen race, a royal priesthood, a holy nation, a redeemed people' (1 Pet. 2:9, 4-5) have a right and obligation by reason of their baptism.

"In the restoration and promotion of the sacred liturgy the full and active participation by all the people is the aim to be considered before all else, for it is the primary and indispensable source from which the faithful are to derive the true Christian spirit. Therefore, in all their apostolic activity, pastors of souls should energetically set about achieving it through the requisite pedagogy" (no. 14).[1]

The Constitution on the Sacred Liturgy goes on to point out the need for liturgical reforms along the following lines:

[1]Unless otherwise noted, the quotations are from the Constitution on the Sacred Liturgy (*Sacrosanctum Concilium*).

"In order that the Christian people may more certainly derive an abundance of graces from the sacred liturgy, holy Mother Church desires to undertake with great care a general restoration of the liturgy itself. For the liturgy is made up of unchangeable elements divinely instituted, and elements subject to change. These latter not only may be changed but ought to be changed with the passage of time, if they have suffered from the intrusion of anything out of harmony with the inner nature of the liturgy or have become less suitable. In this restoration both texts and rites should be drawn up so as to express more clearly the holy things which they signify. The Christian people, as far as is possible, should be able to understand them with ease and take part in them fully, actively, and as a community" (no. 21).

"The faithful should easily understand the sacramental signs, and should eagerly frequent those sacraments which were instituted to nourish the Christian life" (no. 59).

Although the Liturgy "is principally the worship of the divine Majesty, it likewise contains much instruction for the faithful" (no. 33). Modern courses in religion from the grades through college as well as advanced studies in seminaries and graduate schools are careful to give the study of liturgy a prominent place in the development of the spiritual and intellectual aspects of Chrisitan life.

The purpose of this book is to bring together for the first time in one volume those rites which are essential to the planning of liturgical celebrations and which are frequently studied and referred to in theology courses and are of special concern to the laity in general. These rites are as follows:

1. Christian Initiation
A. Rite of Christian Initiation of Adults
B. Rite of Baptism for Children
C. Rite of Reception of Baptized Christians into Full Communion with the Catholic Church
D. Rite of Confirmation
2. Rite of Penance
3. Holy Communion and Worship of the Eucharist outside Mass
4. Blessing of Oils and Consecration of Chrism

5. Rite of Marriage
6. Pastoral Care of the Sick: Rites of Anointing and Viaticum
7. Rite of Funerals

As a further aid to the study of these rites a comprehensive outline of each rite precedes the official text.

Here follows a description of the general principles which guided the Fathers of Vatican II in the reforms of the liturgy: The Constitution on the Sacred Liturgy (*Sacrosanctum Concilium*) states:

"With the passage of time . . . there have crept into the rites of the sacraments and sacramentals certain features which have rendered their nature and purpose far from clear to the people of today. Hence some changes are necessary to adapt them to present-day needs" (no. 62).

The purpose and plan of revision of the liturgical books is closely allied to an enlarged view of the importance of sacred scripture as a source of the liturgy.

"Sacred scripture is of the greatest importance in the celebration of the liturgy. For it is from it that lessons are read and explained in the homily, and psalms are sung. It is from the scriptures that the prayers, collects, and hymns draw their inspiration and their force, and that actions derive their meaning. Hence in order to achieve the restoration, progress, and adaptation of the sacred liturgy it is essential to promote that sweet and living love for sacred scripture to which the venerable tradition of Eastern and Western rites gives testimony" (no. 24).

The Constitution closes its section on the general norms for liturgical reforms with a reiteration of its concern for popular participation:

"To promote active participation, the people should be encouraged to take part by means of acclamations, responses, psalms, antiphons, hymns, as well as by actions, gestures and bodily attitudes. And at the proper time a reverent silence should be observed" (no. 30). Also:

"When the liturgical books are being revised, the people's parts must be carefully indicated by the rubrics" (no. 31). The document gives further "Norms Based on the Educative and Pastoral Nature of the Liturgy." Thus:

". . . the visible signs which the sacred liturgy uses to signify invisible divine things have been chosen by Christ or by the Church. Thus not only when things are read 'which were written for our instruction' (Rom. 15:4), but also when the Church prays or sings or acts, the faith of those taking part is nourished, and their minds are raised to God so that they may offer him their spiritual homage and receive his grace more abundantly" (no. 33).

In accordance with the above principles the Council set up basic guidelines for the reform of specific rites—requirements which were further elaborated by certain post-Vatican II documents.

GUIDELINES FOR THE RITE OF BAPTISM

Certain rites which did not appear in the old ritual and yet stem from the usage of the early Church are restored. Such is the "catechumenate for adults, comprising several distinct steps" which is "to be restored and brought into in use at the discretion of the local ordinary. By this means the time of the catechumenate, which is intended as a period of suitable instruction, may be sanctified by sacred rites to be celebrated at successive intervals of time" (no. 64).

"Both rites for the baptism of adults are to be revised, not only the simpler rite but also, taking into consideration the restored catechumenate, the more solemn rite. A special Mass 'For the conferring of Baptism' is to be inserted into the Roman Missal" (no. 66).

The Constitution continues:

"The rite for the baptism of infants is to be revised, its revision taking into account the fact that those to be baptized are infants. The roles of parents and godparents, and also their duties, should be brought out more clearly in the rite itself" (no. 67).

"The baptismal rite should contain variants, to be used at the discretion of the local ordinary when a large number are to be baptized. Likewise a shorter rite is to be drawn up, especially for mission countries which catechists, and also the faithful in general, may use when there is danger of death and neither priest nor deacon is available (no. 68).

"In place of the rite called 'Rite for supplying what was omitted in the baptism of an infant' a new rite is to be drawn up for converts who have already been validly baptized. It should indicate that they are now admitted to communion with the Church" (no. 69).

"Baptismal water, outside of paschal time, may be blessed within the rite of Baptism itself by an approved shorter formula" (no. 70).

GUIDELINES FOR THE RITE OF CONFIRMATION

"Incorporated into the Church by Baptism, the faithful are appointed by their baptismal character to Christian religious worship; reborn as sons of God, they must profess before men the faith they have received from God through the Church. By the sacrament of Confirmation they are more perfectly bound to the Church and are endowed with the special strength of the Holy Spirit. Hence they are, as true witnesses of Christ, more strictly obliged to spread the faith by word and deed" Dogmatic Constitution on the Church (*Lumen Gentium*), no. 11.

The reasons for the changes and adaptations of the rites of both baptism and confirmation lie in the close relationship between the two sacraments and their function in the Christian life. Thus:

"The rite of Confirmation is to be revised also so that the intimate connection of this sacrament with the whole of the Christian initiation may more clearly appear. For this reason the renewal of baptismal promises should fittingly precede the reception of this sacrament. Confirmation may be conferred within Mass when convenient. For conferring outside Mass, a formula introducing the rite should be drawn up" (no. 71).

GUIDELINES FOR THE RITE OF PENANCE

"Those who approach the sacrament of Penance obtain pardon from God's mercy for the offense committed against him, and are, at the same time reconciled with the Church which they have wounded by their sins and which by charity, by example and by prayer labors for their conversion" *Lumen Gentium,* no. 11.

In this light, then, the Council decreed as follows:
"The rite and formulae of Penance are to be revised so that they more clearly express both the nature and effect of the sacrament" (no. 72).

GUIDELINES FOR THE RITES OF HOLY COMMUNION AND WORSHIP OF THE EUCHARIST OUTSIDE MASS

"Taking part in the eucharist sacrifice, the source and summit of the Christian life, they (the people and priest) offer the divine victim to God and themselves along with it. And so it is that, both in the offering and in Holy Communion, each in his own way, though not of course indiscriminately, has his own part to play in the liturgical action. Then, strengthened by the body of Christ in the eucharistic communion, they manifest in a concrete way that unity of the People of God which this holy sacrament aptly signifies and admirably realizes" *Lumen Gentium,* no. 11.

Moreover, the decree *Presbyterorum Ordinis*—on the Ministry and Life of Priests—declares:

"The house of prayer in which the most holy Eucharist is celebrated and reserved, where the faithful assemble, and where is worshiped the presence of the Son of God our Saviour, offered for us on the sacrificial altar for the help and consolation of the faithful—this house ought to be in good taste and a worthy place for prayer and sacred ceremonial. In it pastors and faithful are called upon to respond with grateful hearts to the gifts of him who through his humanity is unceasingly pouring the divine life into the members of his Body" (no. 5).

These views reflect the teaching and traditions of the Church by stressing the importance of the worship of the reserved Eucharist and the strengthening and healing flowing from the Sacrament even when received outside Mass. The document entitled Instruction on the Worship of the Eucharistic Mystery (S.C.R. *Eucharisticum Mysterium,* May 25, 1967, Chapter II, Section 3C) points out that:

"It is necessary to accustom the faithful to receive communion during the actual celebration of the Eucharist. Even outside Mass, however, priests will not refuse to distribute communion to those who have good reason to ask for it."

A new element in the practice of distributing Communion outside Mass is to give it a more biblical tone. Thus, as noted in the above-mentioned Instruction:

"When, at the prescribed times, communion is distributed outside Mass, if it is judged suitable, a short Bible service may precede it."

The new rite of Holy Communion and Worship of the Eucharist outside Mass clarified some of the traditional practices and encouraged them to be continued as underlined by Pope Paul VI in his encyclical letter *Mysterium Fidei*, September 3, 1965:

"Moreover, in the course of the day the faithful should not omit to visit the Blessed Sacrament, which according to the liturgical laws must be kept in the churches with the greatest possible reverence and in a most honorable location. Such visits are a proof of gratitude, an expression of love to Christ the Lord present in the sacraments, and a duty of the adoration we owe."

The traditional reasons for the reservation of the Eucharist are reiterated and summed up in the document entitled On Holy Communion and the worship of the Eucharistic Mystery Outside Mass (*Eucharistiae Sacramentum*) II, 5:

"The original and primary reason for the reservation of the Eucharist outside Mass is the administration of Viaticum: the distribution of Holy Communion and the adoration of our Lord Jesus Christ present in the Blessed Sacrament are derivative. For in fact the reservation of the sacred species for the benefit of the sick led to the admirable practice of adoring this heavenly food reserved in our churches. This practice of adoration is essentially proper and rational because faith in the real presence of our Lord spontaneously evokes a public and external manifestation of that faith."

GUIDELINES FOR THE RITE OF MARRIAGE

The Dogmatic Constitution on the Church (*Lumen Gentium*) points out:

"Christian married couples help one another to attain holiness in their married life and in the rearing of their children. Hence by reason of their state in life and of their position they have their own gifts in the People of God (cf. 1 Cor. 7:7). From the marriages of Christians there comes the family in which new citizens of human society are born and, by the grace of the Holy Spirit in Baptism, those are made children of God so that the People of God may be perpetuated throughout the centuries. In what might be regarded as the domestic Church, the parents, by word and example, are the first heralds of the faith with regard to their children. They must foster the vocation which is proper to each child, and this with special care if it be to religion" (no. 11).

The Pastoral Constitution on the Church in the Modern World (*Gaudium et Spes*) further illuminates these concepts when it declares:

"Authentic married love is caught up into divine love and is directed and enriched by the redemptive power of Christ and the salvific action of the Church, with the result that the spouses are effectively led to God and are helped and strengthened in their lofty role as fathers and mothers. Spouses, therefore, are fortified and, as it were, consecrated for the duties and dignity of their state by a special sacrament; fulfilling their conjugal and family role by virtue of this sacrament, spouses are penetrated with the spirit of Christ and their whole life is suffused by faith, hope, and charity; thus they increasingly further their own perfection and their mutual sanctification, and together they render glory to God" (no. 48).

It is in the light of these principles which, although traditional in the Church, have received a new impetus through these conciliar pronouncements, that the Council decreed the following:

"The Marriage rite now found in the Roman Ritual is to be revised and enriched so that it will more clearly signify the grace of the sacrament and will emphasize the spouses' duties.

"If any regions use other praiseworthy customs and ceremonies when celebrating the sacrament of Matrimony the sacred Synod earnestly desires that these by all means be retained" (no. 77).

"Matrimony is normally to be celebrated within the Mass after the reading of the gospel and the homily and before 'the prayer of the faithful.' The prayer for the bride, duly amended to remind both spouses of their equal obligation of mutual fidelity, may be said in the vernacular.

"But if the sacrament of Matrimony is celebrated apart from Mass, the epistle and gospel from the nuptial Mass are to be read at the beginning of the rite, and the blessing should always be given to the spouses" (no. 78).

The new rite for the celebration of marriage takes account of the problem of mixed marriages:

"With regard to the liturgical form of the celebration of a mixed marriage, if it is to be taken from the Roman Ritual, use must be made of the ceremonies in the *Rite of Celebration of Marriage* promulgated by our authority, whether it is a question of a marriage between a Catholic and a baptized non-Catholic (39-54) or of a marriage between a Catholic and an unbaptized person (55-66). If, however, the circumstances justify it, a marriage between a Catholic and a baptized non-Catholic can be celebrated, subject to the local Ordinary's consent, according to the rites for the celebration of marriage within Mass (19-38), while respecting the prescription of general law with regard to Eucharistic Communion" Apostolic Letter on Mixed Marriages (*Matrimonia Mixta,* Paul VI, January 7, 1970), no. 11.

GUIDELINES FOR THE RITE OF ANOINTING AND PASTORAL CARE OF THE SICK

The sacrament which has been generally called "extreme unction," is placed in focus by the Dogmatic Constitution on the Church (*Lumen Gentium*):

"By the sacred anointing of the sick and the prayer of the priest the whole Church commends those who are ill to the suffering and glorified Lord that he may raise them up and save them (cf. Jas. 5:14-16). And indeed she exhorts them to contribute to the good of the People of God by freely uniting themselves to the passion and death of Christ (cf. Rom. 8:17; Col. 1:24; Tim. 2:11-12; 1 Pet. 4:13)" (no. 11).

The Council also decreed in the Constitution on the Sacred Liturgy (*Sacrosanctum Concilium*) that:

"'Extreme Unction,' which may also and more fittingly be called 'Anointing of the Sick,' is not a sacrament for those only who are at the point of death. Hence, as soon as anyone of the faithful begins to be in danger of death from sickness or old age, the fitting time for him to receive this sacrament has certainly already arrived" (no. 73).

"In addition to the separate rites for Anointing of the Sick and for Viaticum, a continuous rite shall be prepared in which a sick man is anointed after he has made his confession and before he receives Viaticum" (no. 74).

"The number of the anointings is to be adapted to the occasion, and the prayers which belong to the rite of Anointing are to be revised so as to correspond to the varying conditions of the sick who receive the sacrament" (no. 75).

REVISIONS IN THE RITE OF FUNERALS

It has been pointed out that the rites for Christian burial have stressed gloom rather than the paschal mystery. Christ's resurrection and our own future resurrection should be the theme of Christian death and its expression in the rites of the Church.

The Council, acting along these lines, decree as follows: "Funeral rites should express more clearly the paschal character of Christian death, and should correspond more closely to the circumstances and traditions found in various regions. This also applies to the liturgical color to be used" (no. 81).

"The rite for the Burial of Infants is to be revised, and a special Mass for the occasion should be provided" (no. 82).

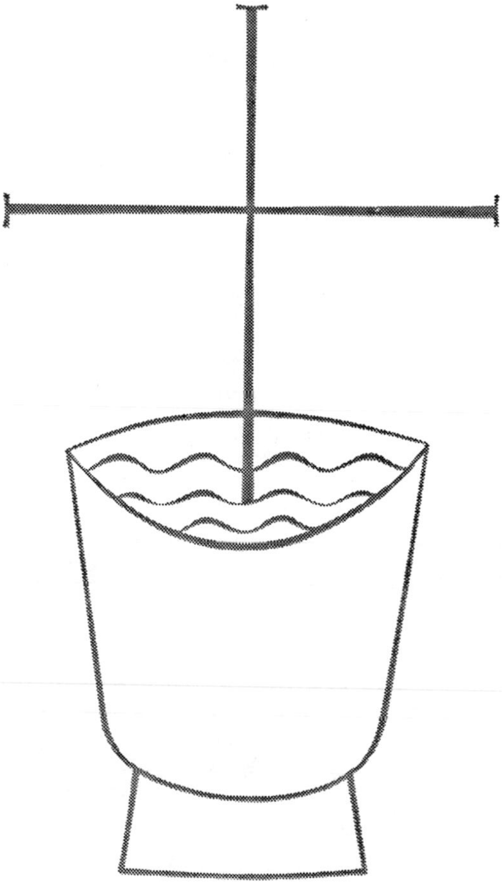

RITE OF CHRISTIAN INITIATION

CHRISTIAN INITIATION

GENERAL INTRODUCTION

1. Through the sacraments of Christian initiation men and women are freed from the power of darkness. With Christ they die, are buried and rise again. They receive the Spirit of adoption which makes them God's sons and daughters and, with the entire people of God, they celebrate the memorial of the Lord's death and resurrection.[1]

2. Through baptism men and women are incorporated into Christ. They are formed into God's people, and they obtain forgiveness of all their sins. They are raised from their natural human condition to the dignity of adopted children.[2] They become a new creation through water and the Holy Spirit. Hence they are called, and are indeed, the children of God.[3]

Signed with the gift of the Spirit in confirmation, Christians more perfectly become the image of their Lord and are filled with the Holy Spirit. They bear witness to him before all the world and eagerly work for the building up of the body of Christ.[4]

Finally they come to the table of the eucharist, to eat the flesh and drink the blood of the Son of Man so that they may have eternal life[5] and show forth the unity of God's people. By offering themselves with Christ, they share in his universal sacrifice: the entire community of the redeemed is offered to God by their high priest.[6] They pray for a greater

[1]II Vatican Council, Decree on the Church's Missionary Activity, *Ad Gentes,* 14.

[2]Romans 8:15; Galatians 4:5; Council of Trent, 6th Session, Decree on Justification, Chapter 4, Denz. 796 (1524).

[3]1 John 3:1.

[4]II Vatican Council, Decree on the Church's Missionary Activity, *Ad Gentes,* 36.

[5]John 6:55.

[6]Saint Augustine, *The City of God,* X, 6: PL 41, 284; II Vatican Council, Dogmatic Constitution on the Church, *Lumen Gentium,* 11; Decree on the Life and Ministry of Priests, *Presbyterorum Ordinis,* 2.

outpouring of the Holy Spirit so that the whole human race may be brought into the unity of God's family.[7]

Thus the three sacraments of Christian initiation closely combine to bring the faithful to the full stature of Christ and to enable them to carry out the mission of the entire people of God in the Church and in the world.[8]

I. DIGNITY OF BAPTISM

3. Baptism is the door to life and to the kingdom of God. Christ offered this first sacrament of the new law to all men that they might have eternal life.[9] He entrusted this sacrament and the gospel to his Church when he told his apostles: "Go, make disciples of all nations, and baptize them in the name of the Father, and of the Son, and of the Holy Spirit."[10] Therefore baptism is, above all, the sacrament of that faith by which men and women, enlightened by the Spirit's grace, respond to the gospel of Christ. That is why the Church believes it is her most basic and necessary duty to inspire all, catechumens, parents of children still to be baptized, and godparents, to that true and living faith by which they adhere to Christ and enter into or confirm their commitment to the new covenant. To accomplish this, the Church prescribes the pastoral instruction of catechumens, the preparation of the children's parents, the celebration of God's word, and the profession of baptismal faith.

4. Further, baptism is the sacrament by which men and women are incorporated into the Church, built into a house where God lives, in the Spirit,[11] into a holy nation and a royal priesthood.[12] It is a sacramental bond of unity linking all who have been signed by it.[13] Because of that unchangeable effect (signified in the Latin liturgy by the anointing of the baptized person with chrism in the presence of God's

[7]II Vatican Council, Dogmatic Constitution on the Church, *Lumen Gentium,* 28.
[8]*Ibid.,* 31.
[9]John 3:5.
[10]Matthew 28:19.
[11]Ephesians 2:22.
[12]1 Peter 2:9.
[13]II Vatican Council, Decree on Ecumenism, *Unitatis Redintegratio,* 22.

people), the rite of baptism is held in highest honor by all Christians. It may never lawfully be repeated once it has been validly celebrated, even if by fellow Christians from whom we are separated.

5. Baptism, the cleansing with water by the power of the living Word,[14] makes us sharers in God's own life[15] and his adopted children.[16] As proclaimed in the prayers for the blessing of the water, baptism is a cleansing water of rebirth,[17] which makes us God's children. The blessed Trinity is invoked over those who are to be baptized. Signed in this name, they are consecrated to the Trinity and enter into fellowship with the Father, the Son, and the Holy Spirit. They are prepared for this high dignity and led to it by the scriptural readings, the prayer of the community, and the threefold profession of faith.

6. Far superior to the purifications of the old law, baptism produces all these effects by the power of the mystery of the Lord's passion and resurrection. Those who are baptized are engrafted in the likeness of Christ's death.[18] They are buried with him, they are given life again with him, and with him they rise again.[19] For baptism recalls and effects the paschal mystery itself, because by means of it men and women pass from the death of sin into life. Its celebration, therefore, should reflect the joy of the resurrection, especially when it takes place during the Easter Vigil or on a Sunday.

II. OFFICES AND MINISTRIES OF BAPTISM

7. Christian instruction and the preparation for baptism are a vital concern of God's people, the Church, which hands on and nourishes the faith it has received from the Apostles. Through the ministry of the Church, adults are called by the Holy Spirit to the gospel, and infants are baptized and brought up in this faith. Therefore it is most important that catechists and other lay people should work with priests and deacons in making preparations for baptism. In the actual celebration, the people of God (represented not only by the

[14]Ephesians 5:26.
[15]2 Peter 1:4.
[16]Romans 8:15; Galatians, 4:5.
[17]Titus 3:5.
[18]Romans 6:4-5.
[19]Ephesians 2:6.

parents, godparents and relatives, but also, as far as possible, by friends, neighbors, and some members of the local church) should take an active part. Thus they will show their common faith and express their joy as the newly baptized are received into the community of the Church.

8. It is a very ancient custom of the Church that an adult is not admitted to baptism without a godparent, a member of the Christian community who will assist him at least in the final preparation for baptism and after baptism will help him persevere in the faith and in his life as a Christian.

In the baptism of children too, the godparent should be present to be added spiritually to the immediate family of the one to be baptized and to represent Mother Church. As occasion offers, he will be ready to help the parents bring up their child to profess the faith and to show this by living it.

9. At least in the final rites of the catechumenate and in the actual celebration of baptism, the godparent is present to testify to the faith of the adult candidate or, together with the parents, to profess the Church's faith, in which the child is being baptized.

10. Pastors of souls should therefore see to it that the godparent, chosen by the catechumen or by the family, is qualified to carry out his proper liturgical functions as specified in no. 9 above. The godparent should:
1) be mature enough to undertake this responsibility;
2) have received the three sacraments of initiation, baptism, confirmation, and the eucharist;
3) be a member of the Catholic Church, canonically free to carry out this office. A baptized and believing Christian from a separated church or community may act as a godparent or Christian witness along with a Catholic godparent, at the request of the parents and in accordance with the norms for various ecumenical cases.

11. The ordinary ministers of baptism are bishops, presbyters, and deacons. At every celebration of this sacrament they should remember that they act in the Church in the name of Christ and by the power of the Holy Spirit. They should therefore be diligent in the ministry of the word of God and in the celebration of the sacraments. They must

avoid any action which the faithful can rightly condemn as favoritism.[20]

12. Bishops are the principal dispensers of the mysteries of God and leaders of the entire liturgical life in the church committed to them.[21] They thus direct the conferring of baptism, by which a sharing in the kingly priesthood of Christ is granted.[22] Therefore they should personally celebrate baptism, especially at the Easter Vigil. The preparation and baptism of adults is commended to them in a special way.

13. It is the duty of parish priests to assist the bishop in the instruction and baptism of the adults entrusted to his care, unless the bishop makes other provisions. It is also their duty, with the assistance of catechists or other qualified lay people, to prepare the parents and godparents of children with appropriate pastoral guidance and to administer baptism to the children.

14. Other priests and deacons, since they are cooperators in the ministry of bishops and parish priests, also prepare candidates for baptism and, with the invitation or consent of the bishop or parish priest, confer the sacrament.

15. The celebrant may be assisted by other priests and deacons and also by the laity in those parts which pertain to them, especially if there are many persons to be baptized. This provision is made in various parts of the rite.

16. In imminent danger of death and especially at the moment of death, when no priest or deacon is available, any member of the faithful, indeed anyone with the right intention, may and sometimes must administer baptism. If it is a question only of danger of death, then the sacrament should be administered by a member of the faithful if possible,

[20] II Vatican Council, Constitution on the Sacred Liturgy, *Sacrosanctum Concilium*, 32; Constitution on the Church in the Modern World, *Gaudium et Spes*, 29.

[21] II Vatican Council, Decree on the Bishops' Pastoral Office, *Christus Dominus*, 15.

[22] II Vatican Council, Dogmatic Constitution on the Church, *Lumen Gentium*, 26.

according to the shorter rite (nos. 157-164). Even in this case a small community should be formed to assist at the rite, or at least one or two witnesses should be present if possible.

17. All lay persons, since they belong to the priestly people, and especially parents and, by reason of their work, catechists, obstetricians, women who are employed as family or social workers or as nurses of the sick, as well as physicians and surgeons, should know the proper method of baptizing in cases of necessity. They should be taught by parish priests, deacons, and catechists. Bishops should provide appropriate means within their diocese for such instruction.

III. REQUIREMENTS FOR THE CELEBRATION OF BAPTISM

18. The water used in baptism should be true water, for the sake of the authentic sacramental symbolism. It should be clean, for reasons of health.

19. The baptismal font, or the vessel in which on occasion the water is prepared for the celebration of the sacrament in the sanctuary, should be very clean and attractive.

20. If the climate requires, provision should be made for the water to be heated beforehand.

21. Except in the case of necessity, the priest or deacon should use only water that has been blessed for the rite. The water consecrated at the Easter Vigil should, if possible, be kept and used throughout the Easter season to signify more clearly the relationship between the sacrament of baptism and the paschal mystery. Outside the Easter season, it is desirable that the water be blessed for each occasion, in order that the words of blessing may clearly express the mystery of salvation which the Church recalls and proclaims. If the baptistry is supplied with flowing water, the blessing will be given to the water as it flows.

22. Either the rite of immersion, which is more suitable as a symbol of participation in the death and resurrection of Christ, or the rite of infusion may lawfully be used in the celebration of baptism.

23. The words for baptism in the Latin Church are: "I baptize you in the name of the Father, and of the Son, and of the Holy Spirit."

24. A suitable place for celebrating the liturgy of the word of God should be provided in the baptistry or in the church.

25. The baptistry is the area where the baptismal font flows or has been placed. It should be reserved for the sacrament of baptism, and should be a worthy place for Christians to be reborn in water and the Holy Spirit. It may be situated in a chapel either inside or outside the church, or in some other part of the church easily seen by the faithful; it should be large enough to accommodate a good number of people. After the Easter season, the Easter candle should be given a place of honor in the baptistry, so that when it is lighted for the celebration of baptism, the candles of the newly baptized may easily be lighted from it.

26. In the celebration, the parts of the rite which are to be performed outside the baptistry should be celebrated in different areas of the church which most conveniently suit the size of the congregation and the several stages of the baptismal liturgy. When the baptistry cannot accommodate all the catechumens and the congregation, the parts of the rite which are customarily performed in the baptistry may be transferred to some other suitable area of the church.

27. As far as possible, all recently born babies should be baptized at a common celebration on the same day. Except for a good reason, baptism should not be celebrated more than once on the same day in the same church.

28. Further details concerning the time of baptism of adults and children will be found in the respective rites. The celebration of the sacrament should always suggest its paschal character.

29. Parish priests should carefully and without delay record in the baptismal register the names of those baptized, the minister, parents and godparents, and the place and date of baptism.

IV. ADAPTATIONS BY CONFERENCES OF BISHOPS

30. According to the Constitution of the Sacred Liturgy (no. 63b), it is within the competence of conferences of bishops to compose for their local rituals a section corresponding to this one in the Roman Ritual, adapted to the needs of their respective regions. When this has been reviewed by the Apostolic See, it should be used in the regions for which it was prepared.

In this connection, it is the responsibility of the conferences of bishops:

1) to determine the adaptations, according to no. 39 of the Constitution on the Sacred Liturgy;

2) carefully and prudently to consider what elements of a country's distinctive culture may suitably be admitted into divine worship. Adaptations considered useful or necessary should then be submitted to the Apostolic See, with whose consent they may be introduced;

3) to retain distinctive elements of existing local rituals as long as they conform with the Constitution on the Sacred Liturgy and correspond to contemporary needs; or to modify these elements;

4) to prepare translations of the texts that genuinely reflect the characteristics of various languages and cultures and to add music for the texts when appropriate;

5) to adapt and augment the introduction contained in the Roman Ritual, so that the ministers may fully understand the meaning of the rites and express this effectively in action;

6) to arrange the material in the various editions of the liturgical books prepared under the guidance of the conferences of bishops so that these books may be best suited for pastoral use.

31. As stated in nos. 37-40 and 65 of the Constitution on the Sacred Liturgy, it is the responsibility of the conferences of bishops in mission countries to judge whether certain initiation ceremonies in use among some peoples can be adapted for the rite of Christian baptism and to decide whether these rites are to be incorporated into it.

32. When the Roman Ritual for baptism provides a choice of several formulas, local rituals may add other formulas of the same kind.

33. The celebration of baptism is greatly enhanced by the use of song. It stimulates a sense of unity among those present, it gives warmth to their common prayer, and it expresses the joy of Easter. Conferences of bishops should encourage and help musical specialists to compose settings for texts suitable for congregational singing at baptism.

V. ADAPTATIONS BY THE MINISTER OF BAPTISM

34. The minister, taking into account existing circumstances and needs, as well as the wishes of the faithful, should freely use the various choices allowed in the rite.

35. In addition to the adaptations which are provided in the Roman Ritual for the dialogue and blessings, the minister may make other adaptations for special circumstances. These adaptations will be indicated more fully in the introduction to the rites of baptism for adults and for children.

RITE OF CHRISTIAN INITIATION OF ADULTS

Second Stage: Rite of Election or Enrollment of Names (133-142)

I Presentation of the Candidates (143-145)

II Examination of Candidates (146)

III Admission or Election (147)

A Prayer for the Elect (148-149)

B Dismissal of the Elect (150)

IV Celebration of the Eucharist (151)

V Period of Purification and Enlightment or Illumination (152-153)

A Scrutinies and Presentations (153)

B Scrutines (154-159)

First Scrutiny (160)
- *Homily (161)*
- *Prayer in Silence (162)*
- *Prayer for the Elect (163)*
- *Exorcism (164)*
- *Dismissal of the Elect (165)*
- *Celebration of the Eucharist (166)*

Second Scrutiny (167)
- *Homily and Prayer in Silence (168-169)*
- *Prayer for the Elect (170)*
- *Exorcism (171)*
- *Dismissal of the Elect (172)*
- *Celebration of the Eucharist (173)*

Third Scrutiny (174)
- *Homily (175)*
- *Prayer in Silence (176)*
- *Prayer for the Elect (177)*
- *Exorcism (178)*
- *Dismissal of the Elect (179)*
- *Celebration of the Eucharist (180)*

C The Presentations (181-182)

Presentation of the Profession of Faith (183-184)
- *Readings and Homily (185)*
- *Presentation of the Profession of Faith (186)*
- *Prayer over the Elect (187)*

Presentation of the Lord's Prayer (188-189)
Readings and Homily (190)
Gospel (191)
Prayer over the Elect (192)

D Preparatory Rites (193)
Recitation of the Profession of Faith (194-195)
Readings and Homily (196-197)
Prayer for the Recitation of the Profession of Faith (198)
Recitation of the Profession of Faith (199)
Rite of Ephphetha or Opening of Ears and Mouth (200-201)
The Choosing of a Christian Name (203)
Reading (204)
Choosing a Name (205)
Anointing with the Oil of Catechumens (206-207)

Third Stage: Celebration of the Sacraments of Initiation (208-209)

I Celebration of Baptism (210-212)

A Instruction by the Celebrant (213)

B Litany (214)

C Blessing the Water (215-216)

D Renunciation (217)

E Anointing with the Oil of Catechumens (218)

F Profession of Faith (219)

G Rite of Baptism (220-222)

II Explanatory Rites (223)

A Anointing after Baptism (224)

B Clothing with the White Garment (225)

C Presentation of the Lighted Candle (226)

III Celebration of Confirmation (227-231)

IV Celebration of the Eucharist (232-234)

V The Period of Post-Baptismal Catechesis or Mystagogia (235-239)

CHAPTER II
SIMPLE RITE OF ADULT INITIATION (240-244)

I. Rite of Reception (245-250)

A. Entry into the Church (251)

II. Liturgy of the Word (252)

A. Readings and Homily (253)

B. Prayer and Penitential Rite (254)

C. Prayer of Exorcism and Anointing of the Catechumen (255-256)

III. Celebration of Baptism

A. Celebrant's Instruction (257)

B. Blessing the Water (258)

C. Renunciation (259)

D. Profession of Faith (260)

E. Rite of Baptism (261-262)

IV. Explanatory Rites

A. Anointing after Baptism (263)

B. Clothing with the White Garment (264)

C. Presentation of the Lighted Candle (265)

V. Celebration of Confirmation (266-270)

VI. Celebration of the Eucharist (271-277)

CHAPTER III
SHORT RITE OF ADULT INITIATION IN PROXIMATE DANGER OF DEATH OR AT THE POINT OF DEATH (278-282)

I. Beginning of the Rite (283-284)

II. Dialogue (285-287)

III. Prayer (288-289)

V. Anointing of Catechumens or Imposition of Hands (340)

VI. Dismissal of the Catechumens (341-342)

Third Stage: Celebration of the Sacraments of Initiation (343-346)

I. Celebration of Baptism (347)

A. Celebrant's Instruction (348)

B. Blessing the Water (349-350)

C. Profession of Faith by the Community (351)

D. Profession of Faith by the Children (352)

E. Renunciation of Sin (353)

F. Anointing with the Oil of Catechumens (354)

G. Profession of Faith (355)

H. Rite of Baptism (356-357)

I. Explanatory Rites

1. Anointing after Baptism (358)
2. Clothing with the White Garment (359)
3. Presentation of the Lighted Candle (360)

II. Celebration of Confirmation (361-365)

III. Celebration of the Eucharist (366-368)

IV. Period of Postbaptismal Catechesis or Mystagogia (369)

CHAPTER VI
VARIOUS TEXTS FOR USE IN THE CELEBRATION OF ADULT INITIATION (370-392)

SACRED CONGREGATION FOR DIVINE WORSHIP

Prot. n. 15/72

DECREE

The Second Vatican Council prescribed the revision of the rite of baptism of adults and decreed that the catechumenate for adults in several stages should be restored. This was to be done so that the period of the catechumenate, a period of appropriate formation, might be sanctified by liturgical rites celebrated at various times. In addition the council decreed that both the solemn and simple rites of adult baptism should be revised in the light of the restored catechumenate.

In observance of these decrees, the Congregation for Divine Worship prepared a new rite for the Christian initiation of adults, which has been approved by Pope Paul VI. The congregation has published this rite and declares the present edition to be the typical edition, to replace the rite of baptism of adults now in the Roman Ritual. It likewise decrees that this new rite may be used at once in Latin and in the vernacular from the day to be indicated by the episcopal conference after it has prepared a translation and had it confirmed by the Apostolic See.

Anything to the contrary notwithstanding.

Congregation for Divine Worship, January 6, 1972, the feast of the Epiphany.

Arturo Cardinal Tabera
Prefect

+ Annibale Bugnini
Secretary

CHRISTIAN INITIATION OF ADULTS

INTRODUCTION

1. The rite of Christian initiation described below is intended for adults. They hear the preaching of the mystery of Christ, the Holy Spirit opens their hearts, and they freely and knowingly seek the living God and enter the path of faith and conversion. By God's help, they will be strengthened spiritually in their preparation and at the proper time they will receive the sacraments fruitfully.

2. This order includes not only the celebration of the sacraments of baptism, confirmation, and the eucharist, but also all the rites of the catechumenate. Approved by the ancient practice of the Church and adapted to contemporary missionary work throughout the world, this catechumenate was so widely requested that the Second Vatican Council decreed its restoration, revision, and accommodation to local traditions.[1]

3. In order to be better suited to the work of the Church and to the circumstances of individuals, parishes, and missions, the rite of initiation first gives the complete or common form, intended for the preparation of a large number of people (see nos. 68-239). By simple changes, pastors may adapt this form for one person. Then, for special cases, there is a simple form, which may be celebrated on a single occasion (see nos. 240-273) or in several parts (see nos. 274-277), as well as a brief form for those in danger of death (see nos. 278-292).

I. STRUCTURE OF THE INITIATION OF ADULTS

4. The initiation of catechumens takes place step by step in the midst of the community of the faithful. Together with the catechumens, the faithful reflect upon the value of the paschal mystery, renew their own conversion, and by their

[1]See Second Vatican Council, Constitution on the Sacret Liturgy, *Sacrosanctum Concilium* [= L], nos. 64-66; Decree on the Missionary Activity of the Church, *Ad gentes* [= M], no. 14; Decree on the Pastoral Office of Bishops, *Christus Dominus* [=EP], no. 14

example lead the catechumens to obey the Holy Spirit more generously.

5. The rite of initiation is suited to the spiritual journey of adults, which varies according to the many forms of God's grace, the free cooperation of the individuals, the action of the Church, and the circumstances of time and place.

6. On this journey, besides the period for making inquiry and maturing (see no. 7, below), there are stages or steps by which the catechumen moves forward, as it were, through a gateway or up another step.

a) First stage: at the point of initial conversion, he wishes to become a Christian and is accepted as a catechumen by the Church.

b) Second stage: when his faith has grown and the catechumenate is almost completed, he is admitted to a more profound preparation for the sacraments.

c) Third stage: after the spiritual preparation is completed, he receives the sacraments by which a Christian is initiated.

These three stages, steps, or gateways are to be considered as major, more serious moments of initiation and are marked by liturgical rites: the first by the rite of becoming a catechumen, the second by the election or choice, and the third by the celebration of the sacraments.

7. These stages lead to periods of investigation and maturation, or the latter prepare for the stages.

a) The first period consists of inquiry by the candidate and evangelization and the precatechumenate on the part of the Church. It ends with entrance into the order of catechumens.

b) The second period, which begins with this entrance into the order of catechumens and may last for several years, includes catechesis and the rites connected with catechesis. It is completed on the day of election.

c) The third period, shorter in length, ordinarily occupies the Lenten preparation for the Easter celebration and the sacraments. It is a time of purification and enlightenment or "illumination."

d) The final period goes through the whole Easter season and is called the post-baptismal catechesis or "mystagogia." It is a time for deepening the Christian experience, for gaining spiritual fruit, and for entering more closely into the life and unity of the community of the faithful.

Thus there are four continuous periods:

—the precatechumenate, a time for hearing the first preaching of the Gospel;

—the catechumenate, set aside for a complete catechesis;

—the period of purification and enlightenment or illumination (Lent) for a more profound spiritual preparation; and

—the postbaptismal catechesis or mystagogia (Easter season), marked with the new experience of the sacraments and of the Christian community.

8. The whole initiation has a paschal character, since the initiation of Christians is the first sacramental sharing in the death and rising of Christ and since, moreover, the time of purification and enlightenment or illumination ordinarily takes place during Lent,[2] with the postbaptismal catechesis or mystagogia during the Easter season. In this way Lent achieves its full force as a profound preparation of the elect, and the Easter Vigil is considered the proper time for the sacraments of initiation.[3] Because of pastoral needs, however, the sacraments of initiation may be celebrated outside these seasons.

A. EVANGELIZATION AND PRECATECHUMENATE

9. Although the rite of initiation begins with admission to the catechumenate, the preceding period or precatechumenate is of great importance and ordinarily should not be omitted. It is a time of evangelization: in faith and constancy the living God is proclaimed, as is Jesus Christ, whom he sent for the salvation of all men. Thus those who are not yet Christians, their hearts opened by the Holy Spirit, may believe and be freely converted to the Lord. They sincerely adhere to him who is the way, the truth, and the life, and who fulfills all their spiritual expectations, indeed goes far beyond them.[4]

[2]See L 109.
[3]This derogates from canon 790 of the Code of Canon Law.
[4]M 13.

10. From evangelization, conducted with the help of God, come faith and initial conversion, by which each one feels himself called away from sin and drawn toward the mystery of God's love. The whole period of the precatechumenate is set aside for this evangelization, so that the true desire of following Christ and seeking baptism may mature.

11. During this time, catechists, deacons and priests, as well as lay persons, suitably explain the Gospel to the candidates. They receive the help they are looking for, so that they may cooperate with God's grace with a pure and certain intention and may meet with the families and communities of Christians with greater ease.

12. In addition to the evangelization that is proper to this period, the episcopal conferences may provide, if necessary and according to local circumstances, a method to receive interested inquirers ("sympathizers"), those who, even if they do not fully believe, show an inclination toward the Christian faith.

1) Such a reception, which is optional and will be carried out without any rite, expresses the inquirers' sound intention rather than faith.

2) The reception will be adapted to local conditions and opportunities. Some candidates need to know and experience the spirit of Christians in a special way. For others, whose catechumenate has been delayed for various reasons, this first external act by them and the community is appropriate.

3) The reception should be carried out at meetings and gatherings of the local community, on a suitable occasion of friendly exchange. The inquirer or sympathizer is presented by a friend, and then he is welcomed and received by the priest or by some other appropriate and worthy member of the community.

13. During the period of the precatechumenate, pastors should help the inquirers with suitable prayers.

B. CATECHUMENATE

14. The rite of becoming a catechumen is of very great importance. Assembling publicly for the first time, the can-

didates make their intention known to the Church; the Church, carrying out its apostolic mission, admits those who intend to become members. God showers his grace on them, since this celebration manifests their desire publicly and the Church expresses their reception and first consecration.

15. Before this step is taken, the candidates are required to be grounded in the basic fundamentals of the spiritual life and Christian teaching:[5] the faith first conceived at the time of the precatechumentate; the initial conversion and desire to change one's life and to enter into contact with God in Christ; thus the first sense of repentance and the practice of calling on God and praying; and the first experience of the society and spirit of Christians.

16. With the help of the sponsors (see no. 42, below), catechists, and deacons, it is the responsibility of pastors to judge the external indications of these dispositions.[6] It is also their duty, in view of the power of sacraments already validly received (see General Introduction, no. 4), to see that a baptized person is not baptized again for any reason whatever.

17. After the celebration of the rite, the names are written at once in the register of catechumens, along with the names of the minister and sponsors and the date and place of admission.

18. From this time on the catechumens, who have been welcomed by the Church with a mother's love and concern, are joined to the Church and are part of the household of Christ.[7] They are nourished by the Church on the word of God and helped by liturgical celebrations. They should be eager, then, to take part in the liturgy of the word and to receive blessings and sacramentals. When two catechumens marry or when a catechumen marries an unbaptized person, the appropriate rite is celebrated.[8] One who dies during the catechumenate receives a Christian burial.

[5]See M 14.
[6]M 13.
[7]See Second Vatican Council, Dogmatic Constitution on the Church, *Lumen gentium* [=E], no. 14; M 14.
[8]*Rite of Marriage,* nos. 55-56.

19. The catechumenate is an extended period during which the candidates are given pastoral formation and are trained by suitable discipline.[9] In this way, the dispositions manifested at the entrance rite into the catechumenate are brought to maturity. This is achieved in four ways:

1) A fitting formation by priests, deacons, or catechists and other lay persons, given in stages and presented integrally, accommodated to the liturgical year and enriched by celebrations of the word, leads the catechumens to a suitable knowledge of dogmas and precepts and also to an intimate understanding of the mystery of salvation in which they desire to share.

2) Familiar with living the Christian way of life and helped by the example and support of sponsors and godparents and the whole community of the faithful, the catechumens will learn to pray to God more easily, to witness to the faith, to be constant in the expectation of Christ in all things, to follow supernatural inspiration in their deeds, and to exercise charity toward neighbors to the point of self-renunciation. Thus formed, "new converts set out on a spiritual journey. Already sharing through faith in the mystery of Christ's death and resurrection, they pass from the old man to the new one made perfect in Christ. This transition, which brings with it a progressive change of outlook and morals, should become evident together with its social consequences and should be gradually developed during the time of the catechumenate. Since the Lord in whom he believes is a sign of contradiction, the convert often experiences human divisions and separations, but he also tastes the joy which God gives without measure."[10]

3) By suitable liturgical rites, Mother Church helps the catechumens on their journey, cleanses them little by little, and strengthens them with God's blessing. Celebrations of the word are encouraged for their benefit, and they may also attend the liturgy of the word with the faithful, thus better preparing themselves for participation in the eucharist in time to come. Ordinarily, however, when they are present in the assembly of the faithful, they should be dismissed in a friendly manner before the eucharistic celebration begins, unless there are difficulties; they must await their baptism

[9]See M 14.
[10]See M 13.

which will bring them into the priestly people and allow them to participate in the Christian worship of the new covenant.

4) Since the Church's life is apostolic, catechumens should also learn how to work actively with others to spread the Gospel and build up the Church by the testimony of their lives and the profession of their faith.[11]

20. The period of time suitable for the catechumenate depends on the grace of God and on various circumstances, such as the plan of instruction to be given, the number of catechists, deacons, and priests, the cooperation of the individual catechumens, the means necessary to reach the place of the catechumenate and to live there, and the help of the local community. Nothing can be determined a priori. The bishop has the responsibility of setting the period of time and directing the discipline of the catechumenate. After considering the conditions of their people and region,[12] episcopal conferences should regulate this matter more specifically.

C. PERIOD OF PURIFICATION AND ENLIGHTENMENT

21. The time of purification and enlightenment or illumination of the catechumens customarily coincides with Lent; both in its liturgy and in its liturgical catechesis, Lent is a memorial or a preparation for baptism and a time of penance.[13] It renews the community of the faithful together with the catechumens and makes them ready to celebrate the paschal mystery which the sacraments of initiation apply to each individual.[14]

22. The second stage of initiation begins the period of purification and enlightenment or illumination, marked by a more intense preparation of heart and spirit. At this stage the Church makes the "election," that is, the choice and admission of the catechumens who because of their dispositions are worthy to take part in the next celebration of the sacraments of initiation. This stage is called election because the admission made by the Church is founded in the elec-

[11]See M 14.
[12]See L 64.
[13]L 109.
[14]See M 14.

tion by God, in whose name the Church acts. It is also called the enrollment or inscription of names because the candidates, as a pledge of fidelity, write their names in the book of the elect.

23. Before the election is celebrated, the candidates are expected to have a conversion of mind and morals, a sufficient knowledge of Christian teaching, and a sense of faith and charity; a consideration of their worthiness is also required. Later, in the actual celebration of the rite, the manifestation of their intention and the decision of the bishop or his delegate should take place in the presence of the community. It is thus clear that the election, which enjoys such great solemnity, is the turning point in the whole catechumenate.

24. From the day of their election and admission, catechumens are called the "elect." They are also called *competentes*, mature catechumens who strive together or contend to receive the sacraments of Christ and the gift of the Holy Spirit. They are also called the enlightened or illumined, because baptism itself is called enlightenment or illumination and by baptism the neophytes are illumined in the light of faith. In our day, other terms may be used which are better adapted to common understanding according to the nature of the languages and civil cultures of various regions.

25. During this period, a more intense preparation of the mind, which involves spiritual recollection more than catechesis, is intended to purify minds and hearts by the examination of conscience and by repentance and also to enlighten those minds and hearts by a deeper knowledge of Christ the Savior. This is accomplished in various rites, especially in the scrutinies and presentations.

1) The scrutinies, which are celebrated solemnly on Sundays, have a twofold purpose: revealing anything that is weak, defective, or sinful in the hearts of the elect, so that it may be healed, and revealing what is upright, strong, and holy, so that it may be strengthened. The scrutinies are intended to free them from sin and the devil and to give them strength in Christ, who is the way, the truth, and the life for his chosen ones.

2) The presentations, by which the Church hands on to the elect its ancient documents of faith and prayer (the profession of faith or the creed and the Lord's Prayer), lead them to enlightenment or illumination. The profession of faith recalls the wonderful work of God for the salvation of man; it deepens the faith and joy of the elect. In the Lord's Prayer, they acknowledge more firmly the new spirit of sonship by which they will call God their Father, especially in the midst of the congregation assembled for the eucharist.

26. In the immediate preparation of the sacraments:

1) The elect should be instructed that on Holy Saturday they should rest from their ordinary work as far as possible, spend the time in prayer and recollection of mind, and fast according to their ability.[15]

2) That same day, if there is a meeting of the elect, some of the immediately preparatory rites may be celebrated, such as the recitation of the profession of faith, the ephphetha or opening of ears and mouth, the choosing of a Christian name, and, if it is to be done, the anointing with the oil of catechumens.

D. SACRAMENTS OF INITIATION

27. The sacraments of baptism, confirmation, and the eucharist are the final stage in which the elect come forward and, with their sins forgiven, are admitted into the people of God, receive the adoption of the sons of God, and are led by the Holy Spirit into the promised fullness of time and, in the eucharistic sacrifice and meal, to the banquet of the Kingdom of God.

a) Celebration of the Baptism of Adults

28. The celebration of baptism, which reaches its high point at the washing with water in the name of the Holy Trinity, is prepared for by the blessing of water and the profession of faith, which are closely connected with the rite of washing with water.

29. The blessing of water recalls the dispensation of the

[15]See L 110.

paschal mystery and the choice of water for the sacramental operation of the mystery. The Holy Trinity is called upon for the first time, water is given a religious meaning, and the working of the divine mystery is shown before all.

30. The rites of the renunciation of sin and the profession of faith also recall, in the active faith of those to be baptized, the same paschal mystery which has been recalled in the blessing of water and briefly professed by the celebrant in the words of baptism. Adults are not saved unless they come forward of their own accord and are willing to accept the gift of God by faith. Baptism is the sacrament of faith, not only the faith of the Church, but also the candidates' own faith, and it is expected that it will be an active faith in them. When they are baptized, they should not receive such a sacrament passively, for of their own will they enter into a covenant with Christ, rejecting their errors and adhering to the true God.

31. As soon as they have professed their living faith in the paschal mystery of Christ, they come forward to receive that mystery expressed in the washing with water. After they have professed faith in the Holy Trinity, the Trinity, called on by the celebrant, brings about the numbering of the elect among the adopted children of God and unites them to his people.

32. Since the washing with water is a sign of mystical sharing in the death and rising of Christ, by which believers in his name die to sin and rise to eternal life, it achieves its full importance in the celebration of baptism. The rite of immersion or of infusion or of pouring is chosen according to what is more suitable in individual cases, so that, according to various traditions and circumstances, it may be understood that the washing is not merely a rite of purification but a sacrament of union with Christ.

33. The anointing with chrism after baptism is a sign of the royal priesthood of the baptized and their enrollment in the fellowship of the people of God. The white robe is a symbol of their new dignity, and the lighted candle shows their vocation of living as befits the children of light.

b) Celebration of the Confirmation of Adults

34. According to the ancient practice maintained in the Roman liturgy, an adult is not to be baptized unless he receives confirmation immediately afterward (see no. 44), provided no serious obstacles exist. This connection signifies the unity of the paschal mystery, the close relationship between the mission of the Son and the pouring out of the Holy Spirit, and the joint celebration of the sacraments by which the Son and the Spirit come with the Father upon those who are baptized.

35. Confirmation is celebrated after the complementary rites of baptism; the postbaptismal anointing is omitted (no. 224).

c) First Sharing in the Eucharist by the Newly Baptized

36. Finally the eucharist is celebrated and for the first time the neophytes have the full right to take part. This is the culminating point of their initiation. In the eucharist, the neophytes who have received the dignity of the royal priesthood have an active part in the general intercessions (prayer of the faithful) and, as far as possible, in the rite of bringing the offerings to the altar. With the whole community they take part in the action of the sacrifice and they say the Lord's Prayer, thus showing the spirit of adoption as God's children which they have received in baptism. Then, by receiving the body that was handed over and the blood that was shed, they confirm the gifts they have received and acquire a foretaste of eternal things.

E. PERIOD OF POSTBAPTISMAL CATECHESIS OR MYSTAGOGIA

37. After this last stage has been completed, the community and the neophytes move forward together, meditating on the Gospel, sharing in the eucharist, and performing works of charity. In this way they understand the paschal mystery more fully and bring it into their lives more and more. The period of postbaptismal catechesis or mystagogia is the final period of initiation of the newly baptized.

38. A fuller, more fruitful understanding of the "mysteries" is acquired by the newness of the account given to the

neophytes and especially by their experience of receiving the sacraments. They have been renewed in mind, have tasted more intimately the good word of God, have shared in the Holy Spirit, and have come to discover the goodness of the Lord. From this experience, which is proper to the Christian and is increased by the way he lives, they draw a new sense of the faith, the Church, and the world.

39. This new frequenting of the sacraments enlightens the neophytes' understanding of the holy scriptures and also increases their knowledge of men and develops the experience in the community itself. As a result, the relationship of the neophyte with the rest of the faithful becomes easier and more beneficial. The time of postbaptismal catechesis is of great importance so that the neophytes, helped by their sponsors, may enter into a closer relationship with the faithful and bring them renewed vision and a new impetus.

40. Since the nature and force proper to this period came from the new, personal experience of the sacraments and of the community, the main place for the postbaptismal catechesis or mystagogia will be the Masses for neophytes, that is, the Sunday Masses of the Easter season. In these celebrations, besides meeting with the community and sharing in the mysteries, the newly baptized will find the readings of the Lectionary appropriate for them, especially the readings, of Year A. For this reason, the whole local community should be invited to these Masses along with the neophytes and their sponsors. The texts for the Masses may be used even when the initiation is celebrated outside the usual time.

II. MINISTRIES AND OFFICES

41. Besides what is explained in the General Introduction (no. 7), the people of God, represented by the local church, should always understand and show that the initiation of adults is its concern and the business of all the baptized.[16]

Therefore the community must always be ready to fulfill its apostolic vocation by giving help to those who need Christ. In the various circumstances of daily life, as in the aposto-

[16]See M 14.

late, each disciple of Christ has the obligation of spreading the faith according to his capability.[17] Hence, the community must help the candidates and catechumens throughout their whole period of initiation, during the precatechumenate, the catechumenate, and the period of postbaptismal catechesis or mystagogia. In particular:

1) During the time of evangelization and the precatechumenate, the faithful should remember that the apostolate of the Church and all its members is directed first to making known to the world the message of Christ through their words and deeds and to communicating his grace.[18] Therefore they will be ready to open up the spirit of the Christian community to the candidates, to invite them into their families, to engage them in private conversation, and to invite them to some community gatherings.

2) The faithful should be present at the celebration of the catechumenate whenever possible and share actively in the responses, prayer, singing, and acclamations.

3) On the day of election, when the community is to be enlarged, the faithful should be sure to give honest and prudent testimony about the catechumens.

4) During Lent, the time of purification and enlightenment or illumination, the faithful should be present at and attentive to the rites of the scrutinies and presentations and give the catechumens the example of their own renewal in the spirit of penance, faith, and charity. At the Easter Vigil, they should renew their own baptismal promises in their hearts.

5) The faithful should take part in the Masses for the newly baptized during the period immediately after baptism, welcome them with charity, and help them to sense the joy of belonging to the community of the baptized.

42. The candidate should be accompanied by a sponsor when he asks to be admitted as a catechumen. This sponsor is to be a man or woman who knows the candidate, helps him, and witnesses to his morals, faith, and intention. It may happen that this sponsor is not to fulfill the function of godparent in the period of purification and enlightenment or illumination and in the period of postbaptismal catechesis or

[17]See E 17.
[18]See Second Vatican Council, decree *Apostolicam Actuositatem*, no. 6.

mystagogia. In this case, another person takes on this responsibility.

43. The godparent,[19] however, who is close to the candidate because of his example, character, and friendship, is delegated by the local Christian community and approved by the priest. He accompanies the candidate on the day of election, in the celebration of the sacraments, and during the period of postbaptismal catechesis. It is his responsibility to show the catechumen in a friendly way the place of the Gospel in his own life and in society, to help him in doubts and anxieties, to give public testimony for him, and to watch over the progress of his baptismal life. Already a friend before the election, this person exercises his office publicly from the day of election when he gives his testimony about the catechumen before the community. His responsibility remains important when the neophyte has received the sacraments and needs to be helped to remain faithful to his baptismal promises.

44. It is for the bishop,[20] in person or through his delegate, to set up, regulate, and promote the pastoral formation of catechumens and to admit the candidates to their election and to the sacraments. It is to be hoped that, if possible, presiding at the Lenten liturgy, he will himself celebrate the rite of election and, at the Easter Vigil, the sacraments of initiation. Finally, as a part of his pastoral care, the bishop should appoint catechists who are truly worthy and properly prepared to celebrate the minor exorcisms.[21]

45. Besides the usual ministry exercised in any celebration of baptism, confirmation, and the eucharist,[22] presbyters have the responsibility of attending to the pastoral and personal care of the catechumens,[23] especially those who seem hesitant and weak, in order to provide for their catechesis with the help of deacons and catechists. They also are to approve the choice of godparents and gladly listen to them and help them. Finally, presbyters should be diligent in the correct celebration and adaptation of the rites

[19]See General Introduction, no. 8.
[20]See L 64.
[21]This abrogates Canon 1153 of the Code of Canon Law.
[22]See General Introduction, nos. 13-15.
[23]See Second Vatican Council, decree *Presbyterorum Ordinis*, no. 6.

throughout the entire rite of Christian initiation (see no. 67, below).

46. When the bishop is absent, the presbyter who baptizes an adult or child of catechetical age should also confer confirmation, unless this sacrament is to be given at another time (see no. 56).[24]

When there are very many to be confirmed, the minister of the sacrament of confirmation may associate other presbyters with himself in its administration.

It is necessary that these presbyters:

a) have a particular function or office in the diocese, namely, that of vicars general, episcopal vicars or delegates, district or regional vicars, or those who by mandate of the ordinary hold equivalent offices;

b) be the parish pastors of the places where confirmation is celebrated or pastors of the places where the candidates belong, or presbyters who did special work in this catechetical preparation.[25]

47. Deacons who are available should be ready to help. If the episcopal conference judges it opportune to have permanent deacons, it should make provision that their number is adequate to permit the stages, periods, and exercises of the catechumenate to take place everywhere when required by pastoral needs.[26]

48. The office of catechists is important for the progress of the catechumens and for the growth of the community. As often as possible, they should have an active part in the rites. When they are teaching, they should see that their instruction is filled with the spirit of the Gospel, adapted to the liturgical signs and the course of the Church year, and enriched by local traditions as far as possible. When so delegated by the bishop, they may perform minor exorcisms (no. 44) and blessings,[27] as mentioned in the Ritual nos. 113-124.

[24]See *Rite of Confirmation*, Introduction, no. 76.
[25]See *Rite of Marriage*, nos. 55-56.
[26]See E 26; M 16.
[27]See L 79.

III. TIME AND PLACE OF INITIATION

49. Ordinarily pastors should make use of the rite of initiation in such a way that the sacraments will be celebrated at the Easter Vigil and the election will take place on the First Sunday of Lent. The other rites should be arranged as explained above (nos. 6-8, 14-40). For serious pastoral needs, however, the plan of the entire rite of initiation may be differently arranged, as indicated below (nos. 58-62).

A. LAWFUL OR CUSTOMARY TIME

50. The following should be noted about the time of celebrating the rite of becoming catechumens:

1) It should not be too early, but should be delayed until the candidates, according to their own dispositions and situation, have had sufficient time to conceive an elementary faith and to show the first signs of conversion (no. 20, above).

2) When the number of candidates is unusually large, the rite should be postponed until the group is large enough for catechesis and the liturgical rites.

3) Two days or, if necessary, three days or period of the year should be set aside for the usual celebration of this rite.

51. The rite of election or enrollment of names should usually be celebrated on the First Sunday of Lent. It may be anticipated somewhat or even celebrated during the week.

52. The scrutinies should take place on the Third, Fourth and Fifth Sundays of Lent or if necessary, on the other Sundays of Lent or even on more suitable weekdays. Three scrutinies should be celebrated, but for serious reasons the bishop may dispense from one of them or even from two in extraordinary circumstances. When time is lacking and the election is anticipated, the first scrutiny may also be held earlier. But in this case, the time of purification and enlightenment or illumination must not be extended beyond eight weeks.

53. By ancient usage, the presentations, since they take place after the scrutinies, belong to the same period of purification and enlightenment or illumination. They are

celebrated during the week. The profession of faith is given during the week after the first scrutiny, and the Lord's Prayer after the third scrutiny. For pastoral reasons, however, to enrich the liturgy of the period of the catchumenate, the presentations may be transferred and celebrated during the catechumenate as rites of transition (see nos. 125-126).

54. Only Holy Saturday, when the elect refrain from work (see no. 26) and spend their time in recollection, the various immediately preparatory rites may be performed: The recitation of the creed, the ephphetha or opening of ears and mouth, the choosing of a Christian name, and even the anointing with the oil of catechumens (see nos. 193-207).

55. The sacraments of the initiation of adults should be celebrated at the Easter Vigil (see nos. 8, 49). If there are very many catechumens, the majority receive the sacraments that night, and the rest may be postponed to the days within the octave of Easter, when they receive the sacraments either in the principal churches or in secondary stations. In this case, either the Mass of the day or the ritual Mass for Christian initiation should be used, with readings from the Easter Vigil.

56. In certain cases, confirmation may be postponed until near the end of the period of postbaptismal catechesis or mystagogia, for example, Pentecost Sunday (see no. 237).

57. The Masses for neophytes are celebrated on all the Sundays after the First Sunday of Easter. The community, the newly baptized and their godparents are urgently invited to participate (see no. 40).

B. OUTSIDE THE CUSTOMARY TIMES

58. The rite of initiation is normally arranged so that the sacraments will be celebrated during the Easter Vigil. Because of unusual circumstances and pastoral needs, however, the rite of election and the period of purification and enlightenment or illumination may be held outside Lent and the sacraments may be celebrated outside the Vigil or Easter Sunday. Even in ordinary circumstances, but only for serious pastoral needs (for example, if there is a very large number of persons to be baptized), apart from the plan of

initiation carried on as usual during Lent, another time for celebrating the sacraments of initiation may be chosen, particularly in the Easter season. In these cases, although the times of the liturgical year are changed, the arrangement of the whole rite with its appropriate intervals remains the same. Adaptations should be made as follows.

59. As far as possible, the sacraments of initiation are celebrated on Sunday, using the Sunday Mass or the proper ritual Mass (see no. 55).

60. The rite of becoming catechumens takes place at a suitable time, as explained in no. 50.

61. The election is celebrated almost six weeks before the sacraments of initiation so that there is sufficient time for the scrutinies and the presentations. Care should be taken that the celebration of the election does not fall on a solemnity of the liturgical year. The readings given in the ritual should be used, and the Mass of the day or the ritual Mass will be celebrated.

62. The scrutinies should not be celebrated on solemnities, but on Sundays or even on weekdays, observing the usual intervals and using the readings given in the ritual. The Mass of the day or the ritual Mass will be celebrated (see no. 374a).

C. PLACES FOR THE RITE OF INITIATION

63. The rites should take place in suitable locations, as indicated in the ritual. Consideration should be given to special needs which arise in secondary stations of missionary regions.

IV. ADAPTATIONS BY EPISCOPAL CONFERENCES WHICH USE THE ROMAN RITUAL

64. Besides the adaptations mentioned in the General Introduction (nos. 30-33), episcopal conferences may make other changes in the rite of initiation of adults.

65. Episcopal conferences may freely choose:

1) To provide, where it seems suitable, some method of receiving interested inquirers (or sympathizers) prior to the catechumenate (see no. 12).

2) Wherever false worship flourishes, to insert the first exorcism and the first renunciation in the rite of becoming catechumens (nos. 79-80).

3) To decree that the gesture of signing the forehead be done in front of the forehead in places where the act of touching may not seem proper (no. 83).

4) Where it is the practice of non-Christian religions to give a new name to the initiated at once, to decree that the new name be given in the rite for becoming catechumens (no. 88).

5) According to local custom, to add auxiliary rites to show that the catechumens have been received into the community (no. 89).

6) Besides the usual rites during the period of the catechumenate (nos. 106-124), to restore the rites of transition by anticipating the presentations (nos. 125-126), the ephphetha or opening of ears and mouth, the recitation of the profession of faith, or even the anointing with the oil of catechumens (nos. 127-129).

7) To decide to omit the anointing with the oil of catechumens (no. 218), to transfer it to the immediately preparatory rites (nos. 206-207), or to use it during the period of catechumenate as a rite of transition (nos. 127-132).

8) To make the formulas of renunciation more detailed and richer (see nos. 80, 217).

V. COMPETENCE OF THE BISHOP

66. For his diocese, the bishop has the responsibility:

1) To set up the formation of the catechumenate and give suitable norms as needed (see no. 44).

2) As circumstances suggest, to decree whether and when the rite of initiation may be celebrated outside the ordinary times (see no. 58).

3) Because of serious obstacles, to dispense from one

scrutiny or even from two scrutinies in extraordinary circumstances (see no. 240).

4) To permit the simple rite to be used in whole or in part (see no. 240).

5) To assign catechists who are truly worthy and properly prepared to give the exorcisms and blessings (see nos. 44, 47).

6) To preside at the rite of election and to ratify personally, or through a delegate, the admission of the elect (see no. 44).

VI. ADAPTATIONS BY THE MINISTER

67. It is for the celebrant to use fully and intelligently the freedom which is given to him either in the General Introduction (no. 34) or in the rubrics of the rite. In many places the manner of acting or praying is intentionally left undetermined or two possibilities are offered, so that the celebrant may accommodate the rite, according to his prudent pastoral judgment, to the circumstances of the candidates and others who are present. The greatest freedom is left in the introductions and intercessions, which may always be shortened, changed, or even increased with new intentions in order to correspond with the circumstances or special situation of the candidates (for example, a sad or joyful event occurring in a family) or of the others present (for example, joy or sorrow common to the parish or town).

The celebrant will also adapt the text by changing the gender and number as needed.

CHAPTER I

RITE OF THE CATECHUMENATE RECEIVED IN STAGES

FIRST STAGE: RITE OF BECOMING CATECHUMENS

68. The rite by which those who wish to become Christians are received as catechumens is celebrated when they have accepted the first proclamation of the living God and already have an elementary faith in Christ the Savior. This presupposes the first evangelization, the beginning of conversion, faith in the meaning of the Church, previous contact with a priest or some members of the community, and some preparation for this liturgical rite.

69. Before candidates are admitted among the catechumens, which is to take place on determined days of the year according to local conditions, a suitable and necessary time for individual cases should be observed for investigating the motives for conversion and, if necessary, for purifying them.

70. It is desirable that the entire Christian community or some part of it, consisting of friends and acquaintances, catechists and priests, should take an active part in the celebration.

71. Sponsors should also be there to present the candidates, their friends, to the Church.

72. The rite, which includes the reception of the candidates, the liturgy of the word and the dismissal, may also be followed by the eucharist.

INTRODUCTORY RITE

73. The candidates, their sponsors and the faithful gather outside the church, or at the entrance, or in a suitable place inside the church, or in another suitable place somewhere else. The priest or deacon goes there, wearing an alb or surplice and a stole or even a cope of festive color. Meanwhile the faithful may sing a psalm or an appropriate song.

FIRST INSTRUCTION

74. The celebrant greets the candidates in a friendly manner. He speaks to them, their sponsors and all present, pointing out the joy and happiness of the Church. He reminds the sponsors and friends of their own experience and religious attitude by which the candidates, following their own spiritual path, have come to this stage.

Then he invites the sponsors and candidates to come forward. While they are coming and taking their places before the priest, an appropriate song may be sung, for example, Psalm 63:1-9.

OPENING DIALOGUE

75. Then the celebrant asks the individual candidates their civil or family name, if necessary, unless their names are already known because of the small number of candidates. This is done in these or similar words:

What is your name?
Candidate: **N.**

They always answer individually, even if the celebrant asks the question only once because of the number of candidates.

If he wishes, the celebrant may call each person by name. Each one answers: **Present.**

When there is a large number of candidates, the remaining questions may always be answered together:

Celebrant:
What do you ask of God's Church?
Candidates: **Faith.**

Celebrant:
What does faith offer you?
Candidates: **Eternal life.**

The celebrant may use other words in asking the candidates about their intentions and may permit them to answer in their own words, for example, after the first question: **What do you ask? What do you desire? For what reason have you come?,** he may receive such answers as: **The grace of Christ,** or **entrance into the Church,** or **eternal life** or other suitable responses. The celebrant will adapt his questions to their answers.

FIRST PROMISE

76. The celebrant, adapting his words as required to the responses given, speaks again to the candidates in these or similar words:

God enlightens every man who comes into the world. Through the world he has created, he makes known the unseen wonders of his love so that man may learn to give thanks to his Creator.

You have followed his light. Now the way of the Gospel opens before you, inviting you to make a new beginning by acknowledging the living God who speaks his words of truth to men. You are called to walk by the light of Christ and to trust in his wisdom. He asks you to submit yourself to him more and more and to believe in him with all your heart. This is the way of faith on which Christ will lovingly guide you to eternal life. Are you ready to enter on this path today under the leadership of Christ?
Candidates: **I am.**

Optional formulas more suitable for other circumstances are given in no. 370.

77. Then he turns to the sponsors and to the entire assembly and asks them in these or similar words:

My brothers and sisters gathered here and you who present these candidates: are you ready to help them come to know and follow Christ?
All: **We are.**

EXORCISM AND RENUNCIATION OF NON-CHRISTIAN WORSHIP

78. Wherever false worship flourishes, whether in worshiping spiritual powers, or in calling on the shades of the dead, or for obtaining benefits from magical arts, episcopal conferences may decide to introduce, in whole or in part, the first exorcism and the first renunciation, as follows. In this case no. 76 is omitted.

79. After a very brief and suitable instruction, the celebrant lightly breathes toward the face of each candidate, and says:

Breathe your Spirit, Lord, and drive out the spirits of evil: command them to depart, for your kingdom is drawing near.

If the breathing, even done lightly, seems unsuitable, it is omitted. The celebrant says the above formula, holding up his right hand toward the candidates. Or he may use another gesture according to the customs of the region, or even say it without any gesture.

If there are many candidates, the celebrant omits the breathing and says the formula once for all.

80. If the episcopal conference judges it suitable to have the candidate openly renounce non-Christian worship and spirits or magical arts, the conference should prepare the formula of question and renunciation, adapted to local circumstances. As long as the formula is not offensive to members of non-Christian religions, it may be presented in these or similar words:

Dear candidates:
With the help of God and in response to his call, you have indicated your intention to worship and serve God alone and his Christ.

Now is the appointed time to renounce in public every power apart from God and every form of worship which does not offer him true honor.

Do you reject every power which sets itself up in opposition to God and his Christ?
Candidates: **We do.**

Celebrant:
Do you renounce your worship of N. and N.?
Candidates: **We do.**

He continues in the same way for each cult to be renounced. Other optional formulas are in no. 371.

81. Then the celebrant turns to the sponsors and the assembly and asks them in these or similar words:

My brothers and sisters gathered here, and you who present these candidates: you have heard them declare their resolve. Do you testify that they have chosen

Christ as Lord and that they wish to serve him alone?
All: **We do.**

Celebrant:
Are you ready to help them come to know and follow Christ?
All: **We are.**

82. The celebrant with hands joined says:

Father of love and mercy,
we thank you in the name of our brothers (and sisters)
who have experienced your guiding presence in their lives.
Today, in the presence of your community,
they are answering your call to faith.

We praise and bless you, Lord!

All: **We praise and bless you, Lord!**

SIGNING OF THE FOREHEAD AND SENSES

83. If there are only a few candidates, the celebrant invites them and their sponsors in these or similar words:

Please come forward, together with your sponsors,
to receive the sign of your new way of life.

With their sponsors, the candidates one by one come to the celebrant. With his thumb he makes a cross on the forehead (or in front of the forehead, if the episcopal conference decides that a touch is not suitable according to the circumstances). While doing this, he says:

N., receive the cross on your forehead:
by this sign of his love (or: **of his triumph)**
Christ will be your strength.
Learn now to know and follow him.

After the celebrant signs the catechumens, the catechists or sponsors, if desired, do the same, unless they are to sign them later, as in no. 85.

84. If the number of candidates is large, the celebrant speaks to them in these or similar words:

Dear candidates:
(If the renunciation preceded: **you have already rejected all false worship and) you have agreed to try our way of life and our hope in Christ. To begin your preparation for baptism, I will now join with your teachers and sponsors in signing you with the cross of Christ. Our whole community will welcome you with love and stand ready to help you.**

Then the celebrant makes the sign of the cross over them all together, while the catechists or sponsors make it over the individual candidates. He says:

Receive the cross on your forehead:
by this sign of his love (or: **of his triumph)**
Christ will be your strength.
Learn now to know and follow him.

85. Then comes the signing of the senses. (In the judgment of the celebrant, this may be omitted in whole or in part.)

The signs are made by the catechists or by the sponsors. (If required by special circumstances, this may be done by several presbyters or deacons.) The formula is always said by the celebrant:

While the ears are being signed:
Receive the sign of the cross on your ears:
may you hear the voice of the Lord.

While the eyes are being signed:
Receive the sign of the cross on your eyes:
may you see with the light of God.

While the lips are being signed:
Receive the sign of the cross on your lips:
may you respond to the word of God.

While the breast is being signed:
Receive the sign of the cross on your breast:
may Christ dwell in your hearts by faith.

While the shoulders are being signed:
Receive the sign of the cross on your shoulders:
may you accept the sweet yoke of Christ.

Without touching them the celebrant alone makes the sign of the cross over the candidates while saying:

I sign all of you in the name of the Father,
and of the Son, ✠ and of the Holy Spirit:
may you live for ever and ever.

Candidates: **Amen.**

When there are few catechumens, the rite of signing may be done over each candidate by the celebrant who says the formula in the singular.

86. The rite of signing the senses (nos. 83-85) may in each instance be suitably concluded by giving praise to Christ, for example:

Glory to you, Lord.

87. Then the celebrant says:

Let us pray.

Father,
we pray for these catechumens N. and N.
who have been signed
with the cross of our Lord Jesus Christ;
by its power, keep them safe.
May they be faithful to your initial teachings
and, by keeping your commandments,
come to be reborn in glory.

We ask this through Christ our Lord.
℟. **Amen.**

Another optional form of the prayer:

Let us pray.

Almighty God,
you have given life to your people
by the death and resurrection of your Son.
May these catechumens take up their cross,
live always by its saving power
and reveal it in their lives.

We ask this through Christ our Lord.
℟. **Amen.**

GIVING THE NEW NAME

88. Where non-Christian religions flourish, which immediately give a new name to those who become members, the episcopal conference may decide that new catechumens may keep the name they already have, or take a Christian name or one familiar in their culture, notwithstanding the rule of canon 761, as long as it has a Christian meaning (in these cases, nos. 203-205 are omitted).

Celebrant:

N., from now on you will also be called N.
Catechumen: **Thank you** (or some other suitable response).

Otherwise it will be enough to explain the Christian meaning of the name his parents gave him.

ADDITIONAL RITES

89. If any customs seem suitable for signifying reception into the community, such as giving salt or some other symbolic act, or even presenting the cross or a holy medal, these may be permitted by the judgment of the episcopal conference, and may be included either before or after the entrance into the church.

ENTRY INTO THE CHURCH

90. After this the celebrant invites the catechumens and their sponsors to enter into the church or other suitable place, using these or similar words:

(N. and N.,) we welcome you into the church
to share with us at the table of God's word.

Then by a gesture he invites the catechumens and sponsors to enter into the church or other suitable place.

Meanwhile, with Psalm 34:2. 3. 6. 9. 10. 11. 16 the antiphon is sung:

Come, my children, and listen to me;
I will teach you the fear of the Lord.

Or some other appropriate song may be sung.

CELEBRATION OF THE WORD OF GOD

91. When the catechumens reach their seats, the celebrant speaks to them briefly, helping them to understand the dignity of God's word which is proclaimed and heard in the church.

Then the book of the scriptures is carried in procession and placed with honor on the lectern and may be incensed.

The celebration of the word of God follows.

READINGS AND HOMILY

92. One or more readings suitable to new catechumens are chosen from those given in the Lectionary for Mass, no. 743. Other appropriate texts and responsorial psalms may be selected from those given below in no. 372.

The homily follows.

PRESENTATION OF THE GOSPELS

93. If the celebrant wishes, books containing the Gospels are given to the catechumens with reverence and dignity. He may use a suitable formula, such as:

Receive the Gospel, the good news of Jesus Christ, the Son of God.

Crosses may also be given unless they were already given as a sign of their reception as catechumens.

The catechumen may respond to the celebrant's words and gift with appropriate words.

PRAYER FOR THE CATECHUMENS

94. Then the sponsors and the whole congregation of the faithful offer this prayer or a similar one for the catechumens:

Celebrant:

These catechumens, our brothers and sisters,
have already traveled a long road.
Let us thank God for his loving care which has brought them to this day
and ask that they may continue to hasten toward complete fellowship
in our Christian way of life.

Reader:

That God our Father reveal his Christ to them more and more with every passing day, let us pray to the Lord:

℟. Lord, hear our prayer.

Reader:

That they undertake with generous hearts and souls whatever God may ask of them, let us pray to the Lord:

℟. Lord, hear our prayer.

Reader:

That they have our sincere and unfailing support every step of the way, let us pray to the Lord:

℟. Lord, hear our prayer.

Reader:

That our community offer them the persuasive witness of unity and generous love, let us pray to the Lord:

℟. Lord, hear our prayer.

Reader:

That both they and we become ever more responsive to the needs of all men, let us pray to the Lord:

℟. Lord, hear our prayer.

Reader:

That they be found ready, in due time, to receive the new birth of baptism and life from the Holy Spirit, let us pray to the Lord:

℟. Lord, hear our prayer.

In the above prayer, the usual petition for the needs of the Church and the whole world is added if the catechumens are to be dismissed and the general intercessions will be omitted in the eucharistic celebration (see no. 97).

CONCLUDING PRAYER

95. After the above prayer, the celebrant extends his hands toward the catechumens and says:

Let us pray.

(God of our fathers and) God of all creation,

keep your servants N. and N. joyful in hope
and faithful in your service.
Lead them, Lord, to the waters of baptism
that give new life.
May the eternal joy you promise
be the reward of all
who spend their lives in good works.

We ask this through Christ our Lord.
℟. **Amen.**

Or another optional prayer:

Let us pray.

God and Father of all creation,
since you created man in your own likeness,
receive with love these men (and women) who come to you today.
May they who have listened to the word in this community
be renewed by its power
and come to reflect the image of Christ
who lives and reigns for ever and ever.
℟. **Amen.**

DISMISSAL OF THE CATECHUMENS

96. Briefly recalling the great joy with which the catechumens were received and urging them to live according to the word they have heard, the celebrant dismisses them in these or similar words:

My dear catechumens: go in peace.
May the Lord be with you always.

Catechumens: **Thanks be to God.**

The group of catechumens goes out but does not disperse. With the help of some of the faithful, they remain together to share their fraternal joy and spiritual experiences.

If for serious reasons they do not leave (see Introduction, no. 19; 3) and must remain with the faithful, they are to be told that even if they are present for the celebration of the eucharist, they cannot take part as baptized persons do.

If the eucharist is not celebrated, an appropriate song may be added, and the faithful and catechumens are dismissed.

CELEBRATION OF THE EUCHARIST

97. If the eucharist follows after the catechumens leave, the general intercessions for the needs of the Church and the whole world begin at once. If required, the profession of faith is then said and the gifts are prepared. For pastoral reasons the general intercessions and the profession of faith may be omitted.

CATECHUMENATE AND ITS RITES

98. The catechumenate or pastoral formation of catechumens continues until they have matured sufficiently in their conversion or faith. If necessary, it may last for several years. By the teaching of the whole Christian life and by an introductory period of appropriate length, the catechumens are well initiated into the mysteries of salvation, in the exercise of Gospel morality and in the sacred rites which are to be celebrated later on. In this way they are introduced into the life of faith, the liturgy and the charity of the people of God.

In special cases, considering the spiritual preparation of the candidate, the local ordinary may decide to shorten the period of the catechumenate; in singular cases, he may allow it to take place in one celebration (no. 240).

99. During this period, instructions should be given to the catechumens, showing them the whole Catholic teaching. Thus their faith should be enlightened, their hearts should be directed toward God, their participation in the liturgical mystery should be encouraged, their apostolic action should be aroused, and their whole life should be nourished according to the Spirit of Christ.

100. Celebrations of the word of God, adapted to the liturgical season and serving both the instruction of the catechumens and the needs of the community, are to be held (see nos. 106-108).

101. The first or minor exorcisms, performed in a prayerful and positive manner, show the catechumens the true nature of the spiritual life as a battle between flesh and spirit, and underline both the importance of self-denial in order to gain the blessings of the Kingdom of God and the continuing need of God's help (nos. 109-118).

102. The blessings signify the love of God and the care of the Church. They are offered to the catechumens so that while they still lack the grace of the sacraments, they may receive from the Church the spirit, joy and peace to continue their work and spiritual journey (see nos. 119-124).

103. Through the years while the catechumens are progressing from the first catechetical gathering, they go on to others, marking their passage with rites as often as this can be meaningful. Therefore it is permitted when desired to anticipate the presentation of the profession of faith or creed and of the Lord's Prayer, and the prayer over the ears and mouth, since time is sometimes lacking for these rites in the final preparation of the catechumens (nos. 125-126). According to local usage and desire, celebrations may be provided for the rite of anointing with the oil of catechumens (see nos. 127-132).

104. During this time, the catechumens should think about finding godparents who will present them to the Church on the day of election (see General Introduction on Christian Initiation, nos. 8-10; above, no. 43).

105. Throughout the year, the whole community should be assembled for some of the celebrations of the catechumenate and for the rites of transition (see nos. 125-132). The community, especially the priests, deacons, catechists, sponsors, godparents, friends and neighbors, will have a part in the initiation of the catechumens.

CELEBRATIONS OF THE WORD OF GOD

106. Special celebrations of the word of God should be held for the benefit of the catechumens. Their main goals will be:

a) to implant in their hearts the teachings they are receiving: the unique morality of the New Testament, the forgiving of injuries and insults, the meaning of sin and repentance, the duties Christians have to carry out in the world, and so on;

b) to give them wise teaching on the different aspects and ways of prayer;

c) to explain the signs, actions and seasons of the liturgy to the catechumens;

d) to lead them gradually into the worship of the whole community.

107. To sanctify the Lord's day, certain provisions are made when the catechumenate is first held:

a) The celebrations for the catechumens, mentioned in no.

106, should be held faithfully on a Sunday, so that the catechumens may become accustomed to take an active and experienced part in them.

b) The first part of the celebration of Sunday Mass is gradually opened to them. If possible, the dismissal of the catechumens should take place after the liturgy of the word, and a petition for them is added in the general intercessions.

108. Celebrations of the word of God may be held after catechesis and for the sake of performing the minor exorcisms. They may also end with blessings as noted below (see nos. 110-119).

MINOR EXORCISMS

109. The minor exorcisms are celebrated by the priest or deacon, or even by a worthy and suitable catechist delegated by the bishop for this ministry. The celebrant extends his hands over the catechumens who bow or kneel, and he says one or two of the prayers given below (nos. 113-118).

110. These take place in the church, the sacristy or the catechumenate center, during a celebration of the word. They may also be held at the beginning or end of the gathering for instructions; on account of special needs, they may be done privately for individual catechumens.

111. Before the catechumenate, during the time of evangelization, the minor exorcisms may be carried out for the spiritual good of interested inquirers (sympathizers) regarding Christianity.

112. The formulas for the minor exorcisms may be used more than once in various circumstances.

PRAYERS OF EXORCISM

113.

Let us pray.

All-powerful and ever-living God,
through your only Son
you promised us the Holy Spirit.
We pray for our brothers (and sisters)

**who present themselves as catechumens.
Keep far from them every evil spirit
and all falsehood and sin,
that they may become temples of your Holy Spirit.
Confirm with your power what we speak in faith,
that our words may not be empty,
but spoken in the strength and grace of your Son
who freed the world from evil.**

We ask this through Christ our Lord.
℟. **Amen.**

114.
Let us pray.

**Lord our God,
you make known to man true life,
you take away evil and strengthen faith,
you renew hope and deepen love.
We pray in the name of your beloved Son,
our Lord Jesus Christ,
and in the power of the Holy Spirit:
remove from our brothers (and sisters)
all unbelief and hesitation in faith,
(the worship of false gods and magic,
witchcraft, and dealings with the dead),
greed and sensuality,
enmity or quarreling,
and all forms of immorality.
Since you have called them
to be holy and sinless in your sight,
renew in them the spirit of faith and reverence,
the spirit of patience and hope,
the spirit of self-control and purity,
the spirit of love and peace.**

We ask this through Christ our Lord.
℟. **Amen.**

115.
Let us pray.

**All-powerful God,
you created man in your image and likeness**

**and formed him in holiness and justice.
Even when he sinned against you,
you did not abandon him,
but in love and wisdom you chose to save him
by the coming of your Son as man.
Save our brothers (and sisters):
free them from all evil and the tyranny of the enemy.
Take from them the spirit of falsehood, greed, and wickedness.
Receive them into your kingdom
and open their hearts to understand your Gospel.
Make them children of the light
and members of your holy Church,
to bear witness to your truth
and to show love to all in obedience to your will.**

We ask this through Christ our Lord.
℟. **Amen.**

116.
Let us pray.

**Lord Jesus Christ,
when ascending and preaching from the hillside
you led your followers from the path of sin
and made known to them the way of happiness of the Kingdom.
Help our brothers (and sisters) who hear the message of the Gospel
and keep them safe from the spirit of selfishness and greed,
from the spirit of pleasure and worldly pride.
As your disciples,
may they see true happiness in poverty and hunger,
in mercy and cleanness of heart.
May they work for peace among men
and joyfully endure persecution.
May they come to share in your Kingdom
and in the forgiveness you promised them.
May they see God in the joy of heaven**

where you live and reign for ever and ever.
℟. Amen.

117.
Let us pray.

God our Father,
Creator and Savior of mankind,
you have given life to these children of yours
and have called them to share your love.
Search their hearts today
and guard them as they look forward to the coming of your Son.
Keep them in your fatherly care
and bring to completion the plan of your love.
By their faithfulness to Christ
may they be counted among his followers on earth
and sing his joyful praise for ever in heaven.

We ask this through Christ our Lord.
℟. Amen.

118.
Let us pray.

God our Father,
you know the secrets of our hearts
and reward us for all we do.
Look with love on the work and progress of our brothers (and sisters).
Strengthen them on their way, increase their faith,
accept their repentance
and give them the abundant blessing of your goodness and justice.
May they share your sacraments on earth
and so come to share your presence for ever in heaven.

We ask this through Christ our Lord.
℟. Amen.

Other prayers of exorcism are given in no. 373.

BLESSING THE CATECHUMENS

119. The blessings mentioned in no. 102 may be given by a priest or deacon or even by a catechist (see no. 48). They extend their hands toward the catechumens and offer one or two of the prayers below (nos. 121-124). After the prayer, the catechumens come to the celebrant, if this can be done conveniently, and he lays his hands on each of them; they then leave.

The blessings are usually given at the end of the liturgy of the word of God. They may be given at the end of a gathering for instruction; on account of special needs, they may be given privately to individual catechumens.

120. Even before the catechumenate, during the time of evangelization, it is permitted to bless those interested inquirers (sympathizers) regarding Christianity for their spiritual good.

121.
Let us pray.

Lord, may these catechumens
come to know the mysteries of your love,
be born again in the waters of baptism,
and be counted among the members of your Church.

We ask this through Christ our Lord.
℟. **Amen.**

122.
Let us pray.

Father, through your holy prophets
you have told all who draw near to you:
"Wash and be cleansed."
And through Christ you have chosen to give us
a birth in the Spirit.
Bless our brothers (and sisters)
as they earnestly prepare themselves for baptism.
Be true to your promise:
make them holy in preparation for your gifts

that they may come to be reborn as your children
and enter the fellowship of your Church.

We ask this through Christ our Lord.
℟. **Amen.**

123.
Let us pray.

All-powerful God,
help our brothers (and sisters)
as they deepen their knowledge of the Gospel of Christ.
May they come to know and love you
and always do your will with generous hearts and willing spirits.
Initiate them into a life of holiness,
and count them among your Church
so that they may share your holy mysteries here on earth
and in the everlasting joy of heaven.

We ask this through Christ our Lord.
℟. **Amen.**

124.
Let us pray.

God our Father,
you have freed the world from falsehood
through the coming of your only Son Jesus Christ.
Give to those who are preparing for baptism
wisdom, holiness, unfailing faith,
and a wholehearted acceptance of your truth.
May they grow daily in goodness
and in due time be born again in baptism,
which brings forgiveness of sins,
and so join us in giving glory to your name.

We ask this through Christ our Lord.
℟. **Amen.**

Other prayers for the blessings are given in no. 374.

RITES BETWEEN STAGES OF THE CATECHUMENATE

125. The presentations may be anticipated because of their benefit during the time of the catechumenate and because of the brevity of the time of purification and enlightenment. They should be celebrated when the catechumens seem to be mature; otherwise, they do not take place.

126. The celebration is described below: the presentation of the profession of faith or creed (nos. 183-187) and of the Lord's Prayer (nos. 188-193). The celebration may conclude with the prayer over the ears and mouth (nos. 200-202), unless there is among the rites of transition the recitation of the profession of faith or creed (nos. 194-199) which begins with the prayer over the ears and mouth. In these cases, the word "catechumens" is used instead of "elect."

127. If it seems desirable to strengthen the catechumens with the first anointing, this is to be given by a priest or deacon.

128. The anointing takes place at the end of the celebration of the word of God and is given to all the catechumens. For special reasons it may also be given privately to individuals. It is also permitted, if desired, to anoint the catechumens several times.

129. In this rite the celebrant uses the oil of catechumens blessed by the bishop in the Chrism Mass; for pastoral reasons, it may be blessed by the priest immediately before the anointing.[1]

RITE OF ANOINTING

130. If the celebrant is using oil blessed by the bishop, he first says one of the minor exorcisms (nos. 113-118). Then he says:

We anoint you with the oil of salvation
in the name of Christ our Savior.

[1]See Rite of Blessing of Oils, Introduction, no. 7.

May he strengthen you with his power,
who lives and reigns for ever and ever.
Catechumens: **Amen.**

Each catechumen is anointed with the oil of catechumens on the breast or on both hands or even on other parts of the body, if this seems desirable. If there is a large number of catechumens, several ministers may be used.

[131.] If the oil is to be blessed by the priest, he uses this prayer:
Lord God, protector of all who believe in you,
bless ✠ this oil
and give the wisdom and strength it signifies
to all who are anointed with it
in preparation for their baptism.
Bring them to a deeper understanding of the Gospel,
help them to accept the challenge of Christian living,
and lead them to the joy of new birth
in the family of your Church.

We ask this through Christ our Lord.
℟. **Amen.**

[132.] Then the celebrant faces the catechumens and says:
We anoint you with the oil of salvation
in the name of Christ our Savior.
May he strengthen you with his power,
who lives and reigns for ever and ever.
Catechumens: **Amen.**

Each catechumen is anointed with the oil of catechumens on the breast or on both hands or even on other parts of the body, if this seems desirable. If there is a large number of catechumens, several ministers may carry out the anointing.

SECOND STAGE: RITE OF ELECTION OR ENROLLMENT OF NAMES

133. At the beginning of Lent, which is the time of the proximate preparation for sacramental initiation, the election or enrollment of names is celebrated. In this rite the Church hears the testimony of the godparents and catechists. After the catechumens reaffirm their intention, then the Church passes judgment on their state of preparation and states whether they may go on to the Easter sacraments.

134. The catechumenate ends with the celebration of the election, thus completing the lengthy formation of the mind and heart. For a person to be enrolled among the elect, he must have enlightened faith and the deliberate intention of receiving the sacraments of the Church. After the election, he is encouraged to advance toward Christ with even greater generosity.

135. For the Church, the election is a matter of great concern for the catechumens. The bishop, presbyters, deacons, catechists, godparents and the whole community, each according to his responsibility, weigh the matter carefully and make their decision on the instruction and growth of the catechumens. Then the elect are received with prayer so that the entire Church may lead them to meet Christ.

136. The godparents are chosen beforehand by the catechumens with the consent of the priest, and as far as possible should be accepted by the community. Now the godparents exercise their first act of ministry: they are called by name at the beginning of the rite and approach with the catechumens (no. 143), and testify in their behalf before the community (no. 144); if desired, they write their names with them in the register (no. 146).

137. As a means to avoid an error in judgment, it would be wise to hold a deliberation on the suitability of the candidates before the liturgical rite is celebrated. This is done by those involved in training the catechumens—presbyters, deacons and catechists—and by the godparents and delegates of the local community. If circumstances permit, the

assembly of catechumens may also take part. This deliberation may take various forms, depending on local conditions and pastoral needs. This acceptance should be noted by the celebrant during the liturgical rite.

138. The celebrant is the bishop or his delegate. However much or little he was involved in the preceding deliberation, it is his responsibility to show in the homily or during the rite the religious and ecclesiastical meaning of the election. He has the responsibility of announcing the Church's decision before all present and hearing their judgment if this is so desired; of asking the catechumens to give a personal expression of their intention; and, acting in the name of Christ and his Church, of admitting the elect. He opens to all the divine mystery shown in the call of the Church and in its liturgical celebration. He reminds the faithful to give good example to the elect, and, together with them, to prepare themselves for the Easter solemnities.

139. Since the sacraments of initiation are celebrated during the Easter solemnities and their preparation belongs to the special nature of Lent, the rite of election should normally take place on the First Sunday of Lent. The final preparation of the mature catechumens is in harmony with the lenten season which will benefit the elect because of its own proper liturgical structure and the community's participation. For urgent pastoral reasons, however (especially in secondary mission stations), it is permitted to celebrate the rite during the preceding or following week.

140. The rite should be held in the church, or, if necessary, in a suitable and fitting place. It should be celebrated within the Mass of the First Sunday of Lent, after the homily.

141. If the rite should happen to be celebrated on another day, it begins with the liturgy of the word. If the readings for the day are not suitable, they should be chosen from among those for the First Sunday of Lent (see Lectionary, nos. 22-24), or from other suitable readings. The proper ritual Mass (no. 374b) may always be celebrated. If the eucharist is not celebrated, the rite ends with the dismissal of all, including the catechumens.

142. The homily, adapted to the circumstances, concerns

not only the catechumens but the whole community of the faithful, so that the baptized members may shine with good example and continue along the way of the paschal mystery together with the elect.

PRESENTATION OF THE CANDIDATES

143. After the homily, the priest, deacon, catechist, or delegate of the community responsible for the initiation of the catechumens presents the elect with these or similar words:

Reverend Father:

As Easter draws near, these catechumens are completing their period of preparation. They have been strengthened by God's grace and supported by this community's example and prayers. Now they request that, after further preparation and the celebration of the scrutinies, they will be allowed to receive the sacraments of baptism, confirmation, and the eucharist.

Celebrant replies:

Those who are to be chosen will please come forward with their godparents.

One by one, they are called by name. Each candidate comes forward with his godparent and stands before the celebrant. If there is a large number of candidates, all are presented at once, for example, by each of the catechists with his own group. The catechists should be encouraged to call their candidates by name in a celebration held some time before they come to the common rite.

144. If the celebrant had no part in the previous deliberation (no. 137), he speaks to the assembly in these or similar words:

God's holy Church wishes to be certain that these catechumens are ready to be admitted among the ranks of the chosen for the coming celebration of Easter.

He turns to the godparents:

And so I ask you godparents: have they faithfully

listened to the word of God proclaimed by the Church?
Godparents: **They have.**

Celebrant:
Have they been true to the word they have received and begun to walk in God's presence?
Godparents: **They have.**

Celebrant:
Have they sought the fellowship of their brothers and sisters and joined with them in prayer?
Godparents: **They have.**

If desired, the celebrant asks the whole congregation for its assent.

[145.] If the celebrant took part in the previous deliberation about the candidates' suitability (no. 137), he may prefer to use these or similar words:

My brothers and sisters:

These catechumens have asked to be admitted into the sacramental life of the Church at Easter. Those who know them judge them to be sincere in their desire. For a long time they have heard the word of Christ and have attempted to shape their conduct accordingly. They have shared in the fellowship and the prayer of their brothers and sisters. Now I wish to inform all here present of our community's decision to call them to the sacraments. Therefore, I ask their godparents to state their opinion once again, so that all may hear.

He turns to the godparents:

As God is your witness, do you consider these candidates worthy to be admitted to the sacraments of Christian initiation?
Godparents: **We do.**

If desired, the celebrant asks the whole congregation for its assent.

EXAMINATION OF CANDIDATES

146. Then the celebrant, facing the candidates, admonishes and questions them in these or similar words:

And now, my dear catechumens, I address myself to you. Your godparents and teachers (and the entire community) have reported favorably about you. Relying on their judgment, the Church in the name of Christ hereby calls you to the Easter sacraments. Now that you have been hearing the voice of Christ for some time, it is for you to express your intention clearly before the whole Church.

Do you wish to receive Christ's sacraments of entry into his Church, the sacraments of baptism, confirmation, and the eucharist?
Catechumens: **We do.**

Celebrant:
Then please give us your names to be enrolled.

The candidates go to the celebrant with the godparents or remain in their place and give their names. There are various ways of enrolling the names. They may be written by each candidate or clearly pronounced and written by the godparent or by the priest. If there is a large number of candidates, a list of names may be given to the celebrant with these or similar words:

These are the names of the elect.

While the enrollment is taking place, an appropriate song, for example, Psalm 16, may be sung.

ADMISSION OR ELECTION

147. Then the celebrant briefly explains the meaning of the rite of enrolling the names. Turning to the candidates, he says in these or similar words:

N. and N., you have been chosen to be initiated into the sacred mysteries at the Easter Vigil.
Catechumens: **Thanks be to God.**
He continues:

Now it is your duty and ours to ask the help of God.

He is always faithful to those he calls. Be faithful to him in return and strive courageously to reach the goal your calling opens up to you.

Then the celebrant turns to the godparents and reminds them in these or similar words:

These catechumens have been entrusted to you in the Lord, and you have given us a favorable report. By your loving care and example continue to help them until they receive the sacraments of God's life.

He invites them to place their hand on the shoulder of the candidate whom they are presenting, or to make some other gesture to indicate this.

PRAYER FOR THE ELECT

148. The community prays for the candidates in these or similar words:

Celebrant:
My brothers and sisters:

Today we begin Lent and look forward to our celebration of the life-giving mysteries of our Lord's suffering, death, and resurrection. These chosen men (and women), whom we lead with us to the Easter sacraments, look to us for an example of Christian life. Let us pray to the Lord for them and for ourselves that we may be strengthened by each other's mutual efforts, and so come to share the joys of Easter.

Reader:
For our catechumens, that they may always remember this day when they were chosen and be thankful for the blessing they have received from heaven, let us pray to the Lord:
℟. **Lord, hear our prayer.**
Reader:
That they may use this lenten season to undertake with us the burden of self-denial and perform works of holiness, let us pray to the Lord:
℟. **Lord, hear our prayer.**

Reader:
For their teachers, that they may always offer the sweetness of God's word to those who are searching for it, let us pray to the Lord:
℟. Lord, hear our prayer.

Reader:
For their godparents, that they may give these catechumens a good example by their consistent living of the Gospel, both in their personal actions and in their duties to society, let us pray to the Lord:
℟. Lord, hear our prayer.

Reader:
For their families, that, far from placing any obstacles in the way of these catechumens, they may assist them to follow the urging of the Holy Spirit, let us pray to the Lord:
℟. Lord, hear our prayer.

Reader:
For our community, that during this Lent we may excel in fidelity to prayer and in charity, let us pray to the Lord:
℟. Lord, hear our prayer.

Reader:
For all who have not yet overcome their hesitation, that they may trust in Christ and one day join our community as brothers and sisters, let us pray to the Lord:
℟. Lord, hear our prayer.

In the above prayer, the usual petition for the needs of the Church and the whole world is added if the catechumens are to be dismissed and the general intercessions will be omitted during the Mass (see no. 151).

Another optional form of this prayer is given in no. 375.

149. The celebrant extends his hands over the elect and concludes with this prayer:

God our Father,
you created the human race

that you might also be the One who makes it ever new.
Count these adopted children
as sons (and daughters) reborn to your new covenant.
Make them children of the promise.
Although they cannot reach eternal life by their own nature,
may they come to share it by the power of your love.

We ask this through Christ our Lord.
℟. **Amen.**

Another optional prayer:

All-powerful Father, God of love,
you wish to make all things new in Christ
and to draw all men to him.
Guide and govern these men (and women),
chosen through the ministry of your Church.
Keep them faithful to their calling,
help them to be built into the Kingdom of your Son,
and prepare them to be sealed with the promised Gift of the Holy Spirit.

We ask this through Christ our Lord.
℟. **Amen.**

DISMISSAL OF THE ELECT

150. The celebrant dismisses the elect with these or similar words:

You have been chosen by God and have entered with us on the way of Lent. May Christ himself be your way, your truth, and your life, especially during the approaching scrutinies when we shall meet with you again. For the present, go in peace.
The elect: **Amen.**

The elect go out. If because of rather serious reasons they cannot leave (see Introduction, no. 19:3) and must remain with the baptized, they are to be reminded that while they are present at the eucharist, they cannot take part in it as baptized people do.

If the eucharist is not celebrated, an appropriate song may be added, and the faithful and the elect are dismissed together.

CELEBRATION OF THE EUCHARIST

151. After the elect leave, the eucharist is celebrated. The general intercessions for the needs of the Church and the whole world begin at once. If necessary, the profession of faith is said, and the gifts are prepared. For pastoral reasons, the general intercessions and the profession of faith may be omitted.

PERIOD OF PURIFICATION AND ENLIGHTENMENT OR ILLUMINATION

152. This period normally falls in Lent and begins with the election. During this time, the catechumens and the local community give themselves to spiritual recollection so that they may prepare themselves for the feast of Easter and for the sacraments of initiation. For this purpose the scrutinies, the presentations and the preparatory rites take place.

SCRUTINIES AND PRESENTATIONS

153. The scrutinies and presentations take place during Lent prior to the sacraments of initiation. By these rites, the spiritual and catechetical preparation of the elect or *competentes* is completed, and it is carried on through the entire period of Lent.

I. SCRUTINIES

154. The purpose of the scrutinies is mainly spiritual, and this is achieved by exorcisms. The scrutinies are intended to purify the catechumens' minds and hearts, to strengthen them against temptation, to purify their intentions, and to make firm their decision, so that they remain more closely united with Christ and make progress in their efforts to love God more deeply.

155. The mature catechumens should have the intention of arriving at an intimate knowledge of Christ and his Church, and they are expected to progress in sincere self-knowledge, in a serious appraisal of self, and in true penance.

156. The rite of exorcism is celebrated by priests or deacons. In it, the Church teaches the elect about the mystery of Christ who frees from sin. By exorcism they are freed from the effects of sin and from the influence of the devil, and they are strengthened in their spiritual journey and open their hearts to receive the gifts of the Savior.

157. To arouse the desire of purification and redemption by Christ, three scrutines are celebrated: either to teach the

catechumens gradually about the mystery of sin, from which the whole world and each person desires to be redeemed, and thus be saved from its present and future effects, or to fill their minds with the meaning of Christ the Redeemer. He is the living water (see Gospel story of the Samaritan woman), light (see Gospel story of the man born blind), resurrection and life (see Gospel story of the raising of Lazarus). During the three scrutinies, they should be making progress in the understanding of sin and in the desire for salvation.

158. The scrutinies are celebrated by a priest or deacon who presides over the community so that the faithful too may benefit from the liturgy of the scrutinies and join in praying for the elect.

159. They take place in the Masses of the scrutinies on the Third, Fourth and Fifth Sundays of Lent. The readings from series A are used, with their chants as assigned in the Lectionary (nos. 745-747). If this cannot be done on the proper Sundays because of pastoral reasons, other Lenten Sundays or even suitable weekdays may be chosen. The first Mass of the scrutinies is always that of the Samaritan woman, the second of the man born blind, and the third of Lazarus.

FIRST SCRUTINY

160. The first scrutiny is celebrated on the Third Sunday of Lent, using the formulas in the Missal and Lectionary (see also nos. 376-377).

HOMILY

161. In the homily the celebrant moves from the scripture readings and explains the meaning of the first scrutiny in the light of the lenten liturgy and of the spiritual journey of the elect.

PRAYER IN SILENCE

162. After the homily the elect and their godparents come

before the celebrant. Looking at the faithful, he invites them to pray in silence for the elect, asking for the spirit of repentance and the understanding of sin, and for the true freedom of the children of God.

Then he turns to the catechumens and invites them to pray in silence. He instructs them to show their spirit of repentance by bowing or kneeling. Then he concludes in these or similar words:

You who have been chosen, bow your heads in prayer (or: **kneel in prayer).**

The elect bow or kneel, and all pray for some time in silence. Then, if desired, all stand.

PRAYER FOR THE ELECT

163. While this prayer is being said for the elect, the godparents place their right hand on the shoulder of the one they are sponsoring.

Celebrant:
The Church has confidently chosen these men and women whose long preparation will be over at Easter. Let us pray that they will be ready and will find Christ in his sacraments.

Reader:
That they may keep the word of God in their hearts and learn to understand it more deeply, let us pray to the Lord:
℟. **Lord, hear our prayer.**

Reader:
That they may learn to know Christ who came to save what had been lost, let us pray to the Lord:
℟. **Lord, hear our prayer.**

Reader:
That they may humbly acknowledge their sinfulness, let us pray to the Lord:
℟. **Lord, hear our prayer.**

Reader:
That they may sincerely reject anything in their lives which is displeasing to Christ or opposed to him, let us pray to the Lord:
℟. **Lord, hear our prayer.**

Reader:
That the Holy Spirit, who searches the hearts of all men, may strengthen their weakness with his power, let us pray to the Lord:
℟. **Lord, hear our prayer.**

Reader:
That the same Holy Spirit may teach them to know the things of God and how to please him, let us pray to the Lord:
℟. **Lord, hear our prayer.**

Reader:
That they and their families may put their hope in Christ and receive peace and holiness from him, let us pray to the Lord:
℟. **Lord, hear our prayer.**

Reader:
That we ourselves in preparation for the feast of Christ's resurrection may amend our hearts and be loving to all men, let us pray to the Lord:
℟. **Lord, hear our prayer.**

Reader:
That throughout the whole world the sick may be restored to health, the broken may be made whole again, the lost be found, and the found be saved, let us pray to the Lord:
℟. **Lord, hear our prayer.**

The celebrant may adapt the introduction and invocations according to various circumstances. The usual petition for the needs of the Church and the whole world is added if the catechumens are to be dismissed and the general intercessions will be omitted in the Mass (see no. 166).
Another optional form of this prayer is given in no. 376.

EXORCISM

164. After the prayer, the celebrant turns to the elect and with hands joined says:

Let us pray.

God our Father,
you sent your Son to be our Savior:
these men (and women) preparing for baptism
thirst for living water as did the Samaritan woman.
May the word of the Lord change their lives too,
and help them to acknowlege the sins and weaknesses
that burden them.
Keep them from relying too much on themselves
and never let the powers of evil deceive them.
Free them from the spirit of falsehood
and help them recognize any evil within themselves,
that with hearts cleansed from sin
they may advance on the way to salvation.

We ask this through Christ our Lord.
℟. **Amen.**

The celebrant then lays his hand in silence on each one of the elect, if this can be done conveniently.

Then he extends his hands over the elect and continues:

Lord Jesus,
you are the fountain we thirst for;
you are the teacher we seek;
you alone are the Holy One.
These chosen ones open their hearts honestly
to confess their failures
and be forgiven.
In your love, free them from evil,
restore their health, satisfy their thirst, and give them
peace.
By the power of your name,
which we call upon in faith,
stay with them and save them.
Command the spirit of evil to leave them,
for you have conquered that spirit by rising to life.

Show your chosen people the way of life in the Holy Spirit
that they may grow closer to the Father and worship him,
for you are Lord for ever and ever.
℟. **Amen.**

Another optional form of the exorcism is given in no. 379.

An appropriate song may be sung, for example, Psalms 7, 26, 32, 38, 39, 40, 51, 115, 130, 139, or 142.

DISMISSAL OF THE ELECT

165. Then the celebrant dismisses the elect:

Go in peace until we meet at the next scrutiny.
May the Lord be with you always.
Elect: **Amen.**

The elect leave. If for rather serious reasons they cannot leave, then the instructions in no. 96 are followed.

If, however, the eucharist is not celebrated, an appropriate song may be added, and the faithful and the elect are dismissed together.

CELEBRATION OF THE EUCHARIST

166. After the elect depart, the eucharist is celebrated. The general intercessions for the needs of the Church and the whole world begin at once. The profession of faith and the preparation of the gifts follow. For pastoral reasons, the general intercessions and the profession of faith may be omitted. A remembrance of the elect and their godparents is made in the eucharistic prayer (see nos. 377, 412).

SECOND SCRUTINY

167. The second scrutiny is celebrated on the Fourth Sunday of Lent, using the formulas in the Missal and Lectionary (see nos. 380-381).

HOMILY

168. In the homily the celebrant moves from the scripture readings and explains the meaning of the second scrutiny in

the light of the lenten liturgy and of the spiritual journey of the elect.

PRAYER IN SILENCE

After the homily the elect and their godparents come before the celebrant.

Looking at the faithful, he invites them to pray in silence for the elect, asking for the spirit of repentance and the understanding of sin, and for the true freedom of the children of God.

169. Then he turns to the catechumens and invites them to pray in silence. He instructs them to show their spirit of repentance by bowing or kneeling. Then he concludes in these or similar words:

You who have been chosen, bow your heads in prayer (or: kneel in prayer).

Then the elect bow or kneel, and all pray for some time in silence. Then, if desired, all stand.

PRAYER FOR THE ELECT

170. While this prayer is being said for the elect, the godparents place their right hand on the shoulder of the one they are sponsoring.

Celebrant:
Let us pray for these men and women whom God has chosen, that their lives may remain centered in him and they may offer convincing witness to the message of eternal life.

Reader:
That they may find and maintain freedom of mind and heart in faithfulness to the truth of Christ, let us pray to the Lord:
℟. Lord, hear our prayer.

Reader:
That they may prefer the foolishness of the cross to the wisdom of the world and seek happiness in God alone, let us pray to the Lord:
℟. Lord, hear our prayer.

Reader:
That the power of the Holy Spirit may fill them with freedom and change their fear into trust, let us pray to the Lord:
℟. **Lord, hear our prayer.**

Reader:
That they may become spiritual men (and women) by striving to do what is holy and just, let us pray to the Lord:
℟. **Lord, hear our prayer.**

Reader:
That all who suffer for their allegiance to Christ may find their strength in him, let us pray to the Lord:
℟. **Lord, hear our prayer.**

Reader:
That families and nations who are hindered from embracing the faith may be granted the freedom to believe the Gospel, let us pray to the Lord:
℟. **Lord, hear our prayer.**

Reader:
That we who are immersed in the world may remain faithful to the spirit of the Gospel, let us pray to the Lord:
℟. **Lord, hear our prayer.**

Reader:
That the whole world, which the Father so loves, may attain complete spiritual freedom in the Church, let us pray to the Lord:
℟. **Lord, hear our prayer.**

The celebrant may adapt the introduction and invocations according to various circumstances. The usual petition for the needs of the Church and the entire world is added if the catechumens are to be dismissed and the general intercessions will be omitted in the Mass (see no. 173).
Another optional formula of this prayer is given in no. 382.

EXORCISM

171. After the prayer, the celebrant turns to the elect and with hands joined says:

Let us pray.

Father of mercy,
you helped the man born blind to believe in your Son
and through that faith to reach the light of your Kingdom.
Free your chosen ones from the falsehoods that surround and blind them.
Let truth be the foundation of their lives.
May they live in your light for ever.

We ask this through Christ our Lord.

℟. **Amen.**

The celebrant then lays his hand in silence on each one of the elect, if this can be done conveniently.

Then he extends his hands over the elect and continues:

Lord Jesus,
you are the true light that enlightens all men.
By the Spirit of truth,
free all who struggle under the yoke of the father of lies.
Arouse the good will of these men (and women)
whom you have chosen for your sacraments.
Grant them to enjoy your light
like the man whose sight you once restored,
and inspire them to become fearless witnesses to the faith,
for you are Lord for ever and ever.
℟. **Amen.**

Another optional form of the exorcism is given in no. 383.

An appropriate song may be sung, for example, Psalms 7, 26, 32, 38, 39, 40, 51, 115, 130, 139, or 142.

DISMISSAL OF THE ELECT

172. Then the celebrant dismisses the elect:

Go in peace until we meet at the next scrutiny.
May the Lord be with you always.
Elect: **Amen.**

The elect leave. If for rather serious reasons they cannot

leave, then the instructions in no. 96 are followed.

If, however, the eucharist is not celebrated, an appropriate song may be added, and the faithful and the elect are dismissed together.

CELEBRATION OF THE EUCHARIST

173. After the elect depart, the eucharist is celebrated. The general intercessions for the needs of the Church and the whole world begin at once. The profession of faith and the preparation of the gifts follow. For pastoral reasons, the general intercessions and the profession of faith may be omitted. A remembrance of the elect and their godparents is made in the eucharistic prayer (see nos. 377, 412).

THIRD SCRUTINY

174. The third scrutiny is celebrated on the Fifth Sunday of Lent, using the formulas in the Missal and Lectionary (see also nos. 384-385).

HOMILY

175. In the homily the celebrant moves from the scripture readings and explains the meaning of the third scrutiny in the light of the lenten liturgy and of the spiritual journey of the elect.

PRAYER IN SILENCE

176. After the homily the elect and their godparents come before the celebrant.

Looking at the faithful, he invites them to pray in silence for the elect, asking for the spirit of repentance and the understanding of sin, and for the true freedom of the children of God.

Then he turns to the catechumens and invites them to pray in silence. He instructs them to show their spirit of repentance by bowing or kneeling. Then he concludes in these or similar words:

You who have been chosen, bow your heads in prayer (or: **kneel in prayer).**

Then the elect bow or kneel, and all pray for some time in silence. Then, if desired, all stand.

PRAYER FOR THE ELECT

177. While this prayer is being said for the elect, the godparents place their right hand on the shoulder of the one they are sponsoring.

Celebrant:

God has chosen these men and women to serve him. Let us pray that they may be united to Christ in his death and resurrection and, by the grace of his sacraments, conquer the bitterness of death.

Reader:

That their faith may strengthen them against the deceits of the world, let us pray to the Lord:
℟. Lord, hear our prayer.

Reader:

That they may remain grateful to God who has rescued them from ignorance and opened to them the hope of salvation, let us pray to the Lord:
℟. Lord, hear our prayer.

Reader:

That the prayers and example of catechumens who have shed their blood for Christ may arouse their hope of eternal life, let us pray to the Lord:
℟. Lord, hear our prayer.

Reader:

That they may reject sin which destroys life, let us pray to the Lord:
℟. Lord, hear our prayer.

Reader:

That all who are saddened by the death of their loved ones may find comfort in Christ, let us pray to the Lord:
℟. Lord, hear our prayer.

Reader:

That we too at Easter may be strengthened by the

hope of rising to life with Christ, let us pray to the Lord:
℟. **Lord, hear our prayer.**

Reader:

That an increase of faith and love may give life to the whole world which God created out of love, let us pray to the Lord:
℟. **Lord, hear our prayer.**

The celebrant may adapt the introduction and invocations according to various circumstances. The usual petition for the needs of the Church and the whole world is added if the catechumens are to be dismissed and the general intercessions will be omitted in the Mass (see no. 180).

Another optional formula of this prayer is given in no. 386.

EXORCISM

178. After the prayer, the celebrant turns to the elect and with hands joined says:

Let us pray.

Father of eternal life,
you are a God, not of the dead, but of the living:
you sent your Son to proclaim the good news of life,
to rescue men from the kingdom of death
and to lead them to resurrection.
Free these chosen people
from the power of the evil spirit who brings death.
May they receive new life from Christ
and bear witness to his resurrection.

We ask this through Christ our Lord.

℟. **Amen.**

The celebrant then lays his hands in silence on each one of the elect, if this can be done conveniently.

Then he extends his hands over the elect and continues:

Lord Jesus,
you raised Lazarus from death
as a sign that you had come to give men life in fullest measure.

Rescue from death all who seek life from your sacraments
and free them from the spirit of evil.
By your Holy Spirit fill them with life;
give them faith, hope and love
that they may live with you always
and come to share the glory of your resurrection,
for you are Lord for ever and ever.
℟. **Amen.**

Another optional form of the exorcism is given in no. 387.

An appropriate song may be sung, for example, Psalms 7, 26, 32, 38, 39, 40, 51, 115, 130, 139 or 142.

DISMISSAL OF THE ELECT

179. Then the celebrant dismisses the elect:

Go in peace, and may the Lord be with you always.
Elect: **Amen.**

The elect leave. If for rather serious reasons they cannot leave, then the instructions in no. 96 are followed. If, however, the eucharist is not celebrated, an appropriate song may be added, and the faithful and the elect are dismissed together.

CELEBRATION OF THE EUCHARIST

180. After the elect depart, the eucharist is celebrated. The general intercessions for the needs of the Church and the whole world begin at once. The profession of faith and the preparation of the gifts follow. For pastoral reasons, the general intercessions and the profession of faith may be omitted. A remembrance of the elect and their godparents is made in the eucharistic prayer (see nos. 377, 412).

II. THE PRESENTATIONS

181. The presentations are to be celebrated after the scrutinies if they have not already taken place (see nos. 125-126). In this way, with the formation of the catechumens completed or under way for a suitable time, the Church entrusts them with the documents which are considered a summary of its faith and prayer from ancient time.

182. It is desirable to have this take place in the presence of the community of the faithful after the liturgy of the word at a weekday Mass with appropriate readings for the presentations.

PRESENTATION OF THE PROFESSION OF FAITH

183. First comes the presentation of the profession of faith or creed, which the elect are to memorize and then render in public (see nos. 194, 199) before they profess their faith in accordance with that creed on the day of their baptism.

184. The presentation of the profession of faith or creed takes place during the week after the first scrutiny. If desired, it may also be celebrated during the catechumenate period (see nos. 125-126).

READINGS AND HOMILY

185. In place of the assigned weekday readings, appropriate passages may be read, for example:

Reading I. **Deuteronomy 6:1-7:**
Listen, Israel: you shall love the Lord your God with all your heart.

Responsorial Psalm: Psalm 19:8. 9. 10. 11.
℟. (John 6:68) **Lord, you have the words of everlasting life.**

Reading II. **Romans 10:8-13:**
By confessing your faith in God you are saved.
or: **1 Corinthians 15:1-8a** (longer) **or 1-4** (shorter):
The Gospel will save you only if you keep believing what I preached to you.

℣. Gospel John 3:16:
God loved the world so much, he gave his only Son, that all who believe in him might have eternal life.

Gospel: **Matthew 16:13-18:**
On this rock I will build my Church.

or: **John 12:44-50:**
I, the light, have come into the world, so that whoever believes in me need not remain in the dark any more.

The celebrant bases his homily on the sacred text and explains the meaning and importance of the creed in relation to the teaching they have received and to the profession of faith they will make in baptism and keep during the rest of their life.

PRESENTATION OF THE PROFESSION OF FAITH

186. After the homily the deacon says:

Those who have been chosen please come forward to receive the Church's profession of faith.

Then the celebrant speaks to them in these or similar words:

My dear friends:
Listen carefully to the words of that faith by which you are to be justified. The words are few, but the mysteries they contain are awe-inspiring. Accept them with a sincere heart and be faithful to them.

The celebrant begins the profession of faith:

I believe in God,
and continues alone or with all the faithful:

the Father almighty,
creator of heaven and earth.

I believe in Jesus Christ, his only Son, our Lord.
He was conceived by the power of the Holy Spirit
and born of the Virgin Mary.
He suffered under Pontius Pilate,
was crucified, died, and was buried.
He descended to the dead.
On the third day he rose again.
He ascended into heaven,
and is seated at the right hand of the Father.
He will come again to judge the living and the dead.

I believe in the Holy Spirit,
the holy catholic Church,
the communion of saints,
the forgiveness of sins,
the resurrection of the body,
and the life everlasting.

If desired, he may also use the Nicene Creed:

We believe in one God,
the Father, the Almighty,
maker of heaven and earth,
of all that is seen and unseen.

We believe in one Lord, Jesus Christ,
the only Son of God,
eternally begotten of the Father,
God from God, Light from Light,
true God from true God,
begotten, not made, one in Being with the Father.
Through him all things were made.
For us men and for our salvation
he came down from heaven:
by the power of the Holy Spirit
he was born of the Virgin Mary, and became man.
For our sake he was crucified under Pontius Pilate;
he suffered, died, and was buried.
On the third day he rose again
in fulfillment of the Scriptures;
he ascended into heaven
and is seated at the right hand of the Father.
He will come again in glory to judge the living and the dead,
and his kingdom will have no end.

We believe in the Holy Spirit, the Lord, the giver of life,
who proceeds from the Father and the Son.
With the Father and the Son he is worshiped and glorified.
He has spoken through the Prophets.
We believe in one, holy, catholic and apostolic Church.
We acknowledge one baptism for the forgiveness of sins.

We look for the resurrection of the dead,
and the life of the world to come. Amen.

PRAYER OVER THE ELECT

187. With these or similar words, the celebrant invites the faithful to pray:

Let us pray for our brothers and sisters who have been chosen for baptism, that God in his mercy may make them responsive to his love, forgive their sins through the waters of new birth, and give them life in Christ Jesus our Lord.

All pray in silence.

Then the celebrant extends his hands over the elect and says:

Father, all-powerful and ever-living God,
fountain of light and truth,
source of eternal love,
hear our prayers for N. and N. your servants.
Cleanse them of sin, make them holy,
give them true knowledge,
firm hope and sound teaching
so that they will be prepared for the grace of baptism.

We ask this through Christ our Lord.
℟. **Amen.**

PRESENTATION OF THE LORD'S PRAYER

188. The Lord's Prayer is also given to the elect. From antiquity it has belonged to those who have received the spirit of adoption of sons in baptism. When the neophytes take part in their first celebration of the eucharist, they will say it together with the rest of the baptized.

189. This presentation takes place during the week after the third scrutiny. If desired, it may also be celebrated even during the catechumenate period (see nos. 125-126). If necessary, it may be left for the preparatory rites (see nos. 193 ff).

READINGS AND HOMILY

190. In place of the assigned weekday readings, appro-

priate passages may be read, for example:

Reading I **Hosea 11:1b, 3-4, 8c-9:**
I have led you with cords of love.

Responsorial Psalm: Psalm 23:1-3a, 3b-4, 5, 6.
℟. (1)
The Lord is my shepherd there is nothing I shall want.

or: Psalm 103:1-2, 8 and 10, 11-12, 13 and 18.
℟. (13)
As a father is kind to his children,
so the Lord is kind to those who fear him.

Reading II **Romans 8:14-17, 26-27:**
You have received the Spirit of sonship and it makes us cry out, "Abba, Father!"
or: **Galatians 4:4-7:**
God has sent the spirit of his son into
our hearts: the spirit that cries, Abba, Father!

Verse before the Gospel: Romans 8:15:
You have received the spirit which makes us God's children,
and in that Spirit we call God our Father.

GOSPEL

191. The deacon says:

Those who wish to learn the Lord's Prayer please come forward.
The celebrant speaks to the elect in these or similar words:

This is how our Lord taught his disciples to pray:

✠ A reading from the holy gospel according to Matthew
At that time, Jesus told his disciples,
When you pray, say:

Our Father. . . .
Matthew 6:9-13

In the homily the celebrant explains the meaning and importance of the Lord's Prayer.

PRAYER OVER THE ELECT

192. With these or similar words, the celebrant invites the faithful to pray:

Let us pray for our brothers and sisters who have been chosen for baptism, that God in his mercy may make them responsive to his love, forgive their sins through the waters of new birth, and give them life in Christ Jesus our Lord.

All pray in silence.

Then the celebrant extends his hands over the elect and says:

Almighty and eternal God,
you continually bless your Church with new
members.
Deepen the faith and understanding
of these candidates chosen for baptism.
Give them a new birth in your living waters
and make them members of your family.

We ask this through Christ our Lord.
℟. **Amen.**

PREPARATORY RITES

193. Whenever the elect can be gathered on Holy Saturday so that they may dispose themselves by recollection and prayer to receive the sacraments, the following rites are suitable. Some or all of them may be used, as desired.

I. RECITATION OF THE PROFESSION OF FAITH

194. By this rite the elect are prepared to profess their baptismal faith and are taught their duty of proclaiming the Gospel message.

195. If because of necessity the profession of faith could not be presented, it is not recited.

READINGS AND HOMILY

196. At the beginning an appropriate song is sung. Then

one of the following passages or another appropriate one is read:

Matthew 16:13-17: You are Christ, the Son of the living God.

John 6:35, 63-71: To whom shall we go? You have the words of eternal life.

When the rite of ephphetha or opening of ears and mouth is celebrated at this time:

Mark 7:31-37: Ephphetha, that is, be opened.

A brief homily is given.

197. If the rite of ephphetha or opening of ears and mouth is used at this time, the celebration continues, beginning with nos. 200-202.

PRAYER FOR THE RECITATION OF THE PROFESSION OF FAITH

198. With hands extended the celebrant says this prayer:

Let us pray.

Lord,
our chosen brothers and sisters
have accepted your loving plan of salvation
and the mysteries of Christ's life.
May they proclaim these mysteries in prayer,
be true to them in faith,
and accomplish your will in their lives.

We ask this through Christ our Lord.
℟. **Amen.**

RECITATION OF THE PROFESSION OF FAITH

199. Then the elect recite the profession of faith:

I believe in God, the Father almighty,
creator of heaven and earth.
I believe in Jesus Christ, his only Son, our Lord.
He was conceived by the power of the Holy Spirit
and born of the Virgin Mary.
He suffered under Pontius Pilate,

was crucified, died, and was buried.
He descended to the dead.
On the third day he rose again.
He ascended into heaven,
and is seated at the right hand of the Father.
He will come again to judge the living and the dead.
I believe in the Holy Spirit,
the holy catholic Church,
the communion of saints,
the forgiveness of sins,
the resurrection of the body,
and the life everlasting. Amen.

If the Nicene creed was used in the presentation (see no. 186), it is also used here.

II. RITE OF EPHPHETHA OR OPENING OF EARS AND MOUTH

200. By its symbolism, this rite shows the need of grace for anyone to be able to hear the word of God and to work for salvation.

READING

201. After an appropriate song, Mark 7:31-37 is read, and the celebrant explains it briefly.

RITE OF EPHPHETHA OR OPENING OF EARS AND MOUTH

202. With his thumb the celebrant touches each of the elect on the right and left ear (of each the elect) and on the closed mouth saying:

Ephphetha: that is, be opened, that you may profess the faith you have heard, to the praise and glory of God.

If there are too many, he uses the whole formula for the first one, and for the rest he says:

Ephphetha: that is, be opened.

III. THE CHOOSING OF A CHRISTIAN NAME

203. Unless it has already been done according to no. 88, a new name may now be given. It must be a Christian name or one in use in that part of the world, as long as it has a Christian meaning. Meanwhile, if circumstances suggest and if there are not many elect, it will be sufficient to explain to each one the Christian meaning of the name already given to him by his parents.

READING

204. After an appropriate song it might be desirable to have a reading which the celebrant explains briefly, for example:

Genesis 17:1-7 You will be called Abraham.
Isaiah 62:1-5 You will be called by a new name.
Revelation 3:11-13 I will write my new name upon him.
Matthew 16:13-18 You are Peter.
John 1:40-42 You will be called Peter.

CHOOSING A NAME

205. The celebrant asks the elect what name he wishes to choose. Then if desired (see no. 203), he says:

N., from now on you will be called N.
Elect: **Thank you** (or some other suitable response).

If necessary, he explains the Christian meaning of the name his parents gave him.

IV. ANOINTING WITH THE OIL OF CATECHUMENS

206. The anointing with the oil of catechumens may be conferred on Holy Saturday if the episcopal conference decides to continue this practice and if it cannot be done during the Easter Vigil because of lack of time. It may be done either separately or with the recitation of the profession of faith or creed; or it may be done before it, to prepare for the profession of faith or creed, or after it, to confirm it.

207. The oil blessed by the bishop in the Chrism Mass is

used. For pastoral reasons,[1] the priest blesses it, saying the following prayer:

Lord God, protector of all who believe in you,
bless ✠ this oil
and give the wisdom and strength it signifies
to all who are anointed with it
in preparation for their baptism.
Bring them to a deeper understanding of the Gospel,
help them to accept the challenge of Christian living,
and lead them to the joy of new birth
in the family of your Church.

We ask this through Christ our Lord.
℟. **Amen.**

Then the celebrant turns to the elect and says:

We anoint you with the oil of salvation
in the name of Christ our Savior.
May he strengthen you with his power,
who lives and reigns for ever and ever.
Elect: **Amen.**

Each elect is anointed with the oil of catechumens on the breast or on both hands or even on other parts of the body, if this seems desirable. If there is a great number of the elect, several ministers may be used.

[1]See Rite of Blessing of Oils, Introduction, no. 7.

THIRD STAGE
CELEBRATION OF THE SACRAMENTS OF INITIATION

208. When the initiation of adults is celebrated as is customary during the Easter Vigil, the sacraments are conferred after the blessing of the water, as noted in the order of the Easter Vigil (no. 44).

209. If it takes place outside the normal time (see Introduction, nos. 58-59), the celebration should be filled with the Easter spirit (General Introduction on Christian Initiation, no. 6), using the ritual Mass from the Missal (see no. 388).

CELEBRATION OF BAPTISM

210. Even when the sacraments of initiation are celebrated outside Easter time, the water is blessed (see General Introduction of Christian Initiation, no. 21), recalling the wonderful works of God from the creation of the world and the human race to the mystery of God's love; then by calling on the Holy Spirit and by the announcing of the death and rising of Christ, the newness of the washing of regeneration by the Lord is taught; through baptism we share in his death and rising and are made the holy people of God.

211. The renunciation of Satan and the profession of faith form one rite which reaches its full strength in the baptism of adults. Since baptism is a sacrament of faith by which the catechumens adhere to God and at the same time are given new life by him, it is fitting that the washing with water is preceded by each person's actions. By these actions, as was prefigured in the covenant of the patriarchs, they renounce sin and Satan completely so that they adhere for ever to the promise of the Savior and the mystery of the Trinity. By this profession, which they make in the presence of the celebrant and the community, they signify their intention, brought to maturity during the catechumenate, of entering into a new covenant with Christ. These adults embrace this faith handed on by the Church with God's help, and in this faith they are baptized.

212. The anointing with the oil of catechumens, which

occurs between the renunciation and the profession of faith, may be anticipated for pastoral need and liturgical benefit.

In this case, it should signify the need of God's strength so that the person who is being baptized, despite the bonds of his past life and overcoming the adversity of the devil, strongly take the step of professing his faith and hold to it without faltering throughout his entire life.

INSTRUCTION BY THE CELEBRANT

213. Before the litany, the candidates and their godparents go to the font. They stand around it in such a way that they do not block the view of the faithful. If there are many to be baptized, they may approach while the litany is being sung.

The celebrant speaks to the assembly and instructs them in these or similar words:

Dear friends: Let us ask God our Father to be merciful to our brothers and sisters N. and N. who are asking for baptism. He has called them and brought them to his hour. May he grant them the riches of his light and strength to follow Christ with courageous hearts and to profess the faith of the Church. May he give them the new life of the Holy Spirit, the Spirit whom we are about to ask to come down upon this water.

LITANY

214. Then the litany is sung. In the litany some names of saints may be added, especially the titular of the church, the local patrons and the saints of those to be baptized.

Lord, have mercy. Lord, have mercy.
Christ, have mercy. Christ, have mercy.
Lord, have mercy. Lord, have mercy.
Holy Mary, Mother of God, pray for us.
Saint Michael, pray for us.
Holy angels of God, pray for us.
Saint John the Baptist, pray for us.
Saint Joseph, pray for us.
Saint Peter and Saint Paul, pray for us.
Saint Andrew, pray for us.
Saint John, pray for us.

Saint Mary Magdalene, pray for us.
Saint Stephen, pray for us.
Saint Ignatius of Antioch, pray for us.
Saint Lawrence, pray for us.
Saint Perpetua and Saint Felicity, pray for us.
Saint Agnes, pray for us.
Saint Gregory, pray for us.
Saint Augustine, pray for us.
Saint Basil, pray for us.
Saint Martin, pray for us.
Saint Benedict, pray for us.
Saint Francis and Saint Dominic, pray for us.
Saint Francis Xavier, pray for us.
Saint John Vianney, pray for us.
Saint Catherine of Siena, pray for us.
Saint Teresa of Avila, pray for us.
All holy men and women, pray for us.
Lord, be merciful. Lord, save your people.
From all evil, Lord, save your people.
From every sin, Lord, save your people.
From everlasting death, Lord, save your people.
By your coming as man, Lord, save your people.
By your death and rising to new life,
Lord, save your people.
By your gift of the Holy Spirit,
Lord, save your people.
Be merciful to us sinners. Lord, hear our prayer.
Give new life to these chosen ones by the grace of baptism, Lord, hear our prayer.
Jesus, Son of the living God,
Lord, hear our prayer.
Christ, hear us, Christ, hear us.
Lord Jesus, hear our prayer,
Lord, Jesus, hear our prayer.

BLESSING THE WATER

215. Then the celebrant turns to the font and blesses the water:

Father,
you give us grace through sacramental signs

which tell us of the wonders of your unseen power.
In baptism we use your gift of water
which you have made a rich symbol of the grace
you give us in this sacrament.
At the very dawn of creation
your Spirit breathed on the waters,
making them the wellspring of all holiness.
The waters of the great flood
you made a sign of the waters of baptism
that make an end of sin
and a new beginning of goodness.
Through the waters of the Red Sea
you led Israel out of slavery
to be an image of God's holy people
set free from sin by baptism.
In the waters of the Jordan
your Son was baptized by John
and anointed with the Spirit.
Your Son willed that water and blood should flow from his side
as he hung upon the cross.
After his resurrection he told his disciples:
"Go out and teach all nations,
baptizing them in the name of the Father, and of the Son, and of the Holy Spirit."

Father,
look now with love upon your Church
and unseal for it the fountain of baptism.
By the power of the Spirit
give to the water of this font
the grace of your Son.
You created man in your own likeness:
cleanse him from sin in a new birth to innocence
by water and the Spirit.

The celebrant touches the water with his right hand and continues:

We ask you, Father, with your Son
to send the Holy Spirit upon the water of this font.
May all who are buried with Christ in the death of baptism

rise also with him to newness of life.

We ask this through Christ our Lord.
All: **Amen.**

Other optional formulas are given in no. 389.

216. During the Easter season, when baptismal water blessed at the Easter Vigil is available, the baptism should have an element of thanksgiving and prayer. In this case, the blessing is given according to the formulas in no. 389, using the variation at the end of the formula.

RENUNCIATION

217. After the font is consecrated, the celebrant questions all the elect together:

A
Celebrant:
Do you reject Satan and all his works and all his empty promises?
Elect: **I do.**

B
Celebrant:
Do you reject Satan?

Elect: **I do.**

Celebrant:
And all his works?
Elect: **I do.**

Celebrant:
And all his empty promises?
Elect: **I do.**

C
Celebrant:
Do you reject sin so as to live in the freedom of God's children?
Elect: **I do.**

Celebrant:
Do you reject the glamor of evil and refuse to be mastered by sin?
Elect: **I do.**

Celebrant:
Do you reject Satan, father of sin and prince of darkness?
Elect: **I do.**

If desired, the celebrant, advised by the godparents of the name of each candidate, asks each of them, choosing any one of the three formulas above.

Besides these three formulas, the episcopal conference may adapt them further, especially where it is necessary for the elect to renounce superstitions, divinations and magical arts (see no. 80).

ANOINTING WITH THE OIL OF CATECHUMENS

218. Unless this anointing took place earlier as one of the preparatory rites (nos. 206-207), the celebrant says:

We anoint you with the oil of salvation
in the name of Christ our Savior.
May he strengthen you with his power,
who lives and reigns for ever and ever.
Elect: **Amen.**

Each of the elect is anointed with the oil of catechumens on the breast or on both hands, or even on other parts of the body, if this seems desirable. If there is a great number of the elect, several ministers may be used.

The episcopal conference may decide to omit this anointing.

PROFESSION OF FAITH

219. Then the celebrant, advised by the godparent of the name of each candidate, asks each one:

N., do you believe in God, the Father almighty, creator of heaven and earth?
Elect: **I do.**

Celebrant:
Do you believe in Jesus Christ, his only Son, our Lord, who was born of the Virgin Mary, was crucified, died, and was buried, rose from the dead, and is now seated at the right hand of the Father?
Elect: **I do.**

Celebrant:
Do you believe in the Holy Spirit, the holy catholic Church, the communion of saints, the forgiveness of sins, the resurrection of the body, and life everlasting?
Elect: **I do.**

After the profession of faith, each candidate is baptized at once.

Where there is a large number to be baptized, the profession of faith may be made by all simultaneously or in several groups.

RITE OF BAPTISM

220. If baptism is by immersion of the whole body or of the head only, decency and decorum should prevail.

Touching the candidate, the celebrant immerses him or his head three times, raising him out of the water each time and baptizing him by using the name of the Trinity only once:

N., I baptize you in the name of the Father,

he immerses him the first time,

and of the Son,

he immerses him the second time,

and of the Holy Spirit.

he immerses him the third time.

Either or both godparents touch the candidate.

After the baptism of each adult, the people may sing a short acclamation (see no. 390).

221. If baptism is done by infusion or pouring, the celebrant takes baptismal water from the font and pours it three times on the bowed head of the candidate, baptizing him in the name of the Trinity:

N., I baptize you in the name of the Father,

he pours water a first time,

and of the Son,

he pours water a second time,

and of the Holy Spirit.

he pours water a third time.

Either or both godparents place their right hand on the right shoulder of the candidate.

After the baptism of each adult, the people may sing a short acclamation (see no. 390).

222. When there is a large number to be baptized, several priests and deacons are distributed among the candidates and baptize them by immersion or by infusion or by pouring, using the form for each person.

While the baptisms are taking place, singing by the people is desirable. There also may be readings or a period of sacred silence.

EXPLANATORY RITES

223. The explanatory rites (nos. 224-226) follow baptism immediately. After these rites, confirmation is customarily celebrated, as described below (nos. 227-231), and thus the anointing after baptism (no. 224) is omitted.

ANOINTING AFTER BAPTISM

[224.] If for some special reason the celebration of confirmation is separated from baptism, then the celebrant anoints the candidates in the usual way after baptism. He says this prayer over all the newly baptized:

God, the Father of our Lord Jesus Christ,
has freed you from all sin,
given you a new birth by water and the Holy Spirit,
and welcomed you into his holy people.
He now anoints you with the chrism of salvation.
As Christ was anointed Priest, Prophet, and King,
so may you live always as a member of his body,
sharing everlasting life.
Newly baptized: **Amen.**

Then the celebrant anoints each one with sacred chrism on the crown of the head, saying nothing.

When a large number is baptized, other presbyters or deacons may anoint some of them with chrism.

CLOTHING WITH THE WHITE GARMENT

225. The celebrant says:

N. and N., you have become a new creation
and have clothed yourselves in Christ.
Take this white garment
and bring it unstained to the judgment seat of our Lord Jesus Christ
so that you may have everlasting life.
Newly baptized: **Amen.**

At the words **Take this white garment** the godparents place the white garment on the neophytes. Another color may be used if local conditions require this.

If so desired, this rite may be omitted.

PRESENTATION OF THE LIGHTED CANDLE

226. The celebrant takes the Easter candle in his hands or touches it, saying:

Godparents, please come forward to give the newly baptized the light of Christ.

The godparents approach, light a candle from the Easter candle and hand it to the neophyte. Then the celebrant says:

You have been enlightened by Christ.
Walk always as children of the light
and keep the flame of faith alive in your hearts.
When the Lord comes, may you go out to meet him
with all the saints in the heavenly kingdom.
Newly baptized: **Amen.**

CELEBRATION OF CONFIRMATION

227. Between the celebration of baptism and confirmation, the congregation may sing an appropriate song.

Confirmation may be celebrated in the sanctuary or in the baptistry, as local circumstances dictate.

228. If baptism is given by a bishop, he should also administer confirmation in the same celebration.

When the bishop is not present, confirmation may be given by the presbyter who conferred baptism.

When there are many to be confirmed, other presbyters may be associated as ministers to give this sacrament, if they are to be delegated for this (see no. 46).

229. The celebrant speaks briefly to the neophytes in these or similar words:

My dear newly baptized:
Born again in Christ by baptism, you have become members of Christ and of his priestly people. Now you are to share in the outpouring of the Holy Spirit among us, the Spirit sent by the Lord upon his apostles at Pentecost and given by them and their successors to the baptized.

The promised strength of the Holy Spirit, which you are to receive, will make you more like Christ, and help you to be witnesses to his suffering, death, and resurrection. It will strengthen you to be active members of the Church and to build up the Body of Christ in faith and love.

Then the celebrant (with the presbyters associated with him as ministers of the sacrament nearby) stands and faces the people and with hands joined says:

Let us pray, dear friends,
to God, the all-powerful Father,
that he will pour out the Holy Spirit
on these newly baptized
to strengthen them with his abundant gifts
and anoint them to be more like Christ his Son.

All pray in silence for a short time.

230. Then the celebrant (and the presbyters associated with him) lay hands upon all who are to be confirmed. The celebrant alone says:

All-powerful God, Father of our Lord Jesus Christ,

by water and the Holy Spirit
you freed your sons (and daughters) from sin
and gave them new life.
Send your Holy Spirit upon them
to be their Helper and Guide.
Give them the spirit of wisdom and understanding,
the spirit of right judgment and courage,
the spirit of knowledge and reverence.
Fill them with the spirit of wonder and awe in your presence.

We ask this through Christ our Lord.
℟. **Amen.**

231. One of the ministers brings the chrism to the celebrant. Each candidate goes to the celebrant, or, according to circumstances, the celebrant may go to the individual candidates. The godparent places his right hand on the candidate's shoulder and gives the candidate's name to the celebrant, or the candidate may give his own name.

The celebrant dips his right thumb in the chrism and makes the sign of the cross on the forehead of the one to be confirmed as he says:

N., be sealed with the Gift of Holy Spirit.
Newly confirmed: **Amen.**

The celebrant adds:
Peace be with you.
Newly confirmed: **And also with you.**

If other presbyters are associated with him in conferring the sacrament, they receive vessels of chrism from the bishop, if he is present.

The candidates go to the celebrant or to the presbyters, or the latter may go to the candidates. The anointing is done as described above.

During the anointing, a suitable song may be sung.

CELEBRATION OF THE EUCHARIST

232. The profession of faith is omitted, and the general

intercessions follow immediately. For the first time the neophytes take part in them. Some of them carry the gifts when they are brought to the altar.

233. In the first eucharistic prayer, the neophytes are mentioned in the **Father, accept this offering** and the godparents in the **Remember, Lord, your people** (no. 377).

If the second, third or fourth eucharistic prayer is used, a special formula is added for the neophytes (no. 391).

234. It is most desirable that the neophytes receive communion under both species, together with their godparents, parents, spouses, and catechists.

Before **This is the Lamb of God** the celebrant may briefly remind the neophytes of the value of this great mystery which is the climax of their initiation and the center of the whole Christian life.

THE PERIOD OF POSTBAPTISMAL CATECHESIS OR MYSTAGOGIA

235. To strengthen the first steps of the neophytes, it is desirable that they be helped carefully and familiarly in all circumstances by the community of the faithful, by their godparents and by their pastors. Great care should be taken that they obtain full and joyful insertion into the life of the community.

236. At Sunday Masses throughout the Easter season, the neophytes should keep their special places among the faithful. All the neophytes should take part in the Mass with their godparents. They should be mentioned in the homily and in the general intercessions.

237. To close the period of postbaptismal catechesis, at the end of the Easter season, around Pentecost, some form of celebration is held, adding external festivities according to local customs.

238. On the anniversary of their baptism, it is desirable that the neophytes gather together again to give thanks to God, to share their spiritual experiences with one another, and to gain new strength.

239. To develop pastoral contact with the new members of his church, the bishop should make sure, especially if he cannot preside at the sacraments of initiation, that at least once a year he meets the newly baptized and presides at a celebration of the eucharist. At this Mass they may receive communion under both species.

CHAPTER II

SIMPLE RITE OF ADULT INITIATION

240. In extraordinary circumstances, when the candidate cannot go through all the stages of initiation, or when the local ordinary, judging that the candidate is sincere in his conversion to Christianity and in his religious maturity, permits him to receive baptism without delay, the bishop may allow this simple rite to be used in individual cases. It may be done in one celebration (nos. 245-273), or one or two of the rites from the catechumenate or from the period of purification and illumination may be carried out before the celebration of the sacraments (nos. 274-277).

241. Before the candidate is baptized, he should choose a godparent (Introduction, no. 43) and spend some time with the local community (Introduction, nos. 12, 19:2). He should be instructed and prepared for a suitable period of time to purify his motives for seeking baptism so that he may become more mature in his conversion and his faith.

242. Besides the presentation and reception of the candidate, the rite expresses his public and firm intention of asking for Christian initiation and the consent of the Church. After an appropriate liturgy of the word, the celebration of all the sacraments of initiation takes place.

243. The rite is usually celebrated during Mass, and suitable readings are chosen. The prayers are taken from the Mass of initiation or from another suitable Mass. After baptism and confirmation, the neophyte takes part in the eucharistic celebration for the first time.

244. As far as possible, the celebration takes place on a Sunday (Introduction, no. 59), with the active participation of the local community.

RITE OF RECEPTION

245. Before the liturgy of the word, the candidate and his

godparent wait outside the entrance of the church or at a suitable spot in the church. The faithful may sing an appropriate psalm or song while the priest, vested for Mass, goes to meet the candidate.

246. The celebrant greets the candidate in a friendly manner. He speaks to him, to his sponsor and to all present, pointing out the joy and happiness of the Church. He reminds the sponsor and friends of their own experiences and religious attitude, as a result of which the candidate, following his own spiritual call, has come to this day.

Then he invites the candidate and his godparent to come forward. While they come and take their places before the priest, an appropriate song may be sung, for example: Psalm 63:1-9.

247. Facing the candidate, the celebrant asks him:

N., what do you ask of God's Church?
Candidate: **Faith.**

Celebrant:
What does faith offer you?
Candidate: **Eternal life.**

The celebrant may use other words in asking the candidate about his intention and may permit him to answer in his own words, for example, after the first question: **What do you ask?** or **What do you desire? For what reason have you come?**, he may receive such answers as: **The grace of Christ,** or **entrance into the Church,** or **eternal life** or other suitable responses. The celebrant will adapt his questions to the answers.

248. The celebrant, adapting his words as required to the responses given, speaks again to the candidate in these or similar words:

This is eternal life: to know the true God and the one he sent, Jesus Christ. God raised him from the dead to be the Lord of life and of all things, seen and unseen. In asking for baptism today you ask for this life. You would not do so unless you had come to know Christ and wanted to be his disciple. Have you completed

your preparation for becoming a Christian? Have you listened to Christ's word and made up your mind to keep his commandments? Have you shared in our way of life and in our prayer?
Candidate: **I have.**

249. The celebrant turns to the godparent and asks:

You are this candidate's godparent. Before God, do you consider him (her) a suitable person to be received today into full communion with the Church?
Godparent: **I do.**

Celebrant:
You have spoken in this candidate's (or: **N's) favor. Will you continue to help him (her) to serve Christ by your words and example?**
Godparent: **I will.**

250. With hands joined the celebrant concludes:

Let us pray.

Father of love and mercy,
we thank you in the name of our brother (sister)
who has experienced your guiding presence in his
(her) life.
Today, in the presence of your Church,
he (she) is answering your call to faith:
let him (her) find joy and fulfillment in his (her) new
life.

We ask this through Christ our Lord.
℟. **Amen.**

ENTRY INTO THE CHURCH

251. The celebrant invites the candidate in these or similar words:

N., we welcome you into the church
to share with us at the table of God's word.

The candidate and his godparent enter the church. Meanwhile an appropriate song may be sung.

LITURGY OF THE WORD

252. When the candidate and his godparent reach their seats and the celebrant comes into the sanctuary, the liturgy of the word begins. The introductory rites of the Mass are omitted.

READINGS AND HOMILY

253. The readings and the responsorial psalm and verse before the Gospel are taken from those listed in no. 388, or they may be chosen from the occurring Sunday or feast. Then the homily is given.

PRAYER AND PENITENTIAL RITE

254. After the homily the candidate and his godparent come before the celebrant. The whole congregation offers this prayer or a similar one:

Let us pray for our brother (sister) who is asking for Christ's sacraments, and for ourselves, sinners that we are: may we all draw nearer to Christ in faith and repentance and walk without tiring in the new life he gives us.

Reader:
That the Lord will kindle in all of us a spirit of true repentance, let us pray to the Lord:
All: **Lord, hear our prayer.**

Reader:
That we, who have been saved by Christ and have died to sin through baptism, may witness to his grace by our manner of life, let us pray to the Lord:
All: **Lord, hear our prayer.**

Reader:
That the Lord will give our brother (sister) sorrow for his (her) sins and trust in God's love as he (she) prepares to meet Christ, his (her) Savior, let us pray to the Lord:
All: **Lord, hear our prayer.**

Reader:
That by following Christ who takes away the sin of the world our brother (sister) will be healed of the

infection of sin and freed from its power, let us pray to the Lord:
All: **Lord, hear our prayer.**

Reader:
That the Holy Spirit will wash him (her) clean from sin and lead him (her) in the way of holiness, let us pray to the Lord:
All: **Lord, hear our prayer.**

Reader:
That through his (her) burial with Christ in baptism he (she) will die to sin and live only for God, let us pray to the Lord:
All: **Lord, hear our prayer.**

Reader:
That on the day of judgment he (she) will come before the Father bearing fruits of holiness and love, we pray to the Lord:
All: **Lord, hear our prayer.**

Reader:
That the world for which the Father gave his beloved Son may believe in his love and turn to him, let us pray to the Lord:
All: **Lord, hear our prayer.**

After the prayer, the candidate bows his head or kneels and joins the congregation in making a general confession. Depending on circumstances, this may be omitted.

PRAYER OF EXORCISM AND ANOINTING OF THE CATECHUMEN

255. Omitting **"May almighty God,"** the celebrant concludes with this prayer:

Almighty God,
you sent your only Son
to rescue us from the slavery of sin
and to give to us the freedom of your children.
We now pray for our brother (sister)
who comes before you, acknowledging his (her)
sinfulness.

He (she) has faced temptation
and been tested by the evil one.
By the passion and resurrection of your Son,
bring him (her) out of the power of darkness.
With the grace of Christ, make him (her) strong
and guide him (her) through life.

We ask this through Christ our Lord.
All: **Amen.**

256. The celebrant continues:

We anoint you with the oil of salvation
in the name of Christ our Savior.
May he strengthen you with his power,
who lives and reigns for ever and ever.
All: **Amen.**

The candidate is anointed with the oil of catechumens on the breast or on both hands or even on other parts of the body, if this seems desirable.

This anointing may be omitted if the episcopal conference so decides. In this case the celebrant says:

May Christ our Savior
strengthen you with his power,
for he is Lord for ever and ever.
All: **Amen.**

He places his hand on the candidate in silence.

CELEBRATION OF BAPTISM

CELEBRANT'S INSTRUCTION

257. The candidate and his godparent go to the font. The celebrant instructs the congregation in these or similar words:

Dear friends: Let us ask God our Father to be merciful to our brother (sister) N. who is asking for baptism. He has called him (her) to this hour. May he grant him (her) the riches of his light and strength to follow Christ with a courageous heart and to profess the faith

of the Church. May he give him (her) the new life of the Holy Spirit, the Spirit whom we are about to ask to come down upon this water.

258. Then the celebrant turns to the font and blesses the water as described in no. 215.

RENUNCIATION

259. After the font is consecrated, the celebrant questions the candidate as described in no. 217.

PROFESSION OF FAITH

260. Then the celebrant asks the candidate the following questions as described in no. 219.

RITE OF BAPTISM

261-262. The rite continues as described in nos. 220 and 221.

EXPLANATORY RITES

ANOINTING AFTER BAPTISM

263. If for some special reason the celebration of confirmation is separated from baptism, then the celebrant anoints the candidate in the usual way after baptism. He says this prayer over the newly baptized:

God, the Father of our Lord Jesus Christ,
has freed you from all sin,
given you a new birth by water and the Holy Spirit,
and welcomed you into his holy people.
He now anoints you with the chrism of salvation.
As Christ was anointed Priest, Prophet, and King,
so may you live always as a member of his body,
sharing everlasting life.
Newly baptized: **Amen.**

Then the celebrant anoints him on the crown of the head with the sacred chrism, in silence.

CLOTHING WITH THE WHITE GARMENT

264. The celebrant says:

N., you have become a new creation
and have clothed yourself in Christ.
Take this white garment
and bring it unstained to the judgment seat of our Lord Jesus Christ
so that you may have everlasting life.

Newly baptized: **Amen.**

At the words **Take this white garment** the godparent places the white garment on the neophyte. Another color may be used if local conditions require this.

If so desired, this rite may be omitted.

PRESENTATION OF THE LIGHTED CANDLE

265. The celebrant takes the Easter candle in his hands or touches it, saying:

Godparent, please come forward to give the newly baptized the light of Christ.

The godparent approaches, lights a candle from the Easter candle and hands it to the neophyte. Then the celebrant says:

You have been enlightened by Christ.
Walk always as a child of the light
and keep the flame of faith alive in your heart.
When the Lord comes, may you go out to meet him
with all the saints in the heavenly kingdom.

Newly baptized: **Amen.**

CELEBRATION OF CONFIRMATION

266. Between the celebration of baptism and confirmation, the congregation may sing an appropriate song.

267. If baptism is given by a bishop, he should also administer confirmation in the same celebration.

When the bishop is not present, confirmation may be given

by the presbyter who conferred baptism.

268. The neophyte stands in front of the celebrant, who speaks to him in these or similar words:

N., born again in Christ by baptism, you have become a member of Christ and of his priestly people. Now you are to share in the outpouring of the Holy Spirit among us, the Spirit sent by the Lord upon his apostles at Pentecost and given by them and their successors to the baptized.

The promised strength of the Holy Spirit which you are to receive will make you more like Christ and help you to be a witness to his suffering, death, and resurrection. It will strengthen you to be an active member of the Church and to build up the Body of Christ in faith and love.

Then the celebrant stands and faces the people and with hands joined says:

Let us pray, dear friends,
to God the all-powerful Father
that he will pour out the Holy Spirit
on the newly baptized,
to strengthen him (her) with his abundant gifts
and anoint him (her) to be a more like Christ, his Son.

All pray in silence for a short time.

269. Then the celebrant lays hands upon the candidate and says:

All-powerful God, Father of our Lord Jesus Christ,
by water and the Holy Spirit
you freed your son (daughter) from sin
and gave him (her) new life.
Send your Holy Spirit upon him (her)
to be his (her) Helper and Guide.
Give him (her) the spirit of wisdom and understanding,
the spirit of right judgment and courage,
the spirit of knowledge and reverence.

Fill him (her) with the spirit of wonder and awe in your presence.

We ask this through Christ our Lord.
℟. **Amen.**

270. The candidate goes to the celebrant. The godparent places his right hand on the candidate's shoulder and gives the candidate's name to the celebrant, or the candidate may give his own name.

The celebrant dips his right thumb in the chrism and makes the sign of the cross on the forehead of the one to be confirmed as he says:

N., be sealed with the Gift of the Holy Spirit.
Newly confirmed: **Amen.**

The celebrant adds:
Peace be with you.
Newly confirmed: **And also with you.**

CELEBRATION OF THE EUCHARIST

271. The profession of faith is omitted, and the general intercessions follow immediately. For the first time the neophyte takes part in them. The neophyte brings the gifts to the altar.

272. In the first eucharistic prayer, the neophyte is mentioned in the **Father, accept his offering,** and the godparent in the **Remember, Lord, your people.** If the second, third or fourth eucharistic prayer is used, a special formula is added for the neophyte (no. 391).

273. It is most desirable that the neophyte receive communion under both kinds, along with his godparent, parents, spouse and catechists.

Before the **Lamb of God,** the celebrant may briefly remind the neophyte of this great mystery which is the climax of his initiation and the center of the whole Christian life.

274. In extraordinary circumstances, such as disease, old age, change of domicile, or a long journey, when:

a) the candidate could not begin the catechumenate with an appropriate rite, or began it and could not complete it with all its rites;

b) and otherwise it would be harmful to his spiritual welfare if he received the first rite and would be deprived of the benefits of a longer preparation, then, with the bishop's permission, it would be advantageous to add one or more elements of the complete rite to the first rite he has received.

275. This additional rite has the advantage of helping a new candidate catch up to those who are more advanced by adding some of the initial ceremonies from the complete rite (such as admission into the catechumenate, minor exorcisms, blessings, and the like); or of helping an individual who began with the others to receive the rites he missed (such as election, rite of purification and illumination, or the sacraments of initiation).

276. Adaptations may be made with pastoral judgment as long as care is taken to connect the preceding and additional rites in this way:
1) by adding a rite, such as rites from the catechumenate (nos. 106-132) and the presentations (nos. 183-192);
2) by dividing and enlarging the rite of reception (nos. 245-251) or the liturgy of the word (nos. 252-256). In the rite of reception, nos. 245-247 may be enlarged along the lines of the rite of admission of catechumens (nos. 73-97); nos. 246-247 may be omitted if desired, and nos. 248-249 may give way to the rite of election. In the liturgy of the word, nos. 253-255 may be adapted to the first or second scrutiny (nos. 160-179), and so on;
3) by using part of the simple rite in place of some of the ceremonies in the complete rite; or, when those interested in Christianity are received (see Introduction, no. 12:3), by joining that ceremony to the rite of admission to the catechumenate (nos. 73-93) and election (nos. 143-151).

277. When this additional rite is used, care should be taken that:
1) the candidate has received a complete formation;
2) the rite is celebrated with the active participation of a congregation;
3) after receiving the sacraments, the neophyte benefits from a period of postbaptismal catechesis, insofar as this is possible.

CHAPTER III

SHORT RITE OF ADULT INITIATION IN PROXIMATE DANGER OF DEATH OR AT THE POINT OF DEATH

278. A person who is in proximate danger of death, whether he is a catechumen or not, may be baptized with the short rite described in nos. 283-294, as long as he is not at the point of death and is able to hear the questions and answer them.

279. If he has already been received as a catechumen, he must promise that when he recovers, he will complete the usual training. If he is not a catechumen, he must show serious signs of conversion to Christ and of renunciation of pagan worship and should not seem to be bound by any obstacles to a moral life, such as "simultaneous" polygamy. Furthermore, he should promise that when his health is restored, he will follow the whole course of initiation suitable to him.

280. This rite is especially suitable for use by catechists and lay persons.

In a case of great urgency, a presbyter or deacon may use this rite. Normally, however, a presbyter or deacon will use the simple rite (nos. 240-273), making the necessary changes because of time and place.

When a presbyter baptizes and has the sacred chrism and sufficient time, he should confer confirmation after baptism. In this case, he omits the anointing with chrism after baptism (no. 263).

If possible, a presbyter or deacon, or even a catechist or lay person with the faculty of distributing communion, should give the eucharist to the neophyte. In this case, the sacrament may be brought before the rite begins and placed with honor on a table covered with a white cloth at the time of celebration.

281. At the point of death, or if death is imminent, since

time is short, the minister omits everything else and pours natural water, even if it is not blessed, on the head of the sick person, saying the usual formula (General Introduction on Christian Initiation, no. 23).

282. If persons who were baptized in danger of death or at the point of death should recover their health, they should be given a suitable formation, received at the church at a fitting time, and then be given the rest of the sacraments of initiation.

In such a case, the guidelines given in nos. 295-305 are followed, with the necessary changes.

BEGINNING OF THE RITE

283. The catechist or lay person greets the family in a friendly manner but briefly. Without delay he speaks with the sick person about his request for baptism and, if he is not a catechumen, about the reasons for his conversion. After deciding to baptize him, he should, if necessary, instruct him briefly.

284. Then he invites the family, the godparent, and some friends and neighbors to gather around the sick person; he selects one or two of these as witnesses. Water, even if it is not blessed, is prepared.

DIALOGUE

285. Going back to the sick person, the minister asks him in these or similar words:

My dear brother (sister), you have asked to be baptized so that as a Christian you may have eternal life. This is eternal life: to know the true God and Jesus Christ whom he has sent. This is the Christian faith; are you aware of this?

Sick person: **I am.**

Minister:

In addition to believing in Jesus Christ, you must intend to follow his commands, as Christians do. Are you aware of this?

Sick person: **I am.**

Minister:
And do you wish to live this Christian life?
Sick person: **I do.**

Minister:
You must therefore promise that after you have recovered your strength you will make an effort to know Christ better and will follow a course of Christian instruction. Do you so promise?
Sick person: **I do.**

286. Turning to the godparent and to the witnesses, the minister asks them in these or similar words:

You have heard his (her) (N.'s) promise. Do you promise, on your part, as his (her) godparent, to remind him (her) of it and to help him (her) learn the teaching of Christ, take part in the life of the community, and become a good Christian?
Sponsor: **I do.**

Minister:
And do you here present bear witness to the promise of your sick brother (sister)?
Witnesses: **We do.**

287. The minister turns to the sick person and says:

Then you shall be baptized into eternal life, as the Lord Jesus commanded.

According to time and circumstances, he reads some words from the gospel, and, if possible, explains them, for example:

John 3:1-6 Unless a man is born again, he will not see the kingdom of heaven.
John 6:44-46 He who believes has eternal life.
Matthew 22:35-40 This is the greatest and first commandment.
Matthew 28:18-20 Teach all nations and baptize them.
Mark 1:9-11 Jesus was baptized by John in the Jordan.

PRAYER

288. The minister invites all to offer this prayer with him:

Let us pray to God our merciful Father for our sick brother (sister) who has asked for the gift of baptism; let us pray for his (her) sponsor and for all his (her) family and friends.

The minister or one of those present offers one or more of the following petitions:

That you, Father, will increase his (her) faith in your Son Christ, our Savior, in faith we ask you:
All: **Lord, hear our prayer.**

Minister:
That you answer his (her) wish to have eternal life and to enter the kingdom of heaven, in faith we ask you:
All: **Lord, hear our prayer.**

Minister:
That you fulfill his (her) hope of knowing you, the Creator of the world and the Father of men, in faith we ask you:
All: **Lord, hear our prayer.**

Minister:
That through baptism you forgive his (her) sins and make him (her) holy, in faith we ask you:
All: **Lord, hear our prayer.**

Minister:
That you grant him (her) the salvation which Christ won for him (her) by his death and resurrection, in faith we ask you:
All: **Lord, hear our prayer.**

Minister:
That in your love you adopt him (her) as your child, in faith we ask you:
All: **Lord, hear our prayer.**

Minister:
That you restore him (her) to health so that he (she) may have the opportunity of knowing and imitating Christ more perfectly, in faith we ask you:
All: **Lord, hear our prayer.**

Minister:
That you keep all of us who have been baptized into the one body of Christ united in faith and love, in faith we ask you:
All: **Lord, hear our prayer.**

The above petitions may be adapted as required.

289. The minister concludes with this prayer:

Father,
look upon the faith and longing of your son
(daughter) N.
By this water you have chosen to give man a new
birth;
by it join N. to Christ
in his suffering, death and resurrection.
Forgive all his (her) sins,
make him (her) your adopted child,
and count him (her) among your holy people.

[When he (she) is well,
may he (she) give thanks in your Church
and be faithful to the teaching of Christ.]

We ask this through Christ our Lord.
℟. **Amen.**

RENUNCIATION OF SIN AND PROFESSION OF FAITH

290. The minister looks at the sick person and asks him to renounce sin and profess the faith:

Do you reject Satan and all his works and all his empty promises?
Sick person: **I do.**

If desired, the minister may use the longer formula (no. 217) and the change mentioned in no. 80. He continues:

Do you believe in God, the Father almighty, creator of heaven and earth?
Sick person: **I do.**

Minister:
Do you believe in Jesus Christ, his only Son, our

Lord, who was born of the Virgin Mary, was crucified, died, and was buried, rose from the dead, and is now seated at the right hand of the Father?
Sick person: **I do.**

Minister:
Do you believe in the Holy Spirit, the holy catholic Church, the communion of saints, the forgiveness of sins, the resurrection of the body, and life everlasting?
Sick person: **I do.**

RITE OF BAPTISM

291. The minister, using the name which the sick person desires to receive, baptizes him, saying:

N., I baptize you in the name of the Father,

he pours the water a first time,

and of the Son,

he pours the water a second time,

and of the Holy Spirit.

he pours the water a third time.

If the minister of baptism is a deacon, he should now anoint him with chrism in the usual way, using the formula in no. 263.

292. If neither confirmation nor holy communion can be given, after baptizing the minister says:

N., God our Father has freed you from your sins, given you a new birth, and made you his son (daughter) in Christ. Soon, God willing, you are to receive the fullness of the Holy Spirit through confirmation, and you will approach the altar of God to share the food of life at the table of his sacrifice. In the Spirit of adoption, whom you have today received, join us now in praying as our Lord himself taught us:

Our Father. . . .

The neophyte and those present join the minister in saying the Lord's Prayer together (no. 294).

RITE OF CONFIRMATION

293. If baptism was conferred by a presbyter, he may also confirm (see no. 280), beginning with an instruction in these or similar words:

N., born again in baptism, you have become a member of Christ and of his priestly people. Now you are to share in the outpouring of the Holy Spirit among us, the Spirit sent by the Lord upon his apostles at Pentecost and given by them and their successors to the baptized.

All pray in silence for a short time.

All-powerful God, Father of our Lord Jesus Christ,
by water and the Holy Spirit
you freed your son (daughter) from sin
and gave him (her) new life.
Send your Holy Spirit upon him (her)
to be his (her) Helper and Guide.
Give him (her) the spirit of wisdom and understanding,
the spirit of right judgment and courage,
the spirit of knowledge and reverence.
Fill him (her) with the spirit of wonder and awe in your presence.

Then the presbyter dips his right thumb in chrism and makes the sign of the cross on the forehead of the person to be confirmed as he says:

N., be sealed with the Gift of the Holy Spirit.
Newly confirmed: **Amen.**

The celebrant adds:
Peace be with you.
Newly confirmed: **And also with you.**

In a case of necessity, it is enough to anoint with chrism, while saying the words **N., be sealed with the Gift of the Holy Spirit.** If possible, he should first lay on hands with the prayer **All-powerful God.**

After confirmation, holy communion may be given to the neophyte as described in no. 294. Otherwise, the celebration ends with the saying of the Lord's Prayer by all.

HOLY COMMUNION

294. If communion is given immediately after confirmation, or after baptism, if confirmation is not conferred, the minister instructs the sick person in these or similar words. If confirmation was given, the words in parentheses are omitted.

N., God the Father has freed you from your sin, given you a new birth, and made you his son (daughter) in Christ. (Soon, God willing, you are to receive the fullness of the Holy Spirit through confirmation.) Before you take the body of Christ in holy communion, join us now, in the Spirit of adoption whom you have today received, and pray with us as our Lord himself taught us to pray:

Our Father. . . .

The minister takes the host, raises it a little, and, facing the neophyte, says:

This is the Lamb of God
who takes away the sins of the world.
Happy are those who are called to his supper.

The neophyte and all present say once:

Lord, I am not worthy to receive you, but only say the word and I shall be healed.

The minister gives communion to the neophyte, saying:

The body of Christ.
The neophyte answers: **Amen.**

He receives communion. The sacrament may be given to all present who wish to receive it.

After communion, the minister says this final prayer:

Father,
almighty and eternal God,
our brother (sister) has received the eucharist

with faith in you and in your healing power.
May the body and blood of Christ
bring him (her) eternal healing in mind and body.

We ask this in the name of Jesus the Lord.
All: **Amen.**

If a sick person receives all or some of the sacraments of initiation while in proximate danger of death and then recovers, he must complete the usual formation, sacraments or rites, he could not receive (see nos. 279, 295-305).

CHAPTER IV

PREPARING UNCATECHIZED ADULTS FOR CONFIRMATION AND THE EUCHARIST

295. The following pastoral suggestions concern adults who were baptized as infants but did not receive further catechetical formation and did not receive confirmation and the eucharist. They may also be used in similar cases, especially for an adult baptized in danger or at the point of death.

Even if these adults have not yet heard the message of the mystery of Christ, their circumstances differ from those of catechumens since they have already become members of the Church and children of God by baptism. Hence their conversion is based on the baptism they have already received, and they must unfold its power.

296. For the same reason as for catechumens, the preparation of these adults requires a long time (Introduction, no. 21) for the faith given to them in baptism to grow and come to maturity by the pastoral teaching given to them. Their Christian life should be strengthened by suitable discipline and the teaching given to them, by contact with the community of believers and by taking part in certain liturgical rites.

297. Their catechetical formation should correspond to the one suggested for catechumens (Introduction, no. 19:1). While teaching them, the priest, deacon or catechist should remember their special situation as adults who have already been enriched by baptism.

298. The Christian community, as it does for catechumens, should help these adults by fraternal love and prayer, and by testifying about their suitability when it is time for them to be admitted to the sacraments (Introduction, nos. 4, 19:2, 23).

299. A sponsor presents the adults to the community.

During the period of formation, each of them chooses a godparent approved by the priest. This godparent acts as the community's delegate for the adult and has the same duties that a godparent has for a catechumen (Introduction, no. 43). The godparent chosen at this time should be the person who acted as the godparent at his baptism, as long as he is truly able to carry out this responsibility.

300. The preparation period is made holy by liturgical actions. The first of these is welcoming the adults into the community, and acknowledging that, because they have been sealed with baptism, they are a part of the community.

301. From this time on they take part in celebrations of the liturgy of the word, both those intended mainly for catechumens and those for all the faithful.

302. To point out God's action in their preparation, some of the rites belonging to the catechumenate may be used if desired. These should reflect the condition of the adults and benefit them spiritually. Such rites would be the presentation of the profession of faith or creed and the Lord's Prayer and even of the Gospels.

303. The period of catechetical formation should be suitably related to the liturgical year; the final part especially should coincide with Lent. During this season time should be set aside for penitential activity which would lead them to the celebration of the sacrament of penance.

304. The climax of their whole formation will normally be the Easter Vigil. Then these adults will profess their baptismal faith, receive the sacrament of confirmation and take part in the eucharist. If confirmation cannot be given at the Easter Vigil because the bishop or the extraordinary minister of the sacrament is not present, it should be given as soon as possible, and insofar as possible during the Easter season.

305. These adults will complete their Christian formation and become fully integrated into the community by experiencing the period of postbaptismal catechesis with the neophytes.

CHAPTER V

RITE OF INITIATION FOR CHILDREN OF CATECHETICAL AGE

306. This rite is intended for children, unbaptized as infants, who have reached the age of reason and are able to be taught and who have been brought by their parents for Christian initiation or have come of their own accord with parental permission. They are suitable candidates if they have developed and nourished their faith and are trying to develop their consciences. They cannot be treated as adults, for they are still children, dependent on their parents or guardians, and still under the strong influence of their companions and society.

307. The initiation of these children requires both a maturity in their own conversion, according to their age, and the help of the education needed for this age. Their initiation is to be adapted to the spiritual progress of the candidates, depending on their increase in faith and on the catechetical instruction they receive. As in the case of adults, their initiation lasts for some years, if necessary, before they receive the sacraments. The various stages and periods of their initiation are enriched by liturgical rites.

308. Since the progress of children in the teaching they receive depends on the help and example of their companions as well as of their parents, both should be taken into consideration.

a) Since the children to be initiated often belong to some group of companions who are now being instructed for confirmation and the eucharist, their advance in Christian initiation is shared and has this catechetical group as its foundation.

b) It is desirable that these children receive as much help and example as possible from their parents whose permission is required for their initiation and for leading a Christian life from this time forward. The period of initiation provides the family a good opportunity to speak with priests and catechists.

309. According to circumstances, it is important that several children in the same situation should be grouped together in the celebrations of this rite so that they may help one another in their progress as catechumens.

310. In setting the times of the celebrations, it is desirable that, insofar as possible, the final period of the preparation will coincide with Lent and that the sacraments be celebrated at the Easter Vigil (Introduction, no. 8). Before children are admitted to the sacraments at Easter, it should be certain that they are ready and that the time is suitable for the order of the catechetical formation they are taking. As far as possible, the candidates should come to the sacraments of initiation while their baptized companions are receiving confirmation or the eucharist.

311. The celebrations take place with the active participation of a congregation, including a suitable number of the faithful, parents, family, classmates and some adult friends. When children of this age are initiated, it is often desirable not to have the whole parish community present; it is enough to have it represented.

312. Episcopal conferences may adapt and add to the rite given here in order to meet local needs and conditions more fully, as well as to provide greater pastoral opportunities.

The adult rite of the presentations (nos. 103, 125, 181-192), adapted to the age of the children, may be added. When the Latin rite is translated, the instructions and prayers should be adapted to the understanding of children. Furthermore, in place of a prayer already translated in the Roman ritual, the episcopal conference may also approve an alternative prayer which says the same things in a way better adapted to children (Introduction on Christian Initiation, no. 32).

313. Ministers using this rite may freely and wisely use the options given to them in the General Introduction (nos. 34-35) and in the Introduction to the Rite of Baptism of Children (no. 31) and Adult Initiation (no. 67).

FIRST STAGE
RITE OF BECOMING CATECHUMENS

314. This rite is celebrated before a small but active congregation so that the children will not become too upset by a large group (see no. 311). When possible, the candidate's parents or guardian should be present. If they cannot come, they should indicate that they have given consent to their children. Their place should be taken by sponsors (no. 42), suitable members of the Church who act on this occasion for the parents and present the children.

315. The celebration takes place in the church or in a suitable place so that according to their age and understanding the children's experience of a warm reception will be increased. The first part, the introductory rite, takes place at the entrance of the church or in another place, according to circumstances. The second part, the liturgy of the word, is celebrated in the church or in a specially chosen place.

RITE OF WELCOME

316. The celebrant comes to the place where the children and their parents, guardians or sponsors are waiting. He greets them in a friendly and simple manner along with those who are present.

FIRST INSTRUCTION

317. The celebrant then speaks to the candidates and their parents, pointing out joy and happiness of the Church. Next, he invites the candidates and their sponsors (if present) to come forward and stand before him.

OPENING DIALOGUE

318. The celebrant questions each child, unless there are many, using these or similar words:

N., What do you wish to become?
Child: **A Christian.**

Celebrant: **Why do you wish to become a Christian?**
Child: **Because I believe in Christ.**

Celebrant:
What does belief in Christ offer you?
Child: **Eternal life.**

The celebrant may use other words in asking the candidates about their intentions and may permit them to answer in their own words: **I want to do the will of God; I want to follow the word of God; I want to be baptized; I ask for faith; I want to be a friend of Jesus Christ; I want to join the Christian family;** etc.

If there is a large number, the celebrant may ask everyone together, draw out some answers and then ask the rest if they agree.

319. The celebrant concludes the dialogue with a brief instruction, adapted to the circumstances and age of the children. He may use these or similar words:

Since you now believe in Christ and wish us to prepare you for baptism, we welcome you with great joy into our Christian family where you will come to know Christ better day by day. Together with us you will strive to live as children of God, for thus has Christ instructed us: Love God with all your heart; love one another as I have loved you.

If desired, the children may repeat these words of Christ to show their consent.

DIALOGUE WITH PARENTS AND CONGREGATION

320. Then the celebrant asks the children if they have asked the consent of their parents or sponsors who presented them. He may do so in this or a similar way.

N. and N.,
go now and ask your parents to come forward with you and give their consent.

The children go to their parents or sponsors and bring them before the celebrant who continues:

Dear parents: Your sons and daughters N. and N. are asking to be prepared for baptism. Do you consent to their request?
Parents: **We do.**

Celebrant:

Are you willing to contribute your part in this preparation for baptism?

Parents: **We are.**

321. Then the celebrant questions all present, using these or similar words:

The important task these young people begin today will require the help of our faith and love. Are you ready, as friends and relatives, to help them in their progress toward baptism?

All: **We are.**

SIGNING WITH THE CROSS

322. Then the celebrant turns to the children and says:

N. and N.,
Christ has called you to become his friends.
May you always keep him in mind and be faithful to him.

And so, I now sign you with the sign of Christians, the cross of Christ.
May this sign be a constant reminder to you of Christ and of his great love for you.

The celebrant moves along in front of them and in silence makes the sign of the cross on each child's forehead.

If desired (see no. 323) he invites the parents and catechists to do the same in silence:

I invite you parents and teachers (N. and N.), since you, too, belong to Christ, to sign them with the sign of Christ.

[323.] If it seems wise, especially if the children are a little older, the sign of the cross may be made on other parts of the body. Only the priest says the words and does the signing.

While signing the ears, the celebrant says:

I sign your ears with the sign of the cross:
may you hear the words of Christ.

While signing the eyes:

**I sign your eyes with the sign of the cross:
may you see the works of Christ.**

While signing the lips:

**I sign your lips with the sign of the cross:
may you speak as Christ would speak.**

While signing the breast:

**I sign your breast with the sign of the cross:
may you welcome Christ into your heart by faith.**

While signing the shoulders:

**I sign your shoulders with the sign of the cross:
may you have the strength of Christ.**

While signing the whole body:

**I sign your whole person with the sign of the cross
in the name of the Father, and of the Son,
✠ and of the Holy Spirit:
may you live with Jesus now and for ever.**
Child: **Amen.**

If desired, the same signing of the senses may be done by the parents (or even by the sponsors) or by the catechists. In this case, the priest alone says the words in the plural form, as in no. 85.

ENTRY INTO THE CHURCH

324. After this the celebrant invites the catechumens to enter into the church, using these or similar words:

Now you may take your place in the Christian assembly. Come, listen to the Lord who speaks to us and join us in prayer to him.

Then the children enter the congregation and take their places with their parents (sponsors) or among their companions, so that it is evident that they now are a part of this congregation.
Meanwhile, Psalm 95 or Psalm 122 or another appropriate song is sung.

LITURGY OF THE WORD

325. The book of scripture is carried in and placed on the lectern with honor. The celebrant may briefly explain the dignity of God's word which is proclaimed and heard in the Christian assembly.
Then a brief service of the word is celebrated.

READINGS AND HOMILY

326. Readings are chosen which can be adapted to the understanding of the catechumens and to their progress in the instruction they and their companions are receiving. Some examples:

Genesis 12:1-4a Abraham is called by God.
Psalm 33:4-5, 12-13, 18-19, 20-22
John 1:35-42 (or 35-39) Behold the Lamb of God. We have found the Messiah.
Ezekiel 36:25-28 A new heart and a new spirit.
Galatians 5:13, 22-23a, 24-25 One commandment and one Spirit.
Mark 12:28c-31 The first commandment.
Luke 8:4-9, 11-15 Parable of the sower.
Luke 19:1-10 Zacchaeus.
John 6:44-47 No one can come to me unless the Father draws him.
John 13:34-35 A new commandment.
John 15:9-11 or 12-17 Love one another.

For other readings, responsorial psalms and verses before the gospel, see no. 388.
After the readings, the celebrant gives a brief homily to illustrate what was read.

327. A period of silence is recommended. The celebrant invites all the children to pray in their hearts. An appropriate song follows.

PRESENTATION OF THE GOSPELS

328. During or after the song, if desired, a book of the Gospels is given to the children. They should be prepared for this by a short but suitable instruction or homily.

PRAYER

329. The following prayer is offered in these or similar words:

Celebrant:

Let us pray for these boys and girls as they draw nearer to God, for they are your sons and daughters, your companions and friends.

Reader:

That you, God our Father, may steadily increase their desire to live with Jesus, for this we pray:
℟. **Lord, hear our prayer.**

Reader:

That their lives in the Church may bring them happiness, for this we pray:
℟. **Lord, hear our prayer.**

Reader:

That you may grant them the courage to persevere in their preparation for baptism, for this we pray:
℟. **Lord, hear our prayer.**

Reader:

That in your love you may keep them safe from the temptation of discouragement and fear, for this we pray:
℟. **Lord, hear our prayer.**

Reader:

That you may grant them the joy of receiving baptism, confirmation, and the eucharist, for this we pray:
℟. **Lord, hear our prayer.**

The celebrant concludes with this prayer:

Lord,
you have filled these young people
with the desire to become perfect Christians.
May they see their hopes and our prayers answered
by reaching you at last.

We ask this through Christ our Lord.
℟. **Amen.**

The celebration ends with a song.
If Mass follows, the catechumens should be dismissed.

SECOND STAGE
SCRUTINIES OR PENITENTIAL RITES

330. These penitential rites, which are among the main stages of the catechumenate for children, are a kind of scrutiny, similar to those in the adult rites (nos. 152-180). Since they are alike in purpose, they may be used and adapted according to the guidelines given for scrutinies (nos. 25:1, 154-159).

331. Since the scrutinies normally belong to the final period of preparation for baptism, the penitential rites require that the children exhibit a degree of faith and understanding that is sufficient for the requirements of baptism.

332. The catechumens take part in these rites along with their godparents and members of the catechetical class. Everything should be adapted to those present so that the penitential celebrations are also of benefit to those who are not catechumens. During this celebration some children who have already been baptized and are members of the catechetical class may receive the sacrament of penance for the first time. In this case, care should be taken to add appropriate instructions, intentions for the prayers and actions referring to these children.

333. The penitential rites are celebrated during Lent if the catechumens are to be initiated at Easter; otherwise, they take place at an appropriate time. At least one celebration is held, and if it can be conveniently done, a second should be added. The formulas of the second celebration are similar to those of the first, using and adapting the texts in nos. 164, 171 and 178 for the prayer and for the exorcism.

INTRODUCTORY RITES

334. The celebrant welcomes the assembly and in a few words explains the meaning of the rite for each group taking part in it: children who are catechumens or already baptized, those receiving the sacrament of penance for the first time today, parents and friends, catechists and priests, and the like.

An appropriate song may be chosen to show the faith and joy experienced because of the mercy of God our Father.

335. The celebrant concludes with this prayer:

Let us pray.

God of mercy and compassion,
you are recognized most clearly
in your readiness to forgive;
our holiness is your glory.
May we who are repentant
be cleansed from sin
and restored to your life once again.

We ask this through Christ our Lord,
℟. **Amen.**

Or:
Lord,
give us your forgiveness and your peace.
May we serve you cleansed of all sins
and with hearts full of confidence and joy.

We ask this through Christ our Lord,
℟. **Amen.**

READING AND HOMILY

336. One or several readings may be read, for example:

Ezekiel 36:25-28 A new heart and a new spirit.
Isaiah 1:16-18 Cleansing of sinners.
Mark 1:1-5, 14-15 Repent and believe the good news.
Mark 2:1-12 Cure of the paralytic.
Luke 15:1-7 Finding the lost sheep.
1 John 1:8-2:2 Jesus Christ is our Savior.

The following readings, usually read at the scrutinies, may be chosen:

John 4:1-14 Samaritan woman.
John 9:1, 6-9, 13-17, 34-39 Curing the man born blind.
John 11:3-7, 17, 20-27, 33b-45 Lazarus is raised from the dead.

If two readings are used, psalms or songs should be used between them (no. 388).

After the readings the celebrant explains the sacred texts in a short homily.

337. During or after the homily, the celebrant disposes the entire congregation to repentance and conversion of heart by periods of silence and by words of encouragement.
If there are baptized children who are members of the catechetical class, the celebrant turns to them and invites them to show by some external sign their faith in Christ the Savior and their sorrow for their sins.

338. After a period of silence to lead all to sincere sorrow, the celebrant invites the congregation to pray.

Let us pray for N. and N. who are preparing themselves for the sacraments of Christian initiation; for N. and N. who will receive God's forgiveness in the sacrament of penance for the first time; and for ourselves, who seek the mercy of Christ.

Reader:
That we may stand before the Lord Jesus with hearts full of gratitude and faith, let us pray to the Lord:
℟. **Lord, hear our prayer.**

Reader:
That we may honestly strive to know our spiritual defects and to recognize our sins, let us pray to the Lord:
℟. **Lord, hear our prayer.**

Reader:
That, mindful of our calling as sons and daughters of God, we may frankly admit our weaknesses and our faults, let us pray to the Lord:
℟. **Lord, hear our prayer.**

Reader:
That we may express heartfelt sorrow for our sins in the presence of Christ Jesus, let us pray to the Lord:
℟. **Lord, hear our prayer.**

Reader:
That we may be delivered from present evils and protected against those yet to come, let us pray to the Lord:
℟. **Lord, hear our prayer.**

Reader:
That we may learn from our Father in heaven to conquer all the sins of man by the power of his divine love, let us pray to the Lord:
℟. **Lord, hear our prayer.**

According to circumstances, the celebrant's instruction and the intentions may be adapted by using the formulas in nos. 378, 382 and 386, with the necessary changes.

EXORCISM

339. Then the celebrant extends his hands over the children and prays:

Father of mercies,
you gave us your beloved Son
to rescue us from the slavery of sin
and to give us the freedom of your children.

Look on these young people
who have experienced temptation
and who know their human weaknesses.
Look on them with love and fulfill their hope in your light;
cleanse them from their sins.
Keep them joyful and at peace
and guide them safely through life.

We ask this through Christ our Lord.
℟. **Amen.**

For another form, see no. 392.

ANOINTING OF CATECHUMENS OR IMPOSITION OF HANDS

340. The celebrant continues:

We anoint you with the oil of salvation
in the name of Christ our Savior.
May he strengthen you with his power,
who lives and reigns for ever and ever.
Children: **Amen.**

Each child is anointed with the oil of catechumens on the

breast or on both hands, or even, if desirable, on other parts of the body.

The episcopal conference may decide to omit this anointing or postpone it until the day of baptism (no. 218). In this case, the celebrant speaks to all the catechumens:

May Christ our Savior
strengthen you with his power,
for he is Lord for ever and ever,
Children: **Amen.**

Then, in silence, the celebrant imposes his hand on each catechumen.

DISMISSAL OF THE CATECHUMENS

341. The celebrant dismisses them with these or similar words:

N. and N., the Lord Jesus has shown you his merciful love in our midst.
Now go in peace.
Children: **Thanks be to God.**

He may send them to their places if they are to remain in church, saying:

N. and N., the Lord Jesus has shown you his merciful love in our midst. Now return to your places and join us in prayer.
Children: **Thanks be to God.**

342. Then the penitential celebration for the baptized children begins. After the celebrant's instruction, the individuals who are to receive the sacrament of penance for the first time do so, and the rest receive after them.
After a song or a prayer of thanksgiving, all leave.

THIRD STAGE
CELEBRATION OF THE SACRAMENTS OF INITIATION

343. To show the paschal character of baptism, this sacrament should be celebrated at the Easter Vigil or on a Sunday when the Church recalls the Lord's resurrection (Introduction to the Rite of Baptism for Children, no. 9), taking into consideration what has been outlined in no. 310.

344. Baptism is celebrated at the Mass in which the neophytes are to share in the eucharist for the first time. Confirmation is given at the same celebration by the bishop or by the presbyter who baptizes.

345. If baptism is celebrated at a time other than the Easter Vigil or Easter Sunday, the Mass of the day or the ritual Mass of Christian initiation is used. The readings are chosen from among those given in no. 388. The readings of the Sunday or feast may also be used.

346. Each child who is a catechumen is accompanied by a godparent who is friendly with him and who has been approved by the priest (Introduction, no. 43).

CELEBRATION OF BAPTISM

347. When the children, parents (or guardians), godparents, classmates, friends and members of the parish have assembled, Mass begins. The liturgy of the word uses the readings mentioned in no. 345. The homily follows.

CELEBRANT'S INSTRUCTION

348. After the homily, the celebrant, catechumens, parents and godparents go to the font. The celebrant speaks to the family, friends and the entire assembly in these or similar words:

My dear brothers and sisters: with the approval of their parents, N. and N. are asking for baptism. Let us humbly ask God, our merciful Father, to admit them among his adopted children in Christ.

BLESSING THE WATER

349-350. Then the celebrant turns to the font and gives this blessing, as described in nos. 215 and 216.

PROFESSION OF FAITH

Profession of faith by the community:
351. Before the children renounce sin and profess their faith, the celebrant may, according to circumstances, invite the parents, godparents and all present to profess their faith:

N. and N. have completed a lengthy preparation and are about to be baptized. From God, who is love, they will receive new life; they will become Christians.

From now on we will have to help them even more than before. This is especially true of you, their parents, who have given them permission to be baptized and who have the primary responsibility for their education. But all of us who have prepared them to meet Christ today must always be ready to be of assistance.

And so, before they profess their faith in the presence of our community, let us, with full deliberation, renew before them our own profession of faith which is the faith of the Church.

All join the celebrant in saying:

I believe in God, the Father almighty,
creator of heaven and earth.

I believe in Jesus Christ, his only Son, our Lord.
He was conceived by the power of the Holy Spirit,
and born of the Virgin Mary.
He suffered under Pontius Pilate,
was crucified, died, and was buried.
He descended to the dead.
On the third day he rose again.
He ascended into heaven,
and is seated at the right hand of the Father.
He will come again to judge the living and the dead.

I believe in the Holy Spirit,
the holy catholic Church,
the communion of saints,
the forgiveness of sins,
the resurrection of the body,
and the life everlasting. Amen.

If desired, the Nicene Creed may be used (no. 186).

Turning to the catechumens, the celebrant says:

N. and N., before you are baptized, reject Satan and profess your faith in the presence of God's Church.

PROFESSION OF FAITH BY THE CHILDREN

352. The celebrant speaks briefly to the children in these or similar words:

N. and N., you have spent much time in preparation, and you are now asking for baptism. Your parents have agreed to your request; your teachers, companions, and friends have helped you; and today all here present promise you the example of their faith and their loving support.

It is for you now, in the presence of the Church, to declare your profession of faith; then you will be baptized.

RENUNCIATION OF SIN

353. The celebrant asks all the catechumens:

A
Celebrant:
Do you reject Satan and all his works and all his empty promises?
Children: **I do.**

Or **B**
Celebrant:
Do you reject sin so as to live in the freedom of God's children?
Children: **I do.**

Celebrant:
Do you reject the glamor of evil and refuse to be mastered by sin?
Children: **I do.**

Celebrant:
Do you reject Satan, father of sin and prince of darkness?
Children: **I do.**

ANOINTING WITH THE OIL OF CATECHUMENS

354. If the anointing with the oil of catechumens has been retained by the episcopal conference and has not already been given, the celebrant says:

We anoint you with the oil of salvation
in the name of Christ our Savior.
May he strengthen you with his power,
who lives and reigns for ever and ever.
Children: **Amen.**

Each child is anointed with oil of catechumens on the breast or on both hands, or even on other parts of the body, if this seems desirable.

If there are many candidates, several ministers may anoint.

PROFESSION OF FAITH

355. Then the celebrant, advised by the godparents of the name of each candidate, asks each one:

N., do you believe in God, the Father almighty, creator of heaven and earth?
Child: **I do.**

Celebrant:
Do you believe in Jesus Christ, his only Son, our Lord, who was born of the Virgin Mary, was crucified, died, and was buried, rose from the dead, and is now seated at the right hand of the Father?
Child: **I do.**

Celebrant:
Do you believe in the Holy Spirit, the holy catholic Church, the communion of saints, the forgiveness of

sins, the resurrection of the body, and life everlasting?
Child: **I do.**

After his profession of faith, each child is baptized at once.

RITE OF BAPTISM

356. The celebrant takes baptismal water from the font and pours it three times on the bowed head of the candidate, baptizing him in the name of the Trinity:

N., I baptize you in the name of the Father,

he pours the water a first time,

and of the Son,

he pours the water a second time,

and of the Holy Spirit.

he pours the water a third time.

The godparent places his right hand on the candidate's right shoulder.

If baptism is by immersion, the celebrant immerses the child or his head three times, raising him out of the water each time and baptizing him with the same words. The requirements of decency and modesty should prevail.
After the baptism of each child, the assembly may sing a short acclamation (see no. 390).

357. If the neophytes are to be confirmed at once, the postbaptismal anointing with chrism (no. 358) is omitted, and the celebration continues with the explanatory rites (nos. 359-360).

EXPLANATORY RITES

ANOINTING AFTER BAPTISM

358. If for some special reason confirmation is separated from baptism, then after baptism the celebrant anoints them with chrism. First he prays over them all:

**God, the Father of our Lord Jesus Christ,
has freed you from sin,
given you a new birth by water and the Holy Spirit,
and welcomed you into his holy people.
He now anoints you with the chrism of salvation.
As Christ was anointed Priest, Prophet, and King,
so may you live always as a member of his body,
sharing everlasting life.**
Newly baptized: **Amen.**

Then the celebrant anoints each child with sacred chrism on the crown of the head, saying nothing.

When a large number of children are baptized, other presbyters or deacons may anoint some of them with chrism.

CLOTHING WITH THE WHITE GARMENT

359. The celebrant says:

**N. and N., you have become a new creation
and have clothed yourselves in Christ.
Take this white garment
and bring it unstained to the judgment seat of our Lord Jesus Christ
that you may have everlasting life.**
Newly baptized: **Amen.**

At the words **Take this white garment,** the godparents place the white garment on the neophytes. Another color may be used if local customs require this.

If desired, this rite may be omitted.

PRESENTATION OF THE LIGHTED CANDLE

360. The celebrant takes the Easter candle in his hands or touches it, saying:

Godparents, please come forward to give the newly-baptized the light of Christ.

The godparents approach, light a candle from the Easter candle and hand it to the neophyte. Then the celebrant says:

**You have been enlightened by Christ.
Walk always as children of the light**

and keep the flame of faith alive in your hearts. When the Lord comes, may you go out to meet him with all the saints in the heavenly kingdom.
Newly baptized: **Amen.**

CELEBRATION OF CONFIRMATION

361. Between the celebration of baptism and confirmation, the congregation may sing an appropriate song.

362. Confirmation may be celebrated in the sanctuary or in the baptistry, as local circumstances dictate.

When there are many to be confirmed, other presbyters may be associated as ministers to give this sacrament, if they are to be delegated for this (see no. 46).

363–365. The celebrant briefly speaks to the candidates as described in nos. 268-270, addressing the candidates as "my dear newly baptized."

CELEBRATION OF THE EUCHARIST

366. The profession of faith is omitted, and the general intercessions follow immediately. For the first time the neophytes take part in them. Some of them carry the gifts when they are brought to the altar.

367. In the first eucharistic prayer, the neophytes are mentioned in the **Father, accept this offering,** and the godparents in the **Remember, Lord, your people.** If the second, third or fourth eucharistic prayer is used, a special formula is added for the neophytes (no. 391).

368. The neophytes may receive communion under both species, together with their parents, godparents and catechists.

Before **This is the Lamb of God** the celebrant may briefly remind the neophytes of the value of this great mystery which is the climax of their initiation and the center of the whole Christian life. He should also pay special attention to those who were baptized earlier and who are now receiving communion for the first time.

PERIOD OF POSTBAPTISMAL CATECHESIS OR MYSTAGOGIA

369. A suitable period of postbaptismal catechesis or mystagogia should be provided for the young neophytes. It should be adapted for them, based on the adult guidelines (nos. 235-239).

CHAPTER VI

VARIOUS TEXTS FOR USE IN THE CELEBRATION OF ADULT INITIATION

FOR THE RITE OF ADMISSION TO THE CATECHUMENATE

370. For no. 76: Formulas for the instruction before the candidate's first promise:

1

Celebrant:

God has created the world and us men; in him all living things have their existence. He fills our minds with light so that we may come to know and worship him. He also sent to us his faithful witness, Jesus Christ, to proclaim to us what he had seen both in heaven and on earth.

You are filled with joy at the coming of Christ. Now is the time to hear his own words so that you may have eternal life by beginning, together with us, to know God and to love your neighbor. Are you ready, with the help of God, to live this kind of life?

Candidates: **I am.**

2

Celebrant:

This is eternal life: to know the true God and Jesus Christ whom he has sent. Christ has been raised up from the dead and appointed by God to be King of life and Lord of all things, seen and unseen.

If you earnestly desire to become his disciples and members of his Church, you must be introduced to the fullness of truth which he has revealed to us. You must learn to make the mind of Christ Jesus your own. You must strive to pattern your life on the teachings of his Gospel, that is to say, you must love the Lord your God and your neighbor, for thus has

Christ commanded, and he has shown us the example.

Do you agree to all these things?
Candidates: **I do.**

371. For no. 80: Another formula for renouncing non-Christian worship:

Celebrant:
My dear candidates:
The true God has called you and led you here. You earnestly desire to worship and serve him alone, and his Son, Jesus Christ. Now, in the presence of this entire community, you must reject all rites and forms of worship that do not offer God true honor. Are you determined never to abandon him and his Son, Jesus Christ, and never to return to the service of other masters?
Candidates: **We are.**

Celebrant:
Christ Jesus, Lord of the living and the dead, has power over all spirits and demons. Are you determined never to abandon him and again serve N. (here he mentions the images worshiped in false rites, such as fetishes)?
Candidates: **We are.**

Celebrant:
Christ Jesus alone has the power to protect men. Are you determined never to abandon him and return to seek (wear, use) N. (here he names objects which are used superstitiously, such as amulets)?
Candidates: **We are.**

Celebrant:
Christ Jesus alone is truth. Are you determined never to abandon him and to seek out soothsayers, magicians, or witch doctors?
Candidates: **We are.**

This formula may be adapted if desired.

372. For no. 92: Scripture readings for the rite of admission of catechumens:

Genesis 12:1-4a
Leave your homeland,
and come into the land I will show you.

John 1:35-42
Behold the Lamb of God.
We have found the Messiah.

Other suitable texts may be chosen.

RESPONSORIAL PSALMS

Ps. 33:4-5, 12-13, 18-19, 20 and 22
(12b): **Happy the people whom God has chosen as his heritage.**

or (22): **Let your mercy come upon us, Lord, for we have hoped in you.**

373. For nos. 113-118: Other prayers of exorcism:

1
Let us pray.

Lord Jesus Christ,
loving Redeemer of mankind,
you alone have the power to save us.
In your Name every knee shall bow
in heaven, on earth, and under the earth.
We pray for these servants of yours
who worship you as the one true God;
send your light into their hearts,
protect them from the hatred of the evil one,
heal in them the wounds of sin,
and strengthen them against temptation.
Give them a love of your commandments
and courage to live always by your Gospel,
and so prepare them to receive your Spirit,
for you live and reign for ever and ever.

2
Let us pray.

Lord Jesus Christ,
sent by the Father and anointed by the Holy Spirit,
you proclaimed the freedom of God's people
and a holy season of forgiveness
when you read from the prophet Isaiah
in the synagogue at Nazareth
and brought his prophecy to fulfillment.
We pray for these servants of yours
who have opened their ears to your word
and their hearts to your love;
may they receive your hour of grace
with joy and thanksgiving.
Enlarge their vision,
lift up their hearts from the things of earth
to the promised glory of heaven.
Free them from the spirit of unbelief
to serve you in faith,
for the Father has given all things into your power
and made you Lord of all.
Give them faith and love
to be obedient to your Spirit
that they may live always
by the hope to which you call them.
Raise them up
to be members of your priestly people
sharing the overflowing joy
of the new Jerusalem,
the city of your peace,
where you live and reign for ever and ever.

3
Let us pray.

Lord Jesus Christ,
when you had calmed the storm
and freed the possessed,
you called a tax collector to follow you.
You chose Matthew
to remind us of your mercy

and of your command to teach all nations.
We pray for these servants of yours
who confess that they are sinners.
In your compassion
save them from the power of the evil one.

Heal in them the wounds of sin
and fill their hearts with your peace.
Keep alive within them the joy and newness of the Gospel
so that they may leave all things and follow you
who lives and reigns for ever and ever.

4

Let us pray.

Lord God,
infinite in wisdom,
you chose Paul as your apostle
to proclaim your Son among the Gentiles.
May these servants of yours
who look forward to baptism
follow in the footsteps of Paul;
may they not be subject to flesh and blood
but follow the inspiration of your grace.
Test their hearts and purify them,
freeing them from all deception.
May they never look back
but always strive toward what is still to come.
May they count everything as loss
for the surpassing worth of knowing Christ your Son,
and so gain him as their reward
who is Lord for ever and ever.

5

Let us pray.

Lord God,
Creator and Redeemer of your holy people,
your great love has inspired these catechumens
to seek and find you;
prepare their hearts today

**to share in your covenant of love,
so that they may follow Christ and receive from him
the living water of salvation.**

We ask this through Christ our Lord.

374. For nos. 121-124: Other prayers for the blessing of catechumens:

1
Let us pray.

**Lord our God,
from the height of heaven
you look with love on the earth below.
Out of pity for the human race
you sent your Son,
Jesus Christ, our Lord and God,
to bring us your gift of salvation.
Look with favor on these catechumens
who bow before you in worship;
prepare them for the rebirth of baptism
which will bring forgiveness of their sins
and clothe them in the garment of incorruptible life.
Bring them into your holy, catholic and apostolic
Church
so that they may join with us
in giving glory to your name.**

We ask this through Christ our Lord.

2
Let us pray.

**Almighty God,
Lord of all,
through your Son
you cast Satan from his throne
and freed mankind from its captivity
by breaking the chains that bound it.
We thank you
in the name of these catechumens
whom you have called.**

Strengthen them in faith
that they may know you, the one true God,
and Jesus Christ, whom you sent to us.
Keep them clean of heart and make them grow in holiness
so that they may receive baptism
and share in the holy mysteries.

We ask this through Christ our Lord.

3
Let us pray.

Lord God,
you desire all men to be saved
and to come to the knowledge of your truth.
In your goodness
fill with faith
the hearts of those who are preparing for baptism;
bring them into the fold of your holy Church
and make them worthy of your gift of eternal life.

We ask this through Christ our Lord.

4
Let us pray.

Almighty Lord and God,
Father of our Savior Jesus Christ,
look with compassion on these servants of yours.
Purify their minds of all remains of false worship
and deepen their love
of your law and your commandments.
Bring them to a full knowledge of your truth
and make them ready for the rebirth of baptism
when they will become the temple of the Holy Spirit.

Grant this through Christ our Lord.

5
Let us pray.

Lord,
look with love on your servants

who reverence your holy name
and bow in worship before you.
Help them to accomplish all that is good;
touch their hearts
so that they may always be mindful
of your mighty works and your commandments
and so give themselves wholly to your covenant of love.

Grant this through Christ our Lord.

374 bis. For no. 141: Ritual Mass for rite of election

INTRODUCTORY RITES

Let hearts rejoice who search for the Lord. Seek the Lord and his strength, seek always the face of the Lord. Ps. 105:3-4

OPENING PRAYER

God our Father,
you always work to save us,
and now we rejoice in the great love
you give to your chosen people.
Protect all who are about to become your children,
and continue to bless those who are already baptized.

Grant this through our Lord Jesus Christ, your Son,
who lives and reigns with you and the Holy Spirit,
one God, for ever and ever.

PRAYER OVER THE GIFTS

Pray, brethren . . .

Ever-living God,
in baptism, the sacrament of our faith,
you restore us to life.
Accept the prayers and gifts of your people;
forgive our sins and fulfill our hopes and desires.

We ask this in the name of Jesus the Lord.

COMMUNION RITE

I will put my law within them, I will write it on their hearts; then I shall be their God, and they will be my people. Jeremiah 31:33

PRAYER AFTER COMMUNION

Let us pray.

Pause for silent prayer, if this has not preceded.

Lord,
may the sacraments we receive
cleanse us of sin and free us from guilt,
for our sins bring us sorrow
but your promise of salvation brings us joy.

We ask this through Christ our Lord.

The Mass of Friday of the Fourth Week of Lent may also be used.

375. For no. 148: Another form of prayer after the election:

That these chosen ones may find joy in daily prayer, for this we pray:
℟. **Lord, hear our prayer.**

That by praying to you often they may live in ever closer union with you, for this we pray:
℟. **Lord, hear our prayer.**

That they may joyfully read your word and ponder it in their hearts, for this we pray:
℟. **Lord, hear our prayer.**

That they may humbly acknowledge their faults and begin energetically to correct them, for this we pray:
℟. **Lord, hear our prayer.**

That they may turn their daily work into an offering pleasing to you, for this we pray:
℟. **Lord, hear our prayer.**

That each day of Lent they may make a conscious effort to please you, for this we pray:
℟. Lord, hear our prayer.

That they may courageously refrain from everything that defiles the heart, for this we pray:
℟. Lord, hear our prayer.

That they may grow to love and seek virtue and holiness of life, for this we pray:
℟. Lord, hear our prayer.

That they may overcome self-seeking and be concerned more for others than for themselves, for this we pray:
℟. Lord, hear our prayer.

That you will protect and bless their families, for this we pray:
℟. Lord, hear our prayer.

That they may share with others the joy they have derived from their faith, for this we pray:
℟. Lord, hear our prayer.

376. For no. 160: Readings for the first scrutiny:

Reading I, **Exodus 17:3-7:**
Give us water to drink.

Resp. Ps.: Psalm 95:1-2. 6-7. 8-9.
(8): **If today you hear his voice, harden not your hearts.**

Reading II, **Romans 5:1-2, 5-8:**
The love of God has been poured into our hearts by the Holy Spirit which has been given to us.

Verse before the Gospel John 4:42 and 15:
Lord, you are truly the Savior of the world; give me living water, that I may never thirst again.

Gospel: **John 4:5-42** (longer) **or 5-15. 19b-26. 39a. 40-42** (shorter):
The water that I shall give will turn into a spring of eternal life.

377. For no. 160: Texts for the Mass when the first scrutiny is celebrated:

OPENING PRAYER

Lord,
you call these chosen ones
to the glory of a new birth in Christ, the second Adam.
Help them to grow in wisdom and love
as they prepare to profess their faith in you.

Grant this through our Lord Jesus Christ, your Son,
who lives and reigns with you and the Holy Spirit,
one God, for ever and ever.

PRAYER OVER THE GIFTS

Pray, brethren . . .

Lord God,
give faith and love to your children
and lead them safely to the supper
you have prepared for them.

We ask this in the name of Jesus the Lord.

When Eucharistic Prayer I is used, the special forms of **Remember, Lord, your people** and **Father, accept this offering** are said:

Remember, Lord, these godparents
who will present your chosen men and women for baptism
(the names of the godparents are mentioned).
Lord, remember all of us . . .

Father,
accept this offering
from your whole family.
We offer it especially for the men and women
you call to share your life
through the living waters of baptism.

[Through Christ our Lord. Amen.]

PRAYER AFTER COMMUNION

Let us pray.

Pause for silent prayer, if this has not preceded.

Lord,
be present in our lives
with your gifts of salvation.
Prepare these men and women for your sacraments
and protect them in your love.

We ask this in the name of Jesus the Lord.

378. For no. 164: Optional form of the prayer for the first scrutiny:

That, like the Samaritan woman, our chosen ones may review their lives before Christ and acknowledge their sins, let us pray to the Lord.
℟. **Lord, hear our prayer.**

That they may be delivered from the spirit of skepticism which leads man astray from the path of Christ, let us pray to the Lord:
℟. **Lord, hear our prayer.**

That while they await the gift of God, they may long with all their hearts for the living water which brings eternal life, let us pray to the Lord:
℟. **Lord, hear our prayer.**

That by accepting the Son of God as their teacher, they may become true adorers of God the Father in spirit and in truth, let us pray to the Lord:
℟. **Lord, hear our prayer.**

That they may share with their friends and fellow men the wonder of their own encounter with Christ, let us pray to the Lord:
℟. **Lord, hear our prayer.**

That all men everywhere who are deprived and in need of the word of God may be able to draw near to the gospel of Christ, let us pray to the Lord:
℟. **Lord, hear our prayer.**

That all of us may be willing to learn from Christ to do the Father's will out of love, let us pray to the Lord:
℟. Lord, hear our prayer.

379. For no. 164: Another form of exorcism for the first scrutiny:

Let us pray.

Father of mercies,
through your Son
you revealed your fatherly care
for the woman of Samaria
and offered salvation to all sinners.
In your great love
look with favor on these chosen ones
who desire to be reborn as your children.
Free them from the slavery of sin;
replace the tyranny of Satan
by the gentle yoke of Jesus.
Protect them in every danger,
keep them faithful to you,
serving you in peace and joy,
and so bring them at last
to the eternal thanksgiving of heaven.

Grant this through Christ our Lord.
℟. Amen.

Lord Jesus,
in the wisdom of your love
you touched the heart of a sinful woman
and taught her to worship your Father
in spirit and in truth.
By your power
free from the deceitfulness of Satan these chosen ones
as they draw near to the fountain of living water.
Touch their hearts with the power of the Holy Spirit
and teach them to adore your Father
with sincere faith inspired by love,
for you live and reign for ever and ever.
℟. Amen.

380. For no. 167: Readings for the second scrutiny:

Reading I, **1 Samuel 16:1b, 6-7, 10-13a**
David is anointed king over Israel.

Resp. Ps. Psalm 23:1-3a. 3b-4, 5, 6
℟. (1): **The Lord is my shepherd, there is nothing I shall want.**

Reading II, **Ephesians 5:8-14**
Rise up from the dead, and Christ will shine on you.

℣. Gos. John 8:12b
I am the light of the world, says the Lord; the man who follows me will have the light of life.

Gospel: **John 9:1-41** longer or **1, 6-9, 13-17, 34-38** shorter
The blind man went off and washed himself and came away with his sight restored.

Another reading which may be chosen: **Exodus 13:21-22.**

381. For no. 167: Texts for the Mass when the second scrutiny is celebrated:

OPENING PRAYER

Almighty and eternal God,
may your Church increase in true joy.
May these candidates for baptism
and all the family of man
be reborn into the life of your kingdom.

We ask this through our Lord Jesus Christ, your Son,
who lives and reigns with you and the Holy Spirit,
one God, for ever and ever.

PRAYER OVER THE GIFTS

Pray, brethren . . .

Lord God,
we offer these gifts
in joy and thanksgiving for our salvation.
May the example of our faith and love
help your chosen ones on their way to salvation.

Grant this through Christ our Lord.

When Eucharistic Prayer I is used, the special forms of **Remember, Lord, your people** and **Father, accept this offering** are said, pages 128-129.

PRAYER AFTER COMMUNION

Let us pray.

Pause for silent prayer, if this has not preceded.

Lord,
be close to your family.
Rule and guide us on our way to your kingdom
and bring us to the joy of salvation.

Grant this through Christ our Lord.

382. For no. 170: Another form of the prayer for the second scrutiny:

That he may dispel darkness and himself be the light that shines in the hearts of our chosen ones, let us pray to the Lord:
℟. **Lord, hear our prayer.**

That he may kindly lead them to his Christ, the light of this world, let us pray to the Lord:
℟. **Lord, hear our prayer.**

That our chosen ones may open their hearts to God and acknowledge him as the source of light and the witness of truth, let us pray to the Lord:
℟. **Lord, hear our prayer.**

That he may heal them and preserve them from the skepticism of this world, let us pray to the Lord:
℟. **Lord, hear our prayer.**

That after having been saved by him, who takes away the sin of the world, they may be freed from the contagious power of sin, let us pray to the Lord:
℟. **Lord, hear our prayer.**

That after having been enlightened by the Holy

Spirit, they may never fail to profess the good news of salvation and share it with others, let us pray to the Lord:
℟. **Lord, hear our prayer.**

That all of us, by the example of our lives, may ourselves become in Christ the light of the world, let us pray to the Lord:
℟. **Lord, hear our prayer.**

That all the inhabitants of the earth may acknowledge the true God as the Creator of all things who bestows upon us men the gift of Spirit and life, let us pray to the Lord:
℟. **Lord, hear our prayer.**

383. For no. 171: Another form of exorcism for the second scrutiny:

Let us pray.

Lord God, unfailing light and Father of lights,
by the death and resurrection of your Christ
you have cast out the darkness of hatred and deceit
and poured out upon the human family
the light of truth and love.

Hear our prayers for the sons and daughters
you have called and chosen to be your very own children.
Help them to pass from darkness to radiance.
Set them free from the power of the prince of darkness
so that they may live for ever as children of light.

We ask this through Christ our Lord.
℟. **Amen.**

Lord Jesus,
at your own baptism
the heavens were opened
and you received the Holy Spirit
to enable you to proclaim the good news to the poor
and to restore sight to the blind.

Pour out that Holy Spirit
on those who long for your sacraments.
Keep them safe from all error, doubt and disbelief.
Lead them along the path of your truth,
heal their blindness
and bring them at last
to the full vision of your glory,
for you live and reign for ever and ever.
℟. **Amen.**

384. For no. 174: Reading for the third scrutiny:

Reading I **Ezekiel 37:12-14**
I shall put my spirit in you, and you will live.

Resp. Ps. **Psalm 130:1-2. 3-4ab. 4c-6. 7-8**
℟. (7): **With the Lord there is mercy,**
and fullness of redemption.

Reading II **Romans 8:8-11**
If the Spirit of him who raised Jesus from the dead is living in you, then he will give life to your own mortal bodies.

Verse before the Gospel **John 11:25a and 26**
I am the resurrection and the life, said the Lord:
he who believes in me will not die for ever.

Gospel **John 11:1-45** (longer) or **3-7. 17. 20-27. 33b-45** (shorter)
I am the resurrection and the life.

385. For no. 174: Texts for the Mass when the third scrutiny is celebrated:

OPENING PRAYER

Lord,
enlighten your chosen ones with the word of life.
Give them a new birth
in the waters of baptism
and make them living members of the Church.

Grant this through our Lord Jesus Christ, your Son,
who lives and reigns with you and the Holy Spirit,
one God, for ever and ever.

PRAYERS OVER THE GIFTS

Pray, brethren . . .

Almighty God,
hear our prayers for these men and women
who have begun to learn the Christian faith,
and by this sacrifice prepare them for baptism.

We ask this through Christ our Lord.

When Eucharistic Prayer I is used, the special forms of **Remember, Lord, your people** and **Father, accept this offering** are said, pages 128-129.

PRAYER AFTER COMMUNION

Let us pray.

Pause for silent prayer, if this has not preceded.

Lord,
may your people be one in spirit
and serve you with all their heart.
Free them from all fear.
Give them joy in your gifts
and love for those who are to be reborn as your children.

We ask this through Christ our Lord.

386. For no. 177: Another form of prayer for the third scrutiny:

That these chosen ones may be given the faith to acknowledge Jesus Christ as the resurrection and the life, we pray to the Lord:
℟. **Lord, hear our prayer.**

That they may be freed from sin to bear the fruit that leads to holiness and eternal life, we pray to the Lord:
℟. **Lord, hear our prayer.**

That by penance they may be loosed from the shackles of sin, and by baptism they may become one with

Christ, dead to sin and forever alive to God, we pray to the Lord.
℟. Lord, hear our prayer.

That they may be filled with the hope of the life-giving Spirit and prepare themselves well for the birth to new life, we pray to the Lord:
℟. Lord, hear our prayer.

That the eucharistic food they are soon to receive may make them one with Christ, the source of life and resurrection, we pray to the Lord:
℟. Lord, hear our prayer.

That all of us may walk in newness of life and show forth to the world the power of the risen Christ, we pray to the Lord:
℟. Lord, hear our prayer.

That all who live on earth may come to find Christ and to know in him the promises of eternal life, we pray to the Lord:
℟. Lord, hear our prayer.

387. For no. 178: Another form of exorcism for the third scrutiny:

Let us pray.

Father,
fountain of all life,
you seek your glory in man fully alive;
you make known your infinite power in the
resurrection of the dead.

Rescue from the power of death these chosen ones
who long to come to life through baptism.
Free them from the power of the devil
who by inducing to sin caused death
and who seeks to ruin the world which you created as
good.
Place them under the power of your beloved Son;
from him may they receive the power of the
resurrection

and bear witness to your glory before all people.

We ask this through Christ our Lord.
℟. **Amen.**

Lord Jesus Christ
you commanded Lazarus to come forth alive from the tomb
and you freed all people from death by your own resurrection.

We pray for your servants
who eagerly approach the waters of new birth and the banquet of life.
Never let the power of death hold them back
who by their faith will share in the victory of your resurrection,
for you live and reign for ever and ever.

388. For nos. 253 and 345: Readings for Christian Initiation apart from the Easter Vigil:

OLD TESTAMENT READING

1. **Genesis 15:1-6, 18a:**
So shall your descendants be. To your descendants I give this land.

2. **Genesis 17:1-8:**
I will establish my covenant between myself and you, and your descendants after you, generation after generation, a covenant in perpetuity.

3. **Genesis 35:1-4. 6-7a:**
Get rid of the foreign gods you have with you.

4. **Deuteronomy 30:15-20:**
Choose life, then, so that you and your descendants may live.

5. **Joshua 24:1-2a. 15-17. 18b-25a:**
We will serve the Lord because he is our God.

6. **2 Kings 5:9-15a:**
Naaman went down and washed himself seven times in the river Jordan and became clean.

7. **Isaiah 44:1-3:**
I will pour my spirit upon your descendants.

8. **Jeremiah 31:31-34:**
In their heart I will write my law.

9. **Ezekiel 36:24-28:**
I shall pour clean water over you and you shall be cleansed of all your sins.

Or the Old Testament readings for the Easter Vigil.

NEW TESTAMENT READING

1. **Acts 2:14a. 36-40a. 41-42:**
Every one of you must be baptized in the name of Jesus Christ.

2. **Acts 8:26-38:**
There is water. What prevents me from being baptized?

3. **Romans 6:3-11** (longer) **or 3-4, 8-11** (shorter):
When we were baptized we joined Jesus in death so that we might walk in the newness of his life.

4. **Romans 8:28-32, 35, 37-39:**
Who can ever come between us and the love of Christ?

5. **1 Corinthians 12:12-13:**
In the one Spirit we were all baptized into one body.

6. **Galatians 3:26-28:**
All baptized in Christ have put on Christ.

7. **Ephesians 1:3-10, 13-14:**
The Father chose us to be his adopted sons through Jesus Christ.

8. **Ephesians 4:1-6:**
There is one Lord, one faith, one baptism.

9. **Colossians 3:9b-17:** As the chosen ones of God, you have put on the new man.

10. **Titus 3:4-7:** We are saved by the cleansing water of rebirth and by being renewed with the Holy Spirit.

11. **Hebrews 10:22-25:** Free our hearts from any trace of bad conscience and wash our bodies with pure water.

12. **1 Peter 2:4-5. 9-10:** You are a chosen race, a royal priesthood.

13. **Revelation 19:1. 5-9a:** Happy are those who are invited to the wedding feast of the Lamb.

RESPONSORIAL PSALM

1. Psalm 8:4-5. 6-7. 8-9 (2a):

O Lord, our God, how wonderful your name in all the earth!

or: Ephesians 5:14:

Wake up and rise from death: Christ will shine upon you!

2. Psalm 23:1-3a. 3b-4. 5. 6 (1):

The Lord is my shepherd; there is nothing I shall want.

or: 1 Peter 2:25:

You were all like lost sheep; but now you have returned to the shepherd of your souls.

3. Psalm 27:1. 4. 8b-9abc. 13-14 (1a):

The Lord is my light and my salvation.

or: Ephesians 5:14:

Wake up and rise from death. Christ will shine upon you!

4. Psalm 32:1-2, 5, 11 (1a):

Happy are those whose sins are forgiven.

or: (11a):

Let the just exult and rejoice in the Lord.

5. Psalm 34:2-3, 6-7, 8-9, 14-15, 16-17, 18-19 (6a):

Come to him and receive his light!

6. Psalm 42:2-3; Psalm 43:3. 4 (Psalm 42:3a):

My soul is thirsting for the living God.

7. Psalm 51:3-4, 8-9, 12-13, 14 and 17 (12a):
Create a clean heart in me, O God.
or: Ezekiel 36:26:
I will give you a new heart, a new spirit within you.

8. Psalm 63:2, 3-4, 5-6, 8-9a (2b):
My soul is thirsting for you, O Lord my God.

9. Psalm 66:1-3a. 8-9, 16-17 (1):
Let all the earth cry out to God with joy.

10. Psalm 89:3-4, 16-17, 21-22, 25 and 27 (2a):
For ever I will sing the goodness of the Lord.

11. Psalm 126:1-2ab, 2cd-3, 4-5, 6 (3):
The Lord has done great things for us; we are filled with joy.

ALLELUIA VERSE AND VERSE BEFORE THE GOSPEL

1. John 3:16:
God loved the world so much, he gave us his only Son,
that all who believe in him might have eternal life.

2. John 8:12:
I am the light of the world, says the Lord;
the man who follows me will have the light of life.

3. John 14:6:
I am the way, the truth, and the life, says the Lord;
no one comes to the Father, except through me.

4. Ephesians 4:5-6:
One Lord, one faith, one baptism.
One God, the Father of all.

5. Colossians 2:12:
In baptism we have died with Christ,
and we have risen to new life in him.

6. Colossians 3:1:
If then you have been raised with Christ, seek the

things that are above,
where Christ is seated at the right hand of God.

7. 2 Timothy 1:10b:
Our Savior Jesus Christ has done away with death
and brought us life through his gospel.

8. 1 Peter 2:9:
You are a chosen race, a royal priesthood, a holy people.
Praise God who called you out of darkness and into his marvelous light.

GOSPEL

1. **Matthew 16:24-27:**
If anyone wishes to follow me, let him deny himself.

2. **Matthew 28:18-20:**
Go and teach all the nations,
baptizing them in the name of the Father, and of the Son,
and of the Holy Spirit.

3. **Mark 1:9-11:**
Jesus was baptized by John in the Jordan.

4. **Mark 10:13-16:**
Anyone who does not welcome the kingdom of God like a little child will never enter it.

5. **Mark 16:15-16. 19-20:**
He who believes and is baptized will be saved.

6. **Luke 24:44-53:**
In the name of Jesus, repentance for the
forgiveness of sins should be preached
to all the nations.

7. **John 1:1-5, 9-14, 16-18:**
He gave power to become children of God
to all who believe in his name.

8. **John 1:29-34:**
Look, there is the Lamb of God
that takes away the sins of the world.

9. **John 3:1-6:**
Unless a man is born from above,
he cannot see the kingdom of God.

10. **John 3:16-21:**
Everyone who believes in him will have everlasting life.

11. **John 12:44-50:**
I, the light, have come into the world.

12. **John 15:1-11:**
Whoever remains in me, and I in him,
bears fruit in plenty.

389. For nos. 215, 216, 258, 349: Another form for the blessing of water:

1.
Celebrant:
Praise to you, almighty God and Father, for you have created water to cleanse and to give life.
All: **Blessed be God** (or some other suitable acclamation by the people).

Celebrant:
Praise to you, Lord Jesus Christ, the Father's only Son, for you offered yourself on the cross, that in the blood and water flowing from your side, and through your death and resurrection, the Church might be born.
All: **Blessed be God.**

Celebrant:
Praise to you, God the Holy Spirit, for you anointed Christ at his baptism in the waters of the Jordan, so that we might all be baptized in you.
All: **Blessed be God.**

Celebrant:
Come to us, Lord, Father of all, and make holy this water which you have created, so that all who are baptized in it may be washed clean of sin and be born again to live as your children.
All: **Hear us, Lord** (or some other suitable invocation).

Celebrant:
Make this water holy, Lord, so that all who are baptized into Christ's death and resurrection by this water may become more perfectly like your Son.
All: **Hear us, Lord.**

The celebrant touches the water with his right hand and continues:

Lord, make holy this water which you have created, so that all those whom you have chosen may be born again by the power of the Holy Spirit and may take their place among your holy people.
All: **Hear us, Lord.**

If the baptismal water has already been blessed, the celebrant omits the invocation **Come to us, Lord** and those which follow it, and says:

You have called your children N. and N. to this cleansing water that they may share in the faith of your Church and have eternal life.
By the mystery of this consecrated water
lead them to a new and spiritual birth.
We ask this through Christ our Lord.

All: **Amen.**

2.
Celebrant:
Father, God of mercy, through these waters of baptism you have filled us with new life as your very own children.

All: **Blessed be God** (or some other suitable acclamation by the people).

Celebrant:
From all who are baptized in water and the Holy Spirit, you have formed one people, united in your Son Jesus Christ.
All: **Blessed be God.**

Celebrant:
You have set us free and filled our hearts with the Spirit of your love so that we may live in your peace.
All: **Blessed be God.**

Celebrant:
You call those who have been baptized to announce the good news of Jesus Christ to people everywhere.
All: **Blessed be God.**

Celebrant:
You have called your children N. and N. to this cleansing water and new birth that by sharing the faith of your Church they might have eternal life. Bless ✠ this water in which they will be baptized. We ask this in the name of Christ our Lord.
All: **Amen.**

If the baptismal water has already been blessed, the celebrant omits this last prayer and says:

You have called your children N. and N. to this cleansing water so that they may share in the faith of your Church and have eternal life. By the mystery of this consecrated water lead them to a new and spiritual birth. We ask this through Christ our Lord.
All: **Amen**

V. ACCLAMATIONS AND HYMNS

390.

ACCLAMATIONS FROM SACRED SCRIPTURE

1. Exodus 15:11
Lord God, who is your equal?
Strong, majestic, and holy!
Worthy of praise, worker of wonders!

2. 1 John 1:5
God is light: in him there is no darkness.

3. 1 John 4:15
God is love; he who lives in love, lives in God.

4. Ephesians 4:6
There is one God, one Father of all;
he is over all, and through all;
he lives in all of us.

5. Psalm 34:6
Come to him and receive his light!

6. see Ephesians 1:4
Blessed be God who chose you in Christ.

7. Ephesians 2:10
You are God's work of art, created in Christ Jesus.

8. 1 John 3:2
You are now God's children, my dearest friends.
What you shall be in his glory has not yet been revealed.

9. 1 John 3:1
Think of how God loves you!
He calls you his own children,
and that is what you are.

10. Revelation 22:14
Happy are those who have washed their robes clean,
washed in the blood of the Lamb!

11. Galatians 3:28
All of you are one,
united in Christ Jesus.

12. Ephesians 5:1-2
Imitate God; walk in his love,
just as Christ loves us.

HYMNS IN THE STYLE OF THE NEW TESTAMENT

13. 1 Peter 1:3-5
Praised be the Father of our Lord Jesus Christ,
a God so merciful and kind!
He has given us a new birth, a living hope,
by raising Jesus his Son from death.
Salvation is our undying inheritance,
preserved for us in heaven,
salvation at the end of time.

14. 1 Timothy 3:16

How great the sign of God's love for us,
Jesus Christ our Lord:
promised before all time began,
revealed in these last days.
He lived and suffered and died for us,
but the Spirit raised him to life.
People everywhere have heard his message
and placed their faith in him.
What wonderful blessings he gives his people;
living in the Father's glory,
he fills all creation
and guides it to perfection.

SONGS FROM ANCIENT LITURGIES

15.

We believe in you, Lord Jesus Christ.
Fill our hearts with your radiance
and make us the children of light!

16.

We come to you, Lord Jesus.
Fill us with your life.
Make us children of the Father
and one in you.

17.

Lord Jesus, from your wounded side
flowed streams of cleansing water;
the world was washed of all its sin,
all life made new again!

18.

The Father's voice calls us above the waters,
the glory of the Son shines on us,
the love of the Spirit fills us with life.

19.

Holy Church of God, stretch out your hand
and welcome your children
newborn of water
and of the Spirit of God.

20.
Rejoice, you newly baptized,
chosen members of the Kingdom.
Buried with Christ in death,
you are reborn in him by faith.

21.
This is the fountain of life,
water made holy by the suffering of Christ,
washing all the world.
You who are washed in this water
have hope of heaven's Kingdom.

391. For no. 233: Commemorations of the neophytes in the eucharistic prayers:

EUCHARISTIC PRAYER II

. . . and all the clergy.
Remember also those who have been baptized (and confirmed) today as members of your family.
Help them to follow Christ your Son with loving hearts.

EUCHARISTIC PRAYER III

. . . gathered here before you.
Strengthen those who have now become your people
by the waters of rebirth
(and the gift of the Holy Spirit).
Help them to walk in newness of life.

EUCHARISTIC PRAYER IV

. . . who take part in this offering,
those here present,
those born again today
by water and the Holy Spirit,
and all your people . . .

392. For no. 339: Another prayer of exorcism in dialogue form:

The celebrant, inviting the children to pray to God with him, says:

God of love, Father of all,
look upon N. and N. who will soon be baptized.
Children: **We have heard the words of Jesus**
and we love them.

Celebrant:
They strive to live as your sons and daughters
but find this a difficult task.
Children: **Father, we want to do always what pleases you,**
but we feel within us an urge to do otherwise.

Celebrant:
Loving Father, free these young people
from the spirit of discouragement and evil
and help them to walk always in your light.
Children: **We want to walk with Jesus**
who gave up his life for us.
Help us, Father, to follow him.

Celebrant:
If they should falter on the way
and do what displeases you,
come to their aid with the power of your strength
that they may rise again
and continue their journey to you,
with Jesus Christ our Lord.
Children: **Father, give us your strength.**

RITE OF BAPTISM FOR CHILDREN

III Celebration of the Sacrament (90)

A Blessing and Invocation of God over Baptismal Water (91-92)

B Renunciation of Sin and Profession of Faith (93-96)

C Baptism (97)
Anointing with Chrism (98)
Clothing with the White Garment (99)
Lighted Candle (100)
Ephphetha or Prayer over Ears and Mouth (101)
Conclusion of the Rite (102)
Lord's Prayer (103-104)
Blessing (105-106)

CHAPTER III
RITE OF BAPTISM FOR A LARGE NUMBER OF CHILDREN

I Reception of the Children (107-111)

II Celebration of God's Word

A Scriptural Readings and Homily (112-113)

B Intercessions (Prayer of the Faithful) (114)

C Prayer of Exorcism (115-116)

III Celebration of the Sacrament (117)

A Blessing and Invocation of God over Baptismal Water (118-119)

B Renunciation of Sin and Profession of Faith (120-123)

C Baptism (124)
Anointing with Chrism (125)
Clothing with White Garment (126)
Lighted Candle (127)

D Conclusion of the Rite
Lord's Prayer (128-129)
Blessing (130-131)

CHAPTER IV
RITE OF BAPTISM FOR CHILDREN ADMINISTERED BY A CATECHIST WHEN NO PRIEST OR DEACON IS AVAILABLE

I Reception of the Children (132-136)

II Celebration of God's Word

A Reading and Homily or Short Talk (137-138)

B Prayer of the Faithful (139-140)

III Celebration of the Sacrament (141)

A Blessing and Invocation of God over Baptismal Water (141-143)

B Renunciation of Sin and Profession of Faith (144-147)

C Baptism (148-151)

D Clothing with White Garment (152)

E Lighted Candle (153)

IV Conclusion of the Rite

A Lord's Prayer and Blessing (154-156)

CHAPTER V
RITE OF BAPTISM FOR CHILDREN IN DANGER OF DEATH WHEN NO PRIEST OR DEACON IS AVAILABLE (157-164)

CHAPTER VI
RITE OF BRINGING A BAPTIZED CHILD TO THE CHURCH

I Reception of the Child (165-171)

II Celebration of God's Word

A Scripture Reading and Homily (172-174)

B Prayer of the Faithful (175)

SACRED CONGREGATION FOR DIVINE WORSHIP

Prot. n. R 23/969

DECREE

The Second Vatican Council decreed that the rite of baptism for children in the Roman Ritual should be revised in order that:
a) the rite might be better adapted to the actual condition of children;
b) the role and responsibilities of parents and godparents might be more clearly expressed;
c) suitable adaptations might be made for the baptism of a large number of people;
d) suitable adaptations might likewise be made for baptism administered by catechists in mission areas or by others in circumstances when the ordinary minister is unavailable;
e) a rite might be provided for use when a child has already been baptized according to the shorter rite, to mark the fact that he has already been received into the Church (Constitution on the Sacred Liturgy, nos. 67-69).

This revision has been carried out by the Consilium for the Implementation of the Constitution on the Sacred Liturgy. Pope Paul VI, by his apostolic authority, has approved this new rite of baptism for children and directs that it should be published to replace the rite given in the Roman Ritual.

Therefore this Sacred Congregation, acting on the express wishes of the Holy Father, publishes this rite to be effective September 8, 1969.

Anything to the contrary notwithstanding.

From the Congregation for Divine Worship, May 5, 1969, Feast of the Ascension.

Benno Card. Gut
Prefect

A. Bugnini
Secretary

BAPTISM FOR CHILDREN

INTRODUCTION

I. IMPORTANCE OF BAPTIZING CHILDREN

1. Children or infants are those who have not yet reached the age of discernment and therefore cannot have or profess personal faith.

2. From the earliest times, the Church, to which the mission of preaching the gospel and of baptizing was entrusted, has baptized children as well as adults. Our Lord said: "Unless a man is reborn in water and the Holy Spirit, he cannot enter the kingdom of God."[1] The Church has always understood these words to mean that children should not be deprived of baptism, because they are baptized in the faith of the Church. This faith is proclaimed for them by their parents and godparents, who represent both the local Church and the whole society of saints and believers: "The Church is at once the mother of all and the mother of each."[2]

3. To fulfill the true meaning of the sacrament, children must later be formed in the faith in which they have been baptized. The foundation of this formation will be the sacrament itself, which they have already received. Christian formation, which is their due, seeks to lead them gradually to learn God's plan in Christ, so that they may ultimately accept for themselves the faith in which they have been baptized.

II. MINISTRIES AND ROLES IN THE CELEBRATION OF BAPTISM

4. The people of God, that is the Church, made present in the local community, has an important part to play in the baptism of both children and adults.

Before and after the celebration of the sacrament, the child has a right to the love and help of the community. During the rite, in addition to the ways of congregational participa-

[1]John 3:5.
[2]Saint Augustine, Epistle 98, 5: PL 33, 362.

tion mentioned in no. 7 of the general introduction, the community exercises its duty when it expresses its assent together with the celebrant after the profession of faith by the parents and godparents. In this way it is clear that the faith in which the children are baptized is not the private possession of the individual family, but it is the common treasure of the whole Church of Christ.

5. Because of the natural relationships, parents have a more important ministry and role in the baptism of infants than the godparents.
1) Before the celebration of the sacrament, it is of great importance that parents, moved by their own faith or with the help of friends or other members of the community, should prepare to take part in the rite with understanding. They should be provided with suitable means such as books, instructions, and catechisms written for families. The parish priest should make it his duty to visit them, or see that they are visited, as a family or as a group of families, and prepare them for the coming celebration by pastoral counsel and common prayer.
2) It is very important that the parents should be present in the celebration in which their child is reborn in water and the Holy Spirit.
3) In the celebration of baptism, the father and mother have special parts to play. They listen to the words addressed to them by the celebrant, they join in prayer along with the congregation, and they exercise a special function when: a) they publicly ask that the child be baptized; b) they sign their child with the sign of the cross after the celebrant; c) they renounce Satan and make their profession of faith; d) they (and especially the mother) carry the child to the font; e) they hold the lighted candle; f) they are blessed with the special prayers for the mothers and fathers.
4) If one of the parents cannot make the profession of faith (if, for example, he is not a Catholic), he may keep silent. All that is asked of him, when he requests baptism for the child, is that he should make arrangements, or at least give permission, for the child to be instructed in the faith of its baptism.
5) After baptism it is the responsibility of the parents, in their gratitude to God and in fidelity to the duty they have undertaken, to enable the child to know God, whose adopted child it has become, to receive confirmation, and to

participate in the holy eucharist. In this duty they are again to be helped by the parish priest by suitable means.

6. Each child may have a godfather and a godmother; the word "godparents" is used in the rite to describe both.

7. In addition to what is said about the ordinary minister of baptism in the general introduction (nos. 11-15), the following should be noted:
1) It is the duty of the priest to prepare families for the baptism of their children and to help them in the task of Christian formation which they have undertaken. It is the duty of the bishop to coordinate such pastoral efforts in the diocese, with the help also of deacons and lay people.
2) It is also the duty of the priest to arrange that baptism is always celebrated with proper dignity and, as far as possible, adapted to the circumstances and wishes of the families concerned. Everyone who performs the rite of baptism should do so with care and devotion; he must also try to be understanding and friendly to all.

III. TIME AND PLACE FOR THE BAPTISM OF CHILDREN

8. As for the time of baptism, the first consideration is the welfare of the child, that it may not be deprived of the benefit of the sacrament; then the health of the mother must be considered, so that, as far as possible she too may be present. Then, as long as they do not interfere with the greater good of the child, there are pastoral considerations such as allowing sufficient time to prepare the parents and for planning the actual celebration to bring out its paschal character:
1) If the child is in danger of death, it is to be baptized without delay, as is laid down in no. 21.
2) In other cases, as soon as possible and even before the child is born, the parents should be in touch with the parish priest concerning the baptism, so that proper preparation may be made for the celebration.
3) An infant should be baptized within the first weeks after birth. The conference of bishops may, for sufficiently serious pastoral reasons, determine a longer interval of time between birth and baptism.
4) When the parents are not yet prepared to profess the faith

or to undertake the duty of bringing up their children as Christians, it is for the parish priest, keeping in mind whatever regulations may have been laid down by the conference of bishops, to determine the time for the baptism of infants.

9. To bring out the paschal character of baptism, it is recommended that the sacrament be celebrated during the Easter Vigil or on Sunday, when the Church commemorates the Lord's resurrection. On Sunday, baptism may be celebrated even during Mass, so that the entire community may be present and the necessary relationship between baptism and eucharist may be clearly seen, but this should not be done too often. Regulations for the celebration of baptism during the Easter Vigil or at Mass on Sunday are set out below.

10. So that baptism may clearly appear as the sacrament of the Church's faith and of admittance into the people of God, it should normally be celebrated in the parish church, which must have a baptismal font.

11. The bishop, after consulting the local parish priest, may permit or direct that a baptismal font be placed in another church or public oratory within the parish boundaries. In these places, too, it is the normal right of the parish priest to celebrate baptism.

12. Except in case of danger, baptism should not be celebrated in private houses.

13. Unless the bishop decides otherwise (see no. 11), baptism should not be celebrated in hospitals, except in cases of emergency or for some other pastoral reason of a pressing kind. Care should always be taken that the parish priest is notified and that the parents are suitably prepared beforehand.

14. While the liturgy of the word is being celebrated, it is desirable that the children should be taken to some other place. Provision should be made for the mothers or godmothers to attend the liturgy of the word; the children should therefore be entrusted to the care of other women.

IV. STRUCTURE OF THE RITE OF BAPTIZING CHILDREN

A. Order of Baptism Celebrated by the Ordinary Minister

15. Baptism, whether for one child, or for several, or even for a larger number, should be celebrated by the ordinary minister and with the full rite when there is no immediate danger of death.

16. The rite begins with the reception of the children. This is to indicate the desire of the parents and godparents, as well as the intention of the Church, concerning the celebration of the sacrament of baptism. These purposes are expressed in action when the parents and the celebrant trace the sign of the cross on the foreheads of the children.

17. Then the liturgy of the word is directed toward stirring up the faith of the parents, godparents, and congregation, and praying in common for the fruits of baptism before the sacrament itself. This part of the celebration consists of the reading of one or more passages from holy scripture; a homily, followed by a period of silence; the prayer of the faithful; and finally a prayer, drawn up in the style of an exorcism, to introduce either the anointing with the oil of catechumens or the laying on of hands.

18. 1) The celebration of the sacrament is immediately preceded by:

a) the solemn prayer of the celebrant, who, by invoking God and recalling his plan of salvation, blesses the water of baptism or commemorates its previous blessing;

b) the renunciation of Satan on the part of parents and godparents, and their profession of faith, to which is added the assent of the celebrant and the community; and the final interrogation of the parents and godparents.

2) The celebration of the sacrament is performed by washing in water, by way of immersion or infusion, according to local custom, and by the invocation of the blessed Trinity.

3) The celebration of the sacrament is completed, first by the anointing with chrism, which signifies the royal priesthood of the baptized and enrollment in the fellowship of God's people; then by the ceremonies of the white garment, lighted candle, and *Ephphetha* (the last of which is optional).

19. After the celebrant speaks of the future reception of the eucharist by the baptized children, the Lord's Prayer, in which God's children pray to their Father in heaven, is recited before the altar. Finally, a prayer of blessing is said over the mothers, fathers, and all present, to ask God's grace in abundance for all.

B. Shorter Rite of Baptism

20. In the shorter rite of baptism designed for the use of catechists,[3] the reception of the children, the celebration of the word of God, or the instruction by the minister, and the prayer of the faithful are retained. Before the font, the minister offers a prayer invoking God and recalling the history of salvation as it relates to baptism. After the baptismal washing, an adapted formula is recited in place of the anointing with chrism, and the whole rite concludes in the customary way. The omissions, therefore, are the exorcism, the anointing with oil of catechumens and with chrism, and the *Ephphetha*.

21. The shorter rite for baptizing a child in danger of death and in the absence of the ordinary minister has a twofold structure:
1) At the moment of death or when there is urgency because of imminent danger of death, the minister,[4] omitting all other ceremonies, pours water (not necessarily blessed but real and natural water), on the head of the child, and pronounces the customary formula.[5]
2) If it is prudently judged that there is sufficient time; several of the faithful may be gathered together, and, if one of them is able to lead the others in a short prayer, the following rite may be used: an explanation by the minister of the sacrament, a short common prayer, the profession of faith by the parents or one godparent, and the pouring of the water with the customary words. But if those present are uneducated, the minister of the sacrament should recite the profession of faith aloud and baptize according to the rite for use at the moment of death.

[3]II Vatican Council, Constitution on the Sacred Liturgy, *Sacrosanctum Concilium*, 68.
[4]General Introduction, 16.
[5]*Ibid.*, 23.

22. In danger of death, the priest or deacon may also use this shorter form if necessary. If there is time and he has the sacred chrism, the parish priest or other priest enjoying the same faculty should not fail to confer confirmation after baptism. In this case he omits the postbaptismal anointing with chrism.

V. ADAPTATIONS BY CONFERENCES OF BISHOPS OR BY BISHOPS

23. In addition to the adaptations provided for in the general introduction (nos. 30-33), the baptismal rite for infants admits other variations, to be determined by the conferences of bishops.

24. As is indicated in the Roman Ritual, the following matters are left to the discretion of the conferences:
1) As local customs may dictate, the questioning about the name of the child may be arranged in different ways: the name may have been given already or may be given during the rite of baptism.
2) The anointing with oil of catechumens may be omitted (nos. 50, 87).
3) The formula of renunciation may be shortened or extended (nos. 57, 94, 121).
4) If the number to be baptized is very great, the anointing with chrism may be omitted (no. 125).
5) The rite of *Ephphetha* may be retained (nos. 65, 101).

25. In many countries parents are sometimes not ready for the celebration of baptism or they ask for their children to be baptized, although the latter will not afterwards receive a Christian education and will even lose the faith. Since it is not enough to instruct the parents and to inquire about their faith in the course of the rite itself, conferences of bishops may issue pastoral directives, for the guidance of parish priests, to determine a longer interval between birth and baptism.

26. It is for the bishop to judge whether in his diocese catechists may give an improvised homily or speak only from a written text.

VI. ADAPTATIONS BY THE MINISTER

27. During meetings to prepare the parents for the baptism of their children, it is important that the instruction should be supported by prayer and religious rites. The various elements provided in the rite of baptism for the celebration of the word of God will prove helpful.

28. When the baptism of children is celebrated as part of the Easter Vigil, the ritual should be arranged as follows:
1) At a convenient time and place before the Easter Vigil, the rite of receiving the children is celebrated. The liturgy of the word may be omitted at the end, according to circumstances, and the prayer of exorcism is said, followed by the anointing with oil of catechumens.
2) The celebration of the sacrament (nos. 56-58, 60-63) takes place after the blessing of the water, as is indicated in the Rite of the Easter Vigil. [See also nos. 93-95, 97-99, or nos. 120-122, 124-126.]
3) The assent of the celebrant and community (no. 59) is omitted, as are the presentation of the lighted candle (no. 64) and the rite of *Ephphetha* (no. 65).
4) The conclusion of the rite (nos. 67-71) is omitted.

29. If baptism takes place during Sunday Mass, the Mass for that Sunday is used, and the celebration takes place as follows:
1) The rite of receiving the children (nos. 33-43) takes place at the beginning of Mass, and the greeting and penitential rite are omitted. [See also nos. 73-80, or nos. 107-111.]
2) In the liturgy of the word:

a) The readings are taken from the Mass of the Sunday or, for special reasons, from those provided in the baptismal rite.

b) The homily is based on the sacred texts, but should take account of the baptism which is to take place.

c) The creed is not said, since the profession of faith by the entire community before baptism takes its place.

d) The general intercessions are taken from those used in the rite of baptism (nos. 47-48). At the end, however, before the invocation of the saints, petitions are added for the universal Church and the needs of the world. [See also nos. 84-85, 114, 217-220.]

3) The celebration of baptism continues with the prayer of

exorcism, anointing, and other ceremonies described in the rite (nos. 49-66). [See also nos. 86-101, or nos. 115-127.]
4) After the celebration of baptism, the Mass continues in the usual way with the offertory.
5) For the blessing at the end of Mass, the priest may use one of the formulas provided in the rite of baptism (nos. 70, 247-249). [See also nos. 105, 130.]

30. If baptism is celebrated during Mass on weekdays, it is arranged in the same way as on Sundays; the readings for the liturgy of the word may be taken from those that are provided in the rite of baptism (nos. 44, 186-194, 204-215).

31. In accordance with no. 34 of the general introduction, the minister may make some adaptations in the rite, as circumstances require, such as:
1) If the child's mother died in childbirth, this should be taken into account in the opening instruction (no. 36), general intercessions (nos. 47, 217-220), and final blessing (nos. 70, 247-248).
2) In the dialogue with the parents (nos. 37-38, 76-77), their answers should be taken into account: if they have not answered **baptism,** but **faith,** or **the grace of Christ,** or **entrance into the Church,** or **everlasting life,** then the minister does not begin by saying **baptism,** but uses **faith,** or **the grace of Christ,** and so forth.
3) The rite of bringing a baptized child to the church (nos. 165-185), which has been drawn up for use only when the child has been baptized in danger of death, should be adapted to cover other contingencies, for example, when children have been baptized during a time of religious persecution or temporary disagreement between the parents.

CHAPTER I

RITE OF BAPTISM FOR SEVERAL CHILDREN

RECEPTION OF THE CHILDREN

32. If possible, baptism should take place on Sunday, the day on which the Church celebrates the paschal mystery. It should be conferred in a communal celebration for all the recently born children, and in the presence of the faithful, or at least of relatives, friends, and neighbors, who are all to take an active part in the rite.

33. It is the role of the father and mother, accompanied by the godparents, to present the child to the Church for baptism.

34. If there are very many children, and if there are several priests or deacons present, these may help the celebrant in the parts referred to below.

35. The people may sing a psalm or hymn suitable for the occasion. Meanwhile the celebrating priest or deacon, vested in alb or surplice, with a stole (with or without a cope) of festive color, and accompanied by the ministers, goes to the entrance of the church or to that part of the church where the parents and godparents are waiting with those who are to be baptized.

36. The celebrant greets all present, and especially the parents and godparents, reminding them briefly of the joy with which the parents welcomed their children as gifts from God, the source of life, who now wishes to bestow his own life on these little ones.

37. First the celebrant questions the parents of each child.

Celebrant:
What name do you give your child? (or: **have you given?)**
Parents: **N.**

Celebrant:
What do you ask of God's Church for N.?
Parents: **Baptism.**

The celebrant may choose other words for this dialogue. The first reply may be given by someone other than the parents if local custom gives him the right to name the child. In the second response the parents may use other words, e.g., **faith** or **the grace of Christ** or **entrance into the Church** or **eternal life.**

38. If there are many children to be baptized, the celebrant asks the names from all the parents together, and each family replies in turn. The second question may also be asked of all together.

Celebrant:
What name do you give each of these children? (or: **have you given?)**
Parents: **N., N.,** etc.

Celebrant:
What do you ask of God's Church for your children?
All: **Baptism.**

39. The celebrant speaks to the parents in these or similar words:
You have asked to have your children baptized. In doing so you are accepting the responsibility of training them in the practice of the faith. It will be your duty to bring them up to keep God's commandments as Christ taught us, by loving God and our neighbor. Do you clearly understand what you are undertaking?
Parents: **We do.**

This response is given by each family individually. But if there are many children to be baptized, the response may be given by all together.

40. Then the celebrant turns to the godparents and addresses them in these or similar words:

Are you ready to help these parents in their duty as Christian mothers and fathers?
All the godparents: **We are.**

41. The celebrant continues:
N. and N. (or, **My dear children**), **the Christian community welcomes you with great joy. In its name I claim you for Christ our Savior by the sign of the cross. I now trace the cross on your foreheads, and invite your parents (and godparents) to do the same.**

He signs each child on the forehead, in silence. Then he invites the parents and (if it seems appropriate) the godparents to do the same.

42. The celebrant invites the parents, godparents, and the others to take part in the liturgy of the word. If circumstances permit, there is a procession to the place where this will be celebrated, during which a song is sung, e.g., Psalm 85:7, 8, 9ab:

Will you not give us life;
and shall not your people rejoice in you?
Show us, O Lord, your kindness,
and grant us your salvation.
I will hear what God proclaims;
the Lord—for he proclaims peace to his people.

43. The children to be baptized may be carried to a separate place, where they remain until the end of the liturgy of the word.

CELEBRATION OF GOD'S WORD

SCRIPTURAL READINGS AND HOMILY

44. One or even two of the following gospel passages are read, during which all may sit if convenient.

John 3:1-6 The meeting with Nicodemus.
Matthew 28:18-20 The apostles are sent to preach the gospel and to baptize.
Mark 1:9-11 The baptism of Jesus.

Mark 10:13-16 Let the little children come to me.

The passages listed in nos. 186-194 and 204-215 may be chosen, or other passages which better meet the wishes or needs of the parents. Between the readings, responsorial psalms or verses may be sung as given in nos. 195-203.

45. After the reading, the celebrant gives a short homily, explaining to those present the significance of what has been read. His purpose will be to lead them to a deeper understanding of the mystery of baptism and to encourage the parents and godparents to a ready acceptance of the responsibilities which arise from the sacrament.

46. After the homily, or in the course of or after the litany, it is desirable to have a period of silence while all pray at the invitation of the celebrant. If convenient, a suitable song follows, e.g., one chosen from nos. 225-245.

INTERCESSIONS (PRAYER OF THE FAITHFUL)

47. Then the prayer of the faithful is said:

Celebrant:
My brothers and sisters,* let us ask our Lord Jesus Christ to look lovingly on these children who are to be baptized, on their parents and godparents, and on all the baptized.

Leader:
By the mystery of your death and resurrection, bathe these children in light, given them the new life of baptism and welcome them into your holy Church.
All: **Lord, hear our prayer.**

Leader:
Through baptism and confirmation, make them your faithful followers and witnesses to your gospel.
All: **Lord, hear our prayer.**

*At the discretion of the priest, other words which seem more suitable under the circumstances, such as **friends** or **dearly beloved** or **brethren,** may be used. This also applies to parallel instances in the liturgy.

Leader:
Lead them by a holy life to the joys of God's kingdom.
All: **Lord, hear our prayer.**

Leader:
Make the lives of their parents and godparents examples of faith to inspire these children.
All: **Lord, hear our prayer.**

Leader:
Keep their families always in your love.
All: **Lord, hear our prayer.**

Leader:
Renew the grace of our baptism in each one of us.
All: **Lord, hear our prayer.**

Other forms may be chosen from nos. 217-220

48. The celebrant next invites all to invoke the saints. At this point, if the children have been taken out, they are brought back.

Holy Mary, Mother of God, pray for us.
Saint John the Baptist, pray for us.
Saint Joseph, pray for us.
Saint Peter and Saint Paul, pray for us.

The names of other saints may be added, especially the patrons of the children to be baptized, and of the church or locality. The litany concludes:

All you saints of God, pray for us.

PRAYER OF EXORCISM AND ANOINTING BEFORE BAPTISM

49. After the invocations, the celebrant says:

A

Almighty and ever-living God,
you sent your only Son into the world
to cast out the power of Satan, spirit of evil,
to rescue man from the kingdom of darkness,

and bring him into the splendor of your kingdom of light.
We pray for these children:
set them free from original sin,
make them temples of your glory,
and send your Holy Spirit to dwell within them.
(We ask this) through Christ our Lord.
All: **Amen.**

Another form of the prayer of exorcism:

B

Almighty God,
you sent your only Son
to rescue us from the slavery of sin,
and to give us the freedom
only your sons and daughters enjoy.
We now pray for these children
who will have to face the world with its temptations,
and fight the devil in all his cunning.
Your Son died and rose again to save us.
By his victory over sin and death,
bring these children out of the power of darkness.
Strengthen them with the grace of Christ,
and watch over them at every step in life's journey.
(We ask this) through Christ our Lord.
All: **Amen.**

50. The celebrant continues:

We anoint you with the oil of salvation
in the name of Christ our Savior;
may he strengthen you
with his power,
who lives and reigns for ever and ever.
All: **Amen.**

He anoints each child on the breast with the oil of catechumens. If the number of children is large, the anointing may be done by several ministers.

51. If, for serious reasons, the conference of bishops so decides, the anointing before baptism may be omitted. [In

the United States, it may be omitted only when the minister of baptism judges the omission to be pastorally necessary or desirable.] In that case the celebrant says once only:

May you have strength in the power of Christ our Savior, who lives and reigns for ever and ever.
All: **Amen.**

And immediately he lays his hand on each child in silence.

52. If the baptistry is located outside the church or is not within view of the congregation, all go there in procession.

If the baptistry is located within view of the congregation, the celebrant, parents, and godparents go there with the children, while the others remain in their places.

If, however, the baptistry cannot accommodate the congregation, the baptism may be celebrated in a suitable place within the church, and the parents and godparents bring the child forward at the proper moment.

Meanwhile, if it can be done suitably, an appropriate song is sung, e.g., Psalm 23:

The Lord is my shepherd; I shall not want.
In verdant pastures he gives me repose;
Beside restful waters he leads me;
he refreshes my soul.
He guides me in right paths
for his name's sake.
Even though I walk in the dark valley
I fear no evil; for you are at my side
With your rod and your staff
that give me courage.
You spread the table before me
in the sight of my foes;
You anoint my head with oil;
my cup overflows.
Only goodness and kindness follow me
all the days of my life;
And I shall dwell in the house of the Lord
for years to come.

CELEBRATION OF THE SACRAMENT

53. When they come to the font, the celebrant briefly reminds the congregation of the wonderful work of God whose plan it is to sanctify man, body and soul, through water. He may use these or similar words:

A

My dear brothers and sisters, we now ask God to give these children new life in abundance through water and the Holy Spirit.

B

My dear brothers and sisters, God uses the sacrament of water to give his divine life to those who believe in him. Let us turn to him, and ask him to pour his gift of life from this font on the children he has chosen.

BLESSING AND INVOCATION OF GOD OVER BAPTISMAL WATER

54. Then, turning to the font, he says the following blessing (outside the Easter season):

A

Father, you give us grace through sacramental signs, which tell us of the wonders of your unseen power.
In baptism we use your gift of water, which you have made a rich symbol of the grace you give us in this sacrament.
At the very dawn of creation your Spirit breathed on the waters, making them the wellspring of all holiness.
The waters of the great flood you made a sign of the waters of baptism, that make an end of sin and a new beginning of goodness.
Through the waters of the Red Sea you led Israel out of slavery, to be an image of God's holy people, set free from sin by baptism.
In the waters of the Jordan your Son was baptized by John and anointed with the Spirit.

Your Son willed that water and blood should flow from his side as he hung upon the cross.
After his resurrection he told his disciples: "Go out and teach all nations, baptizing them in the name of the Father, and of the Son, and of the Holy Spirit."
Father, look now with love upon your Church, and unseal for her the fountain of baptism.
By the power of the Spirit give to the water of this font the grace of your Son.
You created man in your own likeness: cleanse him from sin in a new birth to innocence by water and the Spirit.

The celebrant touches the water with his right hand and continues:

We ask you, Father, with your Son to send the Holy Spirit upon the water of this font. May all who are buried with Christ in the death of baptism rise also with him to newness of life. (We ask this) through Christ our Lord.
All: **Amen.**

Other forms of the blessing, nos. 223-224, may be chosen.

55. During the Easter season, if there is baptismal water which was consecrated at the Easter Vigil, the blessing and invocation of God over the water are nevertheless included, so that this theme of thanksgiving and petition may find a place in the baptism. The forms of this blessing and invocation are those found in nos. 223-224, with the variation indicated at the end of each text.

RENUNCIATION OF SIN AND PROFESSION OF FAITH

56. The celebrant speaks to the parents and godparents in these words:

Dear parents and godparents: You have come here to present these children for baptism. By water and the Holy Spirit they are to receive the gift of new life from God, who is love.

On your part, you must make it your constant care to

bring them up in the practice of the faith. See that the divine life which God gives them is kept safe from the poison of sin, to grow always stronger in their hearts.

If your faith makes you ready to accept this responsibility, renew now the vows of your own baptism. Reject sin; profess your faith in Christ Jesus. This is the faith of the Church. This is the faith in which these children are about to be baptized.

57. The celebrant questions the parents and godparents.

A

Celebrant:
Do you reject Satan?
Parents and godparents: **I do.**

Celebrant:
And all his works?
Parents and godparents: **I do.**

Celebrant:
And all his empty promises?
Parents and godparents: **I do.**

or **B**

Celebrant:
Do you reject sin, so as to live in the freedom of God's children?
Parents and godparents: **I do.**

Celebrant:
Do you reject the glamor of evil, and refuse to be mastered by sin?
Parents and godparents: **I do.**

Celebrant:
Do you reject Satan, father of sin and prince of darkness?
Parents and godparents: **I do.**

According to circumstances, this second form may be expressed with greater precision by the conferences of bishops, especially in places where it is necessary for the parents and godparents to reject superstitious and magical practices used with children.

58. Next the celebrant asks for the threefold profession of faith from the parents and godparents:

Celebrant:
Do you believe in God, the Father almighty, creator of heaven and earth?
Parents and godparents: **I do.**

Celebrant:
Do you believe in Jesus Christ, his only Son, our Lord, who was born of the Virgin Mary, was crucified, died, and was buried, rose from the dead, and is now seated at the right hand of the Father?
Parents and godparents: **I do.**

Celebrant:
Do you believe in the Holy Spirit, the holy catholic Church, the communion of saints, the forgiveness of sins, the resurrection of the body, and life everlasting?
Parents and godparents: **I do.**

59. The celebrant and the congregation give their assent to the profession of faith:

Celebrant:
This is our faith. This is the faith of the Church. We are proud to profess it, in Christ Jesus our Lord.
All: **Amen.**

If desired, some other formula may be used instead, or a suitable song by which the community expresses its faith with a single voice.

BAPTISM

60. The celebrant invites the first of the families to the font. Using the name of the individual child, he questions the parents and godparents.

Celebrant:
Is it your will that N. should be baptized in the faith of the Church, which we have all professed with you?
Parents and godparents: **It is.**

He baptizes the child, saying:

N., I baptize you in the name of the Father,

He immerses the child or pours water upon it.

and of the Son,

He immerses the child or pours water upon it a second time.

and of the Holy Spirit.

He immerses the child or pours water upon it a third time.

He asks the same question and performs the same action for each child.
After each baptism it is appropriate for the people to sing a short acclamation. (See nos. 225-245).

If the baptism is performed by the pouring of water, it is preferable that the child be held by the mother (or father). Where, however, it is felt that the existing custom should be retained, the godmother (or godfather) may hold the child. If baptism is by immersion, the mother or father (godmother or godfather) lifts the child out of the font.

61. If the number of children to be baptized is large, and other priests or deacons are present, these may baptize some of the children in the way described above, and with the same form.

ANOINTING WITH CHRISM

62. Then the celebrant says:

God the Father of our Lord Jesus Christ has freed you from sin, given you a new birth by water and the Holy Spirit, and welcomed you into his holy people. He now anoints you with the chrism of salvation. As Christ was anointed Priest, Prophet, and King, so may you live always as members of his body, sharing everlasting life.
All: **Amen.**

Next, the celebrant anoints each child on the crown of the head with chrism, in silence.
If the number of children is large and other priests or deacons are present, these may anoint some of the children with chrism.

CLOTHING WITH WHITE GARMENT

63. The celebrant says:

(N., N.,) you have become a new creation, and have clothed yourselves in Christ.

See in this white garment the outward sign of your Christian dignity. With your family and friends to help you by word and example, bring that dignity unstained into the everlasting life of heaven.
All: **Amen.**

The white garments are put on the children. A different color is not permitted unless demanded by local custom. It is desirable that the families provide the garments.

LIGHTED CANDLE

64. The celebrant takes the Easter candle and says:

Receive the light of Christ.

Someone from each family (e.g., the father or godfather) lights the child's candle from the Easter candle.

The celebrant then says:

Parents and godparents, this light is entrusted to you to be kept burning brightly. These children of yours have been enlightened by Christ. They are to walk always as children of the light. May they keep the flame of faith alive in their hearts. When the Lord comes, may they go out to meet him with all the saints in the heavenly kingdom.

EPHPHETHA OR PRAYER OVER EARS AND MOUTH

65. If the conference of bishops decides to preserve the practice, the rite of *Ephphetha* follows. [In the United States it may be performed at the discretion of the minister.] The celebrant touches the ears and mouth of each child with his thumb, saying:

The Lord Jesus made the deaf hear and the dumb speak. May he soon touch your ears to receive his word, and your mouth to proclaim his faith, to the praise and glory of God the Father.
All: **Amen.**

66. If the number of children is large, the celebrant says the formula once, but does not touch the ears and mouth.

CONCLUSION OF THE RITE

67. Next there is a procession to the altar, unless the baptism was performed in the sanctuary. The lighted candles are carried for the children.
A baptismal song is appropriate at this time, e.g.:

You have put on Christ,
in him you have been baptized.
Alleluia, alleluia.

Other songs may be chosen from nos. 225-245.

LORD'S PRAYER

68. The celebrant stands in front of the altar and addresses the parents, godparents, and the whole assembly in these or similar words:

Dearly beloved, these children have been reborn in baptism. They are now called children of God, for so indeed they are. In confirmation they will receive the fullness of God's Spirit. In holy communion they will share the banquet of Christ's sacrifice, calling God

their Father in the midst of the Church. In their name, in the Spirit of our common sonship, let us pray together in the words our Lord has given us:

69. All present join the celebrant in singing or saying:

Our Father. . . .

BLESSING

70. The celebrant first blesses the mothers, who hold the children in their arms, then the fathers, and lastly the entire assembly:

A

Celebrant:
God the Father, through his Son, the Virgin Mary's child, has brought joy to all Christian mothers, as they see the hope of eternal life shine on their children. May he bless the mothers of these children. They now thank God for the gift of their children. May they be one with them in thanking him for ever in heaven, in Christ Jesus our Lord.
All: **Amen.**

Celebrant:
God is the giver of all life, human and divine. May he bless the fathers of these children. With their wives they will be the first teachers of their children in the ways of faith. May they be also the best of teachers, bearing witness to the faith by what they say and do, in Christ Jesus our Lord.
All: **Amen.**

Celebrant:
By God's gift, through water and the Holy Spirit, we are reborn to everlasting life. In his goodness, may he continue to pour out his blessings upon all present, who are his sons and daughters. May he make them always, wherever they may be, faithful members of his holy people. May he send his peace upon all who are gathered here, in Christ Jesus our Lord.
All: **Amen.**

Celebrant:
May almighty God, the Father, and the Son, ✠ and the Holy Spirit, bless you.
All: **Amen.**

Other forms of the final blessing, nos. 247, 248, and 249 may be chosen.

B
Celebrant:
May God the almighty Father, who filled the world with joy by giving us his only Son, bless these newly-baptized children. May they grow to be more fully like Jesus Christ our Lord.
All: **Amen.**

Celebrant:
May almighty God, who gives life on earth and in heaven, bless the parents of these children. They thank him now for the gift he has given them. May they always show that gratitude in action by loving and caring for their children.
All: **Amen.**

Celebrant:
May almighty God, who has given us a new birth by water and the Holy Spirit, generously bless all of us who are his faithful children. May we always live as his people, and may he bless all here present with his peace.
All: **Amen.**

Celebrant:
May almighty God, the Father, and the Son, ✠ and the Holy Spirit, bless you.
All: **Amen.**

C
Celebrant:
May God, the source of life and love, who fills the hearts of mothers with love for their children, bless the mothers of these newly-baptized children. As they thank God for a safe delivery, may they find joy in

the love, growth, and holiness of their children.
All: **Amen.**

Celebrant:
May God, the Father and model of all fathers, help these fathers to give good example, so that their children will grow to be mature Christians in all the fullness of Jesus Christ.
All: **Amen.**

Celebrant:
May God, who loves all people, bless all the relatives and friends who are gathered here. In his mercy, may he guard them from evil and give them his abundant peace.
All: **Amen.**

Celebrant:
And may almighty God, the Father, and the Son, ✠ and the Holy Spirit, bless you.
All: **Amen.**

D

Celebrant:
My brothers and sisters, we entrust you all to the mercy and help of God the almighty Father, his only Son, and the Holy Spirit. May he watch over your life, and may we all walk by the light of faith, and attain the good things he has promised us.
Go in peace, and may almighty God, the Father, and the Son, ✠ and the Holy Spirit, bless you.
All: **Amen.**

71. After the blessing, all may sing a hymn which suitably expresses thanksgiving and Easter joy, or they may sing the song of the Blessed Virgin Mary, the Magnificat.

Where there is the practice of bringing baptized infants to the altar of the Blessed Virgin Mary, this custom is observed if appropriate.

CHAPTER II

RITE OF BAPTISM FOR ONE CHILD

RECEPTION OF THE CHILD

72. If possible, baptism should take place on Sunday, the day on which the Church celebrates the paschal mystery. It should be conferred in a communal celebration in the presence of the faithful, or at least of relatives, friends, and neighbors, who are all to take an active part in the rite.

73. It is the role of the father and mother, accompanied by the godparents, to present the child to the Church for baptism.

74. The people may sing a psalm or hymn suitable for the occasion. Meanwhile the celebrating priest or deacon, vested in alb or surplice, with a stole (with or without a cope) of festive color, and accompanied by the ministers, goes to the entrance of the church or to that part of the church where the parents and godparents are waiting with the child.

75. The celebrant greets all present, and especially the parents and godparents, reminding them briefly of the joy with which the parents welcomed this child as a gift from God, the source of life, who now wishes to bestow his own life on this little one.

76. First the celebrant questions the parents:

Celebrant:
What name do you give your child? (or: **have you given?**)
Parents: **N.**

Celebrant:
What do you ask of God's Church for N.?
Parents: **Baptism.**

The celebrant may choose other words for this dialogue. The first reply may be given by someone other than the parents if local custom gives him the right to name the child.

In the second response the parents may use other words, such as, **faith** or **the grace of Christ** or **entrance into the Church** or **eternal life.**

77. The celebrant speaks to the parents in these or similar words:

You have asked to have your child baptized. In doing so you are accepting the responsibility of training him (her) in the practice of the faith. It will be your duty to bring him (her) up to keep God's commandments as Christ taught us, by loving God and our neighbor. Do you clearly understand what you are undertaking?
Parents: **We do.**

78. Then the celebrant turns to the godparents and addresses them in these or similar words:

Are you ready to help the parents of this child in their duty as Christian parents?
Godparents: **We are.**

79. The celebrant continues:

N., the Christian community welcomes you with great joy. In its name I claim you for Christ our Savior by the sign of his cross. I now trace the cross on your forehead, and invite your parents (and godparents) to do the same.

He signs the child on the forehead, in silence. Then he invites the parents and (if it seems appropriate) the godparents to do the same.

80. The celebrant invites the parents, godparents, and the others to take part in the liturgy of the word. If circumstances permit, there is a procession to the place where this will be celebrated, during which a song is sung, e.g., Psalm 85:7, 8, 9ab:

Will you not give us life;
and shall not your people rejoice in you?
Show us, O Lord, your kindness,
and grant us your salvation.

I will hear what God proclaims;
the Lord—for he proclaims peace to his people.

CELEBRATION OF GOD'S WORD

SCRIPTURAL READINGS AND HOMILY

81. One or even two of the following gospel passages are read, during which all may sit if convenient.

John 3:1-6 The meeting with Nicodemus.
Matthew 28:18-20 The apostles are sent to preach the gospel and to baptize.
Mark 1:9-11 The baptism of Jesus.
Mark 10:13-16 Let the little children come to me.

The passages listed in nos. 186-194 and 204-215 may be chosen, or other passages which better meet the wishes or needs of the parents. Between the readings, responsorial psalms or verses may be sung as given in nos. 195-203.

82. After the reading, the celebrant gives a short homily, explaining to those present the significance of what has been read. His purpose will be to lead them to a deeper understanding of the mystery of baptism and to encourage the parents and godparents to a ready acceptance of the responsibilities which arise from the sacrament.

83. After the homily, or in the course of or after the litany, it is desirable to have a period of silence while all pray at the invitation of the celebrant. If convenient, a suitable song follows, such as one chosen from nos. 225-245.

INTERCESSIONS (PRAYER OF THE FAITHFUL)

84. Then the prayer of the faithful is said:

Celebrant:
My dear brothers and sisters, let us ask our Lord Jesus Christ to look lovingly on this child who is to be baptized, on his (her) parents and godparents, and on all the baptized.

Leader:
By the mystery of your death and resurrection, bathe this child in light, give him (her) the new life of baptism and welcome him (her) into your holy Church.
All: **Lord, hear our prayer.**

Leader:
Through baptism and confirmation, make him (her) your faithful follower and a witness to your gospel.
All: **Lord, hear our prayer.**

Leader:
Lead him (her) by a holy life to the joys of God's kingdom.
All: **Lord, hear our prayer.**

Leader:
Make the lives of his (her) parents and godparents examples of faith to inspire this child.
All: **Lord, hear our prayer.**

Leader:
Keep his (her) family always in your love.
All: **Lord, hear our prayer.**

Leader:
Renew the grace of our baptism in each one of us.
All: **Lord, hear our prayer.**

Other forms may be chosen from nos. 217-220.

85. The celebrant next invites all present to invoke the saints.

Holy Mary, Mother of God, pray for us.
Saint John the Baptist, pray for us.
Saint Joseph, pray for us.
Saint Peter and Saint Paul, pray for us.

The names of other saints may be added, especially the patrons of the child to be baptized, and of the church or locality. The litany concludes:

All you saints of God, pray for us.

PRAYER OF EXORCISM AND ANOINTING BEFORE BAPTISM

86. After the invocation, the celebrant says:

**Almighty and ever-living God,
you sent your only Son into the world
to cast out the power of Satan, spirit of evil,
to rescue man from the kingdom of darkness,
and bring him into the splendor of your kingdom of light.
We pray for this child:
set him (her) free from original sin,
make him (her) a temple of your glory,
and send your Holy Spirit to dwell with him (her).
(We ask this) through Christ our Lord.**
All: **Amen.**

For another form of the prayer of exorcism, see no. 221.

87. The celebrant continues:

**We anoint you with the oil of salvation
in the name of Christ our Savior;
may he strengthen you
with his power,
who lives and reigns for ever and ever.**
All: **Amen.**

He anoints the child on the breast with the oil of catechumens.

88. If, for serious reasons, the conference of bishops so decides, the anointing before baptism may be omitted. [In the United States, it may be omitted only when the minister of baptism judges the omission to be pastorally necessary or desirable.] In that case the celebrant says:

May you have strength in the power of Christ our Savior, who lives and reigns for ever and ever.
All: **Amen.**

And immediately he lays his hand on the child in silence.

89. Then they go to the baptistry, or to the sanctuary when baptism is celebrated there on occasion.

CELEBRATION OF THE SACRAMENT

90. When they come to the font, the celebrant briefly reminds the congregation of the wonderful work of God whose plan it is to sanctify man, body and soul, through water. He may use these or similar words:

A

My dear brothers and sisters, we now ask God to give this child new life in abundance through water and the Holy Spirit.

or **B**

My dear brothers and sisters, God uses the sacrament of water to give his divine life to those who believe in him. Let us turn to him, and ask him to pour his gift of life from this font on this child he has chosen.

BLESSING AND INVOCATION OF GOD OVER BAPTISMAL WATER

91. Then, turning to the font, he says the following blessing (outside the Easter season):

Father, you give us grace through sacramental signs, which tell us of the wonders of your unseen power.

In baptism we use your gift of water, which you have made a rich symbol of the grace you give us in this sacrament.

At the very dawn of creation your Spirit breathed on the waters, making them the wellspring of all holiness.

The waters of the great flood you made a sign of the waters of baptism, that make an end of sin and a new beginning of goodness.

Through the waters of the Red Sea you led Israel out of slavery, to be an image of God's holy people, set free from sin by baptism.

In the waters of the Jordan your Son was baptized by John and anointed with the Spirit.

Your Son willed that water and blood should flow from his side as he hung upon the cross.

After his resurrection he told his disciples: "Go out and teach all nations, baptizing them in the name of the Father, and of the Son, and of the Holy Spirit."

Father, look now with love upon your Church, and unseal for her the fountain of baptism.

By the power of the Spirit give to the water of this font the grace of your Son.

You created man in your own likeness: cleanse him from sin in a new birth to innocence by water and the Spirit.

The celebrant touches the water with his right hand and continues:

We ask you, Father, with your Son to send the Holy Spirit upon the water of this font. May all who are buried with Christ in the death of baptism rise also with him to newness of life. (We ask this) through Christ our Lord.
All: **Amen.**

Other forms may be chosen from nos. 223-224.

92. During the Easter season, if there is baptismal water which was consecrated at the Easter Vigil, the blessing and invocation of God over the water are nevertheless included, so that this theme of thanksgiving and petition may find a place in the baptism. The forms of this blessing and invocation are those found in nos. 223-224 with the variation indicated at the end of each text.

RENUNCIATION OF SIN AND PROFESSION OF FAITH

93. The celebrant speaks to the parents and godparents in these words:

Dear parents and godparents: You have come here to present this child for baptism. By water and the Holy Spirit he (she) is to receive the gift of new life from God, who is love.

On your part, you must make it your constant care to bring him (her) up in the practice of the faith. See that the divine life which God gives him (her) is kept safe from the poison of sin, to grow always stronger in his (her) heart.

If your faith makes you ready to accept this responsibility, renew now the vows of your own baptism. Reject sin; profess your faith in Christ Jesus. This is the faith of the Church. This is the faith in which this child is about to be baptized.

94. The celebrant questions the parents and godparents.

A
Celebrant:
Do you reject Satan?
Parents and godparents: **I do.**

Celebrant:
And all his works?
Parents and godparents: **I do.**

Celebrant:
And all his empty promises?
Parents and godparents: **I do.**

or **B**
Celebrant:
Do you reject sin, so as to live in the freedom of God's children?
Parents and godparents: **I do.**

Celebrant:
Do you reject the glamor of evil, and refuse to be mastered by sin?
Parents and godparents: **I do.**

Celebrant:
Do you reject Satan, father of sin and prince of darkness?
Parents and godparents: **I do.**

According to circumstances, this second form may be expressed with greater precision by the conferences of bishops, especially in places where it is necessary for the parents and godparents to reject superstitious and magical practices used with children.

95. Next the celebrant asks for the threefold profession of faith from the parents and godparents:

Celebrant:
Do you believe in God, the Father almighty, creator of heaven and earth?
Parents and godparents: **I do.**

Celebrant:
Do you believe in Jesus Christ, his only Son, our Lord, who was born of the Virgin Mary, was crucified, died, and was buried, rose from the dead, and is now seated at the right hand of the Father?
Parents and godparents: **I do.**

Celebrant:
Do you believe in the Holy Spirit, the holy caltholic Church, the communion of saints, the forgiveness of sins, the resurrection of the body, and life everlasting?
Parents and godparents: **I do.**

96. The celebrant and the congregation give their assent to this profession of faith:

Celebrant:
This is our faith. This is the faith of the Church. We are proud to profess it, in Christ Jesus our Lord.
All: **Amen.**

If desired, some other formula may be used instead, or a suitable song by which the community expresses its faith with a single voice.

BAPTISM

97. The celebrant invites the family to the font and questions the parents and godparents:

Celebrant:
Is it your will that N. should be baptized in the faith of the Church, which we have all professed with you?
Parents and godparents: **It is.**

He baptizes the child, saying:

N., I baptize you in the name of the Father,

He immerses the child or pours water upon it.

and of the Son,

He immerses the child or pours water upon it a second time.

and of the Holy Spirit.

He immerses the child or pours water upon it a third time.

After the child is baptized, it is appropriate for the people to sing a short acclamation. (See nos. 225-245.)

If the baptism is performed by the pouring of water, it is preferable that the child be held by the mother (or father). Where, however, it is felt that the existing custom should be retained, the godmother (or godfather) may hold the child. If baptism is by immersion, the mother or father (godmother or godfather) lifts the child out of the font.

ANOINTING WITH CHRISM

98. Then the celebrant says:

God the Father of our Lord Jesus Christ has freed you from sin, given you a new birth by water and the Holy Spirit, and welcomed you into his holy people. He now anoints you with the chrism of salvation. As Christ was anointed Priest, Prophet, and King, so may you live always as a member of his body, sharing everlasting life.
All: **Amen.**

Then the celebrant anoints the child on the crown of the head with the sacred chrism, in silence.

CLOTHING WITH THE WHITE GARMENT

99. The celebrant says:

N., you have become a new creation, and have clothed yourself in Christ.

See in this white garment the outward sign of your Christian dignity. With your family and friends to help you by word and example, bring that dignity unstained into the everlasting life of heaven.
All: **Amen.**

The white garment is put on the child. A different color is not permitted unless demanded by local custom. It is desirable that the family provide the garment.

LIGHTED CANDLE

100. The celebrant takes the Easter candle and says:

Receive the light of Christ.

Someone from the family (such as the father or godfather) lights the child's candle from the Easter candle.

The celebrant then says:

Parents and godparents, this light is entrusted to you to be kept burning brightly. This child of yours has been enlightened by Christ. He (she) is to walk always as a child of the light. May he (she) keep the flame of faith alive in his (her) heart. When the Lord comes, may he (she) go out to meet him with all the saints in the heavenly kingdom.

EPHPHETHA OR PRAYER OVER EARS AND MOUTH

101. If the conference of bishops decides to preserve the practice, the rite of *Ephphetha* follows. [In the United States it may be performed at the discretion of the minister.] The celebrant touches the ears and mouth of the child with his thumb, saying:

The Lord Jesus made the deaf hear and the dumb speak. May he soon touch your ears to receive his word, and your mouth to proclaim his faith, to the

praise and glory of God the Father.

All: **Amen.**

[If baptism is celebrated during Sunday or weekday Mass, the Mass continues in the usual way with the offertory.]

CONCLUSION OF THE RITE

102. Next there is a procession to the altar, unless the baptism was performed in the sanctuary. The lighted candle is carried for the child.

A baptismal song is appropriate at this time, e.g.:

You have put on Christ,
in him you have been baptized.
Alleluia, alleluia.

Other songs may be chosen from nos. 225-245.

LORD'S PRAYER

103. The celebrant stands in front of the altar, and addresses the parents, godparents, and the whole assembly in these or similar words:

Dearly beloved, this child has been reborn in baptism. He (she) is now called the child of God, for so indeed he (she) is. In confirmation he (she) will receive the fullness of God's Spirit. In holy communion he (she) will share the banquet of Christ's sacrifice, calling God his (her) Father in the midst of the Church. In the name of this child, in the Spirit of our common sonship, let us pray together in the words our Lord has given us:

104. All present join the celebrant in singing or saying:

Our Father. . . .

BLESSING

105. The celebrant first blesses the mother, who holds the child in her arms, then the father, and lastly the entire assembly:

Celebrant:
God the Father, through his Son, the Virgin Mary's child, has brought joy to all Christian mothers, as they see the hope of eternal life shine on their children. May he bless the mother of this child. She now thanks God for the gift of her child. May she be one with him (her) in thanking him for ever in heaven, in Christ Jesus our Lord.
All: **Amen.**

Celebrant:
God is the giver of all life, human and divine. May he bless the father of this child. He and his wife will be the first teachers of their child in the ways of faith. May they be also the best of teachers, bearing witness to the faith by what they say and do, in Christ Jesus our Lord.
All: **Amen.**

Celebrant:
By God's gift, through water and the Holy Spirit, we are reborn to everlasting life. In his goodness, may he continue to pour out his blessings upon these sons and daughters of his. May he make them always, wherever they may be, faithful members of his holy people. May he send his peace upon all who are gathered here, in Christ Jesus our Lord.
All: **Amen.**

Celebrant:
May almighty God, the Father, and the Son, ✠ and the Holy Spirit, bless you.
All: **Amen.**

For other forms of the blessing, see nos. 247-249.

106. After the blessing, all may sing a hymn which suitably expresses thanksgiving and Easter joy, or they may sing the song of the Blessed Virgin Mary, the Magnificat.

Where there is a practice of bringing the baptized child to the altar of the Blessed Virgin Mary, this custom is observed if appropriate.

CHAPTER III

RITE OF BAPTISM FOR A LARGE NUMBER OF CHILDREN

RECEPTION OF THE CHILDREN

107. The people may sing a psalm or hymn suitable for the occasion. Meanwhile the celebrating priest or deacon, vested in alb or surplice, with a stole (with or without a cope) of festive color, and accompanied by the ministers, goes to the entrance of the church or to that part of the church where the parents and godparents are waiting with those who are to be baptized.

108. The celebrant greets all present, and especially the parents and godparents, reminding them briefly of the joy with which the parents welcomed their children as gifts from God, the source of life, who now wishes to bestow his own life on these little ones.

Then the celebrant questions the parents and godparents together:

A

Celebrant:

What name do you want to give your children?

Each family answers in turn, giving the names of the children: **N., N., N.**

Celebrant:

What do you ask of God's Church for these children?

All families together: **Baptism.**

But if there is a very large number to be baptized, he omits the first question and asks:

B

Celebrant:

Parents and godparents, what do you ask for these children?

All families together: **Baptism.**

109. The celebrant speaks to the parents in these or similar words:

You have asked to have your children baptized. In doing so you are accepting the responsibility of training them in the practice of the faith. It will be your duty to bring them up to keep God's commandments as Christ taught us, by loving God and our neighbor. Do you clearly understand what you are undertaking?
All parents together: **We do.**

110. Then the celebrant turns to the godparents and addresses them in these or similar words:

Are you ready to help these parents in their duty as Christian mothers and fathers?
All the godparents: **We are.**

111. The celebrant continues:

My dear children, the Christian community welcomes you with great joy. In its name I claim you for Christ our Savior by the sign of his cross.

He makes the sign of the cross over all the children together, and says:

Parents (or godparents), make the sign of Christ our Savior on the foreheads of your children.

Then the parents (or godparents) sign the children on their foreheads.

CELEBRATION OF GOD'S WORD

SCRIPTURAL READINGS AND HOMILY

112. The celebrant invites the parents, godparents and the others to take part in the liturgy of the word. Matthew 28:18-20 is read, telling how the apostles were sent to preach the gospel and to baptize.

Other passages may also be selected from nos. 44, 186-194, 204-215.

113. After the reading, the celebrant gives a short homily, explaining to those present the significance of what has been read. His purpose will be to lead them to a deeper understanding of the mystery of baptism and to encourage the parents and godparents to a ready acceptance of the responsibilities which arise from the sacrament.

INTERCESSIONS (PRAYER OF THE FAITHFUL)

114. Then the prayer of the faithful is said:

Celebrant:
My dear brothers and sisters, let us ask our Lord Jesus Christ to look lovingly on these children who are to be baptized, on their parents and godparents, and on all the baptized.

Leader:
By the mystery of your death and resurrection, bathe these children in light, give them the new life of baptism and welcome them into your holy Church.
All: **Lord, hear our prayer.**

Leader:
Through baptism and confirmation, make them your faithful followers and witnesses to your gospel.
All: **Lord, hear our prayer.**

Leader:
Lead them by a holy life to the joys of God's kingdom.
All: **Lord, hear our prayer.**

Leader:
Make the lives of their parents and godparents examples of faith to inspire these children.
All: **Lord, hear our prayer.**

Leader:
Keep their families always in your love.
All: **Lord, hear our prayer.**

Leader:
Renew the grace of our baptism in each one of us.
All: **Lord, hear our prayer.**

Other forms may be chosen from nos. 217-220. The invocation of the saints (see no. 48) may be omitted.

PRAYER OF EXORCISM

115. The prayer of the faithful is concluded with the prayer of exorcism:

Almighty and ever-living God,
you sent your only Son into the world
to cast out the power of Satan, spirit of evil,
to rescue man from the kingdom of darkness,
and bring him into the splendor of your kingdom of light.
We pray for these children:
set them free from original sin,
make them temples of your glory,
and send your Holy Spirit to dwell within them.
(We ask this) through Christ our Lord.
All: **Amen.**

For another form of the prayer of exorcism, see no. 221.

Because of the large number of children to be baptized, the celebrant does not anoint them with oil of catechumens. He imposes his hands over all the children at once and says:

May you have strength in the power of Christ our Savior, who lives and reigns for ever and ever.
All: **Amen.**

116. Then they go to the place where baptism is celebrated.

CELEBRATION OF THE SACRAMENT

117. When they come to the font, the celebrant briefly reminds the congregation of the wonderful work of God whose plan it is to sanctify man, body and soul, through water. He may use these or similar words:

My dear brothers and sisters, God uses the sacrament of water to give his divine life to those who believe in him.

Let us turn to him in our faith, and ask him to pour his gift of life from this font on the children he has chosen.

BLESSING AND INVOCATION OF GOD OVER BAPTISMAL WATER

118. Then, turning to the font, he says the following blessing:

Celebrant:

Merciful Father, from the font of baptism you have given us new life as your sons and daughters.
All: **Blessed be God** (or some other suitable acclamation by the people).

Celebrant:

You bring together all who are baptized in water and the Holy Spirit to be one people in Jesus Christ your Son.
All: **Blessed be God.**

Celebrant:

You have made us free by pouring the Spirit of your love into our hearts, so that we will enjoy your peace.
All: **Blessed be God.**

Celebrant:

You have chosen your baptized people to announce with joy the Good News of Christ to all nations.
All: **Blessed be God.**

A

Celebrant:

Come and ✠ bless this water in which your servants are to be baptized. You have called them to the washing of new life in the faith of your Church, so that they may have eternal life. (We ask this) through Christ our Lord.
All: **Amen.**

B

119. During the Easter season, if there is baptismal water already blessed, the celebrant omits the last part of the blessing **Come and bless,** and concludes in this way:

By the mystery of this consecrated water, you bring your servants to spiritual rebirth. You have called them to the washing of new life in the faith of your Church, so that they may have eternal life. (We ask this) through Christ our Lord.
All: **Amen.**

Other forms may be chosen from nos. 223-224.

RENUNCIATION OF SIN AND PROFESSION OF FAITH

120. The celebrant speaks to the parents and godparents in these words:

Dear parents and godparents: You have come here to present these children for baptism. By water and the Holy Spirit they are to receive the gift of new life from God, who is love.

On your part, you must make it your constant care to bring them up in the practice of the faith. See that the divine life which God gives them is kept safe from the poison of sin, to grow always stronger in their hearts.

If your faith makes you ready to accept this responsibility, renew now the vows of your baptism. Reject sin; profess your faith in Christ Jesus. This is the faith of the Church. This is the faith in which these children are about to be baptized.

121. The celebrant questions the parents and godparents.

A
Celebrant:
Do you reject Satan?
Parents and godparents: **I do.**

Celebrant:
And all his works?
Parents and godparents: **I do.**

Celebrant:
And all his empty promises?
Parents and godparents: **I do.**

or **B**
Celebrant:
Do you reject sin, so as to live in the freedom of God's children?
Parents and godparents: **I do.**

Celebrant:
Do you reject the glamor of evil, and refuse to be mastered by sin?
Parents and godparents: **I do.**

Celebrant:
Do you reject Satan, father of sin and prince of darkness?
Parents and godparents: **I do.**

According to circumstances, this second form may be expressed with greater precision by the conferences of bishops, especially in places where it is necessary for the parents and godparents to reject superstitious and magical practices used with children.

122. Next the celebrant asks for the threefold profession of faith from the parents and godparents:

Celebrant:
Do you believe in God, the Father almighty, creator of heaven and earth?
Parents and godparents: **I do.**

Celebrant:
Do you believe in Jesus Christ, his only Son, our Lord, who was born of the Virgin Mary, was crucified, died, and was buried, rose from the dead, and is now seated at the right hand of the Father?
Parents and godparents: **I do.**

Celebrant:
Do you believe in the Holy Spirit, the holy catholic Church, the communion of saints, the forgiveness of

sins, the resurrection of the body, and life everlasting?
Parents and godparents: **I do.**

123. The celebrant and the congregation give their assent to this profession of faith:

Celebrant:
This is our faith. This is the faith of the Church. We are proud to profess it, in Christ Jesus our Lord.
All: **Amen.**

If desired, some other formula may be used instead, or a suitable song by which the community expresses its faith with a single voice.

BAPTISM

124. If there are several ministers because of the large number to be baptized, each of them questions the parents and godparents, using the name of the individual child:

Celebrant:
Is it your will that N. should be baptized in the faith of the Church, which we have all professed with you?
Parents and godparents: **It is.**

He baptizes the child, saying:

N., I baptize you in the name of the Father,

He immerses the child or pours water upon it.

and of the Son,

He immerses the child or pours water upon it a second time.

and of the Holy Spirit.

He immerses the child or pours water upon it a third time.

He asks the same question and performs the same action for each child.

If the baptism is performed by the pouring of water, it is

preferable that the child be held by the mother (or father). Where, however, it is felt that the existing custom should be retained, the godmother (or godfather) may hold the child.

If baptism is by immersion, the mother or father (godmother or godfather) lifts the child out of the font.

While the children are being baptized, the community can make acclamations or sing hymns (see nos. 225-245). Some passages from scripture may also be read, or a sacred silence observed.

ANOINTING WITH CHRISM

125. Then the celebrant says the formula of anointing once for all the children:

God the Father of our Lord Jesus Christ has freed you from sin, given you a new birth by water and the Holy Spirit, and welcomed you into his holy people. He now anoints you with the chrism of salvation. As Christ was anointed Priest, Prophet, and King, so may you live always as members of his body, sharing everlasting life.
All: **Amen.**

Then the ministers anoint each child on the crown of the head with the sacred chrism, in silence. But if the number of children is extremely large, the conferences of bishops may decide that the anointing with chrism may be omitted. [In the United States the anointing may not be omitted.] In this case, an adapted formula is used:

God the Father of our Lord Jesus Christ has freed you from sin, and has given you a new birth by water and the Holy Spirit. He has made you Christians now, and has welcomed you into his holy people. As Christ was anointed Priest, Prophet, and King, so may you live always as members of his body, sharing everlasting life.
All: **Amen.**

CLOTHING WITH WHITE GARMENT

126. The celebrant says:

My dear children, you have become a new creation, and have clothed yourselves in Christ.

See in this white garment the outward sign of your Christian dignity. With your family and friends to help you by word and example, bring that dignity unstained into the everlasting life of heaven.
All: **Amen.**

The white garments are put on the children. A different color is not permitted unless demanded by local custom. It is desirable that the families provide the garments.

LIGHTED CANDLE

127. The celebrant takes the Easter candle and says:

Receive the light of Christ. Parents and godparents, this light is entrusted to you to be kept burning brightly. These children of yours have been enlightened by Christ. They are to walk always as children of the light. May they keep the flame of faith alive in their hearts. When the Lord comes, may they go out to meet him with all the saints in the heavenly kingdom.

Candles are distributed to the families. The head of one family lights his candle from the Easter candle and passes the flame on to the rest. Meanwhile the community sings a baptismal song, such as:

You have put on Christ,
in him you have been baptized.
Alleluia, alleluia.

Other hymns may be chosen from nos. 225-245.

Meanwhile, unless the baptisms were performed in the sanctuary, there is a procession to the altar. The lighted candles are carried for the children.

CONCLUSION OF THE RITE

LORD'S PRAYER

128. The celebrant stands in front of the altar and addresses the parents, godparents, and the whole assembly in these or similar words:

Dearly beloved, these children have been reborn in baptism. They are now called children of God, for so indeed they are. In confirmation they will receive the fullness of God's Spirit. In holy communion they will share the banquet of Christ's sacrifice, calling God their Father in the midst of the Church. In their name, in the spirit of our common sonship, let us pray together in the words our Lord has given us:

129. All present join the celebrant in singing or saying:

Our Father. . . .

BLESSING

130. The celebrant blesses the entire assembly, and dismisses them:

My brothers and sisters, we commend you to the mercy and grace of God our almighty Father, of his only Son, and of the Holy Spirit. May he protect your paths, so that walking in the light of faith, you may come to the good things he has promised us.

May almighty God, the Father, and the Son, ✠ and the Holy Spirit bless you.
All: **Amen.**

For other forms of the blessing, see nos. 70, 247-248.

131. After the blessing, all may sing a hymn which suitably expresses thanksgiving and Easter joy, or they may sing the song of the Blessed Virgin Mary, the Magnificat.

CHAPTER IV

RITE OF BAPTISM FOR CHILDREN ADMINISTERED BY A CATECHIST WHEN NO PRIEST OR DEACON IS AVAILABLE

RECEPTION OF THE CHILDREN

132. While the faithful sing a suitable psalm or hymn, the catechist and the ministers approach the door of the church or the part of the church where the parents, godparents, and the children to be baptized are waiting.

If there is a large group of persons to be baptized, the catechist may be assisted by others in the act of baptism, as noted below.

133. The catechist greets all present, and especially the parents and godparents, reminding them briefly of the joy with which the parents welcomed their children as gifts from God, the source of life, who now wishes to bestow his own life on these little ones.

Then he questions the parents and godparents together in these or similar words:

A

What name do you give your children? (or: **have you given?)**

Each family answers in turn, giving the names of the children: **N., N., N.**

Catechist:

What do you ask of God's Church for these children?

All families together: **Baptism.**

If there are many children to be baptized, the first question is omitted and the catechist asks:

B

Parents and godparents, what do you ask for these children?

All families together: **Baptism.**

134. Then the catechist speaks to the parents:

Parents, you have asked to have your children baptized. In doing so you are accepting the responsibility of training them in the practice of the faith. It will be your duty to bring them up to keep God's commandments as Christ taught us, by loving God and our neighbor. Do you clearly understand what you are undertaking?

All parents together: **We do.**

135. Then turning to the godparents, the catechist asks:

Godparents, are you ready to help these parents in their duty as Christian mothers and fathers?

All the godparents: **We are.**

136. The catechist continues:

My dear children, the Christian community welcomes you with great joy. In its name I claim for you Christ our Savior by the sign of his cross.

He makes the sign of the cross over all the children together, and says:

Parents (or godparents), make the sign of Christ our Savior on the foreheads of your children.

Then the parents (or godparents) sign the children on their foreheads.

CELEBRATION OF GOD'S WORD

READING AND HOMILY OR SHORT TALK

137. The catechist invites the parents, godparents, and the others to take part in the liturgy of the word. Matthew

28:18-20 is read, telling how the apostles were sent to preach the gospel and to baptize.

Other passages may also be selected from nos. 186-194, 204-215. If songs and hymns are sung, see nos. 195-203. After the reading, the catechist can give a brief homily in the way determined by the bishop.

138. In the place of the scripture reading and the homily, the catechist can, if necessary, give this talk:

In baptism, Christ will come to meet these children. He entrusted this sacrament to his Church when he sent forth his apostles with these words: "Go, make disciples of all nations, and baptize them in the name of the Father, and of the Son, and of the Holy Spirit."

As you know, these children will be given countless gifts in this great sacrament: they will be freed from sin; they will become members of the Church; they will become God's children. But since man is unable to accomplish such wonders, we must pray together with humility and faith for these blessings.

May God our Father see in the fellowship of our community the faith of his Church, and hear in our prayer the voice of Jesus his Son. As he promised us through Christ, may he bless these children by the power of his Holy Spirit.

PRAYER OF THE FAITHFUL

139. Then the prayer of the faithful is said:

Catechist:
My dear brothers and sisters, let us ask our Lord Jesus Christ to look lovingly on these children who are to be baptized, on their parents and godparents, and on all the baptized.

Leader:
By the mystery of your death and resurrection, bathe these children in light, give them the new life of baptism and welcome them into your holy Church.
All: **Lord, hear our prayer.**

Leader:
Through baptism and confirmation, make them your faithful followers and witnesses to your gospel.
All: **Lord, hear our prayer.**

Leader:
Lead them by a holy life to the joys of God's kingdom.
All: **Lord, hear our prayer.**

Leader:
Make the lives of their parents and godparents examples of faith to inspire these children.
All: **Lord, hear our prayer.**

Leader:
Keep their families always in your love.
All: **Lord, hear our prayer.**

Leader:
Renew the grace of our baptism in each one of us.
All: **Lord, hear our prayer.**

Other forms may be chosen from nos. 217-220.

Then the catechist invites all present to invoke the saints:

Holy Mary, Mother of God, pray for us.
Saint John the Baptist, pray for us.
Saint Joseph, pray for us.
Saint Peter and Saint Paul, pray for us.

The names of other saints may be added, especially the patrons of the children to be baptized, and of the church or locality. The litany concludes:

All you saints of God, pray for us.

140. The prayer of exorcism and the anointing with oil of catechumens are omitted.

CELEBRATION OF THE SACRAMENT

BLESSING AND INVOCATION OF GOD OVER BAPTISMAL WATER

141. With the parents and godparents carrying the children who are go be baptized, the catechist comes to the font. He invites all to pray:

My dear brothers and sisters, let us ask God to give these children new life in abundance through water and the Holy Spirit.

142. If there is no blessed water available, the catechist stands before the font and says this invocation:

A

Catechist:
Merciful Father, from the font of baptism you have given us new life as your sons and daughters.
All: **Blessed be God** (or some other suitable acclamation by the people).

Catechist:
You bring together all who are baptized in water and the Holy Spirit to be one people in Jesus Christ your Son.
All: **Blessed be God.**

Catechist:
You have made us free by pouring the Spirit of your love into our hearts, so that we will enjoy your peace.
All: **Blessed be God.**

Catechist:
You have chosen your baptized people to announce with joy the Good News of Christ to all nations.
All: **Blessed be God.**

Catechist:
Come and bless this water in which your servants are to be baptized. You have called them to the washing of new life in the faith of your Church, so that they may have eternal life. (We ask this) through Christ our Lord.
All: **Amen.**

143. If blessed water is available, he says the following invocation:

B

Father of our Lord Jesus Christ,
source of all life and love,
you are glorified throughout the world
by the simple joys and daily cares
of mothers and fathers.

In the beauty of a child's birth
and in the mystery of his rebirth to eternal life,
you give us a glimpse of all creation:
it is guided by your fatherly love,
unfolding in fruitfulness to perfection
in Jesus Christ your Son.

In your kindness
hear the prayers of the Church and of these parents.
Look upon these children with love,
and keep them from the power of sin.
Since they are a gift from you, Father,
welcome them into the kingdom of your Son.

You have created this water,
and made it clean, refreshing, and life-giving.
You have made it holy through the baptism of Christ,
that by the power of the Holy Spirit
it may give your people a new birth.

When these children are baptized into the mystery
of Christ's suffering, death, and resurrection,

may they be worthy to become members of your Church,
your very own children.
Father, may they rejoice
with Jesus your Son and the Holy Spirit
for ever and ever.
All: **Amen.**

RENUNCIATION OF SIN AND PROFESSION OF FAITH

144. The catechist speaks to the parents and godparents in these words:

Dear parents and godparents: You have come here to present these children for baptism. By water and the Holy Spirit, they are to receive the gift of new life from God, who is love.

On your part, you must make it your constant care to bring them up in the practice of the faith. See that the divine life which God gives them is kept safe from the poison of sin, to grow always stronger in their hearts.

If your faith makes you ready to accept this responsibility, renew now the vows of your baptism. Reject sin; profess your faith in Christ Jesus. This is the faith of the Church. This is the faith in which these children are about to be baptized.

145. Then he asks them:

A

Catechist:
Do you reject Satan?
Parents and godparents: **I do.**

Catechist:
And all his works?
Parents and godparents: **I do.**

Catechist:
And all his empty promises?
Parents and godparents: **I do.**

or **B**
Catechist:
Do you reject sin, so as to live in the freedom of God's children?
Parents and godparents: **I do.**

Catechist:
Do you reject the glamor of evil, and refuse to be mastered by sin?
Parents and godparents: **I do.**

Catechist:
Do you reject Satan, father of sin and prince of darkness?
Parents and godparents: **I do.**

According to circumstances, this second form may be expressed with greater precision by the conference of bishops, especially in places where it is necessary for the parents and godparents to reject superstitious and magical practices used with children.

146. Then the catechist asks for the threefold profession of faith from the parents and godparents:

Catechist:
Do you believe in God, the Father almighty, creator of heaven and earth?
Parents and godparents: **I do.**

Catechist:
Do you believe in Jesus Christ, his only Son, our Lord, who was born of the Virgin Mary, was crucified, died, and was buried, rose from the dead, and is now seated at the right hand of the Father?
Parents and godparents: **I do.**

Catechist:
Do you believe in the Holy Spirit, the holy catholic Church, the communion of saints, the forgiveness of sins, the resurrection of the body, and life everlasting?
Parents and godparents: **I do.**

147. The catechist and the congregation give their assent to this profession of faith:

Catechist:
This is our faith. This is the faith of the Church. We are proud to profess it, in Christ Jesus our Lord.
All: **Amen.**

If desired, some other formula may be used instead, or a suitable song by which the community expresses its faith with a single voice.

BAPTISM

148. The catechist invites the first of the families to approach the font. Using the name of the individual child, he asks the parents and godparents:

Is it your will that N. should be baptized in the faith of the Church, which we have all professed with you?
Parents and godparents: **It is.**

He baptizes the child, saying:

N., I baptize you in the name of the Father,

He immerses the child or pours water upon it.

and of the Son,

He immerses the child or pours water upon it a second time.

and of the Holy Spirit.

He immerses the child or pours water upon it a third time.

If baptism is performed by the pouring of water, it is preferable that the child be held by the mother or father. Where, however, it is felt that the existing custom should be retained, the godmother or godfather may hold the child. If baptism is by immersion, the parent or godparent lifts the child out of the font.

149. If the number of children to be baptized is large, and other catechists are present, these may baptize some of the children in the way described above, and with the same form (no. 148).

150. While the children are being baptized, the community can make acclamations or sing hymns (see nos. 225-245). Some passages from scripture may also be read, or a sacred silence observed.

151. The anointing with chrism is omitted. The catechist says once for all the newly-baptized children:

God the Father of our Lord Jesus Christ has freed you from sin, and has given you a new birth by water and the Holy Spirit. He has made you Christians now, and has welcomed you into his holy people. As Christ was anointed Priest, Prophet, and King, so may you live always as members of his body, sharing everlasting life.
All: **Amen.**

CLOTHING WITH WHITE GARMENT

152. The catechist says:

My dear children, you have become a new creation, and have clothed yourselves in Christ.

See in this white garment the outward sign of your Christian dignity. With your family and friends to help you by word and example, bring that dignity unstained into the everlasting life of heaven.
All: **Amen.**

The white garments are put on the children. A different color is not permitted unless demanded by local custom. It is desirable that the families provide the garments.

LIGHTED CANDLE

153. The catechist takes the Easter candle and says:

Receive the light of Christ. Parents and godparents, this light is entrusted to you to be kept burning brightly. These children of yours have been enlightened by Christ. They are to walk always as children of the light. May they keep the flame of faith alive in their hearts. When the Lord comes, may they go out to meet him with all the saints in the heavenly kingdom.

Candles are distributed to the families. The head of one family lights his candle from the Easter candle and passes the flame on to the rest. Meanwhile the community sings a baptismal song, such as:

You have put on Christ,
in him you have been baptized.
Alleluia, alleluia.

Other hymns may be chosen from nos. 225-245.

Meanwhile, unless the baptisms were performed in the sanctuary, there is a procession to the altar. The lighted candles are carried for the children.

CONCLUSION OF THE RITE

LORD'S PRAYER

154. The catechist stands in front of the altar and addresses the parents, godparents, and the whole assembly in these or similar words:

Dearly beloved, these children have been reborn in baptism. They are now called children of God, for so indeed they are. In confirmation they will receive the fullness of God's Spirit. In holy communion they will share the banquet of Christ's sacrifice, calling God their Father in the midst of the Church. In their name, in the spirit of common sonship, let us pray together in the words our Lord has given us:

155. All say together:

Our Father. . . .

BLESSING

The catechist blesses the entire assembly and dismisses them:

My brothers and sisters, we commend you to the mercy and grace of God our almighty Father, of his only Son, and of the Holy Spirit. May he protect your paths, so that walking in the light of faith, you may

come to the good things he has promised us.
Go in peace.
All: **Amen.**

156. After the blessing, all may sing a hymn which suitably expresses thanksgiving and Easter joy, or they may sing the canticle of the Blessed Virgin Mary, the Magnificat.

CHAPTER V

RITE OF BAPTISM FOR CHILDREN IN DANGER OF DEATH WHEN NO PRIEST OR DEACON IS AVAILABLE

157. Water, even though not blessed, is prepared for the rite. The parents, godparents, and if possible, some friends and neighbors of the family gather around the sick child. The minister, who is any suitable member of the Church, begins with this brief prayer of the faithful:

Let us ask almighty God to look with mercy on this child who is about to receive the grace of baptism, on his (her) parents and godparents, and on all baptized persons.
Through baptism, welcome this child into your Church.
℟. **Lord, hear our prayer.**

Through baptism, make him (her) one of your adopted children.
℟. **Lord, hear our prayer.**

Through baptism, he (she) is being buried in the likeness of Christ's death. May he (she) also share in the glory of his resurrection.
℟. **Lord, hear our prayer.**

Renew the grace of our baptism in each one of us.
℟. **Lord, hear our prayer.**

May all the followers of Christ, baptized into one body, always live united in faith and love.
℟. **Lord, hear our prayer.**

158. The prayer of the faithful concludes with this prayer:

Father of our Lord Jesus Christ,
source of all life and love,
you know the anxiety of parents
and you lighten their burden
by your fatherly care for all children in danger.

You reveal the depth of your love
by offering them a new and eternal birth.

In your kindness, hear our prayers:
keep this child from the power of sin,
and welcome him (her) with love into the kingdom of your Son.

By water and by the power of the Holy Spirit,
may this child, whom we now call N.,
share in the mystery of Christ's death
so that he (she) may also share in the mystery of Christ's resurrection.

May he (she) become your adopted son (daughter),
and share in the inheritance of Christ.
Grant that he (she) may rejoice in the fellowship of your Church
with your only Son and the Holy Spirit
for ever and ever.
℟. **Amen.**

159. Then they make the profession of faith. The minister says to all present:

A

Let us remember our own baptism, and profess our faith in Jesus Christ. This is the faith of the Church, the faith into which children are baptized.

Then he asks:

Do you believe in God, the Father almighty, creator of heaven and earth?
℟. **I do.**

Minister:
Do you believe in Jesus Christ, his only Son, our Lord, who was born of the Virgin Mary, was crucified, died, and was buried, rose from the dead, and is now seated at the right hand of the Father?
℟. **I do.**

Minister:
Do you believe in the Holy Spirit, the holy catholic Church, the communion of saints, the forgiveness of sins, the resurrection of the body, and life everlasting?
℟. **I do.**

The profession of faith may also be made, if desirable, by reciting the Apostles' Creed:

B

I believe in God, the Father almighty,
Creator of heaven and earth;
and in Jesus Christ, his only Son, our Lord,
who was conceived by the Holy Spirit,
born of the Virgin Mary,
suffered under Pontius Pilate,
was crucified, died, and was buried.
He descended into hell;
the third day he rose again from the dead;
he ascended into heaven,
sitteth at the right hand of God, the Father almighty,
from thence he shall come to judge the living and the dead.
I believe in the Holy Spirit,
the holy Catholic Church,
the communion of saints,
the forgiveness of sins,
the resurrection of the body,
and life everlasting. Amen.

160. Then the minister baptizes the child, saying:

N., I baptize you in the name of the Father,

He pours water upon the child.

and of the Son,

He pours water upon the child a second time.

and of the Holy Spirit.

He pours water upon the child a third time.

161. Omitting all other ceremonies, he may give the white garment to the child. The minister says:

N., you have become a new creation, and have clothed yourself in Christ.

See in this white garment the outward sign of your Christian dignity. May you bring it unstained into the everlasting life of heaven.

162. The celebration concludes with the recitation of the Lord's Prayer:

Our Father. . . .

163. If no one there is capable of directing the prayer, any member of the Church may baptize, after reciting the Apostles' Creed, by pouring water on the child while reciting the customary words (see no. 160, above). The creed may be omitted if necessary.

164. At the moment of death, it is sufficient for the minister to omit all other ceremonies and pour water on the child while saying the usual words (see no. 160, above). It is desirable that the minister, as far as possible, should use one or two witnesses.

CHAPTER VI

RITE OF BRINGING A BAPTIZED CHILD TO THE CHURCH

RECEPTION OF THE CHILD

165. The people may sing a psalm or song suitable for the occasion. Meanwhile the celebrating priest or deacon, vested in alb or surplice, with a stole (with or without a cope) of festive color, and accompanied by the ministers, goes to the entrance of the church where the parents and godparents are waiting with the child.

166. The celebrant greets all present, and especially the parents and godparents. He praises them for having had the child baptized without delay, and thanks God and congratulates the parents on the child's return to health.

167. First the celebrant questions the parents:

Celebrant:
What name have you given the child?
Parents: **N.**

Celebrant:
What do you ask of God's Church, now that your child has been baptized?
Parents: **We ask that the whole community will know that he (she) has been received into the Church.**

The first reply may be given by someone other than the parents if local custom gives him the right to name the child.

In the second response the parents may use other words, such as **that he (she) is a Christian** or **that he (she) has been baptized.**

168. Then the celebrant speaks to the parents in these or similar words:

Celebrant:
Do you realize that in bringing your child to the

Church, you are accepting the duty of raising him (her) in the faith, so that by observing the commandments he (she) will love God and neighbor as Christ taught us?
Parents: **We do.**

169. Then the celebrant turns to the godparents and addresses them in these or similar words:

Are you ready to help the mother and father of this child to carry out their duty as Christian parents?
Godparents: **We are.**

170. The celebrant continues:

N., the Christian community welcomes you with great joy, now that you have recovered your health. We now bear witness that you have been received as a member of the Church. In the name of the community I sign you with the cross of Christ, who gave you a new life in baptism and made you a member of his Church. I invite your parents (and godparents) to do the same.

He signs the child on the forehead, in silence. Then he invites the parents and (if it seems appropriate) the godparents to do the same.

171. The celebrant invites the parents, godparents, and all who are present to take part in the liturgy of the word. If circumstances permit, there is a procession to the place where this will be celebrated, during which a song is sung, such as Psalm 85:7, 8, 9ab:

Will you not give us life;
and shall not your people rejoice in you?
Show us, O Lord, your kindness,
and grant us your salvation.
I will hear what God proclaims:
the Lord—for he proclaims peace to his people.

CELEBRATION OF GOD'S WORD

SCRIPTURAL READINGS AND HOMILY

172. One or even two of the following gospel passages are read, during which all may sit if convenient.

John 3:1-6 The meeting with Nicodemus..
Matthew 28:18-20 The apostles are sent to preach the gospel and to baptize.
Mark 1:9-11 The baptism of Jesus.
Mark 10:13-16 Let the little children come to me.

The passages listed in nos. 186-194 and 204-215 may also be chosen, or other passages which better meet the wishes or needs of the parents, such as the following:

1 Kings 17:17-24
2 Kings 4:8-37

Between the readings, responsorial psalms or verses may be sung, as given in nos. 195-203.

173. After the reading, the celebrant gives a brief homily, explaining to those present the significance of what has been read. His purpose will be to lead them to a deeper understanding of the mystery of baptism and to encourage parents and godparents to a ready acceptance of the responsibilities which arise from the sacrament.

174. After the homily, or in the course of or after the litany, it is desirable to have a period of silence while all pray at the invitation of the celebrant. A suitable hymn may follow, such as one chosen from nos. 225-245.

PRAYER OF THE FAITHFUL

175. Then the prayer of the faithful is said:

Celebrant:
Let us ask our Lord Jesus Christ to look lovingly on this child, on his (her) parents and godparents, and on all the baptized.

Leader:
May this child always show gratitude to God for his (her) baptism and recovery.
All: **Lord, hear our prayer.**

Leader:
Help him (her) always to be a living member of your Church.
All: **Lord, hear our prayer.**

Leader:
Inspire him (her) to hear, follow, and witness to your gospel.
All: **Lord, hear our prayer.**

Leader:
May he (she) come with joy to the table of your sacrifice.
All: **Lord, hear our prayer.**

Leader:
Help him (her) to love God and neighbor as you have taught us.
All: **Lord, hear our prayer.**

Leader:
May he (she) grow in holiness and wisdom by listening to his (her) fellow Christians and following their example.
All: **Lord, hear our prayer.**

Leader:
Keep all your followers united in faith and love for ever.
All: **Lord, hear our prayer.**

176. The celebrant next invites all present to invoke the saints:

Holy Mary, Mother of God, pray for us.
Saint John the Baptist, pray for us.
Saint Joseph, pray for us.
Saint Peter and Saint Paul, pray for us.

The names of other saints may be added, especially the patrons of the child and of the church or locality. The litany concludes:

All you saints of God, pray for us.

Then the celebrant says:

Father of our Lord Jesus Christ,
source of all life and love,
you are glorified by the loving care these parents have shown this child.
You rescue children from danger and save them in baptism.

Your Church thanks you and prays for your child N.
You have brought him (her) out of the kingdom of darkness
and into your marvelous light.
You have made him (her) your adopted child
and a temple of the Holy Spirit.

Help him (her) in all the dangers of this life
and strengthen him (her) in the constant effort to reach your kingdom,
through the power of Christ our Savior.
(We ask this) through Christ our Lord.
All: **Amen.**

FURTHER RITES

ANOINTING WITH CHRISM

178. Then the celebrant says:

God the Father of our Lord Jesus Christ has freed you from sin, given you a new birth by water and the Holy Spirit, and welcomed you into his holy people. He now anoints you with the chrism of salvation. As Christ was anointed Priest, Prophet, and King, so may

you live always as a member of his body, sharing everlasting life.
All: **Amen.**

Then the celebrant anoints the child on the crown of the head with the chrism, in silence.

CLOTHING WITH WHITE GARMENT

179. The celebrant says:

N., you have become a new creation, and have clothed yourself in Christ.

See in this white garment the outward sign of your Christian dignity. With your family and friends to help you by word and example, bring that dignity unstained into the everlasting life of heaven.
All: **Amen.**

LIGHTED CANDLE

180. The celebrant takes the Easter candle and says:

Receive the light of Christ

Someone, such as the father or godfather, lights the child's candle from the Easter candle.

The celebrant then says:

Parents and godparents, this light is entrusted to you to be kept burning brightly. This child of yours has been enlightened by Christ. He (she) is to walk always as a child of the light. May he (she) keep the flame of faith alive in his (her) heart. When the Lord comes, may he (she) go out to meet him with all the saints in the heavenly kingdom.

A baptismal song is appropriate at this time, such as:

You have put on Christ,
in him you have been baptized.
Alleluia, alleluia.

Other songs may be chosen from nos. 225-245.

CONCLUSION OF THE RITE

LORD'S PRAYER

181. The celebrant stands in front of the altar and addresses the parents, godparents, and the whole assembly in these or similar words:

My dear brothers and sisters, this child has been reborn in baptism. He (she) is now called the child of God, for so indeed he (she) is. In confirmation he (she) will receive the fullness of God's Spirit. In holy communion he (she) will share the banquet of Christ's sacrifice, calling God his (her) Father in the midst of the Church. In the name of this child, in the spirit of our common sonship, let us pray together in the words our Lord has given us:

182. All present join the celebrant in singing or saying:

Our Father. . . .

BLESSING

183. The celebrant first blesses the mother, who holds the child in her arms, then the father, and lastly the entire assembly:

Celebrant:
God the Father, through his Son, the Virgin Mary's child, has brought joy to all Christian mothers, as they see the hope of eternal life shine on their children. May he bless the mother of this child. She now thanks God for the gift of her child. May she be one with her son (daughter) in thanking God for ever in heaven, in Christ Jesus our Lord.
All: **Amen.**

Celebrant:
God is the giver of all life, human and divine. May he bless the father of this child. He and his wife will be the first teachers of their child in the ways of faith.

May they also be the best of teachers, bearing witness to the faith by what they say and do, in Christ Jesus our Lord.
All: **Amen.**

Celebrant:
By God's gift, through water and the Holy Spirit, we are reborn to everlasting life. In his goodness, may he continue to pour out his blessings on these sons and daughters of his. May he make them always, wherever they may be, faithful members of his holy people. May he send his peace upon all who are gathered here, in Christ Jesus our Lord.
All: **Amen.**

Celebrant:
May almighty God, the Father, and the Son, ✠ and the Holy Spirit, bless you.
All: **Amen.**

For other forms of the blessing, see nos. 247-249.

184. After the blessing, all may sing a hymn which suitably expresses thanksgiving and Easter joy, or they may sing the song of the Blessed Virgin Mary, the Magnificat.

Where there is the practice of bringing the baptized child to the altar of the blessed Virgin, this custom is observed if appropriate.

185. The above rite is followed even when the baptized child is brought to the church after other difficulties (such as persecution, disagreement between parents) which prevented the celebration of baptism in the church. In such cases, the celebrant should adapt the explanations, readings, intentions in the prayer of the faithful and other parts of the rite to the child's circumstances.

CHAPTER VII

VARIOUS TEXTS FOR USE IN THE CELEBRATION OF BAPTISM FOR CHILDREN

I. SCRIPTURAL READINGS

OLD TESTAMENT READINGS

186. **Exodus 17:3-7** Water from the rock.

187. **Ezekiel 36:24-28** Clean water, a new heart, a renewed spirit.

188. **Ezekiel 47:1-9, 12** The water of salvation.

NEW TESTAMENT READINGS

189. **Romans 6:3-5** Baptism: a sharing in Christ's death and resurrection.

190. **Romans 8:28-32** We have become more perfectly like God's own Son.

191. **1 Corinthians 12:12-13** Baptized in one Spirit to form one body.

192. **Galatians 3:26-28** Now that you have been baptized you have put on Christ.

193. **Ephesians 4:1-6** One Lord, one faith, one baptism.

194. **1 Peter 2:4-5, 9-10** A chosen race, a royal priesthood.

RESPONSORIAL PSALMS

195. Psalm 23:1-3a, 3b-4, 5, 6

℟. (1) **The Lord is my shepherd; there is nothing I shall want.**

196. Psalm 27:1, 4, 8b-9abc, 13-14
℟. (1a) **The Lord is my light and my salvation.**

Or: Ephesians 5:14
Wake up and rise from death:
Christ will shine upon you!

197. Psalm 34:2-3, 6-7, 8-9, 14-15, 16-17, 18-19
℟. (6a) **Come to him and receive his light!**

Or: (9a) **Taste and see the goodness of the Lord.**

ALLELUIA VERSE AND VERSE BEFORE THE GOSPEL

198. John 3:16
God loved the world so much, he gave us his only Son,
that all who believe in him might have eternal life.

199. John 8:12
I am the light of the world, says the Lord;
the man who follows me will have the light of life.

200. John 14:5
I am the way, the truth, and the life, says the Lord;
no one comes to the Father, except through me.

201. Ephesians 4:5-6
One Lord, one faith, one baptism.
One God, the Father of all.

202. 2 Timothy 1:10b
Our Savior Jesus Christ has done away with death,
and brought us life through his gospel.

203. 1 Peter 2:9
You are a chosen race, a royal priesthood, a holy people.
Praise God who called you out of darkness and into his marvelous light.

GOSPELS

204. **Matthew 22:35-40** The first and most important commandment.

205. **Matthew 28:18-20** Christ sends his apostles to teach and baptize.

206. **Mark 1:9-11** The baptism of Jesus.

207. **Mark 10:13-16** Jesus loves children.

208. **Mark 12:28b-34 (longer) or 28b-31 (shorter)** Love God with all your heart.

209. **John 3:1-6** The meeting with Nicodemus.

210. **John 4:5-14** Jesus speaks with the Samaritan woman.

211. **John 6:44-47** Eternal life through belief in Jesus.

212. **John 7:37b-39a** Streams of living water.

213. **John 9:1-7** Jesus heals a blind man who believes in him.

214. **John 15:1-11** Union with Christ, the true vine.

215. **John 19:31-35** The death of Christ, the witness of John the apostle.

II. OTHER FORMS OF THE PRAYER OF THE FAITHFUL

Any one of the following forms given in this baptismal ritual may be used for the prayer of the faithful. Petitions may be added or omitted at will, taking into consideration the special circumstances of each family. The prayer always concludes with the invocation of the saints.

216.
As given in no. 47.

217.
We have been called by the Lord to be a royal priesthood, a holy nation, a people he has acquired for himself. Let us ask him to show his mercy to these children, who are to receive the graces of baptism, to their parents and godparents, and to all the baptized everywhere.

Through baptism, bring these children into your Church.
℟. Lord, hear our prayer.

Throughout their lives, help them to be faithful witnesses to your Son, Jesus Christ, for they are being marked with his cross.
℟. **Lord, hear our prayer.**

As they are being buried in the likeness of Christ's death through baptism, may they also share in the glory of Christ's resurrection.
℟. **Lord, hear our prayer.**

Teach them by the words and example of their parents and godparents, and help them to grow strong as living members of the Church.
℟. **Lord, hear our prayer.**

Renew the grace of baptism in each of us here.
℟. **Lord, hear our prayer.**

May all Christ's followers, baptized into one body, always live united in faith and love.
℟. **Lord, hear our prayer.**

The invocation of the saints follows.

218.
My fellow Christians, let us ask the mercy of Jesus Christ our Lord for these children who will receive the gift of baptism, for their parents and godparents, and for all baptized persons.

Through baptism, make these children God's own sons and daughters.
℟. **Lord, hear our prayer.**

Help these tender branches grow to be more like you, the true vine, and be your faithful followers.
℟. **Lord, hear our prayer.**

May they always keep your commands, walk in your love, and proclaim your Good News to their fellow men.
℟. **Lord, hear our prayer.**

May they be counted as God's friends through your

saving work, Lord Jesus, and may they inherit eternal life.
℟. **Lord, hear our prayer.**

Help their parents and godparents to lead them to know and love God.
℟. **Lord, hear our prayer.**

Inspire all men to share in the new birth of baptism.
℟. **Lord, hear our prayer.**

The invocation of the saints follows.

219.

We have been called by the Lord to be a royal priesthood, a holy nation, a people he has acquired for himself. Let us ask him to show his mercy to these children, who are to receive the graces of baptism, to their parents and godparents, and to all the baptized everywhere.

Through baptism may these children become God's own beloved sons and daughters. We pray to the Lord.
℟. **Lord, hear our prayer.**

Once they are born again of water and the Holy Spirit, may they always live in that Spirit, and make their new life known to their fellow men. We pray to the Lord.
℟. **Lord, hear our prayer.**

Help them to triumph over the deceits of the devil and the attractions of evil. We pray to the Lord.
℟. **Lord, hear our prayer.**

May they love you, Lord, with all their heart, soul, mind and strength, and love their neighbor as themselves. We pray to the Lord.
℟. **Lord, hear our prayer.**

Help all of us here to be models of faith for these children. We pray to the Lord.
℟. **Lord, hear our prayer.**

May all Christ's faithful people, who receive the sign of the cross at baptism, always and everywhere give witness to him by the way they live. We pray to the Lord.
℟. Lord, hear our prayer.

The invocation of the saints follows.

220.

Let us ask Christ's mercy for these children, their parents and godparents, and all baptized Christians. Give them a new birth to eternal life through water and the Holy Spirit.
℟. Lord, hear our prayer.

Help them always to be living members of your Church.
℟. Lord, hear our prayer.

Inspire them to hear and follow your gospel, and to give witness to you by their lives. We ask this, Lord.
℟. Lord, hear our prayer.

May they come with joy to the table of your sacrifice.
℟. Lord, hear our prayer.

Help them to love God and neighbor as you have taught us.
℟. Lord, hear our prayer.

May they grow in holiness and wisdom by listening to their fellow Christians and by following their example.
℟. Lord, hear our prayer.

Let all your followers remain united in faith and love.
℟. Lord, hear our prayer.

The invocation of the saints follows.

III. ANOTHER FORM OF THE PRAYER OF EXORCISM

221.
Almighty God,
you sent your only Son
to rescue us from the slavery of sin,
and to give us the freedom
only your sons and daughters enjoy.

We now pray for these children
who will have to face the world with its temptations,
and fight the devil in all his cunning.

Your Son died and rose again to save us.
By his victory over sin and death,
bring these children out of the power of darkness.
Strengthen them with the grace of Christ,
and watch over them at every step in life's journey.
(We ask this) through Christ our Lord.
All: **Amen.**

IV. BLESSING AND INVOCATION OF GOD OVER BAPTISMAL WATER

222. See the formula in no. 54a.

223. Celebrant:
Praise to you, almighty God and Father, for you have created water to cleanse and give life.
All: **Blessed be God** (or some other suitable acclamation by the people).

Celebrant:
Praise to you, Lord Jesus Christ, the Father's only Son, for you offered yourself on the cross, that in the blood and water flowing from your side, and through

your death and resurrection, the Church might be born.
All: **Blessed be God.**

Celebrant:
Praise to you, God the Holy Spirit, for you anointed Christ at his baptism in the waters of Jordan, so that we might all be baptized into you.
All: **Blessed be God.**

Celebrant:
Come to us, Lord, Father of all, and make holy this water which you have created, so that all who are baptized in it may be washed clean of sin, and be born again to live as your children.
All: **Hear us, Lord** (or some other suitable invocation).

Celebrant:
Make this water holy, Lord, so that all who are baptized into Christ's death and resurrection by this water may become more perfectly like your Son.
All: **Hear us, Lord.**

The celebrant touches the water with his right hand and continues:

Lord, make holy this water which you have created, so that all those whom you have chosen may be born again by the power of the Holy Spirit, and may take their place among your holy people.
All: **Hear us, Lord.**

If the baptismal water has already been blessed, the celebrant omits the invocation **Come to us, Lord** and those which follow it, and says:

You have called your children N., N., to this cleansing water that they may share in the faith of your Church and have eternal life. By the mystery of this consecrated water lead them to a new and spiritual birth. (We ask this) through Christ our Lord.
All: **Amen.**

224. Celebrant:

Father, God of mercy, through these waters of baptism you have filled us with new life as your very own children.

All: **Blessed be God** (or some other suitable acclamation by the people).

Celebrant:

From all who are baptized in water and the Holy Spirit, you have formed one people, united in your Son Jesus Christ.

All: **Blessed be God.**

Celebrant:

You have set us free and filled our hearts with the Spirit of your love, that we may live in your peace.

All: **Blessed be God.**

Celebrant:

You call those who have been baptized to announce the Good News of Jesus Christ to people everywhere.

All: **Blessed be God.**

Celebrant:

You have called your children, N., N., to this cleansing water and new birth that by sharing the faith of your Church they might have eternal life. Bless ✠ this water in which they will be baptized. We ask this in the name of Christ our Lord.

All: **Amen.**

If the baptismal water has already been blessed, the celebrant omits this last prayer and says:

You have called your children N., N., to this cleansing water that they may share in the faith of your Church and have eternal life. By the mystery of this consecrated water lead them to a new and spiritual birth. (We ask this) through Christ our Lord.

All: **Amen.**

V. ACCLAMATIONS AND HYMNS

ACCLAMATIONS FROM SACRED SCRIPTURE

225. Exodus 15:11
Lord God, who is your equal?
Strong, majestic, and holy!
Worthy of praise, worker of wonders!

226. 1 John 1:5
God is light: in him there is no darkness.

227. 1 John 4:16
God is love: he who lives in love, lives in God.

228. Ephesians 4:6
There is one God, one Father of all:
he is over all, and through all:
he lives in all of us.

229. Psalm 34:6
Come to him and receive his light!

230. see Ephesians 1:4
Blessed be God who chose you in Christ.

231. Ephesians 2:10
You are God's work of art, created in Christ Jesus.

232. 1 John 3:2
You are now God's children, my dearest friends.
What you shall be in his glory has not yet been revealed.

233. 1 John 3:1
Think of how God loves you!
He calls you his own children,
and that is what you are.

234. Revelation 22:14
Happy are those who have washed their robes clean:
washed in the blood of the Lamb!

235. Galatians 3:28
All of you are one:
united in Christ Jesus.

236. Ephesians 5:1-2
Imitate God, walk in his love,
just as Christ loves us.

HYMNS IN THE STYLE OF THE NEW TESTAMENT

237. 1 Peter 1:3-5
Praised be the Father of our Lord Jesus Christ:
a God so merciful and kind!
He has given us a new birth, a living hope,
by raising Jesus his Son from death.
Salvation is our undying inheritance,
preserved for us in heaven,
salvation at the end of time.

238.
How great the sign of God's love for us,
Jesus Christ our Lord:
promised before all time began,
revealed in these last days.
He lived and suffered and died for us,
but the Spirit raised him to life.
People everywhere have heard his message
and placed their faith in him.
What wonderful blessings he gives his people:
living in the Father's glory,
he fills all creation
and guides it to perfection.

SONGS FROM ANCIENT LITURGIES

239.
We believe in you, Lord Jesus Christ.
Fill our hearts with your radiance,
and make us the children of light!

240.
We come to you, Lord Jesus.
Fill us with your life,
Make us children of the Father,
and one in you.

241.
Lord Jesus, from your wounded side
flowed streams of cleansing water:
the world was washed of all its sin,
all life made new again!

242.
The Father's voice calls us above the waters,
the glory of the Son shines on us,
the love of the Spirit fills us with life.

243.
Holy Church of God, stretch out your hand
and welcome your children
newborn of water
and of the Spirit of God.

244.
Rejoice, you newly baptized,
chosen members of the kingdom.
Buried with Christ in death,
you are reborn in him by faith.

245.
This is the fountain of life,
water made holy by the suffering of Christ,
washing all the world.
You who are washed in this water
have hope of heaven's kingdom.

VI. FORMS OF THE FINAL BLESSING

246. See the formula in the rite of baptism for several children, no. 70.

247.
Celebrant:
May God the almighty Father, who filled the world with joy by giving us his only Son, bless these newly-baptized children. May they grow to be more fully like Jesus Christ our Lord.
All: **Amen.**

Celebrant:
May almighty God, who gives life on earth and in heaven, bless the parents of these children. They thank him now for the gift he has given them. May they always show that gratitude in action by loving and caring for their children.
All: **Amen.**

Celebrant:
May almighty God, who has given us a new birth by water and the Holy Spirit, generously bless all of us who are his faithful children. May we always live as his people, and may he bless all here present with his peace.
All: **Amen.**

Celebrant:
May almighty God, the Father, and the Son, ✠ and the Holy Spirit, bless you.
All: **Amen.**

248.
Celebrant:
May God, the source of life and love, who fills the hearts of mothers with love for their children, bless the mothers of these newly-baptized children. As they thank God for a safe delivery, may they find joy in the love, growth, and holiness of their children.
All: **Amen.**

Celebrant:
May God, the Father and model of all fathers, help these fathers to give good example, so that their children will grow to be mature Christians in all the fullness of Jesus Christ.
All: **Amen.**

Celebrant:
May God, who loves all people, bless all the relatives and friends who are gathered here. In his mercy, may he guard them from evil and give them his abundant peace.
All: **Amen.**

Celebrant:
And may almighty God, the Father, and the Son, ✠ and the Holy Spirit, bless you.
All: **Amen.**

249.
Celebrant:
My brothers and sisters, we entrust you all to the mercy and help of God the almighty Father, his only Son, and the Holy Spirit. May he watch over your life, and may we all walk by the light of faith, and attain the good things he has promised us.

Go in peace, and may almighty God, the Father, and the Son, ✠ and the Holy Spirit, bless you.
All: **Amen.**

APPENDIX

LITANY OF THE SAINTS

LITANY FOR SOLEMN INTERCESSIONS

In those sections which contain several sets of invocations marked by A and B, one or the other may be chosen as desired. The names of some saints may be added in the proper place such as the patron saint, title of the church, name of the founder, but in a different typeface. Some petitions adapted to the place and need may be added to the petitions for various needs.

I. PETITIONS TO GOD

A

Lord, have mercy
Lord, have mercy
Christ, have mercy
Christ, have mercy
Lord, have mercy
Lord, have mercy

B

God our Father in heaven have mercy on us
God the Son, our redeemer have mercy on us
God the Holy Spirit have mercy on us
Holy Trinity, one God have mercy on us

II. PETITIONS TO THE SAINTS

Holy Mary pray for us
Mother of God pray for us
Most honored of all virgins pray for us
Michael, Gabriel, and Raphael pray for us
Angels of God pray for us

Prophets and Fathers of our Faith

Abraham, Moses and Elijah pray for us
Saint Joseph pray for us
Saint John the Baptist pray for us

Holy patriarchs and prophets pray for us

Apostles and Followers of Christ

Saint Peter and Saint Paul pray for us
Saint Andrew pray for us
Saint John and Saint James pray for us
Saint Thomas pray for us
Saint Matthew pray for us
All holy apostles pray for us
Saint Luke pray for us
Saint Mark pray for us
Saint Barnabas pray for us
Saint Mary Magdalen pray for us
All disciples of the Lord pray for us

Martyrs

Saint Stephen pray for us
Saint Ignatius pray for us
Saint Polycarp pray for us
Saint Justin pray for us
Saint Lawrence pray for us
Saint Cyprian pray for us
Saint Boniface pray for us
Saint Thomas Becket pray for us
Saint John Fisher and Saint Thomas More pray for us
Saint Paul Miki pray for us
Saint Isaac Jogues and Saint John de Brebeuf pray for us
Saint Peter Chanel pray for us
Saint Charles Lwanga pray for us
Saint Perpetua and Saint Felicity pray for us
Saint Agnes pray for us
Saint Maria Goretti pray for us
All holy martyrs for Christ pray for us

Bishops and Doctors

Saint Leo and Saint Gregory pray for us
Saint Ambrose pray for us

Saint Jerome pray for us
Saint Augustine pray for us
Saint Athanasius pray for us
Saint Basil and Saint Gregory pray for us
Saint John Chrysostom pray for us
Saint Martin pray for us
Saint Patrick pray for us
Saint Cyril and Saint Methodius pray for us
Saint Charles Borromeo pray for us
Saint Francis de Sales pray for us
Saint Pius pray for us

Priests and Religious

Saint Anthony pray for us
Saint Benedict pray for us
Saint Bernard pray for us
Saint Francis and Saint Dominic pray for us
Saint Thomas Aquinas pray for us
Saint Ignatius Loyola pray for us
Saint Francis Xavier pray for us
Saint Vincent de Paul pray for us
Saint John Vianney pray for us
Saint John Bosco pray for us
Saint Catherine pray for us
Saint Theresa pray for us
Saint Rose pray for us

Laity

Saint Louis pray for us
Saint Monica pray for us
Saint Elizabeth pray for us
All holy men and women pray for us

III. PETITIONS TO CHRIST

A

Lord, be merciful Lord, save your people
From all evil Lord, save your people
From every sin Lord, save your people
From the snares of the devil
Lord, save your people

From anger and hatred Lord, save your people
From every evil intention Lord, save your people
From everlasting death Lord, save your people
By your coming as man Lord, save your people
By your birth Lord, save your people
By your baptism and fasting
Lord, save your people
By your sufferings and cross
Lord, save your people
By your death and burial Lord, save your people
By your rising to new life Lord, save your people
By your return in glory to the Father
Lord, save your people
By your gift of the Holy Spirit
Lord, save your people
By your coming again in glory
Lord, save your people

B

Christ, Son of the living God have mercy on us
You came into this world have mercy on us
You suffered for us on the cross have mercy on us
You died to save us have mercy on us
You lay in the tomb have mercy on us
You rose from the dead have mercy on us
You returned in glory to the Father
have mercy on us
You sent the Holy Spirit upon your Apostles
have mercy on us
You are seated at the right hand of the Father
have mercy on us
You will come again to judge the living and the dead have mercy on us

IV. PETITIONS FOR VARIOUS NEEDS

A

Lord, be merciful to us Lord, hear our prayer
Give us true repentance Lord, hear our prayer
Strengthen us in your service
Lord, hear our prayer

Reward with eternal life all who do good to us   Lord, hear our prayer
Bless the fruits of the earth and of man's labor   Lord, hear our prayer

B

Lord, show us your kindness
Lord, hear our prayer
Raise our thoughts and desires to you
Lord, hear our prayer
Save us from final damnation
Lord, hear our prayer
Save our friends and all who have helped us
Lord, hear our prayer
Grant eternal rest to all who have died in the faith   Lord, hear our prayer
Spare us from disease, hunger, and war
Lord, hear our prayer
Bring all peoples together in trust and peace
Lord, hear our prayer

C — always used

Guide and protect your holy Church
Lord, hear our prayer
Keep the pope and all the clergy in faithful service to your Church   Lord, hear our prayer
Bring all Christians together in unity
Lord, hear our prayer
Lead all men to the light of the Gospel
Lord, hear our prayer

V. CONCLUSION

A

Christ hear us
Christ hear us

Lord Jesus, hear our prayer
Lord Jesus, hear our prayer

B

Lamb of God, you take away the sins of the world: have mercy on us

Lamb of God, you take away the sins of the world: have mercy on us
Lamb of God, you take away the sins of the world: have mercy on us

PRAYERS

God of love, our strength and protection,
hear the prayers of your Church.
Grant that when we come to you in faith,
our prayers may be answered:
through Christ our Lord.

Or:

Lord God, you know our weakness.
In your mercy
grant that the example of your Saints
may bring us back to love and serve you
through Christ our Lord.

LITANY FOR CONSECRATIONS AND SOLEMN BLESSINGS

In any ceremony, the names of some saints may be added in the proper place in the litany. This may include the patron saint, the saints after whom the church is named, the founder, patrons of those being consecrated, all the apostles in the ordination of a bishop, and so on. Invocations which are more appropriate for individual occasions may also be added to the litany.

Lord, have mercy
Lord, have mercy
Christ, have mercy
Christ, have mercy
Lord, have mercy
Lord, have mercy
Holy Mary, Mother of God pray for us
Saint Michael pray for us
Holy angels of God pray for us
Saint Joseph pray for us

Saint John the Baptist pray for us
Saint Peter and Saint Paul pray for us
Saint Andrew pray for us
Saint John pray for us
Saint Mary Magdalen pray for us
Saint Stephen pray for us
Saint Ignatius pray for us
Saint Lawrence pray for us
Saint Perpetua and Saint Felicity pray for us
Saint Agnes pray for us
Saint Gregory pray for us
Saint Augustine pray for us
Saint Athanasius pray for us
Saint Basil pray for us
Saint Martin pray for us
Saint Benedict pray for us
Saint Francis and Saint Dominic pray for us
Saint Francis Xavier pray for us
Saint John Vianney pray for us
Saint Theresa pray for us
All you saints of God pray for us
Lord, be merciful Lord, save us
From all harm Lord, save us
From every sin Lord, save us
From all temptations Lord, save us
From everlasting death Lord, save us
By your coming among us Lord, save us
By your death and rising to new life Lord, save us
By your gift of the Holy Spirit Lord, save us
Be merciful to us sinners Lord, hear our prayer
Guide and protect your holy Church
Lord, hear our prayer
Keep our pope and all the clergy in faithful service to your Church Lord, hear our prayer
Bring all peoples together in trust and peace
Lord, hear our prayer
Strengthen us in your service
Lord, hear our prayer

SPECIAL INVOCATIONS

WHEN THERE IS BAPTISM DURING THE EASTER VIGIL

Give new life to these chosen ones by the grace of baptism Lord, hear our prayer

ORDINATIONS

Bless these chosen men Lord, hear our prayer
Bless these men and make them holy Lord, hear our prayer
Bless these men, make them holy, and consecrate them for their sacred duties Lord, hear our prayer

Ordination of one person:

Bless this chosen man Lord, hear our prayer
Bless this man and make him holy Lord, hear our prayer
Bless this man, make him holy, and consecrate him for his sacred duties Lord, hear our prayer

DEDICATION OF A CHURCH

Make this church holy and consecrate it to your worship Lord, hear our prayer

Jesus, Son of the living God Lord, hear our prayer
Christ, hear us
Christ, hear us

Lord Jesus, hear our prayer
Lord Jesus, hear our prayer

RITE OF RECEPTION OF BAPTIZED CHRISTIANS INTO FULL COMMUNION WITH THE CATHOLIC CHURCH

FOREWORD

In its constitution on the liturgy, the Second Vatican Council treated two somewhat analagous cases in a single article: (1) children who had been baptized in emergency circumstances and who should later be ritually welcomed into the parish church to signify that they "have already been received into the Church" by baptism, and (2) adults who had been baptized in other churches and ecclesial communities and who are to be ritually welcomed into full communion with the Catholic Church: "And a new rite is to be drawn up for converts who have already been validly baptized; it should indicate that they are now admitted to communion with the Church" (no. 69).

The first mandate was satisfied by a chapter in the *Rite of Baptism for Children* (1969): "Rite of Bringing a Baptized Child to the Church." The present rite deals with the second case and was published as an appendix to the *Ordo Initiationis Christianae Adultorum* (Congregation for Divine Worship, January 6, 1972). In the interval between the constitution on the liturgy and the publication of this ritual, however, it had become evident that the term "convert" or *neo-conversus* may not be appropriately applied to baptized Christians on the occasion of their entering into full Catholic communion.

The term "convert" properly refers to one who comes from unbelief to Christian belief. Although conversion of life is the continuing imperative of Christian believers, the concept of Christian conversion is applied only in reference to Christian initiation—through baptism, confirmation, and the eucharist—rather than to a subsequent change of Christian communion.

The conciliar decree on ecumenism, moreover, employs the expression, "imperfect communion," when speaking of Christian communities "separated from full communion with the Catholic Church." "Men who believe in Christ and have been truly baptized are in communion with the Catholic Church even though the communion is imperfect. The differences that exist in varying degrees . . . do indeed create many obstacles, some serious ones, to full ecclesiastical communion. . . . All who have been justified by faith in baptism are members of Christ's Body and have a right to be called Christian and so are correctly accepted as brothers by the children of the Catholic Church" (no. 3).

Thus the name of the present rite and its contents have been chosen to express, not conversion to Christian faith, but rather admission, reception, and welcome into the fullness of Catholic communion. This is the reason also that the present rite is to be kept entirely distinct from the catechumenate of Christian initiation: "Any confusion between catechumens and candidates for reception into communion should be absolutely avoided" (Introduction, below, no. 5). The rites of the catechumenate and Christian initiation are for unbelievers who come to Christian faith; the present rite is for Christian believers who have been baptized in another church or ecclesial community and who now seek to be received into full communion with the Catholic Church.

CHANGED DISCIPLINE

For the United States, the new rite replaces the discipline in effect since July 20, 1959 (Instruction of the Holy Office; see also decrees of the Plenary Councils of Baltimore: II, no. 242; III, no. 122). This provided, in the case of the reception of already baptized persons, for the abjuration of error by making the profession of faith and for absolution from excommunication; thus admitted to communion, the person could be absolved from his or her sins.

Besides altering the terminology of conversion, the revised rite replaces the discipline described above with one in accord with the directory on ecumenism (May 14, 1967). This includes two substantial changes:

1. The requirement of absolution from excommunication is now suppressed, and no abjuration of heresy is to be made (see nos. 19-20).

2. The previous norm concerning the conditional baptism of the doubtfully baptized has been changed to say that a conditional baptism, "if after serious investigation it seems necessary because of reasonable doubt," is to be celebrated privately (nos. 14-15; see Introduction, below, no. 7).

ELEMENTS OF THE RITE

The revised rite takes place within the eucharistic celebration, after the homily (in which the priest may appropriately speak of the significance of the reception into full communion). It has the following elements:

1. profession of faith by the community and by the person (or persons) to be received into full communion;

2. declaration of reception by the bishop or by the priest who takes his place;

3. sacrament of confirmation (unless the person has been confirmed);

4. general intercessions;

5. sign of peace (which need not be repeated before communion);

6. liturgy of the eucharist, in which the person receives communion for the first time with the members of the Catholic community.

The rite is clearly described in the rubrics (Chapter I, below). It is expected that the reception take place within the Sunday eucharistic celebration of the local church—either with the bishop presiding or, in the ordinary parish or other community celebration, with the priest presiding in the place of the bishop (see Introduction, below, no. 8). Such a celebration gives the full significance of entrance into communion and permits the whole Christian community to express its welcome and unity.

In some personal or family circumstances, the individual may not wish to be received into communion at the public Sunday eucharist. Even then, however, the reception should be part of a eucharistic celebration of some few members of the local community, including friends and others who have helped the baptized person to come into full communion. If even this is impossible, Chapter II describes the rite of reception outside Mass, in the context of a liturgy of the word.

READINGS

In most cases it may be appropriate to take the biblical readings from the Mass of the day and to base the homily, with suitable reference and application to the occasion of reception into full communion, upon these readings. If other readings are desired, they may be taken from the *Lectionary for Mass:*

1. Mass for the unity of Christians (nos. 811-815);

2. Mass for Christian Initiation (nos. 752-756);

3. Readings listed in Chapter III, below. The text of these readings is not reprinted, but the references in the *Lectionary for Mass* have been added for convenience.

INTRODUCTION

1. The rite for the reception of one born and baptized in a separated ecclesial community into full communion with the Catholic Church,[1] according to the Latin rite, is arranged so that no greater burden than necessary is demanded for reception into communion and unity[2] (see Acts 15:28).

2. In the case of Eastern Christians who enter into the fullness of Catholic communion, nothing more than a simple profession of Catholic faith is required, even if they are permitted, upon recourse to the Apostolic See, to transfer to the Latin rite.[3]

3. a. The rite should be seen as a celebration of the Church, with its climax in eucharistic communion. For this reason the rite of reception is generally celebrated within Mass.

b. Anything which has the appearance of triumphalism should be carefully avoided, and the manner of celebrating this Mass should be precisely defined. Both the ecumenical implications and the bond between the candidate and the parish community should be considered. Often it will be more appropriate to celebrate the Mass with only a few relatives and friends. If for a serious reason Mass cannot be celebrated, the reception should take place where possible during a liturgy of the word. The person to be received into full communion should be consulted about the form of reception.

4. If the reception is celebrated outside Mass, the connection with eucharistic communion should be made clear. Mass should be celebrated as soon as possible, so that the newly received person may participate fully with his Catholic brethren for the first time.

5. The baptized Christian is to receive both doctrinal and spiritual preparation, according to pastoral requirements in individual cases, for his/her reception into full communion

[1] See const. on the liturgy, no. 69b; decree on ecumenism, no. 3; Secretariat for the Promotion of Christian Unity, *Directorium*, no. 19: *AAS* 59 (1967) 581.
[2] See decree on ecumenism, no. 18.
[3] See decree on the Eastern Catholic Churches, nos. 25 and 4.

with the Catholic Church. He/she should grow in his/her spiritual adherence to the Church where he/she will find the fullness of his/her baptism.

During the period of preparation the candidate may share in worship according to the norms of the Directory on Ecumenism.

Any confusion between catechumens and candidates for reception into communion should be absolutely avoided.

6. No abjuration of heresy is required of one born and baptized outside the visible communion of the Catholic Church, but only the profession of faith.[4]

7. The sacrament of baptism may not be repeated, and conditional baptism is not permitted unless there is a reasonable doubt about the fact or validity of the baptism already received. If after serious investigation it seems necessary—because of such reasonable doubt—to confer baptism again conditionally, the minister should explain beforehand the reasons why baptism is conferred conditionally in this instance, and he should administer it in the private form.[5]

The local Ordinary shall determine, in individual cases, what rites are to be included or excluded in conditional baptism.

8. It is the office of the bishop to receive baptized Christians into full communion. But the priest to whom he entrusts the celebration of the rite has the faculty of confirming the candidate during the rite of admission,[6] unless the latter has already been validly confirmed.

9. If the profession of faith and reception take place within Mass, the one to be received—with due regard to the individual case—should confess his/her sins beforehand. He/she should first inform the confessor that he/she is about to be received into full communion. Any confessor who is lawfully approved may receive the confession.

[4]See Secretariat for the Promotion of Christian Unity, *Directorium*, nos. 19-20; *AAS* 59 (1967) 581.
[5]*Ibid.*, nos. 14-15: *AAS* 59 (1967) 580.
[6]See *Rite of Confirmation*, Introduction, no. 7.

10. At the reception, the candidate should be accompanied if possible by a sponsor, that is, the man or woman who has had the chief part in bringing him/her to full communion or in preparing him/her. Two sponsors may be permitted.

11. In the eucharistic celebration or, if the reception takes place outside Mass, in the Mass which follows, communion may be received under both kinds by the one received into communion, by his/her sponsors, parents, and spouse, if they are Catholics, by lay catechists who have instructed him/her, and also by all Catholics present, if the numbers or other circumstances suggest this.

12. Conferences of bishops may accommodate the rite of reception to various circumstances, in accord with the constitution on the liturgy (no. 63). The local Ordinary, moreover, may adapt the rite, enlarging or shortening it in view of special personal or local circumstances.[7]

13. The names of those received into full communion should be recorded in a special book, with the date and place of baptism also noted.

[7]See Secretariat for the Promotion of Christian Unity, *Directorium,* no. 19: *AAS,* 59 (1967) 581.

CHAPTER I

RITE OF RECEPTION WITHIN MASS

14. a. If the reception into full communion takes place on a solemnity or on a Sunday, the Mass of the day should be celebrated. On other days the Mass for the unity of Christians may be used.

b. The reception takes place after the homily. In the homily the celebrant should express gratitude to God and should speak of baptism as the basis for reception, of confirmation to be received or already received, and of the eucharist to be celebrated for the first time by the newly received Christian with his Catholic brethren.

c. At the end of the homily the celebrant gives a brief invitation for the candidate to come forward with his/her sponsor and to profess his/her faith with the community. He may use these or similar words:

N., of your own free will you have asked to be received into full communion with the Catholic Church. You have made your decision after careful thought under the guidance of the Holy Spirit. I now invite you to come forward with your sponsor and profess the Catholic faith in the presence of this community. This is the faith in which, for the first time, you will be one with us at the eucharistic table of the Lord Jesus, the sign of the Church's unity.

15. The one to be received then recites the Nicene Creed with the faithful. The profession of faith is always said in this Mass.

Afterwards, at the celebrant's invitation, the one to be received adds:

I believe and profess all that the holy Catholic Church believes, teaches, and proclaims to be revealed by God.

16. The celebrant then says (laying his right hand upon the head of the one to be received, unless confirmation follows):

**N., the Lord receives you into the Catholic Church.
His loving kindness has led you here
so that, in the unity of the Holy Spirit,
you may have full communion with us
in the faith that you have professed
in the presence of his family.**

17. If the one to be admitted has not been confirmed, the celebrant next lays his hands upon the candidate's head and begins the rite of confirmation with prayer.

**All-powerful God, Father of our Lord Jesus Christ,
by water and the Holy Spirit
you freed your son (daughter) from sin
and gave him (her) new life.
Send your Holy Spirit upon him (her)
to be his (her) helper and guide.
Give him (her) the spirit of wisdom and
understanding,
the spirit of right judgment and courage,
the spirit of knowledge and reverence.
Fill him (her) with the spirit of wonder and awe in your
presence.
We ask this through Christ our Lord.**
All: **Amen.**

The sponsor places his right hand upon the shoulder of the candidate.

The celebrant dips his right thumb in the chrism and makes the sign of the cross on the forehead of the one to be confirmed, as he says:

N., be sealed with the Gift of the Holy Spirit.

The newly confirmed responds:

Amen.

The celebrant says:

Peace be with you.

The newly confirmed responds:

And also with you.

18. After the confirmation the celebrant greets the newly received person, taking his/her hands as a sign of friendship and acceptance. With the permission of the Ordinary, another suitable gesture may be substituted depending on local and other circumstances.

If the one received is not confirmed, this greeting follows the formula of reception (no. 16).

19. The general intercessions follow the reception (and confirmation). In the introduction, the celebrant should mention baptism, confirmation, and the eucharist, and express gratitude to God. The one received into full communion is mentioned in the first of the intercessions (see no. 30).

20. After the general intercessions the sponsor and, if only a few persons are present, all the congregation may greet the newly received person in a friendly manner. In this case the sign of peace before communion may be omitted. Finally the one received into communion returns to his/her place.

21. Then Mass continues. It is fitting that communion be received under both kinds by the one received and by the others mentioned in no. 11.

CHAPTER II

RITE OF RECEPTION OUTSIDE MASS

22. If for a serious reason the reception into full communion takes place outside Mass, a liturgy of the word is to be celebrated.

23. The celebrant vests in an alb (or at least in a surplice) and a stole of festive color. First he greets those present.

24. The celebration begins with (an appropriate song and) a reading from Scripture on which the homily is based (see no. 14b).

25. The reception follows, as described above (nos. 14c-19).

26. The general intercessions are concluded with the Lord's Prayer, sung or recited by all present, and the priest's blessing.

27. The sponsor and, if only a few are present, all the congregation may greet the newly received person in a friendly way. Then all depart in peace.

28. If in exceptional circumstances the liturgy of the word cannot be celebrated, everything takes place as above, beginning with the introductory words of the celebrant. He should start with a quotation from scripture (for example, in praise of God's mercy which has led the candidate into full communion) and speak of the eucharistic communion which will soon follow.

CHAPTER III

TEXTS

29. I. BIBLICAL READINGS

The biblical readings for Mass or for the liturgy of the word may be taken in whole or in part from the Mass of the day, the Mass for the unity of Christians (see *Lectionary for Mass*, nos. 811-815), or the Mass for Christian initiation (see *ibid.*, nos. 752-756).

When the rite is celebrated outside Mass, the following texts may be used:

NEW TESTAMENT READINGS

1. **Romans 8:28-39**
He predestined us to become true images of his Son.
(Lectionary for Mass, 110, 482)

2. **1 Corinthians 12:31-13:13**
Love never ends *(Lect., 73)*

3. **Ephesians 1:3-14**
The Father chose us in Christ to be holy and spotless in love.
(Lect., 105)

4. **Ephesians 4:1-7, 11-13**
There is one Lord, one faith, one baptism, one God, the Father of all. *(Lect., 477-478)*

5. **Philippians 4:4-8**
Fill your minds with everything that is holy. *(Lect., 9, 140)*

6. **1 Thessalonians 5:16-24**
May you all be kept blameless, spirit, soul and body, for the coming of our Lord Jesus Christ. *(Lect., 8)*

RESPONSORIAL PSALMS

1. Psalm 27:1, 4, 8b-9abc, 13-14
℟. (1a) **The Lord is my light and my salvation.**

2. Psalm 42:2-3; 43:3,4
℟. (42:3a) **My soul is thirsting for the living God.**

3. Psalm 61:2-3a, 3bc-4, 5-6, 9
℟. (4a) **Lord, you are my refuge.**

4. Psalm 63:2,3-4, 5-6, 8-9
℟. (2b) **My soul is thirsting for you, O Lord my God.**

5. Psalm 65:2-3a, 3b-4, 5, 6
℟. (2a) **It is right to praise you in Zion, O God.**

6. Psalm 121:1-2, 3-4, 5-6, 7-8
℟. (2a) **Our help is from the Lord.**

GOSPELS

1. **Matthew 5:2-12a**
Rejoice and be glad for your reward will be great in heaven. *(Lect., 71)*

2. **Matthew 5:13-16**
Let your light shine before men. *(Lect., 74)*

3. **Matthew 11:25-30**
You have hidden these things from the learned and the clever and revealed them to children. *(Lect., 101)*

4. **John 3:16-21**
Everyone who believes in him will have everlasting life. *(Lect., 269)*

5. **John 14:15-23, 26-27**
My Father will love him, and we will come to him. *(Lect., 56, 285, 58)*

6. **John 15:1-6**
I am the vine and you are the branches. *(Lect., 54)*

30. II. SAMPLE GENERAL INTERCESSIONS

Brothers and sisters: our brother (sister) N. was already united to Christ through baptism (and confirmation). Now, with thanksgiving to God, we have received him (her) into full communion with the Catholic Church (and confirmed him (her) with the gifts of the Holy Spirit). Soon he (she) will share with us at the table of the Lord. Rejoice with the member we have just received into the Catholic Church. With him (her), let us seek the grace and mercy of our Savior.

That N. may have the help and guidance of the Holy Spirit to persevere faithfully in the choice he (she) has made, we pray to the Lord.
℟. Lord, hear our prayer.

That all Christian believers and the communities to which they belong may come to perfect unity, we pray to the Lord.
℟. Lord, hear our prayer.

That the Church (Communion) in which N. was baptized and received his (her) formation as a Christian may always grow in the knowledge of Christ and proclaim him more effectively, we pray to the Lord.
℟. Lord, hear our prayer.

That all whom God's grace has touched may be led to the fullness of truth in Christ, we pray to the Lord.
℟. Lord, hear our prayer.

That those who do not yet believe in Christ the Lord may enter the way of salvation by the light of the Holy Spirit, we pray to the Lord.
℟. Lord, hear our prayer.

That all men may be freed from hunger and war and live in peace and tranquillity, we pray to the Lord.
℟. Lord, hear our prayer.

That we who have received the gift of faith may persevere in it to the end of our lives, we pray to the Lord.
℟. Lord, hear our prayer.

PRAYER

God our Father,
hear the prayers we offer.
May our loving service be pleasing to you.
Grant this through Christ our Lord.
℟. Amen.

31. If the reception is celebrated outside Mass, the transition from the general intercessions to the Lord's Prayer (see no. 26) can be expressed in these or similar words:

Celebrant:

Brothers and sisters,
let us join our prayers together

and offer them to God
as our Lord Jesus Christ taught us to pray.

All:

Our Father . . .

If the person received into full communion is accustomed to the final doxology *For the kingdom,* etc., it should be used in this place.

APPENDIX

RESPONSORIAL PSALMS

1. Ps. 27: 1, 4, 8b-9abc, 13-14
℟. (1a) **The Lord is my light and my salvation.**

The Lord is my light and my salvation;
whom should I fear?
The Lord is my life's refuge;
of whom should I be afraid? ℟.

One thing I ask of the Lord;
this I seek:
To dwell in the house of the Lord
all the days of my life,
That I may gaze on the loveliness of the Lord
and contemplate his temple. ℟.

Your presence, O Lord, I seek.
Hide not your face from me;
do not in anger repel your servant.
You are my helper: cast me not off. ℟.

I believe that I shall see the bounty of the Lord
in the land of the living.
Wait for the Lord with courage;
be stouthearted, and wait for the Lord. ℟.

2. Ps. 42: 2-3; 43: 3, 4
℟. (42: 3a) **My soul is thirsting for the living God.**

As the hind longs for the running waters,
so my soul longs for you, O God. ℟.

Athirst is my soul for God, the living God.
When shall I go and behold the face of God? ℟.

Send forth your light and your fidelity;
they shall lead me on
And bring me to your holy mountain,
to your dwelling-place. ℟.

Then will I go in to the altar of God,
the God of my gladness and joy;

Then will I give you thanks upon the harp,
O God, my God! ℟.

3. Ps. 61: 2-3a, 3bc-4, 5-6, 9
℟. (4a) **Lord, you are my refuge.**

Hear, O God, my cry;
listen to my prayer!
From the earth's end I call to you
as my heart grows faint. ℟.

You will set me high upon a rock; you
will give me rest,
for you are my refuge,
a tower of strength against the enemy.
Oh, that I might lodge in your tent forever,
take refuge in the shelter of your wings! ℟.

You indeed, O God, have accepted my vows;
you granted me the heritage of those
who fear your name.
So will I sing the praises of your name forever,
fulfilling my vows day by day. ℟.

4. Ps. 63: 2, 3-4, 5-6, 8-9
℟. (2b) **My soul is thirsting for you, O Lord my God.**

O God, you are my God whom I seek;
for you my flesh pines and my soul thirsts
like the earth, parched, lifeless and
without water. ℟.

Thus have I gazed toward you in the sanctuary
to see your power and your glory,
For your kindness is a greater good than life;
my lips shall glorify you. ℟.

Thus will I bless you while I live;
lifting up my hands, I will call upon your name.
As with the riches of a banquet shall
my soul be satisfied,
and with exultant lips my mouth shall
praise you. ℟.

You are my help,
and in the shadow of your wings I shout for joy.
My soul clings fast to you;
your right hand upholds me. ℟.

5. Ps. 65: 2-3a, 3b-4, 5, 6
℟. (2a) **It is right to praise you in Zion, O God.**

To you we owe our hymn of praise,
O God, in Zion;
To you must vows be fulfilled,
you who hear prayers. ℟.

To you all flesh must come
because of wicked deeds.
We are overcome by our sins;
it is you who pardon them. ℟.

Happy the man you choose, and bring
to dwell in your courts.
May we be filled with the good things
of your house,
the holy things of your temple! ℟.

With awe-inspiring deeds of justice you answer us,
O God our savior,
The hope of all the ends of the earth
and of the distant seas. ℟.

6. Ps. 121: 1-2, 3-4, 5-6, 7-8
℟. (2a) **Our help is from the Lord.**

I lift up my eyes toward the mountains;
whence shall help come to me?
My help is from the Lord,
who made heaven and earth. ℟.

May he not suffer your foot to slip;
may he slumber not who guards you:
Indeed he neither slumbers nor sleeps,
the guardian of Israel. ℟.

The Lord is your guardian; the Lord
is your shade;
he is beside you at your right hand.

The sun shall not harm you by day,
nor the moon by night. ℟.

The Lord will guard you from all evil;
he will guard your life.
The Lord will guard your coming
and your going,
both now and forever. ℟.

RITE OF CONFIRMATION

RITE OF CONFIRMATION

SACRED CONGREGATION FOR DIVINE WORSHIP

Prot. n. 800/71

DECREE

In the sacrament of confirmation the apostles and the bishops who are their successors hand on to the baptized the special gift of the Holy Spirit, promised by Christ the Lord and poured out upon the apostles at Pentecost. Thus the initiation in the Christian life is completed so that believers are strengthened by power from heaven, made true witnesses of Christ in word and deed, and bound more closely to the Church.

To make "the intimate connection of this sacrament with the whole of Christian initiation" clearer, the Second Vatican Council decreed that the rite of confirmation should be revised.[1]

Now that this work has been completed and approved by Pope Paul VI in the apostolic constitution *Divinae consortium naturae* of August 15, 1971, the Congregation for Divine Worship has published the new Rite of Confirmation. It is to replace the rite now in use in the Roman Pontifical and Ritual. The Congregation declares the present edition to be the typical edition.

Anything to the contrary notwithstanding.

From the Office of the Congregation for Divine Worship, August 22, 1971.

Arturo Cardinal Tabera
prefect

Annibale Bugnini
secretary

[1]See Second Vatican Council, Constitution, *Sacrosanctum Concilium*, no. 71: *AAS*, 56 (1964) 118.

APOSTOLIC CONSTITUTION ON THE SACRAMENT OF CONFIRMATION

PAUL, BISHOP

Servant of the Servants of God For an Everlasting Memorial

The sharing in the divine nature which is granted to men through the grace of Christ has a certain likeness to the origin, development, and nourishing of natural life. The faithful are born anew by baptism, strengthened by the sacrament of confirmation, and finally are sustained by the food of eternal life in the eucharist. By means of these sacraments of Christian initiation, they thus receive in increasing measure the treasures of divine life and advance toward the perfection of charity. It has rightly been written: "The body is washed, that the soul may be cleansed; the body is anointed, that the soul may be consecrated; the body is signed, that the soul too may be fortified; the body is overshadowed by the laying on of hands, that the soul too may be enlightened by the Spirit; the body is fed on the body and blood of Christ, that the soul too should be nourished by God."[1]

Conscious of its pastoral purpose, the Second Vatican Ecumenical Council devoted special attention to these sacraments of initiation. It prescribed that the rites should be suitably revised in order to make them more suited to the understanding of the faithful. Since the *Rite for the Baptism of Children,* revised at the mandate of that General Council and published at our command, is already in use, it is now fitting to publish the rite of confirmation, in order to show the unity of Christian initiation in its true light.

In fact, careful attention and application have been devoted in these last years to the task of revising the manner of celebrating this sacrament. The aim of this work has been that "the intimate connection which this sacrament has with the whole of Christian initiation should be more lucidly set forth."[2] The link between confirmation and the other sacraments of initiation is shown forth more clearly not only by

[1]Tertullian, *De resurrectione mortuorum,* VIII, 3: *CCL,* 2, 931.

[2]See Second Vatican Council, Constitution, *Sacrosanctum Concilium,* no. 71: *AAS,* 56 (1964) 118.

closer association of these sacraments but also by the rite and words by which confirmation is conferred. This is done so that the rite and words of this sacrament may "express more clearly the holy things which they signify. The Christian people, so far as possible, should be able to understand them with ease and take full and active part in the celebration as a community."[3]

For that purpose, it has been our wish also to include in this revision what concerns the very essence of the rite of confirmation, through which the faithful receive the Holy Spirit as a Gift.

The New Testament shows how the Holy Spirit assisted Christ in fulfilling his messianic mission. On receiving the baptism of John, Jesus saw the Spirit descending on him (see Mark 1:10) and remaining with him (see John 1:32). He was impelled by the Spirit to undertake his public ministry as the Messiah, relying on the Spirit's presence and assistance. Teaching the people of Nazareth, he shows by what he said that the words of Isaiah, "The Spirit of the Lord is upon me," referred to himself (see Luke 4:17-21).

He later promised his disciples that the Holy Spirit would help them also to bear fearless witness to their faith even before persecutors (see Luke 12:12). The day before he suffered, he assured his apostles that he would send the Spirit of truth from his Father (see John 15:26) to stay with them "for ever" (John 14:16) and help them to be his witnesses (see John 15:26). Finally, after his resurrection, Christ promised the coming descent of the Holy Spirit: "You will receive power when the Holy Spirit comes down on you; then you are to be my witnesses" (Acts 1:8; see Luke 24:49).

And in fact, on the day of the feast of Pentecost, the Holy Spirit came down in an extraordinary way on the Apostles as they were gathered together with Mary the mother of Jesus and the group of disciples. They were so "filled with" the Holy Spirit (Acts 2:4) that by divine inspiration they began to proclaim "the mighty works of God." Peter regarded the Spirit who had thus come down upon the Apostles as the gift of the messianic age (see Acts 2:17-18). Those who believed the Apostles' preaching were then baptized and they too received "the gift of the Holy Spirit" (Acts

[3] *Ibid.*, no. 21: p. 106.

2:38). From that time on the apostles, in fulfillment of Christ's wish, imparted the gift of the Spirit to the newly baptized by the laying on of hands to complete the grace of baptism. Hence it is that the Letter to the Hebrews lists among the first elements of Christian instruction the teaching about baptisms and the laying on of hands (Hebrews 6:2). This laying on of hands is rightly recognized by Catholic tradition as the beginning of the sacrament of confirmation, which in a certain way perpetuates the grace of Pentecost in the Church.

This makes clear the specific importance of confirmation for sacramental initiation by which the faithful "as members of the living Christ are incorporated into him and made like him through baptism and through confirmation and the eucharist."[4] In baptism, the newly baptized receive forgiveness of sins, adoption as sons of God, and the character of Christ, by which they are made members of the Church and for the first time become sharers in the priesthood of their Savior (see 1 Peter 2:5, 9). Through the sacrament of confirmation, those who have been born anew in baptism receive the inexpressible Gift, the Holy Spirit himself, by which "they are endowed . . . with special strength."[5] Moreover, having received the character of this sacrament, they are "bound more intimately to the Church"[6] and "they are more strictly obliged to spread and defend the faith both by word and by deed as true witnesses of Christ."[7] Finally, confirmation is so closely linked with the holy eucharist[8] that the faithful, after being signed by holy baptism and confirmation, are incorporated fully into the body of Christ by participation in the eucharist.[9]

From ancient times the conferring of the gift of the Holy Spirit has been carried out in the Church with various rites. These rites underwent many changes in the East and the West, while always keeping the significance of a conferring

[4]See Second Vatican Council, decree, *Ad gentes*, no. 36: *AAS*, 58 (1966) 983.

[5]Second Vatican Council, dogmatic constitution *Lumen gentium*, no. 11: *AAS*, 57 (1965) 15.

[6]*Ibid.*

[7]*Ibid.*; see *Ad gentes*, no. 11: *AAS*, 58 (1966) 959-960.

[8]See Second Vatican Council, decree, *Presbyterorum Ordinis*, no. 5: *AAS*, 58 (1966) 997.

[9]See *ibid.*: pp. 997–998.

of the Holy Spirit.[10]

In many Eastern rites, it seems that from early times a rite of anointing, not then clearly distinguished from baptism, prevailed for the conferring of the Holy Spirit. That rite continues in use today in the greater part of the churches of the East.

In the West there are very ancient witnesses concerning the part of Christian initiation which was later distinctly recognized as the sacrament of confirmation. After the baptismal washing and before the eucharistic meal, the performance of many rites is indicated, such as anointing, the laying on of the hand and consignation.[11] These are contained both in liturgical documents[12] and in many testimonies of the Fathers. In the course of the centuries, problems and doubts arose as to what belonged with certainty to the essence of the rite of confirmation. It is fitting to mention at least some of the elements which, from the thirteenth century onwards, in the ecumenical councils and in the documents of the popes, cast light on the importance of anointing while at the same time not allowing the laying on of hands to be obscured.

Our predecessor Innocent III wrote: "By the anointing of the forehead the laying on of the hand is designated, which is otherwise called confirmation, since through it the Holy

[10]See Origen, *De Principiis,* I, 3, 2: *GCS,* 22, 49 sq.; *Comm. in Ep. ad Rom.,* V, 8; *PG,* 14, 1038; Cyril of Jerusalem, *Catech.* XVI, 26; XXI, 1-7: *PG,* 33, 956; 1088-1093.

[11]See Tertullian, *De Baptismo,* VII-VIII: *CCL,* 1, 282 sq.; B. Botte, *La tradition apostolique de Saint Hippolyte: Liturgiewissenschaftliche Quellen und Forschungen,* 39 (Münster in W., 1963) 52-54; Ambrose, *De Sacramentis,* II, 24; III, 2, 8; VI, 2, 9: *CSEL,* 73, pp. 36, 42, 74-75; *De Mysteriis,* VII, 42: *ibid.* p. 106.

[12]*Liber Sacramentorum Romanae Ecclesiae Ordinis Anni circuli,* ed. L. C. Mohlberg: *Rerum Ecclesiasticarum Documenta, Fontes,* IV (Rome, 1960) 75; *Das Sacramentarium Gregorianum nach dem Aachener Urexemplar,* ed. H. Lietzman: *Liturgiegeschichtliche Quellen,* 3 (Münster in W., 1921) 53 sq.; *Liber Ordinum,* ed. M. Ferotin: *Monumenta Ecclesiae Liturgica,* V (Paris, 1904) 33 sq.; *Missale Gallicanum Vetus,* ed. L. C. Mohlberg: *Rerum Ecclesiasticarum Documenta, Fontes,* III (Rome, 1958) 42: *Missale Gothicum,* ed. L. C. Mohlberg: *Rerum Ecclesiasticarum Documenta,* V (Rome, 1961) 67; C. Vogel - R. Elze, *Le Pontifical Romano-Germanique du XII*^e^ *siècle, Le Texte, II; Studi e Testi,* 227 (Vatican City, 1963) 109; M. Andrieu, *Le Pontifical Romain au Moyen-Age,* t. 1, *Le Pontifical Romain du XII*^e^ *siècle: Studi e Testi,* 86 (Vatican City, 1938) 247 sq., 289; t. 2, *Le Pontifical de la Curie Romaine au XIII*^e^ *siècle: Studi e Testi,* 87 (Vatican City, 1940) 452 sq.

Spirit is given for growth and strength."[13] Another of our predecessors, Innocent IV, recalls that the Apostles conferred the Holy Spirit "through the laying on of the hand, which confirmation or the anointing of the forehead represents."[14] In the profession of faith of Emperor Michael Palaeologus, which was read at the Second Council of Lyons, mention is made of the sacrament of confirmation, which "bishops confer by the laying on of the hands, anointing with chrism those who have been baptized."[15] The Decree for the Armenians, issued by the Council of Florence, declares that the "matter" of the sacrament of confirmation is "chrism made of olive oil . . . and balsam,"[16] and, quoting the words of the Acts of the Apostles concerning Peter and John, who gave the Holy Spirit through the laying on of hands (see Acts 8:17), it adds: "in place of that laying on of the hand, in the Church confirmation is given."[17] The Council of Trent, though it had no intention of defining the essential rite of confirmation, only designated it with the name of the holy chrism of confirmation.[18] Benedict XIV made this declaration: "Therefore let this be said, which is beyond dispute: in the Latin Church the sacrament of confirmation is conferred by using sacred chrism or olive oil, mixed with balsam and blessed by the bishop, and by tracing the sign of the cross by the minister of the sacrament on the forehead of the recipient, while the same minister pronounces the words of the form."[19]

Many theologians, taking account of these declarations and traditions, maintained that for valid administration of confirmation there was required only anointing with chrism, done by placing the hand on the forehead. In spite of this, however, in the rites of the Latin Church a laying of hands

[13]Ep. *Cum venisset: PL,* 215, 285. The profession of faith which the same pope prescribed for the Waldensians includes the following: *Confirmationem ab episcopo factam, id est impositionem manuum, sanctam et venerande accipiendam esse censemus: PL,* 215, 1511.

[14]Ep. *Sub Catholicae professione:* Mansi, *Conc. Coll.,* t. 23, 579.

[15]Mansi, *Conc. Coll.,* t. 24, 71.

[16]*Epistolae Pontificiae ad Concilium Florentinum spectantes,* ed. G. Hofmann: *Concilium Florentinun,* vol. I, ser. A. part II (Rome, 1944) 128.

[17]*Ibid.,* 129.

[18]*Concilii Tridentini Actorum pars altera,* ed. S. Ehses: *Concilium Tridentinum,* V, Act. II (Fribourg Br., 1911) 996.

[19]Ep. *Ex quo primum tempore,* 52: *Benedicti XIV. . . . Bullarium,* t. III (Prato, 1847) 320.

upon those to be confirmed was always prescribed before the anointing.

With regard to the words of the rite by which the Holy Spirit is given, it should be noted that, already in the primitive Church, Peter and John, in order to complete the initiation of those baptized in Samaria, prayed for them to receive the Holy Spirit and then laid hands on them (see Acts 8:15-17). In the East, in the fourth and fifth centuries there appear in the rite of anointing the first indications of the words "signaculum doni Spiritus Sancti."[20] These words were quickly accepted by the Church of Constantinople and are still used by the Churches of the Byzantine rite.

In the West, however, the words of this rite, which completed baptism, were not defined until the twelfth and thirteenth centuries. But in the twelfth century Roman Pontifical the formula which later became the common one first occurs: "I sign you with the sign of the cross and confirm you with the chrism of salvation. In the name of the Father and of the Son and of the Holy Spirit."[21]

From what we have recalled, it is clear that in the administration of confirmation in the East and the West, though in different ways, the most important place was occupied by the anointing, which in a certain way represents the apostolic laying on of hands. Since this anointing with chrism well represents the spiritual anointing of the Holy Spirit, who is given to the faithful, we intend to confirm its existence and importance.

As regards the words which are pronounced in confirmation, we have examined with due consideration the dignity of the venerable formula used in the Latin Church, but we judge preferable the very ancient formula belonging to the Byzantine rite, by which the Gift of the Holy Spirit himself is expressed and the outpouring of the Spirit which took place on the day of Pentecost is recalled (see Acts 2:1-4, 38). We therefore adopt this formula, rendering it almost word for word.

[20]See Cyril of Jerusalem, *Catech.* XVIII, 33, 1056; Asterius, Bishop of Amasea, *In parabolam de filio prodigo,* in "Photii Bibliotheca," Cod. 271: *PG,* 104, 213. See also *Epistola cuiusdam Patriarchae Constantinopolitani ad Martyrium Episcopum Antiochenum: PG,* 119, 900.

[21]M. Andrieu, *Le Pontifical Romain au Moyen-Age,* t. 1, *Le Pontifical Romain du XIIe siècle: Studi e Testi,* 86 (Vatican City, 1938) 247.

Therefore, in order that the revision of the rite of confirmation may fittingly embrace also the essence of the sacramental rite, by our supreme apostolic authority we decree and lay down that in the Latin Church the following should be observed for the future:

The Sacrament of Confirmation is conferred through the anointing with chrism on the forehead, which is done by the laying on of the hand, and through the words: "Accipe Signaculum Doni Spiritus Sancti."

Although the laying of hands on the candidates, which is done with the prescribed prayer before the anointing, does not belong to the essence of the sacramental rite, it is nevertheless to be held in high esteem, in that it contributes to the integral perfection of that rite and to a clearer understanding of the sacrament. It is evident that this preceding laying on of hands differs from the laying on of the hand by which the anointing is done on the forehead.

Having established and declared all these elements concerning the essential rite of the sacrament of confirmation, we also approve by our apostolic authority the order for the same sacrament, which has been revised by the Congregation for Divine Worship, after consultation with the Congregations for the Doctrine of the Faith, for the Discipline of the Sacraments, and for the Evangelization of Peoples as regards the matters which are within their competence. The Latin edition of the order containing the new form will come into force as soon as it is published; the editions of the vernacular languages, prepared by the episcopal conferences and confirmed by the Apostolic See, will come into force on the dates to be laid down by the individual conferences. The old order may be used until the end of the year 1972. From January 1, 1973, however, only the new order is to be used by those concerned.

We intend that everything that we have laid down and prescribed should be firm and effective in the Latin Church, notwithstanding, where relevant, the apostolic constitutions and ordinances issued by our predecessors, and other prescriptions, even if worthy of special mention.

Given in Rome, at Saint Peter's, on the fifteenth day of August, the Solemnity of the Assumption of the Blessed Virgin Mary, in the year 1971, the ninth of our pontificate.

PAUL PP. VI

INTRODUCTION

I. DIGNITY OF CONFIRMATION

1. Those who have been baptized continue on the path of Christian initiation through the sacrament of confirmation. In this sacrament they receive the Holy Spirit, who was sent upon the apostles by the Lord on Pentecost.

2. This giving of the Holy Spirit conforms believers more perfectly to Christ and strengthens them so that they may bear witness to Christ for the building up of his body in faith and love. They are so marked with the character or seal of the Lord that the sacrament of confirmation cannot be repeated.

II. OFFICES AND MINISTRIES IN THE CELEBRATION OF CONFIRMATION

3. It is the responsibility of the people of God to prepare the baptized for confirmation. It is the responsibility of the pastors to see that all the baptized come to the fullness of Christian initiation and are carefully prepared for confirmation.

Adult catechumens, who are to be confirmed immediately after baptism, have the help of the Christian community and, in particular, the formation which is given to them during the catechumenate, catechesis, and common liturgical celebrations. Catechists, sponsors, and members of the local church should participate in the catechumenate. The steps of the catechumenate will be appropriately adapted to those who, baptized in infancy, are confirmed only as adults.

The initiation of children into the sacramental life is for the most part the responsibility and concern of Christian parents. They are to form and gradually increase a spirit of faith in the children and, with the help of catechetical institutions, prepare them for the fruitful reception of the sacraments of confirmation and the eucharist. The role of the parents is also expressed by their active participation in the celebration of the sacraments.

4. Attention should be paid to the festive and solemn

character of the liturgical service, especially its significance for the local church, especially if all the candidates are assembled for a common celebration. The whole people of God, represented by the families and friends of the candidates and by members of the local community, will be invited to take part in the celebration and will express its faith in the fruits of the Holy Spirit.

5. Ordinarily there should be a sponsor for each of those to be confirmed. The sponsor brings the candidate to receive the sacrament, presents him to the minister for the anointing, and will later help him to fulfill his baptismal promises faithfully under the influence of the Holy Spirit.

In view of contemporary pastoral circumstances, it is desirable that the godparent at baptism, if present, also be the sponsor at confirmation; canon 796, no. 1 is abrogated. This change expresses more clearly the relationship between baptism and confirmation and also makes the function and responsibility of the sponsor more effective.

Nonetheless the choice of a special sponsor for confirmation is not excluded. Even the parents themselves may present their children for confirmation. It is for the local Ordinary to determine diocesan practice in the light of local circumstances.

6. Pastors will see that the sponsor, chosen by the candidate or his family, is spiritually qualified for the office and satisfies these requirements:

a) that he be sufficiently mature for this role;
b) that he belong to the Catholic Church and have been initiated in the three sacraments of baptism, confirmation, and the eucharist;
c) that he be not prohibited by law from exercising the role of sponsor.

7. The original minister of confirmation is the bishop. Ordinarily the sacrament is administered by the bishop so that there will be a more evident relationship to the first pouring forth of the Holy Spirit on Pentecost. After the apostles were filled with the Holy Spirit, they themselves gave the Spirit to the faithful through the laying on of their hands. Thus the reception of the Spirit through the ministry of the bishop

shows the close bond which joins the confirmed to the Church and the mandate to be witnesses of Christ among men.

In addition to the bishop, the law gives the faculty to confirm to the following:

a) apostolic administrators who are not bishops, prelates or abbots *nullius*, vicars and prefects apostolic, vicars capitular, within the limits of their territory and while they hold office;

b) priests who, in virtue of an office which they lawfully hold, baptize an adult or a child old enough for catechesis or receive a validly baptized adult into full communion with the Church;

c) in danger of death, provided a bishop is not easily available or is lawfully impeded: pastors and parochial vicars; in their absence, their parochial associates; priests who are in charge of special parishes lawfully established; administrators; substitutes; and assistants;[1] in the absence of all of the preceding, any priest who is not subject to censure or canonical penalty.

8. In case of true necessity and special reason, for example, the large number of persons to be confirmed, the minister of confirmation mentioned in no. 7 or the extraordinary minister designated by special indult of the Apostolic See or by law may associate other priests with himself in the administration of this sacrament.

It is required that these priests:

a) have a particular function or office in the diocese, namely, vicars general, episcopal vicars or delegates, district or regional vicars,[2] or those who by mandate of the Ordinary hold equivalent offices; or

b) be the pastors of the places where confirmation is conferred, pastors of the places where the candidates belong, or priests who have had a special part in the catechetical preparation of the candidates.

[1]See canons 451, 471, 476, 216, §4, 472, 474, 475.
[2]See canon 217, §1.

III. CELEBRATION OF THE SACRAMENT

9. The sacrament of confirmation is conferred through the anointing with chrism on the forehead, which is done by the laying on of the hand, and through the words: **Be sealed with the Gift of the Holy Spirit.**

Even though the laying of hands on the candidates with the prayer **All-powerful God** does not pertain to the valid giving of the sacrament, it is to be strongly emphasized for the integrity of the rite and the fuller understanding of the sacrament.

Priests who are sometimes associated with the principal minister in conferring the sacrament join him in laying their hands on all the candidates together, but they do not say the prayer.

The whole rite has a twofold meaning. The laying of hands on the candidates by the bishop and the concelebrating priests is the biblical gesture by which the gift of the Holy Spirit is invoked. This is well adapted to the understanding of the Christian people. The anointing with chrism and the accompanying words express clearly the effects of the giving of the Holy Spirit. Signed with the perfumed oil, the baptized person receives the indelible character, the seal of the Lord, together with the gift of the Spirit, which conforms him more closely to Christ and gives him the grace of spreading the Lord's presence among men.

10. The chrism is consecrated by the bishop in the Mass which is ordinarily celebrated on Holy Thursday for this purpose.

11. Adult catechumens and children who are baptized at an age when they are old enough for catechesis should ordinarily be admitted to confirmation and the eucharist at the same time they receive baptism. If this is impossible, they should receive confirmation in a common celebration (see no. 4). Similarly, adults who were baptized in infancy should, after suitable preparation, receive confirmation and the eucharist in a common celebration.

With regard to children, in the Latin Church the administration of confirmation is generally postponed until about the seventh year. For pastoral reasons, however, especially to strengthen the faithful in complete obedience to Christ the

Lord and in loyal testimony to him, episcopal conferences may choose an age which seems more appropriate, so that the sacrament is given at a more mature age after appropriate formation.

In this case the necessary precautions should be taken so that children will be confirmed at the proper time, even before the use of reason, where there is danger of death or other serious difficulty. They should not be deprived of the benefit of this sacrament.

12. One must be baptized to receive the sacrament of confirmation. In addition, if the baptized person has the use of reason, it is required that he be in a state of grace, properly instructed, and able to renew his baptismal promises.

It is the responsibility of the episcopal conferences to determine more precisely the pastoral methods for the preparation of children for confirmation.

With regard to adults, the same principles should be followed, with suitable adaptations, which are in effect in individual dioceses for the admission of catechumens to baptism and the eucharist. In particular, suitable catechesis should precede confirmation, and there should be sufficient effective relationship of the candidates with the Christian community and with individual members of the faithful to assist in their formation. This formation should be directed toward their giving the witness of a Christian life and exercising the Christian apostolate, while developing a genuine desire to participate in the eucharist (see *Introduction to the Christian Initiation of Adults,* no. 19).

Sometimes the preparation of a baptized adult for confirmation is part of his preparation for marriage. In such cases, if it is foreseen that the conditions for a fruitful reception of confirmation cannot be satisfied, the local Ordinary will judge whether it is better to defer confirmation until after the marriage.

If one who has the use of reason is confirmed in danger of death, he should be prepared spiritually, so far as possible, depending upon the circumstances of the individual case.

13. Ordinarily confirmation takes place within Mass in

order to express more clearly the fundamental connection of this sacrament with the entirety of Christian initiation. The latter reaches its culmination in the communion of the body and blood of Christ. The newly confirmed should therefore participate in the eucharist which completes their Christian initiation.

If the candidates for confirmation are children who have not received the eucharist and are not admitted to their first communion at this liturgical celebration or if there are other special circumstances, confirmation should be celebrated outside Mass. When this occurs, there should first be a celebration of the word of God.

It is fitting that the minister of confirmation celebrate the Mass or, better, concelebrate the Mass, especially with the priests who may join him in the administration of the sacrament.

If the Mass is celebrated by someone else, it is proper that the bishop preside over the liturgy of the word and that he give the blessing at the end of Mass.

Emphasis should be given to the celebration of the word of God which begins the rite of confirmation. It is from the hearing of the word of God that the many-sided power of the Holy Spirit flows upon the Church and upon each one of the baptized and confirmed, and it is by this word that God's will is manifest in the life of Christians.

The saying of the Lord's Prayer by the newly confirmed with the rest of the people is also of very great importance, whether during Mass before communion or outside Mass before the blessing, because it is the Spirit who prays in us, and in the Spirit the Christian says "*Abba,* Father."

14. The pastor should record the names of the minister, those confirmed, parents and sponsors, and the date and place of confirmation in a special book. The notation in the baptismal register should also be made according to law.

15. If the pastor of the newly-confirmed person is not present, the minister should promptly inform him of the confirmation, either personally or through a representative.

IV. ADAPTATIONS IN THE RITE OF CONFIRMATION

16. In virtue of the Constitution on the Sacred Liturgy (art. 63b), episcopal conferences have the right to prepare a title in particular rituals corresponding to this title of the Roman Pontifical on confirmation. This is to be adapted to the needs of individual regions so that, after confirmation of their action by the Apostolic See, the ritual may be used in the territory.[3]

17. The episcopal conference will consider whether, in view of local circumstances and the culture and traditions of the people, it is opportune:

a) to make suitable adaptations of the formulas for the renewal of baptismal promises and professions, either following the text in the rite of baptism or accommodating these formulas to the circumstances of the candidates for confirmation;

b) to introduce a different manner for the minister to give the sign of peace after the anointing, either to each individual or to all the newly confirmed together.

18. The minister of confirmation may introduce some explanations into the rite in individual cases in view of the capacity of candidates for confirmation. He may also make appropriate accommodations in the existing texts, for example, by expressing these in a kind of dialogue, especially with children.

When confirmation is given by a minister who is not a bishop, whether by concession of the general law or by special indult of the Apostolic See, it is fitting for him to mention in the homily that the bishop is the original minister of the sacrament and the reason why priests receive the faculty to confirm from the law or by an indult of the Apostolic See.

V. PREPARATIONS

19. The following should be prepared for confirmation:

a) vestments for the celebration of Mass, for the bishop and for the priests who concelebrate with him; if the bishop

[3]See *Rite of Baptism for Children* (1969), General Instruction on Christian Initiation, nos. 30-33.

does not concelebrate the Mass, he and the priests who may administer confirmation with him should participate in the Mass wearing the vestments for confirmation: alb, stole, and for the minister of confirmation, cope; these vestments are also worn for confirmation outside Mass;

b) chairs for the bishop and the priests;

c) vessel or vessels of chrism;

d) Roman Pontifical or Ritual;

e) preparations for Mass and for communion under both kinds, if it is given in this way;

f) preparations for the washing of the ministers' hands after the anointing.

CHAPTER I

RITE OF CONFIRMATION WITHIN MASS

LITURGY OF THE WORD

20. The liturgy of the word is celebrated in the ordinary way. The readings may be taken in whole or in part from the Mass of the day or from the texts for confirmation in the *Lectionary for Mass* (nos. 763-767) and listed below (nos. 61-65).

SACRAMENT OF CONFIRMATION

PRESENTATION OF THE CANDIDATES

21. After the gospel the bishop and the priests who will be ministers of the sacrament with him take their seats. The pastor or another priest, deacon, or catechist presents the candidates for confirmation, according to the custom of the region. If possible, each candidate is called by name and comes individually to the sanctuary. If the candidates are children, they are accompanied by one of their sponsors or parents and stand before the celebrant.

If there are very many candidates, they are not called by name, but simply take a suitable place before the bishop.

HOMILY OR INSTRUCTION

22. The bishop then gives a brief homily. He should explain the readings and so lead the candidates, their sponsors and parents, and the whole assembly to a deeper understanding of the mystery of confirmation.
He may use these or similar words:

On the day of Pentecost the apostles received the Holy Spirit as the Lord had promised. They also received the power of giving the Holy Spirit to others and so completing the work of baptism. This we read in the Acts of the Apostles. When Saint Paul placed his hands on those who had been baptized, the Holy Spirit came upon them, and they began to speak in

other languages and in prophetic words.

Bishops are successors of the apostles and have this power of giving the Holy Spirit to the baptized, either personally or through the priests they appoint.

In our day the coming of the Holy Spirit in confirmation is no longer marked by the gift of tongues, but we know his coming by faith. He fills our hearts with the love of God, brings us together in one faith but in different vocations, and works within us to make the Church one and holy.

The gift of the Holy Spirit which you are to receive will be a spiritual sign and seal to make you more like Christ and more perfect members of his Church. At his baptism by John, Christ himself was anointed by the Spirit and sent out on his public ministry to set the world on fire.

You have already been baptized into Christ and now you will receive the power of his Spirit and the sign of the cross on your forehead. You must be witnesses before all the world to his suffering, death, and resurrection; your way of life should at all times reflect the goodness of Christ. Christ gives varied gifts to his Church, and the Spirit distributes them among the members of Christ's body to build up the holy people of God in unity and love.

Be active members of the Church, alive in Jesus Christ. Under the guidance of the Holy Spirit give your lives completely in the service of all, as did Christ, who came not to be served but to serve.

So now, before you receive the Spirit, I ask you to renew the profession of faith you made in baptism or your parents and godparents made in union with the whole Church.

RENEWAL OF BAPTISMAL PROMISES

23. After the homily the candidates stand and the bishop questions them:

Do you reject Satan and all his works and all his empty promises?
The candidates respond together: **I do.**

Bishop:
Do you believe in God the Father almighty, creator of heaven and earth?
Candidates: **I do.**

Bishop:
Do you believe in Jesus Christ, his only Son, our Lord,
who was born of the Virgin Mary,
was crucified, died, and was buried,
rose from the dead,
and is now seated at the right hand of the Father?
Candidates: **I do.**

Bishop:
Do you believe in the Holy Spirit,
the Lord, the giver of life,
who came upon the apostles at Pentecost
and today is given to you sacramentally in confirmation?
Candidates: **I do.**

Bishop:
Do you believe in the holy catholic Church,
the communion of saints, the forgiveness of sins,
the resurrection of the body, and life everlasting?
Candidates: **I do.**

The bishop confirms their profession of faith by proclaiming the faith of the Church:

This is our faith. This is the faith of the Church.
We are proud to profess it in Christ Jesus our Lord.

The whole congregation responds: **Amen.**

For **This is our faith,** some other formula may be substituted, or the community may express its faith in a suitable song.

THE LAYING ON OF HANDS

24. The concelebrating priests stand near the bishop. He faces the people and with hands joined, sings or says:

My dear friends:
in baptism God our Father gave the new birth of eternal life
to his chosen sons and daughters.
Let us pray to our Father
that he will pour out the Holy Spirit
to strengthen his sons and daughters with his gifts
and anoint them to be more like Christ the Son of God.

All pray in silence for a short time.

25. The bishop and the priests who will minister the sacrament with him lay hands upon all the candidates (by extending their hands over them). The bishop alone sings or says:
All-powerful God, Father of our Lord Jesus Christ,
by water and the Holy Spirit
you freed your sons and daughters from sin
and gave them new life.
Send your Holy Spirit upon them
to be their Helper and Guide.
Give them the spirit of wisdom and understanding,
the spirit of right judgment and courage,
the spirit of knowledge and reverence.
Fill them with the spirit of wonder and awe in your presence.
We ask this through Christ our Lord.
℟. **Amen.**

THE ANOINTING WITH CHRISM

26. The deacon brings the chrism to the bishop. Each candidate goes to the bishop, or the bishop may go to the individual candidates. The one who presented the candidate places his right hand on the latter's shoulder and gives the candidate's name to the bishop; or the candidate may give his own name.

27. The bishop dips his right thumb in the chrism and makes the sign of the cross on the forehead of the one to be confirmed, as he says:

N., be sealed with the Gift of the Holy Spirit.
The newly confirmed responds: **Amen.**

The bishop says:
Peace be with you.
The newly confirmed responds: **And also with you.**

28. If priests assist the bishop in conferring the sacrament, all the vessels of chrism are brought to the bishop by the deacon or by other ministers. Each of the priests comes to the bishop, who gives him a vessel of chrism.

The candidates go to the bishop or to the priests, or the bishop and priests may go to the candidates. The anointing is done as described above (no. 27).

29. During the anointing a suitable song may be sung. After the anointing the bishop and the priests wash their hands.

GENERAL INTERCESSIONS

30. The general intercessions follow, in this or a similar form determined by the competent authority.

Bishop:
My dear friends:
let us be one in prayer to God our Father
as we are one in the faith, hope, and love his Spirit gives.

Deacon or minister:
For these sons and daughters of God,
confirmed by the gift of the Spirit,
that they give witness to Christ
by lives built on faith and love:
let us pray to the Lord.
℟. **Lord, hear our prayer.**

Deacon or minister:
For their parents and godparents
who led them in faith,
that by word and example they may always encourage them
to follow the way of Jesus Christ:

let us pray to the Lord.
℟. **Lord, hear our prayer.**

Deacon or minister:
For the holy Church of God,
in union with N. our pope, N. our bishop, and all the bishops,
that God, who gathers us together by the Holy Spirit,
may help us grow in unity of faith and love
until his Son returns in glory:
let us pray to the Lord.
℟. **Lord, hear our prayer.**

Deacon or minister:
For all men,
of every race and nation,
that they may acknowledge the one God as Father,
and in the bond of common brotherhood
seek his kingdom,
which is peace and joy in the Holy Spirit:
let us pray to the Lord.
℟. **Lord, hear our prayer.**

Bishop:
God our Father,
you sent your Holy Spirit upon the apostles,
and through them and their successors
you give the Spirit to your people.
May his work begun at Pentecost
continue to grow in the hearts of all who believe.
We ask this through Christ our Lord.

LITURGY OF THE EUCHARIST

31. After the general intercessions the liturgy of the eucharist is celebrated according to the *Order of Mass,* with these exceptions:

a) the profession of faith is omitted, since it has already been made;

b) some of the newly confirmed may join those who bring the gifts to the altar;

c) when Euchaustic Prayer I is used, the special form of **Father, accept this offering** is said.

32. Adults who are confirmed, their sponsors, parents, wives and husbands, and catechists may receive communion under both kinds.

BLESSING

33. Instead of the usual blessing at the end of Mass, the following blessing or prayer over the people is used.

God our Father
made you his children by water and the Holy Spirit:
may he bless you
and watch over you with his fatherly love.
℟. **Amen.**

Jesus Christ the Son of God
promised that the Spirit of truth
would be with his Church for ever:
may he bless you and give you courage
in professing the true faith.
℟. **Amen.**

The Holy Spirit
came down upon the disciples
and set their hearts on fire with love:
may he bless you,
keep you one in faith and love
and bring you to the joy of God's kingdom.
℟. **Amen.**

The bishop adds immediately:
May almighty God bless you,
the Father, and the Son, ✠ and the Holy Spirit.
℟. **Amen.**

PRAYER OVER THE PEOPLE

Instead of the preceding blessing, the prayer over the people may be used.

The deacon or minister gives the invitation in these or similar words:

Bow your heads and pray for God's blessing.

The bishop extends his hands over the people and sings or says:

God our Father,
complete the work you have begun
and keep the gifts of your Holy Spirit
active in the hearts of your people.
Make them ready to live his Gospel
and eager to do his will.
May they never be ashamed
to proclaim to all the world Christ crucified
living and reigning for ever and ever.
℟. **Amen.**

The bishop adds immediately:

And may the blessing of almighty God
the Father, and the Son, ✠ and the Holy Spirit
come upon you and remain with you
for ever.
℟. **Amen.**

CHAPTER II

RITE OF CONFIRMATION OUTSIDE MASS

INTRODUCTORY RITES

ENTRANCE SONG

34. When the candidates, their sponsors and parents, and the whole assembly of the faithful have gathered, the bishop goes to the sanctuary with the priests who assist him, one or more deacons, and the ministers. Meanwhile all may sing a psalm or appropriate song.

35. The bishop makes the usual reverence to the altar with the ministers and greets the people:

Peace be with you.
All: **And also with you.**

OPENING PRAYER

Let us pray.

God of power and mercy,
send your Holy Spirit
to live in our hearts
and make us temples of his glory.
We ask this through our Lord Jesus Christ, your Son,
who lives and reigns with you and the Holy Spirit,
one God, for ever and ever.
℟. **Amen.**

Or:

Lord,
fulfill your promise:
send your Holy Spirit to make us witnesses before the world

to the Good News proclaimed by Jesus Christ, our Lord,
who lives and reigns with you and the Holy Spirit,
one God, for ever and ever.
℟. **Amen.**

Or:

Lord,
send us your Holy Spirit
to help us walk in unity of faith
and grow in the strength of his love
to the full stature of Christ,
who lives and reigns with you and the Holy Spirit,
one God, for ever and ever.
℟. **Amen.**

Or:

Lord,
fulfill the promise given by your Son
and send the Holy Spirit
to enlighten our minds
and lead us to all truth. Grant this through our Lord Jesus Christ,
who lives and reigns with you and the Holy Spirit,
one God, for ever and ever.
℟. **Amen.**

CELEBRATION OF THE WORD OF GOD

36. The celebration of the word of God follows. At least one of the readings suggested for the Mass of confirmation (see nos. 61-65) is read.

37. If two or three readings are chosen, the traditional order is followed, that is, the Old Testament, the Apostle, and the Gospel. After the first and second reading there should be a psalm or song, or a period of silence may be observed.

SACRAMENT OF CONFIRMATION

PRESENTATION OF THE CANDIDATES

38. After the readings the bishop and the priests who will be ministers of the sacrament with him take their seats. The pastor or another priest, deacon, or catechist presents the candidates for confirmation, according to the custom of the region. If possible, each candidate is called by name and comes individually to the sanctuary. If the candidates are children, they are accompanied by one of their sponsors or parents and stand before the celebrant.

If there are very many candidates, they are not called by name, but simply take a suitable place before the bishop.

HOMILY OR INSTRUCTION

39. The bishop then gives a brief homily. He should explain the readings and so lead the candidates, their sponsors and parents, and the whole assembly to a deeper understanding of the mystery of confirmation.

He may use these or similar words:

On the day of Pentecost the apostles received the Holy Spirit as the Lord had promised. They also received the power of giving the Holy Spirit to others and so completing the work of baptism. This we read in the Acts of the Apostles. When Saint Paul placed his hands on those who had been baptized, the Holy Spirit came upon them, and they began to speak in other languages and in prophetic words.

Bishops are successors of the apostles and have this power of giving the Holy Spirit to the baptized, either personally or through the priests they appoint.

In our day the coming of the Holy Spirit in confirmation is no longer marked by the gift of tongues, but we know his coming by faith. He fills our hearts with the love of God, brings us together in one faith but in different vocations, and works within us to make the Church one and holy.

The gift of the Holy Spirit which you are to receive

will be a spiritual sign and seal to make you more like Christ and more perfect members of his Church. At his baptism by John, Christ himself was anointed by the Spirit and sent out on his public ministry to set the world on fire.

You have already been baptized into Christ and now you will receive the power of his Spirit and the sign of the cross on your forehead. You must be witnesses before all the world to his suffering, death, and resurrection; your way of life should at all times reflect the goodness of Christ. Christ gives varied gifts to his Church, and the Spirit distributes them among the members of Christ's body to build up the holy people of God in unity and love.

Be active members of the Church, alive in Jesus Christ. Under the guidance of the Holy Spirit give your lives completely in the service of all, as did Christ, who came not to be served but to serve.

So now, before you receive the Spirit, I ask you to renew the profession of faith you made in baptism or your parents and godparents made in union with the whole Church.

RENEWAL OF BAPTISMAL PROMISES

40. After the homily the candidates stand and the bishop questions them:

Do you reject Satan and all his works and all his empty promises?
The candidates respond together: **I do.**

Bishop:
Do you believe in God the Father almighty, creator of heaven and earth?
Candidates: **I do.**

Bishop:
Do you believe in Jesus Christ, his only Son, our Lord,
who was born of the Virgin Mary,
was crucified, died, and was buried,
rose from the dead,

and is now seated at the right hand of the Father?
Candidates: **I do.**

Bishop:
Do you believe in the Holy Spirit,
the Lord, the giver of life,
who came upon the apostles at Pentecost
and today is given to you sacramentally in confirmation?
Candidates: **I do.**

Bishop:
Do you believe in the holy catholic Church,
the communion of saints, the forgiveness of sins,
the resurrection of the body, and life everlasting?
Candidates: **I do.**

The bishop confirms their profession of faith by proclaiming the faith of the Church:

This is our faith. This is the faith of the Church.
We are proud to profess it in Christ Jesus our Lord.
The whole congregation responds: **Amen.**

For **This is our faith,** some other formula may be substituted, or the community may express its faith in a suitable song.

THE LAYING ON OF HANDS

41. The concelebrating priests stand near the bishop. He faces the people and with hands joined, sings or says:

My dear friends:
in baptism God our Father gave the new birth of eternal life
to his chosen sons and daughters.
Let us pray to our Father
that he will pour out the Holy Spirit
to strengthen his sons and daughters with his gifts
and anoint them to be more like Christ the Son of God.

All pray in silence for a short time.

42. The bishop and the priests who will minister the sacra-

ment with him lay hands upon all the candidates (by extending their hands over them). The bishop alone sings or says:

All-powerful God, Father of our Lord Jesus Christ,
by water and the Holy Spirit
you freed your sons and daughters from sin
and gave them new life.
Send your Holy Spirit upon them
to be their Helper and Guide.
Give them the spirit of wisdom and understanding,
the spirit of right judgment and courage,
the spirit of knowledge and reverence.
Fill them with the spirit of wonder and awe in your presence.
We ask this through Christ our Lord.
℟. **Amen.**

THE ANOINTING WITH CHRISM

43. The deacon brings the chrism to the bishop. Each candidate goes to the bishop, or the bishop may go to the individual candidates. The one who presented the candidate places his right hand on the latter's shoulder and gives the candidate's name to the bishop; or the candidate may give his own name.

44. The bishop dips his right thumb in the chrism and makes the sign of the cross on the forehead of the one to be confirmed, as he says:

N., be sealed with the Gift of the Holy Spirit.
The newly confirmed responds: **Amen.**

The bishop says:
Peace be with you.
The newly confirmed responds: **And also with you.**

45. If priests assist the bishop in conferring the sacrament, all the vessels of chrism are brought to the bishop by the deacon or by other ministers. Each of the priests comes to the bishop, who gives him a vessel of chrism.
The candidates go to the bishop or to the priests, or the bishop and priests may go to the candidates. The anointing is done as described above (no. 44).

46. During the anointing a suitable song may be sung. After the anointing the bishop and the priests wash their hands.

GENERAL INTERCESSIONS

47. The general intercessions follow, in this or a similar form determined by the competent authority.

Bishop:

My dear friends:
let us be one in prayer to God our Father
as we are one in the faith, hope, and love his Spirit gives.

Deacon or minister:

For these sons and daughters of God,
confirmed by the gift of the Spirit,
that they give witness to Christ
by lives built on faith and love:
let us pray to the Lord.
℟. **Lord, hear our prayer.**

Deacon or minister:

For their parents and godparents
who led them in faith,
that by word and example they may always encourage them
to follow the way of Jesus Christ:
let us pray to the Lord.
℟. **Lord, hear our prayer.**

Deacon or minister:

For the holy Church of God,
in union with N. our pope, N. our bishop, and all the bishops,
that God, who gathers us together by the Holy Spirit,
may help us grow in unity of faith and love
until his Son returns in glory:
let us pray to the Lord.
℟. **Lord, hear our prayer.**

Deacon or minister:

For all men,
of every race and nation,

that they may acknowledge the one God as Father,
and in the bond of common brotherhood
seek his kingdom,
which is peace and joy in the Holy Spirit:
let us pray to the Lord.
℟. Lord, hear our prayer.

Bishop:
God our Father,
you sent your Holy Spirit upon the apostles,
and through them and their successors
you give the Spirit to your people.
May his work begun at Pentecost
continue to grow in the hearts of all who believe.
We ask this through Christ our Lord.

LORD'S PRAYER

48. All then say the Lord's Prayer, which the bishop may introduce in these or similar words:

Dear friends in Christ,
let us pray together
as the Lord Jesus Christ has taught.

All:
Our Father. . . .

49. After the Lord's Prayer the bishop blesses all present. Instead of the usual blessing, the following blessing or prayer over the people is used.

God our Father
made you his children by water and the Holy Spirit:
may he bless you
and watch over you with his fatherly love.
℟. Amen.

Jesus Christ the Son of God
promised that the Spirit of truth
would be with his Church for ever:
may he bless you and give you courage
in professing the true faith.
℟. Amen.

The Holy Spirit
came down upon the disciples
and set their hearts on fire with love:
may he bless you,
keep you one in faith and love
and bring you to the joy of God's kingdom.
℟. **Amen.**

The bishop adds immediately:

May almighty God bless you,
the Father, and the Son, ✠ and the Holy Spirit.
℟. **Amen.**

PRAYER OVER THE PEOPLE

Instead of the preceding blessing, the prayer over the people may be used.
The deacon or minister gives the invitation in these or similar words:

Bow your heads and pray for God's blessing.

The bishop extends his hands over the people and sings or says:

God our Father,
complete the work you have begun
and keep the gifts of your Holy Spirit
active in the hearts of your people.
Make them ready to live his Gospel
and eager to do his will.
May they never be ashamed
to proclaim to all the world Christ crucified
living and reigning for ever and ever.
℟. **Amen.**

The bishop adds immediately:

And may the blessing of almighty God
the Father, and the Son, ✠ and the Holy Spirit,
Come upon you and remain with you forever.
℟. **Amen.**

CHAPTER III

RITE OF CONFIRMATION BY A MINISTER WHO IS NOT A BISHOP

50. The minister of confirmation who is not a bishop and who confirms either by concession of the general law or by special indult of the Apostolic See observes the rite described above.

51. If, because of the large number of candidates, other priests join the celebrant in the administration of the sacrament, he chooses them in accord with no. 8 above. These priests should also concelebrate the Mass in which confirmation is conferred.

CHAPTER IV

CONFIRMATION OF A PERSON IN DANGER OF DEATH

52. It is of the greatest importance that the initiation of every baptized Christian be completed by the sacraments of confirmation and the eucharist. The sick person in danger of death who has reached the age of reason should therefore be strengthened by confirmation before he receives the eucharist as viaticum, after the necessary and possible catechesis.

Confirmation in danger of death and anointing of the sick are not ordinarily to be celebrated in a continuous rite.

In the case of a child who has not yet reached the age of reason, confirmation is given in accord with the same principles and norms as for baptism.

53. When circumstances permit, the entire rite described above is followed.

54. In case of urgent necessity, the minister of confirmation lays his hands upon the sick person as he says:

All-powerful God, Father of our Lord Jesus Christ,
by water and the Holy Spirit
you freed your son (daughter) from sin
and gave him (her) new life.
Send your Holy Spirit upon him (her)
to be his (her) Helper and Guide.
Give him (her) the spirit of wisdom and understanding,
the spirit of right judgment and courage,
the spirit of knowledge and reverence.
Fill him (her) with the spirit of wonder and awe in your presence.
We ask this through Christ our Lord.
℟. **Amen.**

55. Then the minister dips his right thumb in the chrism and makes the sign of the cross on the forehead of the one to be confirmed, as he says:

N., be sealed with the Gift of the Holy Spirit.

The newly confirmed responds, if he is able: **Amen.**

Other parts of the preparatory and concluding rites may be added in individual cases, depending on the circumstances.

56. In case of extreme necessity, it is sufficient that the anointing be done with the sacramental form:

N., be sealed with the Gift of the Holy Spirit.

CHAPTER V

TEXTS FOR THE CELEBRATION OF CONFIRMATION

I. MASS FOR THE CELEBRATION OF CONFIRMATION

57. One of the following Masses is celebrated where confirmation is given within Mass or immediately before or after it, except on the Sundays of Advent, Lent and Easter, Solemnities, Ash Wednesday, and the weekdays of Holy Week. Red or white vestments are worn.

A

58.

INTRODUCTORY RITES

Ezekiel 36:25-26

I will pour clean water on you and I will give you a new heart, a new spirit within you, says the Lord.

OPENING PRAYER

God of power and mercy,
send your Holy Spirit
to live in our hearts
and make us temples of his glory.

We ask this through our Lord Jesus Christ, your Son,
who lives and reigns with you and the Holy Spirit,
one God, for ever and ever.
℟. **Amen.**

Or:

Lord,
fulfill your promise.
Send your Holy Spirit
to make us witnesses before the world
to the good news proclaimed by Jesus Christ, our Lord,

**who lives and reigns with you and the Holy Spirit,
one God, for ever and ever.
℟. Amen.**

Another prayer may be chosen from nos. 59, 60.
See Lectionary for Mass, nos. 763–767.

PRAYER OVER THE GIFTS

Pray, brethren . . .

**Lord,
we celebrate the memorial of our redemption
by which your Son won for us the gift of the Holy Spirit.
Accept our offerings,
and send us your Spirit
to make us more like Christ
in bearing witness to the world.**

**We ask this through Christ our Lord.
℟. Amen.**

When Eucharistic Prayer I is used, the special form of **Father, accept this offering** is said.

**Father,
accept this offering
from your whole family
and from those reborn in baptism
and confirmed by the coming of the Holy Spirit.
Protect them with your love and keep them close to you.
[Through Christ our Lord. ℟. Amen.]**

COMMUNION RITE

See Hebrews 6:4

All you who have been enlightened, who have experienced the gift of heaven and who have received your share of the Holy Spirit: rejoice in the Lord.

PRAYER AFTER COMMUNION

Let us pray.

Pause for silent prayer, if this has not preceded.

**Lord,
help those you have anointed by your Spirit
and fed with the body and blood of your Son.
Support them through every trial
and by their works of love.
build up the Church in holiness and joy.
Grant this through Christ our Lord.
℟. Amen.**

SOLEMN BLESSING

**God our Father
made you his children by water and the Holy Spirit:
may he bless you
and watch over you with his fatherly love.
℟. Amen.**

**Jesus Christ the Son of God
promised that the Spirit of truth
would be with his Church for ever:
may he bless you and give you courage
in professing the true faith.
℟. Amen.**

**The Holy Spirit
came down upon the disciples
and set their hearts on fire with love:
may he bless you,
keep you one in faith and love
and bring you to the joy of God's kingdom.
℟. Amen.**

**May almighty God bless you.
the Father, and the Son, ✠ and the Holy Spirit.
℟. Amen.**

Or:

PRAYER OVER THE PEOPLE

**God our Father,
complete the work you have begun
and keep the gifts of your Holy Spirit
active in the hearts of your people.
Make them ready to live his gospel
and eager to do his will.**

May they never be ashamed
to proclaim to all the world Christ crucified
living and reigning for ever and ever.
℟. Amen.

And may the blessing of Almighty God,
the Father, and the Son, ✠ and the Holy Spirit,
come upon you and remain with you for ever.
℟. Amen.

B

59.

INTRODUCTORY RITES

See Romans 5:5; 8:11

The love of God has been poured into our hearts by his Spirit living in us.

OPENING PRAYER

Lord,
send us your Holy Spirit
to help us walk in unity of faith
and grow in the strength of his love
to the full stature of Christ,
who lives and reigns with you and the Holy Spirit,
one God, for ever and ever.
℟. Amen.

Another prayer may be chosen from nos. 58, 60.
See Lectionary for Mass, nos. 763–767.

PRAYER OVER THE GIFTS

Pray, brethren . . .

Lord,
you have signed our brothers and sisters
with the cross of your Son
and anointed them with the oil of salvation.
As they offer themselves with Christ,
continue to fill their hearts with your Spirit.
We ask this through Christ our Lord.
℟. Amen.

When Eucharistic Prayer I is used, the special form of **Father, accept this offering** is said, as in the preceding Mass.

COMMUNION RITE

Psalm 34:6, 9

Look up at him with gladness and smile; taste and see the goodness of the Lord.

PRAYER AFTER COMMUNION

Let us pray.

Pause for silent prayer, if this has not preceded.

Lord,
you give your Son as food
to those you anoint with your Spirit.
Help them to fulfill your law
by living in freedom as your children.
May they live in holiness
and be your witnesses to the world.

We ask this through Christ our Lord.
℟. **Amen.**

II. OTHER PRAYERS

60.

OPENING PRAYER

Lord,
fulfill the promise given by your Son
and send the Holy Spirit
to enlighten our minds and lead us to all truth.
Grant this through our Lord Jesus Christ, your Son,
who lives and reigns with you and the Holy Spirit
one God, for ever and ever.
℟. **Amen.**

PRAYER OVER THE GIFTS

Pray, brethren . . .

Lord,
accept the offering of your family

and help those who receive the gift of your Spirit
to keep him in their hearts
and come to the reward of eternal life.
We ask this in the name of Jesus the Lord.
℟. **Amen.**

PRAYER AFTER COMMUNION

Let us pray.

Pause for silent prayer, if this has not preceded.

Lord,
we have shared the one bread of life.
Send the Spirit of your love
to keep us one in faith and peace.

℟. **Amen.**

III. BIBLICAL READINGS

61. Readings from the Old Testament

1. **Isaiah 11:1-4a**
On him the Spirit of the Lord rests.

2. **Isaiah 42:1-3**
I have endowed my servant with my Spirit.

3. **Isaiah 61:1-3a, 6a, 8b-9**
The Lord God has anointed me and has sent me to bring Good News to the poor, to give them the oil of gladness.

4. **Ezekiel 36:24-28**
I will place a new Spirit in your midst.

5. **Joel 2:23a, 26-30a**
(Hebrew 2:23a; 3:1-3a)
I will pour out my Spirit on all mankind.

62. Readings from the New Testament

1. **Acts 1:3-8**
You will receive the power of the Holy Spirit, and you will be my witnesses.

2. **Acts 2:1-6, 14, 22b-23, 32-33**
They were all filled with the Holy Spirit, and began to speak.

3. **Acts 8:1, 4, 14-17**
They laid hands on them, and they received the Holy Spirit.

4. **Acts 10:1, 33-34a, 37-44**
The Holy Spirit came down on all those listening to the word of God.

5. **Acts 19:1b-6a**
Did you receive the Holy Spirit when you became believers?

6. **Romans 5:1-2, 5-8**
The love of God has been poured into our hearts by the Holy Spirit which has been given to us.

7. **Romans 8:14-17**
The Spirit himself and our spirit bear united witness that we are children of God.

8. **Romans 8:26-27**
The Spirit himself will express our plea in a way that could never be put to words.

9. **1 Corinthians 12:4-13**
There is one and the same Spirit giving to each as he wills.

10. **Galatians 5:16-17, 22-23a, 24-25**
If we live in the Spirit, let us be directed by the Spirit.

11. **Ephesians 1:3a, 4a, 13-19a**
You have been signed with the seal of the Holy Spirit of the promise.

12. **Ephesians 4:1-6**
There is one body, one Spirit, and one baptism.

63. Responsorial Psalms

1. Psalm 22:23-24, 26-27, 28 and 31-32
℟. (23): **I will proclaim your name to my brothers.**
or: (John 15:26-27):
When the Holy Spirit comes to you, you will be my witness.

2. Psalm 23:1-3a, 3b-4, 5-6
℟. (1): **The Lord is my shepherd; there is nothing I shall want.**

3. Psalm 96:1-2a, 2b-3, 9-10a, 11-12
℟. (3): **Proclaim his marvelous deeds to all the nations.**

4. Psalm 104:1ab and 24, 27-28, 30-31, 33-34
℟. (30): **Lord, send out your Spirit, and renew the face of the earth.**

5. Psalm 117:1, 2
℟. (Acts 1:8): **You will be my witnesses to all the world.**
or: **Alleluia.**

6. Psalm 145:2-3, 4-5, 8-9, 10-11, 15-16, 21
℟. (1b): **I will praise your name for ever, Lord.**

64. Alleluia Verse and Verse before the Gospel

1. John 14:16
The Father will send you the Holy Spirit, says the Lord,
to be with you for ever.

2. John 15:26b, 27a
The Spirit of truth will bear witness to me, says the Lord,
and you also will be my witnesses.

3. John 16:13a; 14:26b
When the Spirit of truth comes, he will teach you all truth
and bring to your mind all I have told you.

4. Revelation 1:5a, 6
Jesus Christ, you are the faithful witness, firstborn from the dead;
you have made us a kingdom of priests to serve our God and Father.

5. **Come, Holy Spirit, fill the hearts of your faithful;**
and kindle in them the fire of your love.

6. **Come, Holy Spirit;**
shine on us the radiance of your light.

65. Gospel

1. **Matthew 5:1-12a**
Theirs is the kingdom of heaven.

2. **Matthew 16:24-27**
If anyone wishes to follow me, let him deny himself.

3. **Matthew 25:14-30**
Because you have been faithful in small matters, come into the joy of your master.

4. **Mark 1:9-11**
He saw the Spirit descending and remaining on him.

5. **Luke 4:16-22a**
The Spirit of the Lord is upon me.

6. **Luke 8:4-10a, 11b-15**
Some seed fell into rich soil. These are the people who receive the word and bear fruit in patience.

7. **Luke 10:21-24**
I bless you, Father, for revealing these things to children.

8. **John 7:37b-39**
From the heart of the Lord shall flow fountains of living water.

9. **John 14:15-17**
The Spirit of truth will be with you for ever.

10. **John 14:23-26**
The Holy Spirit will teach you everything.

11. **John 15:18-21, 26-27**
The Spirit of truth who issues from the Father, will be my witness.

12. **John 16:5b-7, 12-13a (Greek 5-7, 12-13a)**
The Spirit of truth will lead you to the complete truth.

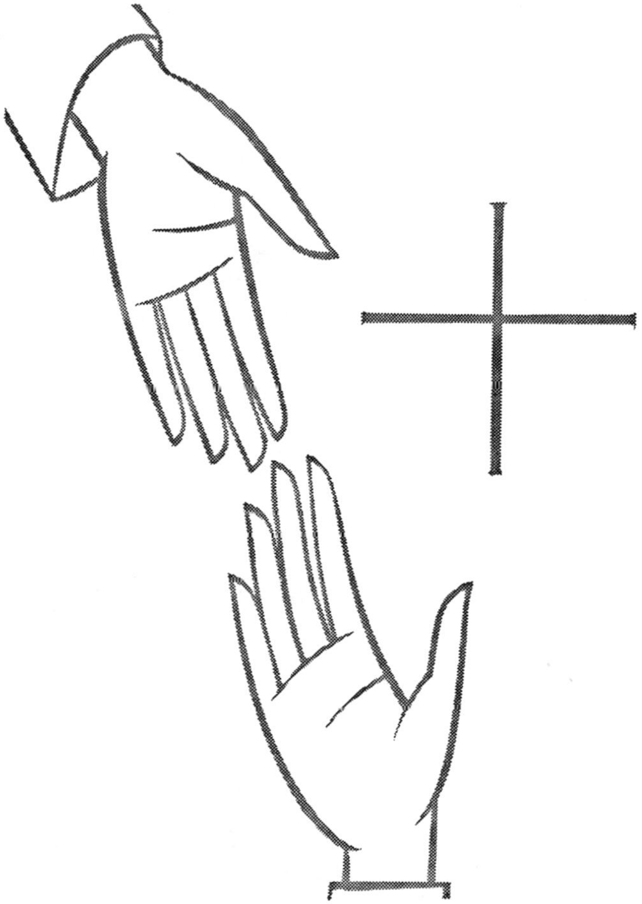

RITE OF PENANCE

RITE OF PENANCE

Decree
Introduction (1-40)

CHAPTER I
RITE OF RECONCILIATION OF INDIVIDUAL PENITENTS

I Reception of the Penitent (41-42)

II Reading of the Word of God (optional) (43)

III Confession of Sins and Acceptance of Satisfaction (44)

IV Prayer of the Penitent and Absolution (45-46)

V Proclamation of Praise of God and Dismissal (47)

CHAPTER II
RITE OF RECONCILIATION OF SEVERAL PENITENTS WITH INDIVIDUAL CONFESSION AND ABSOLUTION

I Introductory Rites

A Song (48)

B Greeting (49)

C Opening Prayer (50)

II Celebration of the Word of God (51)

A Homily (52)

III Examination of Conscience (53)

IV Rite of Reconciliation

A General Confession of Sins (54)

B Individual Confession and Absolution (55)

V Proclamation of Praise for God's Mercy (56)

A Concluding Prayer of Thanksgiving (57)

VI Concluding Rite (58-59)

CHAPTER III
RITE FOR RECONCILIATION OF SEVERAL PENITENTS WITH GENERAL CONFESSION AND ABSOLUTION

I Instruction (60)

II General Confession (61)

III General Absolution (62)

IV Proclamation of Praise and Conclusion (63)

V Short Rite (64-66)

CHAPTER IV
VARIOUS TEXTS USED IN A CELEBRATION OF RECONCILIATION (67-214)

APPENDIX I
ABSOLUTION FROM CENSURES

APPENDIX II
SAMPLE PENITENTIAL SERVICES

APPENDIX III
FORM OF EXAMINATION OF CONSCIENCE

SACRED CONGREGATION FOR DIVINE WORSHIP

Prot. n. 800/73

DECREE

Reconciliation between God and men was brought about by our Lord Jesus Christ in the mystery of his death and resurrection (see Romans 5:10). The Lord entrusted the ministry of reconciliation to the Church in the person of the apostles (see 2 Corinthians 5:18ff). The Church carries this ministry out by bringing the good news of salvation to men and by baptizing them in water and the Holy Spirit (see Matthew 28:19).

Because of human weakness, Christians "turn aside from [their] early love" (see Revelation 2:4) and even break off their friendship with God by sinning. The Lord, therefore, instituted a special sacrament of penance for the pardon of sins committed after baptism (see John 20:21-23), and the Church has faithfully celebrated the sacrament throughout the centuries—in varying ways, but retaining its essential elements.

The Second Vatican Council decreed that "the rite of formulas of penance are to be revised in such a way that they may more clearly express the nature and effects of this sacrament."[1] In view of this the Congregation for Divine Worship has carefully prepared the new *Rite of Penance* so that the celebration of the sacrament may be more fully understood by the faithful.

In this new rite, besides the *Rite for Reconciliation of Individual Penitents,* a *Rite for Reconciliation of Several Penitents* has been drawn up to emphasize the relation of the sacrament to the community. This rite places individual confession and absolution in the context of a celebration of the word of God. Furthermore, for special occasions a *Rite for Reconciliation of Several Penitents with General Confession and Absolution* has been composed in accordance with the Pastoral Norms on

[1]Second Vatican Council, constitution *Sacrosanctum Concilium,* no. 72: *AAS* 56 (1964) 118.

General Sacramental Absolution, issued by the Congregation for the Doctrine of the Faith on June 16, 1972.[2]

The Church is solicitous in calling the faithful to continual conversion and renewal. It desires that the baptized who have sinned should acknowledge their sins against God and their neighbor and have heartfelt repentance for them, and it tries to prepare them to celebrate the sacrament of penance. For this reason the Church urges the faithful to attend penitential celebrations from time to time. This Congregation has therefore made regulations for such celebrations and has proposed examples or specimens which episcopal conferences may adapt to the needs of their own regions.

Accordingly Pope Paul VI has by his authority approved the *Rite of Penance* prepared by the Congregation for Divine Worship and ordered it to be published. It is to replace the pertinent sections of the *Roman Ritual* now in use. The rite in its Latin original is to come into force as soon as it is published, but vernacular versions will be effective from the day determined by the episcopal conferences, after they have approved the translation and received confirmation from the Apostolic See.

Anything to the contrary notwithstanding.

From the office of the Congregation for Divine Worship, December 2, 1973, the First Sunday of Advent.

By special mandate of the Pope

Jean Cardinal Villot
Secretary of State

✠ Annibale Bugnini
Titular Archbishop of Diocletiana
Secretary of the Congregation for Divine Worship

[2]See *AAS* 64 (1972) 510-514.

INTRODUCTION

I

THE MYSTERY OF RECONCILIATION IN THE HISTORY OF SALVATION

1. The Father has shown forth his mercy by reconciling the world to himself in Christ and by making peace for all things on earth and in heaven by the blood of Christ on the cross.[1] The Son of God made man lived among men in order to free them from the slavery of sin[2] and to call them out of darkness into his wonderful light.[3] He therefore began his work on earth by preaching repentance and saying: "Turn away from sin and believe the good news" (Mark 1:15). This invitation to repentance, which had often been sounded by the prophets, prepared the hearts of men for the coming of the Kingdom of God through the voice of John the Baptist who came "preaching a baptism of repentance for the forgiveness of sins" (Mark 1:4).

Jesus, however, not only exhorted men to repentance so that they should abandon their sins and turn wholeheartedly to the Lord,[4] but he also welcomed sinners and reconciled them with the Father.[5] Moreover, by healing the sick he signified his power to forgive sin.[6] Finally, he himself died for our sins and rose again for our justification.[7] Therefore, on the night he was betrayed and began his saving passion,[8] he instituted the sacrifice of the new covenant in his blood for the forgiveness of sins.[9] After his resurrection he sent the Holy Spirit upon the apostles, empowering them to forgive or retain sins[10] and sending

[1]See 2 Corinthians 5:18ff; Colossians 1:20.
[2]See John 8:34-36
[3]See 1 Peter 2:9.
[4]See Luke 15.
[5]Luke 5:20, 27-32; 7:48.
[6]See Matthew 9:2-8.
[7]See Romans 4:25.
[8]See Roman Missal, Eucharistic Prayer III.
[9]See Matthew 26:28.
[10]See John 20:19-23.

them forth to all peoples to preach repentance and the forgiveness of sins in his name.[11]

The Lord said to Peter, "I will give you the keys of the kingdom of heaven, and whatever you bind on earth will be bound in heaven, and whatever you loose on earth will be loosed also in heaven" (Matthew 16:19). In obedience to this command, on the day of Pentecost Peter preached the forgiveness of sins by baptism: "Repent and let every one of you be baptized in the name of Jesus Christ for the forgiveness of your sins" (Acts 2:38).[12] Since then the Church has never failed to call men from sin to conversion and by the celebration of penance to show the victory of Christ over sin.

2. This victory is first brought to light in baptism where our fallen nature is crucified with Christ so that the body of sin may be destroyed and we may no longer be slaves to sin, but rise with Christ and live for God.[13] For this reason the Church proclaims its faith in "the one baptism for the forgiveness of sins."

In the sacrifice of the Mass the passion of Christ is made present; his body given for us and his blood shed for the forgiveness of sins are offered to God again by the Church for the salvation of the world. In the eucharist Christ is present and is offered as "the sacrifice which has made our peace"[14] with God and in order that "we may be brought together in unity"[15] by his Holy Spirit.

Furthermore our Savior Jesus Christ, when he gave to his apostles and their successors power to forgive sins, instituted in his Church the sacrament of penance. Thus the faithful who fall into sin after baptism may be reconciled with God and renewed in grace.[16] The Church "possesses both water and tears: the water of baptism, the tears of penance."[17]

[11] See Luke 24:47
[12] See Acts 3:19, 26; 17:30.
[13] See Romans 6:4-10.
[14] Roman Missal, Eucharistic Prayer III.
[15] Roman Missal, Eucharistic Prayer II.
[16] See Council of Trent, Session XIV, De sacramento Paenitentiae, Chapter I: Denz.-Schön. 1668 and 1670; can. 1: Denz.-Schön. 1701.
[17] St. Ambrose, Letter 41:12: *PL* 16, 1116.

II

THE RECONCILIATION OF PENITENTS IN THE CHURCH'S LIFE

THE CHURCH IS HOLY BUT ALWAYS IN NEED OF PURIFICATION

3. Christ "loved the Church and gave himself up for her to make her holy" (Ephesians 5:25-26), and he united the Church to himself as his bride.[18] He filled her with his divine gifts,[19] because she is his body and fullness, and through her he spreads truth and grace to all.

The members of the Church, however, are exposed to temptation and unfortunately often fall into sin. As a result, "while Christ, 'holy, innocent, and unstained' (Hebrews 7:26), did not know sin (2 Corinthians 5:21) but came only to atone for the sins of the people (see Hebrews 2:17), the Church, which includes within itself sinners and is at the same time holy and always in need of purification, constantly pursues repentance and renewal."[20]

PENANCE IN THE CHURCH'S LIFE AND LITURGY

4. The people of God accomplishes and perfects this continual repentance in many different ways. It shares in the suffering of Christ[21] by enduring its own difficulties, carries out works of mercy and charity,[22] and adopts ever more fully the outlook of the Gospel message. Thus the people of God becomes in the world a sign of conversion to God. All this the Church expresses in its life and celebrates in the liturgy when the faithful confess that they are sinners and ask pardon of God and of their brothers and sisters. This happens in penitential services, in the proclamation of the word of God, in prayer, and in the penitential aspects of the eucharistic celebration.[23]

[18]See Revelation 19:7.
[19]See Ephesians 1:22-23; Second Vatican Council, constitution *Lumen gentium*, no. 7: *AAS* 57 (1965) 9-11.
[20]Second Vatican Council, constitution *Lumen gentium*, no. 8: *ibid.*, 12.
[21]See 1 Peter 4:13.
[22]See 1 Peter 4:8.
[23]See Council of Trent, Session XIV, De sacramento Paenitentiae: Denz.-Schön. 1638, 1740, 1743; Congregation of Rites, instruction *Eucharisticum mysterium*, May 25, 1967, no. 35: *AAS* 59 (1967) 560-561; Roman Missal, *General Instruction*, nos. 29, 30, 56 a. b. g.

In the sacrament of penance the faithful "obtain from the mercy of God pardon for their sins against him; at the same time they are reconciled with the Church which they wounded by their sins and which works for their conversion by charity, example, and prayer."[24]

RECONCILIATION WITH GOD AND WITH THE CHURCH

5. Since every sin is an offense against God which disrupts our friendship with him, "the ultimate purpose of penance is that we should love God deeply and commit ourselves completely to him."[25] Therefore, the sinner who by the grace of a merciful God embraces the way of penance comes back to the Father who "first loved us" (1 John 4:19), to Christ who gave himself up for us,[26] and to the Holy Spirit who has been poured out on us abundantly.[27]

"By the hidden and loving mystery of God's design men are joined together in the bonds of supernatural solidarity, so much so that the sin of one harms the others just as the holiness of one benefits the others."[28] Penance always entails reconciliation with our brothers and sisters who are always harmed by our sins.

In fact, men frequently join together to commit injustice. It is thus only fitting that they should help each other in doing penance so that they who are freed from sin by the grace of Christ may work with all men of good will for justice and peace in the world.

THE SACRAMENT OF PENANCE AND ITS PARTS

6. The follower of Christ who has sinned but who has been moved by the Holy Spirit to come to the sacrament of penance should above all be converted to God with his whole heart. This inner conversion of heart embraces sorrow for sin and the intent to lead a new life. It is expressed

[24]Second Vatican Council, constitution *Lumen gentium*, no. 11: *AAS* 57 (1965) 15-16.

[25]Paul VI, Apostolic Constitution *Paenitemini*, February 17, 1966: *AAS* 58 (1966) 179; See Second Vatican Council, constitution *Lumen gentium*, no. 11: AAS 57 (1965) 15-16.

[26]See Galatians 2:20; Ephesians 5:25.

[27]See Titus 3:6.

[28]Paul VI, Apostolic Constitution *Indulgentiarum doctrina*, January 1, 1967, no. 4: *AAS* 59 (1967) 9; see Pius XII, encyclical *Mystici Corporis*, June 29, 1943: *AAS* 35 (1943) 213.

through confession made to the Church, due satisfaction, and amendment of life. God grants pardon for sin through the Church, which works by the ministry of priests.[29]

a) Contrition

The most important act of the penitent is contrition, which is "heartfelt sorrow and aversion for the sin committed along with the intention of sinning no more."[30] "We can only approach the Kingdom of Christ by *metanoia.* This is a profound change of the whole person by which one begins to consider, judge, and arrange his life according to the holiness and love of God, made manifest in his Son in the last days and given to us in abundance" (see Hebrews 1:2; Colossians 1:19 and *passim*).[31] The genuineness of penance depends on this heartfelt contrition. For conversion should affect a person from within so that it may progressively enlighten him and render him continually more like Christ

b) Confession

The sacrament of penance includes the confession of sins, which comes from true knowledge of self before God and from contrition for those sins. However, this inner examination of heart and the exterior accusation should be made in the light of God's mercy. Confession requires in the penitent the will to open his heart to the minister of God, and in the minister a spiritual judgment by which, acting in the person of Christ, he pronounces his decision of forgiveness or retention of sins in accord with the power of the keys.[32]

c) Act of Penance (Satisfaction)

True conversion is completed by acts of penance or satisfaction for the sins committed, by amendment of conduct, and also by the reparation of injury.[33] The kind and extent of the

[29]See Council of Trent, Session XIV, De sacramento Paenitentiae, Chapter I: Denz.-Schön. 1673-1675.

[30]*Ibid.*, Chapter 4: Denz.-Schön. 1676.

[31]Paul VI, Apostolic Constitution *Paenitemini,* February 17, 1966: *AAS* 58 (1966) 179.

[32]See Council of Trent, Session XIV, De sacramento Paenitentiae, Chapter 5: Denz.-Schön. 1679.

[33]See Council of Trent, Session XIV, De sacramento Paenitentiae, Chapter 8: Denz.-Schön. 1690-1692; Paul VI, Apostolic Constitution *Indulgentiarum doctrina,* January 1, 1967, nos. 2-3: *AAS* 59 (1967) 6-8.

satisfaction should be suited to the personal condition of each penitent so that each one may restore the order which he disturbed and through the corresponding remedy be cured of the sickness from which he suffered. Therefore, it is necessary that the act of penance really be a remedy for sin and a help to renewal of life. Thus the penitent, "forgetting the things which are behind him" (Philippians 3:13), again becomes part of the mystery of salvation and turns himself toward the future.

d) Absolution

Through the sign of absolution God grants pardon to the sinner who in sacramental confession manifests his change of heart to the Church's minister, and thus the sacrament of penance is completed. In God's design the humanity and loving kindness of our Savior have visibly appeared to us,[34] and God uses visible signs to give salvation and to renew the broken covenant.

In the sacrament of penance the Father receives the repentant son who comes back to him, Christ places the lost sheep on his shoulders and brings it back to the sheepfold, and the Holy Spirit sanctifies this temple of God again or lives more fully within it. This is finally expressed in a renewed and more fervent sharing of the Lord's table, and there is great joy at the banquet of God's Church over the son who has returned from afar.[35]

THE NECESSITY AND BENEFIT OF THE SACRAMENT

7. Just as the wound of sin is varied and multiple in the life of individuals and of the community, so too the healing which penance provides is varied. Those who by grave sin have withdrawn from the communion of love with God are called back in the sacrament of penance to the life they have lost. And those who through daily weakness fall into venial sins draw strength from a repeated celebration of penance to gain the full freedom of the children of God.

a) To obtain the saving remedy of the sacrament of penance, according to the plan of our merciful God, the faithful

[34] See Titus 3:4-5.
[35] See Luke 15:7, 10, 32.

must confess to a priest each and every grave sin which they remember upon examination of their conscience.[36]

b) Moreover, frequent and careful celebration of this sacrament is also very useful as a remedy for venial sins. This is not a mere ritual repetition or psychological exercise, but a serious striving to perfect the grace of baptism so that, as we bear in our body the death of Jesus Christ, his life may be seen in us ever more clearly.[37] In confession of this kind, penitents who accuse themselves of venial faults should try to conform more closely to Christ and to follow the voice of the Spirit more attentively.

In order that this sacrament of healing may truly achieve its purpose among Christ's faithful, it must take root in their whole lives and move them to more fervent service of God and neighbor.

The celebration of this sacrament is thus always an act in which the Church proclaims its faith, gives thanks to God for the freedom with which Christ has made us free,[38] and offers its life as a spiritual sacrifice in praise of God's glory, as it hastens to meet the Lord Jesus.

III. OFFICES AND MINISTRIES IN THE RECONCILIATION OF PENITENTS

THE COMMUNITY IN THE CELEBRATION OF PENANCE

8. The whole Church, as a priestly people, acts in different ways in the work of reconciliation which has been entrusted to it by the Lord. Not only does the Church call sinners to repentance by preaching the word of God, but it also intercedes for them and helps penitents with maternal care and solicitude to acknowledge and admit their sins and so obtain the mercy of God who alone can forgive sins. Furthermore, the Church becomes the instrument of the conversion and absolution of the penitent through the ministry entrusted by Christ to the apostles and their successors.[39]

[36]See Council of Trent, Session XIV, De sacramento Paenitentiae, can. 7-8: Denz.-Schön. 1707-1708.
[37]See 2 Corinthians 4:10.
[38]See Galatians 4:31.
[39]See Matthew 18:18; John 20:23.

THE MINISTER OF THE SACRAMENT OF PENANCE

9. a) The Church exercises the ministry of the sacrament of penance through bishops and priests. By preaching God's word they call the faithful to conversion; in the name of Christ and by the power of the Holy Spirit they declare and grant the forgiveness of sins.

In the exercise of this ministry priests act in communion with the bishop and share in his power and office of regulating the penitential discipline.[40]

b) The competent minister of the sacrament of penance is a priest who has the faculty to absolve in accordance with canon law. All priests, however, even though not approved to hear confessions, absolve validly and licitly all penitents who are in danger of death.

THE PASTORAL EXERCISE OF THIS MINISTRY

10. a) In order to fulfill his ministry properly and faithfully the confessor should understand the disorders of souls and apply the appropriate remedies to them. He should fulfill his office of judge wisely and should acquire the knowledge and prudence necessary for this task by serious study, guided by the teaching authority of the Church and especially by fervent prayer to God. Discernment of spirits is a deep knowledge of God's action in the hearts of men; it is a gift of the Spirit as well as the fruit of charity.[41]

b) The confessor should always be ready and willing to hear the confessions of the faithful when they make a reasonable request of him.[42]

c) By receiving the repentant sinner and leading him to the light of the truth the confessor fulfills a paternal function: he reveals the heart of the Father and shows the image of Christ the Good Shepherd. He should keep in mind that he has been entrusted with the ministry of Christ, who mercifully accomplished the saving work of man's redemption and who is present by his power in the sacraments.[43]

[40] See Second Vatican Council, constitution *Lumen gentium,* no. 26: *AAS* 57 (1965) 31-32.

[41] See Philippians 1:9-10.

[42] See Congregation for the Doctrine of the Faith, *Normae pastorales circa absolutionem sacramentalem generali modo impertiendam,* June 16, 1972, No. XII: *AAS* 64 (1972) 514.

[43] See Second Vatican Council, constitution *Sacrosanctum Concilium,* no. 7: *AAS* 56 (1964) 100-101.

d) As the minister of God the confessor comes to know the secrets of another's conscience, and he is bound to keep the sacramental seal of confession absolutely inviolate.

THE PENITENT

11. The acts of the penitent in the celebration of the sacrament are of the greatest importance.

When with proper dispositions he approaches this saving remedy instituted by Christ and confesses his sins, he shares by his actions in the sacrament itself; the sacrament is completed when the words of absolution are spoken by the minister in the name of Christ.

Thus the faithful Christian, as he experiences and proclaims the mercy of God in his life, celebrates with the priest the liturgy by which the Church continually renews itself.

IV
THE CELEBRATION OF THE SACRAMENT OF PENANCE

THE PLACE OF CELEBRATION

12. The sacrament of penance is celebrated in the place and location prescribed by law.

THE TIME OF CELEBRATION

13. The reconciliation of penitents may be celebrated at any time on any day, but it is desirable that the faithful know the day and time at which the priest is available for this ministry. They should be encouraged to approach the sacrament of penance at times when Mass is not being celebrated and especially during the scheduled periods.[44]

The season of Lent is most appropriate for celebrating the sacrament of penance. Already on Ash Wednesday the people of God has heard the solemn invitation "Turn away from sin and believe the good news." It is therefore fitting to have several penitential celebrations during Lent, so that all the faithful may have an opportunity to be reconciled with

[44]See Congregation of Rites, instruction *Eucharisticum mysterium,* May 25, 1967, no. 35: *AAS* 59 (1967) 560-561.

God and their neighbor and so be able to celebrate the paschal mystery in the Easter triduum with renewed hearts.

LITURGICAL VESTMENTS

14. The regulations laid down by the local Ordinaries for the use of liturgical vestments in the celebration of penance are to be observed.

A
RITE FOR THE RECONCILIATION OF INDIVIDUAL PENITENTS

PREPARATION OF PRIEST AND PENITENT

15. Priest and penitent should first prepare themselves by prayer to celebrate the sacrament. The priest should call upon the Holy Spirit so that he may receive enlightenment and charity. The penitent should compare his life with the example and commandments of Christ and then pray to God for the forgiveness of his sins.

WELCOMING THE PENITENT

16. The priest should welcome the penitent with fraternal charity and, if the occasion permits, address him with friendly words. The penitent then makes the sign of the cross, saying: **In the name of the Father, and of the Son, and of the Holy Spirit. Amen.** The priest may also make the sign of the cross with the penitent. Next the priest briefly urges the penitent to have confidence in God. If the penitent is unknown to the priest, it is proper for him to indicate his state in life, the time of his last confession, his difficulties in leading the Christian life, and anything else which may help the confessor in exercising his ministry.

READING THE WORD OF GOD

17. Then the priest, or the penitent himself, may read a text of holy Scripture, or this may be done as part of the preparation for the sacrament. Through the word of God the Christian receives light to recognize his sins and is called to conversion and to confidence in God's mercy.

CONFESSION OF SINS AND THE ACT OF PENANCE

18. The penitent then confesses his sins, beginning, where customary, with a form of general confession: **I confess to almighty God.** If necessary, the priest should help the penitent to make a complete confession; he should also encourage him to have sincere sorrow for his sins against God. Finally, the priest should offer suitable counsel to help the penitent begin a new life and, where necessary, instruct him in the duties of the Christian way of life.

If the penitent has been the cause of harm or scandal to others, the priest should lead him to resolve that he will make appropriate restitution.

Then the priest imposes an act of penance or satisfaction on the penitent; this should serve not only to make up for the past but also to help him to begin a new life and provide him with an antidote to weakness. As far as possible, the penance should correspond to the seriousness and nature of the sins. This act of penance may suitably take the form of prayer, self-denial, and especially service of one's neighbor and works of mercy. These will underline the fact that sin and its forgiveness have a social aspect.

THE PRAYER OF THE PENITENT AND THE ABSOLUTION BY THE PRIEST

19. After this the penitent manifests his contrition and resolution to begin a new life by means of a prayer for God's pardon. It is desirable that this prayer should be based on the words of Scripture.

Following this prayer, the priest extends his hands, or at least his right hand, over the head of the penitent and pronounces the formula of absolution, in which the essential words are: **I absolve you from your sins in the name of the Father, and of the Son, and of the Holy Spirit.** As he says the final words the priest makes the sign of the cross over the penitent. The form of absolution (see no. 46) indicates that the reconciliation of the penitent comes from the mercy of the Father; it shows the connection between the reconciliation of the sinner and the paschal mystery of Christ; it stresses the role of the Holy Spirit in the forgiveness of sins; finally, it underlines the ecclesial aspect of the sacrament because reconciliation with God is asked for and given through the ministry of the Church.

PROCLAMATION OF PRAISE AND DISMISSAL OF THE PENITENT

20. After receiving pardon for his sins the penitent praises the mercy of God and gives him thanks in a short invocation taken from scripture. Then the priest tells him to go in peace.

The penitent continues his conversion and expresses it by a life renewed according to the Gospel and more and more steeped in the love of God, for "love covers over a multitude of sins" (1 Peter 4:8).

SHORT RITE

21. When pastoral need dictates it, the priest may omit or shorten some parts of the rite but must always retain in their entirety the confession of sins and the acceptance of the act of penance, the invitation to contrition (no. 44), and the form of absolution and the dismissal. In imminent danger of death, it is sufficient for the priest to say the essential words of the form of absolution, namely, **I absolve you from your sins in the name of the Father, and of the Son, and of the Holy Spirit.**

B
RITE FOR RECONCILIATION OF SEVERAL PENITENTS WITH INDIVIDUAL CONFESSION AND ABSOLUTION

22. When a number of penitents assemble at the same time to receive sacramental reconciliation, it is fitting that they be prepared for the sacrament by a celebration of the word of God.

Those who will receive the sacrament at another time may also take part in the service.

Communal celebration shows more clearly the ecclesial nature of penance. The faithful listen together to the word of God, which proclaims his mercy and invites them to conversion; at the same time they examine the conformity of their lives with that word of God and help each other through common prayer. After each person has confessed his sins and received absolution, all praise God together for his wonderful deeds on behalf of the people he has gained for himself through the blood of his Son.

If necessary, several priests should be available in suitable places to hear individual confessions and to reconcile the penitents.

INTRODUCTORY RITES

23. When the faithful are assembled, a suitable hymn may be sung. Then the priest greets them, and, if necessary, he or another minister gives a brief introduction to the celebration and explains the order of service. Next he invites all to pray and after a period of silence completes the (opening) prayer.

THE CELEBRATION OF THE WORD OF GOD

24. The sacrament of penance should begin with a hearing of God's word, because through his word God calls men to repentance and leads them to a true conversion of heart.

One or more readings may be chosen. If more than one are read, a psalm, another suitable song, or a period of silence should be inserted between them, so that the word of God may be more deeply understood and heartfelt assent may be given to it. If there is only one reading, it is preferable that it be from the gospel.

Readings should be chosen which illustrate the following:

a) the voice of God calling men back to conversion and ever closer conformity with Christ;

b) the mystery of our reconciliation through the death and resurrection of Christ and through the gift of the Holy Spirit;

c) the judgment of God about good and evil in men's lives as a help in the examination of conscience.

25. The homily, taking its theme from the scriptural text, should lead the penitents to examine their consciences and to turn away from sin and toward God. It should remind the faithful that sin works against God, against the community and one's neighbors, and against the sinner himself. Therefore, it would be good to recall:

a) the infinite mercy of God, greater than all our sins, by which again and again he calls us back to himself;

b) the need for interior repentance, by which we are genuinely prepared to make reparation for sin;

c) the social aspect of grace and sin, by which the actions of individuals in some degree affect the whole body of the Church;

d) the duty to make satisfaction for sin, which is effective because of Christ's work of reparation and requires especially, in addition to works of penance, the exercise of true charity toward God and neighbor.

26. After the homily a suitable period of silence should be allowed for examining one's conscience and awakening true contrition for sin. The priest or a deacon or other minister may help the faithful with brief considerations or a litany, adapted to their background, age, etc.

If it is judged suitable, this communal examination of conscience and awakening of contrition may take the place of the homily. But in this case it should be clearly based on the text of scripture that has just been read.

THE RITE OF RECONCILIATION

27. At the invitation of the deacon or other minister, all kneel or bow their heads and say a form of general confession (for example, **I confess to almighty God**). Then they stand and join in a litany or suitable song to express confession of sins, heartfelt contrition, prayer for forgiveness, and trust in God's mercy. Finally, they say the Lord's Prayer, which is never omitted.

28. After the Lord's Prayer the priests go to the places assigned for confession. The penitents who desire to confess their sins go to the priest of their choice. After receiving a suitable act of penance, they are absolved by him with the form for the reconciliation of an individual penitent.

29. When the confessions are over, the priests return to the sanctuary. The priest who presides invites all to make an act of thanksgiving and to praise God for his mercy. This may be done in a psalm or hymn or litany. Finally, the priest concludes the celebration with prayer, praising God for the great love he has shown us.

DISMISSAL OF THE PEOPLE

30. After the prayer of thanksgiving the priest blesses the faithful. Then the deacon or the priest himself dismisses the congregation.

C
RITE FOR RECONCILIATION OF PENITENTS WITH GENERAL CONFESSION AND ABSOLUTION

THE DISCIPLINE OF GENERAL ABSOLUTION

31. Individual, integral confession and absolution remain the only ordinary way for the faithful to reconcile themselves with God and the Church, unless physical or moral impossibility excuses from this kind of confession.

Particular, occasional circumstances may render it lawful and even necessary to give general absolution to a number of penitents without their previous individual confession.

In addition to cases involving danger of death, it is lawful to give sacramental absolution to several of the faithful at the same time, after they have made only a generic confession but have been suitably called to repentance, if there is grave need, namely when, in view of the number of penitents, sufficient confessors are not available to hear individual confessions properly within a suitable period of time, so that the penitents would, through no fault of their own, have to go without sacramental grace or holy communion for a long time. This may happen especially in mission territories but in other places as well and also in groups of persons when the need is established.

General absolution is not lawful, when confessors are available, for the sole reason of the large number of penitents, as may be on the occasion of some major feast or pilgrimage.[45]

32. The judgment about the presence of the above conditions and the decision concerning the lawfulness of giving general sacramental absolution are reserved to the bishop of the diocese, who is to consult with the other members of the episcopal conference.

Over and above the cases determined by the dioscesan bishop, if any other serious need arises for giving sacramental absolution to several persons together, the priest must have recourse to the local Ordinary beforehand, when this is

[45]Congregation for the Doctrine of the Faith, *Normae pastorales circa absolutionem sacramentalem generali modo impertiendam*, June 16, 1972, no. III: *AAS* 64 (1972) 511.

possible, if he is to give absolution lawfully. Otherwise, he should inform the Ordinary as soon as possible of the need and of the absolution which he gave.[46]

33. In order that the faithful may profit from sacramental absolution given to several persons at the same time, it is absolutely necessary that they be properly disposed. Each one should be sorry for his sins and resolve to avoid committing them again. He should intend to repair any scandal and harm he may have caused and likewise resolve to confess in due time each one of the grave sins which he cannot confess at present. These dispositions and conditions, which are required for the validity of the sacrament, should be carefully recalled to the faithful by priests.[47]

34. Those who receive pardon for grave sins by a common absolution should go to individual confession before they receive this kind of absolution again, unless they are impeded by a just reason. They are strictly bound, unless this is morally impossible, to go to confession within a year. The precept which obliges each of the faithful to confess at least once a year to a priest all the grave sins which he has not individually confessed before also remains in force in this case too.[48]

THE RITE OF GENERAL ABSOLUTION

35. For the reconciliation of penitents by general confession and absolution in the cases provided by law, everything takes place as described above for the reconciliation of several penitents with individual confession and absolution, with the following exceptions:

a) After the homily or during it, the faithful who seek general absolution should be instructed to dispose themselves properly, that is, each one should be sorry for his sins and resolve to avoid committing them again. He should intend to repair any scandal and harm he may have caused and likewise resolve to confess in due time each one of the grave sins which cannot be confessed at present.[49] Some act of penance should be proposed for all; individuals may add to this penance if they wish.

[46] *Ibid.*, no. V: *loc. cit.*, 512.
[47] *Ibid.*, nos. VI and XI: *loc. cit.*, 512, 514.
[48] *Ibid.*, nos. VII and VIII: *loc. cit*, 512-513.
[49] See *Ibid.*, no. VI: *loc. cit.*, 512.

b) The deacon, another minister, or the priest then calls upon the penitents who wish to receive absolution to show their intention by some sign (for example, by bowing their heads, kneeling, or giving some other sign determined by the episcopal conferences). They should also say together a form of general confession (for example, **I confess to almighty God**), which may be followed by a litany or a penitential song. Then the Lord's Prayer is sung or said by all, as indicated in no. 27, above.

c) Then the priest calls upon the grace of the Holy Spirit for the forgiveness of sins, proclaims the victory over sin of Christ's death and resurrection, and gives sacramental absolution to the penitents.

d) Finally, the priest invites the people to give thanks, as described in no. 29, above, and, omitting the concluding prayer, he immediately blesses and dismisses them.

V
PENITENTIAL CELEBRATIONS

NATURE AND STRUCTURE

36. Penitential celebrations are gatherings of the people of God to hear the proclamation of God's word. This invites them to conversion and renewal of life and announces our freedom from sin through the death and resurrection of Christ. The structure of these services is the same as that usually followed in celebrations of the word of God[50] and given in the *Rite for Reconciliation of Several Penitents.*

It is appropriate, therefore, that after the introductory rites (song, greeting, and prayer) one or more biblical readings be chosen with songs, psalms, or periods of silence inserted between them. In the homily these readings should be explained and applied to the congregation. Before or after the readings from scripture, readings from the Fathers or other writers may be selected which will help the community and each person to a true awareness of sin and heartfelt sorrow, in other words, to bring about conversion of life.

After the homily and reflection on God's word, it is desirable that the congregation, united in voice and spirit, pray

[50]See Congregation of Rites, instruction *Inter Oecumenici*, September 26, 1964, nos. 37-39: *AAS* 56 (1964) 110-111.

together in a litany or in some other way suited to general participation. At the end the Lord's Prayer is said, asking God our Father **to forgive us our sins as we forgive those who sin against us . . . and deliver us from evil.** The priest or the minister who presides concludes with a prayer and the dismissal of the people.

BENEFIT AND IMPORTANCE

37. Care should be taken that the faithful do not confuse these celebrations with the celebration of the sacrament of penance.[51] Penitential celebrations are very helpful in promoting conversion of life and purification of heart.[52]

It is desirable to arrange such services especially for these purposes:
—to foster the spirit of penance within the Christian community;
—to help the faithful to prepare for confession which can be made individually later at a convenient time;
—to help children gradually to form their conscience about sin in human life and about freedom from sin through Christ;
—to help catechumens during their conversion.

Penitential celebrations, moreover, are very useful in places where no priest is available to give sacramental absolution. They offer help in reaching that perfect contrition which comes from charity and enables the faithful to attain to God's grace through a desire for the sacrament of penance.[53]

VI
ADAPTATIONS OF THE RITE TO VARIOUS REGIONS AND CIRCUMSTANCES

ADAPTATIONS BY THE EPISCOPAL CONFERENCES

38. In preparing particular rituals episcopal conferences may adapt the rite of penance to the needs of individual regions

[51] See Congregation for the Doctrine of the Faith, *Normae pastorales circa absolutionem sacramentalem generali modo impertiendam,* June 16, 1972, no. X: *AAS* 64 (1972) 513-514.
[52] *Ibid.*
[53] See Council of Trent, Session XIV, De sacramento Paenitentiae, chapter 5: Denz.-Schön. 1677.

so that after confirmation by the Apostolic See the rituals may be used in the respective regions. It is the responsibility of episcopal conferences in this matter:

a) to establish regulations for the discipline of the sacrament of penance, particularly those affecting the ministry of priests and the reservation of sins;

b) to determine more precise regulations about the place proper for the ordinary celebration of the sacrament of penance and about the signs of penance to be shown by the faithful before general absolution (see no. 35, above);

c) to prepare translations of texts adapted to the character and language of each people and also to compose new texts for the prayers of the faithful and the minister, keeping intact the sacramental form.

THE COMPETENCE OF THE BISHOP

39. It is for the diocesan bishop:

a) to regulate the discipline of penance in his diocese,[54] including adaptations of the rite according to the rules proposed by the episcopal conference;

b) to determine, after consultation with the other members of the episcopal conference, when general sacramental absolution may be permitted under the conditions laid down by the Holy See.[55]

ADAPTATIONS BY THE MINISTER

40. It is for priests, and especially parish priests:

a) in reconciling individuals or the community, to adapt the rite to the concrete circumstances of the penitents. The essential structure and the entire form of absolution must be kept, but if necessary they may omit some parts for pastoral reasons or enlarge upon them, may select the texts of readings or prayers, and may choose a place more suitable for the celebration according to the regulations of the episcopal conference, so that the entire celebration may be rich and fruitful;

b) to propose and prepare occasional penitential celebrations during the year, especially in Lent. In order that the

[54]See Second Vatican Council, constitution *Lumen gentium*, no. 26: *AAS* 57 (1965) 31-32.

[55]See Congregation for the Doctrine of the Faith, *Normae pastorales circa absolutionem sacramentalem generali modo impertiendam*, no. V: *AAS* 64 (1972), 512.

texts chosen and the order of the celebration may be adapted to the conditions and circumstances of the community or group (for example, children, sick persons, etc.), they may be assisted by others, including the laity;

c) to decide to give general sacramental absolution preceded by only a generic confession, when a grave necessity not foreseen by the diocesan bishop arises and when recourse to him is not possible. They are obliged to notify the Ordinary as soon as possible of the need and of the fact that absolution was given.

CHAPTER I

RITE FOR RECONCILIATION OF INDIVIDUAL PENITENTS

RECEPTION OF THE PENITENT

41. When the penitent comes to confess his sins, the priest welcomes him warmly and greets him with kindness.

42. Then the penitent makes the sign of the cross which the priest may make also.

In the name of the Father, and of the Son, and of the Holy Spirit. Amen.

The priest invites the penitent to have trust in God, in these or similar words:

May God, who has enlightened every heart,
help you to know your sins
and trust in his mercy.
The penitent answers: **Amen.**

Other forms of reception of the penitent may be chosen from nos. 67-71.

READING OF THE WORD OF GOD (OPTIONAL)

43. Then the priest may read or say from memory a text of Scripture which proclaims God's mercy and calls man to conversion.

A reading may also be chosen from those given in nos. 72-83 and 101-201 for the reconciliation of several penitents. The priest and penitent may choose other readings from scripture.

CONFESSION OF SINS AND ACCEPTANCE OF SATISFACTION

44. Where it is the custom, the penitent says a general formula for confession (for example, **I confess to almighty God**) before he confesses his sins.

If necessary, the priest helps the penitent to make an integral confession and gives him suitable counsel. He urges him to be sorry for his faults, reminding him that through the sacrament of penance the Christian dies and rises with Christ and is thus renewed in the paschal mystery. The priest proposes an act of penance which the penitent accepts to make satisfaction for sin and to amend his life.

The priest should make sure that he adapts his counsel to the penitent's circumstances.

PRAYER OF THE PENITENT AND ABSOLUTION

45. The priest then asks the penitent to express his sorrow, which the penitent may do in these or similar words:

My God,
I am sorry for my sins with all my heart.
In choosing to do wrong
and failing to do good,
I have sinned against you
whom I should love above all things.
I firmly intend, with your help,
to do penance,
to sin no more,
and to avoid whatever leads me to sin.
Our Savior Jesus Christ
suffered and died for us.
In his name, my God, have mercy.

Other prayers of the penitent may be chosen from nos. 85-92.

Or:
Lord Jesus, Son of God
have mercy on me, a sinner.

ABSOLUTION

46. Then the priest extends his hands over the penitent's head (or at least extends his right hand) and says:

God, the Father of mercies,
through the death and resurrection of his Son
has reconciled the world to himself

and sent the Holy Spirit among us
for the forgiveness of sins;
through the ministry of the Church
may God give you pardon and peace,
and I absolve you from your sins
in the name of the Father, and of the Son, ✠
and of the Holy Spirit.
The penitent answers: **Amen.**

PROCLAMATION OF PRAISE OF GOD AND DISMISSAL

47. After the absolution, the priest continues:

Give thanks to the Lord, for he is good.
The penitent concludes: **His mercy endures for ever.**

Then the priest dismisses the penitent who has been reconciled, saying:

The Lord has freed you from your sins. Go in peace.

Or [93]:
May the Passion of our Lord Jesus Christ,
the intercession of the Blessed Virgin Mary,
and of all the saints,
whatever good you do and suffering you endure,
heal your sins,
help you to grow in holiness,
and reward you with eternal life.
Go in peace.

Or:
The Lord has freed you from sin.
May he bring you safely to his kingdom in heaven.
Glory to him for ever.
℟. **Amen.**

Or:

Blessed are those
whose sins have been forgiven,
whose evil deeds have been forgotten.
Rejoice in the Lord,
and go in peace.

Or:

Go in peace,
and proclaim to the world
the wonderful works of God
who has brought you salvation.

CHAPTER II

RITE FOR RECONCILIATION OF SEVERAL PENITENTS WITH INDIVIDUAL CONFESSION AND ABSOLUTION

INTRODUCTORY RITES

SONG

48. When the faithful have assembled, they may sing a psalm, antiphon, or other appropriate song while the priest is entering the church, for example:

Hear us, Lord,
for you are merciful and kind.
In your great compassion,
look on us with love.

Or:

Let us come with confidence before the throne of grace
to receive God's mercy,
and we shall find pardon and strength
in our time of need.

GREETING

49. After the song the priest greets the congregation:

Grace, mercy, and peace be with you
from God the Father
and Christ Jesus our Savior.
℟. And also with you.

Or:

Grace and peace be with you
from God the Father
and from Jesus Christ
who loved us
and washed away our sins in his blood.
℟. Glory to him for ever. Amen.

Or other forms of greeting may be chosen from nos. 94-96.

Then the priest or another minister speaks briefly about the importance and purpose of the celebration and the order of the service.

OPENING PRAYER

50. The priest invites all to pray, using these or similar words:

Brothers and sisters, God calls us to conversion; let us therefore ask him for the grace of sincere repentance.

All pray in silence for a brief period. Then the priest sings or says the prayer:

Lord,
hear the prayers of those who call on you,
forgive the sins of those who confess to you,
and in your merciful love
give us your pardon and your peace.
We ask this through Christ our Lord.
℟. **Amen.**

Or:
Lord,
send your Spirit among us
to cleanse us in the waters of repentance.
May he make of us a living sacrifice
so that in every place,
by his life-giving power,
we may praise your glory
and proclaim your loving compassion.
We ask this through Christ our Lord.
℟. **Amen.**

Other forms of the opening prayer may be chosen from nos. 97-100.

CELEBRATION OF THE WORD OF GOD

51. The celebration of the word follows. If there are several readings a psalm or other appropriate song or even a period of silence should intervene between them, so that everyone may understand the word of God more deeply and give it his heartfelt assent. If there is only one reading, it is preferable that it be from the gospel.

FIRST EXAMPLE

Love is the fullness of the law

FIRST READING:

Deuteronomy 5:1-3, 6-7, 11-12, 16-21a; 6:4-6 Love the Lord your God with all your heart.

RESPONSORIAL PSALM:

Baruch 1:15-22 ℟. (3:2) **Listen and have pity, Lord, because you are merciful.**

SECOND READING:

Ephesians 5:1-14 Walk in love, as Christ loved us.

GOSPEL ACCLAMATION:

John 8:12

I am the light of the world.
The man who follows me will have the light of life.

GOSPEL:

Matthew 22:34-40 On these two commandments the whole law and the prophets depend.

Or :

John 13:34-35; 15:10-13 I give you a new commandment: love one another.

SECOND EXAMPLE

Your mind must be renewed

FIRST READING:

Isaiah 1:10-18 Stop doing what is wrong, and learn to do good.

RESPONSORIAL PSALM:

Psalm 51:1-4, 8-17

℟. (19a) **A humbled heart is pleasing to God.**

SECOND READING:

Ephesians 4:23-32 Your mind must be renewed by a spiritual revolution.

GOSPEL ACCLAMATION:

Matthew 11:28

Come to me, all you that labor and are burdened, and I will give you rest.

GOSPEL:

Matthew 5:1-12 Happy the poor in spirit.

Other optional texts are given in nos. 101-201.

HOMILY

52. The homily which follows is based on the texts of the readings and should lead the penitents to examine their consciences and renew their lives.

EXAMINATION OF CONSCIENCE

53. A period of time may be spent in making an examination of conscience and in arousing true sorrow for sins. The priest, deacon, or another minister may help the faithful by brief statements or a kind of litany, taking into consideration their circumstances, age, etc.

RITE OF RECONCILIATION

GENERAL CONFESSION OF SINS

54. The deacon or another minister invites all to kneel or bow, and to join in saying a general formula for confession (for example, **I confess to almighty God**). Then they stand and say a litany or sing an appropriate song. The Lord's Prayer is always added at the end.

FIRST EXAMPLE

Deacon or Minister:

My brothers and sisters, confess your sins and pray

for each other, that you may be healed.

All say:
I confess to almighty God,
and to you, my brothers and sisters,
that I have sinned through my own fault
They strike their breast:
in my thoughts and in my words,
in what I have done,
and in what I have failed to do;
and I ask blessed Mary, ever virgin,
all the angels and saints,
and you, my brothers and sisters,
to pray for me to the Lord our God.

Deacon or minister:
The Lord is merciful. He makes us clean of heart and leads us out into his freedom when we acknowledge our guilt. Let us ask him to forgive us and bind up the wounds inflicted by our sins.

Give us the grace of true repentance.
℟. **We pray you, hear us.**

Pardon your servants and release them from the debt of sin.
℟. **We pray you, hear us.**

Forgive your children who confess their sins, and restore them to full communion with your Church.
℟. **We pray you, hear us.**

Renew the glory of baptism in those who have lost it by sin.
℟. **We pray you, hear us.**

Welcome them to your altar, and renew their spirit with the hope of eternal glory.
℟. **We pray you, hear us.**

Keep them faithful to your sacraments and loyal in your service.
℟. **We pray you, hear us.**

Renew your love in their hearts, and make them bear witness to it in their daily lives.
℟. **We pray you, hear us.**

Keep them always obedient to your commandments and protect within them your gift of eternal life.
℟. **We pray you, hear us.**

Deacon or minister:
Let us now pray to God our Father in the words Christ gave us, and ask him for his forgiveness and protection from all evil.

All say together:
Our Father . . .

The priest concludes:
Lord,
draw near to your servants
who in the presence of your Church
confess that they are sinners.
Through the ministry of the Church
free them from all sin
so that renewed in spirit
they may give you thankful praise.
We ask this through Christ our Lord.
℟. **Amen.**

SECOND EXAMPLE

Deacon or minister:
Brothers and sisters, let us call to mind the goodness of God our Father, and acknowledge our sins, so that we may receive his merciful forgiveness.

All say:
I confess to almighty God,
and to you, my brothers and sisters,
that I have sinned through my own fault

They strike their breast:
in my thoughts and in my words,
in what I have done,
and in what I have failed to do;
and I ask blessed Mary, ever virgin,
all the angels and saints,
and you, my brothers and sisters,
to pray for me to the Lord our God.

Deacon or minister:
Christ our Savior is our advocate with the Father:
with humble hearts let us ask him to forgive us our sins
and cleanse us from every stain.

You were sent with good news for the poor and healing for the contrite.
℟. **Lord, be merciful to me, a sinner.** Or: **Lord, have mercy.**

You came to call sinners, not the just.
℟. **Lord, be merciful to me, a sinner.** Or: **Lord, have mercy.**

You forgave the many sins of the woman who showed you great love.
℟. **Lord, be merciful to me, a sinner.** Or: **Lord, have mercy.**

You did not shun the company of outcasts and sinners.
℟. **Lord, be merciful to me, a sinner.** Or: **Lord, have mercy.**

You carried back to the fold the sheep that had strayed.
℟. **Lord, be merciful to me, a sinner.** Or: **Lord, have mercy.**

You did not condemn the woman taken in adultery, but sent her away in peace.
℟. **Lord, be merciful to me, a sinner.** Or: **Lord, have mercy.**

You called Zacchaeus to repentance and a new life.
℟. **Lord, be merciful to me, a sinner.** Or: **Lord, have mercy.**

You promised Paradise to the repentant thief.
℟. **Lord, be merciful to me, a sinner.** Or: **Lord, have mercy.**

You are always interceding for us at the right hand of the Father.
℟. **Lord, be merciful to me, a sinner.** Or: **Lord, have mercy.**

Deacon or minister:
Now, in obedience to Christ himself, let us join in prayer to the Father, asking him to forgive us as we forgive others.

All say together:

Our Father . . .

The priest concludes:
Father, our source of life,
you know our weakness.
May we reach out with joy to grasp your hand
and walk more readily in your ways.
We ask this through Christ our Lord.
℟. **Amen.**

For other texts see numbers 202-205.

INDIVIDUAL CONFESSION AND ABSOLUTION

55. Then the penitents go to the priests designated for individual confession, and confess their sins. Each one receives and accepts a fitting act of satisfaction and is absolved. After hearing the confession and offering suitable counsel, the priest extends his hands over the penitent's head (or at least extends his right hand) and gives him absolution. Everything else which is customary in individual confession is omitted.

God, the Father of mercies,
through the death and resurrection of his Son
has reconciled the world to himself

and sent the Holy Spirit among us
for the forgiveness of sins;
through the ministry of the Church
may God give you pardon and peace,
and I absolve you from your sins
in the name of the Father, and of the Son, ✠
and of the Holy Spirit.
The penitent answers: **Amen.**

PROCLAMATION OF PRAISE FOR GOD'S MERCY

56. When the individual confessions have been completed, the other priests stand near the one who is presiding over the celebration. The latter invites all present to offer thanks and encourages them to do good works which will proclaim the grace of repentance in the life of the entire community and each of its members. It is fitting for all to sing a psalm or hymn or to say a litany in acknowledgment of God's power and mercy, for example, the canticle of Mary (Luke 1:46-55), or Psalm 136:1-9, 13-14, 16, 25-26, or one of the psalms as given in no. 206.

CONCLUDING PRAYER OF THANKSGIVING

57. After the song of praise or the litany, the priest concludes the common prayer:

Almighty and merciful God,
how wonderfully you created man
and still more wonderfully remade him.
You do not abandon the sinner
but seek him out with a father's love.
You sent your Son into the world
to destroy sin and death
by his passion,
and to restore life and joy
by his resurrection.
You sent the Holy Spirit into our hearts
to make us your children
and heirs of your kingdom.
You constantly renew our spirit
in the sacraments of your redeeming love,

freeing us from slavery to sin
and transforming us ever more closely
into the likeness of your beloved Son.
We thank you for the wonders of your mercy,
and with heart and hand and voice
we join with the whole Church
in a new song of praise:
Glory to you
through Christ
in the Holy Spirit,
now and for ever.
℟. **Amen.**

Or:
All-holy Father,
you have shown us your mercy
and made us a new creation
in the likeness of your Son.
Make us living signs of your love
for the whole world to see.

We ask this through Christ our Lord.
℟. **Amen.**

Other concluding prayers may be chosen from nos 207-211.

CONCLUDING RITE

58. Then the priest blesses all present:

May the Lord guide your hearts in the way of his love
and fill you with Christ-like patience.
℟. **Amen.**

May he give you strength
to walk in newness of life
and to please him in all things.
℟. **Amen.**

May almighty God bless you,
the Father, and the Son, ✠ and the Holy Spirit.
℟. **Amen.**

Other blessings may be selected from nos. 212-214.

59. The deacon or other minister or the priest himself dismisses the assembly:

The Lord has freed you from your sins. Go in peace.
All answer: **Thanks be to God.**

Any other appropriate form may be used.

CHAPTER III

RITE FOR RECONCILIATION OF SEVERAL PENITENTS WITH GENERAL CONFESSION AND ABSOLUTION

60. For the reconciliation of several penitents with general confession and absolution, in the cases provided for in the law, everything is done as described above for the reconciliation of several penitents with individual absolution, but with the following changes only.

INSTRUCTION

After the homily or as part of the homily, the priest explains to the faithful who wish to receive general absolution that they should be properly disposed. Each one should repent of his sins and resolve to turn away from these sins, to make up for any scandal and harm he may have caused, and to confess individually at the proper time each of the serious sins which cannot now be confessed. Some form of satisfaction should be proposed to all, and each individual may add something if he desires.

GENERAL CONFESSION

61. Then the deacon or other minister or the priest himself invites the penitents who wish to receive absolution to indicate this by some kind of sign. He may say:

Will those of you who wish to receive sacramental absolution please kneel and acknowledge that you are sinners.

Or:

Will those of you who wish to receive sacramental absolution please bow your heads and acknowledge that you are sinners.

Or he may suggest a sign laid down by the episcopal conference.

The penitents say a general formula for confession (for example, **I confess to almighty God**). A litany or appropriate song may follow, as described above for the reconciliation of several penitents with individual confession and absolution (no. 54). The Lord's Prayer is always added at the end.

GENERAL ABSOLUTION

62. The priest then gives absolution, holding his hands extended over the penitents and saying:

God the Father does not wish the sinner to die
but to turn back to him and live.
He loved us first and sent his Son into the world to be its Savior.
May he show you his merciful love and give you peace.
℟. **Amen.**

Our Lord Jesus Christ was given up to death for our sins,
and rose again for our justification.
He sent the Holy Spirit on his apostles
and gave them power to forgive sins.
Through the ministry entrusted to me
may he deliver you from evil
and fill you with his Holy Spirit.
℟. **Amen.**

The Spirit, the Comforter, was given to us for the forgiveness of sins.
In him we approach the Father.
May he cleanse your hearts and clothe you in his glory,
so that you may proclaim the mighty acts of God
who has called you out of darkness into the splendor of his light.
℟. **Amen.**

And I absolve you from your sins
in the name of the Father, and of the Son, ✠

and of the Holy Spirit.
℟. **Amen.**

Or:
God, the Father of mercies,
through the death and resurrection of his Son
has reconciled the world to himself
and sent the Holy Spirit among us
for the forgiveness of sins;
through the ministry of the Church
may God give you pardon and peace,
and I absolve you from your sins
in the name of the Father, and of the Son, ✠
and of the Holy Spirit.
℟. **Amen.**

PROCLAMATION OF PRAISE AND CONCLUSION

63. The priest invites all to thank God and to acknowledge his mercy. After a suitable song or hymn, he blesses the people and dismisses them, as described above, nos. 58-59, but without the concluding prayer (no. 57).

SHORT RITE

64. In case of necessity, the rite for reconciling several penitents with general confession and absolution may be shortened. If possible, there is a brief reading from scripture. After giving the usual instruction (no. 60) and indicating the act of penance, the priest invites the penitents to make a general confession (for example, **I confess to almighty God**), and gives the absolution with the form which is indicated in no. 62.

65. In imminent danger of death, it is enough for the priest to use the form of absolution itself. In this case it may be shortened to the following:

I absolve you from your sins
in the name of the Father, and of the Son, ✠
and of the Holy Spirit.
℟. **Amen.**

66. A person who receives general absolution from grave sins is bound to confess each grave sin at his next individual confession.

CHAPTER IV

VARIOUS TEXTS USED IN THE CELEBRATION OF RECONCILIATION

I. FOR THE RECONCILIATION OF ONE PENITENT

INVITATION TO TRUST IN GOD

67. Ezekiel 33:11

The Lord does not wish the sinner to die
but to turn back to him and live.
Come before him with trust in his mercy.

68. Luke 5:32

May the Lord Jesus welcome you.
He came to call sinners, not the just.
Have confidence in him.

69.

May the grace of the Holy Spirit
fill your heart with light,
that you may confess your sins with loving trust
and come to know that God is merciful.

70.

May the Lord be in your heart
and help you to confess your sins with true sorrow.

71. 1 John 2:1-2

If you have sinned, do not lose heart.
We have Jesus Christ to plead for us with the Father:
he is the Holy One,
the atonement for our sins
and for the sins of the whole world.

SHORT READINGS FROM SCRIPTURE

72. **Let us look on Jesus
who suffered to save us
and rose again for our justification.**
Isaiah 53:4-6

73. **Let us listen to the Lord as he speaks to us:**
Ezekiel 11:19-20

74. **Let us listen to the Lord as he speaks to us:**
Matthew 6:14-15

75. Mark 1:14-15

76. **Let us listen to the Lord as he speaks to us:**
Luke 6:31-38

77. Luke 15:1-7

78. John 10:19-23

79. Romans 5:8-9

80. Ephesians 5:1-2

81. Colossians 1:12-14

82. Colossians 3:8-10, 12-17

83. 1 John 1:6-7, 9

84. A reading may also be chosen from those given in nos. 101-201 for the reconciliation of several penitents. The priest and penitent may choose other readings from scripture.

PRAYER OF THE PENITENT

85. Psalm 25:6-7

**Remember, Lord, your compassion and mercy which you showed long ago.
Do not recall the sins and failings of my youth.
In your mercy remember me, Lord, because of your goodness.**

86. Psalm 50:4-5
**Wash me from my guilt
and cleanse me of my sin.
I acknowledge my offense;
my sin is before me always.**

87. Luke 15:18; 18:13
**Father, I have sinned against you
and am not worthy to be called your son.
Be merciful to me, a sinner.**

88.
**Father of mercy,
like the prodigal son
I return to you and say:
"I have sinned against you
and am no longer worthy to be called your son."
Christ Jesus, Savior of the world,
I pray with the repentant thief
to whom you promised paradise:
"Lord, remember me in your kingdom."
Holy Spirit, fountain of love,
I call on you with trust:
"Purify my heart,
and help me to walk as a child of the light."**

89.
**Lord Jesus,
you opened the eyes of the blind,
healed the sick,
forgave the sinful woman,
and after Peter's denial confirmed him in your love.
Listen to my prayer:
forgive all my sins,
renew your love in my heart,
help me to live in perfect unity with my fellow Christians
that I may proclaim your saving power to all the world.**

90.
Lord Jesus,
you chose to be called the friend of sinners.
By your saving death and resurrection
free me from my sins.
May your peace take root in my heart
and bring forth a harvest
of love, holiness, and truth.

91.
Lord Jesus Christ,
you are the Lamb of God;
you take away the sins of the world.
Through the grace of the Holy Spirit
restore me to friendship with your Father,
cleanse me from every stain of sin
in the blood you shed for me,
and raise me to new life
for the glory of your name.

92.
Lord God,
in your goodness have mercy on me:
do not look on my sins,
but take away all my guilt.
Create in me a clean heart
and renew within me an upright spirit.

Or:
Lord Jesus, Son of God,
have mercy on me, a sinner.

AFTER THE ABSOLUTION

93. In place of the proclamation of God's praise and the dismissal, the priest may say:

May the Passion of our Lord Jesus Christ,
the intercession of the Blessed Virgin Mary and of all the saints,
whatever good you do and suffering you endure,
heal your sins,

help you grow in holiness,
and reward you with eternal life.
Go in peace.

Or:
The Lord has freed you from sin.
May he bring you safely to his kingdom in heaven.
Glory to him for ever.
℟. **Amen.**

Or:
Blessed are those
whose sins have been forgiven,
whose evil deeds have been forgotten.
Rejoice in the Lord,
and go in peace.

Or:
Go in peace,
and proclaim to the world
the wonderful works of God,
who has brought you salvation.

II. FOR THE RECONCILIATION OF SEVERAL PENITENTS

GREETING

94.
Grace, mercy, and peace
from God the Father and Jesus Christ his Son
be with you in truth and love.
℟. **Amen.**

95.
May God open your hearts to his law
and give you peace;
may he answer your prayers
and restore you to his friendship.
℟. **Amen.**

96.
Grace and peace be with you
from God our Father
and from the Lord Jesus Christ
who laid down his life for our sins.
℟. **Glory to him for ever. Amen.**

The greetings from the introductory rites of Mass may also be used.

OPENING PRAYERS

97.
Lord,
turn to us in mercy
and forgive us all our sins
that we may serve you in true freedom.

We ask this through Christ our Lord.
℟. **Amen.**

98.
Lord our God,
you are patient with sinners
and accept our desire to make amends.
We acknowledge our sins
and are resolved to change our lives.
Help us to celebrate this sacrament of your mercy
so that we may reform our lives
and receive from you the gift of everlasting joy.

We ask this through Christ our Lord.
℟. **Amen.**

99.
Almighty and merciful God,
you have brought us together in the name of your Son
to receive your mercy and grace in our time of need.
Open our eyes to see the evil we have done.
Touch our hearts and convert us to yourself.

Where sin has divided and scattered,
may your love make one again;
where sin has brought weakness,

**may your power heal and strengthen;
where sin has brought death,
may your Spirit raise to new life.**

**Give us a new heart to love you,
so that our lives may reflect the image of your Son.
May the world see the glory of Christ
revealed in your Church,
and come to know
that he is the one whom you have sent,
Jesus Christ, your Son, our Lord.**
℟. **Amen.**

100.
**Father of mercies
and God of all consolation,
you do not wish the sinner to die
but to be converted and live.
Come to the aid of your people,
that they may turn from their sins
and live for you alone.
May we be attentive to your word,
confess our sins, receive your forgiveness,
and be always grateful for your loving kindness.
Help us to live the truth in love
and grow into the fullness of Christ, your Son,
who lives and reigns for ever and ever.**
℟. **Amen.**

BIBLICAL READINGS

The following readings are proposed as a help for pastors and others involved in the selection of readings. For diversity, and according to the nature of the group, other readings may be selected.

READINGS FROM THE OLD TESTAMENT

101. **Genesis 3:1-19** She took the fruit of the tree and ate it.

102. **Genesis 4:1-15** Cain set on his brother and killed him.

103. **Genesis 18:17-33** The Lord said: I will not destroy the city for the sake of ten good men.

104. **Exodus 17:1-7** They tempted the Lord saying: Is the Lord here or not?

105. **Exodus 20:1-21** I am the Lord your God . . . you will not have other gods.

106. **Deuteronomy 6:3-9** Love the Lord your God with your whole heart.

107. **Deuteronomy 9:7-19** Your people quickly turned away from the wrong you had showed them.

108. **Deuteronomy 30:15-20** I set before you life and prosperity, death and evil.

109. **2 Samuel 12:1-9, 13** David said to Nathan: I have sinned against the Lord God. Nathan said to David: The Lord has forgiven your sin; you will not die.

110. **Nehemiah 9:1-20** The sons of Israel assembled for a fast and confessed their sins.

111. **Wisdom 1:1-16** Love justice, for wisdom will not enter an evil soul nor live in a body subjected to sin.

112. **Wisdom 5:1-16** The hope of the wicked is like down flying on the wind. The just, however, live for ever.

113. **Sirach 28:1-7** Forgive your neighbor when he hurts you, and then your sins will be forgiven when you pray.

114. **Isaiah 1:2-6, 15-18** I have nourished and educated sons; however they have rebelled against me.

115. **Isaiah 5:1-7** The vineyard became my delight. He looked for grapes, but it yielded wild grapes.

116. **Isaiah 43:22-28** On account of me your iniquities are blotted out.

117. **Isaiah 53:1-12** The Lord laid upon him our guilt.

118. **Isaiah 55:1-11** Let the wicked man forsake his way and return to the Lord, and he will have mercy on him because he is generous in forgiving.

119. **Isaiah 58:1-11** When you give your soul to the hungry and fulfill the troubled soul, your light will rise like dawn from the darkness, and your darkness will be like midday.

120. **Isaiah 59:1-4, 9-15** Your iniquities divide you and your God.

121. **Jeremiah 2:1-13** My people have done two evils: they have abandoned me, the fountain of living water, and have dug for themselves broken cisterns which hold no water.

122. **Jeremiah 7:21-26** Listen to my voice, and I will be your God, and you will be my people.

123. **Ezekiel 11:14-21** I will take the heart of stone from their bodies, and I will give them a heart of flesh, so that they may walk according to my laws.

124. **Ezekiel 18:20-32** If a wicked man turns away from his sins, he shall live and not die.

125. **Ezekiel 36:23-28** I shall sprinkle upon you clean water, put my spirit within you, and make you walk according to my commands.

126. **Hosea 2:16-25** I will make a covenant for them on that day.

127. **Hosea 11:1-11** I took them in my arms, and they did not know that I cured them.

128. **Hosea 14:2-10** Israel, return to the Lord your God.

129. **Joel 2:12-19** Return to me with your whole heart.

130. **Micah 6:1-4, 4-6** Do right and love mercy, and walk humbly with your God.

131. **Micah 7:2-7, 18-20** The Lord will turn back and have mercy on us; he will cast all our sins into the depths of the sea.

132. **Zechariah 1:1-6** Return to me, and I shall return to you.

RESPONSORIAL PSALM

133. Psalm 13

℟. (6a): **All my hope, O Lord, is in your loving kindness.**

134. Psalm 25

℟. (16a): **Turn to me, Lord, and have mercy.**

135. Psalm 31:2-6

℟. (6b): **You have redeemed us, Lord, God of truth.**

136. Psalm 32

℟. (5c): **Lord, forgive the wrong I have done.**

137. Psalm 36

℟. (8): **How precious is your unfailing love, Lord.**

138. Psalm 50: 7-8, 14-23

℟. (23b): **To the upright I will show the saving power of God.**

139. Psalm 51

℟. (14a): **Give back to me the joy of your salvation.**

140. Psalm 73

℟. (28a): **It is good for me to be with the Lord.**

141. Psalm 90

℟. (14): **Fill us with your love, O Lord, and we will sing for joy!**

142. Psalm 95

℟. (8a): **If today you hear his voice, harden not your hearts.**

143. Psalm 119:1, 10-13, 15-16

℟. (1): **Happy are they who follow the law of the Lord!**

144. Psalm 123

℟. (2c): **Our eyes are fixed on the Lord.**

145. Psalm 130

℟. (7bc): **With the Lord there is mercy, and fullness of redemption.**

146. Psalm 139:1-18, 23-24

℟. (23a): **You have searched me, and you know me, Lord.**

147. Psalm 143: 1-11

℟. (10): **Teach me to do your will, my God.**

READINGS FROM THE NEW TESTAMENT

148. **Romans 3:22-26** All men are justified by the gift of God through redemption in Christ Jesus.

149. **Romans 5:6-11** We give glory to God through our Lord Jesus Christ, through whom we have received reconciliation.

150. **Romans 6:2b-13** Consider yourselves dead to sin but alive to God.

151. **Romans 6:16-23** The wages of sin is death; the gift of God is eternal life in Christ Jesus our Lord.

152. **Romans 7:14-25** Unhappy man that I am! Who will free me? Thanks to God through Jesus Christ our Lord.

153. **Romans 12:1-2, 9-19** Be transformed by the renewal of your mind.

154. **Romans 13:8-14** Let us cast away the works of darkness and put on the weapons of light.

155. **2 Corinthians 5:17-21** God reconciled the world to himself through Christ.

156. **Galatians 5:16-24** You cannot belong to Christ unless you crucify the flesh with its passions and concupiscence.

157. **Ephesians 2:1-10** When we were dead to sin, God, on account of his great love for us, brought us to life in Christ.

158. **Ephesians 4:1-3, 17-32** Renew yourself and put on the new man.

159. **Ephesians 5:1-14** You were once in darkness; now you are light in the Lord, so walk as children of light.

160. **Ephesians 6:10-18** Put God's armor on so that you will be able to stand firm against evil.

161. **Colossians 3:1-10, 12-17** If you were raised to life with Christ, aspire to the realm above. Put to death what remains in this earthly life.

162. **Hebrews 12:1-5** You have not resisted to the point of shedding your blood in your struggle against sin.

163. **James 1:22-27** Be doers of the word and not merely listeners.

164. **James 2:14-26** What use is it if someone says that he believes and does not manifest it in works?

165. **James 3:1-12** If someone does not offend in word, he is a perfect man.

166. **1 Peter 1:13-23** You have been redeemed not by perishable goods, gold or silver, but by the precious blood of Jesus Christ.

167. **2 Peter 1:3-11** Be careful so that you may make firm your calling and election.

168. **1 John 1:5-10, 2:1-2** If we confess our sins, he is faithful and just and will forgive our sins and cleanse us from all injustice.

169. **1 John 2:3-11** Whoever hates his brother remains in darkness.

170. **1 John 3:1-24** We know that we have crossed over from death to life because we love our brothers.

171. **1 John 4:16-21** God is love, and he who lives in love, lives in God, and God in him.

172. **Revelation 2:1-5** Do penance and return to your former ways.

173. **Revelation 3:14-22** Because you are lukewarm, neither hot or cold, I will vomit you out of my mouth.

174. **Revelation 20:11-15** All have been judged according to their works.

175. **Revelation 21:1-8** Whoever conquers will inherit all this, and I will be his God, and he will be my son.

176. **Matthew 3:1-12** Repent, for the kingdom of heaven is close at hand.

177. **Matthew 4:12-17** Repent, for the kingdom of heaven is close at hand.

178. **Matthew 5:1-12** When he saw the crowds, he went up to the hill and taught his disciples.

179. **Matthew 5:13-16** Let your light shine before men.

180. **Matthew 5:17-47** But I am speaking to you.

181. **Matthew 9:1-8** Have confidence, my son, your sins are forgiven.

182. **Matthew 9:9-13** I did not come to call the just, but sinners.

183. **Matthew 18:15-20** You have won back your brother.

184. **Matthew 18:21-35** This is the way my heavenly Father will deal with you unless each one forgives his brother from his heart.

185. **Matthew 25:31-46** Whatever you have done to the very least of my brothers, you have done to me.

186. **Matthew 26:69-75** Peter went outside and wept bitterly.

187. **Mark 12:28-34** This is the first commandment.

188. **Luke 7:36-50** Her many sins must have been forgiven her, because she loved much.

189. **Luke 13:1-5** Unless you repent you will all perish as they did.

190. **Luke 15:1-10** Heaven is filled with joy when one sinner turns back to God.

191. **Luke 15:11-32** When he was still far away, his father saw him and was moved with mercy. He ran to him and embraced and kissed him.

192. **Luke 17:1-4** If your brother sins against you seven times a day and returns to you seven times a day and says I am sorry, you must forgive him.

193. **Luke 18:9-14** God, be merciful to me, a sinner.

194. **Luke 19:1-10** The Son of Man has come to seek out and save what was lost.

195. **Luke 23:39-43** Today you will be with me in paradise.

196. **John 8:1-11** Go and sin no more.

197. **John 8:31-36** Everyone who commits sin is a slave of sin.

198. **John 15:1-8** The Father prunes every barren branch, and every branch that bears fruit he makes it bear even more.

199. **John 15:9-14** You are my friends if you do what I command you.

200. **John 19:13-37** They shall look upon him whom they pierced.

201. **John 20:19-23** Receive the Holy Spirit; whose sins you forgive, they are forgiven.

INVITATION OF THE MINISTER FOR THE GENERAL CONFESSION OF SINS

202. If the prayer is directed to the Father:

1

Dear friends in Christ, our merciful Father does not desire the death of the sinner but rather that he should turn back to him and have life. Let us pray that we who are sorry for our past sins may fear no future evil and sin no more.
℟. **Spare us, Lord; spare your people.**

2

God who is infintely merciful pardons all who are repentant and takes away their guilt. Confident in his goodness, let us ask him to forgive all our sins as we confess them with sincerity of heart.
℟. **Lord, hear our prayer.**

3

God gave us his Son for our sins and raised him up to make us holy. Let us humbly pray to the Father.
℟. **Lord, have mercy on your people.**

4

God our Father waits for the return of those who are lost and welcomes them back as his children. Let us pray that we may turn back to him and be received with kindness into his house.
℟. **Lord, do not hold our sins against us.**

Or:

Father, we have sinned in your sight; we are unworthy to be called your children.

5

Our God seeks out what is lost, leads home the abandoned, binds up what is broken and gives strength to the weak; let us ask him to help us.
℟. **Lord, heal our weakness.**

203. If the prayer is directed to Christ:

1

Jesus Christ is the victor over sin and death: in his mercy may he pardon our offenses against God and reconcile us with the Church we have wounded by our sins.
℟. **Lord Jesus, be our salvation.**

2

In his great love Christ willingly suffered and died for our sins and for the sins of all mankind. Let us come before him with faith and hope to pray for the salvation of the world.
℟. **Christ, graciously hear us.**

3

Let us pray with confidence to Christ, the Good Shepherd, who seeks out the lost sheep and carries it back with joy.
℟. **Lord, seek us out and bring us home.**

4

Christ our Lord bore our sins upon the cross and by his suffering has brought us healing, so that we live for God and are dead to sin. Let us pray with humility and trust.
℟. **Lord, to whom shall we go? You have the words of eternal life. We have come to believe and to know that you are the Christ, the Son of God.**

Or:
Have pity on us, and help us.

5
Christ our Lord was given up to death for our sins and rose again for our justification. Let us pray to him with confidence in his goodness.
℟. **You are our Savior**

Or:
Jesus Christ, Son of the living God, have pity on us.

PENITENTIAL INTERCESSIONS

(At least one of the intercessions should always be a petition for a true conversion of heart.)

204. If the prayer is addressed to the Father:

1
—By human weakness we have disfigured the holiness of the Church: pardon all our sins and restore us to full communion with our brethren.
℟. **Lord, hear our prayer.** Or: **Lord, hear us.**

Or another suitable response may be used.

—Your mercy is our hope: welcome us to the sacrament of reconciliation. ℟.

—Give us the will to change our lives, and the lives of others, by charity, good example and prayer. ℟.

—As we make our confession, rescue us from slavery to sin and lead us to the freedom enjoyed by your children. ℟.

—Make us a living sign of your love for all to see: people reconciled with you and with each other. ℟.

—Through the sacrament of reconciliation may we grow in your peace and seek to spread it throughout the world. ℟.

—In this sign of your love you forgive us our sins: may it teach us to love others and to forgive their sins against us. ℟.

—In your mercy clothe us in the wedding garment of grace and welcome us to your table. ℟.

—Forgive us our sins, lead us in the ways of goodness and love, and bring us to the reward of everlasting peace. ℟.

—Give light to our darkness and lead us by your truth. ℟.

—In justice you punish us: in your mercy set us free for the glory of your name. ℟.

—May your power keep safe from all danger those whom your love sets free from the chains of sin. ℟.

—Look on our weakness: do not be angry and condemn, but in your love cleanse, guide and save us. ℟.

—In your mercy free us from the past and enable us to begin a new life of holiness. ℟.

—When we stray from you, guide us back into the way of holiness, love and peace. ℟.

—By your redeeming love overcome our sinfulness and the harm it has brought us. ℟.

—Blot out the sins of the past and fit us for the life that is to come. ℟.

2

The following intercessions may be used with a variable response or with an invariable response as in the *Liturgy of the Hours.*

In your goodness, forgive our sins against the unity of your family,
—make us one in heart, one in spirit.

We have sinned, Lord, we have sinned,
—take away our sins by your saving grace.

Give us pardon for our sins,
—and reconciliation with your Church.

Touch our hearts and change our lives, make us grow always in your friendship,
—help us to make up for our sins against your wisdom and goodness.

Cleanse and renew your Church, Lord,
—may it grow in strength as a witness to you.

Touch the hearts of those who have abandoned you through sin and scandal,
—call them back to you and keep them faithful in your love.

May we show forth in our lives the sufferings of your Son,
—you raised us up to life when you raised him from the dead.

Have mercy on us, Lord, as we praise and thank you,
—with your pardon give us also your peace.

Lord, our sins are many, but we trust in your mercy,
—call us, and we shall turn to you.

Receive us as we come before you with humble and contrite hearts,
—those who trust in you shall never trust in vain.

We have turned away from you and fallen into sin,
—we have followed evil ways and rejected your commandments.

Turn to us, Lord, and show us your mercy; blot out our sins,
—cast them into the depths of the sea.

Restore us, Lord, to your favor, and give us joy in your presence,
—may our glory be to serve you with all our hearts.

205. If the prayer is addressed to Christ:

1
Romans 5:10
—By your death you reconciled us with the Father and brought us salvation.
℟. **Lord, have mercy.** Or: **Christ, hear us.**

Or another suitable response may be used.

Romans 8:34
—You died and rose again, and sit at the right hand of the Father, to make intercession for us. ℟.

1 Corinthians 1:30
—You came from God as our wisdom and justice, our sanctification and redemption. ℟.

1 Corinthians 6:11
—You washed mankind in the Spirit of our God; you made us holy and righteous. ℟.

1 Corinthians 8:12
—You warned us that if we sin against each other we sin against you. ℟.

2 Corinthians 8:9
—Though you were rich you became poor for our sake, so that by your poverty we might become rich. ℟.

Galatians 1:4
—You gave yourself up for our sins to save us from this evil world. ℟.

1 Thessalonians 1:10
—You rose from the dead to save us from the anger that was to come. ℟.

1 Timothy 1:15
—You came into the world to save sinners. ℟.

1 Timothy 2:6
—You gave yourself up to bring redemption to all. ℟.

2 Timothy 1:10
—You destroyed death and gave light to life. ℟.

2 Timothy 4:1
—You will come to judge the living and the dead. ℟.

Titus 2:14
—You gave yourself up for us to redeem us from all sin and to prepare for yourself a holy people, marked as your own, devoted to good works. ℟.

Hebrews 2:17
—You showed us your mercy, and as a faithful high priest in the things of God you made atonement for the sins of the people. ℟.

Hebrews 5:9
—You became the source of salvation for all who obey you. ℟.

Hebrews 9:15
—Through the Holy Spirit you offered yourself to God as a spotless victim, cleansing our consciences from lifeless works. ℟.

Hebrews 9:28
—You were offered in sacrifice to undo the sins of the many. ℟.

1 Peter 3:18
—Once and for all you died for our sins, the innocent one for the guilty. ℟.

1 John 2:2
—You are the atonement for our sins and for the sins of the world. ℟.

John 3:16, 35
—You died that those who believe in you may not perish but have eternal life. ℟.

Matthew 18:11
—You came into the world to seek and save what was lost. ℟.

John 3:17
—You were sent by the Father, not to judge the world but to save it. ℟.

Mark 2:10
—You have power on earth to forgive sins. ℟.

Matthew 11:28
—You invite all who labor and are burdened to come to you to be refreshed. ℟.

Matthew 16:19, 18:18
—You gave your apostles the keys to the kingdom of heaven, the power to bind and to loose. ℟.

Matthew 22:38-40
—You told us that the whole law depends on love of God and of our neighbor. ℟.

John 10:10
—Jesus, life of all mankind, you came into the world to give us life, life in its fullness. ℟.

John 10:11
—Jesus, Good Shepherd, you gave your life for your sheep. ℟.

John 14:6; 8:32, 36
—Jesus, eternal truth, you give us true freedom. ℟.

John 14:6
—Jesus, you are the way to the Father. ℟.

John 11:25
—Jesus, you are the resurrection and life; those who believe in you, even if they are dead, will live. ℟.

John 15:1-2
—Jesus, true vine, the Father prunes your branches to make them bear even greater fruit. ℟.

2

The following intercessions may be used with a variable response or with an invariable response as in the *Liturgy of the Hours.*

Healer of the body and soul, bind up the wounds of our hearts,
—that our lives may grow strong through grace.

Help us to strip ourselves of sin,
—and put on the new life of grace.

Redeemer of the world, give us the spirit of penance and a deeper devotion to your passion,
—so that we may have a fuller share in your risen glory.

May your Mother, the refuge of sinners, intercede for us,
—and ask you in your goodness to pardon our sins.

You forgave the woman who repented,
—show us also your mercy.

You brought back the lost sheep on your shoulders,
—pity us and lead us home.

You promised paradise to the good thief,
—take us with you into your Kingdom.

You died for us and rose again,
—make us share in your death and resurrection.

PROCLAMATION OF PRAISE

206.

Psalm 32:1-7, 10-11

℟. **Rejoice in the Lord and sing for joy, friends of God.**

Psalm 98: 1-9

℟. **The Lord has remembered his mercy.**

Psalm 100:2-5

℟. **The Lord is loving and kind: his mercy is for ever.**

Psalm 119:1, 10-13, 15-16, 18, 33, 105, 169, 170, 174-175.

℟. **Blessed are you, Lord; teach me your decrees.**

Psalm 103:1-4, 8-18

℟. **The mercy of the Lord is from everlasting to everlasting on those who revere him.**

Psalm 145:1-21

℟. **Day after day I will bless you, Lord: I will praise your name for ever.**

Psalm 146:2-10

℟. **I will sing to my God all the days of my life.**

Isaiah 12:1b-6

℟. **Praise the Lord and call upon his name.**

Isaiah 61:10-11

℟. **My spirit rejoices in my God.**

Jeremiah 31:10-14

℟. **The Lord has redeemed his people.**

Daniel 3:52-57

℟. **Bless the Lord, all the works of his hand: praise and glorify him for ever.**

Luke 1:46-55

℟. **The Lord has remembered his mercy.**

Ephesians 1:3-10

℟. **Blessed be God who chose us in Christ.**

Revelation 15:3-4

℟. **Great and wonderful are all your works, Lord.**

CONCLUDING PRAYERS

207.
**Father, all-powerful and ever-living God,
we do well always and everywhere to give you thanks.**

**When you punish us, you show your justice;
when you pardon us, you show your kindness;
yet always your mercy enfolds us.**

When you chastise us, you do not wish to condemn us;
when you spare us, you give us time to make amends for our sins
through Christ our Lord.
℟. Amen.

208.
Lord God,
creator and ruler of your kingdom of light,
in your great love for this world
you gave up your only Son
for our salvation.
His cross has redeemed us,
his death has given us life,
his resurrection has raised us to glory.
Through him we ask you
to be always present among your family.
Teach us to be reverent in the presence of your glory;
fill our hearts with faith,
our days with good works,
our lives with your love;
may your truth be on our lips
and your wisdom in all our actions,
that we may receive the reward of everlasting life.

We ask this through Christ our Lord.
℟. Amen.

209.
Lord Jesus Christ,
your loving forgiveness knows no limits.
You took our human nature
to give us an example of humility
and to make us faithful in every trial.
May we never lose the gifts you have given us,
but if we fall into sin
lift us up by your gift of repentance,
for you live and reign for ever and ever.
℟. Amen.

210.
**Father,
in your love you have brought us
from evil to good and from misery to happiness.
Through your blessings
give the courage of perseverance
to those you have called and justified by faith.**

Grant this through Christ our Lord.
℟. **Amen.**

211.
**God and Father of us all,
you have forgiven our sins
and sent us your peace.
Help us to forgive each other
and to work together to establish peace in the world.**

We ask this through Christ our Lord.
℟. **Amen.**

212.
**And may the blessing of almighty God,
the Father, and the Son, ✠ and the Holy Spirit,
come upon you and remain with you for ever.**
℟. **Amen.**

213.
**May the Father bless us,
for we are his children, born to eternal life.**
℟. **Amen.**

**May the Son show us his saving power,
for he died and rose for us.**
℟. **Amen.**

**May the Spirit give us his gift of holiness
and lead us by the right path,
for he dwells in our hearts.**
℟. **Amen.**

214.
May the Father bless us,
for he has adopted us as his children.
℟. **Amen.**

May the Son come to help us,
for he has received us as brothers and sisters.
℟. **Amen.**

May the Spirit be with us,
for he has made us his dwelling place.
℟. **Amen.**

APPENDIX I

ABSOLUTION FROM CENSURES

1. The form of absolution is not to be changed in respect to sins which are now reserved either in themselves or by reason of a censure. It is enough that the confessor intend to absolve the properly disposed penitent from these reserved sins. Until other provision is made and as may be necessary, the present regulations which make recourse to the competent authority obligatory are to be reserved. Before absolving from sins, however, the confessor may absolve from the censure, using the formula which is given below for absolution from censure outside the sacrament of penance.

2. When a priest, in accordance with the law, absolves a penitent from a censure outside the sacrament of penance, he uses the following formula:

By the power granted to me,
I absolve you
from the bond of excommunication (or **suspension** or **interdict**).
In the name of the Father, and of the Son, ✠
and of the Holy Spirit.
The penitent answers: **Amen.**

DISPENSATION FROM IRREGULARITY

3. When, in accordance with the law, a priest dispenses a penitent from an irregularity, either during confession, after absolution has been given, or outside the sacrament of penance, he says:

By the power granted to me
I dispense you from the irregularity
which you have incurred.
In the name of the Father, and of the Son, ✠
and of the Holy Spirit.
The penitent answers: **Amen.**

APPENDIX II

SAMPLE PENITENTIAL SERVICES

These services have been prepared by the Congregation for Divine Worship to help those who prepare or lead penitential celebrations.

PREPARING PENITENTIAL CELEBRATIONS

1. Penitential celebrations, mentioned in the *Rite of Penance* (nos. 36-37), are beneficial in fostering the spirit and virtue of penance among individuals and communities; they also help in preparing for a more fruitful celebration of the sacrament of penance. However, the faithful must be reminded of the difference between these celebrations and sacramental confession and absolution.[1]

2. The particular conditions of life, the manner of speaking, and the educational level of the congregation or special group should be taken into consideration. Thus liturgical commissions[2] and individual Christian communities preparing these celebrations should choose the texts and format most suited to the circumstances of each particular group.

3. To this end, several examples of penitential celebrations are given below. These are models and should be adapted to the specific conditions and needs of each community.

4. When the sacrament of penance is celebrated in these services, it follows the readings and homily, and the rite of reconciling several penitents with individual confession and absolution is used (nos. 54-59, *Rite of Penance*); when permitted by law, the rite for general confession and absolution is used (nos. 60-63, *Rite of Penance*).

I. PENITENTIAL CELEBRATIONS DURING LENT

5. Lent is the principal time of penance both for individual Christians and for the whole Church. It is therefore desira-

[1]See Congregation for the Doctrine of the Faith, *Normae pastorales circa absolutionem sacramentalem generali modo impertiendam,* June 16, 1972, no. X: *AAS* 64 (1972) 513.

[2]See Congregation of Rites, Instruction *Inter Oecumenici,* September 26, 1964, no. 39: *AAS* (1964) 110.

ble to prepare the Christian community for a fuller sharing in the paschal mystery by penitential celebrations during Lent.[1]

6. Texts from the lectionary and sacramentary may be used in these penitential celebrations; the penitential nature of the liturgy of the word in the Masses for Lent should be considered.

7. Two outlines of penitential celebrations suitable for Lent are given here. The first emphasizes penance as strengthening or restoring baptismal grace; the second shows penance as a preparation for a fuller sharing in the Easter mystery of Christ and his Church.

FIRST EXAMPLE

PENANCE LEADS TO A STRENGTHENING OF BAPTISMAL GRACE

8. a) After an appropriate song and the greeting by the minister, the meaning of this celebration is explained to the people. It prepares the Christian community to recall their baptismal grace at the Easter Vigil and to reach newness of life in Christ through freedom from sins.

9. b) Prayer

My brothers and sisters, we have neglected the gifts of our baptism and fallen into sin. Let us ask God to renew his grace within us as we turn to him in repentance.

Let us kneel (or: **Bow your heads before God).**
All pray in silence for a brief period.
Let us stand (or: **Raise your heads).**

Lord Jesus,
you redeemed us by your passion
and raised us to new life in baptism.
Protect us with your unchanging love
and share with us the joy of your resurrection,
for you live and reign for ever and ever.
℟. **Amen.**

[1]See Second Vatican Council, constitution *Sacrosanctum concilium,* no. 109; Paul VI, Apostolic Constitution *Paenitemini,* February 17, 1966, no. IX: *AAS* 58 (1966) 185.

10. c) Readings

First Reading
1 Corinthians 10:1-13
All this that happened to the people of Moses in the desert was written for our benefit.

Responsorial Psalm
Psalm 106:6-10, 13-14, 19-22
℟. (4): **Lord, remember us,**
for the love you bear your people.

Gospel
Luke 15:4-7
Share my joy: I have found my lost sheep.

or
Luke 15:11-32
Your brother here was dead, and has come to life.

11. d) Homily
The celebrant may speak about:
—the need to fulfill the grace of baptism by living faithfully the Gospel of Christ (see 1 Corinthians 10:1-13);
—the seriousness of sin committed after baptism (see Hebrews 6:4-8);
—the unlimited mercy of our God and Father who continually welcomes those who turn back to him after having sinned (see Luke 15);
—Easter as the feast when the Church rejoices over the Christian initiation of catechumens and the reconciliation of penitents.

12. e) Examination of conscience.
After the homily, the examination of conscience takes place; a sample text is given in Appendix III. A period of silence should always be included so that each person may personally examine his conscience. In a special way the people should examine their conscience on the baptismal promises which will be renewed at the Easter Vigil.

13. f) Act of repentance
The deacon (or another minister, if there is no deacon) speaks to the assembly:

My brothers and sisters, the hour of God's favor draws near, the day of his mercy and of our salvation, when death was destroyed and eternal life began. This is the season for planting new vines in God's vineyard, the time for pruning the vines to ensure a richer harvest.

We all acknowledge that we are sinners. We are moved to penance, encouraged by the example and prayers of our brothers and sisters. We admit our guilt and say: "Lord, I acknowledge my sins; my offenses are always before me. Turn away your face, Lord, from my sins, and blot out all my wrong-doing. Give me back the joy of your salvation and give me a new and steadfast spirit."

We are sorry for having offended God by our sins. May he be merciful and hear us as we ask to be restored to his friendship and numbered among the living who share the joy of Christ's risen life.

Then the priest sprinkles the congregation with holy water, while all sing (say):

Cleanse us, Lord, from all our sins;
Wash us, and we shall be whiter than snow.

Then the priest says:
Lord our God,
you created us in love
and redeemed us in mercy.
While we were exiled from heaven
by the jealousy of the evil one,
you gave us your only Son,
who shed his blood to save us.
Send now your Holy Spirit
to breathe new life into your children,
for you do not want us to die
but to live for you alone.
You do not abandon those who abandon you;
correct us as a Father
and restore us to your family.

Lord,
your sons and daughters stand before you
in humility and trust.
Look with compassion on us
as we confess our sins.
Heal our wounds;
stretch out a hand of pity
to save us and raise us up.
Keep us free from harm
as members of Christ's body,
as sheep of your flock,
as children of your family.
Do not allow the enemy
to triumph over us
or death to claim us for ever,
for you raised us to new life in baptism.

Hear, Lord, the prayers we offer from contrite hearts.
Have pity on us as we acknowledge our sins.
Lead us back to the way of holiness.
Protect us now and always
from the wounds of sin.
May we ever keep safe in all its fullness
the gift your love once gave us
and your mercy now restores.

We ask this through our Lord Jesus Christ, your Son,
who lives and reigns with you and the Holy Spirit,
one God for ever and ever.
℟. **Amen.**

The celebration ends with an appropriate song and the dismissal of the people.

SECOND EXAMPLE

PENANCE PREPARES FOR A FULLER SHARING IN THE PASCHAL MYSTERY OF CHRIST FOR THE SALVATION OF THE WORLD

14. a) After an appropriate song and the greeting by the

minister, the faithful are briefly reminded that they are linked with each other in sin and in repentance so that each should take his calling to conversion as an occasion of grace for the whole community.

15. b) Prayer

My brothers and sisters, let us pray that by penance we may be united with Christ, who was crucified for our sins, and so share with all mankind in his resurrection.

Let us kneel (or: **Bow your heads before God).**
All pray in silence for a brief period.
Let us stand (or: **Raise your heads).**

Lord, our God and Father,
through the passion of your Son
you gave us new life.
By our practice of penance
make us one with him in his dying
so that we and all mankind
may be one with him
in his resurrection.

We ask this through Christ our Lord.
℟. **Amen.**

Or:
Almighty and merciful Father,
send your Holy Spirit
to inspire and strengthen us,
so that by always carrying
the death of Jesus in our bodies
we may also show forth the power of his risen life.

We ask this through Christ our Lord.
℟. **Amen.**

16. c) Readings

First Reading
Isaiah 53:1-7, 10-12
He is the one who bore our sufferings.

Responsorial Psalm
Psalm 22:2-3, 7-9, 18-28
℟. **Father, your will be done.**

Second Reading
1 Peter 2:20-25
You had gone astray but now you have come back to the shepherd and guardian of your souls.

Gospel
Verse before the gospel
Glory to you, Lord; you were given up to death for our sins and rose again for our justification. Glory to you, Lord.
Or an appropriate song may be sung.

Mark 10:32-45 (or short form: **Mark 10:32-34, 42-45)**
Now we are going up to Jerusalem, and the Son of Man will be handed over.

17. d) Homily
The celebrant may speak about:
—sin, by which we offend God and also Christ's body, the Church, whose members we became in baptism;
—sin as a failure of love for Christ who in the paschal mystery showed his love for us to the end;
—the way we affect each other when we do good or choose evil;
—the mystery of vicarious satisfaction by which Christ bore the burden of our sins, so that by his wounds we would be healed (see Isaiah 53; 1 Peter 2:24);
—the social and ecclesial dimension of penance by which individual Christians share in the work of converting the whole community;
—the celebration of Easter as the feast of the Christian community which is renewing itself by the conversion or repentance of each member, so that the Church may become a clearer sign of salvation in the world.

18. e) Examination of conscience
After the homily, the examination of conscience takes place; a sample text is given in Appendix III. A period of silence should always be included so that each person may personally examine his conscience.

19. f) Act of repentance
After the examination of conscience, all say together:

I confess to almighty God,
and to you, my brothers and sisters,
that I have sinned through my own fault.
They strike their breast:
in my thoughts and in my words,
in what I have done,
and in what I have failed to do;
and I ask blessed Mary, ever virgin,
all the angels and saints,
and you, my brothers and sisters,
to pray for me to the Lord our God.

As a sign of conversion and charity toward others, it should be suggested that the faithful give something to help the poor to celebrate the feast of Easter with joy; or they might visit the sick, or make up for some injustice in the community, or perform similar works.

Then the Lord's Prayer may be said, which the priest concludes in this way:

Deliver us, Father, from every evil
as we unite ourselves through penance
with the saving passion of your Son.
Grant us a share
in the joy of the resurrection of Jesus
who is Lord for ever and ever.
℟. **Amen.**

Depending on circumstances, the general confession may be followed by a form of devotion such as adoration of the cross or the way of the cross, according to local customs and the wishes of the people.

At the end, an appropriate song is sung, and the people are sent away with a greeting or blessing.

II. PENITENTIAL CELEBRATIONS DURING ADVENT

20. a) After an appropriate song and the greeting by the minister, the meaning of the celebration is explained in these or similar words:

My brothers and sisters, Advent is a time of preparation, when we make ready to celebrate the mystery of our Lord's coming as man, the beginning of our redemption. Advent also moves us to look forward with renewed hope to the second coming of Christ, when God's plan of salvation will be brought to fulfillment. We are reminded too of our Lord's coming to each one of us at the hour of our death. We must make sure that he will find us prepared for his coming, as the gospel tells us: "Blessed are those servants who are found awake when the Lord comes" Luke 12:37. **This service of penance is meant to make us ready in mind and heart for the coming of Christ, which we are soon to celebrate in the Mass of Christmas.**

Or:

Now it is time for you to wake from sleep, for our salvation is nearer to us than it was when we first believed. The night is ending; the day draws near. Let us then cast off the deeds of darkness and put on the armor of light. Let us live honestly as people do in the daylight, not in carousing and drunkenness, not in lust and debauchery, not in quarreling and jealousy. But rather let us put on the Lord Jesus Christ and give no thought to the desires of the flesh. Romans 13:11-12.

21. b) Prayer

My brothers and sisters, we look forward to celebrating the mystery of Christ's coming on the feast of Christmas. Let us pray that when he comes he may find us awake and ready to receive him.

All pray in silence for a brief period.

Lord our God,
maker of the heavens,
as we look forward to the coming of our redeemer
grant us the forgiveness of our sins.

We ask this through Christ our Lord.
℟. **Amen.**

Or:

Eternal Son of God,
creator of the human family
and our redeemer,
come at last among us
as the child of the immaculate Virgin,
and redeem the world.
Reveal your loving presence
by which you set us free from sin
in becoming one like us
in all things but sin,
for you live and reign for ever and ever.
℟. **Amen.**

22. c) Readings

First Reading
Malachi 3:1-7a
The Lord whom you seek will come to his temple.

Responsorial Psalm
Psalm 85:1-13
℟. (8) **Lord, let us see your kindness, and grant us your salvation.**

Second Reading
Revelation 21:1-12
He will wipe away all the tears from their eyes.

Gospel
Verse before the gospel
I am coming quickly, says the Lord, and I will repay each man.
Come, Lord Jesus.

Or:

The Spirit and the Bride say: "Come."
Let all who hear answer: "Come."
Come, Lord Jesus.

Or another appropriate song may be sung.

Matthew 3:1-12
Repent, for the kingdom of heaven is close at hand.

Or:
Luke 3:3-17
All mankind shall see the salvation of God.

23. d) Examination of conscience
After the homily, the examination of conscience takes place; a sample text is given in Appendix III. A period of silence should always be included so that each person may personally examine his conscience.

24. e) Act of repentance
The act of repentance follows the examination of conscience. All may say the **I confess to almighty God** or the intercessions as in no. 60.

The Lord's Prayer is said or sung, and is concluded by the presiding minister in this way:

Lord our God,
on the first day of creation
you made the light
that scatters all darkness.
Let Christ, the light of lights,
hidden from all eternity,
shine at last on your people
and free us from the darkness of sin.
Fill our lives with good works
as we go out to meet your Son,
so that we may give him a fitting welcome.

We ask this through Christ our Lord.
℟. **Amen.**

Or:

Almighty and eternal God,
you sent your only-begotten Son
to reconcile the world to yourself.
Lift from our hearts
the oppressive gloom of sin,
so that we may celebrate
the approaching dawn of Christ's birth
with fitting joy.

We ask this through Christ our Lord.
℟. **Amen.**

At the end, a song is sung, and the people are sent away with a greeting or blessing.

III. COMMON PENITENTIAL CELEBRATIONS

I. SIN AND CONVERSION

25. a) After an appropriate song (for example Psalm 139:1-12, 16, 23-24) and greeting, the minister who presides briefly explains the meaning of the readings. Then he invites all to pray. After a period of silence, he concludes the prayer in this way:

Lord Jesus,
you turned and looked on Peter
when he denied you for the third time.
He wept for his sin
and turned again to you in sincere repentance.
Look now on us and touch our hearts,
so that we also may turn back to you
and be always faithful in serving you,
for you live and reign for ever and ever.
℟. **Amen.**

26. b) Readings

First Reading
Luke 22:31-34
I tell you, Peter: the cock will not crow today before you deny me three times.

A short period of silence follows the reading.

Second Reading
Luke 22:54-62
Peter went out and wept bitterly.

Responsorial Psalm
Psalm 32:10, 15-27, 20 or Psalm 52 or another appropriate song.
℟. **My trust is in you, O Lord.**

Gospel
John 21:15-19
Simon, son of John, do you love me?

27. c) Homily
The celebrant may speak about:
—the trust we must put in God's grace, not in our own powers;
—the faithfulness by which we as baptized Christians must live as true and faithful followers of the Lord;
—our weakness by which we often fall into sin and refuse to give witness to the gospel;
—the mercy of the Lord, who welcomes as a friend the one who turns to him with his whole heart.

28. d) Examination of conscience
After the homily, the examination of conscience takes place; a sample text is given in Appendix III. A period of silence should always be included so that each person may personally examine his conscience.

29. e) Act of repentance
After the examination of conscience, the presiding minister invites all to prayer in these or similar words:

God gives us an example of love: when we were sinners he first loved us and took pity on us. Let us turn to him with a sincere heart, and in the words of Peter say to him:
℟. **Lord, you know all things; you know that I love you.**

A short period of silence should follow each invocation.

Each invocation may be said by different individuals, the rest answering.

—Lord, like Peter we have relied on our own strength rather than on grace. Look on us, Lord, and have mercy.
℟. **Lord, you know all things; you know that I love you.**

—Our pride and foolishness have led us into temptation. Look on us, Lord, and have mercy.
℟. **Lord, you know all things; you know that I love you.**

—We have been vain and self-important. Look on us, Lord, and have mercy.
℟. **Lord, you know all things; you know that I love you.**

—We have at times been pleased rather than saddened by the misfortunes of others. Look on us, Lord, and have mercy.
℟. **Lord, you know all things; you know that I love you.**

—We have shown indifference for those in need instead of helping them. Look on us, Lord, and have mercy.
℟. **Lord, you know all things; you know that I love you.**

—We have been afraid to stand up for justice and truth. Look on us, Lord, and have mercy.
℟. **Lord, you know all things; you know that I love you.**

—We have repeatedly broken the promises of our baptism and failed to be your disciples. Look on us, Lord, and have mercy.
℟. **Lord, you know all things; you know that I love you.**

—Let us now pray to the Father in the words Christ gave us and ask forgiveness for our sins:
Our Father . . .

30. f) After an appropriate song, the presiding minister says the final prayer and dismisses the people:

Lord Jesus, our Savior,
you called Peter to be an apostle;
when he repented of his sin
you restored him to your friendship
and confirmed him as first of the apostles.
Turn to us with love
and help us to imitate Peter's example.
Give us strength to turn from our sins
and to serve you in the future
with greater love and devotion,
for you live and reign for ever and ever.
℟. **Amen.**

II. THE SON RETURNS TO THE FATHER

31. a) After an appropriate song and the greeting by the minister, the theme of the celebration is explained to the community. Then he invites all to pray. After a period of silence, he says:

Almighty God,
you are the Father of us all.
You created the human family
to dwell for ever with you
and to praise your glory.
Open our ears to hear your voice
so that we may return to you
with sincere repentance for our sins.
Teach us to see in you our loving Father,
full of compassion for all who call to you for help.
We know that you punish us only to set us free from evil
and that you are ready to forgive us our sins.

Restore your gift of salvation
which alone brings true happiness,
so that we may all return to our Father's house
and share your table
now and for ever.
℟. **Amen.**

32. b) Readings

First Reading
Ephesians 1:3-7
He chose us from all eternity to be his adopted sons and daughters.

Responsorial Psalm
Psalm 27:1, 4, 7-10, 13-14
℟. **The Lord is my light and my help.**

Gospel
Luke 15:11-32
His father saw him and was filled with pity.

33. c) Homily
The minister may speak about:
—sin as a turning away from the love that we should have for God our Father;
—the limitless mercy of our Father for his children who have sinned;
—the nature of true conversion;
—the forgiveness we should extend to our brothers;
—the eucharistic banquet as the culmination of our reconciliation with the Church and with God.

34. d) Examination of conscience
After the homily, the examination of conscience takes place; a sample text is given in Appendix III. A period of silence should always be included so that each person may personally examine his conscience.

35. e) Act of repentance
After the examination of conscience, the presiding minister invites all to pray:

Our God is a God of mercy, slow to anger and full of patience. He is the father who welcomes his son when he returns from a distant country. Let us pray to him with trust in his goodness:
℟. **We are not worthy to be called your children.**

—By our misuse of your gifts we have sinned against you.
℟. **We are not worthy to be called your children.**

—By straying from you in mind and heart we have sinned against you.
℟. **We are not worthy to be called your children.**

—By forgetting your love we have sinned against you.
℟. **We are not worthy to be called your children.**

—By indulging ourselves, while neglecting our true good and the good of our neighbor, we have sinned against you.
℟. **We are not worthy to be called your children.**

—By failing to help our neighbor in his need we have sinned against you.
℟. **We are not worthy to be called your children.**

—By being slow to forgive we have sinned against you.
℟. **We are not worthy to be called your children.**

—By failing to remember your repeated forgiveness we have sinned against you.
℟. **We are not worthy to be called your children.**

Members of the congregation may add other invocations. A brief period of silence should follow each invocation. It may be desirable to have different individuals say each invocation.

—Let us now call upon our Father in the words that Jesus gave us, and ask him to forgive us our sins: Our Father . . .

36. f) After an appropriate song, the presiding minister says the final prayer and dismisses the people:

God our Father,
you chose us to be your children,
to be holy in your sight
and happy in your presence.
Receive us as a loving Father
so that we may share the joy and love
of your holy Church.

We ask this through Christ our Lord.
℟. **Amen.**

III. THE BEATITUDES

37. a) After an appropriate song and greeting of the minister, the person presiding explains briefly the meaning of the readings. Then he invites all to pray. After a period of silence, he says:

Lord,
open our ears and our hearts today
to the message of your Son,
so that through the power of his death and resurrection
we may walk in newness of life.

We ask this through Christ our Lord.
℟. **Amen.**

38. b) Readings

First Reading
1 John 1:5-9
If we say that we have no sin, we are deceiving ourselves.

Responsorial Psalm (See Isaiah 35:4)
Psalm 146:5-10
℟. **Lord, come and save us.**

Gospel
Matthew 5:1-10
Happy are the poor in spirit, for theirs is the kingdom of heaven.

39. c) Homily
The minister may speak about:
—sin, by which we ignore the commandments of Christ and act contrary to the teaching of the beatitudes;
—the firmness of our faith in the words of Jesus;
—our faithfulness in imitating Christ in our private lives, in the Christian community, and in human society;
—each beatitude.

40. d) Examination of conscience
After the homily, the examination of conscience takes place; a sample text is given in Appendix III. A period of silence should always be included so that each person may personally examine his conscience.

41. e) Act of repentance
After the examination of conscience, the presiding minister invites all to pray in these or similar words:

My brothers and sisters, Jesus Christ has left an example for us to follow. Humbly and confidently let us ask him to renew us in spirit so that we may shape our lives according to the teaching of his Gospel.

—Lord Jesus Christ, you said:
"Blessed are the poor in spirit,
for theirs is the kingdom of heaven."
Yet we are preoccupied with money and worldly goods
and even try to increase them at the expense of justice.
Lamb of God, you take away the sin of the world:
℟. Have mercy on us.

—Lord Jesus Christ, you said:
"Blessed are the gentle,
for they shall inherit the earth."
Yet we are ruthless with each other,
and our world is full of discord and violence.
Lamb of God, you take away the sin of the world:
℟. Have mercy on us.

—Lord Jesus Christ, you said:
"Blessed are those who mourn,
for they shall be comforted."
Yet we are impatient under our own burdens
and unconcerned about the burdens of others.
Lamb of God, you take away the sin of the world:
℟. Have mercy on us.

—Lord Jesus Christ, you said:
"Blessed are those who hunger and thirst for justice,
for they shall be filled."
Yet we do not thirst for you, the fountain of all holiness,
and are slow to spread your influence
in our private lives or in society.
Lamb of God, you take away the sin of the world:
℟. Have mercy on us.

—Lord Jesus Christ, you said:
"Blessed are the merciful,
for they shall receive mercy."
Yet we are slow to forgive
and quick to condemn.
Lamb of God, you take away the sin of the world:
℟. Have mercy on us.

—Lord Jesus Christ, you said:
"Blessed are the clean of heart,
for they shall see God."
Yet we are prisoners of our senses and evil desires
and dare not raise our eyes to you.
Lamb of God, you take away the sin of the world:
℟. Have mercy on us.

—Lord Jesus Christ, you said:
"Blessed are the peacemakers,
for they shall be called children of God."
Yet we fail to make peace in our families,
in our country, and in the world.
Lamb of God, you take away the sin of the world:
℟. Have mercy on us.

—Lord Jesus Christ, you said:
"Blessed are those who are persecuted
for the sake of justice,
for the kingdom of heaven is theirs."
Yet we prefer to practice injustice
rather than suffer for the sake of right;
we discriminate against our neighbors
and oppress and persecute them.
Lamb of God, you take away the sin of the world:
℟. **Have mercy on us.**

—Now let us turn to God our Father and ask him to free us from evil and prepare us for the coming of his kingdom:
Our Father . . .

42. f) After an appropriate song, the presiding minister says the final prayer and dismisses the people:

Lord Jesus Christ,
gentle and humble of heart,
full of compassion and maker of peace,
you lived in poverty
and were persecuted in the cause of justice.
You chose the cross as the path to glory
to show us the way to salvation.
May we receive with joyful hearts
the word of your Gospel
and live by your example
as heirs and citizens of your kingdom,
where you live and reign for ever and ever.
℟. **Amen.**

IV. FOR CHILDREN

43. This service is suitable for younger children, including those who have not yet participated in the sacrament of penance.

Theme:

GOD COMES TO LOOK FOR US

44. The penitential celebration should be prepared with the children so that they will understand its meaning and purpose, be familiar with the songs, have at least an elementary knowledge of the biblical text to be read, and know what they are to say and in what order.

45. a) Greeting
When the children have come together in the church or some other suitable place, the celebrant greets them in a friendly manner. Briefly he reminds them why they have come together and recounts the theme of the service. After the greeting, an opening song may be sung.

46. b) Reading
The celebrant may give a short introduction to the reading in these or similar words:

My dear children, each one of us has been baptized, and so we are all sons and daughters of God. God loves us as a Father, and he asks us to love him with all our hearts. He also wants us to be good to each other, so that we may all live happily together.

But people do not always do what God wants. They say: "I will not obey! I am going to do as I please." They disobey God and do not want to listen to him. We, too, often act like that.

That is what we call sin. When we sin we turn our backs on God. If we do something really bad we cut ourselves off from God; we are complete strangers to him.

What does God do when someone turns away from him? What does he do when we leave the path of goodness that he has shown us, when we run the risk of losing the life of grace he has given us? Does God turn away from us when we turn away from him by our sins?

Here is what God does, in the words of Jesus himself:

47. Only one text of Scripture should be read.

Luke 15:1-7
Heaven is filled with joy when one sinner turns back to God.

48. c) Homily
The homily should be short, proclaiming God's love for us and preparing the ground for the examination of conscience.

49. d) Examination of conscience
The celebrant should adapt the examination to the children's level of understanding by brief comments. There should be a suitable period of silence (see Appendix III).

50. e) Act of repentance
This litany may be said by the celebrant or by one or more of the children, alternating with all present. Before the response, which may be sung, all should observe a brief pause.

God our Father,

——Sometimes we have not behaved as your children should.
℟. **But you love us and come to us.**

——We have given trouble to our parents and teachers.
℟. **But you love us and come to us.**

——We have quarrelled and called each other names.
℟. **But you love us and come to us.**

——We have been lazy at home and in school, and have not been helpful to our parents (brothers, sisters, friends).
℟. **But you love us and come to us.**

——We have thought too much of ourselves and have told lies.
℟. **But you love us and come to us.**

——We have not done good to others when we had the chance.
℟. **But you love us and come to us.**

Now with Jesus, our brother, we come before our Father in heaven and ask him to forgive our sins: Our Father . . .

51. f) Act of contrition and purpose of amendment
Sorrow may be shown by some sign, for example, individual children may come to the altar or another suitable place with a candle, and light it there; if necessary, a server may help. Each child says in his own words:

Father,
I am sorry for all my sins:
for what I have done
and for what I have failed to do.
I will sincerely try to do better
especially . . .
(he mentions his particular resolution).
Help me to walk by your light.

In place of the candle, or in addition to it, the children may prepare a written prayer or resolution and place it on the altar or on a table designated for this purpose.

If the number of children or other circumstances do not allow for this, the celebrant asks the children present to say the above prayer together, along with a general resolution.

52. g) Prayer of the celebrant

God our Father always seeks us out
when we walk away from the path of goodness.
He is always ready to forgive
when we have sinned.
May almighty God have mercy on us,
forgive us our sins,
and bring us to everlasting life.
℟. **Amen.**

53. The minister invites the children to express their thanks to God. They may do this by an appropriate hymn.

Then he dismisses them.

V. FOR YOUNG PEOPLE

54. The penitential celebration should be prepared with the young people so that with the celebrant, they may choose or compose the texts and songs. The readers, cantors or choir should be chosen from among them.

Theme:

RENEWAL OF OUR LIVES ACCORDING TO THE CHRISTIAN VOCATION

55. a) Greeting
This may be given in these or similar words:

Dear friends, we have come here to do penance and to make a fresh start as Christians. Many people see in penance only its difficult side, and its emphasis on sorrow. But it has also a more joyful side, and it looks more to the future than to the past.

Through penance God calls us to a new beginning. He helps us to find our true freedom as his sons and daughters. When Jesus invites us to repentance, he is inviting us to take our place in his Father's kingdom. This is what he teaches us in the parable about the merchant who came across a pearl of great value and sold everything he had in order to buy it.

If we follow our Lord's advice we exchange our past life for one far more valuable.

Then a song is sung; it should stress the call to a new life or following God's call with an eager heart (for example, Psalm 40:1-9).
℟. **Here am I, Lord; I come to do your will.**

56. b) Prayer

Lord our God,
you call us out of darkness into light,

out of self-deception into truth,
out of death into life.
Send us your Holy Spirit
to open our ears to your call.
Fill our hearts with courage
to be true followers of your Son.
We ask this through Christ our Lord.
℟. **Amen.**

57. c) Readings

First Reading
Romans 7:18-25
Unhappy man am I! Who will free me? Thanks to God through Jesus Christ our Lord.

or:
Romans 8:19-23
We know that by turning everything to their good, God cooperates with all those who love him.

A song is sung, or a brief period of silence is observed.

Gospel
Matthew 13:44-46
He sold all that he had and bought the field.

58. d) Homily
The celebrant may speak about:
——the law of sin which in us struggles against God;
——the necessity of giving up the way of sin so that we may enter the kingdom of God.

59. e) Examination of conscience
After the homily, the examination of conscience takes place; a sample text is given in Appendix III. A period of silence should always be included so that each person may personally examine his conscience.

60. f) Act of repentance
Christ our Lord came to call sinners into his Father's kingdom. Let us now make an act of sorrow in our hearts and resolve to avoid sin in the future.

After a brief period of silence, all say together:
I confess to almighty God,
and to you, my brothers and sisters,
that I have sinned through my own fault
They strike their breast:
in my thoughts and in my words,
in what I have done,
and in what I have failed to do;
and I ask blessed Mary, ever virgin,
all the angels and saints,
and you, my brothers and sisters,
to pray for me to the Lord our God.

Minister:
Lord our God,
you know all things.
You know that we want to be more generous
in serving you and our neighbor.
Look on us with love and hear our prayer.

Reader:
Give us the strength to turn away from sin.
℟. **Hear our prayer.**

Help us to be sorry for our sins and to keep our resolutions.
℟. **Hear our prayer.**

Forgive our sins and have pity on our weakness.
℟. **Hear our prayer.**

Give us trust in your goodness and make us generous in serving you.
℟. **Hear our prayer.**

Help us to be true followers of your Son and living members of his Church.

Minister:
God does not want the sinner to die, but to turn to him and live. May he be pleased that we have confessed our sinfulness, and may he show us his mercy as we pray in obedience to his Son.

All say together:
Our Father . . .

61. The celebration ends with an appropriate song and the dismissal.

VI. FOR THE SICK

62. According to the condition of the sick people and the suitability of the place, the minister goes to the sick, gathered in one room, or else he brings them together in the sanctuary or church. He should adapt carefully the texts and their number to the condition of those who take part in the service. Since in most instances none of the sick will be able to act as reader, the minister should, if possible, invite another person to carry out this office.

Theme:

THE TIME OF SICKNESS IS A TIME OF GRACE

63. a) Greeting
He may greet them in these or similar words:

My dear friends, when Jesus came to preach repentance, he was bringing us good news, for he was proclaiming to us God's love and mercy. Again and again God comes to our help so that we may turn to him and live our lives entirely in his service. Penance is his gift, a gift we should accept with gratitude. Keeping this in mind, let us open our hearts to God with great simplicity and humility and ask to be reconciled with him as we now forgive each other.

If possible, a penitential song is sung by the sick persons, or by a choir.

64. b) Prayer
Lord our God,
source of all goodness and mercy,
we come together as your family
to ask your forgiveness

and the forgiveness of each other.
Give us true sorrow for our sins
and loving trust in your compassion
so that we may acknowledge our sins
with sincere hearts.
Through this celebration
restore us to fuller union with yourself
and with our neighbor
so that we may serve you with greater generosity.

We ask this through Christ our Lord.
℟. **Amen.**

65. c) Readings
The readings may be introduced in these or similar words:

Many people enjoy good health and other blessings and accept them as a matter of course, with no sense of gratitude. In time of sickness we discover that all these are great gifts, and that without them we easily lose heart. God allows us to experience sickness in order to test our faith. What is more, if we see our suffering as a share in Christ's suffering, it can be of great value both to ourselves and to the Church. The time of sickness is not then wasted or meaningless. It is in fact a time of grace if we accept it as God wants us to accept it. This celebration is meant to help us to do so. We shall therefore listen to God's word, examine our conscience, and pray with sincere hearts.

66. First Reading
James 5:13-16
The prayer of faith will save the sick man.

Responsorial Psalm
Between the readings, a psalm may be said or sung alternately, for example, Psalm 130 or Psalm 51.

Gospel
Mark 2:1-12
The Son of Man has authority on earth to forgive sins.

67. d) Homily
It is fitting that the celebrant speak of sickness, dwelling not so much on sickness of the body as on sickness of the soul. He should emphasize the power of Jesus and his Church to forgive sins and the value of suffering offered for others.

68. e) Examination of conscience
After the homily, the examination of conscience takes place; a sample text is given in Appendix III. A period of silence should always be included so that each person may personally examine his conscience.

The following questions may be added but adapted to the condition of the sick:

——Do I trust God's goodness and providence, even in times of stress and illness?
——Do I give in to sickness, to despair, to other unworthy thoughts and feelings?
——Do I fill my empty moments with reflection on life and with prayer to God?
——Do I accept my illness and pain as an opportunity for suffering with Christ, who redeemed us by his passion?
——Do I live by faith, confident that patience in suffering is of great benefit to the Church?
——Am I thoughtful of others and attentive to my fellow patients and their needs?
——Am I grateful to those who look after me and visit me?
——Do I give a good Christian example to others?
——Am I sorry for my past sins, and do I try to make amends for them by my patient acceptance of weakness and illness.

69. f) Act of repentance
After a moment of silence, all say together:

I confess to almighty God,
and to you, my brothers and sisters,
that I have sinned through my own fault

They strike their breast:
in my thoughts and in my words,
in what I have done,
and in what I have failed to do;
and I ask blessed Mary, ever virgin,
all the angels and saints,
and you, my brothers and sisters,
to pray for me to the Lord our God.

Reader:
Lord our God, we bear the name of your Son and call you Father. We are sorry for our sins against you and against our brothers and sisters.
℟. **Give us true repentance and sincere love for you and for our neighbor.**

Lord Jesus Christ, you redeemed us by your passion and cross and gave us an example of patience and love. We are sorry for our sins against you, and especially for failing to serve you and our brothers and sisters.
℟. **Give us true repentance and sincere love for you and for our neighbor.**

Holy Spirit, Lord, you speak to us in the Church and in our conscience and inspire within us the desire to do good. We are sorry for our sins against you, and especially for our obstinate refusal to obey you.
℟. **Give us true repentance and sincere love for you and for our neighbor.**

Minister:
Let us ask God our Father to forgive us and to free us from evil:
Our Father . . .

70. Then, if possible, the choir or the assembled people sing a song, and the service concludes with a prayer of thanksgiving:

71.
God of consolation and Father of mercies,

you forgive the sinner who acknowledges his guilt:
℟. **We praise you and thank you.**

God of consolation and Father of mercies,
you give to those who suffer hardship or pain
a share in the sufferings of your Son
for the salvation of the world:
℟. **We praise you and thank you.**

God of consolation and Father of mercies,
you look with love on those who are troubled or in sorrow;
you give them hope of salvation
and the promise of eternal life:
℟. **We praise you and thank you.**

Let us pray.
Lord,
your goodness and mercy are boundless.
Look on your sons and daughters
gathered here in the name of your Son.
We thank you for all your gifts
and ask you to keep us always as your family,
full of living faith, firm hope,
and sincere love for you and for our neighbor.
We ask this through Christ our Lord.
℟. **Amen.**

72. In place of the prayer, the service may end with a blessing.

May the God of peace
fill your hearts with every blessing.
May he sustain you
with his gifts of hope and consolation,
help you to offer your lives in his service,
and bring you safely to eternal glory.
May almighty God,
the Father, and the Son, ✠ and the Holy Spirit,
grant you all that is good.
℟. **Amen.**

73. The minister dismisses the assembly, or invites those present to a friendly visit with the sick.

APPENDIX III

FORM OF EXAMINATION OF CONSCIENCE

1. This suggested form for an examination of conscience should be completed and adapted to meet the needs of different individuals and to follow local usages.

2. In an examination of conscience, before the sacrament of penance, each individual should ask himself these questions in particular:

1. What is my attitude to the sacrament of penance? Do I sincerely want to be set free from sin, to turn again to God, to begin a new life, and to enter into a deeper friendship with God? Or do I look on it as a burden, to be undertaken as seldom as possible?

2. Did I forget to mention, or deliberately conceal, any grave sins in past confessions?

3. Did I perform the penance I was given? Did I make reparation for any injury to others? Have I tried to put into practice my resolution to lead a better life in keeping with the Gospel?

3. Each individual should examine his life in the light of God's word.

I. The Lord says: "You shall love the Lord your God with your whole heart."

1. Is my heart set on God, so that I really love him above all things and am faithful to his commandments, as a son loves his father? Or am I more concerned about the things of this world? Have I a right intention in what I do?

2. God spoke to us in his Son. Is my faith in God firm and secure? Am I wholehearted in accepting the Church's teaching? Have I been careful to grow in my understanding of the faith, to hear God's word, to

listen to instructions on the faith, to avoid dangers to faith? Have I been always strong and fearless in professing my faith in God and the Church? Have I been willing to be known as a Christian in private and public life?

3. **Have I prayed morning and evening? When I pray, do I really raise my mind and heart to God or is it a matter of words only? Do I offer God my difficulties, my joys, and my sorrows? Do I turn to God in time of temptation?**

4. **Have I love and reverence for God's name? Have I offended him in blasphemy, swearing falsely, or taking his name in vain? Have I shown disrespect for the Blessed Virgin Mary and the saints?**

5. **Do I keep Sundays and feast days holy by taking a full part, with attention and devotion, in the liturgy, and especially in the Mass? Have I fulfilled the precept of annual confession and of communion during the Easter season?**

6. **Are there false gods that I worship by giving them greater attention and deeper trust than I give to God: money, superstition, spiritism, or other occult practices?**

II. The Lord says: "Love one another as I have loved you."

1. **Have I a genuine love for my neighbors? Or do I use them for my own ends, or do to them what I would not want done to myself? Have I given grave scandal by my words or actions?**

2. **In my family life, have I contributed to the well-being and happiness of the rest of the family by patience and genuine love? Have I been obedient to parents, showing them proper respect and giving them help in their spiritual and material needs? Have I been careful to give a Christian upbringing to my children, and to help them by good example and by**

exercising authority as a parent? Have I been faithful to my husband (wife) in my heart and in my relations with others?

3. Do I share my possessions with the less fortunate? Do I do my best to help the victims of oppression, misfortune, and poverty? Or do I look down on my neighbor, especially the poor, the sick, the elderly, strangers, and people of other races?

4. Does my life reflect the mission I received in confirmation? Do I share in the apostolic and charitable works of the Church and in the life of my parish? Have I helped to meet the needs of the Church and of the world and prayed for them: for unity in the Church, for the spread of the Gospel among the nations, for peace and justice, etc.?

5. Am I concerned for the good and prosperity of the human community in which I live, or do I spend my life caring only for myself? Do I share to the best of my ability in the work of promoting justice, morality, harmony, and love in human relations? Have I done my duty as a citizen? Have I paid my taxes?

6. In my work or profession am I just, hard-working, honest, serving society out of love for others? Have I paid a fair wage to my employees? Have I been faithful to my promises and contracts?

7. Have I obeyed legitimate authority and given it due respect?

8. If I am in a position of responsibility or authority, do I use this for my own advantage or for the good of others, in a spirit of service?

9. Have I been truthful and fair, or have I injured others by deceit, calumny, detraction, rash judgment, or violation of a secret?

10. Have I done violence to others by damage to life or limb, reputation, honor, or material possessions? Have I involved them in loss? Have I been responsi-

ble for advising an abortion or procuring one? Have I kept up hatred for others? Am I estranged from others through quarrels, enmity, insults, anger? Have I been guilty of refusing to testify to the innocence of another because of selfishness?

11. Have I stolen the property of others? Have I desired it unjustly and inordinately? Have I damaged it? Have I made restitution of other people's property and made good their loss?

12. If I have been injured, have I been ready to make peace for the love of Christ and to forgive, or do I harbor hatred and the desire for revenge?

III. Christ our Lord says: "Be perfect as your Father is perfect."

1. Where is my life really leading me? Is the hope of eternal life my inspiration? Have I tried to grow in the life of the Spirit through prayer, reading the word of God and meditating on it, receiving the sacraments, self-denial? Have I been anxious to control my vices, my bad inclinations and passions, e.g., envy, love of food and drink? Have I been proud and boastful, thinking myself better in the sight of God and despising others as less important than myself? Have I imposed my own will on others, without respecting their freedom and rights?

2. What use have I made of time, of health and strength, of the gifts God has given me to be used like the talents in the Gospel? Do I use them to become more perfect every day? Or have I been lazy and too much given to leisure?

3. Have I been patient in accepting the sorrows and disappointments of life? How have I performed mortification so as to "fill up what is wanting to the sufferings of Christ"? Have I kept the precept of fasting and abstinence?

4. **Have I kept my senses and my whole body pure and chaste as a temple of the Holy Spirit consecrated for resurrection and glory, and as a sign of God's faithful love for men and women, a sign that is seen most perfectly in the sacrament of matrimony? Have I dishonored my body by fornication, impurity, unworthy conversation or thoughts, evil desires, or actions? Have I given in to sensuality? Have I indulged in reading, conversation, shows, and entertainments that offend against Christian and human decency? Have I encouraged others to sin by my own failure to maintain these standards? Have I been faithful to the moral law in my married life?**

5. **Have I gone against my conscience out of fear or hypocrisy?**

6. **Have I always tried to act in the true freedom of the sons of God according to the law of the Spirit, or am I the slave of forces within me?**

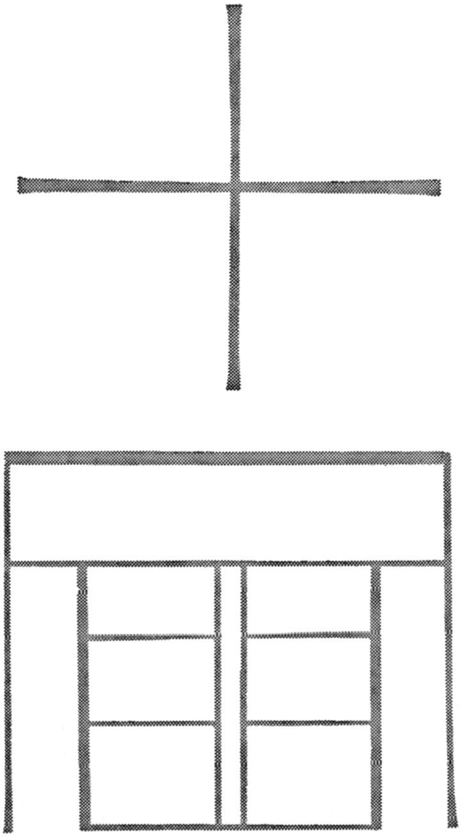

HOLY COMMUNION
AND WORSHIP OF THE EUCHARIST
OUTSIDE MASS

HOLY COMMUNION AND WORSHIP OF THE EUCHARIST OUTSIDE MASS

Decree
General Introduction (1-12)

CHAPTER I
HOLY COMMUNION OUTSIDE MASS

Introduction

I The Relationship Between Communion outside Mass and

II The Time of Communion outside Mass (16)

III The Minister of Communion (17)

IV The Place of Communion outside Mass (18)

V Regulations for Giving Communion (19-22)

VI Dispositions for Communion (23-25)

Rite of Distributing Holy Communion Outside Mass

I The Long Rite with the Celebration of the Word (26)

A Introductory Rites
Greeting (27)
Penitential Rite (28)

B Celebration of the Word of God (29)

C Holy Communion (30-37)
Concluding Prayer (38)

D Concluding Rite (39-41)

II The Short Rite with the Celebration of the Word (42)

A Introductory Rites
Greeting (43)
Penitential Rite (43 cont.)

B The Short Form of the Reading of the Word (44)

C Holy Communion (45-49)
Concluding Prayer (50)

D Concluding Rite (51-53)

CHAPTER II
ADMINISTRATION OF COMMUNION AND VIATICUM TO THE SICK BY AN EXTRAORDINARY MINISTER (54-55)

I The Ordinary Rite of Communion of the Sick

A Introductory Rite
Greeting (56)
Penitential Rite (57)

B The Short Form of the Reading of the Word (58)

C Holy Communion (59-61)
Concluding Prayer (62)

D Concluding Rite (63)

II Short Rite of Communion of the Sick (64-67)

III Viaticum

A Introductory Rite (68-69)
Penitential Rite (70)

B The Short Form of the Reading of the Word (71)

C Profession of the Baptismal Faith (72)

D Prayer for the Sick Person (73)

E Viaticum (74-77)

F Concluding Rite
Concluding Prayer (78)

CHAPTER III
FORMS OF WORSHIP OF THE HOLY EUCHARIST (79-81)

I Explanation of Exposition of the Holy Eucharist

SACRED CONGREGATION FOR DIVINE WORSHIP

Prot. no. 900/73

DECREE

The sacrament of the eucharist was entrusted by Christ to his bride, the Church, as spiritual nourishment and as a pledge of eternal life. The Church continues to receive this gift with faith and love.

The celebration of the eucharist in the sacrifice of the Mass is the true origin and purpose of the worship shown to the eucharist outside Mass. The principal reason for reserving the sacrament after Mass is to unite, through sacramental communion, the faithful unable to participate in the Mass, especially the sick and the aged, with Christ and the offering of his sacrifice.

In turn, eucharistic reservation, which became customary in order to permit the reception of communion, led to the practice of adoring this sacrament and offering to it the worship which is due to God. This cult of adoration is based upon valid and solid principles. Moreover, some of the public and communal forms of this worship were instituted by the Church itself.

The rite of Mass has been revised and, in the instruction *Eucharisticum mysterium* of May 25, 1967, regulations have been published "on the practical arrangements for the cult of this sacrament even after Mass and its relationship to the proper ordering of the sacrifice of the Mass in the light of the regulations of the Second Vatican Council, and of other documents of the Apostolic See on this matter."[1] Now the Congregation for Divine Worship has revised the rites, "Holy Communion and the Worship of the Eucharist Outside Mass."

These rites, approved by Pope Paul VI, are now published in this edition, which is declared to be the *editio typica*. They are to replace the rites which appear in the Roman Ritual at

[1]See Congregation of Rites, instruction *Eucharisticum mysterium,* no. 3g: *AAS* 59 (1967) 543.

the present time. They may be used at once in Latin; they may be used in the vernacular from the day set by the episcopal conferences for their territory, after the conferences have prepared a vernacular version and have obtained the confirmation of the Holy See.

Anything to the contrary notwithstanding.

From the office of the Congregation for Divine Worship, June 21, 1973, the feast of Corpus Christi.

Arturo Cardinal Tabera
Prefect

✠ Annibale Bugnini
Titular Archbishop of Diocletiana
Secretary

HOLY COMMUNION AND WORSHIP OF THE EUCHARIST OUTSIDE MASS

GENERAL INTRODUCTION

I. THE RELATIONSHIP BETWEEN EUCHARISTIC WORSHIP OUTSIDE MASS AND THE EUCHARISTIC CELEBRATION

1. The celebration of the eucharist is the center of the entire Christian life, both for the Church universal and for the local congregations of the Church. "The other sacraments, all the ministries of the Church, and the works of the apostolate are united with the eucharist and are directed toward it. For the holy eucharist contains the entire spiritual treasure of the Church, that is, Christ himself, our passover and living bread. Through his flesh, made living and life-giving by the Holy Spirit, he offers life to men, who are thus invited and led to offer themselves, their work, and all creation together with him."[1]

2. "The celebration of the eucharist in the sacrifice of the Mass," moreover, "is truly the origin and the goal of the worship which is shown to the eucharist outside Mass."[2] Christ the Lord "is offered in the sacrifice of the Mass when he becomes present sacramentally as the spiritual food of the faithful under the appearance of bread and wine." And, "once the sacrifice is offered and while the eucharist is reserved in churches and oratories, he is truly Emmanuel, 'God with us'. He is in our midst day and night; full of grace and truth, he dwells among us."[3]

3. No one therefore may doubt "that all the faithful show this holy sacrament the veneration and adoration which is due to God himself, as has always been customary in the Catholic Church. Nor is the sacrament to be less the object

[1]Second Vatican Council, decree *Presbyterorum ordinis*, no. 5

[2]Congregation of Rites, instruction *Eucharisticum mysterium*, no. 3e: *AAS* 59 (1967) 542.

[3]*Ibid.*, no. 36: *loc. cit.* 541; Paul VI, encyclical *Mysterium fidei*, near the end: *AAS* 57 (1965) 771.

of adoration because it was instituted by Christ the Lord to be received as food."[4]

4. In order to direct and to encourage devotion to the sacrament of the eucharist correctly, the eucharistic mystery must be considered in all its fullness, both in the celebration of Mass and in the worship of the sacrament which is reserved after Mass to extend the grace of the sacrifice.[5]

II. THE PURPOSE OF EUCHARISTIC RESERVATION

5. The primary and original reason for reservation of the eucharist outside Mass is the administration of viaticum. The secondary reasons are the giving of communion and the adoration of our Lord Jesus Christ who is present in the sacrament. The reservation of the sacrament for the sick led to the praiseworthy practice of adoring this heavenly food in the churches. This cult of adoration rests upon an authentic and solid basis, especially because faith in the real presence of the Lord leads naturally to external, public expression of that faith.[6]

6. In the celebration of Mass the chief ways in which Christ is present in his Church gradually become clear. First he is present in the very assembly of the faithful, gathered together in his name; next he is present in his word, when the Scriptures are read in the Church and explained; then in the person of the minister; finally and above all, in the eucharistic sacrament. In a way that is completely unique, the whole and entire Christ, God and man, is substantially and permanently present in the sacrament. This presence of Christ under the appearance of bread and wine "is called real, not to exclude other kinds of presence as if they were not real, but because it is real *par excellence.*"[7]

Therefore, to express the sign of the eucharist, it is more in harmony with the nature of the celebration that, at the altar

[4]Congregation of Rites, instruction *Eucharisticum mysterium,* no. 3f: *AAS* 59 (1967) 543.

[5]See *ibid.*, no. 3g: *loc. cit.* 543.

[6]See *ibid.*, no. 49: *loc. cit.* 566-567.

[7]Paul VI, encyclical *Mysterium fidei: AAS* 57 (1965) 764; see Congregation of Rites, instruction *Eucharisticum mysterium,* no. 55: *AAS* 59 (1967) 568-569.

where Mass is celebrated, there should if possible be no reservation of the sacrament in the tabernacle from the beginning of Mass. The eucharistic presence of Christ is the fruit of the consecration and should appear to be such.[8]

7. The consecrated hosts are to be frequently renewed and reserved in a ciborium or other vessel, in a number sufficient for the communion of the sick and others outside Mass.[9]

8. Pastors should see that churches and public oratories where, according to law, the holy eucharist is reserved, are open every day at least for some hours, at a convenient time, so that the faithful may easily pray in the presence of the blessed sacrament.[10]

III. THE PLACE OF EUCHARISTIC RESERVATION

9. The place for the reservation of the eucharist should be truly preeminent. It is highly recommended that the place be suitable also for private adoration and prayer so that the faithful may easily, fruitfully, and constantly honor the Lord, present in the sacrament, through personal worship.

This will be achieved more easily if the chapel is separate from the body of the church, especially in churches where marriages and funerals are celebrated frequently and churches which are much visited by pilgrims or because of their artistic and historical treasures.

10. The holy eucharist is to be reserved in a solid tabernacle. It must be opaque and unbreakable. Ordinarily there should be only one tabernacle in a church; this may be placed on an altar or, at the discretion of the local Ordinary, in some other noble and properly ornamented part of the church other than an altar.[11]

The key to the tabernacle where the eucharist is reserved must be kept most carefully by the priest in charge of the

[8]See Congregation of Rites, instruction *Eucharisticum mysterium: AAS* (1967) 568-569.

[9]See Roman Missal, General Instruction, nos. 285 and 292.

[10]See Congregation of Rites, instruction *Eucharisticum mysterium*, no. 51: *AAS* 59 (1967) 567.

[11]See *ibid.*, nos. 52-53: *loc. cit.*, 567-568.

church or oratory or by a special minister who has received the faculty to give communion.

11. The presence of the eucharist in the tabernacle is to be shown by a veil or in another suitable way determined by the competent authority.

According to traditional usage, an oil lamp or lamp with a wax candle is to burn constantly near the tabernacle as a sign of the honor which is shown to the Lord.[12]

IV. THE COMPETENCE OF EPISCOPAL CONFERENCES

12. It is for episcopal conferences, in the preparation of particular rituals in accord with the Constitution on the Liturgy (no. 63b), to accommodate this title of the Roman Ritual to the needs of individual regions so that, their actions having been confirmed by the Apostolic See, the ritual may be followed in the respective regions.

In this matter it will be for the conferences:
a) to consider carefully and prudently what elements, if any, of popular traditions may be retained or introduced, provided they can be harmonized with the spirit of the liturgy, and then to propose to the Apostolic See the adaptations they judge necessary or useful; these may be introduced with the consent of the Apostolic See;
b) to prepare translations of texts which are truly accommodated to the character of various languages and the mentality of various cultures; they may add texts, especially for singing, with appropriate melodies.

Liturgical texts, which are used in respect of a man, may be used with a change of gender for a woman also. And in either case the singular may be changed into the plural.

[12]See *ibid.*, no. 57: *loc. cit.*, 569.

CHAPTER I

HOLY COMMUNION OUTSIDE MASS

INTRODUCTION

I. THE RELATIONSHIP BETWEEN COMMUNION OUTSIDE MASS AND THE SACRIFICE

13. Sacramental communion received during Mass is the more perfect participation in the eucharistic celebration. The eucharistic sign is expressed more clearly when the faithful receive the body of the Lord from the same sacrifice after the communion of the priest.[1] Therefore, recently baked bread, for the communion of the faithful, should ordinarily be consecrated in every eucharistic celebration.

14. The faithful should be encouraged to receive communion during the eucharistic celebration itself.

Priests, however, are not to refuse to give communion to the faithful who ask for it even outside Mass.[2]

In fact it is proper that those who are prevented from being present at the community's celebration should be refreshed with the eucharist. In this way they may realize that they are united not only with the Lord's sacrifice but also with the community itself and are supported by the love of their brothers and sisters.

Pastors should see that an opportunity to receive the eucharist is given to the sick and aged, even though not gravely sick or in imminent danger of death, frequently and, if possible, daily, especially during the Easter season. It is lawful to minister communion under the appearance of wine to those who cannot receive the consecrated bread.[3]

15. The faithful should be instructed carefully that, even when they receive communion outside Mass, they are

[1]See Second Vatican Council, constitution *Sacrosanctum Concilium*, no. 55.
[2]See Congregation of Rites, instruction *Eucharisticum mysterium*, no. 33a: *AAS* 59 (1967) 559-560.
[3]See *ibid.*, nos. 40-41: *loc. cit.*, 562-563.

closely united with the sacrifice which perpetuates the sacrifice of the cross. They are sharers in the sacred banquet in which "by communion in the body and blood of the Lord the people of God shares in the blessings of the paschal sacrifice, renews the new covenant once made by God with men in the blood of Christ, and by faith and hope prefigures and anticipates the eschatological banquet in the kingdom of the Father, proclaiming the death of the Lord until he comes."[4]

II. THE TIME OF COMMUNION OUTSIDE MASS

16. Communion may be given outside Mass on any day and at any hour. It is proper, however, to determine the hours for giving communion, with a view to the convenience of the faithful, so that the celebration may take place in a fuller form and with greater spiritual benefit.

Nevertheless:
a) on Holy Thursday, communion may be given only during Mass; communion may be brought to the sick at any hour of the day;
b) on Good Friday communion may be given only during the celebration of the Passion of the Lord; communion may be brought to the sick who cannot participate in the celebration at any hour of the day;
c) on Holy Saturday communion may be given only as viaticum.[5]

III. THE MINISTER OF COMMUNION

17. It is, first of all, the office of the priest and the deacon to minister holy communion to the faithful who ask to receive it.[6] It is most fitting, therefore, that they give a suitable part of their time to this ministry of their order, depending on the needs of the faithful.

It is the office of an acolyte who has been properly instituted to give communion as a special minister when the priest and

[4]*Ibid.*, no. 3a: *loc. cit.*, 541-542.
[5]See Roman Missal, typical edition 1970; *Missa vespertina in Cena Domini*, 243; *Celebratio Passionis Domini*, 250, no. 3; *Sabbato sancto*, 265.
[6]See Congregation of Rites, instruction *Eucharisticum mysterium*, no. 31: *AAS* 59 (1967).

deacon are absent or impeded by sickness, old age, or pastoral ministry or when the number of the faithful at the holy table is so great that the Mass or other service may be unreasonably protracted.[7]

The local Ordinary may give other special ministers the faculty to give communion whenever it seems necessary for the pastoral benefit of the faithful and a priest, deacon, or acolyte is not available.[8]

IV. THE PLACE OF COMMUNION OUTSIDE MASS

18. The place where communion outside Mass is ordinarily given is a church or oratory in which the eucharist is regularly celebrated or reserved or a church, oratory, or other place where the local community regularly gathers for the liturgical assembly on Sundays or other days. Communion may be given, however, in other places, including private homes, when it is a question of the sick, prisoners, or others who cannot leave the place without danger or serious difficulty.

V. REGULATIONS FOR GIVING COMMUNION

19. When communion is given in a church or oratory, a corporal is to be placed on the altar, which is already covered with a cloth.[9] A communion plate is to be used.

When communion is given in other places, a suitable table is to be prepared and covered with a cloth; candles are also to be provided.

20. The minister of communion, if he is a priest or deacon, is to be vested in an alb, or a surplice over a cassock, and a stole.

Other ministers should wear either the liturgical vesture which may be traditional in their region or the vestment which is appropriate for this ministry and has been approved by the Ordinary.

[7]See Paul VI, apostolic letter *Ministeria quaedam,* August 15, 1972, no. VI: *AAS* 64 (1972) 532.

[8]See Congregation for the Discipline of the Sacraments, instruction *Immensae caritatis,* January 29, 1973, 1, I and II.

[9]See Roman Missal, *General Instruction,* no. 269.

The eucharist for communion outside a church is to be carried in a pyx or other covered vessel; the vesture of the minister and the manner of carrying the eucharist should be appropriate and in accord with local circumstances.

21. In giving communion the custom of placing the particle of consecrated bread on the tongue of the communicant is to be maintained because it is based on tradition of several centuries.

Episcopal conferences, however, may decree, their actions having been confirmed by the Apostolic See, that communion may also be given in their territories by placing the consecrated bread in the hands of the faithful, provided there is no danger of irreverence or false opinions about the eucharist entering the minds of the faithful.[10]

The faithful should be instructed that Jesus Christ is Lord and Savior and that, present in the sacrament, he must be given the same worship and adoration which is to be given to God.[11]

In either case, communion must be given by the competent minister, who shows the particle of consecrated bread to the communicant and gives it to him, saying, **The body of Christ,** to which the communicant replies **Amen.**

In the case of communion under the appearance of wine, the regulations of the instruction *Sacramentali Communione* of June 29, 1970, are to be followed exactly.[12]

22. Fragments which may remain after communion are to be reverently gathered and placed in a ciborium or in a vessel with water.

Likewise, if communion is given under the appearance of wine, the chalice or other vessel is to be washed with water. The water used for cleansing the vessels may be drunk or poured out in a suitable place.

[10]See Congregation for Divine Worship, instruction *Memoriale Domini,* May 29, 1969: *AAS* 61 (1969) 541-555.

[11]See Congregation for the Discipline of the Sacraments, instruction *Immensae caritatis,* January 21, 1973, no. 4.

[12]See no. 6: *AAS* 62 (1970) 665-666.

VI. DISPOSITIONS FOR COMMUNION

23. The eucharist continuously makes present among men the paschal mystery of Christ. It is the source of every grace and of the forgiveness of sins. Nevertheless, those who intend to receive the body of the Lord must approach it with a pure conscience and proper dispositions of soul if they are to receive the effects of the paschal sacrament.

On this account the Church prescribes "that no one conscious of mortal sin, even though he seems to be contrite, may go to the holy eucharist without previous sacramental confession."[13] In urgent necessity and if no confessor is available, he should simply make an act of perfect contrition with the intention of confessing individually, at the proper time, the mortal sins which he cannot confess at present.

It is desirable that those, who receive communion daily or very often, go to the sacrament of penance at regular intervals, depending on their circumstances.

Besides this, the faithful should look upon the eucharist as an antidote which frees them from daily faults and keeps them from mortal sins; they should also understand the proper way to use the penitential parts of the liturgy, especially at Mass.[14]

24. Communicants are not to receive the sacrament unless they have fasted for one hour from solid food and beverages, with the exception of water.

The period of the eucharistic fast, that is, abstinence from food or alcoholic drink, is reduced to about a quarter of an hour for:
1) the sick who are living in hospitals or at home, even if they are not confined to bed;
2) the faithful of advanced age, even if not bedridden, whether they are confined to their homes because of old age or live in a nursing home;

[13]See Council of Trent, Session XIII, Decree on the Eucharist, 7: Denz.-Schön. 1646-1647; *ibid.*, Session XIV *Canones de sacramento Paenitentiae*, 9: Denz-Schön. 1709; Congregation for the Doctrine of the Faith, *Normae pastorales circa absolutionem sacramentalem generali modo impertiendam*, June 16, 1972, introduction and no. VI: *AAS* 64 (1972) 510 and 512.

[14]See Congregation of Rites, instruction *Eucharisticum mysterium*, no. 35: *AAS* 59 (1967) 561.

3) sick priests, even if not bedridden, or elderly priests, whether they are to celebrate Mass or to receive communion;
4) persons who care for the sick or aged, and the family of the sick or aged, who wish to receive communion with them, when they cannot conveniently observe the fast of one hour.[15]

25. The union with Christ, to which the sacrament is directed, should be extended to the whole of Christian life. Thus the faithful, constantly reflecting upon the gift they have received, should carry on their daily work with thanksgiving, under the guidance of the Holy Spirit, and should bring forth fruits of rich charity.

So that they may continue more easily in the thanksgiving which is offered to God in an excellent manner through the Mass, it is recommended that each one who has been refreshed by communion should remain in prayer for a period of time.[16]

[15]See Congregation for the Discipline of the Sacraments, instruction *Immensae caritatis*, January 29, 1973, no. 3.
[16]See Congregation of Rites, instruction *Eucharisticum mysterium*, no. 38: *AAS* (1967) 562.

RITE OF DISTRIBUTING HOLY COMMUNION OUTSIDE MASS

1. THE LONG RITE WITH THE CELEBRATION OF THE WORD

26. This rite is to be used chiefly when Mass is not celebrated or when communion is not distributed at scheduled times. The purpose is that the people should be nourished by the word of God. By hearing it they learn that the marvels it proclaims reach their climax in the paschal mystery of which the Mass is a sacramental memorial and in which they share by communion. Nourished by God's word, they are led on to grateful and fruitful participation in the saving mysteries.

INTRODUCTORY RITES

27. After the people have assembled and preparations for the service (see nos. 19-20) are complete, all stand for the greeting of the minister.

GREETING

If he is a priest or deacon, he says:

The grace of our Lord Jesus Christ and the love of God and the fellowship of the Holy Spirit be with you all.
The people answer: **And also with you.**

Or:
The Lord be with you.
The people answer: **And also with you.**

If the minister is not a priest or deacon, he greets those present with these or similar words:

Brothers and sisters,
the Lord invites us (you) to his table
to share in the body of Christ:
bless him for his goodness.
The people answer: **Blessed be God for ever.**

Another form of greeting, no. 189, may be chosen.

Any other customary forms of greeting from scripture may be used.

PENITENTIAL RITE

28. The penitential rite follows, and the minister invites the people to recall their sins and to repent of them in these words:

My brothers and sisters,
to prepare ourselves for this celebration,
let us call to mind our sins.

A pause for silent reflection follows.

All say:
I confess to almighty God,
and to you, my brothers and sisters,
that I have sinned through my own fault
They strike their breast:
in my thoughts and in my words,
in what I have done,
and in what I have failed to do;
and I ask blessed Mary, ever virgin,
all the angels and saints,
and you, my brothers and sisters,
to pray for me to the Lord our God.

The minister concludes:
May almighty God have mercy on us,
forgive us our sins,
and bring us to everlasting life.
The people answer: **Amen.**

Other forms of the penitential rite, no. 190 or 191, may be chosen.

CELEBRATION OF THE WORD OF GOD

29. The Liturgy of the Word now takes place as at Mass. Texts are chosen for the occasion either from the Mass of the day or from the votive Masses of the Holy Eucharist or the Precious Blood, the readings from which are in the Lection-

ary. A list of these passages can be found in nos. 113-153 of this Ritual. The Lectionary offers a wide range of readings which may be drawn upon for particular needs, such as the votive Mass of the Sacred Heart. See nos. 154-158 below.

There may be one or more readings, the first being followed by a psalm or some other chant or by a period of silent prayer.

The celebration of the word ends with the general intercessions.

HOLY COMMUNION

30. After the prayer the minister goes to the place where the sacrament is reserved, takes the ciborium or pyx containing the body of the Lord, places it on the altar and genuflects. He then introduces the Lord's Prayer in these or similar words:

Let us pray with confidence to the Father in the words our Savior gave us:

He continues with the people:

Our Father. . . .

31. The minister may invite the people in these or similar words:

Let us offer each other the sign of peace.

All make an appropriate sign of peace, according to local custom.

32. The minister genuflects. Taking the host, he raises it slightly over the vessel or pyx and, facing the people, says:

This is the Lamb of God
who takes away the sins of the world.
Happy are those who are called to his supper.

The communicants say once:

Lord, I am not worthy to receive you,
but only say the word and I shall be healed.

33. If the minister receives communion, he says quietly:

May the body of Christ bring me to everlasting life.

He reverently consumes the body of Christ.

34. Then he takes the vessel or pyx and goes to the communicants. He takes a host for each one, raises it slightly, and says:

The body of Christ.

The communicant answers: **Amen,**
and receives communion.

35. During the distribution of communion, a hymn may be sung.

36. After communion the minister puts any particle left on the plate into the pyx, and he may wash his hands. He returns any remaining hosts to the tabernacle and genuflects.

37. A period of silence may now be observed, or a psalm or song of praise may be sung.

38. The minister then says the concluding prayer:
Let us pray.

Lord Jesus Christ,
you gave us the eucharist
as the memorial of your suffering and death.
May our worship of this sacrament of your body and blood
help us to experience the salvation you won for us
and the peace of the kingdom
where you live with the Father and the Holy Spirit,
one God, for ever and ever.
The people answer: **Amen.**
Other prayers, nos. 210-222, may be chosen.

CONCLUDING RITE

39. If the minister is a priest or deacon, he extends his

hands and, facing the people, says:

The Lord be with you.
The people answer: **And also with you.**

He blesses the people with these words:

May almighty God bless you,
the Father, and the Son, ✠ and the Holy Spirit.
The people answer: **Amen.**

Instead of this formula a solemn blessing or prayer over the people may be used, as in the concluding rite of Mass in the Roman Missal.

40. If the minister is not a priest or deacon, he invokes God's blessing and, crossing himself, says:

May the Lord bless us,
protect us from all evil
and bring us to everlasting life.

or:

May the almighty and merciful God bless and protect us,
the Father, and the Son, ✠ and the Holy Spirit.
The people answer: **Amen.**

41. Finally the minister says:

Go in the peace of Christ.
The people answer: **Thanks be to God.**

Then after the customary reverence, the minister leaves.

2. THE SHORT RITE WITH THE CELEBRATION OF THE WORD

42. This form of service is used when the longer, more elaborate form is unsuitable, especially when there are only one or two for communion and a true community celebration is impossible.

INTRODUCTORY RITES

43. When everything is ready (see nos. 19-20), the minister greets the communicants.

GREETING

[27]
If he is a priest or deacon, he says:

The grace of our Lord Jesus Christ and the love of God and the fellowship of the Holy Spirit be with you all.
The people answer: **And also with you.**

Or:
The Lord be with you.
The people answer: **And also with you.**

If the minister is not a priest or deacon, he greets those present with these or similar words:

Brothers and sisters,
the Lord invites us (you) to his table
to share in the body of Christ:
bless him for his goodness.
The people answer: **Blessed be God for ever.**

Another form of greeting, no. 189, may be chosen:

The grace and peace of God our Father and the Lord Jesus Christ be with you.
The people answer: **Blessed be the God and Father of our Lord Jesus Christ.**
or:
And also with you.

Any other customary forms of greeting from scripture may be used.

PENITENTIAL RITE

The penitential rite follows, and the minister invites the people to recall their sins and to repent of them in these words [28]:

My brothers and sisters,
to prepare ourselves for this celebration,
let us call to mind our sins.

A pause for silent reflection follows.

All say:
I confess to almighty God,
and to you, my brothers and sisters,
that I have sinned through my own fault
They strike their breast:
in my thoughts and in my words,
in what I have done,
and in what I have failed to do;
and I ask blessed Mary, ever virgin,
all the angels and saints,
and you, my brothers and sisters,
to pray for me to the Lord our God.

The minister concludes:
May almighty God have mercy on us,
forgive us our sins,
and bring us to everlasting life.
The people answer: **Amen.**

Other forms of the penitential rite, no. 190 or 191, may be chosen.

THE SHORT FORM OF THE READING OF THE WORD

44. Omitting the celebration of the word of God, the minister or other person should read a short scriptural text referring to the bread of life.
John 6:54-55
John 6:54-58

John 14:6
John 14:23
John 15:4
1 Corinthians 11:26
1 John 4:16

See nos. 133ff. for a further selection of texts.

HOLY COMMUNION

45. The minister takes the ciborium or pyx containing the body of the Lord, places it on the altar, and genuflects. He then introduces the Lord's Prayer in these or similar words:

Let us pray with confidence to the Father
in the words our Savior gave us:

He continues with the people:

Our Father. . . .

46. The minister genuflects. Taking the host, he raises it slightly over the vessel or pyx and, facing the people, says:

This is the Lamb of God
who takes away the sins of the world.
Happy are those who are called to his supper.

The communicants say once:
Lord, I am not worthy to receive you,
but only say the word and I shall be healed.

47. If the minister receives communion, he says quietly:

May the body of Christ bring me to everlasting life.

He reverently consumes the body of Christ.

48. Then he takes the vessel or pyx and goes to the communicants. He takes a host for each one, raises it slightly, and says:

The body of Christ.

The communicant answers: **Amen,** and receives communion.

49. After communion the minister puts any particles left on the plate into the pyx, and he may wash his hands. He returns any remaining hosts to the tabernacle and genuflects.

A period of silence may now be observed, or a psalm or song of praise may be sung.

50. The minister then says the concluding prayer:

Let us pray.

Lord Jesus Christ,
you gave us the eucharist as the memorial of your suffering and death.
May our worship of this sacrament of your body and blood
help us to experience the salvation you won for us
and the peace of the kingdom
where you live with the Father and the Holy Spirit,
one God, for ever and ever.
The people answer: **Amen.**

Other prayers, nos. 210-222, may be chosen.

CONCLUDING RITE

51. If the minister is a priest or deacon, he extends his hands and, facing the people, says:

The Lord be with you.
The people answer: **And also with you.**

He blesses the people with these words:

May almighty God bless you,
the Father, and the Son, ✠ and the Holy Spirit.
The people answer: **Amen.**

52. If the minister is not a priest or deacon, he invokes God's blessing, and crossing himself says:

May the Lord bless us,
protect us from all evil
and bring us to everlasting life.

or:

May the almighty and merciful God bless and protect us,
the Father, and the Son, and the Holy Spirit.

The people answer: **Amen.**

53. Finally the minister says:

Go in the peace of Christ.

The people answer: **Thanks be to God.**

Then after the customary reverence, the minister leaves.

CHAPTER II

ADMINISTRATION OF COMMUNION AND VIATICUM TO THE SICK BY AN EXTRAORDINARY MINISTER

54. A priest or deacon administers communion or viaticum to the sick in the manner prescribed by the *Rite of Anointing and Pastoral Care of the Sick.* When an acolyte or an extraordinary minister, duly appointed, gives communion to the sick, the rite here described is followed.

55. Those who cannot receive communion in the form of bread may receive it in the form of wine. The precioius blood must be carried to the sick person in a vessel so secured as to eliminate all danger of spilling. The sacrament should be administered with due regard to the individual concerned, and the rite for giving communion under both kinds provides a choice of methods. If all the precious blood is not consumed, the minister himself must consume it and then wash the vessel as required.

1. THE ORDINARY RITE OF COMMUNION OF THE SICK

INTRODUCTORY RITE

GREETING

56. Wearing the appropriate vestments (see no. 20), the minister approaches the sick person and greets him and the others present in a friendly manner. He may use this greeting:

Peace to this house and to all who live in it.

Any other customary form of greeting from scripture may be used. Then he places the sacrament on the table, and all adore it.

PENITENTIAL RITE

57. The minister invites the sick person and those present to recall their sins and to repent of them in these words:

My brothers and sisters,
to prepare ourselves for this celebration,
let us call to mind our sins.

A pause for silent reflection follows.

All say:
I confess to almighty God,
and to you, my brothers and sisters,
that I have sinned through my own fault
They strike their breast:
in my thoughts and in my words,
in what I have done,
and in what I have failed to do;
and I ask blessed Mary, ever virgin,
all the angels and saints,
and you, my brothers and sisters,
to pray for me to the Lord our God.

The minister concludes:
May almighty God have mercy on us,
forgive us our sins,
and bring us to everlasting life.
The people answer: **Amen.**

Other forms of the penitential rite, no. 190 or 191, may be chosen.

THE SHORT FORM OF THE READING OF THE WORD

58. A brief passage from sacred scripture (see no. 71) may then be read by one of those present or by the minister himself.
John 6:54-58
John 14:6
John 14:23

John 15:4
John 15:5
1 Corinthians 11:26
1 John 4:16

See the *Rite of Anointing and Pastoral Care of the Sick* (nos. 247ff. or 153ff.) for a further selection of texts.

HOLY COMMUNION

59. The minister then introduces the Lord's Prayer in these or similar words:

Now let us pray together to the Father in the words given us by our Lord Jesus Christ.

He continues with the people:
Our Father. . . .

60. Then the minister shows the holy eucharist, saying:

This is the Lamb of God
who takes away the sins of the world.
Happy are those who are called to his supper.

The sick person and the other communicants say once:

Lord, I am not worthy to receive you,
but only say the word and I shall be healed.

61. The minister goes to the sick person and, showing him the sacrament, says:

The body of Christ (or: **The blood of Christ**).

The sick person answers: **Amen,** and receives communion.

Others present then receive in the usual manner.

62. After communion the minister washes the vessel as usual. A period of silence may now be observed.

The minister then says the concluding prayer:

Let us pray.

**God our Father, almighty and eternal,
we confidently call upon you,
that the body [and blood] of Christ
which our brother (sister) has received
may bring him (her)
lasting health in mind and body.**

We ask this through Christ our Lord.
The people answer: **Amen.**

Other prayers, nos. 210-222, may be chosen.

CONCLUDING RITE

63. Then the minister invokes God's blessing, and crossing himself says:

**May the Lord bless us,
protect us from all evil
and bring us to everlasting life.**

or:

May the almighty and merciful God bless and protect us, the Father, and the Son, and the Holy Spirit.
The people answer: **Amen.**

2. SHORT RITE OF COMMUNION OF THE SICK

64. This shorter rite is to be used when communion is given in different rooms of the same building, such as a hospital. Elements taken from the ordinary rite may be added according to circumstances.

65. The rite may begin in the church or chapel or in the first room, where the minister says the following antiphon:

**How holy this feast
in which Christ is our food:
his passion is recalled,**

grace fills our hearts,
and we receive a pledge of the glory to come.

Other antiphons, nos. 201-203, may be chosen.

66. Then the minister may be escorted by someone carrying a candle. He says to all the sick persons in the same room or to each communicant individually:

This is the Lamb of God
who takes away the sins of the world.
Happy are those who are called to his supper.

The one who is to receive communion then says once:

Lord, I am not worthy to receive you,
but only say the word and I shall be healed.

He receives communion in the usual manner.

67. The rite is concluded with a prayer (see no. 62) which may be said in the church or chapel or in the last room:

Let us pray.

God our Father, almighty and eternal,
we confidently call upon you,
that the body [and blood] of Christ
which our brother (sister) has received
may bring him (her)
lasting health in mind and body.

We ask this through Christ our Lord.
The people answer: **Amen.**

Other prayers, nos. 210-222, may be chosen.

3. VIATICUM

INTRODUCTORY RITE

68. Wearing the appropriate vestments (see no. 20) the minister approaches the sick person and greets him and the

others present in a friendly manner. He may use this greeting:

Peace to this house and to all who live in it.

Any other customary form of greeting from scripture may be used. Then he places the sacrament on the table, and all adore it.

69. Afterward the minister addresses those present, using the following instruction or one better suited to the sick person's condition:

My brothers and sisters:

Before our Lord Jesus Christ passed from this world to return to his Father, he gave us the sacrament of his body and blood. This is the promise of our resurrection, the food and drink for our journey as we pass from this life to join him. United in the love of Christ, let us ask God to give strength to our brother (sister).

A period of silent prayer then follows.

70. The minister invites the sick person and all present to recall their sins and to repent of them in these words:

My brothers and sisters,
to prepare ourselves for this celebration,
let us call to mind our sins.

A pause for silent reflection follows.

All say:
I confess to almighty God,
and to you, my brothers and sisters,
that I have sinned through my own fault
They strike their breast:
in my thoughts and in my words,
in what I have done,
and in what I have failed to do;
and I ask blessed Mary, ever virgin,
all the angels and saints,
and you, my brothers and sisters,
to pray for me to the Lord our God.

The minister concludes:
May almighty God have mercy on us,
forgive us our sins,
and bring us to everlasting life.
The people answer: **Amen.**

Other forms of the penitential rite, no. 190 or 191, may be chosen.

THE SHORT FORM OF THE READING OF THE WORD

71. It is most fitting that one of those present or the minister himself read a brief text from scripture:
John 6:54-58
John 14:6
John 14:23
John 15:4
1 Corinthians 11:26
1 John 4:16

See the *Rite of Anointing and Pastoral Care of the Sick* (nos. 247ff. or 153ff.) for a further selection of texts.

PROFESSION OF BAPTISMAL FAITH

72. It is desirable that the sick person renew his baptismal profession of faith before he receives viaticum. The minister gives a brief instruction and then asks the following questions:

Do you believe in God, the Father almighty, creator of heaven and earth?
℟. **I do.**

Do you believe in Jesus Christ, his only Son, our Lord, who was born of the Virgin Mary, was crucified, died, and was buried, rose from the dead, and is now seated at the right hand of the Father?
℟. **I do.**

Do you believe in the Holy Spirit, the holy Catholic Church, the communion of saints, the forgiveness

of sins, the resurrection of the body, and life everlasting?
℟. **I do.**

PRAYER FOR THE SICK PERSON

73. If the condition of the sick person permits, a brief litany is recited in these or similar words. The sick person, if he is able, and all present respond:

My brothers and sisters, let us pray with one mind and heart to our Lord Jesus Christ:

Lord, you loved us to the end, and you accepted death that we might have life: hear our prayer for our brother (sister).
℟. **Lord, hear our prayer.**

Lord, you said: "He who eats my flesh and drinks my blood has eternal life": hear our prayer for our brother (sister).
℟. **Lord, hear our prayer.**

Lord, you invite us to the banquet of your kingdom, where there will be no more pain or mourning, no more sorrow or separation: hear our prayer for our brother (sister).
℟. **Lord, hear our prayer.**

VIATICUM

74. The minister introduces the Lord's Prayer in these or similar words:

Now let us pray together to the Father in the words given us by our Lord Jesus Christ.

All continue:
Our Father. . . .

75. Then the minister shows the holy eucharist to those present, saying:

This is the Lamb of God

who takes away the sins of the world.
Happy are those who are called to his supper.

The sick person and all who are to receive communion say once:

Lord, I am not worthy to receive you,
but only say the word and I shall be healed.

76. The minister goes to the sick person and, showing him the sacrament, says:

The body of Christ (or: **The blood of Christ**).

The sick person answers: **Amen.**
Immediately, or after giving communion, the minister adds:

May the Lord Jesus Christ protect you and lead you to eternal life.
The sick person answers: **Amen.**

Others present then receive communion in the usual manner.

77. After communion the minister washes the vessel as usual. Then a period of silence may be observed.

CONCLUDING RITE

78. The minister says the concluding prayer:
Let us pray.
Father,
your son, Jesus Christ, is our way, our truth, and our life.
Our brother (sister) N. entrusts himself (herself) to you
with full confidence in all your promises.
Refresh him (her) with the body and blood of your Son
and lead him (her) to your kingdom in peace.
We ask this through Christ our Lord.
The people answer: **Amen.**

For another prayer, no. 223 may be chosen.

CHAPTER III

FORMS OF WORSHIP OF THE HOLY EUCHARIST

79. The eucharistic sacrifice is the source and culmination of the whole Christian life. Both private and public devotion toward the eucharist, therefore, including the devotion outside Mass, are strongly encouraged when celebrated according to the regulations of lawful authority.

In the arrangement of devotional services of this kind, the liturgical seasons should be taken into account. Devotions should be in harmony with the sacred liturgy in some sense, take their origin from the liturgy, and lead the people back to the liturgy.[1]

80. When the faithful honor Christ present in the sacrament, they should remember that this presence is derived from the sacrifice and is directed toward sacramental and spiritual communion.

The same piety which moves the faithful to eucharistic adoration attracts them to a deeper participation in the paschal mystery. It makes them respond gratefully to the gifts of Christ who by his humanity continues to pour divine life upon the members of his body. Living with Christ the Lord, they achieve a close familiarity with him and in his presence pour out their hearts for themselves and for those dear to them; they pray for peace and for the salvation of the world. Offering their entire lives with Christ to the Father in the Holy Spirit, they draw from this wondrous exchange an increase of faith, hope and love. Thus they nourish the proper disposition to celebrate the memorial of the Lord as devoutly as possible and to receive frequently the bread given to us by the Father.

The faithful should make every effort to worship Christ the Lord in the sacrament, depending upon the circumstances

[1]See Congregation of Rites, instruction *Eucharisticum mysterium,* no. 58: *AAS* 59 (1967) 569.

of their own life. Pastors should encourage them in this by example and word.[2]

81. Prayer before Christ the Lord sacramentally present extends the union with Christ which the faithful have reached in communion. It renews the covenant which in turn moves them to maintain in their lives what they have received by faith and by sacraments. They should try to lead their whole lives with the strength derived from the heavenly food, as they share in the death and resurrection of the Lord. Everyone should be concerned with good deeds and with pleasing God so that he or she may imbue the world with the Christian spirit and be a witness of Christ in the midst of human society.[3]

[2]See *ibid.*, no. 50: *loc. cit.*, 567.
[3]See *ibid.*, no. 13: *loc. cit.*, 549.

1. EXPOSITION OF THE HOLY EUCHARIST

INTRODUCTION

I. RELATIONSHIP BETWEEN EXPOSITION AND MASS

82. Exposition of the holy eucharist, either in the ciborium or in the monstrance, is intended to acknowledge Christ's marvelous presence in the sacrament. Exposition invites us to the spiritual union with him that culminates in sacramental communion. Thus it fosters very well the worship which is due to Christ in spirit and in truth.

This kind of exposition must clearly express the cult of the blessed sacrament in its relationship to the Mass. The plan of the exposition should carefully avoid anything which might somehow obscure the principal desire of Christ in instituting the eucharist, namely, to be with us as food, medicine, and comfort.[4]

83. During the exposition of the blessed sacrament, the celebration of Mass is prohibited in the body of the Church. In addition to the reasons given in no. 6, the celebration of the eucharistic mystery includes in a more perfect way the internal communion to which exposition seeks to lead the faithful.

If exposition of the blessed sacrament is extended for an entire day or over several days, it is to be interrupted during the celebration of Mass. Mass may be celebrated in a chapel distinct from the area of exposition if at least some members of the faithful remain in adoration.[5]

II. REGULATIONS FOR EXPOSITION

84. A single genuflection is made in the presence of the blessed sacrament, whether reserved in the tabernacle or exposed for public adoration.

85. For exposition of the blessed sacrament in the monstrance, four to six candles are lighted, as at Mass, and

[4]See *ibid.*, no. 60: *loc. cit.*, 570.
[5]See *ibid.*, no. 61: *loc. cit.*, 570-571.

incense is used. For exposition of the blessed sacrament in the ciborium, at least two candles should be lighted, and incense may be used.

Lengthy Exposition

86. In churches where the eucharist is regularly reserved, it is recommended that solemn exposition of the blessed sacrament for an extended period of time should take place once a year, even though this period is not strictly continuous. In this way the local community may reflect more profoundly upon this mystery and adore Christ in the sacrament.

This kind of exposition, however, may take place, with the consent of the local Ordinary, only if suitable numbers of the faithful are expected to be present.[6]

87. For a grave and general necessity the local Ordinary may direct that a more extended period of supplication before the blessed sacrament exposed take place in churches where the faithful assemble in large numbers.[7]

88. If a period of uninterrupted exposition is not possible, because of too few worshipers, the blessed sacrament may be replaced in the tabernacle during the periods which have been scheduled and announced beforehand. This reposition may not take place more often than twice during the day, for example, about noon and at night.

The following form of simple reposition may be observed: the priest or deacon, vested in an alb, or a surplice over a cassock, and a stole, replaces the blessed sacrament in the tabernacle after a brief period of adoration and a prayer said with those present. The exposition of the blessed sacrament may take place in the same manner (at the scheduled time.)[8]

Brief Period of Exposition

89. Shorter expositions of the eucharist are to be arranged in such a way that the blessing with the eucharist is preceded by a suitable period for readings of the word of

[6]See *ibid.*, no. 63: *loc. cit.*, 571.
[7]See *ibid.*, no. 64: *loc. cit.*, 572.
[8]See *ibid.*, no. 65: *loc. cit.*, 572.

God, songs, prayers, and sufficient time for silent prayer.[9]

Exposition which is held exclusively for the giving of benediction is prohibited.

Adoration in Religious Communities

90. According to the constitutions and regulations of their institute, some religious communities and other groups have the practice of perpetual eucharistic adoration or adoration over extended periods of time. It is strongly recommended that they pattern this holy practice in harmony with the spirit of the liturgy. Thus, when the whole community takes part in adoration before Christ the Lord, readings, songs, and religious silence may foster effectively the spiritual life of a community. This will promote among the members of the religious house the spirit of unity and brotherhood which the eucharist signifies and effects, and the cult of the sacrament may express a noble form of worship.

The form of adoration in which one or two members of the community take turns before the blessed sacrament is also to be maintained and is highly commended. In accordance with the life of the institute, as approved by the Church, the worshipers adore Christ the Lord in the sacrament and pray to him in the name of the whole community and of the Church.

III. THE MINISTER OF EXPOSITION

91. The ordinary minister for exposition of the eucharist is a priest or deacon. At the end of the period of adoration, before the reposition, he blesses the people with the sacrament.

In the absence of a priest or deacon or if they are lawfully impeded, the following persons may publicly expose and later repose the holy eucharist for the adoration of the faithful:

a) an acolyte or special minister of communion;

b) a member of a religious community or of a lay association of men or women which is devoted to eucharistic adoration, upon appointment by the local Ordinary.

Such ministers may open the tabernacle and also, if suitable, place the ciborium on the altar or place the host in the

[9]See *ibid.*, no. 66: *loc. cit.*, 572.

monstrance. At the end of the period of adoration, they replace the blessed sacrament in the tabernacle. It is not lawful, however, for them to give the blessing with the sacrament.

92. The minister, if he is a priest or deacon, should vest in an alb or a surplice over a cassock, and a stole.

Other ministers should wear either the liturgical vestments which are usual in the region or the vesture which is suitable for this ministry and which has been approved by the Ordinary.

The priest or deacon should wear a white cope and humeral veil to give the blessing at the end of adoration, when the exposition takes place with the monstrance; in the case of exposition in the ciborium, the humeral veil should be worn.

RITE OF EUCHARISTIC EXPOSITION AND BENEDICTION

EXPOSITION

93. After the people have assembled, a song may be sung while the minister comes to the altar. If the holy eucharist is not reserved at the altar where the exposition is to take place, the minister puts on a humeral veil and brings the sacrament from the place of reservation; he is accompanied by servers or by the faithful with lighted candles.

The ciborium or monstrance should be placed upon the table of the altar which is covered with a cloth. If exposition with the monstrance is to extend over a long period, a throne in an elevated position may be used, but this should not be too lofty or distant.[10] After exposition, if the monstrance is used, the minister incenses the sacrament. If the adoration is to be lengthy, he may then withdraw.

94. In the case of more solemn and lengthy exposition, the host should be consecrated in the Mass which immediately precedes the exposition and after communion should be placed in the monstrance upon the altar. The Mass ends with the prayer after communion, and the concluding rites are omitted. Before the priest leaves, he may place the blessed sacrament on the throne and incense it.

ADORATION

95. During the exposition there should be prayers, songs, and readings to direct the attention of the faithful to the worship of Christ the Lord.

To encourage a prayerful spirit, there should be readings from scripture with a homily or brief exhortations to develop a better understanding of the eucharistic mystery. It is also desirable for the people to respond to the word of God by singing and to spend some periods of time in religious silence.

96. Part of the liturgy of the hours, especially the principal

[10]See *ibid.*, no. 62: *loc. cit.*, 571.

hours, may be celebrated before the blessed sacrament when there is a lengthy period of exposition. This liturgy extends the praise and thanksgiving offered to God in the eucharistic celebration to the several hours of the day; it directs the prayers of the Church to Christ and through him to the Father in the name of the whole world.

BENEDICTION

97. Toward the end of the exposition the priest or deacon goes to the altar, genuflects, and kneels. Then a hymn or other eucharistic song is sung.[11] Meanwhile the minister, while kneeling, incenses the sacrament if the exposition has taken place with the monstrance.

98. Afterward the minister rises and sings or says:

Let us pray.

After a brief period of silence, the minister continues:

Lord Jesus Christ,
you gave us the eucharist
as the memorial of your suffering and death.
May our worship of this sacrament of your body and blood
help us to experience the salvation you won for us
and the peace of the kingdom
where you live with the Father and the Holy Spirit,
one God, for ever and ever.
All respond: **Amen.**

Other prayers, nos. 224-229, may be chosen.

99. After the prayer the priest or deacon puts on the humeral veil, genuflects, and takes the monstrance or ciborium. He makes the sign of the cross over the people with the monstrance or ciborium, in silence.

REPOSITION

100. After the blessing the priest or deacon who gave the

[11]See below, nos. 192-199.

blessing, or another priest or deacon, replaces the blessed sacrament in the tabernacle and genuflects. Meanwhile the people may sing or say an acclamation, and the minister then leaves.

2. EUCHARISTIC PROCESSIONS

101. When the eucharist is carried through the streets in a solemn procession with singing, the Christian people give public witness of faith and devotion through the sacrament.

It is for the local Ordinary, however, to judge whether this is opportune in today's circumstances, and to determine the time, place, and order of such processions, so that they may be conducted with dignity and without loss of reverence to the sacrament.[12]

102. The annual procession on the feast of Corpus Christi, or on an appropriate day near this feast, has a special importance and meaning for the pastoral life of the parish or city. It is therefore desirable to continue this procession, in accordance with the law, when today's circumstances permit and when it can truly be a sign of common faith and adoration.

In the principal districts of large cities there may be additional eucharistic processions for pastoral reasons at the discretion of the local Ordinary. If the procession cannot be held on the feast of Corpus Christi, it is fitting to hold some kind of public celebration for the entire city or its principal districts in the cathedral church or other appropriate places.

103. It is fitting that a eucharistic procession begin after the Mass in which the host to be carried in the procession has been consecrated. A procession may also take place, however, at the end of a lengthy period of public adoration.

104. Eucharistic processions should be arranged in accordance with local customs concerning the decoration of the streets and the order followed by the participants. In the course of the procession there may be stations where the eucharistic blessing is given, if this custom is in effect and is of pastoral advantage. Songs and prayers should be so directed that all proclaim their faith in Christ and direct their attention to the Lord alone.

105. The priest who carries the blessed sacrament may

[12]See Congregation of Rites, instruction *Eucharisticum mysterium*, no. 59: *AAS* 59 (1967) 570.

wear the vestments used for the celebration of Mass if the procession takes place immediately afterward, or he may vest in a white cope.

106. Lights, incense, and the canopy under which the priest carrying the blessed sacrament walks should be used in accordance with local customs.

107. It is fitting that the procession should go from one church to another. Nevertheless, if local circumstances require, the procession may return to the same church where it began.

108. At the end of the procession benediction with the blessed sacrament should be given in the church where the procession ends or at another appropriate place. Then the blessed sacrament is reposed.

3. EUCHARISTIC CONGRESSES

109. Eucharistic congresses have been introduced into the life of the Church in recent years as a special manifestation of eucharistic worship. They should be considered as a kind of station to which a particular community invites an entire local church or to which an individual local church invites other churches of a single region or nation or even of the entire world. The purpose is that together the members of the church join in the deepest profession of some aspect of the eucharistic mystery and express their worship publicly in the bond of charity and unity.

Such congresses should be a genuine sign of faith and charity by reason of the total participation of the local church and the association with it of the other churches.

110. Both the local church and other churches should undertake studies beforehand concerning the place, theme, and program of the congress. These studies will lead to the consideration of genuine needs and will foster the progress of theological studies and the good of the local church. Specialists in theological, biblical, liturgical, pastoral, and humane studies should help in this research.

111. In preparation for a eucharistic congress, primary consideration should be given to the following:

a) a thorough catechesis concerning the eucharist, especially as the mystery of Christ living and working in the Church, accommodated to the capacity of different groups;

b) more active participation in the liturgy in order to encourage a religious hearing of the word of God and the spirit of brotherhood and community;[13]

c) research and promotion of social undertakings for human development and the proper distribution of property, including temporal property, following the example of the primitive Christian community.[14] Thus the ferment of the Gospel, as a force in the growth of contemporary society and as the pledge of the future kingdom,[15] may be diffused

[13]Second Vatican Council, constitution *Sacrosanctum Concilium,* nos. 41-52; constitution *Lumen gentium,* no. 26.

[14]See Acts 4:32.

[15]Second Vatican Council, constitution *Sacrosanctum Concilium,* no. 47; decree *Unitatis redintegratio,* no. 15.

in some measure at the eucharistic table.

112. The celebration of the congress should follow these criteria:[16]

a) the celebration of the eucharist should be the true center and high point of the congress to which all the efforts and the various devotional services should be directed;

b) celebrations of the word of God, catechetical meetings, and public conferences should be planned to investigate thoroughly the theme of the congress and to propose clearly the practical aspects to be carried out;

c) there should be an opportunity for common prayers and extended adoration in the presence of the blessed sacrament exposed at designated churches which are especially suited to this form of piety;

d) the regulations concerning eucharistic processions[17] should be observed for the procession in which the blessed sacrament is carried through the streets of the city with common hymns and prayers, taking into account local social and religious conditions.

[16]See Congregation of Rites, instruction *Eucharisticum mysterium*, no. 67: *AAS* 59 (1967) 572-573.

[17]See above, nos. 101-108.

CHAPTER IV

TEXTS FOR USE IN THE RITE OF DISTRIBUTING HOLY COMMUNION OUTSIDE MASS AND IN THE WORSHIP AND PROCESSION OF THE BLESSED SACRAMENT

1. BIBLICAL READINGS

READINGS FROM THE OLD TESTAMENT

113. **Genesis 14:18-20**
Melchisedech brought bread and wine.

114. **Exodus 12:21-27**
When the Lord sees the blood on the door, he will pass over your home.

115. **Exodus 16:2-4, 12-15**
I will rain bread from heaven upon you.

116. **Exodus 24:3-8**
This is the blood of the covenant that the Lord God has made with you.

117. **Deuteronomy 8:2-3, 15b-16a**
He gave you food which you and your fathers did not know.

118. **1 Kings 19:4-8**
Strengthened by the food, he walked to the mountain of the Lord.

119. **Proverbs 9:1-6**
Come and eat my bread, drink the wine I have prepared.

READINGS FROM THE NEW TESTAMENT

120. **Acts 2:42-47**
They continued in fellowship with the apostles and in the breaking of the bread.

121. **Acts 10:34a, 37-43**
After he was raised from the dead, we ate and drank with him.

122. **1 Corinthians 10:16-17**
Though we are many, we are one bread and one body.

123. **1 Corinthians 11:23-26**
Each time you eat this bread and drink this cup, you are proclaiming the death of the Lord Jesus.

124. **Hebrews 9:11-15**
The blood of Christ purifies our hearts from sin.

125. **Hebrews 12:18-19, 22-24**
Jesus brings you to the Father by shedding his blood for you.

126. **1 Peter 1:17-21**
You have been redeemed by the precious blood of Jesus Christ.

127. **1 John 5:4-7a, 8b**
The Spirit, the water, and the blood give witness.

128. **Revelation 1:5-8**
Because he loves us, he has saved us from sin with his blood.

129. **Revelation 7:9-14**
They have washed their robes in the blood of the Lamb.

RESPONSORIAL PSALM

130. Psalm 23:1-3, 4, 5, 6
℟. (1): **The Lord is my shepherd; there is nothing I shall want.**

131. Psalm 34:2-3, 4-5, 6-7, 8-9
℟. (9a): **Taste and see the goodness of the Lord.**

132. Psalm 40:2 and 4ab, 7-8a, 8b-9, 10
℟. (8a and 9a): **Here I am, Lord; I come to do your will.**

133. Psalm 78:3-4a and 7ab, 23-24, 25, 54
℟. (24b): **The Lord gave them bread from heaven.**

134. Psalm 110: 1, 2, 3, 4
℟. (4bc): **You are a priest for ever, in the line of Melchisedech.**

135. Psalm 116:12-13, 15 and 16bc, 17-18
℟. (13): **I will take the cup of salvation, and call on the name of the Lord.**

or (1 Corinthians 10:16): **Our blessing-cup is a communion with the blood of Christ.**

136. Psalm 145:10-11, 15-16, 17-18
℟. (see 16): **The hand of the Lord feeds us; he answers all our needs.**

137. Psalm 148:12-13, 14-15, 19-20
℟. (12a): **Praise the Lord, Jerusalem.**
or (John 6:58c): **Whoever eats this bread will live for ever.**

ALLELUIA VERSE AND VERSE BEFORE THE GOSPEL

138. John 6:51
I am the living bread from heaven, says the Lord;
if anyone eats this bread he will live for ever.

139. John 6:56
Whoever eats my flesh and drinks my blood, says the Lord, will live in me and I in him.

140. John 6:57
As the living Father sent me, and I live because of the Father, so he who eats me will live because of me.

141. See Revelation 1:5ab
Jesus Christ, you are the faithful witness, firstborn from the dead.

142. Revelation 5:9
You are worthy, O Lord, to receive the book and open its seals.

GOSPEL

143. **Mark 14:12-16, 22-26**
This is my body. This is my blood.

144. **Mark 15:16-20**
They dressed Jesus up in purple and put a crown of thorns on him.

145. **Luke 9:11b-17**
All the people ate and were satisfied.

146. **Luke 22:39-44**
His sweat became like drops of blood falling to the ground.

147. **Luke 24:13-35** (longer) **or 13-16, 28-35** (shorter)
They recognized him at the breaking of the bread.

148. **John 6:1-15**
They gave the people all the food they wanted.

149. **John 6:24-35**
If you come to me, you will never be hungry. He who believes in me will never know thirst.

150. **John 6:41-51**
I am the living bread from heaven.

151. **John 6:51-58**
My flesh and blood are true food and drink.

152. **John 19:31-37**
When they pierced his side with a spear, blood and water flowed out.

153. **John 21:1-14**
Jesus took the bread and gave it to them.

READING FROM THE VOTIVE MASS OF THE SACRED HEART

READINGS FROM THE OLD TESTAMENT

154. **Exodus 34:4b-7a, 8-9**
Our God is merciful and compassionate.

155. **Deuteronomy 7:6-11**
God has chosen you because he loves you.

156. **Deuteronomy 10:12-22**
God loves his chosen ones and their children.

157. **Isaiah 49:13-15**
Even if a mother forgets her child, I will never forget you.

158. **Jeremiah 31:1-4**
I have loved you with a love that will never end.

159. **Ezekiel 34:11-16**
I will take care of my flock.

160. **Hosea 11:1b, 3-4, 8c-9 (Hebrew 1, 3-4, 8c-9)**
My heart is saddened at the thought of parting.

READINGS FROM THE NEW TESTAMENT

161. **Romans 5:5-11**
God has poured out his love into our hearts.

162. **Ephesians 1:3-10**
He has lavished his rich graces upon us.

163. **Ephesians 3:8-12**
God has given me the privilege of proclaiming the riches of Christ to all the nations.

164. **Ephesians 3:14-19**
I pray that you will grasp the unbounded love of Christ.

165. **Philippians 1:8-11**
May your life be filled with the perfection which comes through Jesus Christ.

166. **1 John 4:7-16**
We love God because he has loved us first.

167. **Revelation 3:14b, 20-22**
I will come to eat with you.

168. **Revelation 5:6-12**
You brought us back to God by shedding your blood for us.

RESPONSORIAL PSALM

169. Isaiah 12:2-3, 4bcd, 5-6
℟. (3): **You will draw water joyfully from the springs of salvation.**

170. Psalm 23:1-3, 4, 5, 6
℟. (1): **The Lord is my shepherd; there is nothing I shall want.**

171. Psalm 25:4bc-5ab, 6-7bc, 8-9, 10, 14
℟. (6a): **Remember your mercies, O Lord.**

172. Psalm 33:1-2, 4-5, 11-12, 18-19, 20-21
℟. (5b): **The earth is full of the goodness of the Lord.**

173. Psalm 34:2-3, 4-5, 6-7
℟. (9a): **Taste and see the goodness of the Lord.**

174. Psalm 103:1-2, 3-4, 6-7, 8, 10
℟. (17): **The Lord's kindness is everlasting to those who fear him.**

ALLELUIA VERSE AND VERSE BEFORE THE GOSPEL

175. See Matthew 11:25

Blessed are you, Father, Lord of heaven and earth;
you have revealed to little ones the mysteries of the kingdom.

176. Matthew 11:28

Come to me, all you that labor and are burdened,
and I will give you rest, says the Lord.

177. Matthew 11:29ab

Take my yoke upon you;
learn from me, for I am gentle and lowly in heart.

178. John 10:14

I am the good shepherd, says the Lord;
I know my sheep, and mine know me.

179. John 15:9

As the Father has loved me, so have I loved you;
remain in my love.

180. 1 John 4:10b

God first loved us
and sent his Son to take away our sins.

GOSPEL

181. **Matthew 11:25-30**
I am gentle and humble of heart.

182. **Luke 15:1-10**
Heaven is filled with joy when one sinner turns back to God.

183. **Luke 15:1-3, 11-32**
We are celebrating because your brother has come back from death.

184. **John 10:11-18**
A good shepherd is ready to die for his flock.

185. **John 15:1-8**
Live in me as I live in you.

186. **John 15:9-17**
Love one another as much as I love you.

187. **John 17:20-26**
Father, you loved them as you loved me.

188. **John 19:31-37**
When they pierced his side with a spear, blood and water flowed out.

2. FORMS OF GREETING

189.
The grace and peace of God our Father and the Lord Jesus Christ be with you.

The people answer:
Blessed be the God and Father of our Lord Jesus Christ.

or:
And also with you.

3. FORMS OF THE PENITENTIAL RITE

190. The minister invites the people to recall their sins and to repent of them in these words:

My brothers and sisters,
to prepare ourselves for this celebration,
let us call to mind our sins.

A pause for silent reflection follows.

The minister says:
Lord, we have sinned against you.
The people answer: **Lord, have mercy.**

Minister:
Lord, show us your mercy and love.
The people answer: **And grant us your salvation.**

The minister concludes:
May almighty God have mercy on us,
forgive us our sins,
and bring us to everlasting life.
The people answer: **Amen.**

191. The minister invites the people to recall their sins and to repent of them in these words:

My brothers and sisters,
to prepare ourselves for this celebration,
let us call to mind our sins.

After a brief silence the minister, or someone else, makes the following or other invocations:

Minister:
You brought us to salvation by your paschal mystery:
Lord, have mercy.
The people answer: **Lord, have mercy.**

Minister:
You renew among us the wonders of your passion:
Christ, have mercy.
The people answer: **Christ, have mercy.**

Minister:
You give us your body to make us one with your Easter sacrifice:
Lord, have mercy.
The people answer: **Lord, have mercy.**

The minister concludes:
May almighty God have mercy on us,
forgive us our sins,
and bring us to everlasting life.
The people answer: **Amen.**

4. HYMNS

At benediction, which concludes the service of adoration, especially the short form, singing may be confined to the last part, beginning with the words: **Tantum ergo.**

Pange, Lingua
192. Pange, lingua, gloriosi

Sacris sollemniis
193. Sacris sollemniis iuncta sint gaudia

Verbum Supernum
194. Verbum supernum prodiens

Jesu, Nostra Redemptio
195. Jesu, nostra redemptio

Aeterne Rex Altissime
196. Aeterne rex altissime

Lauda, Sion
197. This sequence may be sung either in its entirety or beginning at the words: Ecce panis.

Adoro Te Devote
198. Adoro te devote, latens veritas,

Ubi Caritas
199. Ubi caritas est vera, Deus ibi est
A further choice of chants can be found in the Liturgy of the Hours.

5. ANTIPHONS

200.
How holy this feast
in which Christ is our food:
his passion is recalled,
grace fills our hearts,
and we receive a pledge of the glory to come.

201.
How gracious you are, Lord:
your gift of bread from heaven
reveals a Father's love and brings us perfect joy.
You fill the hungry with good things
and send away empty the rich in their pride.

202.
Body of Jesus, born of the Virgin Mary,
body bowed in agony,
raised upon the cross
and offered for us in sacrifice,
body pierced and flowing with blood and water,
come at the hour of our death

as our living bread,
the foretaste of eternal glory:
come, Lord Jesus,
loving and gracious Son of Mary.

203.

I am the living bread
come down from heaven.
If anyone eats this bread
he shall live for ever.
The bread I will give is my flesh
for the life of the world.

6. RESPONSORIES

204.

While they were at table, Jesus took bread,
said the blessing, broke the bread,
and gave it to his disciples saying:
Take this, all of you, and eat it: this is my body.

℣. Those who dwell with me said: Who will give us flesh to eat?
Take this, all . . .

205.

I am the bread of life: your fathers ate the manna in the desert and they are dead;
this is the bread which comes down from heaven; whoever eats it will not die.

℣. I am the living bread which has come down from heaven;
whoever eats this bread will live for ever.
This is the . . .

206.

See in this bread the body that hung on the cross;
see in this cup the blood that flowed from his side.
Take and eat the body of Christ; take and drink his blood.

For now you are members of Christ.

℣. Receive the bond of love and be united; receive the price of your salvation and know your worth.
For now you . . .

207.
We though many are one bread, one body; for we all share one bread and one cup.

℣. You have made us live in peace in your house, O Lord;
in your kindness you have prepared a banquet for the poor.
For we all . . .

208.
A man prepared a banquet and sent his servants to tell the guests:
Come, all is ready.

℣. Eat my bread and drink my wine.
Come, all is ready.

209.
The living Father has sent me and I have life from the Father.
He who eats me, has life from me.

℣. The Lord has fed him on the bread of life and understanding.
He who eats . . .

7. PRAYERS AFTER COMMUNION

210.
Father,
you have brought to fulfillment the work of our redemption
through the Easter mystery of Christ your Son.
May we who faithfully proclaim his death and resurrection in these sacramental signs

experience the constant growth of your salvation in our lives.

We ask this through Christ our Lord.

211.
Lord,
you have nourished us with one bread from heaven.
Fill us with your Spirit,
and make us one in peace and love.

We ask this through Christ our Lord.

212.
Lord,
may our sharing at this holy table make us holy.
By the body and blood of Christ
join all your people in brotherly love.

We ask this through Christ our Lord.

213.
Father,
you give us food from heaven.
By our sharing in this mystery
teach us to judge wisely the things of earth
and to love the things of heaven.

Grant this through Christ our Lord.

214.
Lord,
we give thanks for these holy mysteries
which bring to us here on earth
a share in the life to come,
through Christ our Lord.

215.
All-powerful God,
you renew us with your sacraments.
Help us to thank you by lives of faithful service.

We ask this through Christ our Lord.

216.
God our Father,
you give us a share in the one bread and the one cup
and make us one in Christ.
Help us to bring your salvation and joy
to all the world.

We ask this through Christ our Lord.

217.
Lord,
you renew us at your table with the bread of life.
May this food strengthen us in love
and help us to serve you in each other.

We ask this in the name of Jesus the Lord.

218.
Lord,
we thank you for the nourishment you give us
through your holy gift.
Pour out your Spirit upon us
and in the strength of this food from heaven
keep us single-minded in your service.

We ask this in the name of Jesus the Lord.

219.
Lord,
we are renewed by the breaking of one bread.
Keep us in your love
and help us to live the new life Christ won for us.

Grant this in the name of Jesus the Lord.

During the Easter Season the prayers in nos. 220-222 are preferred:

220.
Lord,
you have nourished us with your Easter sacraments.
Fill us with your Spirit
and make us one in peace and love.

We ask this through Christ our Lord.

221.
Lord,
may this sharing in the sacrament of your Son
free us from our old life of sin
and make us your new creation.

We ask this in the name of Jesus the Lord.

222.
Almighty and ever-living Lord,
you restored us to life
by raising Christ from death.
Strengthen us by this Easter sacrament;
may we feel its saving power in our daily life.

We ask this through Christ our Lord.

223. Another prayer after Viaticum:

Lord,
you are the source of eternal health
for those who believe in you.
May our brother (sister) N.,
who has been refreshed
with food and drink from heaven,
safely reach your kingdom of light and life.

We ask this through Christ our Lord.

8. PRAYERS AT BENEDICTION OF THE BLESSED SACRAMENT

224.
Lord our God,
in this great sacrament
we come into the presence of Jesus Christ, your Son,
born of the Virgin Mary
and crucified for our salvation.
May we who declare our faith in this fountain of love and mercy
drink from it the water of everlasting life.

We ask this through Christ our Lord.

225.
**Lord our God,
may we always give due honor
to the sacramental presence of the Lamb who was slain for us.
May our faith be rewarded
by the vision of his glory,
who lives and reigns for ever and ever.**

226.
**Lord our God,
you have given us the true bread from heaven.
In the strength of this food
may we live always by your life
and rise in glory on the last day.**

We ask this through Christ our Lord.

227.
**Lord,
give to our hearts
the light of faith and the fire of love,
that we may worship in spirit and in truth
our God and Lord, present in this sacrament,
who lives and reigns for ever and ever.**

228.
**Lord,
may this sacrament of new life
warm our hearts with your love
and make us eager
for the eternal joy of your kingdom.**

We ask this through Christ our Lord.

229.
**Lord our God,
teach us to cherish in our hearts
the paschal mystery of your Son
by which you redeemed the world.
Watch over the gifts of grace
your love has given us**

and bring them to fulfillment
in the glory of heaven.

We ask this through Christ our Lord.

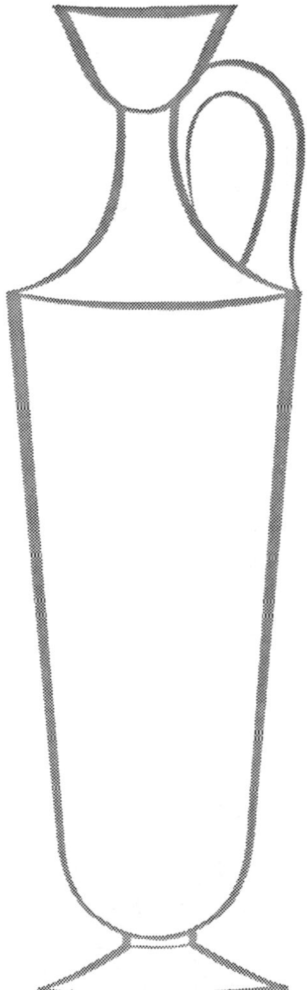

RITE OF THE BLESSING OF OILS
RITE OF CONSECRATING THE CHRISM

RITE OF THE BLESSING OF OILS
RITE OF CONSECRATING THE CHRISM

Decree
Introduction (1-12)

BLESSING OF OILS AND CONSECRATION OF THE CHRISM

I Preparations (13)

II Rite of Blessing (14-19)

III Blessing of the Oil of the Sick (20)

IV Blessing of the Oil of Catechumens (21-22)

V Consecration of the Chrism (23)

A Invitation (24)

B Consecratory Prayer (24-26)

Conclusion (27-28)

SACRED CONGREGATION FOR DIVINE WORSHIP

Prot. n. 3133/70

DECREE

Since the Holy Week rites of the Roman Missal have been revised, it seemed appropriate to make the necessary adaptations in the rites of the blessing of the oil of catechumens and the oil of the sick and of consecrating the chrism, for use in the chrism Mass.

Therefore the Sacred Congregation for Divine Worship has revised these rites and, with the approval of Pope Paul VI, publishes them to be used in place of those now given in the Roman Pontifical.

It is the responsibility of the conferences of bishops to prepare vernacular editions of these rites and to present them to this Congregation for confirmation.

Anything to the contrary notwithstanding.

From the Sacred Congregation for Divine Worship,
December 3, 1970.

Benno Cardinal Gut
prefect

A. Bugnini
secretary

INTRODUCTION

1. The bishop is to be considered as the high priest of his flock. The life in Christ of his faithful is in some way derived and dependent upon the bishop.[1]

The chrism Mass is one of the principal expressions of the fullness of the bishop's priesthood and signifies the close unity of the priests with him. During the Mass, which he concelebrates with priests from various sections of the diocese, the bishop consecrates the chrism and blesses the other oils. The newly baptized are anointed and confirmed with the chrism consecrated by the bishop. Catechumens are prepared and disposed for baptism with the second oil. And the sick are anointed in their illness with the third oil.

2. The Christian liturgy has assimilated this Old Testament usage of anointing kings, priests, and prophets with consecratory oil because the name of Christ, whom they prefigured, means "the anointed of the Lord."

Chrism is a sign: by baptism Christians are plunged into the paschal mystery of Christ; they die with him, are buried with him, and rise with him;[2] they are sharers in his royal and prophetic priesthood. By confirmation Christians receive the spiritual anointing of the Spirit who is given to them.

By the oil of catechumens the effect of the baptismal exorcisms is extended. Before they go to the font of life to be reborn the candidates for baptism are strengthened to renounce sin and the devil.

By the use of the oil of the sick, to which Saint James is a witness,[3] the sick receive a remedy for the illness of mind and body, so that they may have strength to bear suffering and resist evil and obtain the forgiveness of sins.

I. THE OILS

3. The matter proper for the sacraments is olive oil or, ac-

[1]See II Vatican Council, Constitution on the Sacred Liturgy, *Sacrosanctum Concilium,* no. 42.
[2]*Ibid.,* no. 6.
[3]James 5:14

cording to circumstances, other plant oil.

4. Chrism is made of oil and perfumes or other sweet smelling matter.

5. The preparation of the chrism may take place privately before the rite of consecration or may be done by the bishop during the liturgical service.

II. THE MINISTER

6. The consecration of the chrism belongs to the bishop alone.

7. If the use of the oil of catechumens is retained by the conferences of bishops, it is blessed by the bishop with the other oils during the chrism Mass.

In the case of the baptism of adults, however, priests have the faculty to bless the oil of catechumens before the anointing in the designated stage of the catechumenate.

8. The oil used for anointing the sick must be blessed for this purpose by the bishop or by a priest who has this faculty, either from the law or by special concession of the Apostolic See.

The law itself permits the following to bless the oil of the sick:

a) those whom the law equates with diocesan bishops;
b) in case of true necessity, any priest.

III. TIME OF BLESSING

9. The blessing of the oil and the consecration of the chrism are ordinarily celebrated by the bishop at the chrism Mass celebrated on Holy Thursday morning.

10. If it is difficult for the clergy and people to assemble with the bishop on Holy Thursday morning, the blessing may be held on an earlier day, near Easter, with the celebration of the proper chrism Mass.

IV. PLACE OF THE BLESSING IN THE MASS

11. According to the tradition of the Latin liturgy, the blessing of the oil of the sick takes place before the end of the eucharistic prayer; the blessing of the oil of catechumens and the consecration of the chrism, after communion.

12. For pastoral reasons, however, the entire rite of blessing may be celebrated after the liturgy of the word, according to the order described below.

BLESSING OF OILS AND CONSECRATION OF THE CHRISM

PREPARATIONS

13. For the blessing of oils the following preparations are made in addition to what is needed for Mass:

In the sacristy or other appropriate place:
—vessels of oils;
—balsam or perfume for the preparation of the chrism if the bishop wishes to mix the chrism during the liturgical service;
—bread, wine, and water for Mass, which are carried with the oils before the preparation of the gifts.

In the sanctuary:
—table for the vessels of oil, placed so that the people may see the entire rite easily and take part in it;
—chair for the bishop, if the blessing takes place in front of the altar.

RITE OF BLESSING

14. The chrism Mass is always concelebrated. It is desirable that there be some priests from the various sections of the diocese among the priests who concelebrate with the bishop and are his witnesses and the co-workers in the ministry of the holy chrism.

15. The preparation of the bishop, the concelebrants, and other ministers, their entrance into the church, and everything from the beginning of Mass until the end of the liturgy of the word take place as indicated in the rite of concelebration. The deacons who take part in the blessing of oils walk ahead of the concelebrating priests to the altar.

16. After the renewal of commitment to priestly service the deacons and ministers appointed to carry the oils or, in their absence, some priests and ministers together with the faithful who will carry the bread, wine, and water, go in procession to the sacristy or other place where the oils and other offerings have been prepared. Returning to the altar, they follow this order: first the minister carrying the vessel of

balsam, if the bishop wishes to prepare the chrism, then the minister with the vessel for the oil of the catechumens, if it is to be blessed, the minister with the vessel for the oil of the sick, lastly a deacon or priest carrying the oil for the chrism. The ministers who carry the bread, wine, and water for the celebration of the eucharist follow them.

17. During the procession through the church, the choir leads the singing of the hymn "O Redeemer" or some other appropriate song, in place of the offertory song.

18. When the procession comes to the altar or the chair, the bishop receives the gifts. The deacon who carries the vessel of oil for the chrism shows it to the bishop, saying in a loud voice: **The oil for the holy chrism.** The bishop takes the vessel and gives it to one of the assisting deacons to place on the table. The same is done by those who carry the vessels for the oil of the sick and the oil of the catechumens. The first says: **The oil of the sick;** the second says: **The oil of catechumens.** The bishop takes the vessels in the same way, and the ministers place them on the table.

19. Then the Mass continues, as in the rite of concelebration, until the end of the eucharistic prayer, unless the entire rite of blessing takes place immediately (see no. 12). In this case everything is done as described below (no. 26).

BLESSING OF THE OIL OF THE SICK

20. Before the bishop says **Through Christ our Lord/you give us all these gifts** in Eucharistic Prayer I, or the doxology **Through him** in the other eucharistic prayers, the one who carried the vessel for oil of the sick brings it to the altar and holds it in front of the bishop while he blesses the oil. The bishop says or sings this prayer:

Lord God, loving Father,
you bring healing to the sick
through your Son Jesus Christ.
Hear us as we pray to you in faith,
and send the Holy Spirit, man's Helper and Friend,
upon this oil, which nature has provided
to serve the needs of men.

**May your blessing ✠
come upon all who are anointed with this oil,
that they may be freed from pain and illness
and made well again in body, mind, and soul.
Father, may this oil be blessed for our use
in the name of our Lord Jesus Christ
(who lives and reigns with you for ever and ever.
℟. Amen.)**

The conclusion **Who lives and reigns with you** is said only when this blessing takes place outside the eucharistic prayer.

When Eucharistic Prayer I is used, the beginning of the prayer **Through Christ our Lord/you give us all these gifts** is changed to: **Through whom you give us all these gifts.**

After the blessing, the vessel with the oil of the sick is returned to its place, and the Mass continues until the communion rite is completed.

BLESSING OF THE OIL OF CATECHUMENS

21. After the prayer after communion, the ministers place the oils to be blessed on a table suitably located in the center of the sanctuary. The concelebrating priests stand around the bishop on either side, in a semicircle, and the other ministers stand behind him. The bishop then blesses the oil of catechumens, if it is to be blessed, and consecrates the chrism.

22. When everything is ready, the bishop faces the people and, with his hands extended, sings or says the following prayer:

**Lord God, protector of all who believe in you,
bless ✠ this oil
and give wisdom and strength
to all who are anointed with it
in preparation for their baptism.
Bring them to a deeper understanding of the gospel,
help them to accept the challenge of Christian living,
and lead them to the joy of new birth**

in the family of your Church.
We ask this through Christ our Lord.
℟. **Amen.**

CONSECRATION OF THE CHRISM

23. Then the bishop pours the balsam or perfume in the oil and mixes the chrism in silence, unless this was done beforehand.

24. After this he sings or says the invitation:

Let us pray
that God our almighty Father
will bless this oil
so that all who are anointed with it
may be inwardly transformed
and come to share in eternal salvation.

CONSECRATORY PRAYER

25. Then the bishop may breathe over the opening of the vessel of chrism. With his hands extended, he sings or says one of the following consecratory prayers.

God our maker,
source of all growth in holiness,
accept the joyful thanks and praise
we offer in the name of your Church.

In the beginning, at your command,
the earth produced fruit-bearing trees.
From the fruit of the olive tree
you have provided us with oil for holy chrism.
The prophet David sang of the life and joy
that the oil would bring us in the sacraments of your love.

After the avenging flood,
the dove returning to Noah with an olive branch
announced your gift of peace.
This was a sign of a greater gift to come.
Now the waters of baptism wash away the sins of men,

and by the anointing with olive oil
you make us radiant with your joy.

At your command,
Aaron was washed with water,
and your servant Moses, his brother,
anointed him priest.
This too foreshadowed greater things to come.
After you Son, Jesus Christ our Lord,
asked John for baptism in the waters of Jordan,
you sent the Spirit upon him
in the form of a dove
and by the witness of your own voice
you declared him to be your only, well-beloved Son.
In this you clearly fulfilled the prophecy of David,
that Christ would be anointed with the oil of gladness
beyond his fellow men.

All the celebrants extend their right hands toward the chrism, without saying anything, until the end of the prayer.

And so, Father, we ask you to bless ✠ this oil you
have created.
Fill it with the power of your Holy Spirit
through Christ your Son.
It is from him that chrism takes its name
and with chrism you have anointed
for yourself priests and kings,
prophets and martyrs.

Make this chrism a sign of life and salvation
for those who are to be born again in the waters of
baptism.
Wash away the evil they have inherited from sinful
Adam,
and when they are anointed with this holy oil
make them temples of your glory,
radiant with the goodness of life
that has its source in you.

Through this sign of chrism
grant them royal, priestly, and prophetic honor,

**and clothe them with incorruption.
Let this be indeed the chrism of salvation
for those who will be born again of water and the
Holy Spirit.
May they come to share eternal life
in the glory of your kingdom.
We ask this through Christ our Lord.
℟. Amen.**

Or:

**Father, we thank you for the gifts
you have given us in your love:
we thank you for life itself and for the sacraments
that strengthen it and give it fuller meaning.**

**In the Old Covenant you gave your people
a glimpse of the power of this holy oil
and when the fullness of time had come
you brought that mystery to perfection
in the life of our Lord Jesus Christ, your Son.**

**By his suffering, dying, and rising to life
he saved the human race.
He sent your Spirit to fill the Church
with every gift needed to complete your saving work.**

**From that time forward,
through the sign of holy chrism,
you dispense your life and love to men.
By anointing them with the Spirit,
you strengthen all who have been reborn in baptism.
Through that anointing
you transform them into the likeness of Christ your
Son
and give them a share
in his royal, priestly, and prophetic work.**

All the concelebrants extend their right hands toward the chrism without saying anything, until the end of the prayer.

**And so, Father, by the power of your love,
make this mixture of oil and perfume
a sign and source ✠ of your blessing.**

Pour out the gifts of your Holy Spirit
on our brothers and sisters who will be anointed with it.
Let the splendor of holiness shine on the world
from every place and thing
signed with this oil.

Above all, Father, we pray
that through this sign of your anointing
you will grant increase to your Church
until it reaches the eternal glory
where you, Father, will be the all in all,
together with Christ your Son,
in the unity of the Holy Spirit,
for ever and ever.
℟. **Amen.**

26. When the entire rite of blessing of oils is to be celebrated after the liturgy of the word, at the end of the renewal of commitment to priestly service the bishop goes with the concelebrants to the table where the blessing of the oil of the sick and of the oil of the chrism are to take place, and everything is done as described above (nos. 20-25).

27. After the final blessing of the Mass, the bishop puts incense in the censer, and the procession to the sacristy is arranged.

The blessed oils are carried by the ministers immediately after the cross, and the choir and people sing some verses of the hymn "O Redeemer" or some other appropriate song.

28. In the sacristy the bishop may instruct the priests about the reverent use and safe custody of the holy oils.

RITE OF MARRIAGE

RITE OF MARRIAGE

CHAPTER III
RITE FOR CELEBRATING MARRIAGE BETWEEN A CATHOLIC AND AN UNBAPTIZED PERSON

I Rite of Welcome and Liturgy of the Word (55-57)

II Rite of Marriage (58-59)

A Consent (60-61)

B Blessing and Exchange of Rings (62-63)

III General Intercessions and Nuptial Blessings (64-65)

IV Conclusion of the Celebration (66)

CHAPTER IV
TEXTS FOR USE IN THE MARRIAGE RITE AND IN THE WEDDING MASS (67-127)

SACRED CONGREGATION OF RITES

Prot. n. R 23/969

DECREE

The rite for celebrating marriage has been revised according to the decrees of the Constitution on the Sacred Liturgy, in order that this richer rite would more clearly signify the grace of the sacrament and that the responsibilities of the married couple would be better taught. This revision has been carried out by the Consilium for the Implementation of the Constitution on the Sacred Liturgy.

By his apostolic authority, Pope Paul VI has approved this rite and directs that it be published. Therefore this sacred Congregation, acting on the special mandate of the Holy Father, publishes this rite and directs that it be used from July 1, 1969.

Anything to the contrary notwithstanding.

From the Congregation of Rites, March 19, 1969, solemnity of Saint Joseph, husband of the Blessed Virgin Mary.

Benno Card. Gut
Prefect of S.R.C.
President of the Consilium

✠ Ferdinando Antonelli
Titular Archbishop of Idicra
Secretary of S.R.C.

INTRODUCTION

IMPORTANCE AND DIGNITY OF THE SACRAMENT OF MATRIMONY

1. Married Christians, in virtue of the sacrament of matrimony, signify and share in the mystery of that unity and fruitful love which exists between Christ and his Church;[1] they help each other to attain to holiness in their married life and in the rearing and education of their children; and they have their own special gift among the people of God.[2]

2. Marriage arises in the covenant of marriage, or irrevocable consent, which each partner freely bestows on and accepts from the other. This intimate union and the good of the children impose total fidelity on each of them and argue for an unbreakable oneness between them. Christ the Lord raised this union to the dignity of a sacrament so that it might more clearly recall and more easily reflect his own unbreakable union with his Church.[3]

3. Christian couples, therefore, nourish and develop their marriage by undivided affection, which wells up from the fountain of divine love, while, in a merging of human and divine love, they remain faithful in body and in mind, in good times as in bad.[4]

4. By their very nature, the institution of matrimony and wedded love are ordained for the procreation and education of children and find in them their ultimate crown. Therefore, married Christians, while not considering the other purposes of marriage of less account, should be steadfast and ready to cooperate with the love of the Creator and Savior, who through them will constantly enrich and enlarge his own family.[5]

5. A priest should bear in mind these principles of faith,

[1]Ephesians 5:32
[2]1 Corinthians 7:7; II Vatican Council, Dogmatic Constitution on the Church, *Lumen Gentium*, 11.
[3]II Vatican Council, Constitution on the Church in the Modern World, *Gaudium et Spes*, 48.
[4]*Ibid.*, 48, 49.
[5]*Ibid.*, 48, 50.

both in his instructions to those about to be married and when giving the homily during the marriage ceremony. He should relate his instructions to the texts of the sacred readings.[6]

The bridal couple should be given a review of the fundamentals of Christian doctrine. This may include instruction on the teachings about marriage and the family, on the rites used in the celebration of the sacrament itself, and on the prayers and readings. In this way the bridegroom and the bride will receive far greater benefit from the celebration.

6. In the celebration of marriage (which normally should be within the Mass), certain elements should be stressed, especially the liturgy of the word, which shows the importance of Christian marriage in the history of salvation and the duties and responsibility of the couple in caring for the holiness of their children. Also of supreme importance are the consent of the contracting parties, which the priest asks and receives; the special nuptial blessing for the bride and for the marriage covenant; and finally, the reception of holy communion by the groom and the bride, and by all present, by which their love is nourished and all are lifted up into communion with our Lord and with one another.[7]

7. Priests should first of all strengthen and nourish the faith of those about to be married, for the sacrament of matrimony presupposes and demands faith.[8]

CHOICE OF RITE

8. In a marriage between a Catholic and a baptized person who is not Catholic, the regulations which appear below in the rite of marriage outside Mass (nos. 39-54) shall be observed. If suitable, and if the Ordinary of the place gives permission, the rite for celebrating marriage within Mass (nos. 19-38) may be used, except that, according to the

[6] II Vatican Council, Constitution on the Sacred Liturgy, *Sacrosanctum Concilium*, 52; S.C.R. Instruction *Inter Oecumenici*, no. 54: *AAS* 56 (1964) 890.

[7] II Vatican Council, Decree on the Apostolate of the Laity, *Apostolicam actuositatem*, 3: Dogmatic Constitution on the Church, *Lumen Gentium*, 12.

[8] II Vatican Council, Constitution on the Sacred Liturgy, *Sacrosanctum Concilium*, 59.

general law, communion is not given to the non-Catholic.

In a marriage between a Catholic and one who is not baptized, the rite which appears in nos. 55-66 is to be followed.

9. Furthermore, priests should show special consideration to those who take part in liturgical celebrations or hear the gospel only on the occasion of a wedding, either because they are not Catholics, or because they are Catholics who rarely, if ever, take part in the eucharist or seem to have abandoned the practice of their faith. Priests are ministers of Christ's gospel to everyone.

10. In the celebration of matrimony, apart from the liturgical laws providing for due honors to civil authorities, no special honors are to be paid to any private persons or classes of person, whether in the ceremonies or by external display.[9]

11. Whenever marrriage is celebrated during Mass, white vestments are worn and the wedding Mass is used. If the marriage is celebrated on a Sunday or solemnity, the Mass of the day is used with the nuptial blessing and, where appropriate, the special final blessing.

The liturgy of the word is extremely helpful in emphasizing the meaning of the sacrament and the obligations of marriage. When the wedding Mass may not be used, one of the readings in nos. 67-105 should be chosen, except from Holy Thursday to Easter and on the feasts of Christmas, Epiphany, Ascension, Pentecost, Corpus Christi, and other holydays of obligation. On the Sundays of the Christmas season and throughout the year, in Masses which are not parish Masses, the wedding Mass may be used without change.

When a marriage is celebrated during Advent or Lent or other days of penance, the parish priest should advise the couple to take into consideration the special nature of these times.

[9]*Ibid.*, 32.

PREPARATION OF LOCAL RITUALS

12. In addition to the faculty spoken of below in no. 17 for regions where the Roman Ritual for matrimony is used, particular rituals shall be prepared, suitable for the customs and needs of individual areas, according to the principle of art. 63b and 77 of the Constitution on the Sacred Liturgy. These are to be reviewed by the Apostolic See.
In making adaptations, the following points must be remembered:

13. The formulas of the Roman Ritual may be adapted or, as the case may be, filled out (including the questions before the consent and the actual words of consent).
When the Roman Ritual has several optional formulas, local rituals may add other formulas of the same type.

14. Within the rite of the sacrament of matrimony, the arrangement of its parts may be varied. If it seems more suitable, even the questions before the consent may be omitted as long as the priest asks and receives the consent of the contracting parties.

15. After the exchange of rings, the crowning or veiling of the bride may take place according to local custom.

In any region where the joining of hands or the blessing or exchange of rings does not fit in with the practice of the people, the conference of bishops may allow these rites to be omitted or other rites substituted.

16. As for the marriage customs of nations that are now receiving the gospel for the first time, whatever is good and is not indissolubly bound up with superstition and error should be sympathetically considered and, if possible, preserved intact. Sometimes the Church admits such things into the liturgy itself, as long as they harmonize with its true and authentic spirit.[10]

RIGHT TO PREPARE A COMPLETELY NEW RITE

17. Each conference of bishops may draw up its own marriage rite suited to the usages of the place and people and

[10] *Ibid.*, 37.

approved by the Apostolic See. The rite must always conform to the law that the priest assisting at such marriages must ask for and receive the consent of the contracting parties,[11] and the nuptial blessing should always be given.[12]

18. Among peoples where the marriage ceremonies customarily take place in the home, sometimes over a period of several days, these customs should be adapted to the Christian spirit and to the liturgy. In such cases the conference of bishops, according to the pastoral needs of the people, may allow the sacramental rite to be celebrated in the home.

[11] *Ibid.*, 77.
[12] *Ibid.*, 78.

CHAPTER I
RITE FOR CELEBRATING MARRIAGE DURING MASS

ENTRANCE RITE

19. At the appointed time, the priest, vested for Mass, goes with the ministers to the door of the church or, if more suitable, to the altar. There he meets the bride and bridegroom in a friendly manner, showing that the Church shares their joy.

Where it is desirable that the rite of welcome be omitted, the celebration of marriage begins at once with the Mass.

20. If there is a procession to the altar, the ministers go first, followed by the priest, and then the bride and the bridegroom. According to local custom, they may be escorted by at least their parents and the two witnesses. Meanwhile, the entrance song is sung.

LITURGY OF THE WORD

21. The liturgy of the word is celebrated according to the rubrics. There may be three readings, the first of them from the Old Testament.

22. After the gospel, the priest gives a homily drawn from the sacred text. He speaks about the mystery of Christian marriage, the dignity of wedded love, the grace of the sacrament and the responsibilities of married people, keeping in mind the circumstances of this particular marriage.

RITE OF MARRIAGE

23. All stand, including the bride and bridegroom, and the priest addresses them in these or similar words:

My dear friends,* you have come together in this church so that the Lord may seal and strengthen your love in the presence of the Church's minister and this community. Christ abundantly blesses this love. He has already consecrated you in baptism and now he enriches and strengthens you by a special sacrament so that you may assume the duties of marriage in mutual and lasting fidelity. And so, in the presence of the Church, I ask you to state your intentions.

24. The priest then questions them about their freedom of choice, faithfulness to each other, and the acceptance and upbringing of children:

N. and N., have you come here freely and without reservation to give yourselves to each other in marriage?

Will you love and honor each other as man and wife for the rest of your lives?

The following question may be omitted if, for example, the couple is advanced in years.

Will you accept children lovingly from God, and bring them up according to the law of Christ and his Church?

Each answers the questions separately.

CONSENT

25. The priest invites the couple to declare their consent:

Since it is your intention to enter into marriage, join your right hands, and declare your consent before God and his Church.

They join hands.

*At the discretion of the priest, other words which seem more suitable under the circumstances, such as **friends** or **dearly beloved** or **brethren** may be used. This also applies to parallel instances in the liturgy.

The bridegroom says:

I, N., take you, N., to be my wife. I promise to be true to you in good times and in bad, in sickness and in health. I will love you and honor you all the days of my life.

The bride says:

I, N., take you, N., to be my husband. I promise to be true to you in good times and in bad, in sickness and in health. I will love you and honor you all the days of my life.

If, however, it seems preferable for pastoral reasons, the priest may obtain consent from the couple through questions.

First he asks the bridegroom:
N., do you take N. to be your wife? Do you promise to be true to her in good times and in bad, in sickness and in health, to love her and honor her all the days of your life?
The bridegroom: **I do.**

Then he asks the bride:
N., do you take N. to be your husband? Do you promise to be true to him in good times and in bad, in sickness and in health, to love him and honor him all the days of your life?
The bride: **I do.**

If pastoral necessity demands it, the conference of bishops may decree, in virtue of the faculty in no. 17, that the priest should always obtain the consent of the couple through questions.

In the dioceses of the United States, the following form may also be used:

I, N., take you, N., for my lawful wife, to have and to hold, from this day forward, for better, for worse, for

richer, for poorer, in sickness and in health, until death do us part.

I, N., take you, N., for my lawful husband, to have and to hold, from this day forward, for better, for worse, for richer, for poorer, in sickness and in health, until death do us part.

If it seems preferable for pastoral reasons for the priest to obtain consent from the couple through questions, in the dioceses of the United States the following alternative form may be used:

N., do you take N. for your lawful wife (husband), to have and to hold, from this day forward, for better, for worse, for richer, for poorer, in sickness and in health, until death do you part?
The bride (bridegroom): **I do.**

26. Receiving their consent, the priest says:

You have declared your consent before the Church.
May the Lord in his goodness strengthen your consent
and fill you both with his blessings.
What God has joined, men must not divide.
℟. **Amen.**

BLESSING AND EXCHANGE OF RINGS

27. Priest:

May the Lord bless ✠ these rings
which you give to each other
as the sign of your love and fidelity.
℟. **Amen.**

Other forms of the blessing of the rings, nos. 110 or 111, may be chosen.

28. The bridegroom places his wife's ring on her ring finger. He may say:

N., take this ring as a sign of my love and fidelity. In the name of the Father, and of the Son, and of the Holy Spirit.

The bride places her husband's ring on his ring finger. She may say:

N., take this ring as a sign of my love and fidelity. In the name of the Father, and of the Son, and of the Holy Spirit.

29. The general intercessions (prayer of the faithful) follow, using formulas approved by the conference of bishops. If the rubrics call for it, the profession of faith is said after the general intercessions.

LITURGY OF THE EUCHARIST

30. The Order of Mass is followed, with the following changes. During the offertory, the bride and bridegroom may bring the bread and wine to the altar.

31. Proper preface (see nos. 115-117).

32. When the Roman canon is used, the special **Hanc igitur** is said (no. 118).

NUPTIAL BLESSING

33. After the Lord's Prayer, the prayer **Deliver us** is omitted. The priest faces the bride and bridegroom and, with hands joined, says:

My dear friends, let us turn to the Lord and pray
that he will bless with his grace this woman (or N.)
now married in Christ to this man (or N.)
and that (through the sacrament of the body and blood of Christ,)
he will unite in love the couple he has joined in this holy bond.

All pray silently for a short while. Then the priest extends his hands and continues:

Father, by your power you have made everything out of nothing.
In the beginning you created the universe
and made mankind in your own likeness.

You gave man the constant help of woman
so that man and woman should no longer be two,
but one flesh,
and you teach us that what you have united
may never be divided.

Or:

Father, you have made the union of man and wife so holy a mystery
that it symbolizes the marriage of Christ and his Church.

Or:

Father, by your plan man and woman are united,
and married life has been established
as the one blessing that was not forfeited by original sin
or washed away in the flood.

Look with love upon this woman, your daughter,
now joined to her husband in marriage.
She asks your blessing.
Give her the grace of love and peace.
May she always follow the example of the holy women
whose praises are sung in the scriptures.

May her husband put his trust in her
and recognize that she is his equal
and the heir with him to the life of grace.
May he always honor her and love her
as Christ loves his bride, the Church.

Father, keep them always true to your commandments.
Keep them faithful in marriage
and let them be living examples of Christian life.

Give them the strength which comes from the gospel
so that they may be witnesses of Christ to others.
(Bless them with children
and help them to be good parents.

May they live to see their children's children.)
And, after a happy old age,
grant them fullness of life with the saints
in the kingdom of heaven.

We ask this through Christ our Lord.
℟. **Amen.**

34. If one or both of the parties will not be receiving communion, the words in the introduction to the nuptial blessing, **through the sacrament of the body and blood of Christ,** may be omitted.

If desired, in the prayer **Father, by your power,** two of the first three paragraphs may be omitted, keeping only the paragraph which corresponds to the reading of the Mass.

In the last paragraph of this prayer, the words in parentheses may be omitted whenever circumstances suggest it, if, for example, the couple is advanced in years.

Other forms of the nuptial blessing, no. 120 or 121, may be chosen.

35. At the words **Let us offer each other the sign of peace,** the married couple and all present show their peace and love for one another in an appropriate way.

36. The married couple may receive communion under both kinds.

BLESSING AT THE END OF MASS

37. Before blessing the people at the end of Mass, the priest blesses the bride and bridegroom, using one of the forms in nos. 125-127.

Or:
In the dioceses of the United States, the following form may be used:

May almighty God, with his Word of blessing, unite your hearts in the never-ending bond of pure love.
℟. **Amen.**

May your children bring you happiness, and may

your generous love for them be returned to you, many times over.
℟. **Amen.**

May the peace of Christ live always in your hearts and in your home.
May you have true friends to stand by you, both in joy and in sorrow.
May you be ready and willing to help and comfort all who come to you in need.
And may the blessings promised to the compassionate be yours in abundance.
℟. **Amen.**

May you find happiness and satsifaction in your work.
May daily problems never cause you undue anxiety, nor the desire for earthly possessions dominate your lives.
But may your hearts' first desire be always the good things waiting for you in the life of heaven.
℟. **Amen.**

May the Lord bless you with many happy years together, so that you may enjoy the rewards of a good life.
And after you have served him loyally in his kingdom on earth, may he welcome you to his eternal kingdom in heaven.
℟. **Amen.**

And may almighty God bless you all, the Father, and the Son, ✝ and the Holy Spirit.
℟. **Amen.**

38. If two or more marriages are celebrated at the same time, the questioning before the consent, the consent itself, and the acceptance of consent shall always be done individually for each couple; the rest, including the nuptial blessing, is said once for all, using the plural form.

CHAPTER II
RITE FOR CELEBRATING MARRIAGE OUTSIDE MASS[13]

ENTRANCE RITE AND LITURGY OF THE WORD

39. At the appointed time, the priest, wearing surplice and white stole (or a white cope, if desired), proceeds with the ministers to the door of the church, or, if more suitable, to the altar. There he greets the bride and bridegroom in a friendly manner, showing that the Church shares their joy.

Where it is desirable that the rite of welcome be omitted, the celebration of matrimony begins at once with the liturgy of the word.

40. If there is a procession to the altar, the ministers go first, followed by the priest, and then the bride and the bridegroom. According to local custom, they may be escorted by at least their parents and the two witnesses. Meanwhile, the entrance song is sung.

Then the people are greeted, and the prayer is offered, unless a brief pastoral exhortation seems more desirable.[14] See nos. 106-109.

41. The liturgy of the word takes place in the usual manner. There may be three readings, the first of them from the Old Testament. See nos. 67-105.

42. After the gospel, the priest gives a homily drawn from the sacred text. He speaks about the mystery of Christian marriage, the dignity of wedded love, the grace of the sacrament, and the responsibilities of married people, keeping in mind the circumstances of this particular marriage.

[13]According to the words of the Constitution on the Sacred Liturgy, *Sacrosanctum Concilium*, repeated in no. 6 of the introduction above, the celebration of marriage normally takes place during Mass. Nevertheless, a good reason can excuse from the celebration of Mass (Sacred Congregation of Rites, Instruction, *Inter Oecumenici*, no. 70: *AAS* 56 [1964] 893), and sometimes even urges that Mass should be omitted. In this case the rite for celebrating marriage outside Mass should be used.

[14]Sacred Congregation of Rites, Instruction, *Inter Oecumenici*, no. 74: *AAS* 56 (1964) 894.

RITE OF MARRIAGE

43. All stand, including the bride and bridegroom, and the priest addresses them in these or similar words:

My dear friends, you have come together in this church so that the Lord may seal and strengthen your love in the presence of the Church's minister and this community. Christ abundantly blesses this love. He has already consecrated you in baptism and now he enriches and strengthens you by a special sacrament so that you may assume the duties of marriage in mutual and lasting fidelity. And so, in the presence of the Church, I ask you to state your intentions.

44. The priest then questions them about their freedom of choice, faithfulness to each other, and the acceptance and upbringing of children:

If two or more marriages are celebrated at the same time, see no. 38, above.

N. and N., have you come here freely and without reservation to give yourselves to each other in marriage?

Will you love and honor each other as man and wife for the rest of your lives?

The following question may be omitted if, for example, the couple is advanced in years.

Will you accept children lovingly from God, and bring them up according to the law of Christ and his Church?

Each answers the questions separately.

CONSENT

45. The priest invites them to declare their consent:

Since it is is your intention to enter into marriage, join your right hands, and declare your consent before God and his Church.

They join hands.

The bridegroom says:

I, N., take you, N., to be my wife. I promise to be true to you in good times and in bad, in sickness and in health. I will love you and honor you all the days of my life.

The bride says:

I, N., take you, N., to be my husband. I promise to be true to you in good times and in bad, in sickness and in health. I will love you and honor you all the days of my life.

If, however, it seems preferable for pastoral reasons, the priest may obtain consent from the couple through questions. First he asks the bridegroom:

N., do you take N. to be your wife? Do you promise to be true to her in good times and in bad, in sickness and in health, to love her and honor her all the days of your life?

The bridegroom: **I do.**

Then he asks the bride:

N., do you take N. to be your husband? Do you promise to be true to him in good times and in bad, in sickness and in health, to love him and honor him all the days of your life?

The bride: **I do.**

If pastoral necessity demands it, the conference of bishops may decree, in virtue of the faculty in no. 17, that the priest should always obtain the consent of the couple through questions.

In the dioceses of the United States, the following form may also be used:

I, N., take you, N., for my lawful wife, to have and to hold, from this day forward, for better, for worse, for richer, for poorer, in sickness and in health, until death do us part.

I, N., take you N., for my lawful husband, to have and to hold, from this day forward, for better, for

worse, for richer, for poorer, in sickness and in health, until death do us part.

If it seems preferable for pastoral reasons for the priest to obtain consent from the couple through questions, in the dioceses of the United States the following alternative form may be used:

N., do you take N. for your lawful wife (husband), to have and to hold, from this day forward, for better, for worse, for richer, for poorer, in sickness and in health, until death do you part?
The bride (bridegroom): **I do.**

46. Receiving their consent, the priest says:

You have declared your consent before the Church. May the Lord in his goodness strengthen your consent and fill you both with his blessings.

What God has joined, men must not divide.
℟. **Amen.**

BLESSING AND EXCHANGE OF RINGS

47. Priest:

May the Lord bless ✠ these rings which you give to each other as the sign of your love and fidelity.
℟. **Amen.**

For other forms of the blessing of rings, see nos. 110, 111.

48. The bridegroom places his wife's ring on her ring finger. He may say:

N., take this ring as a sign of my love and fidelity. In the name of the Father, and of the Son, and of the Holy Spirit.

The bride places her husband's ring on his ring finger. She may say:

N., take this ring as a sign of my love and fidelity. In

the name of the Father, and of the Son, and of the Holy Spirit.

GENERAL INTERCESSIONS AND NUPTIAL BLESSINGS

49. The general intercessions (prayer of the faithful) and the blessing of the couple take place in this order:

a) First the priest uses the invitatory of any blessing of the couple [see the first part of no. 33, 120, and 121] or any other, taken from the approved formulas for the general intercessions.

b) Immediately after the invitatory, there can be either a brief silence, or a series of petitions from the prayer of the faithful with responses by the people. All the petitions should be in harmony with the blessing which follows, but should not duplicate it.

c) Then, omitting the prayer that concludes the prayer of the faithful, the priest extends his hands and blesses the bride and bridegroom.

50. This blessing may be **Father, by your power,** (no. 33) or another from nos. 120 or 121.

CONCLUSION OF THE CELEBRATION

51. The entire rite can be concluded with the Lord's Prayer and the blessing, whether with the simple form, **May almighty God,** or with one of the forms in nos. 125-127.

52. If two or more marriages are celebrated at the same time, the questioning before the consent, the consent itself and the acceptance of consent shall always be done individually for each couple; the rest, including the nuptial blessing, is said once for all using the plural form.

53. The rite described above should be used by a deacon who, when a priest cannot be present, has been delegated by the bishop or pastor to assist at the celebration of marriage, and to give the Church's blessing.[15]

54. If Mass cannot be celebrated and communion is to be distributed during the rite, the Lord's Prayer is said first. After

[15]Paul VI, motu proprio, *Sacrum Diaconatus Ordinem,* June 18, 1967, no. 22, 4: *AAS* 59 (1967) 702.

communion, a reverent silence may be observed for a while, or a psalm or song of praise may be sung or recited. Then comes the prayer, **Lord, we who have shared** (no. 123, if only the bride and bridegroom receive), or the prayer, **God, who in this wondrous sacrament** or other suitable prayer.

The rite ends with a blessing, either the simple formula, **May almighty God bless you,** or one of the forms in nos. 125-127.

CHAPTER III
RITE FOR CELEBRATING MARRIAGE BETWEEN A CATHOLIC AND AN UNBAPTIZED PERSON

If marriage is celebrated between a Catholic and unbaptized person (either a catechumen or a non-Christian), the rite may be performed in the church or some other suitable place and takes the following form.

RITE OF WELCOME AND LITURGY OF THE WORD

55. At the appointed time, the priest, wearing surplice and white stole (or a white cope if desired), proceeds with the ministers to the door of the church or to another appropriate place and greets the bride and the bridegroom.

Where it is desirable that the rite of welcome be omitted, the celebration of marriage begins at once with the liturgy of the word.

56. The liturgy of the word takes place in the usual manner. There may be three readings, the first of them from the Old Testament. If circumstances make it more desirable, there may be a single reading. See nos. 67-105.

57. A homily, drawn from the sacred text, is given and should speak of the obligations of marriage and other appropriate points.

RITE OF MARRIAGE

58. All stand, including the bride and the bridegroom. The priest addresses them in these or similar words:

My dear friends, you have come together in this church so that the Lord may seal and strengthen your love in the presence of the Church's minister and this community. In this way you will be strengthened to keep mutual and lasting faith with each other and to carry out the other duties of marriage. And so, in the presence of the Church, I ask you to state your intentions.

59. The priest then questions them about their freedom of choice, faithfulness to each other, and the acceptance and upbringing of children:

N. and N., have you come here freely and without reservation to give yourselves to each other in marriage?

Will you love and honor each other as man and wife for the rest of your lives?

The following question may be omitted if, for example, the couple is advanced in years.

Will you accept children lovingly from God, and bring them up according to the law of Christ and his Church?

Each answers the questions separately.

CONSENT

60. The priest invites them to declare their consent:

Since it is your intention to enter into marriage, join your right hands, and declare your consent before God and his Church.

They join hands.

The bridegroom says:

I, N., take you, N., to be my wife. I promise to be true to you in good times and in bad, in sickness and in health. I will love you and honor you all the days of my life.

The bride says:

I, N., take you, N., to be my husband. I promise to be true to you in good times and in bad, in sickness and in health. I will love you and honor you all the days of my life.

If, however, it seems perferable for pastoral reasons, the priest may obtain consent from the couple through questions. First he asks the bridegroom:

N., do you take N. to be your wife? Do you promise

to be true to her in good times and in bad, in sickness and in health, to love her and honor her all the days of your life?
The bridegroom: **I do.**

Then he asks the bride:

N., do you take N. to be your husband? Do you promise to be true to him in good times and in bad, in sickness and in health, to love him and honor him all the days of your life?
The bride: **I do.**

If pastoral necessity demands it, the conference of bishops may decree, in virtue of the faculty in no. 17, that the priest should always obtain the consent of the couple through questions.

In the dioceses of the United States, the following form may also be used:

I, N., take you, N., for my lawful wife, to have and to hold, from this day forward, for better, for worse, for richer, for poorer, in sickness and in health, until death do us part.

I, N., take you, N., for my lawful husband, to have and to hold, from this day forward, for better, for worse, for richer, for poorer, in sickness and in health, until death do us part.

If it seems preferable for pastoral reasons for the priest to obtain consent from the couple through questions, in the dioceses of the United States the following alternative form may be used:

N., do you take N. for your lawful wife (husband), to have and to hold, from this day forward, for better, for worse, for richer, for poorer, in sickness and in health, until death do you part?
The bride (bridegroom): **I do.**

61. Receiving their consent, the priest says:

You have declared your consent before the Church. May the Lord in his goodness strengthen your consent

and fill you both with his blessings.

What God has joined, men must not divide.
℟. **Amen.**

BLESSING AND EXCHANGE OF RINGS

62. If circumstances so require, the blessing and exchange of rings can be omitted. If this rite is observed, the priest says:

May the Lord bless ✠ these rings which you give to each other as the sign of your love and fidelity.
℟. **Amen.**

For other forms of the blessing of rings, see nos. 110-111.

63. The bridegroom places his wife's ring on her ring finger. He may say:

N., take this ring as a sign of my love and fidelity. In the name of the Father, and of the Son, and of the Holy Spirit.

The bride places her husband's ring on his ring finger. She may say:

N., take this ring as a sign of my love and fidelity. In the name of the Father, and of the Son, and of the Holy Spirit.

GENERAL INTERCESSIONS AND NUPTIAL BLESSINGS

64. If circumstances so require, the blessing of the bride and bridegroom can be omitted. If used, it is combined with the general intercessions (prayer of the faithful) in this order:

a) First the priest uses the invitatory of any blessing of the couple (see the first part of nos. 33, 120, and 121) or any other, taken from any approved formula for the general intercessions.

b) Immediately after the invitatory, there can be either a brief period of silence, or a series of petitions from the prayer of the faithful with responses by the people. All the petitions should be in harmony with the blessing which follows, but should not duplicate it.

c) Then, omitting the prayer that concludes the prayer of the faithful, the priest blesses the bride and the bridegroom:

65. Facing them, he joins his hands and says:

My brothers and sisters, let us ask God for his continued blessings upon this bridegroom and his bride.

All pray silently for a short while. Then the priest extends his hands and continues:

Holy Father, creator of the universe,
maker of man and woman in your likeness,
source of blessing for married life,
we humbly pray to you for this bride
who today is united with her husband in the bond of marriage.

May your fullest blessing come upon her and her husband
so that they may together rejoice in your gift of married love.
May they be noted for their good lives,
(and be parents filled with virtue).

Lord, may they both praise you when they are happy
and turn to you in their sorrows.
May they be glad that you help them in their work,
and know that you are with them in their need.
May they reach old age in the company of their friends,
and come at last to the kingdom of heaven.
We ask this through Christ our Lord.
℟. **Amen.**

CONCLUSION OF THE CELEBRATION

66. The rite may be concluded with the Lord's Prayer (or, if the nuptial blessing has been omitted, another prayer by the priest) and a blessing using the customary form, **May almighty God bless you** or another formula from nos. 125-127.

CHAPTER IV

TEXTS FOR USE IN THE MARRIAGE RITE AND IN THE WEDDING MASS

I. SCRIPTURE READINGS

In the wedding Mass and in marriages celebrated without Mass, the following selections may be used:

OLD TESTAMENT READINGS

67. **Genesis 1:26-28, 31a**
Male and female he created them.

68. **Genesis 2:18-24**
And they will be two in one flesh.

69. **Genesis 24:48-51, 58-67**
Isaac loved Rebekah, and so he was consoled for the loss of his mother.

70. **Tobit 7:9-10, 11-15**
May God join you together and fill you with his blessings.

71. **Tobit 8:5-10**
May God bring us to old age together.

72. **Song of Songs 2:8-10, 14, 16a; 8:6-7a**
For love is as strong as death.

73. **Ecclesiasticus 26:1-4, 16-21 (Greek 1-4, 13-16)**
Like the sun rising is the beauty of a good wife in a well-kept house.

74. **Jeremiah 31:31-32a, 33-34a**
I will make a new covenant with the House of Israel and Judah.

NEW TESTAMENT READINGS

75. **Romans 8:31b-35, 37-39**
Who will separate us from the love of Christ?

76. **Romans 12:1-2, 9-18** (longer) or **Romans 12:1-2, 9-13** (shorter)

Offer to God your bodies as a living and holy sacrifice, truly pleasing to him.

77. **1 Corinthians 6:13c-15a, 17-20**
Your body is a temple of the Spirit.

78. **1 Corinthians 12:31; 13:8a**
If I am without love, it will do me no good whatever.

79. **Ephesians 5:2a, 21-33** (longer) or **2a, 25-32** (shorter)
This mystery has many implications, and I am saying it applies to Christ and the Church.

80. **Colossians 3:12-17**
Above all have love, which is the bond of perfection.

81. **1 Peter 3:1-9**
You should agree with one another, be sympathetic and love the brothers.

82. **1 John 3:18-24**
Our love is to be something real and active.

83. **1 John 4:7-12**
God is love.

84. **Revelation 19:1, 5-9a**
Happy are those who are invited to the wedding feast of the Lamb.

RESPONSORIAL PSALMS

85. Psalm 33:12 and 18, 20-21, 22
℟. (5b) **The earth is full of the goodness of the Lord.**

86. Psalm 34:2-3, 4-5, 6-7, 8-9
℟. (2a) **I will bless the Lord at all times.**
Or: (9a) **Taste and see the goodness of the Lord.**

87. Psalm 103:1-2, 8 and 13, 17-18a
℟. (8a) **The Lord is kind and merciful.**
Or: (17) **The Lord's kindness is everlasting to those who fear him.**

88. Psalm 112:1-2, 3-4, 5-7a, 7bc-8, 9
℟. (1b) **Happy are those who do what the Lord commands.**
Or: **Alleluia.**

89. Psalm 128:1-2, 3, 4-5
℟. (1a) **Happy are those who fear the Lord.**

Or: (4) **See how the Lord blesses those who fear him.**

90. Psalm 145:8-9, 10 and 15, 17-18
℟. (9a) **The Lord is compassionate to all his creatures.**

91. Psalm 148:1-2, 3-4, 9-10, 11-12ab, 12c-14a
℟. (12c) **Let all praise the name of the Lord.**
Or: **Alleluia.**

ALLELUIA VERSE AND VERSE BEFORE THE GOSPEL

92. 1 John 4:8 and 11
God is love;
let us love one another as he has loved us.

93. 1 John 4:12
If we love one another
God will live in us in perfect love.

94. 1 John 4:16
He who lives in love, lives in God, and God in him.

95. 1 John 4:7b
Everyone who loves is born of God and knows him.

GOSPELS

96. **Matthew 5:1-12**
Rejoice and be glad, for your reward will be great in heaven.

97. **Matthew 5:13-16**
You are the light of the world.

98. **Matthew 7:21, 24-29** (longer) or **21, 24-25** (shorter)
He built his house on rock.

99. **Matthew 19:3-6**
So then, what God has united, man must not divide.

100. **Mathew 22:35-40**
This is the greatest and the first commandment. The second is similar to it.

101. **Mark 10:6-9**
They are no longer two, therefore, but one body.

102. **John 2:1-11**
This was the first of the signs given by Jesus; it was given at Cana in Galilee.

103. **John 15:9-12**
Remain in my love.

104. **John 15:12-16**
This is my commandment: love one another.

105. **John 17:20-26** (longer) or **20-23** (shorter)
May they be completely one.

II. OPENING PRAYERS

106.
Father,
you have made the bond of marriage
a holy mystery,
a symbol of Christ's love for his Church.
Hear our prayers for N. and N.
With faith in you and in each other
they pledge their love today.
May their lives always bear witness
to the reality of that love.

We ask this through our Lord Jesus Christ, your Son,
who lives and reigns with you and the Holy Spirit,
one God, for ever and ever.

107.
Father,
hear our prayers for N. and N.,
who today are united in marriage before your altar.
Give them your blessing.
and strengthen their love for each other.

We ask this through our Lord Jesus Christ, your Son,
who lives and reigns with you and the Holy Spirit,
one God, for ever and ever.

108.
Almighty God,
hear our prayers for N. and N.,
who have come here today

to be united in the sacrament of marriage.
Increase their faith in you and in each other,
and through them bless your Church (with Christian children).

We ask this through our Lord Jesus Christ, your Son,
who lives and reigns with you and the Holy Spirit,
one God, for ever and ever.

109.
Father,
when you created mankind
you willed that man and wife should be one.
Bind N. and N.
in the loving union of marriage;
and make their love fruitful
so that they may be living witnesses
to your divine love in the world.

We ask this through our Lord Jesus Christ, your Son,
who lives and reigns with you and the Holy Spirit,
one God, for ever and ever.

III. BLESSING OF RINGS

110.
Lord, bless these rings which we bless ✠ in your name.
Grant that those who wear them
may always have a deep faith in each other.
May they do your will
and always live together
in peace, good will, and love.

We ask this through Christ our Lord.
℟. **Amen.**

111.
Lord,
bless ✠ and consecrate N. and N.

in their love for each other.
May these rings be a symbol
of true faith in each other,
and always remind them of their love.

We ask this through Christ our Lord.
℟. Amen.

IV. PRAYERS OVER THE GIFTS

112.
Lord,
accept our offering
for this newly-married couple, N. and N.
By your love and providence you have brought them together;
now bless them all the days of their married life.

We ask this through Christ our Lord.

113.
Lord,
accept the gifts we offer you
on this happy day.
In your fatherly love
watch over and protect N. and N.,
whom you have united in marriage.

We ask this through Christ our Lord.

114.
Lord,
hear our prayers
and accept the gifts we offer for N. and N.
Today you have made them one in the sacrament of marriage.
May the mystery of Christ's unselfish love,
which we celebrate in this eucharist,
increase their love for you and for each other.

We ask this through Christ our Lord.

V. PREFACES

115.

**Father, all-powerful and ever-living God,
we do well always and everywhere to give you thanks.
By this sacrament your grace unites man and woman
in an unbreakable bond of love and peace.**

**You have designed the chaste love of husband and wife
for the increase both of the human family
and of your own family born in baptism.**

**You are the loving Father of the world of nature;
you are the loving Father of the new creation of grace.
In Christian marriage you bring together the two orders of creation:
nature's gift of children enriches the world
and your grace enriches also your Church.**

**Through Christ the choirs of angels
and all the saints
praise and worship your glory.
May our voices blend with theirs
as we join in their unending hymn:**

116.

**Father, all-powerful and ever-living God,
we do well always and everywhere to give you thanks
through Jesus Christ our Lord.**

**Through him you entered into a new covenant with your people.
You restored man to grace in the saving mystery of redemption.
You gave him a share in the divine life
through his union with Christ.
You made him an heir of Christ's eternal glory.**

This outpouring of love in the new covenant of grace

is symbolized in the marriage covenant
that seals the love of husband and wife
and reflects your divine plan of love.

And so, with the angels and all the saints in heaven
we proclaim your glory
and join in their unending hymn of praise:

117.
Father, all-powerful and ever-living God,
we do well always and everywhere to give you thanks.

You created man in love to share your divine life.
We see his high destiny in the love of husband and wife,
which bears the imprint of your own divine love.

Love is man's origin,
love is his constant calling,
love is his fulfillment in heaven.

The love of man and woman
is made holy in the sacrament of marriage,
and becomes the mirror of your everlasting love.

Through Christ the choirs of angels
and all the saints
praise and worship your glory.
May our voices blend with theirs
as we join in their unending hymn:

VI. HANC IGITUR

118. The words in parentheses may be omitted if desired.

Father, accept this offering
from your whole family
and from N. and N., for whom we now pray.
You have brought them to their wedding day:
grant them (the gift and joy of children and)

a long and happy life together.

[Through Christ our Lord. Amen.]

VII. NUPTIAL BLESSING

119.

Father, by your power, with the proper invitatory, as in no. 33.

120. In the following prayer, either the paragraph **Holy Father, you created mankind,** or the paragraph **Father, to reveal the plan of your love,** may be omitted, keeping only the paragraph which corresponds to the reading of the Mass.

The priest faces the bride and bridegroom and, with hands joined, says:

Let us pray to the Lord for N. and N.
who come to God's altar at the beginning of their married life
so that they may always be united in love for each other
(as now they share in the body and blood of Christ).

All pray silently for a short while. Then the priest extends his hands and continues:

Holy Father, you created mankind in your own image
and made man and woman to be joined as husband and wife
in union of body and heart
and so fulfill their mission in this world.

Father, to reveal the plan of your love,
you made the union of husband and wife
an image of the covenant between you and your people.
In the fulfillment of this sacrament,
the marriage of Christian man and woman
is a sign of the marriage between Christ and the Church.

Father, stretch out your hand, and bless N. and N.

Lord, grant that as they begin to live this sacrament
they may share with each other the gifts of your love
and become one in heart and mind
as witnesses to your presence in their marriage.
Help them to create a home together
(and give them children to be formed by the gospel
and to have a place in your family).

Give your blessings to N., your daughter,
so that she may be a good wife (and mother),
caring for the home,
faithful in love for her husband,
generous and kind.
Give your blessings to N., your son,
so that he may be a faithful husband
(and a good father).
Father, grant that as they come together to your table on earth,
so they may one day have the joy of sharing your feast in heaven.

We ask this through Christ our Lord.
℟. **Amen.**

121. The priest faces the bride and bridegroom and, with hands joined, says:

My dear friends, let us ask God
for his continued blessings upon this bridegroom and his bride (or N. and N.).

All pray silently for a short while. Then the priest extends his hands and continues:

Holy Father, creator of the universe,
maker of man and woman in your own likeness,
source of blessing for married life,
we humbly pray to you for this woman
who today is united with her husband in this sacrament of marriage.

May your fullest blessing come upon her and her husband
so that they may together rejoice in your gift of married love
(and enrich your Church with their children).

Lord, may they both praise you when they are happy
and turn to you in their sorrows.
May they be glad that you help them in their work
and know that you are with them in their need.
May they pray to you in the community of the Church,
and be your witnesses in the world.
May they reach old age in the company of their friends,
and come at last to the kingdom of heaven.

We ask this through Christ our Lord.
℟. **Amen.**

VIII. PRAYERS AFTER COMMUNION

122.
Lord,
in your love
you have given us this eucharist
to unite us with one another and with you.
As you have made N. and N.
one in this sacrament of marriage
(and in the sharing of the one bread and the one cup),
so now make them one in love for each other.

We ask this through Christ our Lord.

123.
Lord,
we who have shared the food of your table
pray for our friends N. and N.,
whom you have joined together in marriage.
Keep them close to you always.
May their love for each other

proclaim to all the world
their faith in you.

We ask this through Christ our Lord.

124.
Almighty God,
may the sacrifice we have offered
and the eucharist we have shared
strengthen the love of N. and N.,
and give us all your fatherly aid.

We ask this through Christ our Lord.

IX. BLESSING AT THE END OF MASS

125.
God the eternal Father keep you in love with each other,
so that the peace of Christ may stay with you
and be always in your home.
℟. **Amen.**

May (your children bless you,)
your friends console you
and all men live in peace with you.
℟. **Amen.**

May you always bear witness to the love of God in this world
so that the afflicted and the needy
will find in you generous friends,
and welcome you into the joys of heaven.
℟. **Amen.**

And may almighty God bless you all,
the Father, and the Son, ✠ and the Holy Spirit.
℟. **Amen.**

126.
May God, the almighty Father,
give you his joy

and bless you (in your children).
℟. **Amen.**

May the only Son of God have mercy on you
and help you in good times and in bad.
℟. **Amen.**

May the Holy Spirit of God
always fill your hearts with his love.
℟. **Amen.**

And may almighty God bless you all,
the Father, and the Son, ✠ and the Holy Spirit.
℟. **Amen.**

127.
May the Lord Jesus, who was a guest at the wedding in Cana,
bless you and your families and friends.
℟. **Amen.**

May Jesus, who loved his Church to the end,
always fill your hearts with his love.
℟. **Amen.**

May he grant that, as you believe in his resurrection,
so you may wait for him in joy and hope.
℟. **Amen.**

And may almighty God bless you all,
the Father, and the Son, ✠ and the Holy Spirit.
℟. **Amen.**

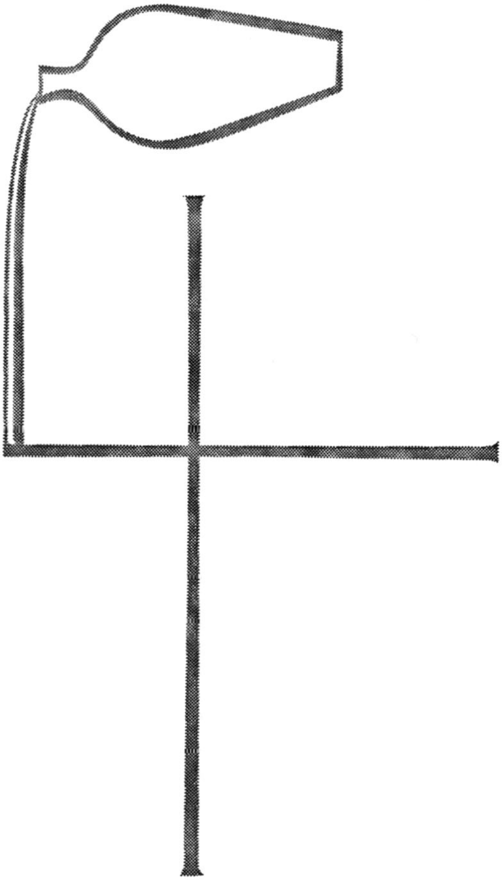

PASTORAL CARE OF THE SICK:

RITES OF ANOINTING AND VIATICUM

PASTORAL CARE OF THE SICK: RITES OF ANOINTING AND VIATICUM

CHAPTER III
COMMUNION OF THE SICK

Introduction (71-80)

I Communion in Ordinary Circumstances

A Introductory Rites
Greeting (81)
Sprinkling with Holy Water (82)
Penitential Rite (83)

B Liturgy of the Word
Reading (84)
Response (85)
General Intercessions (86)

C Liturgy of Holy Communion
The Lord's Prayer (87)
Communion (88)
Silent Prayer (89)
Prayer after Communion (90)

D Concluding Rite
Blessing (91)

II Communion in a Hospital or Institution

A Introductory Rite
Antiphon (92)

B Liturgy of Holy Communion
Greeting (93)
Lord's Prayer (94)
Communion (95)

C Concluding Rite
Concluding Prayer (96)

CHAPTER IV
ANOINTING OF THE SICK

Introduction (97-110)

I Anointing outside Mass

Introduction (111-114)

A Introductory Rites
Greeting (115)
Sprinkling with Holy Water (116)
Instruction (117)
Penitential Rite (118)

B Liturgy of the Word
Reading (119)
Response (120)

C Liturgy of Anointing
Litany (121)
Laying on of Hands (122)
Prayer over the Oil (123)
Anointing (124)
Prayer after Anointing (125)
The Lord's Prayer (126)

D Liturgy of Holy Communion
Communion (127)
Silent Prayer (128)
Prayer after Communion (129)

E Concluding Rite
Blessing (130)

II Anointing within Mass

Introduction (131-134)

A Introductory Rites
Reception of the Sick (135)
Opening Prayer (136)

B Liturgy of the Word (137)

C Liturgy of Anointing
Litany (138)
Laying on of Hands (139)
Prayer over the Oil (140)
Anointing (141)
Prayer after Anointing (142)
Liturgy of the Eucharist (143)
  Prayer over the Gifts (144)
  Eucharistic Prayer (145)
Prayer after Communion (146)

D Concluding Rites
Blessing (147)
Dismissal (148)

III Anointing in a Hospital or Institution

Introduction (149-153)

A Introductory Rites
Greeting (154)
Instruction (155)

B Liturgy of Anointing
Laying on of Hands (156)
Anointing (157)
The Lord's Prayer (158)
Prayer after Anointing (159)

C Concluding Rite
Blessing (160)

PART II
PASTORAL CARE OF THE DYING

Introduction (161-174)

CHAPTER V
CELEBRATION OF VIATICUM

Introduction (175-188)

I Viaticum within Mass

A Liturgy of the Word
Homily (189)
Baptismal Profession of Faith (190)
Litany (191)

B Liturgy of the Eucharist
Sign of Peace (192)
Communion as Viaticum (193)

C Concluding Rites
Blessing (194)
Apostolic Pardon (195)
Dismissal (196)

CHAPTER VIII
RITES FOR EXCEPTIONAL CIRCUMSTANCES

PART III
READINGS, RESPONSES, AND VERSES FROM SACRED SCRIPTURE (297-298)

APPENDIX
RITES FOR RECONCILIATION OF INDIVIDUAL PENITENTS (299)

A Reception of Penitents
Invitation to Trust (300)
Revelation of State of Life (301)

B Liturgy of Reconciliation
Confession of Sins (302)
Acceptance of Satisfaction (303)
Penitent's Prayer of Sorrow (304)
Absolution (305)

SACRED CONGREGATION FOR DIVINE WORSHIP

Prot. no. 1501/72

DECREE

When the Church cares for the sick, it serves Christ himself in the suffering members of his Mystical Body. When it follows the example of the Lord Jesus, who "went about doing good and healing all" (Acts 10:38), the Church obeys his command to care for the sick (see Mark 16:18).

The Church shows this solicitude not only by visiting those who are in poor health but also by raising them up through the sacrament of anointing and by nourishing them with the eucharist during their illness and when they are in danger of death. Finally, the Church offers prayers for the sick to commend them to God, especially in the last crisis of life.

To make the meaning of the sacrament of anointing clearer and more evident, Vatican Council II decreed: "The number of the anointings is to be adapted to the circumstances; the prayers that belong to the rite of anointing are to be so revised that they correspond to the varying conditions of the sick who receive the sacrament."[1] The Council also directed that a continuous rite be prepared according to which the sick person is anointed after the sacrament of penance and before receiving viaticum.[2]

In the Apostolic Constitution *Sacram Unctionem infirmorum* of 30 November 1972, Pope Paul VI established a new sacramental form of anointing and approved the *Ordo Unctionis infirmorum eorumque pastoralis curae*. The Congregation for Divine Worship prepared this rite and now issues it, declaring this to be the *editio typica* so that it may replace the pertinent sections that are now in the Roman Ritual.

Anything to the contrary notwithstanding.

[1]Vatican Council II, Constitution on the Liturgy, art. 75: *Acta Apostolicae Sedis* (AAS) 56 (1964) 119.
[2]See ibid., art. 74: AAS 119.

From the office of the Congregation for Divine Worship, 7 December 1972.

Arturo Cardinal Tabera
Prefect

✠ Annibale Bugnini
Titular Archbishop of Diocletiana
Secretary

APOSTOLIC CONSTITUTION

SACRAMENT OF THE ANOINTING OF THE SICK

PAUL, BISHOP

Servant of the Servants of God
For an Everlasting Memorial

The Catholic Church professes and teaches that the anointing of the sick is one of the seven sacraments of the New Testament, that it was instituted by Christ our Lord, "intimated in Mark (6:13) and through James, the apostle and brother of the Lord, recommended to the faithful and made known: 'Is there anyone sick among you? Let him send for the presbyters of the Church and let them pray over him, anointing him with oil in the name of the Lord. The prayer of faith will save the sick man and the Lord will raise him up. If he has committed any sins, they will be forgiven him' (James 5:14-15)."[1]

From ancient times there is evidence of the anointing of the sick in the Church's tradition, particularly in the liturgical tradition, both in the East and in the West. Worthy of special note are the letter which Innocent I, our predecessor, addressed to Decentius, Bishop of Gubbio,[2] and also the ancient prayer used for blessing the oil of the sick, "Lord, . . . send the Holy Spirit, our Helper and Friend. . . ." This prayer was inserted in the eucharistic prayer[3] and is still preserved in the Roman Pontifical.[4]

In the course of centuries of liturgical tradition, the parts of the body to be anointed with holy oil were more explicitly defined in different ways. Several formularies of prayer were

[1]Council of Trent, sess. 14, De Extrema Unctione, cap. 1 (see also can. 1): *Concilium Tridentinum* (CT), vol. 7, pt. 1, 355-356; Denz.-Schön. 1695, 1716.
[2]See Innocent I, Ep. *Si Instituta Ecclesiastica,* cap. 8:PL 20, 559-561; Denz.-Schön. 216.
[3]See L.C. Mohlberg, ed., *Liber Sacramentorum Romanae Aecclesiae Ordinis Anni Circuli* in *Rerum Ecclesiasticarum Documenta, Fontes* 4 (Rome, 1960) 61; J. Deshusses, ed., *Le Sacramentaire Grégorien,* in *Spicilegium Friburgense* 16 (Fribourg, 1971) 172. See also B. Botte, ed., *La Tradition Apostolique de Saint Hippolyte* in *Liturgiewissenschaftliche Quellen und Forschungen* 39 (Münster-W., 1963) 18-19; E. Lanne, ed., *Le Grand Euchologie du Monastère Blanc* in *Patrologia Orientalis* 28, pt. 2 (Paris, 1958) 392-395.
[4]See Roman Pontifical, *Rite of Blessing Oils, Rite of Consecrating the Chrism,* no. 20 [*The Sacramentary* (*The Roman Missal*) Appendix II].

added to accompany the anointings and these are contained in the liturgical books of various Churches. In the Church of Rome during the Middle Ages the custom prevailed of anointing the sick on the senses with the formulary: *Per istam sanctam Unctionem, et suam piissimam misericordiam, indulgeat tibi Dominus quidquid deliquisti*, with the name of each sense added.[5]

In addition, the teaching concerning the sacrament of anointing is expounded in the documents of the ecumenical Councils of Florence, Trent especially, and Vatican II.

After the Council of Florence had described the essential elements of the sacrament of the anointing of the sick,[6] the Council of Trent declared that it was of divine institution and explained what is taught in the Letter of James concerning holy anointing, especially about the reality signified and the effects of the sacrament: "This reality is in fact the grace of the Holy Spirit, whose anointing takes away sins, if any still remain, and the remnants of sin; this anointing also raises up and strengthens the soul of the sick person, arousing a great confidence in the divine mercy; thus sustained, the sick person may more easily bear the trials and hardships of sickness, more easily resist the temptations of the devil 'lying in wait for his heel' (Genesis 3:15), and sometimes regain bodily health, if this is expedient for the health of the soul."[7] The same Council also declared that these words of the apostle state with sufficient clarity that "this anointing is to be given to the sick, especially those who are in such a serious condition as to appear to have reached the end of their life. For this reason it is also called the sacrament of the dying."[8] Finally, the Council declared that the presbyter is the proper minister of the sacrament.[9]

Vatican Council II adds the following: " 'Extreme unction,' which may also and more properly be called 'anointing of the sick,' is not a sacrament for those only who are at the point of

[5]See M. Andrieu, *Le Pontifical Romain au Moyen-Age*, vol. 1, *Le Pontifical Romain du XII siècle* in *Studi e Testi* 86 (Vatican City, 1938) 267-268; vol. 2, *Le Pontifical de la Curie Romaine au XIIIe siècle* in *Studi e Testi* 87 (Vatican City, 1940) 491-492.
[6]See Council of Florence, *Decr. pro Armeniis*: G. Hofmann, *Concilium Florentinum*, vol. 1, pt. 2 (Rome, 1944) 130; Denz.-Schön. 1324-1325.
[7]Council of Trent, sess. 14, De Extrema Unctione, cap. 2: CT 7, 1, 356; Denz.-Schön, 1696.
[8]Ibid., cap. 3: CT, ibid.; Denz.-Schön. 1698.
[9]See ibid., cap. 3, can. 4: CT, ibid.; Denz-Schön. 1697, 1719.

death. Hence, as soon as any one of the faithful begins to be in danger of death from sickness or old age, the fitting time for that person to receive this sacrament has certainly already arrived."[10] The use of this sacrament is a concern of the whole Church: "By the sacred anointing of the sick and the prayer of its presbyters, the whole Church commends the sick to the suffering and glorified Lord so that he may raise them up and save them (see James 5:14-16). The Church exhorts them, moreover, to contribute to the welfare of the whole people of God by associating themselves willingly with the passion and death of Christ (see Romans 8:17; Colossians 1:24; 2 Timothy 2:11-12; 1 Peter 4:13)."[11]

All these considerations had to be weighed in revising the rite of anointing in order better to adapt to present-day conditions those elements which were subject to change.[12]

We have thought fit to modify the sacramental form in such a way that, by reflecting the words of James, it may better express the effects of the sacrament.

Since olive oil, which has been prescribed until now for the valid celebration of the sacrament, is unobtainable or difficult to obtain in some parts of the world, we have decreed, at the request of a number of bishops, that from now on, according to circumstances, another kind of oil can also be used, provided it is derived from plants, and is thus similar to olive oil.

As regards the number of anointings and the parts of the body to be anointed, it has seemed opportune to simplify the rite.

Therefore, since this revision in certain points touches upon the sacramental rite itself, by our apostolic authority we establish that the following is to be observed for the future in the Latin rite:

The sacrament of the anointing of the sick is given to those who are seriously ill by anointing them on the forehead and hands with blessed olive oil or, according to circumstances, with another blessed plant oil and saying once only these words:

[10] Vatican Council II, Constitution on the Liturgy, art. 73: AAS 56 (1964) 118-119.
[11] Vatican Council II, Dogmatic Constitution on the Church, no. 11: AAS 57 (1965) 15.
[12] See Vatican Council II, Constitution on the Liturgy, art. 1: AAS 56 (1964) 97.

"Through this holy anointing
May the Lord in His love and mercy help you
with the grace of the Holy Spirit.

"May the Lord who frees you from sin
save you and raise you up."*

In the case of necessity, however, it is sufficient that a single anointing be given on the forehead or, because of the particular condition of the sick person, on another suitable part of the body, while the whole sacramental form is said.

The sacrament may be repeated if the sick person recovers after being anointed and then again falls ill or if during the same illness the person's condition becomes more serious.

Having made these decisions and declarations about the essential rite of the sacrament of the anointing of the sick, by our apostolic authority we also approve the *Ordo Unctionis infirmorum eorumque pastoralis curae,* which has been revised by the Congregation for Divine Worship. At the same time, where necessary we amend the prescriptions of the Code of Canon Law or other laws hitherto in force or we repeal them; other prescriptions and laws, which are neither repealed nor amended by the above-mentioned rite, remain valid and in force. The Latin edition containing the new rite will come into force as soon as it is published; the vernacular editions, prepared by the conferences of bishops and confirmed by the Apostolic See, will come into force on the dates to be laid down by the individual conferences. The old rite may be used until 31 December 1973. From 1 January 1974, however, only the new rite is to be used by those concerned.

We intend that everything we have laid down and prescribed should be firm and effective in the Latin rite, notwithstanding, where relevant, the apostolic constitutions and ordinances issued by our predecessors and other prescriptions, even if worthy of special mention.

Given at Rome, at Saint Peter's, 30 November 1972, the tenth year of our pontificate.

PAUL VI

**Latin*: Per istam sanctam unctionem et suam piissimam misericordiam, adiuvette Dominus gratia Spiritus Sancti, ut a peccatis liberatum te salvet atque propitius allevet.

NATIONAL CONFERENCE OF CATHOLIC BISHOPS UNITED STATES OF AMERICA

DECREE

In accord with the norms established by decree of the Sacred Congregation of Rites *"Cum, nostra aetate"* (27 January 1966), *Pastoral Care of the Sick: Rites of Anointing and Viaticum* is declared to be the vernacular *editio typica* of the *Ordo Unctionis Infirmorum eorumque pastoralis curae* for the dioceses of the United States of America, and may be published by authority of the National Conference of Catholic Bishops.

Pastoral Care of the Sick: Rites of Anointing and Viaticum was canonically approved by the National Conference of Catholic Bishops in plenary assembly on 18 November 1982 and was subsequently confirmed by the Apostolic See by decree of the Sacred Congregation for the Sacraments and Divine Worship on 11 December 1982 (Prot. CD 1207/82).

On 1 September 1983 *Pastoral Care of the Sick: Rites of Anointing and Viaticum* may be published and used in celebrations for the sick and dying. The mandatory effective date has been established by the conference of bishops as 27 November 1983, the First Sunday of Advent. From that day forward no other vernacular versions of these rites may be used.

Given at the General Secretariat of the National Conference of Catholic Bishops, Washington, D.C., on 28 January 1983, the Memorial of Saint Thomas Aquinas, priest and doctor.

✠ John R. Roach
Archbishop of Saint Paul and Minneapolis
President
National Conference of Catholic Bishops

Daniel F. Hoye
General Secretary

FOREWORD

The purpose of this Foreword is to draw attention to the special features of *Pastoral Care of the Sick: Rites of Anointing and Viaticum,* approved by the National Conference of Catholic Bishops on November 18, 1982 and confirmed by the Sacred Congregation for the Sacraments and Divine Worship on December 11, 1982 (Prot. CD 1207/82).

While the material in this volume is substantially a translation of the Latin *editio typica* of the *Ordo Unctionis Infirmorum eorumque pastoralis curae* promulgated by the Apostolic Constitution of Paul VI, *Sacram Unctionem infirmorum*, of November 30, 1972, at the request of the member and associate member episcopal conferences of the Joint International Commission on English in the Liturgy, the Latin edition has been expanded and adapted for greater pastoral effectiveness.

This expansion and adaptation includes original English texts which address pastoral circumstances not foreseen in the Latin edition nor in the provisional English edition of 1973. Also included in this volume are texts from other approved parts of the Roman Ritual, e.g. *Rite of Funerals, Rite of Christian Initiation of Adults*, etc.

The texts in this volume have been arranged "in a format that will be as suitable as possible for pastoral use" (General Introduction 38*f*.). Finally, as the General Introduction notes, "whenever the Roman Ritual gives several alternative texts, particular rituals may add other texts of the same kind" (no. 39).

In undertaking the pastoral rearrangement of *Ordo Unctionis Infirmorum eorumque pastoralis curae* it was necessary to depart from the numbering system employed in the Latin edition. The General Introduction corresponds exactly to the Latin introduction. Beginning with number 42, however, the present numbering system diverges from the Latin system. The new numbering system appears at the left-hand side of the page. The corresponding reference number from the Latin edition appears in the right-hand margin.

1. In the case of the rubrics or the introduction to the parts or chapters of this book, the reference number from the Latin edition indicates that the text is either a direct translation or

that it is derived from the numbered material in the Latin. In the case of liturgical texts, the reference number from the Latin edition indicates that the text is translated from the Latin text cited. Reference numbers from the Latin edition appear only once, at the beginning of the appropriate material, unless this is interrupted by material from another reference number or by the insertion of a newly composed text. In this case, the previous reference number is repeated.

2. A text having a number on the left but no reference number in the right-hand margin is newly composed.

3. A reference number in the right-hand margin that is preceded by a letter indicates a text which has been taken from a rite other than the *Ordo Unctionis Infirmorum eorumque pastoralis curae.*

a. Texts with reference numbers preceded by the letter "E" are taken from *Holy Communion and Worship of the Eucharist outside Mass.*
b. "F" indicates texts from the *Rite of Funerals.*
c. "I" indicates texts from *Christian Initiation of Adults.*
d. "P" indicates texts taken from the *Rite of Penance.*

This new edition of *Pastoral Care of the Sick: Rites of Anointing and Viaticum* is commended to the Church and its ministers who care for the sick and dying members of the Body of Christ in the confident hope of the Lord's constant compassionate love for them.

John S. Cummins, Bishop of Oakland
Chairman
The Bishops' Committee on the Liturgy
National Conference of Catholic Bishops

27 November 1983
First Sunday of Advent

GENERAL INTRODUCTION

HUMAN SICKNESS AND ITS MEANING IN THE MYSTERY OF SALVATION

1. Suffering and illness have always been among the greatest problems that trouble the human spirit. Christians feel and experience pain as do all other people; yet their faith helps them to grasp more deeply the mystery of suffering and to bear their pain with greater courage. From Christ's words they know that sickness has meaning and value for their own salvation and for the salvation of the world. They also know that Christ, who during his life often visited and healed the sick, loves them in their illness.

2. Although closely linked with the human condition, sickness cannot as a general rule be regarded as a punishment inflicted on each individual for personal sins (see John 9:3). Christ himself, who is without sin, in fulfilling the words of Isaiah took on all the wounds of his passion and shared in all human pain (see Isaiah 53:4–5). Christ is still pained and tormented in his members, made like him. Still, our afflictions seem but momentary and slight when compared to the greatness of the eternal glory for which they prepare us (see 2 Corinthians 4:17).

3. Part of the plan laid out by God's providence is that we should fight strenuously against all sickness and carefully seek the blessings of good health, so that we may fulfill our role in human society and in the Church. Yet we should always be prepared to fill up what is lacking in Christ's sufferings for the salvation of the world as we look forward to creation's being set free in the glory of the children of God (see Colossians 1:24; Romans 8:19–21).

Moreover, the role of the sick in the Church is to be a reminder to others of the essential or higher things. By their witness the sick show that our mortal life must be redeemed through the mystery of Christ's death and resurrection.

4. The sick person is not the only one who should fight against illness. Doctors and all who are devoted in any way to caring for the sick should consider it their duty to use all the means which in their judgment may help the sick, both

physically and spiritually. In so doing, they are fulfilling the command of Christ to visit the sick, for Christ implied that those who visit the sick should be concerned for the whole person and offer both physical relief and spiritual comfort.

CELEBRATION OF THE SACRAMENTS FOR THE SICK AND THE DYING

ANOINTING OF THE SICK

5. The Lord himself showed great concern for the bodily and spiritual welfare of the sick and commanded his followers to do likewise. This is clear from the gospels, and above all from the existence of the sacrament of anointing, which he instituted and which is made known in the Letter of James. Since then the Church has never ceased to celebrate this sacrament for its members by the anointing and the prayer of its priests, commending those who are ill to the suffering and glorified Lord, that he may raise them up and save them (see James 5:14-16). Moreover, the Church exhorts them to associate themselves willingly with the passion and death of Christ (see Romans 8:17),[1] and thus contribute to the welfare of the people of God.[2]

Those who are seriously ill need the special help of God's grace in this time of anxiety, lest they be broken in spirit and, under the pressure of temptation, perhaps weakened in their faith.

This is why, through the sacrament of anointing, Christ strengthens the faithful who are afflicted by illness, providing them with the strongest means of support.[3]

The celebration of this sacrament consists especially in the laying on of hands by the priests of the Church, the offering of the prayer of faith, and the anointing of the sick with oil made holy by God's blessing. This rite signifies the grace of the sacrament and confers it.

[1]See also Colossians 1:24; 2 Timothy 2:11-12; 1 Peter 4:13.

[2]See Council of Trent, sess. 14, De Extrema Unctione, cap. 1: Denz.-Schön. 1695; Vatican Council II, Dogmatic Constitution on the Church, no. 11: AAS 57 (1965) 15.

[3]See Council of Trent, sess. 14, De Extrema Unctione, cap. 1: Denz-Schön. 1694.

6. This sacrament gives the grace of the Holy Spirit to those who are sick: by this grace the whole person is helped and saved, sustained by trust in God, and strengthened against the temptations of the Evil One and against anxiety over death. Thus the sick person is able not only to bear suffering bravely, but also to fight against it. A return to physical health may follow the reception of this sacrament if it will be beneficial to the sick person's salvation. If necessary, the sacrament also provides the sick person with the forgiveness of sins and the completion of Christian penance.[4]

7. In the anointing of the sick, which includes the prayer of faith (see James 5:15), faith itself is manifested. Above all this faith must be made actual both in the minister of the sacrament and, even more importantly, in the recipient. The sick person will be saved by personal faith and the faith of the Church, which looks back to the death and resurrection of Christ, the source of the sacrament's power (see James 5:15),[5] and looks ahead to the future kingdom that is pledged in the sacraments.

Recipients of the Anointing of the Sick

8. The Letter of James states that the sick are to be anointed in order to raise them up and save them.[6] Great care and concern should be taken to see that those of the faithful whose health is seriously* impaired by sickness or old age receive this sacrament.[7]

A prudent or reasonably sure judgment, without scruple, is sufficient for deciding on the seriousness of an illness;[8] if necessary a doctor may be consulted.

[4]See ibid., prooem. and cap. 2: Denz.-Schön. 1694 and 1696.
[5]See St. Thomas Aquinas, *In 4 Sententiarum,* d. 1, q. 1, a. 4, quaestiuncula 3.
[6]See Council of Trent, sess. 14, De Extrema Unctione, cap. 2: Denz.-Schön. 1698.
[7]See Vatican Council II, Constitution on the Liturgy, art, 73: AAS 56 (1964) 118-119.
[8]See Pius XI, Epist. *Explorata res,* 2 February 1923: AAS 15 (1923) 103-107.
*The word *periculose* has been carefully studied and rendered as "seriously," rather than as "gravely," "dangerously," or "perilously." Such a rendering will serve to avoid restrictions upon the celebration of the sacrament. On the one hand, the sacrament may and should be given to anyone whose health is seriously impaired; on the other hand, it may not be given indiscriminately or to any person whose health is not seriously impaired.

9. The sacrament may be repeated if the sick person recovers after being anointed and then again falls ill or if during the same illness the person's condition becomes more serious.

10. A sick person may be anointed before surgery whenever a serious illness is the reason for the surgery.

11. Elderly people may be anointed if they have become notably weakened even though no serious illness is present.

12. Sick children may be anointed if they have sufficient use of reason to be strengthened by this sacrament.

13. In public and private catechesis, the faithful should be educated to ask for the sacrament of anointing and, as soon as the right time comes, to receive it with full faith and devotion. They should not follow the wrongful practice of delaying the reception of the sacrament. All who care for the sick should be taught the meaning and purpose of the sacrament.

14. The sacrament of anointing may be conferred upon sick people who, although they have lost consciousness or the use of reason, would, as Christian believers, probably have asked for it were they in control of their faculties.[9]

15. When a priest has been called to attend those who are already dead, he should not administer the sacrament of anointing. Instead, he should pray for them, asking that God forgive their sins and graciously receive them into the kingdom. But if the priest is doubtful whether the sick person is dead, he may give the sacrament conditionally (no. 269).[10]

Minister of the Anointing of the Sick

16. The priest is the only proper minister of the anointing of the sick.[11]

This office is ordinarily exercised by bishops, parish priests (pastors) and their assistants, priests who are responsible for

[9]See *Codex Iuris Canonici* (CIC), can. 943.
[10]See ibid., can. 941.
[11]See Council of Trent, sess. 14, De Extrema Unctione, cap. 3 and can. 4. Denz.-Schön. 1697 and 1719; see also CIC, can, 938.

the sick or aged in hospitals, and superiors of clerical religious institutes.[12]

17. These ministers have the pastoral responsibility both of preparing and helping the sick and others who are present, with the assistance of religious and laity, and of celebrating the sacrament.

The local Ordinary has the responsibility of supervising celebrations at which sick persons from various parishes or hospitals may come together to receive the sacrament.

18. Other priests also confer the sacrament of anointing with the consent of the ministers mentioned in no. 16. Presuming such consent in case of necessity, a priest need only inform the parish priest (pastor) or hospital chaplain later.

19. When two or more priests are present for the anointing of a sick person, one of them may say the prayers and carry out the anointings, saying the sacramental form. The others may take the remaining parts, such as the introductory rites, readings, invocations, or instructions. Each priest may lay hands on the sick person.

Requirements for Celebrating the Anointing of the Sick

20. The matter proper for the sacrament is olive oil or, according to circumstances, other oil derived from plants.[13]

21. The oil used for anointing the sick must be blessed for this purpose by the bishop or by a priest who has this faculty, either from the law or by special concession of the Apostolic See.

The law itself permits the following, besides a bishop, to bless the oil of the sick:

a. those whom the law equates with diocesan bishops;
b. in case of true necessity, any priest.[14]

The oil of the sick is ordinarily blessed by the bishop on Holy Thursday.[15]

[12]See CIC, can. 938.
[13]See Roman Pontifical, *Rite of Blessing of Oils, Rite of Consecrating the Chrism,* Introduction, no. 3. [*The Sacramentary (The Roman Missal)* Appendix II].
[14]See ibid., no. 8.
[15]See ibid., no. 9.

22. If a priest in accord with no. 21b, is to bless the oil during the rite, he may bring the unblessed oil with him, or the family of the sick person may prepare the oil in a suitable vessel. If any of the oil is left after the celebration of the sacrament, it should be absorbed in cotton (cotton wool) and burned.

If the priest uses oil that has already been blessed (either by the bishop or by a priest), he brings it with him in the vessel in which it is kept. This vessel, made of suitable material, should be clean and should contain sufficient oil (soaked in cotton [cotton wool] for convenience). In this case, after celebrating the sacrament the priest returns the vessel to the place where it is kept with proper respect. He should make sure that the oil remains fit for use and should replenish it from time to time, either yearly when the bishop blesses the oil on Holy Thursday or more frequently if necessary.

23. The sick person is anointed on the forehead and on the hands. It is appropriate to divide the sacramental form so that the first part is said while the forehead is anointed, the latter part while the hands are anointed.

In case of necessity, however, it is sufficient that a single anointing be given on the forehead or, because of the particular condition of the sick person, on another suitable part of the body, while the whole sacramental form is said.

24. Depending on the culture and traditions of different peoples, the number of anointings may be increased and the place of anointing may be changed. Directives on this should be included in the preparation of particular rituals.

25. The following is the sacramental form with which the anointing of the sick is given in the Latin rite:

Through this holy anointing
may the Lord in his love and mercy help you
with the grace of the Holy Spirit.

May the Lord who frees you from sin
save you and raise you up.

VIATICUM FOR THE DYING

26. When in their passage from this life Christians are strengthened by the body and blood of Christ in viaticum,

they have the pledge of the resurrection that the Lord promised "Those who eat my flesh and drink my blood have eternal life, and I will raise them up on the last day" (John 6:54).

When possible, viaticum should be received within Mass so that the sick person may receive communion under both kinds. Communion received as viaticum should be considered a special sign of participation in the mystery which is celebrated in the eucharist: the mystery of the death of the Lord and his passage to the Father.[16]

27. All baptized Christians who are able to receive commuion are bound to receive viaticum by reason of the precept to receive communion when in danger of death from any cause. Priests with pastoral responsibility must see that the celebration of this sacrament is not delayed, but that the faithful are nourished by it while still in full possession of their faculties.[17]

28. It is also desirable that during the celebration of viaticum, Christians renew the faith professed at their baptism, by which they became adopted children of God and coheirs of the promise of eternal life.

29. The ordinary ministers of viaticum are the parish priest (pastor) and his assistants, the priest who is responsible for the sick in hospitals, and the superior of a clerical religious institute. In case of necessity, any other priest with at least the presumed permission of the competent minister may give viaticum.

If no priest is available, viaticum may be brought to the sick by a deacon or by another member of the faithful, either a man or a woman, who by the authority of the Apostolic See has been duly appointed by the bishop to give the eucharist to the faithful. In this case, a deacon follows the rite prescribed in the ritual; other ministers use the rite they ordinarily follow for distributing communion, but with the

[16]See Congregation of Rites, Instruction *Eucharisticum mysterium*, 25 May 1967, nos. 36, 39, 41:AAS 59 (1967) 561, 562, 563; Paul VI, Motu Proprio *Pastorale munus*, 30 November 1963, [I] no. 7: AAS 56 1964) 7; CIC, can. 822, § 4.

[17]See Congregation of Rites, Instruction *Eucharisticum mysterium*, 25 May 1967, no. 39: AAS 59 (1967) 562.

special words given in the ritual for the rite for viaticum (no. 207).

CONTINUOUS RITE

30. For special cases, when sudden illness or some other cause has unexpectedly placed one of the faithful in proximate danger of death, a continuous rite is provided by which the sick person may be given the sacraments of penance, anointing, and the eucharist as viaticum in a single celebration.

If death is imminent and there is not enough time to celebrate the three sacraments in the manner already described, the sick person should be given an opportunity to make a sacramental confession, even if it has to be a generic confession. After this the person should be given viaticum, since all the faithful are bound to receive this sacrament if they are in danger of death. Then, if there is sufficient time, the sick person should be anointed.

The sick person who, because of the nature of the illness, cannot receive communion should be anointed.

31. If the sick person is to be strengthened by the sacrament of confirmation, nos. 238, 246, 276, 290, and 291 of this ritual should be consulted.

In danger of death, provided the bishop is not easily available or is lawfully impeded, the law gives the faculty to confirm to the following: parish priests (pastors) and parochial vicars; in their absence, associate pastors; priests who are in charge of special parishes lawfully established, administrators, substitute priests, and assistant priests (coadjutors); in the absence of all of the preceding, any priest who is not under censure or canonical penalty.[18]

OFFICES AND MINISTRIES FOR THE SICK

32. If one member suffers in the Body of Christ, which is the Church, all the members suffer with that member (1 Corinthians 12:26).[19] For this reason, kindness shown toward the sick and works of charity and mutual help for the relief of

[18]See Roman Pontifical, *Rite of Confirmation*, Introduction, no. 7c.
[19]See Vatican Council II, Dogmatic Constitution on the Church, no. 7: AAS 57 (1965) 9-10.

every kind of human want are held in special honor.[20] Every scientific effort to prolong life[21] and every act of care for the sick, on the part of any person, may be considered a preparation for the Gospel and a sharing in Christ's healing ministry.[22]

33. It is thus especially fitting that all baptized Christians share in this ministry of mutual charity within the Body of Christ by doing all that they can to help the sick return to health, by showing love for the sick, and by celebrating the sacraments with them. Like the other sacraments, these too have a community aspect, which should be brought out as much as possible when they are celebrated.

34. The family and friends of the sick and those who take care of them in any way have a special share in this ministry of comfort. In particular, it is their task to strengthen the sick with words of faith and by praying with them, to commend them to the suffering and glorified Lord, and to encourage them to contribute to the well-being of the people of God by associating themselves willingly with Christ's passion and death.[23] If the sickness grows worse, the family and friends of the sick and those who take care of them have the responsibility of informing the parish priest (pastor) and by their kind words of prudently disposing the sick for the reception of the sacraments at the proper time.

35. Priests, particularly parish priests (pastors) and the others mentioned in no. 16, should remember that it is their duty to care for the sick by personal visits and other acts of kindness.[24] Especially when they give the sacraments, priests should stir up the hope of those present and strengthen their faith in Christ who suffered and is glorified. By bringing the Church's love and the consolation of faith, they comfort believers and raise the minds of others to God.

[20]See Vatican Council II, Decree on the Apostolate of the Laity, no. 8: AAS 58 (1966) 845.

[21]See Vatican Council II, Pastoral Constitution on the Church in the Modern World, no. 18: AAS 58 (1966) 1038.

[22]See Vatican Council II, Dogmatic Constitution on the Church, no. 28: AAS 57 (1965) 34.

[23]See ibid., no. 21: AAS 57 (1965) 24.

[24]See CIC, can. 468, § 1.

36. It is important that all the faithful, and above all the sick, be aided by suitable catechesis in preparing for and participating in the sacraments of anointing and viaticum, especially if the celebration is to be carried out communally. In this way they will understand more fully what has been said about the anointing of the sick and about viaticum, and the celebration of these sacraments will nourish, strengthen, and manifest faith more effectively. For the prayer of faith which accompanies the celebration of the sacrament is nourished by the profession of this faith.

37. When the priest prepares for the celebration of the sacraments, he should ask about the condition of the sick person. He should take this information into account, for example, in planning the rite, in choosing readings and prayers, and in deciding whether he will celebrate Mass when viaticum is to be given. As far as possible, he should arrange all this with the sick person and the family beforehand, when he explains the meaning of the sacraments.

ADAPTATIONS BELONGING TO THE CONFERENCES OF BISHOPS

38. In virtue of the Constitution on the Liturgy (art. 63b), the conferences of bishops have the right to prepare a section in particular rituals corresponding to the present section of the Roman Ritual and adapted to the needs of the different parts of the world. This section is for use in the regions concerned once the *acta* have been reviewed by the Apostolic See.

The following are the responsibilities of the conferences of bishops in this regard:

a. to decide on the adaptations dealt with in the Constitution on the Liturgy, article 39;

b. to weigh carefully and prudently what elements from the traditions and culture of individual peoples may be appropriately admitted into divine worship, then to propose to the Apostolic See adaptations considered useful or necessary that will be introduced with its consent;

c. to retain elements in the rites of the sick that now exist in particular rituals, as long as they are compatible with the

Constitution on the Liturgy and with contemporary needs; or to adapt any of these elements;

d. to prepare translations of the texts so that they are truly adapted to the genius of different languages and cultures and to add, whenever appropriate, suitable melodies for singing;

e. to adapt and enlarge, if necessary, this Introduction in the Roman Ritual in order to encourage the conscious and active participation of the faithful;

f. to arrange the material in the editions of liturgical books prepared under the direction of the conferences of bishops in a format that will be as suitable as possible for pastoral use.

39. Whenever the Roman Ritual gives several alternative texts, particular rituals may add other texts of the same kind.

ADAPTATIONS BY THE MINISTER

40. The minister should take into account the particular circumstances, needs, and desires of the sick and of other members of the faithful and should willingly use the various opportunities that the rites provide.

a. The minister should be especially aware that the sick tire easily and that their physical condition may change from day to day and even from hour to hour. For this reason the celebration may be shortened if necessary.

b. When there is no group of the faithful present, the priest should remember that the Church is already present in his own person and in the one who is ill. For this reason he should try to offer the sick person the love and help of the Christian community both before and after the celebration of the sacrament. He may ask another Christian from the local community to do this if the sick person will accept this help.

c. Sick persons who regain their health after being anointed should be encouraged to give thanks for the favor received by participating in a Mass of thanksgiving or by some other suitable means.

41. The priest should follow the structure of the rite in the celebration, while accommodating it to the place and the people involved. The penitential rite may be part of the

introductory rite or take place after the reading from Scripture. In place of the thanksgiving over the oil, the priest may give an instruction. This alternative should be considered when the sick person is in a hospital and other sick people present do not take part in the celebration of the sacrament.

PART I

PASTORAL CARE OF THE SICK

INTRODUCTION
Lord, your friend is sick.

42. The rites in Part I of *Pastoral Care of the Sick: Rites of Anointing and Viaticum* are used by the Church to comfort the sick in time of anxiety, to encourage them to fight against illness, and perhaps to restore them to health. These rites are distinct from those in the second part of this book, which are provided to comfort and strengthen a Christian in the passage from this life.

43. The concern that Christ showed for the bodily and 5
spiritual welfare of those who are ill is continued by the 33 42
Church in its ministry to the sick. This ministry is the 43
common responsibility of all Christians, who should visit the sick, remember them in prayer, and celebrate the sacraments with them. The family and friends of the sick, doctors and others who care for them, and priests with pastoral responsibilities have a particular share in this ministry of comfort. Through words of encouragement and faith they can help the sick to unite themselves with the sufferings of Christ for the good of God's people.

Remembrance of the sick is especially appropriate at common worship on the Lord's Day, during the general intercessions at Mass and in the intercessions at Morning Prayer and Evening Prayer. Family members and those who are dedicated to the care of the sick should be remembered on these occasions as well.

44. Priests have the special task of preparing the sick to 43
celebrate the sacrament of penance (individually or in a communal celebration), to receive the eucharist frequently if their condition permits, and to celebrate the sacrament of anointing at the appropriate time. During this preparation it will be especially helpful if the sick person, the priest, and the family become accustomed to praying together. The priest should provide leadership to those who assist him in the care of the sick, especially deacons and other ministers of the eucharist.

The words "priest," "deacon," and "minister" are used advisedly. Only in those rites which must be celebrated by a priest is the word "priest" used in the rubrics (that is, the sacrament of penance, the sacrament of the anointing of the sick, the celebration of viaticum within Mass). Whenever it is clear that, in the absence of a priest, a deacon may preside at a particular rite, the words "priest or deacon" are used in the rubrics. Whenever another minister is permitted to celebrate a rite in the absence of a priest or deacon, the word "minister" is used in the rubrics, even though in many cases the rite will be celebrated by a priest or deacon.

45. The pastoral care of the sick should be suited to the nature and length of the illness. An illness of short duration in which the full recovery of health is a possibility requires a more intensive ministry, whereas illness of a longer duration which may be a prelude to death requires a more extensive ministry. An awareness of the attitudes and emotional states which these different situations engender in the sick is indispensable to the development of an appropriate ministry.

VISITS TO THE SICK

46. Those who visit the sick should help them to pray, 45
sharing with them the word of God proclaimed in the assembly from which their sickness has separated them. As the occasion permits, prayer drawn from the psalms or from other prayers or litanies may be added to the word of God. Care should be taken to prepare for a future visit during which the sick will receive the eucharist.

VISITS TO A SICK CHILD

47. What has already been said about visiting the sick and praying with them (see no. 46) applies also in visits to a sick child. Every effort should be made to know the child and to accommodate the care in keeping with the age and comprehension of the child. In these circumstances the minister should also be particularly concerned to help the child's family.

48. If it is appropriate, the priest may discuss with the parents the possibility of preparing and celebrating with the child the sacraments of initiation (baptism, confirmation, eucharist). The priest may baptize and confirm the child (see *Rite of Confirmation,* no. 7b). To complete the process of

initiation, the child should also receive first communion. (If the child is a proper subject for confirmation, then he or she may receive first communion in accordance with the practice of the Church.) There is no reason to delay this, especially if the illness is likely to be a long one.

49. Throughout the illness the minister should ensure that the child receives communion frequently, making whatever adaptations seem necessary in the rite for communion of the sick (Chapter III).

50. The child may be anointed if he or she has sufficient use 12
of reason to be strengthened by the sacrament of anointing. The rites provided (Chapter IV) are to be used and adapted.

COMMUNION OF THE SICK

51. Because the sick are prevented from celebrating the eucharist with the rest of the community, the most important visits are those during which they receive holy communion. In receiving the body and blood of Christ, the sick are united sacramentally to the Lord and are reunited with the eucharistic community from which illness has separated them.

ANOINTING OF THE SICK

52. The priest should be especially concerned for those 5
whose health has been seriously impaired by illness or old 6 8
age. He will offer them a new sign of hope: the laying on of hands and the anointing of the sick accompanied by the prayer of faith (James 5:14). Those who receive this sacrament in the faith of the Church will find it a true sign of comfort and support in time of trial. It will work to overcome the sickness, if this is God's will.

53. Some types of mental sickness are now classified as 5
serious. Those who are judged to have a serious mental 9
illness and who would be strengthened by the sacrament may be anointed (see no. 5). The anointing may be repeated in accordance with the conditions for other kinds of serious illness (see no. 9).

CHAPTER I

VISITS TO THE SICK

INTRODUCTION

I was sick, and you visited me.

54. The prayers contained in this chapter follow the common pattern of reading, response, prayer, and blessing. This pattern is provided as an example of what can be done and may be adapted as necessary. The minister may wish to invite those present to prepare for the reading from Scripture, perhaps by a brief introduction or through a moment of silence. The laying on of hands may be added by the priest, if appropriate, after the blessing is given. 45

55. The sick should be encouraged to pray when they are alone or with their families, friends, or those who care for them. Their prayer should be drawn primarily from Scripture. The sick person and others may help to plan the celebration, for example, by choosing the prayers and readings. Those making these choices should keep in mind the condition of the sick person. 44

The passages found in this chapter and those included in Part III speak of the mystery of human suffering in the words, works, and life of Christ. Occasionally, for example, on the Lord's Day, the sick may feel more involved in the worship of the community from which they are separated if the readings used are those assigned for that day in the lectionary. Prayers may also be drawn from the psalms or from other prayers or litanies. The sick should be helped in making this form of prayer, and the minister should always be ready to pray with them.

56. The minister should encourage the sick person to offer his or her sufferings in union with Christ and to join in prayer for the Church and the world. Some examples of particular intentions which may be suggested to the sick person are: for peace in the world; for a deepening of the life of the Spirit in the local Church; for the pope and the bishops; for people suffering in a particular disaster. 43

READING

57. The word of God is proclaimed by one of those present or by the minister. An appropriate reading from Part III or one of the following readings may be used:

A Acts of the Apostles 3:1-10 162
In the name of Jesus and the power of his Church, there is salvation—even liberation from sickness.

B Matthew 8:14-17 206
Jesus fulfills the prophetic figure of the servant of God taking upon himself and relieving the sufferings of God's people.

RESPONSE

58. A brief period of silence may be observed after the reading of the word of God. An appropriate psalm from Part III or one of the following psalms may be used:

A Psalm 102 193
℟. **O Lord, hear my prayer and let my cry come to you.**

B Psalm 27 186
℟. **The Lord is my light and my salvation.**

The minister may then give a brief explanation of the reading, applying it to the needs of the sick person and those who are looking after him or her.

THE LORD'S PRAYER

59. The minister introduces the Lord's Prayer in these or similar words:

Now let us offer together the prayer our Lord Jesus Christ taught us:

All say:

Our Father . . .

60. The minister says a concluding prayer. One of the following may be used:

A

Father,
your Son accepted our sufferings
to teach us the virtue of patience in human illness.
Hear the prayers we offer for our sick brother/sister.

May all who suffer pain, illness, or disease
realize that they have been chosen to be saints
and know that they are joined to Christ
in his suffering for the salvation of the world.

We ask this through Christ our Lord.
℟. Amen.

B
All-powerful and ever-living God,
the lasting health of all who believe in you,
hear us as we ask your loving help for the sick;
restore their health,
that they may again offer joyful thanks in your Church.

Grant this through Christ our Lord.
℟. Amen.

C
All-powerful and ever-living God,
we find security in your forgiveness.
Give us serenity and peace of mind;
may we rejoice in your gifts of kindness
and use them always for your glory and our good.

We ask this in the name of Jesus the Lord.
℟. Amen.

BLESSING

61. The minister may give a blessing. One of the following may be used:

A
All praise and glory is yours, Lord our God,
for you have called us to serve you in love.
Bless N.
so that he/she may bear this illness
in union with your Son's obedient suffering.
Restore him/her to health,
and lead him/her to glory.

We ask this through Christ our Lord.
℟. Amen.

B For an elderly person

All praise and glory are yours, Lord our God,
for you have called us to serve you in love.
Bless all who have grown old in your service
and give N. strength and courage
to continue to follow Jesus your Son.

We ask this through Christ our Lord.
℟. Amen.

If the minister is a priest or deacon, he immediately concludes:

May the blessing of almighty God, 238
the Father, and the Son, ✛ and the Holy Spirit,
come upon you and remain with you for ever.
℟. Amen.

The priest may lay hands upon the sick person's head. 45

A minister who is not a priest or deacon invokes God's blessing and makes the sign of the cross on himself or herself, while saying:

May the Lord bless us,
protect us from all evil,
and bring us to everlasting life.
℟. Amen.

The minister may then trace the sign of the cross on the sick person's forehead. E40

CHAPTER II

VISITS TO A SICK CHILD

INTRODUCTION

Let the children come to me; do not keep them back from me.

62. The following readings, prayers, and blessings will help the minister to pray with sick children and their families. They are provided as an example of what can be done and may be adapted as necessary. The minister may wish to invite those present to prepare for the reading from Scripture, perhaps by a brief introduction or through a moment of silence.

63. If the child does not already know the minister, the latter should seek to establish a friendly and easy relationship with the child. Therefore, the greeting which begins the visit should be an informal one.

64. The minister should help sick children to understand that the sick are very special in the eyes of God because they are suffering as Christ suffered and because they can offer their sufferings for the salvation of the world.

65. In praying with the sick child the minister chooses, together with the child and the family if possible, suitable elements of common prayer in the form of a brief liturgy of the word. This may consist of a reading from Scripture, simple one-line prayers taken from Scripture which can be repeated by the child, other familiar prayers such as the Lord's Prayer, the Hail Mary, litanies, or a simple form of the general intercessions. The laying on of hands may be added by the priest, if appropriate, after the child has been blessed.

READING

66. One of the following readings may be used for a brief liturgy of the word. Other readings may be chosen, for example: Mark 5:21-23, 35-43, *Jesus raises the daughter of Jairus and gives her back to her parents;* Mark 9:14-27, *Jesus cures a boy and gives him back to his father;* Luke 7:11-15, *Jesus raises a young*

man, the only son of his mother, and gives him back to her; John 4:46-53, *Jesus gives his second sign by healing an official's son.* In addition, other stories concerning the Lord's healing ministry may be found suitable, especially if told with the simplicity and clarity of one of the children's versions of Scripture.

A Mark 9:33-37
Jesus proposes the child as the ideal of those who would enter the kingdom.

B Mark 10:13-16
Jesus welcomes the children and lays his hands on them.

RESPONSE

67. After the reading of the word of God, time may be set apart for silent reflection if the child is capable of this form of prayer. The minister should also explain the meaning of the reading to those present, adapting it to their circumstances.

The minister may then help the child and the family to respond to the word of God. The following short responsory may be used:

Jesus, come to me.
—Jesus, come to me.

Jesus, put your hand on me.
—Jesus, put your hand on me.

Jesus, bless me.
—Jesus, bless me.

THE LORD'S PRAYER

68. The minister introduces the Lord's Prayer in these or similar words:

Let us pray to the Father using those words which Jesus himself used:

All say:

Our Father . . .

CONCLUDING PRAYER

69. The minister says a concluding prayer. One of the following may be used:

A
God of love,
ever caring,
ever strong,
stand by us in our time of need.

Watch over your child N. who is sick,
look after him/her in every danger,
and grant him/her your healing and peace.

We ask this in the name of Jesus the Lord.
℟. **Amen.**

B
Father,
in your love
you gave us Jesus
to help us rise triumphant over grief and pain.

Look on your child N. who is sick
and see in his/her sufferings those of your Son.

Grant N. a share in the strength you granted your Son
that he/she too may be a sign
of your goodness, kindness, and loving care.

We ask this in the name of Jesus the Lord.
℟. **Amen.**

BLESSING

70. The minister makes a sign of the cross on the child's forehead, saying one of the following:

A
N., when you were baptized,
you were marked with the cross of Jesus.
I (we) make this cross ✠ on your forehead
and ask the Lord to bless you,
and restore you to health.
℟. **Amen.**

B
All praise and glory is yours, heavenly God,
for you have called us to serve you in love.

Have mercy on us and listen to our prayer
as we ask you to help N.

Bless ✠ your beloved child,
and restore him/her to health
in the name of Jesus the Lord.
℟. **Amen.**

Each one present may in turn trace the sign of the cross on the child's forehead, in silence.

If the minister is a priest or deacon, he concludes as described on page 628.

The priest may then lay hands upon the sick child, in silence. 45

A minister who is not a priest or deacon concludes as described on page 628.

CHAPTER III

COMMUNION OF THE SICK

INTRODUCTION

Whoever eats this bread will live for ever.

71. This chapter contains two rites: one for use when communion can be celebrated in the context of a liturgy of the word; the other, a brief communion rite for use in more restrictive circumstances, such as in hospitals. 59

72. Priests with pastoral responsibilities should see to it that the sick or aged, even though not seriously ill or in danger of death, are given every opportunity to receive the eucharist frequently, even daily, especially during the Easter season. They may receive communion at any hour. Those who care for the sick may receive communion with them, in accord with the usual norms. To provide frequent commuion for the sick, it may be necessary to ensure that the community has a sufficient number of ministers of communion. The communion minister should wear attire appropriate to this ministry. 43 46 47 49

The sick person and others may help to plan the celebration, for example, by choosing the prayers and readings. Those making these choices should keep in mind the condition of the sick person. The readings and the homily should help those present to reach a deeper understanding of the mystery of human suffering in relation to the paschal mystery of Christ.

73. The faithful who are ill are deprived of their rightful and accustomed place in the eucharistic community. In bringing communion to them the minister of communion represents Christ and manifests faith and charity on behalf of the whole community toward those who cannot be present at the eucharist. For the sick the reception of communion is not only a privilege but also a sign of support and concern shown by the Christian community for its members who are ill.

The links between the community's eucharistic celebration, especially on the Lord's Day, and the communion of the sick are intimate and manifold. Besides remembering the sick in the general intercessions at Mass, those present should be reminded occasionally of the significance of communion in the lives of those who are ill: union with Christ in his struggle with evil, his prayer for the world, and his love for the Father, and union with the community from which they are separated.

The obligation to visit and comfort those who cannot take part in the eucharistic assembly may be clearly demonstrated by taking communion to them from the community's eucharistic celebration. This symbol of unity between the community and its sick members has the deepest significance on the Lord's Day, the special day of the eucharistic assembly.

74. When the eucharist is brought to the sick, it should be 46
carried in a pyx or small closed container. Those who are with 47 48
the sick should be asked to prepare a table covered with a 95
linen cloth upon which the blessed sacrament will be placed. Lighted candles are prepared and, where it is customary, a vessel of holy water. Care should be taken to make the occasion special and joyful.

Sick people who are unable to receive communion under the form of bread may receive it under the form of wine alone. If the wine is consecrated at a Mass not celebrated in the presence of the sick person, the blood of the Lord is kept in a properly covered vessel and is placed in the tabernacle after communion. The precious blood should be carried to the sick in a vessel which is closed in such a way as to eliminate all danger of spilling. If some of the precious blood remains, it should be consumed by the minister, who should also see to it that the vessel is properly purified.

75. If the sick wish to celebrate the sacrament of penance, it is 60
preferable that the priest make himself available for this 65
during a previous visit.

76. If it is necessary to celebrate the sacrament of penance 51
during the rite of communion, it takes the place of the 65
penitential rite.

COMMUNION IN ORDINARY CIRCUMSTANCES

77. If possible, provision should be made to celebrate Mass in the homes of the sick, with their families and friends gathered

around them. The Ordinary determines the conditions and requirements for such celebrations.

COMMUNION IN A HOSPITAL OR INSTITUTION

78. There will be situations, particularly in large institutions 59
with many communicants, when the minister should consider alternative means so that the rite of communion of the sick is not diminished to the absolute minimum. In such cases the following alternatives should be considered: (a) where possible, the residents or patients may be gathered in groups in one or more areas; (b) additional ministers of communion may assist.

When it is not possible to celebrate the full rite, the rite for communion in a hospital or institution may be used. If it is convenient, however, the minister may add elements from the rite for ordinary circumstances, for example, a Scripture reading.

79. The rite begins with the recitation of the eucharistic 61
antiphon in the church, the hospital chapel, or the first room visited. Then the minister gives communion to the sick in their individual rooms.

80. The concluding prayer may be said in the church, the 63
hospital chapel, or the last room visited. No blessing is given.

COMMUNION IN ORDINARY CIRCUMSTANCES

INTRODUCTORY RITES

GREETING

81. The minister greets the sick person and the others present. One of the following may be used: 49

A

The peace of the Lord be with you always.
℟. And also with you.

B

Peace be with you (this house) and with all who live here.
℟. And also with you.

C

The grace of our Lord Jesus Christ and the love of God and the fellowship of the Holy Spirit be with you all. 230
℟. And also with you.

D

The grace and peace of God our Father and the Lord Jesus Christ be with you. 231
℟. And also with you.

The minister then places the blessed sacrament on the table and all join in adoration. 49

SPRINKLING WITH HOLY WATER

82. If it seems desirable, the priest or deacon may sprinkle the sick person and those present with holy water. One of the following may be used: 50

A

Let this water call to mind our baptism into Christ, who by his death and resurrection has redeemed us.

B

Like a stream in parched land,
may the grace of the Lord
refresh our lives.

If the sacrament of penance is now celebrated (see Appendix p. 737), the penitential rite is omitted. 51

PENITENTIAL RITE

83. The minister invites the sick person and all present to join in the penitential rite, using these or similar words: 52

A

My brothers and sisters, to prepare ourselves for this celebration, let us call to mind our sins.

B

My brothers and sisters, let us turn with confidence to the Lord and ask his forgiveness for all our sins.

After a brief period of silence, the penitential rite continues, using one of the following: 52

A

Lord Jesus, you healed the sick:
Lord, have mercy.
℟. Lord, have mercy.

Lord Jesus, you forgave sinners:
Christ, have mercy.
℟. Christ, have mercy.

Lord Jesus, you give us yourself to heal us and bring us strength:
Lord, have mercy.
℟. Lord, have mercy.

B All say: 52

I confess to almighty God,
and to you, my brothers and sisters,
that I have sinned through my own fault

They strike their breast.

in my thoughts and in my words,
in what I have done,
and in what I have failed to do;
and I ask blessed Mary, ever virgin,
all the angels and saints,
and you, my brothers and sisters,
to pray for me to the Lord our God.

The minister concludes the penitential rite with the following:

May almighty God have mercy on us,
forgive us our sins,
and bring us to everlasting life.
℟. **Amen.**

LITURGY OF THE WORD

READING

84. The word of God is proclaimed by one of those present or by the minister. An appropriate reading from Part III or one of the following readings may be used: 53

A John 6:51
B John 6:54-58
C John 14:6
D John 15:5
E John 4:16

RESPONSE

85. A brief period of silence may be observed after the reading of the word of God. 53

The minister may then give a brief explanation of the reading, applying it to the needs of the sick person and those who are looking after him or her.

GENERAL INTERCESSIONS

86. The general intercessions may be said. With a brief introduction the minister invites all those present to pray. After the intentions the minister says the concluding prayer. It is desirable that the intentions be announced by someone other than the minister.

LITURGY OF HOLY COMMUNION

THE LORD'S PRAYER

87. The minister introduces the Lord's Prayer in these or similar words: 54

A

Now let us pray as Christ the Lord has taught us:

B

And now let us pray with confidence as Christ our Lord commanded:

All say:

Our Father . . .

COMMUNION

88. The minister shows the eucharistic bread to those present, saying: 55

A

This is the bread of life.
Taste and see that the Lord is good.

B

This is the Lamb of God 55
who takes away the sins of the world.
Happy are those who are called to his supper.

The sick person and all who are to receive communion say:

Lord, I am not worthy to receive you,
but only say the word and I shall be healed.

The minister goes to the sick person and, showing the blessed sacrament, says: 56

The body of Christ.

The sick person answers: "Amen," and receives communion.

Then the minister says:

The blood of Christ.

The sick person answers: "Amen," and receives communion.

Others present who wish to receive communion then do so in the usual way.

After the conclusion of the rite, the minister cleanses the vessel as usual. 57

SILENT PRAYER

89. Then a period of silence may be observed. 57

PRAYER AFTER COMMUNION

90. The minister says a concluding prayer. One of the following may be used: 57

Let us pray.

Pause for silent prayer, if this has not preceded.

A

God our Father, 235
you have called us to share the one bread and one cup
and so become one in Christ.

Help us to live in him
that we may bear fruit,
rejoicing that he has redeemed the world.

We ask this through Christ our Lord.
℟. **Amen.**

B

All-powerful God, 236
we thank you for the nourishment you give us
through your holy gift.

Pour out your Spirit upon us
and in the strength of this food from heaven
keep us single-minded in your service.

We ask this in the name of Jesus the Lord.
℟. **Amen.**

C

All-powerful and ever-living God, 57
may the body and blood of Christ your Son
be for our brother/sister N.
a lasting remedy for body and soul.

We ask this through Christ our Lord.
℟. **Amen.**

CONCLUDING RITE

BLESSING

91. The priest or deacon blesses the sick person and the others present, using one of the following blessings. If, however, any of the blessed sacrament remains, he may bless the sick person by making a sign of the cross with the blessed sacrament, in silence. 58

A

May God the Father bless you. 79
℟. Amen.

May God the Son heal you.
℟. Amen.

May God the Holy Spirit enlighten you.
℟. Amen.

May almighty God bless you,
the Father, and the Son, ✛ and the Holy Spirit,
℟. Amen.

B

May the Lord be with you to protect you. 237
℟. Amen.

May he guide you and give you strength.
℟. Amen.

May he watch over you, keep you in his care,
and bless you with his peace.
℟. Amen.

May almighty God bless you,
the Father, and the Son, ✛ and the Holy Spirit.
℟. Amen.

C

May the blessing of almighty God, 238
the Father, and the Son, ✛ and the Holy Spirit,
come upon you and remain with you for ever.
℟. Amen.

A minister who is not a priest or deacon invokes God's blessing and makes the sign of the cross on himself or herself, while saying: E40

A

May the Lord bless us,
protect us from all evil,
and bring us to everlasting life.
℟. **Amen.**

B

May the almighty and merciful God bless and protect us,
the Father, and the Son, ✠ and the Holy Spirit.
℟. **Amen.**

COMMUNION IN A HOSPITAL OR INSTITUTION

INTRODUCTORY RITE

ANTIPHON

92. The rite may begin in the church, the hospital chapel, or 61
the first room, where the minister says one of the following antiphons:

A

How holy this feast
in which Christ is our food:
his passion is recalled;
grace fills our hearts;
and we receive a pledge of the glory to come.

B

How gracious you are, Lord: E201
your gift of bread from heaven
reveals a Father's love and brings us perfect joy.
You fill the hungry with good things
and send the rich away empty.

C

I am the living bread E203
come down from heaven.
If you eat this bread
you will live for ever.
The bread I will give is my flesh
for the life of the world.

If it is customary, the minister may be accompanied by a 62
person carrying a candle.

LITURGY OF HOLY COMMUNION

GREETING

93. On entering each room, the minister may use one of the 49
following greetings:

A

The peace of the Lord be with you always.
℟. And also with you.

B

The grace of our Lord Jesus Christ and the love of God 230
and the fellowship of the Holy Spirit be with you all.
℟. And also with you.

The minister then places the blessed sacrament on the table, and all join in adoration. 49

If there is time and it seems desirable, the minister may proclaim a Scripture reading from those found in no. 84 or those appearing in Part III. 59

THE LORD'S PRAYER

94. When circumstances permit (for example, when there are not many rooms to visit), the minister is encouraged to lead the sick in the Lord's Prayer. The minister introduces the Lord's Prayer in these or similar words: 59

A

Jesus taught us to call God our Father, and so we have the courage to say:

B

Now let us pray as Christ the Lord has taught us:

All say:

Our Father . . .

COMMUNION

95. The minister shows the eucharistic bread to those present, saying: 62

A

This is the Lamb of God
who takes away the sins of the world.
Happy are those who hunger and thirst,
for they shall be satisfied.

B

This is the bread of life,
Taste and see that the Lord is good.

The rite then continues as described in no. 88.

CONCLUDING RITE

CONCLUDING PRAYER

96. The concluding prayer may be said either in the last room visited, in the church, or chapel. One of the following may be used. 63

Let us pray.

Pause for silent prayer.

A

God our Father, 235
you have called us to share the one bread and one cup
and so become one in Christ.

Help us to live in him
that we may bear fruit,
rejoicing that he has redeemed the world.

We ask this through Christ our Lord.
℟. Amen.

B

All-powerful and ever-living God, 57
may the body and blood of Christ your Son
be for our brothers and sisters
a lasting remedy for body and soul.
We ask this through Christ our Lord.
℟. Amen.

C

All-powerful God, 236
we thank you for the nourishment you give us
through your holy gift.

Pour out your Spirit upon us
and in the strength of this food from heaven
keep us single-minded in your service.

We ask this in the name of Jesus the Lord.
℟. Amen.

The blessing is omitted and the minister cleanses the vessel as usual. 63

CHAPTER IV

ANOINTING OF THE SICK

INTRODUCTION

Do not be worried or distressed. Have faith in God, and faith in me.

97. The sacrament of anointing is the proper sacrament for 8
those Christians whose health is seriously impaired by 80
sickness or old age. It may be celebrated in the home, in a hospital or institution, or in church. This chapter contains three rites for use in these varying circumstances: anointing outside Mass, anointing within Mass, and anointing in a hospital or institution. Several sick persons may be anointed within the rite especially if the celebration takes place in a church or hospital. While the sacrament will be celebrated more frequently outside Mass, the celebration may also take place within Mass.

98. In the course of his visits to the sick, the priest should try 3
to explain two complementary aspects of this sacrament: 5 64
through the sacrament of anointing the Church supports the 85
sick in their struggle against illness and continues Christ's messianic work of healing. All who are united in the bond of a common baptism and a common faith are joined together in the body of Christ since what happens to one member affects all. The sacrament of anointing effectively expresses the share that each one has in the sufferings of others. When the priest anoints the sick, he is anointing in the name and with the power of Christ himself (see Mark 6:13). On behalf of the whole community, he is ministering to those members who are suffering. This message of hope and comfort is also needed by those who care for the sick, especially those who are closely bound in love to them. There should be opportunity for suitable preparation over a period of time for the benefit of the sick themselves and of those who are with them.

99. The priest should ensure that the abuse of delaying the 8
reception of the sacrament does not occur, and that the 13
celebration takes place while the sick person is capable of active participation. However, the intent of the conciliar

reform (Constitution on the Liturgy, art. 73) that those needing the sacrament should seek it at the beginning of a serious illness should not be used to anoint those who are not proper subjects for the sacrament. The sacrament of the anointing of the sick should be celebrated only when a Christian's health is seriously impaired by sickness or old age.

Because of its very nature as a sign, the sacrament of the anointing of the sick should be celebrated with members of the family and other representatives of the Christian community whenever this is possible. Then the sacrament is seen for what it is—a part of the prayer of the Church and an encounter with the Lord. The sign of the sacrament will be further enhanced by avoiding undue haste in prayer and action.

100. The priest should inquire about the physical and 37
spiritual condition of the sick person and he should become 64 66
acquainted with the family, friends, and others who may be present. The sick person and others may help to plan the celebration, for example, by choosing the readings and prayers. It will be especially helpful if the sick person, the priest, and the family become accustomed to praying together.

In the choice of readings the condition of the sick person should be kept in mind. The readings and the homily should help those present to reach a deeper understanding of the mystery of human suffering in relation to the paschal mystery of Christ.

The sick person who is not confined to bed may take part in the sacrament of anointing in a church, chapel, or other appropriate place. He or she should be made comfortable and there should be room for relatives and friends. In hospitals and other institutions the priest should consider all who will be present for the celebration: whether they are able to take part; whether they are very weak; and, if they are not Catholic, whether they might be offended.

101. If the sick person wishes to celebrate the sacrament of 65
penance, it is preferable that the priest make himself available 86
for this during a previous visit. If it is necessary to celebrate

the sacrament of penance during the rite of anointing, it takes the place of the penitential rite. The priest should also arrange for the continued pastoral care of the sick, especially for frequent opportunities to receive communion.

102. The sacrament of anointing may be repeated: 9

a. when the sick person recovers after being anointed and, at 11
a later time, becomes sick again;
b. when during the same illness the condition of the sick person becomes more serious.

In the case of a person who is chronically ill, or elderly and in a weakened condition, the sacrament of anointing may be repeated when in the pastoral judgment of the priest the condition of the sick person warrants the repetition of the sacrament.

103. A sick person who recovers after being anointed should 40c
be encouraged to give thanks for the favors received, especially by participating in a Mass of thanksgiving.

CELEBRATING THE SACRAMENT OF ANOINTING

104. There are three distinct and integral aspects to the celebration of this sacrament: the prayer of faith, the laying on of hands, and the anointing with oil.

105. *Prayer of faith:* The community, asking God's help for the sick, makes its prayer of faith in response to God's word and in a spirit of trust (see James 5:14-15). In the rites for the sick, it is the people of God who pray in faith. The entire Church is made present in this community—represented by at least the priest, family, friends, and others—assembled to pray for those to be anointed. If they are able, the sick persons should also join in this prayer.

106. *Laying on of hands:* The gospels contain a number of instances in which Jesus healed the sick by the laying on of hands or even by the simple gesture of touch. The ritual has restored to major significance the gesture of the laying on of hands with its several meanings. With this gesture the priest indicates that this particular person is the object of the Church's prayer of faith. The laying on of hands is clearly a

sign of blessing, as we pray that by the power of God's healing grace the sick person may be restored to health or at least strengthened in time of illness. The laying on of hands is also an invocation: the Church prays for the coming of the Holy Spirit upon the sick person. Above all, it is the biblical gesture of healing and indeed Jesus' own usual manner of healing: "They brought the sick with various diseases to him; and he laid hands on every one of them and healed them" (Luke 4:40).

107. *Anointing with oil:* The practice of anointing the sick with oil signifies healing, strengthening, and the presence of the Spirit.

In the gospel of Mark the disciples were sent out by the Lord to continue his healing ministry: "They anointed many sick people with oil and cured them" (Mark 6:13). And Saint James witnesses to the fact that the Church continued to anoint the sick with oil as both a means and a sign of healing (James 5:14). The Church's use of oil for healing is closely related to its remedial use in soothing and comforting the sick and in restoring the tired and the weak. Thus the sick person is strengthened to fight against the physically and spiritually debilitating effects of illness. The prayer for blessing the oil of the sick reminds us, furthermore, that the oil of anointing is the sacramental sign of the presence, power, and grace of the Holy Spirit.

If the anointing is to be an effective sacramental symbol, there should be a generous use of oil so that it will be seen and felt by the sick person as a sign of the Spirit's healing and strengthening presence. For the same reason, it is not desirable to wipe off the oil after the anointing.

ANOINTING OF THE SICK WITH A LARGE CONGREGATION

108. The rites for anointing outside Mass and anointing 67
within Mass may be used to anoint a number of people within 83 84
the same celebration. These rites are appropriate for large 85
gatherings of a diocese, parish, or society for the sick, or for pilgrimages. These celebrations should take place in a church, chapel, or other appropriate place where the sick and others can easily gather. On occasion, they may also take place in hospitals and other institutions.

If the Ordinary decides that many people are to be anointed in the same celebration, either he or his delgate should ensure that all disciplinary norms concerning anointing are observed, as well as the norms for pastoral preparation and liturgical celebration. In particular, the practice of indiscriminately anointing numbers of people on these occasions simply because they are ill or have reached an advanced age is to be avoided. Only those whose health is seriously impaired by sickness or old age are proper subjects for the sacrament. The Ordinary also designates the priests who will take part in the celebration of the sacrament.

The full participation of those present must be fostered by every means, especially through the use of appropriate songs, so that the celebration manifests the Easter joy which is proper to this sacrament.

109. The communal rite begins with a greeting followed by a 87
reception of the sick (see no. 135), which is a sympathetic 91
expression of Christ's concern for those who are ill and of the role of the sick in the people of God.

Before the rite of dismissal the blessing is given. The celebration may conclude with an appropriate song.

110. If there are large numbers of sick people to be anointed, 67
other priests may assist the celebrant. Each priest lays hands 90
on some of the sick and anoints them, using the sacramental form. Everything else is done once for all, and the prayers are said in the plural by the celebrant. After the sacramental form has been heard at least once by those present, suitable songs may be sung while the rest of the sick are being anointed.

ANOINTING OUTSIDE MASS

INTRODUCTION

He has borne our sickness and endured our suffering.

111. The rite which follows provides for the celebration of the sacrament of anointing outside Mass. This celebration takes place in the home, in a hospital or institution, or in church. Appropriate vestments should be worn by the priest. 68

112. The priest should inquire beforehand about the physical and spiritual condition of the sick person and he should become acquainted with the family, friends, and others who may be present. If possible, he should involve them in the preparation for the celebration, for example, in the choice of the readings and prayers, and he should explain to them the significance of the sacrament. Since the liturgical texts appear in the singular, they must be adapted in gender and number for a celebration in which two or more people are anointed. 64 85

113. If the sick person wishes to celebrate the sacrament of penance, it is preferable that the priest make himself available for this during a previous visit. If it is necessary for the sick person to confess during the celebration of the sacrament of anointing, this takes the place of the penitential rite. 65 86

114. If communion is to be given during the celebration, this occurs after the liturgy of anointing. 78

INTRODUCTORY RITES

GREETING

115. The priest greets the sick person and the others present. One of the greetings in no. 81 may be used. 68

If communion is to take place during the rite, the priest then places the blessed sacrament on the table, and all join in adoration. 68

SPRINKLING WITH HOLY WATER

116. If it seems desirable, the priest may sprinkle the sick person and those present with holy water. One of the following may be used: 69

A

The Lord is our shepherd
and leads us to streams of living water.

B

Like a stream in parched land,
may the grace of the Lord
refresh our lives.

C

Let this water call to mind our baptism into Christ, 69
who by his death and resurrection has redeemed us.

INSTRUCTION

117. Then he addresses those present in these or similar words: 70

My dear friends, we are gathered here in the name of our Lord Jesus Christ who is present among us. As the gospels relate, the sick came to him for healing; moreover, he loves us so much that he died for our sake. Through the apostle James, he has commanded us: "Are there any who are sick among you? Let them send for the priests of the Church, and let the priests pray over them, anointing them with oil in the name of the Lord; and the prayer of faith will save the sick persons, and the Lord will raise them up; and if they have committed any sins, their sins will be forgiven them."

Let us therefore commend our sick brother/sister N. to the grace and power of Christ, that he may save him/her and raise him/her up.

If the sacrament of penance is now celebrated (see Appendix, p. 737) the penitential rite is omitted. 65

PENITENTIAL RITE

118. The priest invites the sick person and all present to join in the penitential rite, using these or similar words: 52 88

A

My brothers and sisters, to prepare ourselves for this holy anointing, let us call to mind our sins.

B

My brothers and sisters, as we prepare to celebrate this holy sacrament, let us acknowledge our failings and ask the Lord for pardon and strength.

C

My brothers and sisters, let us turn with confidence to the Lord and ask his forgiveness for all our sins.

D

Coming together as God's family, with confidence let us ask the Lord's forgiveness, for he is full of gentleness and compassion.

After a brief period of silence, the penitential rite continues, using one of the following:

A All say:

I confess to almighty God, 52
and to you, my brothers and sisters, 74
that I have sinned through my own fault

They strike their breast.

in my thoughts and in my words,
in what I have done,
and in what I have failed to do;
and I ask blessed Mary, ever virgin,
all the angels and saints,
and you, my brothers and sisters,
to pray for me to the Lord our God.

B

Lord Jesus, you healed the sick:
Lord, have mercy.
℟. Lord, have mercy.

Lord Jesus, you forgave sinners:
Christ, have mercy.
℟. Christ, have mercy.

Lord Jesus, you give us yourself to heal us and bring us strength:
Lord, have mercy.
℟. Lord, have mercy.

C

By your paschal mystery 233
you have won for us salvation:
Lord, have mercy.
℟. Lord, have mercy.

You renew among us now
the wonders of your passion:
Christ, have mercy.
℟. Christ, have mercy.

When we receive your body,
you share with us your paschal sacrifice:
Lord, have mercy.
℟. Lord, have mercy.

The priest concludes the penitential rite with the following: 52

May almighty God have mercy on us,
forgive us our sins,
and bring us to everlasting life.
℟. Amen.

LITURGY OF THE WORD

READING

119. The word of God is proclaimed by one of those present or by the priest. An appropriate reading from Part III or one of the following readings may be used:

A

Matthew 11:25-30 207
Childlike confidence in the goodness of God will bring us the "rest" that only Jesus can give.

B

Mark 2:1-12 210
Much more important than the health of our bodies is the peace and consolation of the presence of Jesus who can forgive us our sins and reconcile us with God.

C

Luke: 18b-23 214
The healing hand of Christ is a sign of the presence of God; that same hand is extended to us in this sacrament now, to console and strengthen us.

RESPONSE

120. A brief period of silence may be observed after the reading of the word of God. 72 89

The priest may then give a brief explanation of the reading, applying it to the needs of the sick person and those who are looking after him or her.

LITURGY OF ANOINTING

LITANY

121. The priest may adapt or shorten the litany according to the condition of the sick person. 73 90

My brothers and sisters, in our prayer of faith let us appeal to God for our brother/sister N. 70

Come and strengthen him/her through this holy anointing: Lord, have mercy.
℟. Lord, have mercy.

Free him/her from all harm: Lord, have mercy. ℟.

Free him/her from sin and all temptation: Lord, have mercy. ℟.

Relieve the sufferings of all the sick [here present]: Lord, have mercy. ℟.

Assist all those dedicated to the care of the sick: Lord, have mercy. ℟.

Give life and health to our brother/sister N., on whom we lay our hands in your name: Lord, have mercy. ℟.

LAYING ON OF HANDS

122. In silence, the priest lays his hands on the head of the sick person. 74 90

PRAYER OVER THE OIL

123. The priest says a prayer of thanksgiving over blessed oil or he may bless the oil himself (see no. 21), using one of the following: 75

Thanksgiving over Blessed Oil—If the oil is already blessed, the priest says the following prayer of thanksgiving over it:

Praise to you, God, the almighty Father.
You sent your Son to live among us
and bring us salvation.
℟. **Blessed be God who heals us in Christ.**

Praise to you, God, the only-begotten Son.
You humbled yourself to share in our humanity
and you heal our infirmities. ℟.

Praise to you, God, the Holy Spirit, the Consoler.
Your unfailing power gives us strength
in our bodily weakness. ℟.

God of mercy,
ease the sufferings and comfort the weakness of your servant N.,
whom the Church anoints with this holy oil.

We ask this through Christ our Lord.
℟. **Amen.**

Blessing of Oil—When the priest blesses the oil during the rite, he uses the following blessing:

Let us pray.

God of all consolation,
you chose and sent your Son to heal the world.
Graciously listen to our prayer of faith:
send the power of your Holy Spirit, the Consoler,
into this precious oil, this soothing ointment,
this rich gift, this fruit of the earth.

Bless this oil ✠ and sanctify it for our use.

Make this oil a remedy for all who are anointed with it;
heal them in body, in soul, and in spirit,
and deliver them from every affliction.

We ask this through our Lord Jesus Christ, your Son,
who lives and reigns with you and the Holy Spirit,
one God, for ever and ever.
℟. **Amen.**

Other forms of the blessing may be found on pp. 666–667 and 712.

ANOINTING

124. The priest anoints the sick person with the blessed oil. 76

First he anoints the forehead, saying:

Through this holy anointing
may the Lord in his love and mercy help you
with the grace of the Holy Spirit.
℟. Amen.

Then he anoints the hands, saying:

May the Lord who frees you from sin
save you and raise you up.
℟. Amen.

The sacramental form is said only once, for the anointing of the forehead and hands, and is not repeated.

Depending upon the culture and traditions of the place, as 23
well as the condition of the sick person, the priest may also 24
anoint additional parts of the body, for example, the area of pain or injury. He does not repeat the sacramental form.

PRAYER AFTER ANOINTING

125. The priest says one of the following prayers: 77 90

Let us pray.

A General

Father in heaven,
through this holy anointing
grant N. comfort in his/her suffering.

When he/she is afraid, give him/her courage,
when afflicted, give him/her patience,
when dejected, afford him/her hope,
and when alone, assure him/her of the support
of your holy people.

We ask this through Christ our Lord.
℟. Amen.

B General

Lord Jesus Christ, our Redeemer, 77
by the grace of your Holy Spirit
cure the weakness of your servant N.

Heal his/her sickness and forgive his/her sins;
expel all afflictions of mind and body;
mercifully restore him/her to full health,
and enable him/her to resume his/her former duties,
for you are Lord for ever and ever.
℟. Amen.

C In extreme or terminal illness

Lord Jesus Christ, 77
you chose to share our human nature,
to redeem all people, and to heal the sick.

Look with compassion upon your servant N.,
whom we have anointed in your name with this holy oil
for the healing of his/her body and spirit.

Support him/her with your power,
comfort him/her with your protection,
and give him/her the strength to fight against evil.

Since you have given him/her a share in your own passion,
help him/her to find hope in suffering,
for you are Lord for ever and ever.
℟. Amen.

D In advanced age

God of mercy, 243
look kindly on your servant
who has grown weak under the burden of years.
In this holy anointing
he/she asks for healing in body and soul.

Fill him/her with the strength of your Holy Spirit.
Keep him/her firm in faith and serene in hope,
so that he/she may give us all an example of patience
and joyfully witness to the power of your love.

We ask this through Christ our Lord.
℟. Amen.

E Before surgery

God of compassion,
our human weakness lays claim to your strength.

We pray that through the skills of surgeons and nurses
your healing gifts may be granted to N.

May your servant respond to your healing will
and be reunited with us at your altar of praise.

Grant this through Christ our Lord.
℟. Amen.

F For a child
God our Father,
we have anointed your child N.
with the oil of healing and peace.

Caress him/her,
Shelter him/her,
and keep him/her in your tender care.

We ask this in the name of Jesus the Lord.
℟. Amen

G For a young person
God our healer,
in this time of sickness you have come
to bless N. with your grace.

Restore him/her to health and strength,
make him/her joyful in spirit,
and ready to embrace your will.

Grant this through Christ our Lord.
℟. Amen.

THE LORD'S PRAYER

126. The priest introduces the Lord's Prayer in these or similar words: 78

A

Now let us offer together the prayer our Lord Jesus Christ taught us:

B

And now let us pray with confidence as Christ our Lord commanded:

All say:

Our Father . . .

If the sick person does not receive communion, the rite concludes with a blessing as in no. 130. 79

LITURGY OF HOLY COMMUNION

COMMUNION

127. The priest shows the eucharistic bread to those present, saying: 55

A

This is the Lamb of God
who takes away the sins of the world.
Come to me, all you that labor and are burdened,
and I will refresh you.

B

These are God's holy gifts to his holy people:
receive them with thanksgiving.

C

This is the bread of life.
Taste and see that the Lord is good.

The rite then continues as described in no. 88.

SILENT PRAYER

128. Then a period of silence may be observed. 57

PRAYER AFTER COMMUNION

129. The priest says a concluding prayer. One of the following may be used: 57

Let us pray.

Pause for silent prayer, if this has not preceded.

A

All-powerful God,
through the paschal mystery of Christ your Son 234
you have completed the work of our redemption.

May we, who in these sacramental signs
proclaim his death and resurrection,
grow in the experience of your saving power.

We ask this through Christ our Lord.
℟. Amen.

B

All-powerful God, 236
we thank you for the nourishment you give us
through your holy gift.

Pour out your Spirit upon us
and in the strength of this food from heaven
keep us single-minded in your service.

We ask this in the name of Jesus the Lord.
℟. Amen.

C

All-powerful and ever-living God, 57
may the body and blood of Christ your Son
be for our brother/sister N.
a lasting remedy for body and soul.

We ask this through Christ our lord.
℟. Amen.

CONCLUDING RITE

BLESSING

130. The priest blesses the sick person and the others 58
present, using one of the following blessings. If, however, 79
any of the blessed sacrament remains, he may bless the sick person by making a sign of the cross with the blessed sacrament, in silence.

A

May the Lord be with you to protect you. 237
℟. Amen.

May he guide you and give you strength.
℟. Amen.

May he watch over you, keep you in his care,
and bless you with his peace.
℟. Amen.

May almighty God bless you,
the Father, and the Son, ✠ and the Holy Spirit.
℟. Amen.

B
May God the Father bless you. 79
℟. Amen.

May God the Son heal you.
℟. Amen.

May God the Holy Spirit enlighten you.
℟. Amen.

May almighty God bless you,
the Father, and the Son, ✠ and the Holy Spirit.
℟. Amen.

C
May the God of all consolation 79
bless you in every way
and grant you hope all the days of your life.
℟. Amen.

May God restore you to health
and grant you salvation.
℟. Amen.

May God fill your heart with peace
and lead you to eternal life.
℟. Amen.

May almighty God bless you,
the Father, and the Son, ✠ and the Holy Spirit.
℟. Amen.

D
May the blessing of almighty God, 238
the Father, and the Son, ✠ and the Holy Spirit,
come upon you and remain with you for ever.
℟. Amen.

ANOINTING WITHIN MASS

INTRODUCTION

If one member suffers, all share in those sufferings.

131. When the condition of the sick person permits, and 80
especially when communion is to be received, the sacrament of anointing may be celebrated within Mass. The following rite provides for such a celebration, which takes place in a church or, with the consent of the Ordinary, in a suitable place in the home of the sick person or in the hospital.

132. This rite may be used to anoint a number of people 67
within the same celebration (see nos. 108-110). It is especially 83
appropriate for large gatherings of a diocese, parish, or society for the sick, or for pilgrimages. Since the liturgical texts appear in the plural, they must be adapted in gender and number for a celebration in which one person is anointed.

133. The priest should ensure that the sick who wish to 65
celebrate the sacrament of penance have a convenient 86
opportunity to do so before Mass.

134. When the ritual Mass for the anointing of the sick is 81
celebrated, the priest wears white vestments. The readings are taken from *The Lectionary for Mass* (2nd edition, nos. 790-795) or from Part III, unless the sick person and those involved with the priest in planning the liturgy choose other readings from Scripture.

The ritual Mass for the anointing of the sick is not permitted during the Easter triduum, on the solemnities of Christmas, Epiphany, Ascension, Pentecost, Corpus Christi, or on a solemnity which is a holy day of obligation. On these occasions, the texts and readings are taken from the Mass of the day. Although the ritual Mass is also excluded on the Sundays of Advent, Lent, and the Easter season, on solemnities, Ash Wednesday, and the weekdays of Holy Week, one of the readings may be taken from the Scripture texts indicated above, and the special form of the final blessing may be used.

INTRODUCTORY RITES

RECEPTION OF THE SICK

135. After the greeting the priest welcomes the sick in these or similar words: 92

A

We have come together to celebrate the sacraments of anointing and eucharist. Christ is always present when we gather in his name; today we welcome him especially as physician and healer. We pray that the sick may be restored to health by the gift of his mercy and made whole in his fullness.

B

Christ taught his disciples to be a community of love. In praying together, in sharing all things, and in caring for the sick, they recalled his words: "Insofar as you did this to one of these, you did it to me." We gather today to witness to this teaching and to pray in the name of Jesus the healer that the sick may be restored to health. Through this eucharist and anointing we invoke his healing power.

OPENING PRAYER

136. Afterward the priest, with hands joined, sings or says:

Let us pray.

All pray in silence for a brief period.

A

Father,
you raised your Son's cross
as the sign of victory and life.

May all who share in his suffering
find in these sacraments
a source of fresh courage and healing.

We ask this through our Lord Jesus Christ, your Son,
who lives and reigns with you and the Holy Spirit,
one God, for ever and ever.
℟. **Amen.**

B

God of compassion,
you take every family under your care
and know our physical and spiritual needs.

Transform our weakness by the strength of your grace
and confirm us in your covenant
so that we may grow in faith and love.

We ask this through our Lord Jesus Christ, your Son,
who lives and reigns with you and the Holy Spirit,
one God, for ever and ever.
℟. Amen.

LITURGY OF THE WORD

137. The liturgy of the word is celebrated in the usual way 92
according to the instructions in no. 134. The general 82a 89
intercessions are omitted since they are included in the litany.

In the homily the celebrant should show how the sacred text speaks of the meaning of illness in the history of salvation and of the grace given by the sacrament of anointing.

A brief period of silence may follow the homily.

LITURGY OF ANOINTING

LITANY

138. The priest may adapt or shorten the litany according to 73
the condition of the sick persons. 82b

Let us pray to God for our brothers and sisters and for all those who devote themselves to caring for them. 241

Bless N. and N. and fill them with new hope and strength: Lord, have mercy.
℟. Lord, have mercy.

Relieve their pain: Lord, have mercy. ℟.

Free them from sin and do not let them give way to temptation: Lord, have mercy. ℟.

Sustain all the sick with your power: Lord, have mercy. ℟.

Assist all who care for the sick: Lord, have mercy. ℟.

Give life and health to our brothers and sisters on whom we lay our hands in your name: Lord, have mercy. ℟.

LAYING ON OF HANDS

139. In silence, the priest lays his hands on the head of each sick person. If there are several priests present, each one lays hands on some of the sick. 74 82b 90

PRAYER OVER THE OIL

140. The priest says a prayer of thanksgiving over blessed oil or he may bless the oil himself (see no. 21), using one of the following: 75 75b 82b

Thanksgiving over Blessed Oil—If the oil is already blessed, the priest says the following prayer of thanksgiving over it:

Praise to you, God, the almighty Father.
You sent your Son to live among us
and bring us salvation.
℟. Blessed be God who heals us in Christ.

Praise to you, God, the only-begotten Son.
You humbled yourself to share in our humanity
and you heal our infirmities. ℟.

Praise to you, God, the Holy Spirit, the Consoler.
Your unfailing power gives us strength
in our bodily weakness. ℟.

God of mercy,
ease the sufferings and comfort the weakness of your servants
whom the Church anoints with this holy oil.

We ask this through Christ our Lord.
℟. Amen.

Blessing of Oil—When the priest blesses the oil during the rite, he uses one of the following blessings: 75

A

This blessing is found on page 656.

B

Praise to you, God, the almighty Father. 242
You sent your Son to live among us
and bring us salvation.
℟. Blessed be God who heals us in Christ.

Praise to you, God, the only-begotten Son.
You humbled yourself to share in our humanity
and you heal our infirmities. ℟.

Praise to you, God, the Holy Spirit, the Consoler.
Your unfailing power gives us strength
in our bodily weakness. ℟.

Almighty God,
come to our aid and sanctify this oil
which has been set apart for healing your people.
May the prayer of faith and the anointing with oil
free them from every affliction.

We ask this through Christ our Lord.
℟. Amen.

ANOINTING

141. The priest anoints the sick person with the blessed oil. If 76
there are large numbers of sick people to be anointed, other 90
priests may assist the celebrant. Each priest anoints some of the sick, using the sacramental form as described in no. 124.

PRAYER AFTER ANOINTING

142. The priest says one of the following prayers A-D, as in 82c
no. 125.

LITURGY OF THE EUCHARIST

143. The Order of Mass then continues with the liturgy of the 82c
eucharist.

PRAYER OVER THE GIFTS

144. With hands extended, the priest sings or says:

A

Merciful God,
as these simple gifts of bread and wine
will be transformed into the risen Lord,
so may he unite our sufferings with his
and cause us to rise to new life.

We ask this through Christ our Lord.
℟. Amen.

B

Lord,
we bring you these gifts,
to become the health-giving body and blood of your Son.

In his name
heal the ills which afflict us
and restore to us the joy of life renewed.

We ask this through Christ our Lord.
℟. Amen.

EUCHARISTIC PRAYER

145. The priest begins the eucharistic prayer. With hands extended he sings or says:

The Lord be with you.
℟. And also with you.

Lift up your hearts.
℟. We lift them up to the Lord.

Let us give thanks to the Lord our God.
℟. It is right to give him thanks and praise.

Father, all-powerful and ever-living God,
we do well always and everywhere to give you thanks,
for you have revealed to us
in Christ the healer
your unfailing power and steadfast compassion.

In the splendor of his rising
your Son conquered suffering and death
and bequeathed to us his promise
of a new and glorious world,

where no bodily pain will afflict us
and no anguish of spirit.

Through your gift of the Spirit,
you bless us, even now,
with comfort and healing,
strength and hope,
forgiveness and peace.

In this supreme sacrament of your love
you give us the risen body of your Son:
a pattern of what we shall become
when he returns again at the end of time.

In gladness and joy
we unite with the angels and saints
in the great canticle of creation,
as we say (sing):

Holy, holy, holy Lord, God of power and might,
heaven and earth are full of your glory.
Hosanna in the highest.
Blessed is he who comes in the name of the Lord.
Hosanna in the highest.

Special Intercessions—The following embolisms may be used with Eucharistic Prayers I, II, and III.

When Eucharistic Prayer I is used, the special form of "Father, accept this offering," is said:

Father, accept this offering
from your whole family,
and especially from those who ask for healing
of body, mind, and spirit.
Grant us your peace in this life,
save us from final damnation,
and count us among those you have chosen.

When Eucharistic Prayer II is used, after the words "and all the clergy," there is added:

Remember also those who ask for healing
in the name of your Son,
that they may never cease to praise you
for the wonders of your power.

When Eucharistic Prayer III is used, after the words "the family you have gathered here," there is added:

Hear especially the prayers of those who ask for healing
in the name of your Son,
that they may never cease to praise you
for the wonders of your power.

PRAYER AFTER COMMUNION

146. With hands extended, the priest sings or says:

Let us pray.

Pause for silent prayer, if this has not preceded.

A
Merciful God,
in celebrating these mysteries
your people have received the gifts of unity and peace.

Heal the afflicted
and make them whole
in the name of your only Son,
who lives and reigns for ever and ever.
℟. Amen.

B
Lord,
through these sacraments
you offer us the gift of healing.

May this grace bear fruit among us
and make us strong in your service.

We ask this through Christ our Lord.
℟. Amen.

CONCLUDING RITES

BLESSING

147. Then the priest blesses the sick persons and others present, using one of the following:

A

May the God of all consolation 79
bless you in every way
and grant you hope all the days of your life.
℟. Amen.

May God restore you to health
and grant you salvation.
℟. Amen.

May God fill your heart with peace
and lead you to eternal life.
℟. Amen.

May almighty God bless you,
the Father, and the Son, ✠ and the Holy Spirit.
℟. Amen.

B

May the Lord be with you to protect you. 237
℟. Amen.

May he guide you and give you strength.
℟. Amen.

May he watch over you, keep you in his care,
and bless you with his peace.
℟. Amen.

May almighty God bless you,
the Father, and the Son, ✠ and the Holy Spirit.
℟. Amen.

C

May the blessing of almighty God, 238
the Father, and the Son, ✠ and the Holy Spirit,
come upon you and remain with you for ever.
℟. Amen.

DISMISSAL

148. The deacon (or the priest) then dismisses the people and commends the sick to their care.

ANOINTING IN A HOSPITAL OR INSTITUTION

INTRODUCTION

Have faith in God, and faith in me.

149. Although the sacrament of anointing should be celebrated whenever possible in accordance with the full rites already given, the special circumstances of hospital ministry often make it necessary to abbreviate the rite. The rite which follows is a simplification of the anointing rite and preserves its central elements. It is intended for those occasions when only the priest and sick person are present and the complete rite cannot be celebrated.

150. The priest should inquire beforehand about the physical 64
and spiritual condition of the sick person in order to plan the celebration properly and choose the appropriate prayers. If possible he should involve the sick person in this preparation, and should explain the significance of the sacrament.

151. If the sick person wishes to celebrate the sacrament of 65
penance, it is preferable that the priest make himself available for this during a previous visit. If it is necessary, this may take place during the introductory rites.

152. The circumstances of an emergency room or casualty ward of a hospital may make the proper celebration of the sacrament difficult. If the condition of the sick person does not make anointing urgent, the priest may find it better to wait for a more appropriate time to celebrate the sacrament.

153. The priest should arrange for the continued pastoral care of the sick person, especially for frequent opportunities to receive communion.

INTRODUCTORY RITES

GREETING

154. The priest greets the sick person. One of the following 68
may be used:

A

The peace of the Lord be with you always.
℟. And also with you.

B

The grace and peace of God our Father and the Lord Jesus Christ be with you. 231
℟. And also with you.

INSTRUCTION

155. The priest may prepare the sick person for the liturgy of anointing with an instruction (see no. 117) or with the following prayer: 70

Lord God, 239
you have said to us through your apostle James:
"Are there people sick among you?
Let them send for the priests of the Church,
and let the priests pray over them
anointing them with oil in the name of the Lord.
The prayer of faith will save the sick persons,
and the Lord will raise them up.
If they have committed any sins,
their sins will be forgiven them."

Lord,
we have gathered here in your name
and we ask you to be among us,
to watch over our brother/sister N.
We ask this with confidence,
for you live and reign for ever and ever.
℟. Amen.

If the sick person so wishes, the sacrament of penance may now be celebrated (see Appendix, p. 737). 65

LITURGY OF ANOINTING

LAYING ON OF HANDS

156. In silence, the priest lays his hands on the head of the sick person. 74

ANOINTING

157. The rite is as described in no. 124. 76

THE LORD'S PRAYER

158. The priest introduces the Lord's Prayer in these or similar words: 78

A

Now let us pray to God as our Lord Jesus Christ taught us:

B

And now let us pray with confidence as Christ our Lord commanded:

All say:

Our Father . . .

PRAYER AFTER ANOINTING

159. The priest says one of the prayers given in no. 125. 77

CONCLUDING RITE

BLESSING

160. Then the priest blesses the sick person, using one of the following: 79

A

May the blessing of almighty God, 238
the Father, and the Son, ✠ and the Holy Spirit,
come upon you and remain with you for ever.
℟. **Amen.**

B

May God the Father bless you. 79
℟. **Amen.**

May God the Son heal you.
℟. **Amen.**

May God the Holy Spirit enlighten you.
℟. **Amen.**

May almighty God bless you,
the Father, and the Son, + and the Holy Spirit.
℟. **Amen.**

PART II

PASTORAL CARE OF THE DYING

INTRODUCTION

When we were baptized in Christ Jesus we were baptized into his death . . . so that as Christ was raised from the dead by the Father's glory, we too might live a new life.

161. The rites in Part II of *Pastoral Care of the Sick: Rites of Anointing and Viaticum* are used by the Church to comfort and strengthen a dying Christian in the passage from this life. The ministry to the dying places emphasis on trust in the Lord's promise of eternal life rather than on the struggle against illness which is characteristic of the pastoral care of the sick.

The first three chapters of Part II provide for those situations in which time is not a pressing concern and the rites can be celebrated fully and properly. These are to be clearly distinguished from the rites contained in Chapter Eight, "Rites for Exceptional Circumstances," which provide for the emergency situations sometimes encountered in the ministry to the dying.

162. Priests with pastoral responsibilities are to direct the 142
efforts of the family and friends as well as other ministers of the local Church in the care of the dying. They should ensure that all are familiar with the rites provided here.

The words "priest," "deacon," and "minister" are used advisedly. Only in those rites which must be celebrated by a priest is the word "priest" used in the rubrics (that is, the sacrament of penance, the sacrament of the anointing of the sick, the celebration of viaticum within Mass). Whenever it is clear that, in the absence of a priest, a deacon may preside at a particular rite, the words "priest or deacon" are used in the rubrics. Whenever another minister is permitted to celebrate a rite in the absence of a priest or deacon, the word "minister" is used in the rubrics, even though in many cases the rite will be celebrated by a priest or deacon.

163. The Christian community has a continuing 138
responsibility to pray for and with the person who is dying. Through its sacramental ministry to the dying the community

helps Christians to embrace death in mysterious union with the crucified and risen Lord, who awaits them in the fullness of life.

CELEBRATION OF VIATICUM

164. A rite for viaticum within Mass and another for viaticum outside Mass are provided. If possible, and with the permission of the Ordinary, viaticum should take place within the full eucharistic celebration, with the family, friends, and other members of the Christian community taking part. The rite for viaticum outside Mass is used when the full eucharistic celebration cannot take place. Again, if it is possible, others should take part. 94

COMMENDATION OF THE DYING

165. The second chapter of Part II contains a collection of prayers for the spiritual comfort of the Christian who is close to death. These prayers are traditionally called the commendation of the dying to God and are to be used according to the circumstances of each case.

PRAYERS FOR THE DEAD

166. A chapter has also been provided to assist a minister who has been called to attend a person who is already dead. A priest is not to administer the sacrament of anointing. Instead, he should pray for the dead person, using prayers such as those which appear in this chapter. He may find it necessary to explain to the family of the person who is dead that sacraments are celebrated for the living, not for the dead, and that the dead are effectively helped by the prayers of the living. 15

RITES FOR EXCEPTIONAL CIRCUMSTANCES

167. Chapter VIII, "Rites for Exceptional Circumstances," contains rites which should be celebrated with a person who has suddenly been placed in proximate or immediate danger of death. They are for emergency circumstances and should be used only when such pressing conditions exist.

CARE OF A DYING CHILD

168. In its ministry to the dying the Church must also respond to the difficult circumstances of a dying child. Although no specific rites appear in Part II for the care of a

dying child, these notes are provided to help bring into focus the various aspects of this ministry.

169. When parents learn that their child is dying, they are often bewildered and hurt. In their love for their son or daughter, they may be beset by temptations and doubts and find themselves asking: Why is God taking this child from us? How have we sinned or failed that God would punish us in this way? Why is this innocent child being hurt?

Under these trying circumstances, much of the Church's ministry will be directed to the parents and family. While pain and suffering in an innocent child are difficult for others to bear, the Church helps the parents and family to accept what God has allowed to happen. It should be understood by all beforehand that this process of acceptance will probably extend beyond the death of the child. The concern of the Christian community should continue as long as necessary.

Concern for the child must be equal to that for the family. Those who deal with dying children observe that their faith matures rapidly. Though young children often seem to accept death more easily than adults, they will often experience a surprisingly mature anguish because of the pain which they see in their families.

170. At such a time, it is important for members of the Christian community to come to the support of the child and the family by prayer, visits, and other forms of assistance. Those who have lost children of their own have a ministry of consolation and support to the family. Hospital personnel (doctors, nurses, aides) should also be prepared to exercise a special role with the child as caring adults. Priests and deacons bear particular responsibility for overseeing all these elements of the Church's pastoral ministry. The minister should invite members of the community to use their individual gifts in this work of communal care and concern.

171. By conversation and brief services of readings and prayers, the minister may help the parents and family to see that their child is being called ahead of them to enter the kingdom and joy of the Lord. The period when the child is dying can become a special time of renewal and prayer for the family and close friends. The minister should help them to see that the child's sufferings are united to those of Jesus for the salvation of the whole world.

172. If it is appropriate, the priest should discuss with the parents the possibility of preparing and celebrating with the child the sacraments of initiation (baptism, confirmation, eucharist). The priest may baptize and confirm the child (see *Rite of Confirmation*, no. 7b). To complete the process of initiation, the child should also receive first communion.

According to the circumstances, some of these rites may be celebrated by a deacon or lay person. So that the child and family may receive full benefit from them, these rites are normally celebrated over a period of time. In this case, the minister should use the usual rites, that is, the *Rite of Baptism for Children*, the *Rite of Confirmation*, and if suitable, the *Rite of Penance*. Similarly, if time allows, the usual rites for anointing and viaticum should be celebrated.

173. If sudden illness or an accident has placed an uninitiated child in proximate danger of death, the minister uses "Christian Initiation for the Dying" (p. 719), adapting it for use with a child.

174. For an initiated child or a child lacking only the sacrament of confirmation, who is in proximate danger of death, the "Continuous Rite of Penance, Anointing, and Viaticum" (p. 708) may be used and adapted to the understanding of the child. If death is imminent it should be remembered that viaticum rather than anointing is the sacrament for the dying.

CHAPTER V

CELEBRATION OF VIATICUM

INTRODUCTION

I am going to prepare a place for you; I shall come back and take you with me.

175. This chapter contains a rite for viaticum within Mass and a rite for viaticum outside Mass. The celebration of the eucharist as viaticum, food for the passage through death to eternal life, is the sacrament proper to the dying Christian. It is the completion and crown of the Christian life on this earth, signifying that the Christian follows the Lord to eternal glory and the banquet of the heavenly kingdom.

The sacrament of the anointing of the sick should be celebrated at the beginning of a serious illness. Viaticum, celebrated when death is close, will then be better understood as the last sacrament of Christian life.

176. Priests and other ministers entrusted with the spiritual 93
care of the sick should do everything they can to ensure that those in proximate danger of death receive the body and blood of Christ as viaticum. At the earliest opportunity, the necessary preparations should be given to the dying person, family, and others who may take part.

177. Whenever it is possible, the dying Christian should be 36
able to receive viaticum within Mass. In this way he or she 101
shares fully, during the final moments of this life, in the eucharistic sacrifice, which proclaims the Lord's own passing through death to life. However, circumstances, such as confinement to a hospital ward or the very emergency which makes death imminent, may frequently make the complete eucharistic celebration impossible. In this case, the rite for viaticum outside Mass is appropriate. The minister should wear attire appropriate to this ministry.

178. Because the celebration of viaticum ordinarily takes place in the limited circumstances of the home, a hospital, or other institution, the simplifications of the rite for Masses in small gatherings may be appropriate. Depending on the condition of the dying person, every effort should be made to

involve him or her, the family, friends, and other members of the local community in the planning and celebration. Appropriate readings, prayers, and songs will help to foster the full participation of all. Because of this concern for participation, the minister should ensure that viaticum is celebrated while the dying person is still able to take part and respond.

179. A distinctive feature of the celebration of viaticum, 28
whether within or outside Mass, is the renewal of the 108
baptismal profession of faith by the dying person. This occurs after the homily and replaces the usual form of the profession of faith. Through the baptismal profession at the end of earthly life, the one who is dying uses the language of his or her initial commitment, which is renewed each Easter and on other occasions in the Christian life. In the context of viaticum, it is a renewal and fulfillment of initiation into the Christian mysteries, baptism leading to the eucharist.

180. The rites of viaticum within and outside Mass may 99d
include the sign of peace. The minister and all who are 114
present embrace the dying Christian. In this and in other parts of the celebration the sense of leave-taking need not be concealed or denied, but the joy of Christian hope, which is the comfort and strength of the one near death, should also be evident.

181. As an indication that the reception of the eucharist by 26
the dying Christian is a pledge of resurrection and food for 95 96
the passage through death, the special words proper to viaticum are added: "May the Lord Jesus Christ protect you and lead you to eternal life." The dying person and all who are present may receive communion under both kinds. The sign of communion is more complete when received in this manner because it expresses more fully and clearly the nature of the eucharist as a meal, one which prepares all who take part in it for the heavenly banquet (see General Instruction of *The Roman Missal,* no. 240).

The minister should choose the manner of giving communion under both kinds which is suitable in the particular case. If the wine is consecrated at a Mass not celebrated in the presence of the sick person, the blood of the Lord is kept in a properly covered vessel and is placed in the tabernacle after communion. The precious blood should be carried to the sick person in a vessel which is closed in such a way as to eliminate all danger of spilling. If some of the precious blood remains after communion, it should be consumed by the minister, who should also see to it that the vessel is properly purified.

The sick who are unable to receive under the form of bread may receive under the form of wine alone. If the wine is consecrated at a Mass not celebrated in the presence of the sick person, the instructions given above are followed.

182. In addition to these elements of the rites which are to be given greater stress, special texts are provided for the general intercessions or litany and the final solemn blessing.

183. It often happens that a person who has received the eucharist as viaticum lingers in a grave condition or at the point of death for a period of days or longer. In these circumstances he or she should be given the opportunity to receive the eucharist as viaticum on successive days, frequently if not daily. This may take place during or outside Mass as particular conditions permit. The rite may be simplified according to the condition of the one who is dying.

VIATICUM WITHIN MASS

184. When viaticum is received within Mass, the ritual Mass 97
for Viaticum or the Mass of the Holy Eucharist may be 99f
celebrated. The priest wears white vestments. The readings may be taken from *The Lectionary for Mass* (2nd edition, nos. 796-800) or from Part III of this ritual, unless the dying person and those involved with the priest in planning the liturgy choose other readings from Scripture.

A ritual Mass is not permitted during the Easter triduum, on the solemnities of Christmas, Epiphany, Ascension, Pentecost, Corpus Christi, or on a solemnity which is a holy day of obligation. On these occasions, the texts and readings are taken from the Mass of the day. Although the Mass for Viaticum or the Mass of the Holy Eucharist are also excluded on the Sundays of Advent, Lent, and the Easter season, on solemnities, Ash Wednesday, and the weekdays of Holy Week, one of the readings may be taken from the biblical texts indicated above. The special form of the final blessing may be used and, at the discretion of the priest, the apostolic pardon may be added.

185. If the dying person wishes to celebrate the sacrament of penance, it is preferable that the priest make himself available for this during a previous visit. If this is not possible, the sacrament of penance may be celebrated before Mass begins (see Appendix, p. 737). 98

VIATICUM OUTSIDE MASS

186. Although viaticum celebrated in the context of the full eucharistic celebration is always preferable, when it is not possible the rite for viaticum outside Mass is appropriate. This rite includes some of the elements of the Mass, especially a brief liturgy of the word. Depending on the circumstances and the condition of the dying person, this rite should also be a communal celebration. Every effort should be made to involve the dying person, family, friends, and members of the local community in the planning and celebration. The manner of celebration and the elements of the rite which are used should be accommodated to those present and the nearness of death.

187. If the dying person wishes to celebrate the sacrament of penance and this cannot take place during a previous visit, it should be celebrated before the rite of viaticum begins, especially if others are present. Alternatively, it may be celebrated during the rite of viaticum, replacing the penitential rite. At the discretion of the priest, the apostolic pardon may be added after the penitential rite or after the sacrament of penance. 100

188. An abbreviated liturgy of the word, ordinarily consisting of a single biblical reading, gives the minister an opportunity to explain the word of God in relation to viaticum. The sacrament should be described as the sacred food which strengthens the Christian for the passage through death to life in sure hope of the resurrection. 107

VIATICUM WITHIN MASS

LITURGY OF THE WORD

HOMILY

189. After the gospel a brief homily on the sacred text may be given in which the priest explains the meaning and importance of viaticum. 99a

BAPTISMAL PROFESSION OF FAITH

190. If the sick person is to renew his or her baptismal profession of faith, this should be done at the conclusion of the homily. This renewal takes the place of the usual profession of faith in the Mass. 99b

The priest gives a brief introduction and then asks the following questions: 108

N., do you believe in God, the Father almighty,
creator of heaven and earth?
℟. I do.

Do you believe in Jesus Christ, his only Son, our Lord,
who was born of the Virgin Mary,
was crucified, died, and was buried,
rose from the dead,
and is now seated at the right hand of the Father?
℟. I do.

Do you believe in the Holy Spirit,
the holy catholic Church, the communion of saints,
the forgiveness of sins, the resurrection of the body,
and life everlasting?
℟. I do.

LITANY

191. The priest may adapt or shorten the litany according to the condition of the sick person. The litany may be omitted if the sick person has made the profession of faith and appears to be tiring. 99c

My brothers and sisters, with one heart let us call on our Savior Jesus Christ. 109

You loved us to the very end and gave yourself over to death in order to give us life. For our brother/sister, Lord, we pray:
℟. Lord, hear our prayer.

You said to us: "All who eat my flesh and drink my blood will live forever." For our brother/sister, Lord, we pray: ℟.

You invite us to join in the banquet where pain and sorrow, sadness and separation will be no more. For our brother/sister, Lord, we pray: ℟.

LITURGY OF THE EUCHARIST

SIGN OF PEACE

192. The priest and those present may give the sick person 99d
the sign of peace at the usual place in the Order of Mass.

COMMUNION AS VIATICUM

193. The sick person and all present may receive communion 99e
under both kinds. When the priest gives communion to the sick person, he uses the form for viaticum.

The priest genuflects, takes the eucharistic bread, raises it slightly and, facing those present, says:

A

Jesus Christ is the food for our journey;
he calls us to the heavenly table.

B

This is the Lamb of God 111
who takes away the sins of the world.
Happy are those who are called to his supper.

C

These are God's holy gifts to his holy people:
receive them with thanksgiving.

The sick person and all who are to receive communion say: 111

Lord, I am not worthy to receive you,
but only say the word and I shall be healed.

The priest goes to the sick person and, showing the blessed sacrament, says: 112

The body of Christ.

The sick person answers: "Amen."

Then the priest says:

The blood of Christ.

The sick person answers: "Amen."

Immediately, or after giving communion to the sick person, the priest adds:

May the Lord Jesus Christ protect you
and lead you to eternal life.
℟. Amen.

Others present who wish to receive communion then do so in the usual way.

CONCLUDING RITES

BLESSING

194. At the end of Mass the priest may use one of the blessings B, A, or C, in no. 91. 99f

APOSTOLIC PARDON

195. The priest may add the apostolic pardon for the dying. 99f

Through the holy mysteries of our redemption, 106
may almighty God release you from all punishments
in this life and in the life to come.

May he open to you the gates of paradise
and welcome you to everlasting joy.
℟. Amen.

DISMISSAL

196. The deacon (or priest) then dismisses the people.

VIATICUM OUTSIDE MASS

INTRODUCTORY RITES

GREETING

197. The minister greets the sick person and the others present as described in no. 115. 101

The minister then places the blessed sacrament on the table, and all join in adoration. 101

SPRINKLING WITH HOLY WATER

198. If it seems desirable, the priest or deacon may sprinkle the sick person and those present with holy water. One of the following may be used: 102

A

Let this water call to mind our baptism into Christ,
who by his death and resurrection has redeemed us.

B

The Lord is our shepherd
and leads us to streams of living water.

INSTRUCTION

199. Afterward the minister addresses those present, using the following instruction or one better suited to the sick person's condition. 103

My brothers and sisters, before our Lord Jesus Christ passed from this world to return to the Father, he left us the sacrament of his body and blood. When the hour comes for us to pass from this life and join him, he strengthens us with this food for our journey and comforts us by this pledge of our resurrection.

If the sacrament of penance is now celebrated (see Appendix, p. 737), the penitential rite is omitted. In case of necessity, this may be a generic confession. 104

PENITENTIAL RITE

200. The minister invites the sick person and all present to join in the penitential rite, using these or similar words: 105

A

My brothers and sisters, to prepare ourselves for this celebration, let us call to mind our sins.

B

My brothers and sisters, let us turn with confidence to the Lord and ask his forgiveness for all our sins.

After a brief period of silence, the penitential rite continues, using prayer A or C in no. 118. 105

The minister concludes the penitential rite with the following: 105

May almighty God have mercy on us,
forgive us our sins,
and bring us to everlasting life.
℟. Amen.

APOSTOLIC PARDON

201. At the conclusion of the sacrament of penance or the penitential rite, the priest may give the apostolic pardon for the dying, using one of the following: 106

A

Through the holy mysteries of our redemption,
may almighty God release you from all punishments
in this life and in the life to come.

May he open to you the gates of paradise
and welcome you to everlasting joy.
℟. Amen.

B

By the authority which the Apostolic See has given me,
I grant you a full pardon and the remission of all your sins
in the name of the Father, and of the Son, ✠ and of the Holy Spirit.
℟. Amen.

LITURGY OF THE WORD

READING

202. The word of God is proclaimed by one of those present 107

or by the minister. An appropriate reading from Part III or one of the following may be used:

A John 6:54-55
B John 14:23
C John 15:4
D 1 Corinthians 11:26

HOMILY

203. Depending on circumstances, the minister may then give a brief explanation of the reading. 107

BAPTISMAL PROFESSION OF FAITH

204. The rite is as described in no. 190. 108

LITANY

205. The rite is as described in no. 191. 109

LITURGY OF VIATICUM

THE LORD'S PRAYER

206. The minister introduces the Lord's Prayer as in no. 126. 110

COMMUNION AS VIATICUM

207. The sick person and all present may receive communion under both kinds. When the minister gives communion to the sick person, the form for viaticum is used. 99e

The minister shows the eucharistic bread to those present, saying: 111

A
Jesus Christ is the food for our journey;
he calls us to the heavenly table.

B
This is the bread of life.
Taste and see that the Lord is good.

The rite then proceeds as described in no. 193. 111 112

After the conclusion of the rite, the minister cleanses the vessel as usual. 113

SILENT PRAYER

208. Then a period of silence may be observed. 113

PRAYER AFTER COMMUNION

209. The minister says a concluding prayer. One of the following may be used: 114

Let us pray.

Pause for silent prayer, if this has not preceded.

A

God of peace, 259
you offer eternal healing to those who believe in you;
you have refreshed your servant N.
with food and drink from heaven:
lead him/her safely into the kingdom of light.

We ask this through Christ our Lord.
℟. Amen.

B

All-powerful and ever-living God, 57
may the body and blood of Christ your Son
be for our brother/sister N.
a lasting remedy for body and soul.

We ask this through Christ our Lord.
℟. Amen.

C

Father, 114
your son, Jesus Christ, is our way, our truth, and our life.
Look with compassion on your servant N.
who has trusted in your promises.
You have refreshed him/her with the body and blood of your Son:
may he/she enter your kingdom in peace.

We ask this through Christ our Lord.
℟. Amen.

CONCLUDING RITES

BLESSING

210. The priest or deacon blesses the sick person and the others present, using one of the blessings in no. 91. If, 114

however, any of the blessed sacrament remains, he may bless the sick person by making a sign of the cross with the blessed sacrament, in silence.

A minister who is not a priest or deacon invokes God's blessing and makes the sign of the cross on himself or herself, as described on page 642. E40

SIGN OF PEACE

211. The minister and the others present may then give the sick person the sign of peace. 114

CHAPTER VI

COMMENDATION OF THE DYING

INTRODUCTION

Into your hands, Lord, I commend my spirit.

212. In viaticum the dying person is united with Christ in his passage out of this world to the Father. Through the prayers for the commendation of the dying contained in this chapter, the Church helps to sustain this union until it is brought to fulfillment after death.

213. Christians have the responsibility of expressing their 138
union in Christ by joining the dying person in prayer for 142
God's mercy and for confidence in Christ. In particular, the presence of a priest or deacon shows more clearly that the Christian dies in the communion of the Church. He should assist the dying person and those present in the recitation of the prayers of commendation and, following death, he should lead those present in the prayer after death. If the priest or deacon is unable to be present because of other serious pastoral obligations, other members of the community should be prepared to assist with these prayers and should have the texts readily available to them.

214. The minister may choose texts from among the prayers, 139
litanies, aspirations, psalms, and readings provided in this 140
chapter, or others may be added. In the selection of these texts the minister should keep in mind the condition and piety of both the dying person and the members of the family who are present. The prayers are best said in a slow, quiet voice, alternating with periods of silence. If possible, the minister says one or more of the brief prayer formulas with the dying person. These may be softly repeated two or three times.

215. These texts are intended to help the dying person, if still 139
conscious, to face the natural human anxiety about death by imitating Christ in his patient suffering and dying. The Christian will be helped to surmount his or her fear in the hope of heavenly life and resurrection through the power of Christ, who destroyed the power of death by his own dying.

Even if the dying person is not conscious, those who are

present will draw consolation from these prayers and come to a better understanding of the paschal character of Christian death. This may be visibly expressd by making the sign of the cross on the forehead of the dying person, who was first signed with the cross at baptism.

216. Immediately after death has occurred, all may kneel while one of those present leads the prayers given on pp. 700–703. 141

SHORT TEXTS

217. One or more of the following short texts may be recited with the dying person. If necessary, they may be softly repeated two or three times. 140

Romans 8:35 143
Who can separate us from the love of Christ?

Romans 14:8
Whether we live or die, we are the Lord's.

2 Corinthians 5:1
We have an everlasting home in heaven.

1 Thessalonians 4:17
We shall be with the Lord for ever.

1 John 3:2
We shall see God as he really is.

1 John 3:14
We have passed from death to life
because we love each other.

Psalm 25:1
To you, Lord, I lift up my soul.

Psalm 27:1
The Lord is my light and my salvation.

Psalm 27:13
I believe that I shall see the goodness of the Lord
in the land of the living.

Psalm 42:3
My soul thirsts for the living God.

Psalm 23:4
Though I walk in the shadow of death,
I will fear no evil,
for you are with me.

Matthew 25:34
Come, blessed of my Father,
says the Lord Jesus,
and take possession of the kingdom
prepared for you.

Luke 23:43
The Lord Jesus says,
today you will be with me in paradise.

John 14:2
In my Father's home
there are many dwelling places,
says the Lord Jesus.

John 14:2-3
The Lord Jesus says,
I go to prepare a place for you,
and I will come again to take you to myself.

John 17:24
I desire that where I am,
they also may be with me,
says the Lord Jesus.

John 6:40
Everyone who believes in the Son
has eternal life.

Psalm 31:5a
Into your hands, Lord,
I commend my spirit.

Acts 7:59
Lord Jesus, receive my spirit.

Holy Mary, pray for me.

Saint Joseph, pray for me.

Jesus, Mary, and Joseph,
assist me in my last agony.

READING

218. The word of God is proclaimed by one of those present or by the minister. Selections from Part III or from the following readings may be used: 144

A Job 19:23-27a
Job's act of faith is a model for our own; God is the God of the living.

B Psalm 23
C Psalm 25
D Psalm 91
E Psalm 121
F 1 John 4:16

G Revelation 21:1-5a, 6-7
God our Father is the God of newness and life; it is his desire that we should come to share his life with him.

H Matthew 25:1-13
Jesus bid us be prepared for our ultimate destiny, which is eternal life.

I Luke 22:39-46
Jesus is alive to our pain and sorrow, because faithfulness to his Father's will cost him life itself.

J Luke 23:44-49
Jesus' death is witnessed by his friends.

K Luke 24:1-8
Jesus is alive; he gives us eternal life with the Father.

L John 6:37-40
Jesus will raise his own from death and give them eternal life.

M John 14:1-6, 23, 27
The love of Jesus can raise us up from the sorrow of death to the joy of eternal life.

LITANY OF THE SAINTS

219. When the condition of the dying person calls for the use 145
of brief forms of prayer, those who are present are encouraged to pray the litany of the saints—or at least some of its invocations—for him or her. Special mention may be made of the patron saints of the dying person, of the family, and of the parish. The litany may be said or sung in the usual way. Other customary prayers may also be used.

One of the following litanies may be used:

A

Lord, have mercy	**Lord, have mercy**
Christ, have mercy	**Christ, have mercy**
Lord, have mercy	**Lord, have mercy**
Holy Mary, Mother of God	**pray for him/her**
Holy angels of God	**pray for him/her**

Abraham, our father in faith	**pray for him/her**
David, leader of God's people	**pray for him/her**
All holy patriarchs and prophets	**pray for him/her**
Saint John the Baptist	**pray for him/her**
Saint Joseph	**pray for him/her**
Saint Peter and Saint Paul	**pray for him/her**
Saint Andrew	**pray for him/her**
Saint John	**pray for him/her**
Saint Mary Magdalene	**pray for him/her**
Saint Stephen	**pray for him/her**
Saint Ignatius	**pray for him/her**
Saint Lawrence	**pray for him/her**
Saint Perpetua and Saint Felicity	**pray for him/her**
Saint Agnes	**pray for him/her**
Saint Gregory	**pray for him/her**
Saint Augustine	**pray for him/her**
Saint Athanasius	**pray for him/her**
Saint Basil	**pray for him/her**
Saint Martin	**pray for him/her**
Saint Benedict	**pray for him/her**
Saint Francis and Saint Dominic	**pray for him/her**
Saint Francis Xavier	**pray for him/her**
Saint John Vianney	**pray for him/her**
Saint Catherine	**pray for him/her**
Saint Teresa	**pray for him/her**

Other saints may be included here.

All holy men and women	**pray for him/her**
Lord, be merciful	**Lord, save your people**
From all evil	**Lord, save your people**
From every sin	**Lord, save your people**
From Satan's power	**Lord, save your people**
At the moment of death	**Lord, save your people**
From everlasting death	**Lord, save your people**
On the day of judgment	**Lord, save your people**
By your coming as man	**Lord, save your people**
By your suffering and cross	**Lord, save your people**

By your death and rising to new life	**Lord, save your people**
By your return in glory to the Father	**Lord, save your people**
By your gift of the Holy Spirit	**Lord, save your people**
By your coming again in glory	**Lord, save your people**
Be merciful to us sinners	**Lord, hear our prayer**
Bring N. to eternal life, first promised to him/her in baptism	**Lord, hear our prayer**
Raise N. on the last day, for he/she has eaten the bread of life	**Lord, hear our prayer**
Let N. share in your glory, for he/she has shared in your suffering and death	**Lord, hear our prayer**
Jesus, Son of the living God	**Lord, hear our prayer**
Christ, hear us	**Christ, hear us**
Lord Jesus, hear our prayer	**Lord Jesus, hear our prayer**

B

A brief form of the litany may be prayed. Other saints may be added, including the patron saints of the dying person, of the family, and of the parish; saints to whom the dying person may have a special devotion may also be included.

Holy Mary, Mother of God	**pray for him/her**
Holy angels of God	**pray for him/her**
Saint John the Baptist	**pray for him/her**
Saint Joseph	**pray for him/her**
Saint Peter and Saint Paul	**pray for him/her**

Other saints may be included here.

All holy men and women	**pray for him/her**

PRAYER OF COMMENDATION

220. When the moment of death seems near, some of the 145
following prayers may be said:

A

Go forth, Christian soul, from this world 146
in the name of God the almighty Father,
who created you,
in the name of Jesus Christ, Son of the living God,
who suffered for you,
in the name of the Holy Spirit,
who was poured out upon you,
go forth, faithful Christian.

May you live in peace this day,
may your home be with God in Zion,
with Mary, the virgin Mother of God,
with Joseph, and all the angels and saints.

B

I commend you, my dear brother/sister, to almighty God, 147
and entrust you to your Creator.
May you return to him
who formed you from the dust of the earth.
May holy Mary, the angels, and all the saints
come to meet you as you go forth from this life.
May Christ who was crucified for you
bring you freedom and peace.
May Christ who died for you,
admit you into his garden of paradise.
May Christ, the true Shepherd,
acknowledge you as one of his flock.
May he forgive all your sins,
and set you among those he has chosen.
May you see your Redeemer face to face,
and enjoy the vision of God for ever.
℟. **Amen.**

C

Welcome your servant, Lord, into the place of salvation 148
which because of your mercy he/she rightly hoped for.
℟. **Amen,** or ℟. **Lord, save your people.**

Deliver your servant, Lord, from every distress. ℟.

Deliver your servant, Lord, as you delivered Noah from the flood. ℟.

Deliver your servant, Lord, as you delivered Abraham from Ur of the Chaldees. ℟.

Deliver your servant, Lord, as you delivered Job from his sufferings. ℟.

Deliver your servant, Lord, as you delivered Moses from the hand of the Pharaoh. ℟.

Deliver your servant, Lord, as you delivered Daniel from the den of lions. ℟.

Deliver your servant, Lord, as you delivered the three young men from the fiery furnace. ℟.

Deliver your servant, Lord, as you delivered Susanna from her false accusers. ℟.

Deliver your servant, Lord, as you delivered David from the attacks of Saul and Goliath. ℟.

Deliver your servant, Lord, as you delivered Peter and Paul from prison. ℟.

Deliver your servant, Lord, through Jesus our Savior, who suffered death for us and gave us eternal life. ℟.

D

Lord Jesus Christ, Savior of the world, 149
we pray for your servant N.,
and commend him/her to your mercy.
For his/her sake you came down from heaven;
receive him/her now into the joy of your kingdom.

For though he/she has sinned,
he/she has not denied the Father, the Son, and the Holy Spirit,
but has believed in God
and has worshiped his/her Creator.
℟. Amen.

E The following antiphon may be said or sung: 150
Hail, holy Queen, Mother of mercy,
hail, our life, our sweetness, and our hope.
To you we cry, the children of Eve;
to you we send up our sighs,
mourning and weeping in this land of exile.
Turn, then, most gracious advocate,

your eyes of mercy toward us;
lead us home at last
and show us the blessed fruit of your womb, Jesus:
O clement, O loving, O sweet Virgin Mary.

PRAYER AFTER DEATH

221. When death has occurred, one or more of the following prayers may be said: 151

A

Saints of God, come to his/her aid!
Come to meet him/her, angels of the Lord!
℟. Receive his/her soul and present him/her to God the Most High.

May Christ, who called you, take you to himself;
may angels lead you to Abraham's side. ℟.

Give him/her eternal rest, O Lord,
and may your light shine on him/her for ever. ℟.

The following prayer is added:

Let us pray.

All-powerful and merciful God,
we commend to you N., your servant.
In your mercy and love,
blot out the sins he/she has committed through human weakness.
In this world he/she has died:
let him/her live with your for ever.

We ask this through Christ our Lord.
℟. Amen.

B Psalm 130 F163
℟. My soul hopes in the Lord.

The following prayer is added: F30

Let us pray.

God of love,
welcome into your presence
your son/daughter N., whom you have called from this life.
Release him/her from all his/her sins,

bless him/her with eternal light and peace,
raise him/her up to live for ever with all your saints
in the glory of the resurrection.

We ask this through Christ our Lord.
℟. Amen.

C Psalm 23
℟. Lord, remember me in your kingdom. F145

The following prayer is added: F33

Let us pray.

God of mercy,
hear our prayers and be merciful
to your son/daughter N., whom you have called from this life.
Welcome him/her into the company of your saints,
in the kingdom of light and peace.

We ask this through Christ our Lord.
℟. Amen.

D
Almighty and eternal God, F167
hear our prayers for your son/daughter N.,
whom you have called from this life to yourself.

Grant him/her light, happiness, and peace.
Let him/her pass in safety through the gates of death,
and live for ever with all your saints
in the light you promised to Abraham
and to all his descendants in faith.

Guard him/her from all harm
and on that great day of resurrection and reward
raise him/her up with all your saints.
Pardon his/her sins
and give him/her eternal life in your kingdom.

We ask this through Christ our Lord.
℟. Amen.

E
Loving and merciful God, F168
we entrust our brother/sister to your mercy.

You loved him/her greatly in this life:
now that he/she is freed from all its cares,
give him/her happiness and peace for ever.

The old order has passed away:
welcome him/her now into paradise
where there will be no more sorrow,
no more weeping or pain,
but only peace and joy
with Jesus, your Son,
and the Holy Spirit
for ever and ever
℟. Amen.

F
God of our destiny, F48
into your hands we commend our brother/sister.
We are confident that with all who have died in Christ
he/she will be raised to life on the last day
and live with Christ for ever.

[We thank you for all the blessings
you gave him/her in this life
to show your fatherly care for all of us
and the fellowship which is ours with the saints
in Jesus Christ.]

Lord, hear our prayer:
welcome our brother/sister to paradise
and help us to comfort each other
with the assurance of our faith
until we all meet in Christ
to be with you and with our brother/sister for ever.

We ask this through Christ our Lord.
℟. Amen.

PRAYER FOR THE FAMILY AND FRIENDS

222. One of the following prayers may be said:

Let us pray. 834

A For the family and friends F34
God of all consolation,
in your unending love and mercy for us

you turn the darkness of death
into the dawn of new life.
Show compassion to your people in their sorrow.

[Be our refuge and our strength
to lift us from the darkness of this grief
to the peace and light of your presence.]

Your Son, our Lord Jesus Christ,
by dying for us, conquered death
and by rising again, restored life.

May we then go forward eagerly to meet him,
and after our life on earth
be reunited with our brothers and sisters
where every tear will be wiped away.

We ask this through Christ our Lord.
℟. Amen.

B For the deceased person and for the family and friends F169
Lord Jesus, our Redeemer,
you willingly gave yourself up to death
so that all people might be saved
and pass from death into a new life.
Listen to our prayers,
look with love on your people
who mourn and pray for their brother/sister N.

Lord Jesus, holy and compassionate:
forgive N. his/her sins.
By dying you opened the gates of life
for those who believe in you:
do not let our brother/sister be parted from you,
but by your glorious power
give him/her light, joy, and peace in heaven
where you live for ever and ever.
℟. Amen.

For the solace of those present the minister may conclude these prayers with a simple blessing or with a symbolic gesture, for example, signing the forehead with the sign of the cross. A priest or deacon may sprinkle the body with holy water.

CHAPTER VII

PRAYERS FOR THE DEAD

INTRODUCTION

I want those you have given me to be with me where I am.

223. This chapter contains prayers for use by a minister who 15
has been called to attend a person who is already dead. A priest is not to administer the sacraments of penance or anointing. Instead, he should pray for the dead person using these or similar prayers.

224. It may be necessary to explain to the family of the person who is dead that sacraments are celebrated for the living, not for the dead, and that the dead are effectively helped by the prayers of the living.

225. To comfort those present the minister may conclude these prayers with a simple blessing or with a symbolic gesture, for example, making the sign of the cross on the forehead. A priest or deacon may sprinkle the body with holy water.

GREETING

226. The minister greets those who are present, offering them sympathy and the consolation of faith, using one of the following or similar words:

A

In this moment of sorrow
the Lord is in our midst
and comforts us with his word:
Blessed are the sorrowful; they shall be consoled.

B

Praised be God, the Father of our Lord Jesus Christ,
the Father of mercies,
and the God of all consolation!
He comforts us in all our afflictions
and thus enables us to comfort those who are in trouble,
with the same consolation
we have received from him.

PRAYER

227. The minister then says one of prayers D or E in no. 221.

READING

228. The word of God is proclaimed by one of those present or by the minister. An appropriate reading from Part III or one of the following readings may be used:

A Luke 23:44-46

B John 11:3-7, 17, 20-27, 33-36, 41-44

LITANY

229. Then one of those present may lead the others in praying a brief form of the litany of the saints. (The full form of the litany of the saints may be found in no. 219.) Other saints may be added, including the patron saints of the dead person, of the family, and of the parish; saints to whom the deceased person may have had a special devotion may also be included.

Saints of God, come to his/her aid!
Come to meet him/her, angels of the Lord!

Holy Mary, Mother of God	**pray for him/her**
Saint Joseph	**pray for him/her**
Saint Peter and Saint Paul	**pray for him/her**

The following prayer is added:

God of mercy, F33
hear our prayers and be merciful
to your son/daughter N., whom you have called from this life.
Welcome him/her into the company of your saints,
in the kingdom of light and peace.

We ask this through Christ our Lord.
℟. Amen.

THE LORD'S PRAYER

230. The minister introduces the Lord's Prayer in these or similar words:

A

With God there is mercy and fullness of redemption;
let us pray as Jesus taught us to pray:

B

Let us pray for the coming of the kingdom as Jesus taught us:

All say:

Our Father . . .

PRAYER OF COMMENDATION

231. The minister then concludes with the following prayer:

Lord Jesus, our Redeemer, F169
you willingly gave yourself up to death
so that all people might be saved
and pass from death into a new life.
Listen to our prayers,
look with love on your people
who mourn and pray for their brother/sister N.

Lord Jesus, holy and compassionate:
forgive N. his/her sins.
By dying you opened the gates of life
for those who believe in you:
do not let our brother/sister be parted from you,
but by your glorious power
give him/her light, joy, and peace in heaven
where you live for ever and ever.
℟. Amen.

For the solace of those present the minister may conclude these prayers with a simple blessing or with a symbolic gesture, for example, signing the forehead with the sign of the cross. A priest or deacon may sprinkle the body with holy water.

CHAPTER VIII

RITES FOR EXCEPTIONAL CIRCUMSTANCES

INTRODUCTION

I am the gateway. Whoever enters through me will be safe.

232. The rites contained in this section are exclusively for use in exceptional circumstances. In all other cases, the more developed forms of pastoral care ought to be employed for the greater benefit of those members of the community who are dying and for the greater consolation of those who are close to them.

The exceptional circumstances for which these rites are provided arise when there is a genuine necessity, for example, when sudden illness or an accident or some other cause has placed one of the faithful in the proximate or immediate danger of death.

CONTINUOUS RITE

233. A "Continuous Rite of Penance, Anointing, and Viaticum" has been set out so that these sacraments may be given together in a single celebration. If the person is unable to receive holy communion, the priest can use this rite, omitting the liturgy of viaticum.

RITE FOR EMERGENCIES

234. If death seems imminent and there is not enough time to 116
celebrate the three sacraments in the manner given in the continuous rite, the priest should proceed with the "Rite for Emergencies."

CHRISTIAN INITIATION

235. This chapter also includes "Christian Initiation for the Dying," which contains the rites for baptism, confirmation, and viaticum. It is to be used when ministering to an uninitiated or partially initiated person.

CONTINUOUS RITE OF PENANCE, ANOINTING, AND VIATICUM

INTRODUCTION

He will wipe away all tears from their eyes; there will be no more death, and no more mourning or sadness.

236. This rite has been provided for use when sudden illness, an accident, or some other cause has placed one of the faithful in danger of death. It makes possible the reception of the three sacraments of penance, anointing, and viaticum in a single celebration. It is not only for use at the point of death, but even possibly a day or so before when time or the condition of the dying person will not allow a more developed celebration of these sacraments over a period of time. In its pastoral ministry the Church always seeks to be as complete as possible, and with this continuous rite those who are in danger of death are prepared to face it sustained by all the spiritual means available to the Church. 30

237. The priest should be guided by the condition of the dying person in deciding how much of this rite should be celebrated and where it should be appropriately shortened or adapted. If the dying person wishes to celebrate the sacrament of penance, this should take place before the anointing and reception of communion as viaticum. If necessary, the dying person may confess at the beginning of the celebration, before the anointing. Otherwise, the penitential rite should be celebrated. 115 116

If the danger of death is imminent, the priest should anoint immediately with a single anointing and then give viaticum. If the circumstances are extreme, he should give viaticum immediately (see no. 30), without the anointing. The "Rite for Emergencies" has been designed for this situation. Christians in danger of death are bound by the precept of receiving communion so that in their passage from this life, they may be strengthened by the body of Christ, the pledge of the resurrection.

238. It is preferable not to celebrate the sacrament of confirmation and the sacrament of the anointing of the sick in 117

a continuous rite. The two anointings can cause some confusion between the two sacraments. However, if the dying person has not been confirmed this sacrament may be celebrated immediately before the blessing of the oil of the sick. In this case, the imposition of hands which is part of the liturgy of anointing is omitted.

INTRODUCTORY RITES

GREETING

239. The priest greets the sick person and the others present. 118
One of the following may be used as described in no. 81.

If communion as viaticum is celebrated during the rite, the 118
priest then places the blessed sacrament on the table, and all join in adoration.

INSTRUCTION

240. If the occasion requires, the priest speaks to the sick 119
person about the celebration of the sacraments.

Depending on the circumstances, he reads a brief gospel text or an instruction to invite the sick person to repentance and the love of God.

A Matthew 11:28-30
B John 6:40

C The priest may use the following instruction, or one 119
better adapted to the sick person's condition:

Beloved in Christ, the Lord Jesus is with us at all times, warming our hearts with his sacramental grace. Through his priests he forgives the sins of the repentant; he strengthens the sick through holy anointing; to all who watch for his coming, he gives the food of his body and blood to sustain them on their last journey, confirming their hope of eternal life. Our brother/sister has asked to receive these three sacraments: let us help him/her with our love and our prayers.

LITURGY OF PENANCE

SACRAMENT OF PENANCE

241. If the sick person so wishes, the sacrament of penance is 120
celebrated; in case of necessity, the confession may be generic.

The priest extends his hands over the penitent's head (or at F46
least extends his right hand) and says:

God, the Father of mercies,
through the death and resurrection of his Son
has reconciled the world to himself
and sent the Holy Spirit among us
for the forgiveness of sins;
through the ministry of the Church
may God give you pardon and peace,
and I absolve you from your sins
in the name of the Father, and of the Son, ✠
and of the Holy Spirit.
℟. **Amen.**

PENITENTIAL RITE

242. If there is no celebration of the sacrament of penance, 121
the penitential rite takes place as usual. The priest invites the sick person and all present to join in the penitential rite using these or similar words:

A

My brothers and sisters, let us turn with confidence to the Lord and ask his forgiveness for all our sins.

B

My brothers and sisters, to prepare ourselves for this celebration, let us call to mind our sins.

After a brief period of silence, the penitential rite continues, as described in no. 118, A or C.

APOSTOLIC PARDON

243. At the conclusion of the sacrament of penance or the 122
penitential rite, the priest may give the apostolic pardon for the dying, as described in no. 201.

BAPTISMAL PROFESSION OF FAITH

244. If the condition of the sick person permits, the baptismal profession of faith follows. The priest gives a brief introduction and then asks the following questions, as described in no. 190. 108 123

The priest may sprinkle the sick person with holy water after the renewal of the baptismal profession of faith.

LITANY

245. The litany may be adapted to express the intentions of the sick person and of those present. The sick person, if able, and all present respond. One of the following may be used:

A

You bore our weakness and carried our sorrows: 240
Lord, have mercy.
℟. Lord, have mercy.

You felt compassion for the crowd,
and went about doing good and healing the sick:
Christ, have mercy.
℟. Christ, have mercy.

You commanded your apostles
to lay their hands on the sick in your name:
Lord, have mercy.
℟. Lord, have mercy.

B

Let us pray, dear friends, for our brother/sister N., whom the Lord at this hour is refreshing with the sacraments. 123

That the Lord may look on our brother/sister and see in him/her the face of his own suffering Son, we pray:
℟. Lord, hear our prayer.

That the Lord may help N. in this moment of trial, we pray: ℟.

That the Lord may watch over N., and keep him/her ever in his love, we pray: ℟.

That the Lord may give N. strength and peace, we pray: ℟.

LITURGY OF CONFIRMATION

246. It is highly appropriate that the initiation of every baptized Christian be completed by the sacraments of confirmation and the eucharist. If the sacrament of confirmation is celebrated in the same rite, the priest continues as indicated in "Christian Initiation for the Dying," no. 290. In such a case, the laying on of hands which belongs to the anointing of the sick (see no. 247) is omitted. 124

LITURGY OF ANOINTING

LAYING ON OF HANDS

247. In silence, the priest then lays his hands on the head of the sick person. 125

PRAYER OVER THE OIL

248. In some situations the priest may bless the oil himself (see no. 21). Otherwise, he says a prayer of thanksgiving over oil already blessed. 75

Thanksgiving over Blessed Oil—If the oil is already blessed, the priest says the following prayer of thanksgiving over it, as described in no. 123. 127

Blessing of Oil—When the priest is to bless the oil during the rite, he uses the following blessing: 126

Bless, ✠ Lord, your gift of oil
and our brother/sister N.
that it may bring him/her relief.

Other forms of the blessing may be found on pp. 666–667.

ANOINTING

249. The priest anoints the sick person with the blessed oil, as described in no. 124. 128

When viaticum is celebrated the following prayer is omitted. 134

PRAYER AFTER ANOINTING

250. The priest says one of the following prayers: 134

A

Lord Jesus Christ, Redeemer of the world, 244
you have shouldered the burden of our weakness

and borne our sufferings in your own passion and death.

Hear this prayer for our sick brother/sister N.
whom you have redeemed.
Strengthen his/her hope of salvation
and sustain him/her in body and soul,
for you live and reign for ever and ever.
℟. Amen.

B See Prayer D, in no. 125. 243

LITURGY OF VIATICUM

THE LORD'S PRAYER

251. The priest introduces the Lord's Prayer in these or similar words: 129

A

Jesus taught us to call God our Father, and so we have the courage to say:

B

And now let us pray with confidence as Christ our Lord commanded:

All say:

Our Father . . .

COMMUNION AS VIATICUM

252. The sick person and all present may receive communion under both kinds. When the priest gives communion to the sick person, the form for viaticum is used, as described in no. 193. 99e 130 131

After the conclusion of the rite, the priest cleanses the vessel as usual. 132

SILENT PRAYER

253. Then a period of silence may observed. 132

PRAYER AFTER COMMUNION

254. The priest says a concluding prayer. One of the following may be used: 133

Let us pray.

Pause for silent prayer, if this has not preceded.

A See Prayer C, in no. 209.
B See Prayer A, in no. 209.

CONCLUDING RITES

BLESSING

255. The priest blesses the sick person and the others present, using one of the following blessings. If, however, any of the blessed sacrament remains, he may bless the sick person by making a sign of the cross with the blessed sacrament, in silence. 133

A See Blessing A in no. 91.
B See Blessing C in no. 91.

SIGN OF PEACE

256. The priest and the others present may then give the sick person the sign of peace. 133

257. If the person recovers somewhat, the priest or other minister may continue to give further pastoral care, bringing viaticum frequently, and using other prayers and blessings from the rite of visiting the sick.

258. When death has occurred, prayers may be offered for the dead person and for the family and friends. These are given on pp. 700–703. This may be done in any suitable place, including a hospital chapel or prayer room.

RITE FOR EMERGENCIES

INTRODUCTION

I am at your side always.

259. There are extreme circumstances in which not even the continuous rite can be celebrated. These occur when the danger of death from injury or illness is sudden and unexpected or when the priest is not called to exercise his ministry until the person is at the point of death.

260. In such a situation of emergency the priest should offer every possible ministry of the Church as reverently and expeditiously as he can. He may be able to provide only the barest minimum of sacramental rites and forms of prayer, but even then he should add other appropriate prayers from the ritual to help the dying person and those who may be present.

261. If the dying person wishes, the sacrament of penance is 30
celebrated first. If necessary, the confession may be generic. 116
Because of the emergency situation, viaticum follows immediately. Christians in danger of death are bound by the precept to receive communion. If there is still sufficient time, the anointing of the sick may then be celebrated. The brief rite which follows has been provided for the celebration of these sacraments in such a situation. The priest should judge, in light of the particular circumstances, how much or how little of this rite is possible.

262. After the celebration of the abbreviated rite for emergencies, the priest should continue in prayer with the dying person, if possible, and with the family and friends, as suggested in the "Commendation of the Dying" (p. 692). When death has occurred, some of the prayers suggested at the end of the "Commendation of the Dying" may be said with the family and friends.

263. When a priest has been called to attend a person who is 15
already dead, he is not to administer the sacrament of 135
anointing. Instead, he should pray for the dead person, asking that God forgive his or her sins and graciously receive him or her into the kingdom. It is appropriate that he lead the

family and friends, if they are present, in some of the prayers suggested at the end of the "Commendation of the Dying," as already mentioned. Sometimes the priest may find it necessary to explain to the family of the person who has died that sacraments are celebrated for the living, not for the dead, and that the dead are effectively helped by the prayers of the living.

If the priest has reason to believe that the person is still living, he may anoint him or her conditionally. In this case, the sacramental form is introduced with the words: "If life is in you: . . ."

SACRAMENT OF PENANCE

264. If the sick person so wishes, the sacrament of penance is 120
celebrated; in case of necessity, the confession may be generic.

The rite is as described in no. 241.

APOSTOLIC PARDON

265. The priest may give the apostolic pardon for the dying, 122
as described in no. 195.

THE LORD'S PRAYER

266. The priest introduces the Lord's Prayer: 129

Jesus taught us to call God our Father, and so we have the courage to say:

All say:

Our Father . . .

COMMUNION AS VIATICUM

267. The priest goes to the sick person and, showing the 131
blessed sacrament, says:

The body of Christ,

The sick person answers: "Amen."

Then the priest says:

The blood of Christ.

The sick person answers: "Amen."

Immediately, or after giving communion to the sick person, the priest adds the form for viaticum:

May the Lord Jesus Christ protect you
and lead you to eternal life.
℟. Amen.

Others present who wish to receive communion then do so in the usual way.

PRAYER BEFORE ANOINTING

268. The priest says: 135

Let us ask the Lord to come to our brother/sister N.
with his merciful love, and grant him/her relief
through this holy anointing. In faith we pray:
℟. Lord, hear our prayer.

ANOINTING

269. The priest anoints the sick person with the blessed oil,* 128
as described in no. 124. 135

CONCLUDING PRAYER

270. The priest says one of the following prayers: 134b

A

Father, 246
you readily take into account
every stirring of good will,
and you never refuse to pardon the sins
of those who seek your forgiveness.

Have mercy on your servant N.,
who has now entered the struggle of his/her final agony.
May this holy anointing and our prayer of faith
comfort and aid him/her in body and soul.
Forgive all his/her sins,
and protect him/her with your loving care.

*If the priest is anointing the sick person conditionally, the sacramental form is introduced with the words: "If life is in you: . . ." 135

We ask this, Father, through your Son Jesus Christ,
because he has won the victory over death,
opened the way to eternal life,
and now lives and reigns with you for ever and ever.
℟. **Amen.**

B When anointing and viaticum are given together: 245
Lord God, merciful Father,
comforter of the afflicted,
look kindly on your servant N., who trusts in you.
Though now weighed down with grievous distress,
may he/she find relief through this holy anointing;
and may the food he/she has received,
the body and blood of your Son, Jesus Christ,
refresh and strengthen him/her for his/her journey to life.

We ask this through Christ our Lord.
℟. **Amen.**

BLESSING

271. The priest blesses the sick person: 133

May the blessing of almighty God, 238
the Father, and the Son, ✠ and the Holy Spirit,
come upon you and remain with you for ever.
℟. **Amen.**

SIGN OF PEACE

272. The priest and the others present may then give the sick person the sign of peace. 133

273. If the person recovers somewhat, the priest or other minister may continue to give further pastoral care, bringing viaticum frequently, and using other prayers and blessings from the rite of visiting the sick.

274. When death has occurred, prayers may be offered for the dead person and for the family and friends. These are given on pp. 700–703. This may be done in any suitable place, including a hospital chapel or prayer room.

CHRISTIAN INITIATION FOR THE DYING

INTRODUCTION

By becoming coheirs with Christ, we share in his sufferings; we will also share in his glory.

275. The rites of Christian initiation are normally celebrated over a period of time. This allows the dying person, family, and friends to benefit fully from their celebration. In such circumstances the rite of *Christian Initiation of Adults* should be used.

276. Anyone, catechumen or not, who is in danger of death I278
may be baptized with the short rite that follows, as long as I280
such a person is not at the point of death and is able to hear and answer the questions. When no priest or deacon is available, any member of the faithful may baptize.

If the sacred chrism is at hand and there is time, a priest who baptizes should confer confirmation after the baptism; in this case the postbaptismal anointing with chrism is omitted.

Also whenever possible the priest or deacon, as well as a catechist or layperson having permission to distribute communion, should give the eucharist to the person newly baptized (with the special words proper to viaticum). In this case the sacrament may be brought before the celebration of the rite and placed reverently on a table covered with a white cloth.

277. When a person is at the point of death or when time is I281
pressing because death is imminent, the minister, omitting everything else, pours natural water (even if not blessed) on the head of the sick person, while saying the usual sacramental form (see General Introduction to *Christian Initiation*, no. 23).

278. One already admitted as a catechumen must make a I279
promise to complete the usual catechesis upon recovering. One not a catechumen must give serious indication of being converted to Christ and of renouncing pagan worship and must not be seen to be attached to anything that conflicts with the moral life (for example, "simultaneous" polygamy, etc.). The person must also make a promise to go through the complete cycle of initiation upon recovering.

279. If persons who were baptized in proximate danger of death or at the point of death should recover their health, they should be given a suitable formation, be received at the church at a fitting time, and be given the rest of the sacraments of initiation. I282

CARE OF A DYING CHILD

280. As far as possible, the *Rite of Baptism for Children* and the *Rite of Confirmation* are celebrated in the usual way. The eucharist completes the sacraments of initiation. A dying child with the use of reason shares the common responsibility of receiving viaticum. It is also desirable that an even younger child complete his or her initiation by reception of the eucharist, in accord with the practice of the Church.

INTRODUCTORY RITES

GREETING

281. The minister greets the family and then speaks with the sick person about the request for baptism and, if the sick person is not a catechumen, about the reasons for conversion. After deciding to baptize him or her, the minister should, if necessary, instruct the person briefly. I283 I284

Then the minister invites the family, the godparent, and some friends and neighbors to gather around the sick person, and selects one or two of these as witnesses. Water, even if it is not blessed, is prepared.

DIALOGUE

282. The minister addresses the sick person in these or similar words: I285

Dear brother/sister, you have asked to be baptized because you wish to have eternal life. This is eternal life: to know the one, true God and Jesus Christ, whom he has sent. This is the faith of Christians. Do you acknowledge this?
℟. **I do.**

As well as professing your faith in Jesus Christ, you must also be willing to follow his commands, as Christians do. Are you willing to accept this?
℟. **I am.**

And are you prepared to live as Christians do?
℟. I am.

[Promise, therefore, that once you have recovered your strength, you will try to know Christ better and follow a course of Christian formation. Do you so promise?
℟. I do.]

Turning to the godparent and to the witnesses, the minister asks them the following questions in these or similar words: 1286

You have heard N.'s promise. As his/her godparent do you promise to remind him/her of it and to help him/her to learn the teaching of Christ, to take part in the life of our community, and to bear witness as a true Christian?
℟. I do.

And will the rest of you, who have witnessed this promise, assist him/her in fulfilling it?
℟. We will.

The minister turns to the sick person and says: 1287

Therefore you will now be baptized into eternal life, in accordance with the command of our Lord Jesus.

LITURGY OF THE WORD

GOSPEL

283. According to time and circumstances, the minister reads some words from the gospel and explains them. One of the following may be used: 1287

A
Matthew 22:35-40
This is the greatest and first commandment.

B
John 6:44-47
Whoever believes has eternal life.

LITANY

284. The minister may adapt or shorten the litany according to the condition of the sick person. The litany may be omitted if the sick person appears to be tiring. 1288

Let us pray to the God of mercy for our sick brother/sister who has asked for the gift of baptism; let us pray for his/her godparent and for all his/her family and friends.

Father, increase his/her faith in Christ, your Son and our Saviour; in faith we make our prayer:
℟. Lord, hear us.

Grant his/her desire to have eternal life and enter the kingdom of heaven; in faith we make our prayer: ℟.

Fulfill his/her hope of knowing you, the creator of the world and the Father of all; in faith we make our prayer: ℟.

Through baptism forgive his/her sins and make him/her holy; in faith we make our prayer: ℟.

Grant him/her the salvation which Christ won by his death and resurrection; in faith we make our prayer: ℟.

In your love adopt him/her into your family; in faith we make our prayer: ℟.

[Restore him/her to health so that he/she may have the time to know and imitate Christ more perfectly; in faith we make our prayer: ℟.]

Keep united in faith and love all who have been baptized into the one body of Christ; in faith we make our prayer: ℟.

The minister concludes with the following prayer: I289

Father,
look kindly upon the faith and longing of your servant, N.;
through this water
by which you have chosen to give us new birth
join him/her to Christ's death and resurrection.

Forgive all his/her sins,
adopt him/her as your own,
and count him/her among your holy people.

[Grant also that he/she may be restored to health,
to render you thanks in your Church,
and grow in faithfulness to the teaching of Christ.]

We ask this through Christ our Lord.
℟. Amen.

LITURGY OF CHRISTIAN INITIATION

RENUNCIATION OF SIN

285. The minister first asks the sick person to renounce sin. 1290

Do you reject Satan,
and all his works,
and all his empty promises?
℟. I do.

PROFESSION OF FAITH

286. A profession of faith is then made. One of the following may be used. In the case of a child, the Apostles' Creed may be more appropriate. 1290

A See no. 190

B

I believe in God, the Father almighty, creator of heaven and earth.

I believe in Jesus Christ, his only Son, our Lord.
He was conceived by the power of the Holy Spirit and born of the Virgin Mary.
He suffered under Pontius Pilate, was crucified, died, and was buried.
He descended to the dead.
On the third day he rose again.
He ascended into heaven, and is seated at the right hand of the Father.
He will come again to judge the living and the dead.

I believe in the Holy Spirit,
the holy catholic Church,
the communion of saints,

the forgiveness of sins,
the resurrection of the body,
and the life everlasting. Amen

BAPTISM

287. The minister, using the name which the sick person desires to receive, baptizes him or her, saying: 1291

N., I baptize you in the name of the Father,

The minister pours water a first time.

and of the Son,

The minister pours water a second time.

and of the Holy Spirit.

The minister pours water a third time.

ANOINTING AFTER BAPTISM

288. If the minister of baptism is a priest or deacon and confirmation does not take place, he should now anoint the neophyte with chrism in the usual way. He says the following prayer over the newly baptized: 1263 1291

God, the Father of our Lord Jesus Christ, 1263
has freed you from sin,
given you a new birth by water and the Holy Spirit,
and welcomed you into his holy people.

He now anoints you with the chrism of salvation.

As Christ was anointed Priest, Prophet, and King, so may you live always as a member of his body, sharing everlasting life.
℟. Amen.

289. If neither confirmation nor viaticum can be given, after baptizing, the minister says: 1292

N., God our Father has freed you from your sins, has given you a new birth, and made you his son/daughter in Christ. Soon, God willing, you will receive the fullness of the Holy Spirit through confirmation, and will approach the altar of God to share the food of life at the table of his sacrifice. In the spirit of that

adoption which you have received today, join us now in praying as our Lord himself taught us:

All say:

Our Father . . .

The rite concludes with the blessing, no. 295.

CONFIRMATION

290. If baptism was conferred by a priest, he may also confirm (see rite of *Christian Initiation of Adults,* no. 280), beginning with an instruction in these or similar words: 1293

My dear newly baptized, born again in Christ by baptism, you have become a member of Christ and of his priestly people. Now you are to share in the outpouring of the Holy Spirit among us, the Spirit sent by the Lord upon his apostles at Pentecost and given by them and their successors to the baptized.

All pray in silence for a short time. The priest lays hands upon the candidate and says: 136

All-powerful God, Father of our Lord Jesus Christ,
by water and the Holy Spirit
you freed your son/daughter from sin
and gave him/her new life.

Send your Holy Spirit upon him/her
to be his/her helper and guide.

Give him/her the spirit of wisdom and understanding,
the spirit of right judgment and courage,
the spirit of knowledge and reverence.
Fill him/her with the spirit of wonder and awe in your presence.

Then the priest dips his right thumb in chrism and makes the sign of the cross on the forehead of the person to be confirmed as he says:

N., be sealed with the Gift of the Holy Spirit.
℟. **Amen.**

The priest adds: 1293

Peace be with you.
℟. **And also with you.**

291. In a case of necessity, it is enough to anoint with chrism, while saying the words: "N., be sealed with the Gift of the Holy Spirit." If possible, the priest should first lay hands upon the sick person with the prayer: "All-powerful God." After confirmation, viaticum, if possible, should be given to the neophyte. Otherwise, the celebration ends with the recitation of the Lord's Prayer by all present. 137 1293

THE LORD'S PRAYER

292. The minister instructs the sick person in these or similar words. If confirmation was given, the words in brackets are omitted. 1294

N., God our Father has freed you from your sins, has given you a new birth, and made you his son/daughter in Christ. [Soon, God willing, you will receive the fullness of the Holy Spirit through confirmation.] Before you partake of the body of the Lord, and in the spirit of that adoption which you have received today, join us now in praying as our Lord himself taught us:

All say:

Our Father . . .

COMMUNION AS VIATICUM

293. The minister shows the eucharistic bread to those present, saying: 130

A

Jesus Christ is the food for our journey;
he calls us to the heavenly table.

B

This is the Lamb of God 130
who takes away the sins of the world. 131
Happy are those who are called to his supper.

The rite then proceeds as described in no. 193.

PRAYER AFTER COMMUNION

294. The minister says a concluding prayer. 133

Let us pray.

Pause for silent prayer, if this has not preceded. 1294

Father,
almighty and eternal God,
our brother/sister has received the eucharist
with faith in you and in your healing power.
May the body and blood of Christ
bring him/her eternal healing in mind and body.

We ask this in the name of Jesus the Lord.
℟. **Amen.**

CONCLUDING RITES

BLESSING

295. The priest or deacon blesses the sick person and the others present, using one of the following blessings. If, however, any of the blessed sacrament remains, he may bless the sick person by making a sign of the cross with the blessed sacrament, in silence. 133

A Blessing B, no. 147.
B Blessing C, no. 147.

A minister who is not a priest or deacon invokes God's blessing and makes the sign of the cross on himself or herself, as described on p. 642. E40

SIGN OF PEACE

296. The minister and the others present may then give the sick person the sign of peace. 133

PART III

READINGS, RESPONSES, AND VERSES FROM SACRED SCRIPTURE

297. The following readings may be used in the Mass for the sick, in the visitation of the sick, or when praying for the sick. The selection should be made according to pastoral need, and special attention should be given to the physical and spiritual condition of the sick persons for whom the readings are used. Certain readings are indicated as more suitable for the dying. 152

OLD TESTAMENT READINGS

A 1 Kings 19:4-8 153
God strengthens and sustains his servants.

B Job 3:3, 11-17, 20-23 154
Why should the sufferer be born to see the light?

C Job 7:1-4, 6-11 155
Remember that our life is like the wind, and yet we are destined for eternal life with God.

D Job 7:12-21 156
What are we, that you make much of us?

E (For the dying) Job 19:23-27a 157
I know that my Redeemer lives.

F Wisdom 9:1, 9-18 158
Who could know your counsel? We ask to share in God's wisdom.

G Isaiah 35:1-10 159
Strengthen the feeble hands.

H Isaiah 52:13-53:12 160
He bore our sufferings himself.

I Isaiah 61:1-3a 161
The spirit of the Lord is upon me to comfort all who mourn.

NEW TESTAMENT READINGS

EASTER SEASON

A **Acts 3:1-10** 162
In the name of Jesus, stand up and walk.

B **Acts 3:11-16** 163
Faith in Jesus has given this man perfect health.

C **Acts 4:8-12** 164
There is no other name but the name of Jesus by which we are saved.

D **Acts 13:32-39** 165
The one whom God raised from the dead will never see corruption of the flesh.

OTHER SEASONS

E **Romans 8:14-17** 166
If we suffer with him, we will be glorified with him.

F **Romans 8:18-27** 167
We groan while we wait for the redemption of our bodies. The Spirit enables us to pray in our suffering.

G **Romans 8:31b-35, 37-39** 168
Nothing can come between us and the love of Christ.

H **Romans 12:1-2**
All our lives, even our suffering and pain, are caught up in the offering of Christ in obedience to the will of our Father.

I **1 Corinthians 1:18-25** 169
God's weakness is stronger than human strength.

J **1 Corinthians 12:12-22, 24b-27** 170
If one member suffers, all the members suffer.

K **1 Corinthians 15:1-4**
The death and resurrection of Christ, the basis of our faith.

L (for the dying) **1 Corinthians 15:12-20** 171
Christ has been raised from the dead; through him has come the resurrection of us all.

M **2 Corinthians 4:16-18** 172
Though our body is being weakened, our spirit is renewed.

N (for the dying) **2 Corinthians 5:1, 6-10** 173
We have an everlasting home in heaven.

O **Galatians 4:12-19** 174
My illness gave me the opportunity to bring the Gospel to you.

P **Philippians 2:25-30** 175
He was ill and almost died but God took pity on him.

Q **Colossians 1:22-29** 176
In my flesh I fill up what is lacking in the sufferings of Christ for the sake of his body.

R **Hebrews 4:14-16; 5:7-9** 177
Jesus identified himself with us totally; he suffered, and through his suffering discovered the will of the Father.

S **James 5:13-16** 178
This prayer, made in faith, will save the sick person.

T **1 Peter 1:3-9** 179
You will rejoice even though for a short time you must suffer.

U **1 John 3:1-2** 180
What we shall be has not yet been revealed.

V **Revelation 21:1-7** 181
There will be no more death or mourning, sadness or pain.

W (for the dying) **Revelation 22:17, 20-21** 182
Come, Lord Jesus.

RESPONSORIAL PSALMS

A Isaiah 38: The cry of a suffering person and joy in God's strength. 183

℟. **You saved my life, O Lord; I shall not die.**

B Psalm 6: A suffering person who cries to God for strength. 184
℟. **Have mercy on me, Lord; my strength is gone.**

C Psalm 25: A prayer for forgiveness and salvation. 185
℟. **To you, O Lord, I lift my soul.**

D Psalm 27: Trust in God in time of suffering. 186
℟. **Put your hope in the Lord; take courage and be strong.**

E Psalm 34: God is the salvation of those who trust in him. 187
℟. **The Lord is near to broken hearts.**
or: **Taste and see the goodness of the Lord.**

F Psalms 42 and 43: Nostalgia and longing to be with God. 188
℟. **Like a deer that longs for running streams, my soul longs for you, my God.**

G Psalm 63: A prayer of desire to be with God. 189
℟. **My soul is thirsting for you, O Lord my God.**

H Psalm 71: God is our hope in all our trials. 190
℟. **My God, come quickly to help me.**
or: **My lips, my very soul will shout for joy: you have redeemed me!**

I Psalm 86: Prayer of those who are in distress. 191
℟. **Listen, Lord, and answer me.**
or: **God, you are merciful and kind; turn to me and have mercy.**

J Psalm 90: Our God is eternal, strong, with power to save us. 192
℟. **In every age, O Lord, you have been our refuge.**

K Psalm 102: The prayer of those who want to be united with God. 193
℟. **O Lord, hear my prayer and let my cry come to you.**

L Psalm 103: Praise and thanks to God for his merciful love. 194
℟. **O bless the Lord, my soul.**
or: **The Lord is kind and merciful; slow to anger, and rich in compassion.**

M Psalm 123: God is the hope of his people. 195
℟. **Our eyes are fixed on the Lord, pleading for his mercy.**

N Psalm 143: A prayer for help in time of trouble. 196
℟. **O Lord, hear my prayer.**
or: **For the sake of your name, O Lord, save my life.**

ALLELUIA VERSE AND VERSE BEFORE THE GOSPEL

A Psalm 33 192
Lord, let your mercy be on us,
as we place our trust in you.

B Matthew 5:4 198
Happy are they who mourn;
they shall be comforted.

C Matthew 8:17 199
He bore our sickness,
and endured our suffering.

D Matthew 11:28 200
Come to me, all you that labor and are burdened,
and I will give you rest, says the Lord.

E 2 Corinthians 1:3b-4a 201
Blessed be the Father of mercies and the God of all comfort,
who consoles us in all our afflictions.

F Ephesians 1:3 202
Blessed be God, the Father of our Lord Jesus Christ,
for he has blessed us with every spiritual gift in Christ.

G James 1:12 203
Blessed are they who stand firm when trials come;
when they have stood the test, they will win the crown of life.

GOSPELS

A Matthew 5:1-12a 204
Rejoice and be glad, for your reward is great in heaven.

B Matthew 8:1-4 205
If you wish to do so, you can cure me.

C **Matthew 8:5-17** 206
He bore our infirmities.

D **Matthew 11:25-30** 207
Come to me, all you who labor.

E **Matthew 15:29-31** 208
Jesus heals large crowds.

F **Matthew 25:31-40** 209
As often as you did it to the least of these who belong to me, you did it to me.

G **Mark 2:1-12** 210
Seeing their faith, Jesus said to the sick man: Your sins are forgiven.

H **Mark 4:35-41** 211
Why are you so fearful? Why do you not have faith?

I **Mark 10:46-52** 212
Jesus, Son of David, have mercy on me.

J **Mark 16:15-20** 213
They will place their hands on the sick and they will recover.

K **Luke 7:18b-23** 214
Go tell John what you have seen.

L **Luke 10:5-6, 8-9** 215
Heal the sick, Jesus commanded his followers.

M **Luke 10:25-37** 216
Who is my neighbor?

N **Luke 11:5-13** 217
Ask and it will be given to you.

O **Luke 12:35-44** 218
Happy are those whom the master finds watching when he returns.

P **Luke 18:9-14** 219
O God, be merciful to me, a sinner.

Q (for the dying) **John 6:35-40** 220
It is the will of my Father that what he has given me will not perish.

R (for the dying) **John 6:53-58** 221
Whoever eats this bread has eternal life.

S John 9:1-7 222
The blind man has not sinned; it was to let God's work show forth in him.

T John 10:11-18 223
The good shepherd lays down his life for his sheep.

MASS FOR VIATICUM

298. The following texts may be used when celebrating the Mass for Viaticum.

OLD TESTAMENT READINGS

A 1 Kings 19:4-8 247
Strengthened by that food, he walked to the mountain of God.

B Job 19:23-27a
Job's act of faith is a model for our own: God is the God of the living.

NEW TESTAMENT READINGS

A 1 Corinthians 10:16-17
Though we are many, we are one bread and body.

B 1 Corinthians 11:23-26 248
When you eat this bread and drink this cup, you proclaim the death of the Lord.

C Revelation 3:14b, 20-22
I will come and share his meal, side by side.

D Revelation 22:17, 20-21
Come, Lord Jesus!

RESPONSORIAL PSALMS

A Psalm 23 249
℟. **Though I walk in the valley of darkness, I fear no evil, for you are with me.**
or: **The Lord is my shepherd; there is nothing I shall want.**

B Psalm 34 250
℟. **Taste and see the goodness of the Lord.**

C Psalms 42 and 43 251
℟. **My soul is thirsting for the living God: when shall I see him face to face?**

D Psalm 116 252

℟. **I will walk in the presence of the Lord, in the land of the living.**
or: **I will take the cup of salvation and call on the name of the Lord.**
or: **Alleluia.**

E Psalm 145

℟. **The Lord is near to all who call on him.**

ALLELUIA VERSE AND VERSE BEFORE THE GOSPEL

A John 6:51 253

I am the living bread from heaven, says the Lord;
whoever eats this bread will live for ever.

B John 6:54 254

All who eat my flesh and drink my blood have eternal life, says the Lord;
and I will raise them up on the last day.

C John 10:9 255

I am the gate, says the Lord;
whoever enters through me will be safe and find pasture.

D John 11:25; 14:6 256

I am the resurrection and the life, says the Lord;
no one comes to the Father except through me.

GOSPELS

A John 6:41-51a 257

I am the bread of life that comes down from heaven.

B John 6:51-58 258

All who eat this bread will live for ever and I will raise them up on the last day.

APPENDIX

RITE FOR RECONCILIATION OF INDIVIDUAL PENITENTS

299. This form for celebrating the sacrament of penance is for use when it is necessary in the following cases: during communion of the sick; during the celebration of anointing; during the celebration of viaticum. As far as possible, the indications contained in the pastoral notes preceding these various rites should be observed.

RECEPTION OF THE PENITENT

INVITATION TO TRUST

300. Using one of the following forms, or other similar words, the priest invites the sick person to have trust in God: P42

A

May the grace of the Holy Spirit P69
fill your heart with light,
that you may confess your sins with loving trust
and come to know that God is merciful.
℟. **Amen.**

B

May the Lord be in your heart P70
and help you to confess your sins with true sorrow.
℟. **Amen.**

C

The Lord does not wish the sinner to die P67
but to turn back to him and live.
Come before him with trust in his mercy.
℟. **Amen.**

REVELATION OF STATE OF LIFE

301. At this point, if the sick person is unknown to the priest, it is proper for the sick person to indicate his or her state in life, the time of the last confession, difficulties in leading the Christian life, and anything else which may help the priest to exercise his ministry.

LITURGY OF RECONCILIATION

CONFESSION OF SINS

302. Where it is the custom, the sick person may say a general formula for confession (for example, "I confess to almighty God . . .") before confessing his or her sins. P44

The sick person then confesses his or her sins. If circumstances call for it, a generic confession is sufficient.

If necessary, the priest helps the person to make an integral confession and gives suitable counsel; he should make sure that such counsel is adapted to the circumstances.

The priest urges the sick person to sorrow for sins, underlining that through the sacrament of penance the Christian dies and rises with Christ and is thus renewed in the paschal mystery.

ACCEPTANCE OF SATISFACTION

303. Where it is opportune, the priest proposes an act of penance which the sick person accepts to make satisfaction for sin and to amend his or her life. The act of penance should serve not only to make up for the past, but also to help begin a new life and provide an antidote to weakness. P44

As far as possible, the penance should correspond to the seriousness and nature of the sins.

This act of penance may suitably take the form of prayer, self-denial, and especially the uniting of sufferings with those of Christ for the salvation of the world. This will underline the fact that sins and their forgiveness have a social aspect, and will emphasize the important role the sick have in praying with and for the rest of the community.

PENITENT'S PRAYER OF SORROW

304. The priest then asks the sick person to express his or her sorrow; this may be done using one of the following prayers or any other act of contrition which may be familiar to the penitent. P45

A

Lord Jesus, P89
you opened the eyes of the blind,
healed the sick,
forgave the sinful woman,
and after Peter's denial confirmed him in your love.
Listen to my prayer, forgive all my sins,
renew your love in my heart,
help me to live in perfect unity with my fellow Christians
that I may proclaim your saving power to all the world.

B

Father of mercy, P88
like the prodigal son I return to you and say:
"I have sinned against you and am no longer worthy to be called your son."
Christ Jesus, Savior of the world,
I pray with the repentant thief to whom you promised Paradise:
"Lord, remember me in your Kingdom."
Holy Spirit, fountain of love, I call on you with trust:
"Purify my heart, and help me to walk as a child of light."

ABSOLUTION

305. Then the priest extends his hands over the head of the penitent (or at least extends his right hand); care should be taken that this gesture is not confused with the laying on of hands during anointing. He says: P46

God, the Father of mercies,
through the death and resurrection of his Son
has reconciled the world to himself
and sent the Holy Spirit among us
for the forgiveness of sins;
through the ministry of the Church
may God give you pardon and peace,
and I absolve you from your sins
in the name of the Father, and of the Son, ✠
and of the Holy Spirit.
℟. **Amen.**

He concludes by saying: P47

The Lord has freed you from sin. P93
May he bring you safely to his kingdom in heaven.
Glory to him for ever.
℟. **Amen.**

RITE OF FUNERALS

RITE OF FUNERALS

D Procession to the Church (35)
(If the station in the home is not held, the priest meets the cortege at the door of the church.) (36)

II Second Station: In the Church (37-38)

A Mass
Rite at the Entrance to the Church (for the United States)
Liturgy of the Word and Other Rites of the Mass (39-45)

B Final Commendation and Farewell (If celebrated after Mass, see Introductory Note, above.) (46)
Sprinkling of the Body with Holy Water (47)[1]
Prayer (48)
Removal of the Body (49-51)
Procession to the Cemetery (52)

III Third Station: A. At the Grave or Tomb (If the final commendation has been celebrated after Mass.)

A Blessing of the Grave or Tomb (If this has not been done) (53)

B Final Commendation and Farewell (If not celebrated at end of Mass, see nos. 46-48 above.) (54)

C Burial (55)
Reading and Responsorial Psalm (For use in the United States)
Prayer of the Faithful (56) (Prayers for those present, for use in the United States.)
Conclusion (57)

IV Third Station: B. At the Grave or Tomb (With final commendation and farewell)

A Blessing of the Grave or Tomb (If this has not been done previously—, see no. 53, above.)

B Final Commendation and Farewell (Special scripture reading and responsorial psalm for use in the United States, see no. 46, above.)

C Sprinkling of the Body with Holy Water (with special prayers for use in the United States; see no. 47, above.)
Prayer (See no. 48, above.)
Conclusion (57)

[1]With special options for the United States

V Reception of the Funeral at the Church when the Funeral Liturgy Does not Take Place at Once (58)

CHAPTER III
SECOND PLAN OF THE FUNERAL RITE WITH STATION IN THE CEMETERY CHAPEL AND AT THE GRAVE OR TOMB (59)

I First Station: In the Cemetery Chapel

A Greeting (60)

B Responsory or Other Song (61)

C Liturgy of the Word (62-64)

D Final Commendation and Farewell (65-69)[2]

E Procession to the Grave or Tomb (70)

II Second Station: A. At the Grave or Tomb (If the final commendation has already been celebrated after the liturgy of the word at the First Station.)

A Blessing of the Grave or Tomb (If this has not been done previously. The rite is as described in nos. 53 and 54, above.) (71)

B Burial (72)

Optional Scripture Reading and Responsorial Psalm

C Homily (optional) (73)

D Final Commendation and Farewell (74)[3]

E Prayer of the Faithful (75) (with special prayers for use in the United States)

F Conclusion (76)

III Second Station: B. At the Grave or Tomb (with final commendation and farewell)

A Blessing of the Grave or Tomb (If this has not been done previously. The rite is as described in nos. 53 and 54, above.

[2]This rite is the same as that given in nos 46-49, above. The rite, however, may be deferred until it is celebrated at the grave or tomb.

[3]If this rite is celebrated at the grave, the following prayer, no. 75, is omitted, and the funeral rites are concluded, as above, in nos. 65-67.

B Final Commendation and Farewell (See no. 46, above.)

Reading and Responsorial Psalm (For use in the United States)
Sprinkling of the Body with Holy Water (See no. 47, above, including special prayers for use in the United States.)

Concluding Prayers (See no. 48, above.) (With special prayers for use in the United States for those present.)

Conclusion (76)

CHAPTER IV
THIRD PLAN IF THE FUNERAL RITE IS CELEBRATED IN THE HOME OF THE DECEASED (77-79)

CHAPTER V
FUNERALS OF CHILDREN (80-82)

I First Station: In the Home of the Deceased (See nos. 32-34, above.)

A Procession to the Church (See nos. 35-36, above.)

II Second Station: In the Church (See nos. 37-38, above.)

A Mass
Rite at the Entrance of the Church
Greeting (For use in the United States) and other rites (See nos. 39-45, above.)

B Final Commendation and Farewell (If celebrated after Mass, see nos. 48-51, above. Special prayers for use in the United States.)

C Procession to the Cemetery (See no. 52, above.)

III Third Station: A. At the Grave or Tomb (If the final commendation has been celebrated after Mass.)

A Blessing of the Grave or Tomb (If this has not been done previously.)

B Burial (See nos. 53-57, above, with special prayers for use in the United States.)

IV Third Station: B. At the Grave or Tomb (with final commendation and farewell. See no. 54, above.)

A Blessing of the Grave or Tomb (If this has not been done previously.)

B Final Commendation and Farewell (See no. 46, above, with special prayers for use in the United States.)

C Sprinkling of the Body with Holy Water (See nos. 47-48, above, with special prayers for the United States.)

D Conclusion (See no. 57, above.)

V Reception of the Funeral at the Church when the Funeral Liturgy does not Take Place at Once (See no. 58, above.)

CHAPTER VI
VARIOUS TEXTS USED IN THE ORDER OF FUNERALS FOR ADULTS (83-202)

CHAPTER VII
VARIOUS TEXTS FOR FUNERALS OF BAPTIZED CHILDREN (203-237)

SACRED CONGREGATION FOR DIVINE WORSHIP

Prot. n. 720/69

DECREE

It has been the Church's custom in the funeral rites not only to commend the dead to God but also to support the Christian hope of the people and give witness to its faith in the future resurrection of the baptized with Christ.

For this reason the Second Vatican Council in its Constitution on the Liturgy directed that the funeral services be revised to express more clearly the paschal character of Christian death, and that the rite for the burial of infants be given a special Mass (art. 81-82).

The Consilium for the Implementation of the Constitution on the Liturgy prepared these rites and offered them for experiment in various regions of the world. Now Pope Paul VI, by his apostolic authority, has approved the rites and directed that they be published for the use of all who follow the Roman Ritual.

This Congregation for Divine Worship, at the direction of the pope, therefore promulgates the Rite of Funerals and decrees that it shall take effect beginning June 1, 1970.

The Congregation decrees, moreover, that, if funeral services are celebrated in Latin, either this rite or the one in the Roman Ritual may be used until June 1, 1970; only this new Rite of Funerals may be used from that date.

It is for the individual conferences of bishops, after a translation has been prepared and has been confirmed by this Congregation, to determine another date prior to June 1 for the new rite to go into effect, according to circumstances.

Anything to the contrary notwithstanding.

From the Sacred Congregation for Divine Worship, August 15, 1969, the solemnity of the Assumption.

Benno Card. Gut
Prefect

A. Bugnini
Secretary

FOREWORD

This edition of the *Rite of Funerals,* for use in the dioceses of the United States, is for the most part an English translation of the *Ordo Exsequiarum,* in the version prepared by the International Committee on English in the Liturgy, approved by the National Conference of Catholic Bishops, and confirmed by the Apostolic See.

To this have been added adaptations for the United States, in accord with nos. 21 and 22 of the Introduction, made by the episcopal conference and approved by the Apostolic See. Such adaptations have been clearly indicated by inclusion in brackets or boxes or by a phrase referring to their use in this country (see Introduction, no. 21, 6).

For the convenience of the minister, the optional alternative texts—found in Chapter VI—have also been printed in Chapter II, which is the rite ordinarily followed in the United States. For completeness, rites or variants never or rarely used in this country (funeral processions, funeral in the home, etc.) have been included in this edition.

The principal rearrangement of the text occurs at the end of Chapter II. Since the final commendation may take place either after the funeral Mass ("First Station") or at the grave or tomb ("Third Station"), it has been printed in its entirety in both places. If the rite of commendation is celebrated in the church after Mass, the first form (A) of the Third Station is followed at the grave or tomb. If the rite of commendation is postponed, the alternative form (B) of the Third Station is followed at the grave or tomb.

In the case of optional alternative texts, the choice has been indicated by the use of the letters A, B, C, etc. The numbering of prayers and rubrics in the *Ordo Exsequiarum* has been retained for purposes of simpler cross reference.

In addition, an introductory note has been placed at the head of some chapters. These notes are intended to suggest the principal alternatives available in the planning of the service by the priest together with the family of the deceased person and others (see Introduction, nos. 23–25).

INTRODUCTION

1. In the funeral rites the Church celebrates the paschal mystery of Christ. Those who in baptism have become one with the dead and risen Christ will pass with him from death to life, to be purified in soul and welcomed into the fellowship of the saints in heaven. They look forward in blessed hope to his second coming and the bodily resurrection of the dead.

The Church therefore celebrates the eucharistic sacrifice of Christ's passover for the dead, and offers prayers and petitions for them. In the communion of all Christ's members, the prayers which bring spiritual help to some may bring to others a consoling hope.

2. In celebrating the funeral rites of their brothers and sisters, Christians should certainly affirm their hope in eternal life, but in such a way that they do not seem to neglect or ignore the feeling and practice of their own time and place. Family traditions, local customs, groups established to take care of funerals, anything that is good may be used freely, but anything alien to the Gospel should be changed so that funeral rites for Christians may proclaim the paschal faith and the spirit of the Gospel.

3. The bodies of the faithful, which were temples of the Holy Spirit, should be shown honor and respect, but any kind of pomp or display should be avoided. Between the time of death and burial there should be sufficient opportunities for the people to pray for the dead and profess their own faith in eternal life.

Depending on local custom, the significant times during this period would seem to be the following: the vigil in the home of the deceased; the time when the body is laid out; the assembly of the relatives and, if possible, the whole community, to receive hope and consolation in the liturgy of the word, to offer the eucharistic sacrifice, and to bid farewell to the deceased in the final commendation, followed by the carrying of the body to the grave or tomb.

4. The rite of funerals for adults has been arranged in three plans to take into account conditions in all parts of the world.

a) the first plan provides for three stations: in the home of the deceased, in the church, and at the cemetery;
b) the second plan has two stations: in the cemetery chapel and at the grave;
c) the third plan has one station: at the home of the deceased.

5. The first plan is the one found until now in the Roman Ritual. Ordinarily it includes three stations, at least when celebrated in rural areas. These stations are in the home of the deceased, in the church, and at the cemetery, with two intervening processions. Such processions, however, are uncommon or inconvenient for various reasons, especially in large cities. On the other hand, priests are frequently unable to lead the services in the home and at the cemetery because of the limited number of clergy or the distance from the church to the cemetery. The faithful themselves should therefore be urged to recite the appointed prayers and psalms in the absence of a priest or deacon; if this is impossible, the stations in the home and at the cemetery may be omitted.

6. According to this first plan, the station in the church usually includes the celebration of the funeral Mass. The latter is prohibited only during the triduum of Holy Week, on solemnities, and on the Sundays of Advent, Lent, and the Easter season. For pastoral reasons the funeral rites may be celebrated in church on such days but without Mass (which should be celebrated on another day if possible). In such cases the celebration of the liturgy of the word is prescribed. Thus the station in the church will always include the liturgy of the word, with or without the eucharistic sacrifice, and will be completed by the rite formerly called the "absolution" of the deceased and now called the "final commendation and farewell."

7. The second plan has only two stations, in the cemetery chapel and at the grave. The eucharistic celebration is not provided for, but it will take place, in the absence of the body, either before or after the funeral.

8. The funeral rite, according to the third plan, is to be celebrated in the home of the deceased. In some places this plan is not at all useful, but in some regions it is actually

necessary. In view of the variety of circumstances, specific points have not been considered, but it seemed desirable to mention this rite so that it may include elements common to the others, for example, in the liturgy of the word and in the rite of final commendation and farewell. For the rest the conferences of bishops may make their own arrangements.

9. When particular rituals are prepared in harmony with the new Roman Ritual, the conference of bishops may retain the three plans for funeral rites, change the order, or omit one or other of them. It may be that in a country a single plan, for example, the first one with three stations, is the only one in use and therefore should be retained to the exclusion of the others; in another country all three plans may be necessary. The conference of bishops, after considering pastoral needs, will make suitable arrangements.

10. After the funeral Mass the rite of final commendation and farewell is celebrated.

This rite is not to be understood as a purification of the dead—which is effected rather by the eucharistic sacrifice—but as the last farewell with which the Christian community honors one of its members before the body is buried. Although in death there is a certain separation, Christians, who are members of Christ and are one in him, can never be really separated by death.[1]

The priest introduces this rite with an invitation to pray: then follow a period of silence, the sprinkling with holy water, the incensation, and the song of farewell. The text and melody of the latter should be such that it may be sung by all present and be experienced as the climax of this entire rite.

The sprinkling with holy water, which recalls the person's entrance into eternal life through baptism, and the incensation, which honors the body of the deceased as a temple of the Holy Spirit, may also be considered signs of farewell.

The rite of final commendation and farewell is to be held only in the funeral celebration itself, that is, with the body present.

[1]Cf. Simeon of Thessalonica, *De ordine sepulturae:* P.G. 155, 685 B.

In the United States, however, although the rite of final commendation at the catafalque or pall is excluded, it is permitted to celebrate the funeral service, including the commendation, in those cases where it is physically or morally impossible for the body of the deceased person to be present.

11. In celebrations for the dead, whether the funeral service or any other, emphasis should be given to the biblical readings. These proclaim the paschal mystery, support the hope of reunion in the kingdom of God, teach respect for the dead, and encourage the witness of Christian living.

12. The Church employs the prayer of the psalms in the offices for the dead to express grief and to strengthen genuine hope. Pastors must therefore try by appropriate catechesis to lead their communities to understand and appreciate at least the chief psalms of the funeral liturgy. When pastoral considerations indicate the use of other sacred songs, these should reflect a "warm and living love for sacred scripture"[2] and a liturgical spirit.

13. In the prayers, too, the Christian community expresses its faith and intercedes for adults who have died so that they may enjoy eternal happiness with God. This is the happiness which deceased children, made sons of adoption through baptism, are believed to enjoy already. Prayers are offered for the parents of these infants, as for the relatives of all the dead, so that in their sorrow they may experience the consolation of faith.

14. In places where, by particular law, endowment, or custom, the Office of the Dead is usually said not only at the funeral rites but also apart from them, this office may continue to be celebrated with devotion. In view of the demands of modern life and pastoral considerations, a vigil or celebration of God's word (nos. 27-29) may take the place of the office.

15. Christian funeral rites are permitted for those who choose to have their bodies cremated unless it is shown that

[2]II Vatican Council, Constitution on the Sacred Liturgy, *Sacrosanctum Concilium*, n. 24.

they have acted for reasons contrary to Christian principles. See the norms in the Instruction of the Sacred Congregation of the Holy Office, de cadaverum crematione, May 8, 1963, nos. 2-3.[3]

These funeral rites should be celebrated according to the plan in use for the region but in a way that does not hide the Church's preference for the custom of burying the dead in a grave or tomb, as the Lord himself willed to be buried. In the case of cremation any danger of scandal or confusion should be removed.

The rites ordinarily performed at the cemetery chapel or at the grave or tomb may be used in the crematory building. If there is no other suitable place for the rites, they may be celebrated in the crematory hall itself, provided that the danger of scandal and religious indifferentism is avoided.

OFFICES AND MINISTRIES TOWARD THE DEAD

16. In funeral celebrations all who belong to the people of God should keep in mind their office and ministry: the parents or relatives, those who take care of funerals, the Christian community as a whole, and finally the priest. As teacher of the faith and minister of consolation, the priest presides over the liturgical service and celebrates the eucharist.

17. Priests and all others should remember that, when they commend the dead to God in the funeral liturgy, it is their duty to strengthen the hope of those present and to foster their faith in the paschal mystery and the resurrection of the dead. In this way the compassionate kindness of Mother Church and the consolation of the faith may lighten the burden of believers without offending those who mourn.

18. In preparing and arranging funeral celebrations priests should consider the deceased and the circumstance of his life and death and be concerned also for the sorrow of the relatives and their Christian needs. Priests should be especially aware of persons, Catholic or non-Catholic, who seldom or never participate in the eucharist or who seem to

[3]Cf. *AAS* 56 (1964) 822–823.

have lost their faith, but who assist at liturgical celebrations and hear the Gospel on the occasion of funerals. Priests must remember that they are ministers of Christ's Gospel to all men.

19. The funeral rites, except the Mass, may be celebrated by a deacon. If pastoral necessity demands, the conference of bishops may, with the permission of the Holy See, permit a lay person to celebrate the service.

In the absence of a priest or deacon, it is urged that in the funeral rites according to the first plan the stations in the home of the deceased and at the cemetery be conducted by lay persons; the same holds for vigil services for the dead.

In the United States, the local ordinary may depute a lay person, in the absence of a priest or deacon, to lead the station in the church (i.e., the liturgy of the word and the commendation).

20. Apart from distinctions based on liturgical function and sacred orders and the honors due to civil authorities according to liturgical law, no special honors are to be paid to any private persons or classes of persons, whether in the ceremonies or by external display.[4]

ADAPTATIONS BY THE CONFERENCES OF BISHOPS

21. In accordance with article 63b of the Constitution on the Sacred Liturgy, the conferences of bishops have the right to prepare a section of their particular rituals, which will correspond to this section of the Roman Ritual but is adapted to the needs of each region. After review by the Apostolic See it may be used in the regions for which it has been prepared.

In making this adaptation, it is for the conferences of bishops:
1) To define the adaptations, within the limits stated in this section of the Roman Ritual.
2) To consider carefully and prudently which elements from

[4]Cf. II Vatican Council, Constitution on the Sacred Liturgy, *Sacrosanctum Concilium*, n. 32.

the traditions and cultures of individual countries may be appropriately admitted and to submit such other adaptations, which they feel to be useful or necessary, to the Apostolic See, by whose consent they may be introduced.
3) To retain or adapt special elements of existing particular rituals, if any, provided that they can be brought into harmony with the Constitution on the Liturgy and contemporary needs.
4) To prepare translations of texts which are truly suited to the genius of the various languages and cultures, adding, when appropriate, melodies for singing.
5) To adapt and supplement the introductory material of the Roman Ritual so that the ministers will fully understand the significance of the rites and celebrate them effectively.
6) To arrange the material in the liturgical books prepared under the direction of the conferences of bishops so that the order is best suited to pastoral purposes. None of the material contained in this typical edition is to be omitted.

If it seems advisable to add rubrics and texts, they should be distinguished typographically from the rubrics and texts of the Roman Ritual.

22. In preparing particular rituals for funerals, it is for the conferences of bishops:
1) To arrange the rite according to one or more plans, as indicated above in no. 9.
2) To substitute, if preferred, texts from Chapter VI for those which appear in the basic rite.
3) To add, according to the rule in no. 21, 6, other formulas of the same kind whenever the Roman Ritual provides a choice of texts.
4) To judge whether lay persons are to be deputed to celebrate the funeral rites (see above, no. 19).
5) To decree, if there are pastoral reasons, that the sprinkling with holy water and the incensation may be omitted or another rite substituted.

In the United States, the use of holy water may not ordinarily be omitted, but it should be explained with reference to Christian baptism. The use of incense may be omitted. Neither holy water nor incense should ordinarily be used more than once during the station in the church.

6) To determine the liturgical color for funerals in accordance with popular feeling. The color should not be offensive to human sorrow but should express Christian hope enlightened by the paschal mystery.

In the United States, white, violet, or black vestments may be worn at funeral services and at other offices and Masses for the dead.

THE FUNCTION OF THE PRIEST IN PREPARING AND PLANNING THE CELEBRATION

23. The priest should consider the various circumstances, and in particular the wishes of the family and the community. He should make free use of the choices afforded in the rite.

24. The rite for each plan is so described that it may be celebrated very simply. On the other hand, a generous selection of texts is given for use according to circumstances. For example:
1) In general, all the texts are interchangeable and may be chosen, with the help of the community or family, to reflect the individual situation.
2) Some elements of the rite are not obligatory but may be freely added, for example, the prayer for the mourners at the home of the deceased.
3) In keeping with liturgical tradition, greater freedom of choice is given in the case of texts for processions.
4) Whenever a psalm, indicated or preferred for liturgical reasons, may offer some pastoral difficulty, another psalm is provided for optional use. In addition, one or other psalm verse which seems pastorally unsuitable may be omitted.
5) Since the text of the prayers is always given in the singular, masculine form, the gender and number must be adapted.
6) In the prayers, the lines within parentheses may be omitted.
[If an individual prayer or other text is clearly not appropriate to the circumstances of the deceased person, it is the responsibility of the priest to make the necessary adaptation.]

25. The celebration of the funeral liturgy with meaning and dignity and the priest's ministry to the dead presuppose an integral understanding of the Christian mystery and the pastoral office.

Among other things, the priest should:
1) Visit the sick and the dying, as indicated in the relevant section of the Roman Ritual.
2) Teach the significance of Christian death.
3) Show loving concern for the family of the deceased person, support them in the time of sorrow, and as much as possible involve them in planning the funeral celebration and the choice of the options made available in the rite.
4) Integrate the liturgy for the dead with the whole parish liturgical life and the pastoral ministry.

CHAPTER I

VIGIL FOR THE DECEASED AND PRAYER WHEN THE BODY IS PLACED ON THE BIER

INTRODUCTORY NOTE

FOR THE UNITED STATES

This chapter includes two kinds of service of prayer which may be followed at appropriate times during the period from death to the funeral rite itself (which is given in Chapter II). These are:

1) A wake service or vigil in the form of a celebration of the word of God. This may take place in the home of the deceased person, in a funeral parlor or chapel, or even in the church. In the absence of a priest or deacon, it should be led by a lay person.

An appropriate pattern or structure of such a vigil is suggested in nos. 26-29 of this chapter, from the *Ordo Exsequiarum*. The choice of texts is left to the one who presides, in consultation with the family of the deceased and others.

2) Prayer at other times before the funeral rite.

The second part of Chapter I (nos. 30-31) suggests appropriate psalms, readings, and prayers at various times when the family, friends, and neighbors of the deceased or other members of the community assemble at the coffin. Such brief prayer may be suitable, according to local usage, when the body has been prepared and placed in the coffin, when the coffin is placed on the bier, when the family first comes together for prayer at the coffin, when the coffin is closed, or—especially if the station in the home (Chapter II, nos. 32-36) is omitted—before the body is taken to the church. It is appropriate that the priest make a selection of such prayers available for use by the family of the deceased.

VIGIL OR CELEBRATION OF THE WORD FOR THE DECEASED

26. According to local custom, a vigil or celebration of God's word may be held in the home of the deceased, under the leadership of a priest or a lay person. In this case the station in the home, mentioned below in nos. 32 and the following, may be omitted.

27. This celebration may be arranged as follows: after an introductory explanation, a psalm and prayer may be said, as indicated in nos. 33-34; these are followed by a reading from among those listed in nos. 83-107, 128-144.

After the reading, the priest may give a homily.

The vigil concludes with the general intercessions and the Lord's Prayer or with some other suitable prayer (see nos. 56, 167-169).

28. Other scripture readings may be used, especially those which express and develop the Christian view of death. The readings may be interspersed with songs, especially from the psalms or from the Office of the Dead.

29. This vigil may also take place in the church at a suitable time, provided it is not held immediately before the funeral Mass lest the funeral service be too burdensome and the liturgy of the word duplicated.

GREETING

Matthew 11:28

"Come to me, all you who are weary and find life burdensome, and I will refresh you."

Or Sirach 2:6:

Trust God and he will help you; make straight your ways and hope in him.

Or 2 Corinthians 1:3-4:

Praised be God, the Father of our Lord Jesus Christ, the Father of mercies, and the God of all consolation! He comforts us in all our afflictions and thus enables us to comfort those who are in trouble, with the same consolation we have received from him.

If it is the custom, he sprinkles the body with holy water.

PSALM

Psalm 130
Out of the depths, with a response after each verse, for example:
I cry to you, O Lord.
Or:
My soul hopes in the Lord. [162-163]

Or Psalm 23
The Lord is my shepherd, with the response:
Lord, remember, me in your kingdom. [145]

Or Psalm 114-115:12
When Israel came forth from Egypt, with the response:
May Christ make you welcome in paradise. [152]

Or another appropriate psalm with responsorial verse or biblical invocation.

PRAYER

After this he adds:

℣. **The Lord be with you.**
℟. **And also with you.**

[33]
Let us pray.

Lord,
hear our prayers and be merciful
to your son (daughter) N., whom you have called from this life.
Welcome him (her) into the company of your saints,
in the kingdom of light and peace.
(We ask this) through Christ our Lord.
℟. **Amen.**

Other prayers from nos. 167-169 may be substituted.

The following prayer for the mourners, number 34, may be said after or even before the above prayer for the deceased:

**Father,
God of all consolation,
in your unending love and mercy for us
you turn the darkness of death
into the dawn of new life.**

**Show compassion to your people in their sorrow.
(Be our refuge and our strength
to lift us from the darkness of this grief
to the peace and light of your presence.)**

**Your Son, our Lord Jesus Christ,
by dying for us, conquered death
and by rising again, restored life.**

**May we then go forward eagerly to meet him,
and after our life on earth
be reunited with our brothers and sisters
where every tear will be wiped away.
(We ask this) through Christ our Lord.**
℟. **Amen.**

Another prayer may be chosen (no. 169).

READING

A reading from among those listed in nos. 83-107 or nos. 128-144 follows.

HOMILY

After the reading, the priest may give a homily.

GENERAL INTERCESSIONS

[200]

God, the almighty Father, raised Christ his Son from the dead; with confidence we ask him to save his people, living and dead.

Our brother (sister), N., was given the promise of eternal life in baptism; Lord, give him (her) communion with your saints for ever.
℟. **Lord, hear our prayer.**

N. ate the bread of eternal life, the body of Christ; raise him (her) up, Lord, at the last day.
℟. **Lord, hear our prayer.**

For a priest
Our brother, N., was a priest on earth; welcome him, Lord, into the sanctuary of heaven.
℟. **Lord, hear our prayer.**

We pray for our brothers and sisters, our relatives, for all who were close to us and good to us; Lord, give them the reward of their goodness.
℟. **Lord, hear our prayer.**

We pray for all who have died in the hope of rising again; welcome them, Lord, into the light of your presence.
℟. **Lord, hear our prayer.**

We pray for all who have gathered here to worship in faith; Lord, make us one in your kingdom.
℟. **Lord, hear our prayer.**

Or another form of general intercession, no. 201, may be chosen.

Then the LORD'S PRAYER or the following prayer is added:

PRAYER

Lord,
hear our prayers for our dead brothers and sisters;
forgive them their sins,
and bring them to the fullness of your salvation.
(We ask this) through Christ our Lord.
℟. **Amen.**

Or some other suitable prayer (see no. 56, nos. 167-169).

PRAYER WHEN THE BODY IS PLACED ON THE BIER

30. When the body of the deceased is placed on the bier, the following may be said:
Psalm 130
Out of the depths, with a response after each verse, for example:

I cry to you, O Lord.
Or:
My soul hopes in the Lord. [162-163]

Or Psalm 23
The Lord is my shepherd, with the response:
Lord, remember me in your kingdom. [145]

Or Psalm 114-115:12
When Israel came forth from Egypt, with the response:
May Christ make you welcome in paradise. [152]

In the United States
Or Psalm 51
Have mercy on me, O God. [148]

Or Psalm 26
Do me justice, O Lord. [146a]

Or another appropriate psalm with a responsorial verse, biblical invocations, or a brief scripture reading:

Then the LORD'S PRAYER or the following prayer is said:

Let us pray.

Lord,
welcome into your presence
your son (daughter) N., whom you have called from this life.
Release him (her) from all his (her) sins,
bless him (her) with eternal light and peace,
raise him (her) up to live for ever with all your saints
in the glory of the resurrection.
(We ask this) through Christ our Lord.
℟. **Amen.**

Other prayers from nos. 167-169 may be substituted.

31. Wherever customary, when the body of the deceased is laid out or other acts of piety are performed, a similar form of prayer may be used.

CHAPTER II

FIRST PLAN OF THE FUNERAL RITE WITH STATIONS IN THE HOME OF THE DECEASED, IN THE CHURCH, AND AT THE CEMETERY

INTRODUCTORY NOTE FOR THE UNITED STATES

Because this first plan or form of the funeral rite, with the celebration of the funeral Mass in the church before the burial, is usual in the United States, as far as possible optional alternative texts have been reprinted at the proper places. It is understood that the ritual processions (from the home to the church and from the church to the cemetery) do not ordinarily take place in this country; the chants or psalms appointed for these processions may thus be sung according to circumstances, for example, if the entrance of the congregation into the church or the recession after the funeral Mass is prolonged.

The principal parts of the rite, called stations, are:
a) the service in the home of the deceased person, the funeral parlor, a chapel or other place where the body of the deceased has been placed during the period before the funeral rite;
b) the eucharistic celebration in the church;
c) the rite of burial.

There are two major options in the complete funeral rite, which—like other elements of the preparations and planning—should be determined by the priest in consultation with the family of the deceased and others (see Introduction, no. 23):

1) The first station in the home of the deceased person or elsewhere is not customary in most parts of the United States. It may, however, be celebrated under the leadership of a lay person in the absence of a priest or deacon or it may be replaced by a brief station or rite at the entrance of the church or it may be entirely omitted.

It is usual in many parts of the United States for the priest and ministers to meet the funeral procession at the church entrance—instead of celebrating the first station in the home of the deceased or elsewhere. This rite has therefore been printed in full. Moreover, several optional symbolic rites have been added, for use at the discretion of the priest and in accord with local practice: sprinkling of the body with holy water, covering the coffin with a white pall, carrying of the Easter candle through the church.
2) After the funeral Mass, the rite of final commendation may take place in the church or may be postponed and celebrated at the place of burial. Ordinarily this choice should depend on the local practice:

a) if only a small number of the congregation at the funeral Mass will participate in the third station at the place of burial, it is preferable to celebrate the final commendation in the church immediately after Mass;

b) if almost all the members of the congregation will be present at the place of burial, the final commendation may be celebrated there rather than immediately after Mass.

Other options and alternatives are indicated in the course of Chapter II, for example, the celebration of only the liturgy of the word and the final commendation, when there can be no eucharistic celebration.

If the deceased person has chosen that his body be cremated, the funeral rite is not changed except as indicated in the Introduciton, no. 15.

For the funerals of children, the same order of the service or sequence of rites is followed, but approprite prayers and other texts are chosen. See Chapters V, VII, VIII.

FIRST STATION: IN THE HOME OF THE DECEASED

32. The priest vests in an alb or surplice and a stole of the color for funerals, with a cope of the same color if he wishes. He goes to the home of the deceased with the ministers who carry the cross and holy water. Local circumstances should be considered, especially if the station takes place in a hospital.

[It is desirable that, in the absence of a priest or deacon, a lay person should lead the station in the home.]

33. Upon entering the house, the priest greets those present and offers them his sympathy and the consolation of faith, using words from the scriptures, for example:

GREETING

Matthew 11:28

"Come to me, all you who are weary and find life burdensome, and I will refresh you."

Or Sirach 2:6

Trust God and he will help you; make straight your ways and hope in him.

Or 2 Corinthians 1:3-4

Praised be God, the Father of our Lord Jesus Christ, the Father of mercies, and the God of all consolation! He comforts us in all our afflictions and thus enables us to comfort those who are in trouble, with the same consolation we have received from him.

If it is the custom, he sprinkles the body with holy water.

PSALM

Then he may say:

Psalm 130
Out of the depths, with a response after each verse, for example:
I cry to you, O Lord.
Or:
My soul hopes in the Lord. [162-163]

P 9 1952 Ritual

Or Psalm 23
The Lord is my shepherd, with the response:
Lord, remember me in your kingdom. [145]

Or Psalm 114-115:12
When Israel came forth from Egypt, with the response:
May Christ make you welcome in paradise. [152]

Or another appropriate psalm with responsorial verse or biblical invocations.

PRAYER

After this he adds:

℣. The Lord be with you.
℟. And also with you.

Let us pray.

Lord,
hear our prayers and be merciful
to your son (daughter) N., whom you have called from this life.
Welcome him (her) into the company of your saints,
in the kingdom of light and peace.
(We ask this) through Christ our Lord.
℟. Amen.

Or Another prayer may be chosen, nos. 167, 168 or 169.

34. The following prayer for the mourners may be said after or even before the above prayer for the deceased:

Father,
God of all consolation,
in your unending love and mercy for us
you turn the darkness of death
into the dawn of new life.

Show compassion to your people in their sorrow.
(Be our refuge and our strength
to lift us from the darkness of this grief
to the peace and light of your presence.)

Your Son, our Lord Jesus Christ,
by dying for us, conquered death
and by rising again, restored life.

May we then go forward eagerly to meet him,
and after our life on earth
be reunited with our brothers and sisters
where every tear will be wiped away.
(We ask this) through Christ our Lord
℟. Amen.

Another prayer may be chosen, 169.

PROCESSION TO THE CHURCH

35. If the body is taken to the church in a procession, this should be arranged according to local custom. The procession is led by a minister carrying a cross, and the priest walks in front of the bier.

The following may be sung during the procession:

Psalm 115
I love the Lord because he has heard. [154]

Antiphon
May the choir of angels welcome you and lead you to Abraham's side. Where Lazarus is poor no longer, may you have everlasting rest. [153]

Or Antiphon
I heard a voice from heaven saying: Happy are those who die in the Lord. [151]

Psalm 51
Have mercy on me, O God, with the antiphon:
Give him (her) eternal rest, O Lord, and may your light shine on him (her) for ever. [148]

Or Antiphon
Lord, may our brother (sister), whom you have called to yourself, find happiness in the glory of your saints. [149]

Or Antiphon
The bones that were crushed shall leap for joy before the Lord. [150]

Psalm 121
I lift up my eyes toward the mountains. [158]

Psalm 122
I rejoiced because they said to me. [159]

Psalm 123
To you I lift up my eyes. [160]

Psalm 126
When the Lord brought back the captives of Zion. [161]

Psalm 132
Remember, O Lord, for David. [164]

Psalm 134
Come, bless the Lord. [165]

Other appropriate songs or customary prayers may also be used.

36. If the station in the home is not held, the priest goes to the entrance of the church and there greets those present, offering them his sympathy. If it is the custom, he sprinkles the body with holy water and he may say one or more of the prayers given above for the station in the home.

SECOND STATION: IN THE CHURCH

37. Ordinarily for the entrance into the church, and for the beginning of Mass, there should be only one song, according to the norms in the General Instruction on the Order of Mass. If, however, a particular pastoral reason requires two chants, one of the responsories in numbers 47 and 187-191 may be used.

[It is appropriate that the paschal candle be carried in the entrance procession.]

38. The custom of placing the body of the deceased in the position which he occupied in the liturgical assembly may be continued, namely, the faithful facing the altar and sacred ministers facing the people.

The gospel book, the Bible, or a cross may be placed on the coffin. A second cross is not to be placed near the coffin if the altar cross can be easily seen from the body of the church. Lighted candles may be placed about the coffin or the paschal candle alone may be placed at the head of the deceased.

MASS

RITE AT THE ENTRANCE OF THE CHURCH

In the United States, the priest accompanied by the ministers, may begin the rite at the door of the church, using one of the apostolic greetings of the Mass.

GREETING

The grace of our Lord Jesus Christ and the love of God and the fellowship of the Holy Spirit be with you all.
People: **And also with you.**

Or:

The grace and peace of God our Father and the Lord Jesus Christ be with you.
People: **Blessed be God, the Father of our Lord Jesus Christ.**

Or: **And also with you.**

Or:

The Lord be with you.
People: **And also with you.**

Or: 2 Corinthians 1:3-4:
Praised be God, the Father of our Lord Jesus Christ, the Father of mercies, and the God of all consolation! He comforts us in all our afflictions and thus enables us to comfort those who are in trouble, with the same consolation we have received from him.
People: **Blessed be God, the Father of our Lord Jesus Christ.**

The priest may then sprinkle the body with holy water, saying these or similar words:

I bless the body of N., with the holy water that recalls his (her) baptism of which Saint Paul writes: All of us who were baptized into Christ Jesus were baptized into his death. By baptism into his death we were buried together with him, so that just as Christ was raised from the dead by the glory of the Father, we too might live a new life. For if we have been united with him by likeness to his death, so shall we be united with him by likeness to his resurrection.

A white pall, in remembrance of the baptismal garment, may then be placed on the coffin by the pallbearers or others, and the priest may say these or similar words:

On the day of his (her) baptism, N. put on Christ. In the day of Christ's coming, may he (she) be clothed with glory.

In the United States, if the introductory rites have taken place at the church door, the priest venerates the altar and goes to his chair. The penitential rite is omitted, and the priest sings or says the opening prayer.

39. After the introductory rites, the liturgy of the word is celebrated. Three readings may be used, the first of them from the Old Testament.

[It is desirable that the first and second readings be read by relatives or friends of the deceased person.]

If a fuller rite is desired for the funeral Mass, the psalms in the Roman Gradual or the Simple Gradual for the several parts of Mass may be sung.

40. If the Simple Gradual is used, the **alleluia** may be omitted for pastoral reasons.

41. A brief homily should be given after the gospel, but without any kind of funeral eulogy.

[The homily may properly include an expression of praise and gratitude to God for his gifts, particularly the gift of a Christian life, to the deceased person. The homily should relate Christian death to the paschal mystery of the Lord's victorious death and resurrection and to the hope of eternal life.]

42. The general intercessions (prayer of the faithful) take place after the homily.

43. Where it is customary, the procession of the faithful at the preparation of the gifts may be retained in funeral Masses, provided it is kept within the limits of the offertory rite and its eucharistic meaning is explained to the faithful.

[It is desirable that members of the family or friends of the deceased person participate in the usual offering of the bread and wine for the celebration of the eucharist, together with other gifts for the needs of the Church and of the poor.]

In the United States, if incense is used, the priest, after incensing the gifts and the altar, may incense the body. The deacon or another minister then incenses the priest and people.

44. It is recommended that the faithful, especially the members of the family, take part in the eucharistic sacrifice offered for the deceased by receiving holy communion.

In the United States, communion may be given under both kinds, in accordance with the judgment of the Ordinary, to members of the faithful present at funeral Masses.

45. If the liturgy of the word is celebrated without the eucharistic sacrifice, the greeting and opening prayer are said after the entrance song, unless for pastoral reasons brief introductory remarks seem more appropriate.

The liturgy of the word follows in the usual manner. Three readings may be used, the first of them from the Old Testament. A brief homily should be given after the gospel, but without any kind of funeral eulogy. For pastoral reasons there may be only one reading, followed by the homily.

After the homily the general intercessions (prayer of the faithful) are said, and concluded either with a prayer by the priest or the Lord's Prayer recited by all present.

FINAL COMMENDATION AND FAREWELL

If celebrated after Mass

46. After the prayer after communion or, if the eucharistic sacrifice is not celebrated, after the liturgy of the word, the priest, vested in a chasuble or cope, begins the rite of final commendation and farewell.[1]

The priest stands near the coffin with the ministers who have the holy water and incense. [If the body was sprinkled with holy water at the entrance to the church at the beginning of Mass, the sprinkling is ordinarily omitted in the rite of commendation. If the body was incensed at the preparation of the gifts during Mass, the incensation is ordinarily omitted in the rite of commendation.] He faces the people and introduces the rite in these or similar words:

[1] See nos. 50 and 54.

With faith in Jesus Christ,
we reverently bring the body of our brother (sister)
to be buried in its human imperfection.

Let us pray with confidence to God,
who gives life to all things,
that he will raise up this mortal body
to the perfection and the company of the saints.

May God give him (her) a merciful judgment
and forgive all his (her) sins.
May Christ, the Good Shepherd,
lead him (her) safely home
to be at peace with God our Father.
And may he (she) be happy for ever
with all the saints
in the presence of the eternal King.

Or another introduction may be chosen, nos. 183, 184, 185 or 186.

Then all pray in silence for a little while.

According to local custom, the conference of bishops may permit the relatives of the deceased to give some words of greeting after the period of silent prayer.

47. The body is sprinkled with holy water and incensed, or this may be done after the song of farewell.

℣. **Saints of God, come to his (her) aid!**
Come to meet him (her), angels of the Lord!
℟. **Receive his (her) soul and present him (her) to God the Most High.**

℣. **May Christ, who called you, take you to himself;**
may angels lead you to Abraham's side.
℟. **Receive his (her) soul and present him (her) to God the Most High.**

℣. **Give him (her) eternal rest, O Lord,**
and may your light shine on him (her) for ever.
℟. **Receive his (her) soul and present him (her) to God the Most High.**

Another responsory may be chosen from nos. 187-191, or some other song may be used. If no singing is possible, it is recommended that prayers for the deceased be said by all present, for example, at least some invocations.

In the United States

If neither a responsory nor the above mentioned prayers or invocations are possible, one of the following may be added:

Priest:

Peace be with those who have left us and have gone to God.

Deacon or another minister:

May N. be at peace. May he (she) be with God.

All:

May he (she) be with the living God.
May he (she) be with the immortal God.
May he (she) be in God's hands.

Deacon:

May he (she) sleep in peace.

All:

May he (she) live in peace.

Deacon:

May he (she) be where the name of God is great.

All:

May he (she) be with the living God now and on the day of judgment.
May he (she) live with God.
May he (she) live in eternal light.

Deacon:

May he (she) live in the peace of the Lord.

All:

May he (she) live forever in peace.
With God in peace.

Or:

The deacon or another minister may lead the following part of the litany.

By your coming as man Lord, save your people
By your birth Lord, save your people

By your baptism and fasting Lord, save your people
By your sufferings and cross Lord, save your people
By your death and burial Lord, save your people
By your rising to new life Lord, save your people
By your return in glory to the Father Lord, save your people
By your gift of the Holy Spirit Lord, save your people
By your coming again in glory Lord, save your people

48. Then the priest says the prayer:

Father,
into your hands we commend our brother (sister).
We are confident that with all who have died in Christ
he (she) will be raised to life on the last day
and live with Christ for ever.
(We thank you for all the blessings
you gave him (her) in this life
to show your fatherly care for all of us
and the fellowship which is ours with the saints
in Jesus Christ.)

Lord, hear our prayer:
welcome our brother (sister) to paradise
and help us to comfort each other
with the assurance of our faith
(until we all meet in Christ
to be with you and with our brother (sister) for ever.)
(We ask this) through Christ our Lord.
℟. **Amen.**

Or prayer no. 192 may be chosen.

49. After the prayer, while the body is being taken away, the antiphons in no. 50 may be sung.

50. If the priest and the congregation accompany the

funeral to the cemetery, the final commendation and farewell may be celebrated at the grave or tomb itself. In this case, after the prayer after communion or, if the eucharistic liturgy is not celebrated, after the liturgy of the word, the body is taken away. Meanwhile one or other of these antiphons may be used:

May the angels lead you into paradise;
may the martyrs come to welcome you
and take you to the holy city,
the new and eternal Jerusalem.

Or:

May the choir of angels welcome you.
Where Lazarus is poor no longer,
may you have eternal rest.

Another antiphon no. 166 may be chosen.

Psalms or other appropriate verses may be sung with these antiphons.

51. If the priest cannot accompany the funeral procession to the cemetery, the prayers which follow may be said by lay persons, according to the circumstances and pastoral needs.

PROCESSION TO THE CEMETERY

52. During the procession to the cemetery, the following may be sung:

Psalm 118
Give thanks to the Lord, for he is good, with the antiphon:
Open for me the gates of holiness;
I will go in and praise the Lord. [155]

Or Antiphon:
This is the door of the Lord; the just shall enter it. [156]

Psalm 42
As the hind longs for the running waters, with the antiphon:
I will go to the glorious shrine of God, to the dwelling place of my lord. [147]

Psalm 93
The Lord is king, with the antiphon:

Of earth you formed me, with flesh you covered me;
Lord, my Redeemer, raise me up again at the last day.
[151]

Psalm 25
To you I lift up my soul, O Lord, with the antiphon:
Lord, see the depth of my misery and grief, and forgive me all my sins. [146]

Or parts of Psalm 119
Happy are they whose way is blameless. [157]

A
THIRD STATION: AT THE GRAVE OR TOMB

If the final commendation has been celebrated after Mass

[It is desirable that, in the absence of a priest or deacon, a lay person should lead the station in the cemetery.]

53. If the grave or tomb has not been blessed, it is blessed before the body is placed in it:

Let us pray.

Lord Jesus Christ,
by the three days you lay in the tomb
you made holy the graves of all who believe in you;
and even though their bodies lie in the earth,
they trust that they, like you, will rise again.

Give our brother (sister) peaceful rest in this grave,
until that day when you,
the resurrection and the life,
will raise him (her) up in glory.
Then may he (she) see the light of your presence,
Lord Jesus,
in the kingdom where you live for ever and ever.
℟. **Amen.**

Or another prayer may be chosen, nos. 193, 194, or 195.

After the prayer the priest, if it is the custom, sprinkles the body and the grave or tomb with holy water and incenses them, unless this is to be done during the rite of final commendation.

54. If the priest and congregation accompany the funeral to the cemetery, the final commendation and farewell may be celebrated at the grave or tomb itself, as described in nos. 46-48. In this case the funeral rites are concluded with the rite of commendation. [See B, Third Station at the Grave or Tomb, Final Commendation and Farewell.]

55. Depending on local custom, the burial takes place immediately or at the end of the rite. While the body is being placed in the grave or tomb, or at another suitable moment, the priest may say:

Since almighty God has called our brother (sister) N.
from this life to himself,
we commit his (her) body
to the earth from which it was made.

Christ was the first to rise from the dead,
and we know that he will raise up our mortal bodies
to be like his in glory.

We commend our brother (sister) to the Lord:
may the Lord receive him (her) into his peace
and raise up his (her) body on the last day.

A reading from scripture, and a responsorial psalm may then be said, especially if there is some interval between the station in the church and the burial. The reading and psalm may be included in the rite of final commendation, for a similar reason, if this takes place at the grave or tomb.

READING

John 12:23-26
Or: **John 12:35-36:**

RESPONSORIAL PSALM

Psalm 62

Antiphon: **Only in God is my soul at rest; from him comes my hope.**

Psalm 93

Antiphon: **Of earth you formed me, with flesh you covered me; Lord, my Redeemer, raise me up again at the last day.**

56. Then the priest may say, in whole or in part, the following prayer of the faithful, or a similar one:

Let us pray for our brother (sister)
to our Lord Jesus Christ,
who said:
"I am the resurrection and the life.
The man who believes in me will live
even if he dies,
and every living person
who puts his faith in me
will never suffer eternal death."

He (she) was nourished with your body and blood:
grant him (her) a place at the table in your heavenly kingdom.
We ask this in faith:
℟. **Lord, hear our prayer.**

Lord, you wept at the death of Lazarus, your friend:
comfort us in our sorrow.
We ask this in faith:
℟. **Lord, hear our prayer.**

You raise the dead to life:
give our brother (sister) eternal life.
We ask this in faith:
℟. **Lord, hear our prayer.**

You promised paradise to the thief who repented:
bring our brother (sister) to the joys of heaven.
We ask this in faith:
℟. **Lord, hear our prayer.**

Our brother (sister) was washed clean in baptism and anointed with the oil of salvation:
give him (her) fellowship with all your saints.
We ask this in faith:
℟. **Lord, hear our prayer.**

Comfort us in our sorrow at the death of our brother (sister):
let our faith be our consolation and eternal life our hope.

We ask this in faith:
℟. **Lord, hear our prayer.**

Then all say the LORD'S PRAYER together, or the priest says the following prayer:

Lord,
listen to our prayers for our brother (sister).
As he (she) always desired to do your will,
so in your mercy forgive
whatever wrong he (she) may have done.
By his (her) Christian faith he (she) was united
with all your believing people.
Now, in love and mercy
give him (her) a place with your angels and saints.
We ask this through Christ our Lord.
℟. **Amen.**

Or another prayer may be chosen, no. 196, 197, 198, 199, 34, or 169.

℣. **Give him (her) eternal rest, O Lord.**
℟. **And may your light shine on him (her) for ever.**

In the United States, if a prayer for those present is desired, no. 34 or 169 may be added.

57. At the end of the entire rite, an appropriate song may be sung, according to local custom.

B
THIRD STATION: AT THE GRAVE OR TOMB

FINAL COMMENDATION AND FAREWELL

(If the final commendation is to be celebrated at the grave or tomb)

If the priest and congregation accompany the funeral to the cemetery, the final commendation and farewell may be celebrated at the grave or tomb itself, as described in nos. 46-48. In this case the funeral rites are concluded with the rite of commendation.

If the grave or tomb has not been blessed, it is blessed before the body is placed in it, as described in no. 53.

FINAL COMMENDATION AND FAREWELL

The priest stands near the coffin with the ministers who have the holy water and incense. He faces the people and introduces the rite as described in no. 46.

A reading from scripture, and a responsorial psalm (see no. 55) may then be said, especially if there is some interval between the station in the church and the burial.

The body is sprinkled with holy water and incensed, or this may be done after the song of farewell, as described in nos. 47 and 48.

57. At the end of the entire rite, an appropriate song may be sung, according to local custom.

RECEPTION OF THE FUNERAL AT THE CHURCH WHEN THE FUNERAL LITURGY DOES NOT TAKE PLACE AT ONCE

58. When the body of the deceased is brought to the church some time before the funeral liturgy is to be celebrated, the rite may be arranged as follows:

The priest receives the funeral procession at the church door with the sprinkling of holy water and the prayer mentioned in no. 33.

While the body is being carried into the church, one of the responsories in nos. 187-191 may be sung.

After this John 14:1-6 (no. 143) or another passage indicated below in nos. 83-107, 128-144 is read.

After the reading a psalm taken from those mentioned above in no. 35 is said, or the prayer of the faithful in a short form.

The entire rite is completed with the Lord's Prayer.
Then the body is placed in the chapel used for this purpose.

CHAPTER III

SECOND PLAN OF THE FUNERAL RITE WITH STATIONS IN THE CEMETERY CHAPEL AND AT THE GRAVE OR TOMB

59. This plan of the funeral rites does not provide for a Mass as a part of the funeral. A Mass will be celebrated, however, at some suitable time, without the body present, either before or after the funeral. The funeral Mass may be celebrated in the home of the deceased, if the local Ordinary judges this to be appropriate in particular circumstances.

FIRST STATION: IN THE CEMETERY CHAPEL

60. The priest vests in an alb or surplice and stole of the color for funerals, with a cope of the same color if he wishes. He goes with the ministers to the bier, where the funeral party is waiting. The priest greets those present and offers them his sympathy and the consolation of faith.

61. Then one of the responsories in nos. 47 and 187-191 or another appropriate song is sung.

LITURGY OF THE WORD

62. After this John 14:1-6 (no. 143) or another reading from nos. 128-144 is read.

63. If circumstances suggest, an epistle or a reading from the Old Testament, from nos. 83-107, may be read before the gospel. In this case one of the psalms indicated above in no. 33 is said or sung with its antiphon between the readings.

64. After the reading or readings, there should be a brief homily, unless this takes place at the grave or tomb.

FINAL COMMENDATION AND FAREWELL

65-69. The rite of final commendation and farewell follows, as described in nos. 46-48, unless it is to be celebrated at the grave or tomb.

PROCESSION TO THE GRAVE OR TOMB

70. During the procession to the grave or tomb, psalms and antiphons, as described in no. 52, may be sung.

A
SECOND STATION: AT THE GRAVE OR TOMB

(If the final commendation has been celebrated after the First Station)

71-72. If the grave or tomb has not been blessed, it is blessed before the body is placed in it, as described in nos. 53-55.

73. If there is to be a homily at the grave or tomb, it is given at this point.

74. If the final commendation and farewell is also celebrated at the grave, it takes the place of the following prayer of the faithful. In this case the funeral rites are concluded with the rite of commendation, nos. 65-67.

75. Then the priest may say, in whole or in part, the prayer of the faithful, or a similar one as described in no. 56.

76. At the end of the entire rite, an appropriate song may be sung, according to local custom.

B

For B, Second Station at the Grave or Tomb, Final Commendation and Farewell, see pp. 683-684.

CHAPTER IV

THIRD PLAN OF THE FUNERAL RITE CELEBRATED IN THE HOME OF THE DECEASED

77. Depending on local custom, when the body of the deceased is laid out, when it is placed on the bier, or whenever other acts of piety are celebrated between the time of death and the principal funeral service, the prayers, readings, and songs may be used as indicated in no. 30 or in a similar manner, with texts taken from Chapter VI.

78. The liturgy of the word in the form of a vigil may be held in the home of the deceased, as mentioned above in nos. 26-28. The several aspects of the meaning of Christian death, mentioned in nos. 1 and 2, should be clearly expressed.

For pastoral reasons the local Ordinary may permit the funeral Mass to be celebrated in the home of the deceased.

79. The rite of final commendation and farewell is celebrated according to the first plan, nos. 46-48.

CHAPTER V

FUNERALS OF CHILDREN

80. The funeral rites for baptized children who die before the age of reason are arranged according to the different plans of funerals described in Chapters II, III, and IV. The special texts given below in nos. 203-230 are to be used.

81. The liturgical color should be festive and with a paschal significance.

82. If a child whom the parents wished to be baptized should die before baptism, the local Ordinary, taking into consideration pastoral circumstances, may permit the funeral to be celebrated either in the home of the child (see above, Chapter IV) or even according to the plan of funeral rites customarily used for other funerals in the region (see above, Chapters II and III). In either case, the special texts given below in nos. 231-237 are to be used.

When funerals of this kind are celebrated, the doctrine of the necessity of baptism should not be weakened in the catechesis of the faithful.

FIRST STATION: IN THE HOME OF THE DECEASED

The rite begins as described in nos. 32 and 33.

PRAYER

Then the priest adds:

℣. **The Lord be with you.**
℟. **and also with you.**

One of the prayers in no. 223, 224, 235, 236, or 226, is said, according to the circumstances.

The prayer for the mourners, nos. 225 or 226 may be said after or even before the above prayer for the deceased.

PROCESSION TO THE CHURCH

The rite takes place as described in no. 35 and 36.

SECOND STATION: IN THE CHURCH

The rite takes place as described in nos. 37-45.

FINAL COMMENDATION AND FAREWELL

(If celebrated after Mass)

The rite takes place as described in no. 46, with an introduction from nos. 227, 228, or 237, according to the circumstances.

The other texts may be chosen from those in the rite for baptized children.

Then all pray in silence for a little while.

According to local custom, the conference of bishops may permit the relatives of the deceased to give some words of greeting after the period of silent prayer.
The body is sprinkled with holy water and incensed, or this may be done after the song of farewell, as described in no. 47.

Then the priest says one of the prayers, no. 223 or 224.

The rite concludes as described in nos. 49 and 50.

PROCESSION TO THE CEMETERY

The rite takes place as described in no. 52.

A

THIRD STATION: AT THE GRAVE OR TOMB

(If the final commendation has been celebrated after Mass)
The rite takes place as described in no. 53, with the prayer, no. 230.

The rite continues as described in nos. 54 and 55.

Then the priest may say, in whole or in part, the following

prayer of the faithful, or a similar one [the petitions in brackets are omitted according to the circumstances of the deceased child].

**Let us pray for our brother (sister)
to our Lord Jesus Christ,
who said:
"I am the resurrection and the life.
The man who believes in me will live
even if he dies,
and every living person
who puts his faith in me
will never suffer eternal death."**

**Lord, you wept at the death of Lazarus, your friend:
comfort us in our sorrow.
We ask this in faith:
℟. Lord, hear our prayer.**

**You raise the dead to life:
give our brother (sister) eternal life.
We ask this in faith:
℟. Lord, hear our prayer.**

**[You promised paradise to the thief who repented:
bring our brother (sister) to the joys of heaven.
We ask this in faith:
℟. Lord, hear our prayer.]**

**[Our brother (sister) was washed clean in baptism
and anointed with the oil of salvation:
give him (her) fellowship with all your saints.
We ask this in faith:
℟. Lord, hear our prayer.]**

**[He (she) was nourished with your body and blood:
grant him (her) a place at the table in your heavenly kingdom.
We ask this in faith:
℟. Lord, hear our prayer.]**

**Comfort us in our sorrow at the death of our brother (sister):
let our faith be our consolation**

and eternal life our hope.
We ask this in faith:
℟. **Lord, hear our prayer.**

Then all say the LORD'S PRAYER together, or the priest says one of the prayers, no. 223, 224, 235, 236, or 226, according to the circumstances.

The prayer for the mourners no. 225 or 226 may be said after or even before the above prayer for the deceased.

At the end of the entire rite, an appropriate song may be sung, according to local custom.

B
THIRD STATION: AT THE GRAVE OR TOMB

If the final commendation is to be celebrated at the grave or tomb

If the priest and congregation accompany the funeral to the cemetery, the final commendation and farewell may be celebrated at the grave or tomb itself, as described in nos. 46-48. In this case the funeral rites are concluded with the rite of commendation.

If the grave or tomb has not been blessed, it is blessed before the body is placed in it according to the rites described in no. 53 using prayer no. 230.

The priest stands near the coffin with the ministers who have the holy water and incense. He faces the people and introduces the rite using prayers no. 227, 228, or 237, according to circumstances, or similar words.

The other texts may be chosen from those in the rite for baptized children.

Then all pray in silence for a little while.

According to local custom, the conference of bishops may permit the relatives of the deceased to give some words of greeting after the period of silent prayer.

A reading from scripture, and a responsorial psalm may then be said, especially if there is some interval between the station in the church and the burial as described in no. 55.

The body is sprinkled with holy water and incensed, or this may be done after the song of farewell. See no. 229.

Another responsory may be chosen from nos. 187-191, or some other song may be used. If no singing is possible, it is recommended that prayers for the deceased be said by all present, for example, at least some invocations.

(In the United States)

If neither a responsory nor the above mentioned prayers or invocations are possible, one of the prayers given on pages 662-665 may be added:

Then the priest says one of the prayers for a deceased child, no. 223, 224, 225, 236, and for the mourners, no. 225 or 226, according to the rite described in no. 34.

At the end of the rite an appropriate song may be sung according to local custom.

CHAPTER VI

VARIOUS TEXTS USED IN THE ORDER OF FUNERALS FOR ADULTS

I. SCRIPTURE READINGS

OLD TESTAMENT READING

83. **Job 19:1, 23-27a**
I know that my redeemer lives

84. **Wisdom 3:1-9** (longer) **or 1-6** (shorter)
He accepted them as a holocaust.

85. **Wisdom 4:7-15**
A blameless life is a ripe old age.

86. **Isaiah 25:6a, 7-9**
The Lord God will destroy death for ever.

87. **Lamentations 3:17-26**
It is good to wait in silence for the Lord God to save.
The Hebrew letters are omitted.

88. **Daniel 12:1-3**
Of those who lie sleeping in the dust of the earth many will awake.

89. **2 Maccabees 12:43-46**
It is good and holy to think of the dead rising again.

NEW TESTAMENT READING

90. **Acts 10:34-43** (longer) **or 34-36, 42-43** (shorter)
God has appointed Jesus to judge everyone, alive and dead.

91. **Romans 5:5-11**
Having been justified by his blood, we will be saved from God's anger through him.

92. **Romans 5:17-21**
However great the number of sins committed, grace was even greater.

93. **Romans 6:3-9** (longer) **or 3-4, 8-9** (shorter)
Let us walk in newness of life.

94. **Romans 8:14-23**
We wait for our bodies to be set free.

95. **Romans 8:31b-35, 37-39**
Nothing can really come between us and the love of Christ.

96. **Romans 14:7-9, 10b-12**
Alive or dead, we belong to the Lord.

97. **1 Corinthians 15:20-24a, 25-28** (longer), **20-23** (shorter)
All men will be brought to life in Christ.

98. **1 Corinthians 15:51-57**
Death is swallowed up in victory.

99. **2 Corinthians 5:1, 6-10**
We have an everlasting home in heaven.

100. **Philippians 3:20-21**
Jesus will transfigure these wretched bodies of ours to be like his glorious body.

101. **1 Thessalonians 4:13-18**
We shall stay with the Lord for ever.

102. **2 Timothy 2:8-13**
If we have died with him, then we shall live with him.

103. **1 John 3:1-2**
We shall see him as he really is.

104. **1 John 3:14-16**
We have passed out of death and into life because we love the brothers.

105. **Revelation 14:13**
Happy are those who die in the Lord.

106. **Revelation 20:11—21:1**
The dead have been judged according to their works.

107. **Revelation 21:1-5a, 6b-7**
There will be no more death.

RESPONSORIAL PSALM

108. Psalm 23:1-3a, 3b-4, 5, 6
℟. (1): **The Lord is my shepherd; there is nothing I shall want.**

or: (4a): **Though I walk in the valley of darkness, I fear no evil, for you are with me.**

109. Psalm 25:6-7bc, 17-18, 20-21
℟. (1b): **To you, O Lord, I lift my soul.**
or: (3b): **No one who waits for you, O Lord, will ever be put to shame.**

110. Psalm 27:1, 4, 7 and 8b and 9a, 13-14.
℟. (1a): **The Lord is my light and my salvation.**
or: (13): **I believe that I shall see the good things of the Lord in the land of the living.**

111. Psalm 42:2, 3, 5bcd; Psalm 43:3, 4, 5
℟. (Psalm 42:3): **My soul is thirsting for the living God: when shall I see him face to face?**

112. Psalm 63:2-3a, 3bc-4, 5-6, 8-9
℟. (2b): **My soul is thirsting for you, O Lord my God.**

113. Psalm 103:8 and 10, 13-14, 15-16, 17-18
℟. (8a): **The Lord is kind and merciful.**
or: (Psalm 38:39a): **The salvation of the just comes from the Lord.**

114. Psalm 115:5, 6; Psalm 116:10-11, 15-16ac
℟. (Psalm 115:9): **I will walk in the presence of the Lord, in the land of the living.**
or: **Alleluia.**

115. Psalm 122:1-2, 3-4a, 4b-5, 6-7, 8-9.
℟. (1): **I rejoiced when I heard them say: let us go to the house of the Lord.**
or: **Let us go rejoicing to the house of the Lord.**

116. Psalm 130:1-2, 3-4ab, 4c-6, 7-8
℟. (1): **Out of the depths, I cry to you, Lord.**
or: (see 5): **I hope in the Lord, I trust in his word.**

117. Psalm 143:1-2, 5-6, 7ab and 8ab, 10
℟. (1a): **O Lord, hear my prayer.**

ALLELUIA VERSE AND VERSE BEFORE THE GOSPEL

118. Matthew 11:25
Blessed are you, Father, Lord of heaven and earth;

you have revealed to little ones the mysteries of the kingdom.

119. Matthew 25:34

Come, you whom my Father has blessed, says the Lord;
inherit the kingdom prepared for you since the foundation of the world.

120. John 3:16

God loved the world so much, he gave us his only Son,
that all who believe in him might have eternal life.

121. John 6:39

This is the will of my Father, says the Lord,
that I should lose nothing of all that he has given to me,
and that I should raise it up on the last day.

122. John 6:40

This is the will of my Father, says the Lord,
all who believe in the Son will have eternal life
and I will raise them to life again on the last day.

123. John 11:25a, 26

I am the resurrection and the life, said the Lord:
he who believes in me will not die for ever.

124. Philippians 3:20

Our true home is in heaven,
and Jesus Christ whose return we long for
will come from heaven to save us.

125. 2 Timothy 2:11-12a

If we die with Christ, we shall live with him,
and if we are faithful to the end, we shall reign with him.

126. Revelation 1:5-6

Jesus Christ is the firstborn of the dead;
glory and kingship be his for ever and ever. Amen.

127. Revelation 14:13

Happy are those who have died in the Lord;
let them rest from their labors for their good deeds go with them.

GOSPEL

128. **Matthew 5:1-12a**
Rejoice and be glad, for your reward will be great in heaven.

129. **Matthew 11:25-30**
You have hidden these things from the learned and have revealed them to children.

130. **Matthew 25:1-13**
Look, the bridegroom is coming; go out and meet him.

131. **Matthew 25:31-46**
Come, you whom my Father has blessed.

132. **Mark 15:33-39; 16:1-6** (longer) **or 15:33-39** (shorter)
Jesus gave a loud cry and breathed his last.

133. **Luke 7:11-17**
Young man, I say to you, get up.

134. **Luke 12:35-40**
Be like men waiting for the arrival of their master.

135. **Luke 23:33, 39-43**
Today you will be with me in paradise.

136. **Luke 23:44-49, 24:1-6a** (longer) **or 23:44-49** (shorter)
Father, into your hands I commit my spirit.

137. **Luke 24:13-35** (longer) **or 13-16, 28-35** (shorter)
Was it not necessary that the Christ should suffer and so enter into his glory?

138. **John 6:37-40**
Whoever believes in Jesus has eternal life and I will raise him up on the last day.

139. **John 6:51-59 (Greek 51-58)**
Anyone who eats this bread will live for ever; and I will raise him up on the last day.

140. **John 11:17-27** (longer) **or 21-27** (shorter)
I am the resurrection and the life.

141. **John 11:32-45**
Lazarus, come out.

142. **John 12:23-38** (longer) **or 23-26** (shorter)
If a grain of wheat falls on the ground and dies, it yields a rich harvest.

143. **John 14:1-6**
There are many rooms in my Father's house.

144. **John 17:24-26**
Father, I want those you have given me to be with me where I am.

II. PSALMS AND ANTIPHONS

For convenience the psalms mentioned in this rite, together with antiphons, are indicated here.

145. Psalm 23 The Lord, Shepherd and Host
Psalm: **Lord, remember me in your kingdom.**

146. Psalm 25 Prayer for Guidance and Help
Ant.: **Lord, see the depth of my misery and grief, and forgive me all my sins.**

146a. [In the United States] Psalm 26 Prayer of an Innocent Man
Antiphon: **Redeem me and have pity on me.**

147. Psalm 42 Desire for God in His Temple.
Antiphon: **I will go to the glorious shrine of God, to the dwelling place of my Lord.**

148. Psalm 51 The Miserere: Prayer of Repentance.
Antiphon: **Give him (her) eternal rest, O Lord, and may your light shine on him (her) for ever.**

149. Psalm 51
Antiphon: **Lord, may our brother (sister), whom you have called to yourself, find happiness in the glory of your saints.**

150. Psalm 51
Antiphon: **The bones that were crushed shall leap for joy before the Lord.**

150a. [In the United States] Psalm 62 Trust in God Alone
Antiphon: **Only in God is my soul at rest, from him comes my hope.**

151. Psalm 93 The Glory of the Lord's Kingdom.
Antiphon: **Of earth you formed me, with flesh you**

covered me; Lord, my Redeemer, raise me up again at the last day.

152. Psalm 114 The Lord's Wonders at the Exodus.
Psalm 115: 1-12 The Greatness and Goodness of the True God.
Responsorial Psalm: **May Christ make you welcome in paradise.**

153. Psalm 116(A) Thanksgiving to God for Help in Need.
Antiphon: **May the choir of angels welcome you and lead you to Abraham's side. Where Lazarus is poor no longer, may you have everlasting rest.**

154. Psalm 116(B)
Antiphon: **I heard a voice from heaven saying: Happy are those who die in the Lord.**

155. Psalm 118 Hymn of Thanksgiving to the Savior of Israel.
Antiphon: **Open for me the gates of holiness; I will go in and praise the Lord.**

156. Psalm 118
Antiphon: **This is the door of the Lord; the just shall enter it.**

157. Psalm 119 Praise of God's Law.

158. Psalm 121 The Lord Our Guardian.

159. Psalm 122 The Pilgrim's Greeting to Jerusalem.

160. Psalm 123 Israel's Prayer in Persecution.

161. Psalm 126 The People's Prayer for Full Restoration.

162-163. Psalm 130 Prayer for Pardon and Mercy.
Responsorial Psalm: **I cry to you, O Lord.**
Or: **My soul hopes in the Lord.**

164. Psalm 132 The Pact Between David and the Lord.

165. Psalm 134 Exhortations to the Night Watch to Bless the Lord.

166. The following antiphon may be used while the body of the deceased is being carried from the church.

**I am the resurrection and the life.
The man who believes in me will live
even if he dies,
and every living person
who puts his faith in me
will never suffer eternal death.**

III. PRAYERS FOR THE STATION IN THE HOME OF THE DECEASED

Even if it is indicated for a particular part of the funeral service, any of the following prayers may be used at other parts of the rite, provided the character of the text is taken into account.

167. For the deceased person

**Almighty Father,
eternal God,
hear our prayers
for your son (daughter) N.
whom you have called from this life to yourself.
Grant him (her) light, happiness, and peace.
Let him (her) pass in safety through the gates of death,
and live for ever with all your saints
in the light you promised to Abraham
and to all his descendants in faith.
Guard him (her) from all harm
and on that great day of resurrection and reward
raise him (her) up with all your saints.
Pardon his (her) sins
and give him (her) eternal life in your kingdom.
We ask this through Christ our Lord.**
℟. **Amen.**

168. For the deceased person

**Father,
we entrust our brother (sister) to your mercy.
You loved him (her) greatly in this life:
now that he (she) is freed from all its cares,
give him (her) happiness and peace for ever.**

The old order has passed away:
welcome him (her) now into paradise
where there will be no more sorrow,
no more weeping or pain,
but only peace and joy
with Jesus, your Son,
and the Holy Spirit
for ever and ever.
℟. **Amen.**

169. For the deceased person and for tne mourners
Lord Jesus,
our Redeemer,
you willingly gave yourself up to death
so that all people might be saved
and pass from death into a new life.
Listen to our prayers,
look with love on your people
who mourn and pray for their dead brother (sister).
Lord Jesus, you alone are holy and compassionate:
forgive our brother (sister) his (her) sins.
By dying you opened the gates of life
for those who believe in you:
do not let our brother (sister) be parted from you,
but by your glorious power
give him (her) light, joy, and peace in heaven
where you live for ever and ever.
℟. **Amen.**

IV. PRAYERS FOR THE LITURGY OF THE WORD

In addition to these prayers, any prayer from the Mass for the dead may be chosen.

The texts are ordinarily written to refer to a single deceased person and should be changed when used for several persons.

170.
Lord God,
almighty Father,

our faith testifies that your Son
died for us and rose to life again.
May our brother (sister) N. share in this mystery:
as he (she) has gone to his (her) rest believing in Jesus,
may he (she) come through him to the joy of the resurrection.
We ask this through Christ our Lord.
℟. **Amen.**

171.
Lord God,
you are the glory of believers
and the life of the just.
Your Son redeemed us
by dying and rising to life again.
Since our brother (sister) N. believed in the mystery
of our own resurrection,
let him (her) share the joys and blessings
of the life to come.
We ask this through Christ our Lord.
℟. **Amen.**

172.
Lord God, almighty Father,
you have made the cross for us a sign of strength
and marked us as yours in the sacrament of the resurrection.
Now that you have freed our brother (sister) from this mortal life,
make him (her) one with your saints in heaven.
We ask this through Christ our Lord.
℟. **Amen.**

173.
Lord, hear our prayers.
By raising your Son from the dead, you have given us faith.
Strengthen our hope that N., our brother (sister),
will share in his resurrection.

We ask this through Christ our Lord.
℟. **Amen.**

174.
In your presence, Lord, those who die still live,
and our bodies do not perish in death,
but are transformed by your power.
Listen to our prayers
and welcome your son (daughter) N.
to the company of Abraham, our father in faith,
and raise him (her) up on the last day,
the day of judgment.
In your love cleanse him (her)
from every sin he (she) has committed
during his (her) life on earth.
We ask this through Christ our Lord.
℟. **Amen.**

175.
Lord, we ask your mercy for your son (daughter) N.
Welcome him (her) into your love
and forgive whatever wrong he (she) may have done
during his (her) life on earth.
Free him (her) from the chains of death
and let him (her) enter into life.
We ask this through Christ our Lord.
℟. **Amen.**

176.
Help us, Lord, to receive and understand your gospel,
so that we may find light in this darkness,
faith in our doubts,
and comfort for one another in your saving words.
We ask this through Christ our Lord.
℟. **Amen.**

177. For a young person
Lord God, the days allotted to each of us
are in your fatherly care.
Though we are saddened

that our brother (sister) N. was with us for so short a time,
we entrust him (her) to you with confidence.
May he (she) live, radiant and for ever young
in the happiness of your kingdom.
We ask this through Christ our Lord.
℟. **Amen.**

178. For one who worked in the service of the Gospel
Lord, hear our prayers for your son (daughter) N.,
who labored so generously
to bring your Gospel to the world.
May he (she) be the more worthy to share the rewards of your kingdom.
We ask this through Christ our Lord.
℟. **Amen.**

179. For one who suffered a long illness
Lord God, in his (her) suffering and long illness
our brother (sister) N. served you faithfully
by imitating the patience of your Son, Jesus Christ.
May he (she) also share in the reward of his glory
for ever and ever.
℟. **Amen.**

180. For one who died suddenly
Lord, as we mourn the sudden death of our brother (sister) N.,
comfort us with the great power of your love
and strengthen us in our faith
that he (she) is with you for ever.
We ask this through Christ our Lord.
℟. **Amen.**

181. For parents
God, you command us to honor father and mother;
in your mercy forgive the sins of my (our) parents
and let me (us) one day see them again
in the radiance of eternal joy.
We ask this through Christ our Lord.
℟. **Amen.**

182. For a married couple
**Lord, pardon the sins of your servants N. and N.
In this life they were joined in true married love.
Now let the fullness of your own love
unite them for life eternal.
We ask this through Christ our Lord.**
℟. **Amen.**

V. INTRODUCTION TO THE FINAL COMMENDATION AND FAREWELL

183.
Our brother (sister) has gone to his (her) rest in the peace of Christ. With faith and hope in eternal life, let us commend him (her) to the loving mercy of our Father, and assist him (her) with our prayers. He (she) became God's son (daughter) through baptism and was often fed at the table of our Lord. May the Lord now welcome him (her) to the table of God's children in heaven, and, with all the saints, may he (she) inherit the promise of eternal life.

Let us also pray to the Lord for ourselves. May we who mourn be reunited one day with our brother (sister). Together may we meet Christ Jesus when he, who is our life, shall appear in his glory.

184.
Since almighty God has called our brother (sister) N. from this life to himself, we commit his (her) body to the earth from which it was made.

Christ was the first to rise from the dead, and we know that he will raise up our mortal bodies to be like his in glory.

We commend our brother (sister) to the Lord: may the Lord receive him (her) into his peace and raise up his (her) body on the last day.

185.
Before we part, let us take leave of our brother

(sister). May this last farewell express the depth of our love for him (her), ease our sadness, and strengthen our hope. We know that one day we shall greet him (her) with joy where the love of Christ, which overcomes all things, will destroy even death itself.

186.
Our prayers now are ended, and we bid our last farewell. There is sadness in the parting, but it should fill us with new hope, for one day we shall see our brother (sister) again and enjoy his (her) love. By God's mercy, we who leave this church today in sorrow will be reunited in the joy of God's kingdom. Let us comfort one another in the faith of Jesus Christ.

VI. RESPONSORIES FOR THE FINAL COMMENDATION AND FAREWELL

187.
Lord, you shed your blood for our brother (sister); welcome him (her) into your presence;* do not forget, Lord, that we are dust, and man is like grass, like a flower of the field.

℣. The Lord is merciful and kind, patient and rich in mercy;* do not forget, Lord, that we are dust, and man is like grass, like a flower of the field.

188.
You knew me, Lord, before I was born, for you made me in your likeness;* now I return you my soul, for you are my maker.

℣. My sins, Lord, make me afraid, and bring me shame; do not condemn me when you come in judgment;* now I return you my soul, for you are my maker.

189.
I know that my Redeemer lives, and on the last day I

shall rise again;* in my body I shall look on God, my Savior.

℣. **I myself shall see him; my own eyes will gaze on him;* in my body I shall look on God, my Savior.**

℣. **This is the hope I cherish in my heart;* in my body I shall look on God, my Savior.**

190.
Lord, you raised Lazarus from the dead;* forgive our brother (sister), and give him (her) a resting-place in peace.

℣. **Give him (her) eternal rest, O Lord, and may your light shine on him (her) for ever;* forgive our brother (sister), and give him (her) a resting-place in peace.**

191.
Lord, lead me out of the ways of darkness; you broke down the gates of death, and visited the prisoners of darkness;* you brought them light to let them see your face.

℣. **They cried out in welcome: "Redeemer, you have come at last!"* you brought them light to let them see your face.**

℣. **Give him (her) eternal rest, O Lord, and may your light shine on him (her) for ever;* you brought them light to let them see your face.**

VII. ANOTHER PRAYER AT END OF FINAL COMMENDATION AND FAREWELL

192.
**We commend our brother (sister) N. to you, Lord.
Now that he (she) has passed from this life,
may he (she) live on in your presence.
In your mercy and love,
forgive whatever sins he (she) may have committed
through human weakness.
We ask this through Christ our Lord.**
℟. **Amen.**

VII. PRAYERS FOR THE BLESSING OF THE GRAVE OR TOMB

193.
Lord God, through your mercy
those who have lived in faith
find eternal peace.
Bless this grave
and send your angel to watch over it.
Forgive the sins of our brother (sister)
whose body we bury here.
Welcome him (her) into your presence,
and with your saints let him (her) rejoice in you for ever.
We ask this through Christ our Lord.
℟. **Amen.**

194.
Lord God, we give you thanks and praise
for you created the earth and the heavens
and set the stars in their places.
When mankind was caught in the snare of death
you set us free through baptism.
In fulfillment of your will
our Lord Jesus Christ
conquered death and rose to life
to bring salvation and resurrection to those who belong to him by faith.
We ask you, Lord, to bless this grave.
Give our brother (sister) peace and rest,
and on the day of judgment
raise him (her) up to eternal life
with all your saints.
We ask this through Christ our Lord.
℟. **Amen.**

195.
Lord God,
when we were justly condemned for our sins
you taught us repentance
so that we might rise again to life.

You gave Abraham, our father in faith,
a burial place in the promised land.
You inspired Joseph of Arimathea
to bury Jesus in the tomb he had made for himself.
With sorrow for our sins,
we earnestly ask you to bless this grave
prepared for the burial of our brother (sister).
We commit his (her) body to the earth,
and ask you to welcome him (her) to the joys of paradise.
We ask this through Christ our Lord.
℟. **Amen.**

IX. CONCLUDING PRAYERS AT THE CEMETERY

196.
Lord God, you always listen to sincere prayers.
We have celebrated the funeral rite of our brother (sister)
and now we ask you to grant him (her) a share in that blessed reward
which you have prepared for all the saints.
We ask this through Christ our Lord.
℟. **Amen.**

197.
Lord God, giver of life and resurrection,
you desire that sinful men should turn to you in prayer.
Accept the prayers
which in our sorrow we offer for your son (daughter) N.
Save him (her) from eternal death,
and welcome him (her) to the joys of your saints in paradise.
We ask this through Christ our Lord.
℟. **Amen.**

198.
God, your days are without end,

your mercies beyond counting.
Help us always to remember
that life is short
and the day of our death is known to you alone.
May your Holy Spirit lead us
to live in holiness and justice all our days.
Then, after serving you in the fellowship of your Church,
with strong faith, consoling hope, and perfect love for all,
may we joyfully come to your kingdom.
We ask this through Christ our Lord.
℟. **Amen.**

199.
Almighty God,
through the death of your Son on the cross,
you have overcome death for us.
Through his burial and resurrection from the dead
you have made the grave a holy place
and restored to us eternal life.
We pray for those who died believing in Jesus
and are buried with him in the hope of rising again.
God of the living and the dead,
may those who faithfully believed in you on earth
praise you for ever in the joy of heaven.
We ask this through Christ our Lord.
℟. **Amen.**

X. OTHER FORMS OF THE PRAYERS OF THE FAITHFUL

200. For use at Mass or liturgy of the word

God, the almighty Father, raised Christ his Son from the dead; with confidence we ask him to save his people, living and dead.

Our brother (sister), N., was given the promise of eternal life in baptism; Lord, give him (her) communion with your saints for ever.
℟. **Lord, hear our prayer.**

N. ate the bread of eternal life, the body of Christ; raise him (her) up, Lord, at the last day.
℟. **Lord, hear our prayer.**

(for a priest) **Our brother, N., was a priest on earth; welcome him, Lord, into the sanctuary of heaven.**
℟. **Lord, hear our prayer.**

We pray for our brothers and sisters, our relatives, for all who were close to us and good to us; Lord, give them the reward of their goodness.
℟. **Lord, hear our prayer.**

We pray for all who have died in the hope of rising again; welcome them, Lord, into the light of your presence.
℟. **Lord, hear our prayer.**

We pray for all who have gathered here to worship in faith; Lord, make us one in your kingdom.
℟. **Lord, hear our prayer.**

PRAYER

Lord,
hear our prayers for our dead brothers and sisters;
forgive them their sins,
and bring them to the fullness of your salvation.
We ask this through Christ our Lord.
℟. **Amen.**

201. For use at Mass or a liturgy of the word

My dear friends, we join in prayer for our deceased brother (sister); let us pray also for the Church, for peace in the world, and for ourselves.
℟. **Hear us, Lord, and have mercy.**

We pray to the Father for the bishops and priests of the Church; may he give them strength to be examples of what they preach.
℟. **Hear us, Lord, and have mercy.**

We pray for all in public office; may they work for justice and true peace.
℟. **Hear us, Lord, and have mercy.**

We pray for all who suffer in mind or body; may they realize that God is always with them.
℟. Hear us, Lord, and have mercy.

We pray that God may free our brother (sister), N., from punishment and darkness.
℟. Hear us, Lord, and have mercy.

We pray that in his mercy God may forgive all his (her) sins.
℟. Hear us, Lord, and have mercy.

We pray that God may give him (her) peace and light for ever.
℟. Hear us, Lord, and have mercy.

We pray that God may give him (her) joy in the company of all his saints.
℟. Hear us, Lord, and have mercy.

We pray for our deceased relatives and for all who have done good to us; may God welcome them into the radiant light of his presence.
℟. Hear us, Lord, and have mercy.

We pray for all who died in faith; may the Lord welcome them into his presence.
℟. Hear us, Lord, and have mercy.

PRAYER

Let us pray.

Lord God, Creator and Redeemer,
release our departed brothers and sisters from all punishment;
in answer to our prayers,
give them the pardon they have always desired.
We ask this through Christ our Lord.
℟. Amen.

202. For use at the grave or tomb

Dear friends, God is the Father of mercies. Let us pray to him for our brothers and sisters who have died in Christ.

In your goodness, forgive them their sins.
℟. Lord, hear our prayer.

Remember their good works done in faith.
℟. Lord, hear our prayer.

Welcome them into eternal life
℟. Lord, hear our prayer.

Let us pray also for those who mourn our brother's (sister's) death;
comfort them in their sorrow.
℟. Lord, hear our prayer.

Fill the emptiness in their hearts with the presence of your love.
℟. Lord, hear our prayer.

Increase their faith and strengthen their hope.
℟. Lord, hear our prayer.

Let us pray also for ourselves in our pilgrimage through life;
strengthen us and keep us faithful in your service.
℟. Lord, hear our prayer.

Fill our hearts with the hope for heaven.
℟. Lord, hear our prayer.

PRAYER

Let us pray.

Almighty, ever-living God,
you watch over the living and the dead
and are merciful to all who are marked as your children
by their faith and good works.
We pray for our friends, living and dead;
in your goodness
grant them pardon for their sins
through the prayers of all your saints.
We ask this through Christ our Lord.
℟. Amen.

CHAPTER VII

VARIOUS TEXTS FOR FUNERALS OF BAPTIZED CHILDREN

I. SCRIPTURE READINGS

OLD TESTAMENT READING

203. **Isaiah 25:6a, 7-9**
The Lord God will destroy death for ever.

204. **Lamentations 3:17-26**
It is good to wait in silence for the Lord God to save.
The Hebrew letters are omitted

NEW TESTAMENT READING

205. **Romans 6:3-4, 8-9**
We believe that we shall return to life with Christ.

206. **Romans 14:7-9**
Alive or dead we belong to the Lord.

207. **1 Corinthians 15:20-23**
All men will be brought to life in Christ.

208. **Ephesians 1:3-5**
The Father chose us in Christ, before the creation of the world to be holy.

209. **1 Thessalonians 4:13—14, 18**
We shall stay with the Lord for ever.

210. **Revelation 7:9-10, 15-17**
God will wipe away all tears from their eyes.

211. **Revelation 21:1a, 3-5a**
There will be no more death.

RESPONSORIAL PSALM

212. Psalm 23:1-3a, 3b-4, 5, 6
℟. (1): **The Lord is my shepherd; there is nothing I shall want.**

213. Psalm 25:4bc-5ab, 6 and 7bc, 20-21
℟. (1b): **To you, O Lord, I lift my soul.**

214. Psalm 42:2, 3, 5bcd; Psalm 43:3, 4, 5
℟. (Psalm 42:3): **My soul is thirsting for the living God: when shall I see him face to face?**

215. Psalm 148:1-2, 11-12ab, 12c-14a, 14bcd
℟. (12c): **Let all praise the name of the Lord.**
or: **Alleluia.**

ALLELUIA VERSE AND VERSE BEFORE THE GOSPEL

216. Matthew 11:25
Blessed are you, Father, Lord of heaven and earth;
you have revealed to little ones the mysteries of the kingdom.

217. John 6:39
This is the will of my Father, says the Lord,
that I should lose nothing of all that he has given to me,
and that I should raise it up on the last day.

218. 2 Corinthians 1:3b-4a
Blessed be the Father of mercies and the God of all comfort,
who consoles us in all our afflictions.

GOSPEL

219. **Matthew 11:25-30**
You have hidden these things from the learned and revealed them to children.

220. **John 6:37-40 or 37-39**
This is the will of my Father, that I should lose nothing of all that he has given to me.

221. **John 6:51-59 (Greek 51-58)**
Anyone who eats this bread will live for ever; and I will raise him up on the last day.

222. **John 11:32-38, 40**
If you believe you will see the glory of God.

II. PRAYERS

223. For a deceased child

Lord, hear the prayers for N. we offer in our sorrow.
As we believe that this child, N., is now living in your kingdom,
so one day may we join him (her)
and together share the joy of eternal life.
We ask this through Christ our Lord.
℟. **Amen.**

224. For a deceased child

Father, we entrust to you this child
whom you loved so much in this life.
Welcome him (her) into paradise
where there will be no more sorrow,
no more weeping or pain,
but only peace and joy
with your Son and the Holy Spirit
for ever and ever.
℟. **Amen.**

225. For the mourners

Lord, comfort this family in their sorrow.
You cleansed this child in the waters of baptism
and gave him (her) new life.
May we one day join him (her)
and share heaven's joys for ever.
We ask this through Christ our Lord.
℟. **Amen.**

226. For the mourners

Lord, may the prayers of Mary, the mother of God, assist us.
As she stood by the cross while her Son was dying,
so may she sustain these parents in their grief,
bring them the comfort of her own faith
and by her prayers, help them to eternal life.
We ask this through Christ our Lord.
℟. **Amen.**

III. INTRODUCTIONS TO THE FINAL COMMENDATION AND FAREWELL

227.

God, our Father, has made this child his adopted son (daughter) through baptism. Now, in his wisdom, he has called him (her) to himself. We reverently bury his (her) body knowing that one day it will rise again to a new life that never ends. We believe that this child has already entered eternal life. May God strengthen and comfort his (her) parents and friends, and make us all long for the joys of heaven.

228.

With faith in Jesus Christ, we reverently bring the body of this child to be buried in its human imperfection. Let us pray with confidence to God who gives life to all things, that he will raise up this mortal body to the perfection and the company of the saints.

IV. RESPONSORY FOR THE FINAL COMMENDATION AND FAREWELL

229.

I know that my Redeemer lives, and on the last day I shall rise again;* in my body I shall look on God, my Savior.

℣. **I myself shall see him; my own eyes will gaze on him;* in my body I shall look on God, my Savior.**

℣. **This is the hope I cherish in my heart;* in my body I shall look on God, my Savior.**

V. BLESSING OF THE GRAVE

230.

Lord God, through your mercy
those who have lived in faith

find eternal peace.
Bless this grave
and send your angel to watch over it.
As we bury the body of this child
welcome him (her) into your presence,
and with your saints let him (her) rejoice in you for ever.
We ask this through Christ our Lord.
℟. **Amen.**

CHAPTER VIII

VARIOUS TEXTS FOR FUNERALS OF CHILDREN WHO DIE BEFORE BAPTISM

I. SCRIPTURE READINGS

231. **Isaiah 25:6a, 7-8a**
The Lord God will destroy death for ever.

232. **Lamentations 3:17-26**
It is good to wait in silence for the Lord God to save.
The Hebrew letters are omitted

233. Psalm 25:4bc-5ab, 6 and 7bc, 17 and 20.
℟. (1b): **To you, O Lord, I lift my soul.**
or (3b): **No one who waits for you, O Lord, will ever be put to shame.**

234. **Mark 15:33-46**
Jesus gave a loud cry and breathed his last.

II. PRAYERS

235.

Lord, listen to the prayers
of this family that has faith in you.
In their sorrow at the death of this child,
may they find hope in your infinite mercy.
We ask this through Christ our Lord.
℟. Amen.

236.

Father of all consolation,
from whom nothing is hidden,
you know the faith of these parents
who mourn the death of their child.
May they find comfort in knowing
that you have taken him (her)
into your loving care.
We ask this through Christ our Lord.
℟. Amen.

Another prayer, no. 226.

III. INTRODUCTION TO THE FINAL COMMENDATION AND FAREWELL

237.

Let us commend this child to the Lord,
and support his (her) parents in their sorrow with our love and prayers.

The other texts may be chosen from those in the rite for baptized children.